Elder Law

Aspen Casebook Series

Elder Law
Practice, Policy, and Problems

NINA A. KOHN
Syracuse University College of Law

Wolters Kluwer
Law & Business

Published by Wolters Kluwer Law & Business in New York.

Wolters Kluwer Law & Business serves customers worldwide with CCH, Aspen Publishers, and Kluwer Law International products. (www.wolterskluwerlb.com)

To contact Customer Service, e-mail customer.service@wolterskluwer.com, call 1-800-234-1660, fax 1-800-901-9075, or mail correspondence to:

Wolters Kluwer Law & Business
Attn: Order Department
PO Box 990
Frederick, MD 21705

Printed in the United States of America.

1 2 3 4 5 6 7 8 9 0

ISBN 978-1-4548-3781-7

Library of Congress Cataloging-in-Publication Data

Kohn, Nina A., author.
    Elder law: practice, policy, and problems / Nina A. Kohn, Syracuse University College of Law.—First edition.
        pages cm
    Includes bibliographical references and index.
    ISBN 978-1-4548-3781-7 (alk. paper)
1. Older people—Legal status, laws, etc.—United States. I. Title.
    KF390.A4K67 2014
    342.7308'774—dc23

                                                                                                2013041079

SUSTAINABLE FORESTRY INITIATIVE

Certified Sourcing
www.sfiprogram.org
SFI-01234

SFI label applies to the text stock

About Wolters Kluwer Law & Business

Wolters Kluwer Law & Business is a leading global provider of intelligent information and digital solutions for legal and business professionals in key specialty areas, and respected educational resources for professors and law students. Wolters Kluwer Law & Business connects legal and business professionals as well as those in the education market with timely, specialized authoritative content and information-enabled solutions to support success through productivity, accuracy and mobility.

Serving customers worldwide, Wolters Kluwer Law & Business products include those under the Aspen Publishers, CCH, Kluwer Law International, Loislaw, ftwilliam.com and MediRegs family of products.

CCH products have been a trusted resource since 1913, and are highly regarded resources for legal, securities, antitrust and trade regulation, government contracting, banking, pension, payroll, employment and labor, and healthcare reimbursement and compliance professionals.

Aspen Publishers products provide essential information to attorneys, business professionals and law students. Written by preeminent authorities, the product line offers analytical and practical information in a range of specialty practice areas from securities law and intellectual property to mergers and acquisitions and pension/benefits. Aspen's trusted legal education resources provide professors and students with high-quality, up-to-date and effective resources for successful instruction and study in all areas of the law.

Kluwer Law International products provide the global business community with reliable international legal information in English. Legal practitioners, corporate counsel and business executives around the world rely on Kluwer Law journals, looseleafs, books, and electronic products for comprehensive information in many areas of international legal practice.

Loislaw is a comprehensive online legal research product providing legal content to law firm practitioners of various specializations. Loislaw provides attorneys with the ability to quickly and efficiently find the necessary legal information they need, when and where they need it, by facilitating access to primary law as well as state-specific law, records, forms and treatises.

ftwilliam.com offers employee benefits professionals the highest quality plan documents (retirement, welfare and non-qualified) and government forms (5500/PBGC, 1099 and IRS) software at highly competitive prices.

MediRegs products provide integrated health care compliance content and software solutions for professionals in healthcare, higher education and life sciences, including professionals in accounting, law and consulting.

Wolters Kluwer Law & Business, a division of Wolters Kluwer, is headquartered in New York. Wolters Kluwer is a market-leading global information services company focused on professionals.

For OHM, a source of endless joy.

Summary of Contents

Contents

Preface

There are many reasons to study elder law. First, elder law is one of the fastest growing legal specialties, and thus represents an expanding job market. Second, elder law attorneys report unusually high levels of job satisfaction, which they tend to attribute to the ability to directly help their clients and to the relationships they form with their clients and with other professionals. Third, elder law addresses a wide range of interesting and politically charged topics. As the cases and problems you will consider in this text illustrate, the field is rich with human drama, compelling family sagas, and complex policy challenges. Finally—no matter who you are—you are aging, your family is aging, and your friends are aging (have you ever met anyone getting younger?). Even if you never practice elder law, a basic understanding of elder law is likely to be useful in your personal life.

But what is elder law? Unlike many other areas of the law, elder law is not defined by a particular set of legal doctrines or theories, but rather by the client population it seeks to serve. Elder law therefore includes a broad range of substantive legal topics of particular importance to older adults ranging from planning for the possibility of future disability, to obtaining benefits from programs such as Medicaid and Social Security, to avoiding and addressing elder abuse and exploitation. Elder law is also an unusually dynamic area of law as it is shaped by ever-changing state and federal policies surrounding old-age and old-age entitlement programs.

This text reflects the nature of the field by combining a client-focused approach with in-depth discussions of important elder law-related policy issues. Its aim is to provide students with the specific knowledge as well as the conceptual background that they need to understand the key legal issues facing older adults and those who represent them. The text is thus meant to be both practical and theoretical, both straightforward and intellectually rigorous.

To this end, the text weaves together narrative with cases, statutes, commentaries, and problems to create a comprehensive, tightly organized text that facilitates engaged teaching and active learning. A central feature of the text is that it is replete with opportunities for students to apply what they are learning. Specifically, it contains: (1) *questions* that ask for students to critique specific policies or test students' formal legal reasoning skills, (2) *problems* that allow students to apply what they have read to hypothetical client situations, and (3) *exercises* that provide an opportunity for students to engage in activities or outside research on the topics they are studying. The questions and problems are designed so that they can be used either during in-class discussions or outside of class by students studying independently. Likewise, most exercises can be used either as in-class activities or as writing assignments.

The substantive coverage of the book reflects those subjects that students could expect to encounter in an elder law practice. Special attention is paid to issues identified by elder law attorneys and professors as often under-appreciated (e.g., ethics, changes associated with aging, and aging network services) as well as emerging areas of interest (e.g., international dimensions of elder law and modern Medicaid planning techniques). Since many of the laws and regulations that form the legal framework for elder law practice are subject to frequent political debate and legislative amendment, the text aims to ensure that readers understand the overarching structures of the systems they study, not just the current rules that apply to them.

Chapter 1 introduces the reader to elder law as a specialty and to the study of aging more broadly. Recognizing that most students will have little previous age-related training, it provides a "crash course" in gerontology. This includes an overview of the physical, psychological, and social changes associated with aging, a concise discussion of the demographic characteristics of the United States' elderly population, and an introduction to the aging services network.

Chapter 2 focuses on the practice of elder law. It surveys different models of elder law practice and considers the ethical challenges that elder law attorneys face in working with older clients and their families.

Chapter 3 explores the role that age plays in the U.S. legal system. The chapter is designed to facilitate a "big picture" discussion to which students and teachers can refer when discussing old-age entitlement programs and age-specific legislation in subsequent chapters. It begins with a discussion of the constitutionality and desirability of age-based classifications in the law. It then explores age discrimination in a variety of contexts including medical care, safety statutes, and employment. It concludes by highlighting the debate on the proposed Convention on the Rights of Older Persons.

Chapter 4 focuses on advance planning and surrogate decision-making. It covers legal and practical issues surrounding guardianship, durable powers of attorney, representative payees, and advance directives. It also highlights ethical issues involved when representing clients with appointed surrogates. Since advance planning is a key element of elder law practice, the chapter also contains multiple document drafting and review exercises.

Chapter 5 considers how older adults obtain and maintain income in older age, and especially after retirement. It covers Social Security benefits, strategies for maximizing them, and disputes over them. It also covers private pensions, savings, Supplemental Security Income benefits, and military retirement and veterans' pension benefits. In addition, it highlights the role of family support and duties under filial responsibility laws.

Chapters 6 and 7 are the longest chapters in the text, reflecting the fact that both address complex topics that are central to elder law practice. Students and teachers alike should therefore expect that it will take longer to work through these chapters than the others in the text.

Chapter 6 focuses on financing health care in older age. It includes substantial discussions of both Medicare and Medicaid coverage. As Medicaid planning has historically been a very significant component of elder law practice, it includes discussions of both the ethics of Medicaid planning and of Medicaid planning techniques. In addition, Chapter 6 addresses long-term care insurance and employer-provided health care benefits.

Chapter 7 focuses on the housing options for older adults. Recognizing that most older adults wish to remain in their homes, it begins with a discussion of aging in place and the legal tools that can be employed to facilitate it. It then explores specialized housing arrangements (including nursing homes, assisted living facilities, and continuing care retirement communities) and the rights of those residing in them. The decision to separate a discussion of rights of those residing in long-term care settings from the financing of care in those settings (a topic covered in Chapter 6) recognizes that long-term care settings are the home of those who reside in them, and that the issues residents face extend far beyond how to pay for the care they are receiving. The chapter ends with a discussion of protections from disability discrimination in housing that can be used to protect the choices of older adults across housing settings. Notably, the integration of disability law throughout Chapter 7 recognizes the close relationship between elder law and disability law—a closeness that the practicing elder law bar is increasingly capitalizing upon by expanding elder law practices into "elder law and special needs" practices.

Chapter 8 addresses the important topic of elder abuse and neglect. It details the phenomenon of elder mistreatment, including warning signs for attorneys. It then explores legal strategies for addressing elder abuse. Finally, it explores the thorny legal and moral issues surrounding elder abuse, including how to determine who should be held responsible for caring for older adults and how the law should treat self-neglect.

Chapters 9 and 10 explore two topics that—although regularly encountered by elder law attorneys and of importance to older adults—are currently less central to most elder law practices. Thus, instructors offering a two-credit elder law course may wish to omit portions of Chapter 9 and perhaps all of Chapter 10, or assign them as optional reading. Chapter 9 focuses on representing dying clients and end-of-life issues. It addresses the emotional and practical challenges associated with counseling terminally ill clients, explores the legal contours of the right to refuse life-sustaining care (including food and drink), discusses constitutional and statutory approaches to physician-assisted suicide, and highlights the role of hospice care and the Medicare hospice benefit. Finally, Chapter 10 focuses on grandparenting and grandparents' rights. It discusses grandparents' ability to obtain visitation with grandchildren, as well as the legal rights of grandparents raising or caring for grandchildren, and supports available to them. It concludes with a discussion of grandparents' rights to receive care from grandchildren, bringing the discussion of intergenerational responsibilities full circle.

Throughout the book, omissions in edited materials are indicated using ellipses, with the exception that footnotes and endnotes, internal references, and parallel citations are deleted without any notation. In addition, the author has taken the liberty of making slight changes in the formatting of excerpted court opinions (e.g., adding italics to case names) in the interest of uniformity and readability.

Nina A. Kohn
November 2013

Acknowledgments and Gratitude

The author is grateful to the many individuals who generously provided feedback on earlier drafts of this casebook and shared their subject matter expertise including Naomi Cahn, Eric Carlson, Marie-Therese Connolly, Stephen Gordon, Richard Kaplan, Barry Kozak, Katherine Pearson, Thaddeus Pope, Suzanne Scheller, Terry Turnipseed, Page Ulrey, Erica Wood, and Stephanie Woodward.

Thanks is also due to Jill Cramer, Marissa Nossick, Emily Parker, Ed Thater, and the staff of the Barclay Law School Library at Syracuse University for their research assistance; to Anne Hensberry for her administrative assistance; and to Rick Mixter, John Devins, Tom Daughhetee, and the team at Aspen Publishers for helping to make this book a reality. In addition, the author benefited from the support and encouragement of Dean Hannah Arterian and the Syracuse University College of Law, and the Syracuse University Judith Greenberg Seinfeld Distinguished Faculty Fellows Program.

Finally, the author thanks the multiple generations of her family for their love, support, and implicit reminders of the importance of elder care. A special thanks is extended to Miriam Adams, Roger Kohn, and Jeffrey Milder.

stored in an electronic database or retrieval system without the express written consent of the American Bar Association. Reprinted with permission.

American Council of Trusts and Estates Counsel, Commentary on MRPC 1.14. Reprinted with permission.

Ed St. Aubin et al., *Elder and End-of-Life Medical Issues: Legal Context, Psychological Issues, and Recommendations to Attorneys Serving Seniors*, 7 MARQ. ELDER'S ADVISOR 259 (2006). Reprinted with the permission of Marquette University Law School Elder's Advisor. Originally published in 7 MARQ. ELDER'S ADVISOR, Spring 2006 at 259.

Debra Lyn Bassett, *Three's a Crowd: A Proposal to Abolish Joint Representation*, 32 RUTGERS L.J. 387 (2001). Reprinted with permission.

Kathy L. Cerminara, *Hospice & Health Care Reform: Improving Care at the End of Life*, 17 WIDENER L. REV. 443 (2011). Reprinted with permission.

Israel Doron & Itai Apter, *The Debate Around the Need for an International Convention on the Rights of Older Persons*, 50 GERONTOLOGIST 586 (2010). Reprinted with permission.

Lawrence A. Frolik, *The Client's Desire to Age in Place: Our Role as Elder Law Attorneys*, 15 NAELA Q. 6 (2002). Reprinted with permission.

Stephen M. Golant, *Commentary: Irrational Exuberance for the Aging in Place of Vulnerable Low-Income Homeowners*, 20 J. AGING & SOC. POL'Y 379 (2008). Reprinted with permission.

Susan G. Haines & John J. Campbell, *Defects, Due Process, and Protective Proceedings: Are Our Probate Codes Unconstitutional?*, 14 QUINNIPIAC PROB. L.J. 57 (1999). Reprinted with permission.

HomeShare Vermont, Sample Homesharing Agreement. Reprinted with permission.

Richard A. Kaplan, *Rethinking Medicare's Payroll Tax After Health Care Reform*, TAXES—THE TAX MAGAZINE 55 (2011). Reprinted with permission.

Richard Kaplan, *Top Ten Myths of Medicare*, 20 ELDER L.J. 1 (2012). Reprinted with permission.

Daniela Kraieman, *Consumer Direction in Medicaid Long-Term Care: Autonomy, Commodification of Family Labor, and Community Resilience*, 19 AM. U. J. GENDER SOC. POL'Y & L. 671 (2011). Reprinted with permission.

John A. Miller, *Voluntary Impoverishment to Obtain Government Benefits*, 13 CORNELL J.L. & PUB. POL'Y 81 (2003). Reprinted with permission.

Kathryn Moore, *The Future of Social Security: Principles to Guide Reform*, 41 JOHN MARSHALL L. REV. 1061 (2008). Reprinted with permission.

Thaddeus Pope & Lindsey Anderson. *Voluntarily Stopping Eating and Drinking: A Legal Treatment Option at the End of Life*, 17 WIDENER L. REV. 363 (2011). Reprinted with permission.

Benjamin Templin, *Social Security Reform: Should the Retirement Age Be Increased?*, 89 OR. L. REV. 1179 (2011). Reprinted with permission.

Sidney D. Watson, *From Almhouses to Nursing Homes and Community Care: Lessons from Medicaid's History*, 26 GA. ST. U. L. REV. 937 (2010). Reprinted with permission.

Jennifer Wright, *Practical Concerns in Elder Law Mediation*, THE HENNEPIN LAWYER 21 (2011). Published May 2011 in The Hennepin Lawyer, membership publication of the Hennepin County Bar Association. Used with permission.

Washington, District of Columbia Bar Association, Ethics Opinion 353 (2010). Reprinted with permission.

Jessica Dixon Weaver, *Grandma in the White House: Support for Intergenerational Caregiving*, 43 SETON HALL L. REV. 1 (2013). Reprinted with permission.

Elder Law

CHAPTER 1

Introduction to Elder Law and the Aging Process

A. INTRODUCTION

Populations worldwide are aging, and the U.S. population is no exception. The elderly population in the United States has expanded significantly and today over 40 million people, or approximately 13 percent of the country's population, are at least 65 years old. The elderly population in the United States is expected to continue to grow dramatically in the coming decades, rising to over 72 million people age 65 and older by 2030.

The emerging field of elder law is poised to play a key role in responding to the needs of this growing population. Elder law is a legal specialty focused on counseling and representing older persons or their representatives on later-in-life planning and other legal issues of particular importance to older adults. Although the field is still young—it was almost unknown two decades ago—it is rapidly growing. This growth appears to reflect a burgeoning market for elder law services. In a recent national study, 93 percent of elder law attorneys surveyed reported that elder law is a growing field, nearly three-quarters felt that more elder law attorneys are needed, and the vast majority described the field as one with ample job opportunities.

Elder law is closely related to estate planning. Indeed, many elder law practitioners have transitioned to elder law after practicing in the field of trusts and estates law. A key difference between the two subjects is that elder law focuses on a broader range of issues and concerns. In addition, whereas estate planning places significant emphasis on the management and distribution of their resources following death, elder law focuses primarily on individuals' needs while they are living. To capture this difference, some elder law practitioners refer to their practice area as "life care planning" or "life services planning." These alternative terms also reflect the fact that many elder law attorneys also provide representation with regards to special needs planning for younger persons with disabilities.

B. AN OVERVIEW OF THE FIELD OF ELDER LAW

Elder law is practiced in a wide variety of settings—from large private law firms, to solo practices, to legal aid offices, to government agencies administering laws affecting older adults, to prosecutors' offices. The typical private elder law practice focuses on planning for later-in-life needs through individual client counseling and document drafting, and on helping clients obtain benefits, such as insurance coverage for health care services.

Elder law has traditionally been defined by the client population it serves, rather than by a specific set of legal doctrines. As such, elder law attorneys work with a broad range of substantive legal issues. Issues that elder law attorneys frequently address include:

■ Planning for potential future disability, including Medicaid planning,
■ Guardianship and other forms of surrogate decision-making,
■ Health care benefits,
■ Social Security,
■ End-of-life issues, and
■ Elder abuse.

Many elder law attorneys, especially those practicing in the non-profit sector, also frequently deal with issues related to nursing home rights and litigation, senior housing, and pensions. Accordingly, the elder law attorney can expect to use a wide range of legal strategies to meet client objectives in a wide range of legal issues.

Elder law is increasingly defined not only by the population it serves, however, but also by the holistic, interdisciplinary manner in which it does so. Elder law attorneys tend to embrace an integrated approach to planning for their clients' needs, recognizing that clients' legal needs interrelate with their non-legal needs and goals. Elder law attorneys are also inclined to work in an interdisciplinary manner with other professionals to meet their clients' needs. As Charles Sabatino, the director of the ABA Commission on Law and Aging, has explained:

> Social workers, geriatricians, other health practitioners, geriatric case managers, financial planners, and others all serve as allies in the legal planning work of elder law attorneys. Often, elder law practices function as an entry point for clients into aging and disability networks and community resources. Experienced elder law attorneys know how to connect to and provide the supportive services their clients might need.

Charles P. Sabatino, *Elder Law 2009-2039?*, 30 BIFOCAL 105 (July 2009).

To successfully practice in such a varied and interdisciplinary field, an elder law attorney must have a broad range of knowledge both about the law and about aging, as well as a diverse set of problem-solving skills. Accordingly, this book explores a wide range of legal problems that affect older adults, and encourages readers to think creatively and holistically about how to address the problems that older adults face.

Part of what makes elder law practice highly satisfying for many attorneys is that these tasks can have significant lifestyle and civil rights implications for older adults. For example, by helping clients plan for long-term care and its financial implications, elder law attorneys can help older adults increase their control over their health care, living arrangements, and resources. Similarly, by helping older adults execute advance directives, elder law attorneys enhance their clients' abilities to determine future life choices and how those choices are made.

Consistent with the interactive and client-focused nature of the field, attorneys tend to be attracted to elder law because of the high level of human interaction it affords. In a recent national survey, elder law attorneys reported that the most satisfying aspect of elder practice is the opportunity to help people, followed by the level of meaningful client interaction and the opportunity to engage in a multidisciplinary practice. This likely reflects the fact that elder law attorneys work closely with individuals on matters of great personal importance and, in so doing, frequently come to know not only their clients and their clients' immediate situations, but also their clients' life history and family.

C. AN OVERVIEW OF AGING

The client-centered and often holistic nature of elder law practice means that elder law attorneys frequently bring together legal and non-legal resources to meet client needs. Thus, to be most effective, an elder law practitioner must have an understanding of the aging process and individuals' needs and desires as they age, as well as the community resources that may be available to help satisfy those needs and desires. This subsection therefore provides a demographic overview of the aging population, an overview of the aging process, and an introduction to the network of social services designed to support older adults.

1. Characteristics of the U.S. Elderly Population

The elderly population is a diverse one. Part of this diversity stems from the fact that it includes people of a broad range of ages. The term elderly is typically used to describe all those age 65 and over, as is the case in this text. Yet, the average person who reaches age 65 will live an additional 18.8 years (20 years for women; 17.3 years for men). Over this period of time, the individual's goals and needs are likely to evolve significantly. It is therefore important for those working with older adults to have a sense of some of the general characteristics of the elderly population, as well as how those characteristics may vary based on chronological age and other factors. Accordingly, in describing the elderly population, this sub-section also highlights some of the variability within it.

a. Size

The U.S. population is aging. This aging can be conceptualized in several different ways. First, there is an overall numerical increase in the total number of older adults. According to the 2010 U.S. Census, there were more than 40 million people age 65 and older living in the United States, a 15 percent increase from a decade earlier. Second, there is an increase in the average age of the population. The 2010 Census found that the median age increased from 35.3 years to 37.2 years between 2000 and 2010. Finally, there is an increase in the ratio of older adults to younger persons. The 2010 Census found that people over the age of 65 compose 13 percent of the U.S. population, as compared to 12.4 percent a decade earlier. In short, regardless of which figure is used, the conclusion is the same: the American population is aging. This aging is attributable to several different factors, including the aging of the Baby Boom generation and increases in longevity.

The fastest growing group of older adults are the "oldest of the old," a term typically used to refer to those age 85 and older (although occasionally to refer to those 80 and older or those 90 and older). To give a sense of the growth of the population of those who are very old: in 1980, those age 90 and older constituted only 2.8 percent of those age 65 and older; today, they constitute 4.7 percent of it; and by 2050, they are expected to constitute 10 percent of it.

As a consequence of the population aging, the balance between generations is changing such that the number of younger people relative to older people is decreasing. One figure that aims to quantify this changing balance is the "old age dependency ratio." The old age dependency ratio is determined by dividing the number of people age 65 and over by the number of people of "productive age" (commonly age 18 to 64). The rationale for this calculation is that it represents the ratio of the population that is of "dependent age" to the population that is of working age. This reasoning is increasingly outdated because older Americans increasingly delay retirement beyond age 65 and younger Americans increasingly delay entry into the workforce. Nevertheless, the old age dependency ratio is frequently treated as an important economic indicator because it provides an indication of the ability of the population to support its aging members. Currently, the old age dependency ratio is increasing. In 2010, the old age dependency ratio was 20.7, an increase from 20.1 a decade earlier. This means that there were an additional 6 persons age 65 or older for every 1,000 "working age" adults.

The aging trends seen in the United States are part of a worldwide aging phenomenon. According to the World Health Organization, during the 50-year period spanning the years 2000 to 2050, the proportion of the world population age 60 and older is expected to double from 11 percent to 22 percent. During that same period of time, the total number of people over the age of 60 is expected to more than triple, growing from 605 million in the year 2000 to 2 billion by 2050. The most rapid growth of older adults is in the developing world, and the oldest of the old are the fastest growing segment of the older population in many countries.

For additional information on the changing structure of the aging population, KEVIN KINSELLA & WAN HE, U.S. CENSUS BUREAU & NAT'L INST. ON AGING, P95/09-1, AN AGING WORLD: 2008 (2009), *available at* http://www.census.gov/prod/2009pubs/p95-09-1.pdf; and WAN HE & MARK N. MUENCHRATH, U.S. CENSUS BUREAU, ACS-17, 90+ IN THE UNITED STATES: 2006-2008 (2011).

b. Demographics

The elderly population is disproportionately female because women live longer than men. The average life expectancy of women in the United States is approximately 81, whereas it is only 76 for men. Thus, women tend to outlive men by an average of 5 years. The gap between the number of women and men increases with age; according to the 2010 Census, by the age of 90 there are more than twice as many women as men.

The older population in the United States is also disproportionately Caucasian relative to the general population. In part, this reflects racial differences in life expectancies. For example, African Americans have an average life expectancy of 74.5 (71 for men, 78 for women), compared to a life expectancy of 78.8 for Caucasians. Hispanics, by contrast, have slightly greater life expectancies than non-Hispanic Caucasians.

Like younger adults, most older adults live in community-based settings. Only approximately 1.5 million people in the United States, or 4.1 percent of the population over the age of 65, live in an institution such as a nursing home. That percentage, however, rises as people age. Approximately 13 percent of those age 85 and older are institutionalized.

Older adults, contrary to some popular perceptions, are not disproportionately poor by most calculations. Older adults experience somewhat lower rates of poverty than the adult population as a whole, in large part because most older adults receive Social Security income that provides them with a financial safety net. However, as discussed in Chapter 5, nearly 10 percent of the elderly in the United States live in poverty and another approximately 6 percent are "near poor," meaning that they have incomes within 125 percent of the poverty level. Poverty among the elderly population disproportionately affects persons of color, with Hispanic, African-American, and Asian older adults experiencing significantly greater poverty rates than Caucasian older adults. Indeed, poverty rates for African-American and Hispanic older adults are more than twice those for Caucasian older adults. These higher poverty rates reflect a lifetime of economic disadvantage as economic disadvantages in younger life have a cumulative effect that snowballs in later age.

c. Social Supports

A common myth about aging is that older people are typically alone and isolated. Fortunately, contrary to this stereotype, many older people are embedded in rich social and family networks. The extent of these social networks, however, is affected by a variety of demographic factors. For example, older women are less likely to have a spouse than older men due to women's longer life expectancies and the fact that they historically have tended to marry men who are older than they are. Similarly, lesbian, gay, bisexual, and transgender (LGBT) individuals typically have less support from members of their biological families, and are more likely to have social support networks that consist predominantly of other older adults as opposed to intergenerational support networks.

While older adults increasingly live alone, many older adults live with a spouse. In addition, many older adults live near adult children. A 2010 study found that approximately half of mothers with adult children live no more than ten miles from an adult child. Proximity to an adult child varied by different demographic characteristics. For example, mothers with daughters and mothers with larger families were more likely to have a child who lives within ten miles of them; by contrast, white mothers were less likely than black and Hispanic mothers to have a child living within a ten-mile radius. *See* Suzanne Bianchi et al., *Geographic Dispersion and the Well-Being of the Elderly* (University of Michigan Retirement Research Center Working Paper No. 2010-234, 2010).

2. The Aging Process

The process of aging is marked by physical, psychological, and social changes. However, the nature, effect, and timing of these changes vary within the older population. Some of this variability is highly individualistic, such as that which stems from differences in individuals' genetic makeup. Other variability is highly correlated with an individual's lifestyle and socioeconomic status. The effect of these changes depends on many factors, including older adults' ability to adapt to them. Fortunately, many older adults become skilled at developing strategies for compensating for physical and cognitive declines, as well as for social changes.

a. Physical Changes

As individuals age, they experience a vast array of physical changes. Typical changes include declines in the functioning of the immune system (making them more vulnerable to disease) and declines in organ functioning (including in major organs such as the heart, lungs, and the skin). Critical systems such as the nervous system and the endocrine system also experience changes, including reduced responsiveness.

Among the most tangible physical changes that individuals experience as a result of aging are sensory changes. Older adults typically experience declines in vision, including declines in the ability to see in low-light situations, reduced ability to focus on objects nearby and thus to read without corrective lenses, and changes in ability to distinguish between different levels of brightness and different colors. Older adults also typically experience declines in hearing, including the loss of the ability to hear certain frequencies of sound and a decline in the ability to differentiate among similar sounds. In addition, as people age, their other senses—taste, smell, and touch—typically become less sensitive, making it harder to differentiate among stimuli. As with other physical changes associated with aging, sensory declines are typically not a sudden event, but rather part of a life-long aging process. For example, while changes in hearing are typically most evident in older age, the diminishment of the ability to hear begins around age 20.

As a result of physical changes, certain conditions that are uncommon among younger individuals are common among older ones. For example, according to the Centers for Disease Control and Prevention (CDC), in 2010 approximately 20 percent of those age 65 and older in the United States had coronary heart disease, compared to only 7 percent of those aged 45 to 64 and 1.2 percent of those aged 18 to 44. However, the fact that the risk of acquiring a condition increases with age does not mean that most persons with that condition are elderly. For example, the likelihood of having arthritis generally increases as people age, and approximately half of those over the age of 65 have the condition. Nevertheless, two-thirds of those who have been diagnosed by a doctor as having arthritis are actually under the age of 65.

The physical changes associated with aging can significantly affect individuals' abilities to function within their environments. Sensory changes can undermine the ability of older adults to effectively and efficiently perceive the world around them, as well as to effectively communicate their needs and wishes to their family and caregivers. Changes in muscles and joints can reduce mobility and coordination leading to both difficulty getting places and difficulty performing important tasks. Changes in the neurologic system can contribute to a wide range of challenges such as dizziness and falls (due to decreased ability to compensate for changes in blood pressure after standing up), as well as difficulty with fine motor tasks (such as those needed to write a check or comb one's hair). Other changes in organ functioning can result in an overall reduced sense of energy with which to perform a wide range of tasks. Decreasing quality and quantity of sleep is commonly seen in the elderly and can contribute to overall fatigue and poor concentration.

While many physical changes are the predictable result of the aging process, there is great variability in the physical experience of aging. The extent to which any particular individual experiences these changes, and the timing of those changes, depends on many factors. Aging processes are influenced not only by environmental and lifestyle factors but also by genetic ones. Moreover, not all disabilities that older people have are age-related or even acquired later than life. Some older adults were born with a disability or acquired one as a child or young adult. Recognizing this is important because the experience of living with a disability, and the ability of an individual to adapt to a disability, may vary based on when the disability was acquired. That is, the experience of aging *with* disability may be very different from that of aging *into* disability.

b. Psychological Changes

As people age, they experience a variety of psychological changes. Although individuals experiencing normal aging typically retain the ability to learn and engage in complex problem-solving throughout their lives, aging is associated with predictable declines in certain types of cognitive functioning. These changes can have a significant impact on older adults' well-being. Declines in cognitive functioning are associated with reduced quality of life, declines in physical and mental health, and increases in depression and social isolation.

A common type of cognitive decline associated with aging is a decline in the speed with which individuals process information. Similarly, aging is associated with increased difficulty in dividing attention or switching attention between competing tasks.

Perhaps the most feared area of cognitive decline is memory. Indeed, concerns about loss of memory are rampant among older adults, although there is often little correlation between an individual's actual memory ability and their perception of their own memory. Certain types of memory are more affected by aging than others. In general, older adults have the most difficulty with memory tasks for which there are relatively few cues. Accordingly, they are likely to experience a more significant decline in their ability to recall (i.e., to remember something when presented with a cue or asked a question—such as, what is the capital of France?) than their ability to recognize (i.e., to discern whether an answer is correct—e.g., which of these cities is the capital of France?).

While most of the cognitive changes associated with aging are cognitive declines, some abilities appear to actually improve with age. Although it is difficult to measure, some older adults experience improved judgment or wisdom as they age. This is consistent with findings that certain types of intelligence may improve with age. Older adults typically experience declines in *fluid intelligence*, i.e., the ability to reason abstractly and to identify patterns or relationships between stimuli. By contrast, they do not typically experience declines in *crystallized intelligence*, or knowledge-based intelligence. Indeed, as people age, they may actually experience improved crystallized intelligence as the result of having acquired greater experience and knowledge through their lives.

As with physical changes, psychological changes associated with aging tend to vary based on lifestyle, environmental, and genetic factors. Certain behaviors such as social engagement and mental and physical activity, for example, appear to reduce the likelihood of experiencing dementia. Similarly, there is some research to suggest that eating foods high in antioxidants and omega-3 fatty acids can also support cognitive well-being and help protect against dementia. Several cardiovascular risk factors are also associated with an increased risk of cognitive decline, including high blood pressure.

Gerontologists distinguish between cognitive changes associated with normal aging and cognitive changes that are associated with age-related diseases. For example, although many older people experience depression, depression is not considered a normal part of aging. Similarly, the term "dementia" is often used when referring to memory and thinking-related problems associated with old age. However, dementia is an umbrella term that refers to a group of symptoms that undermine social or intellectual functioning to the extent that they interfere with daily functioning. The most common cause of dementia is Alzheimer's disease, accounting for an estimated 60 to 80 percent of all cases, but other types of dementia, such as vascular dementia, Lewy Body dementia, and frontotemporal lobe dementia, are also quite common. Although the prevalence of dementia increases with age, the majority of older adults do not suffer from dementia. Just under 5 percent of people in their 70s have dementia; compared with approximately a quarter of those in their 80s and just over a third (37%) of those age 90 and older. As a result, gerontologists widely agree that dementia should be considered a pathology and not part of "normal" aging.

c. Social Changes

Aging is associated with a variety of changes in individuals' social experiences. One reason for this is that as people age they typically find themselves in new roles. In part, this is the result of giving up old roles. For example, role losses commonly result from retirement, which may entail both losing a role in the workforce (i.e., employee or manager) and a professional identity (i.e., teacher, truck driver, or attorney). Role changes may also be triggered by changes within an individual's family or social circle, such as the death of a spouse or partner or the birth of a grandchild.

Another reason why aging affects one's social experience is that it is associated with changes in an individual's social networks, and the experience of aging depends in large part on an individual's social environment. Greater availability of social support is associated with a higher standard of living, better physical and psychological health, reduced risk of institutionalization, and even reduced mortality.

The extent to which age affects social experiences also depends, in part, on society's beliefs about age. Age functions as a social category and thus its effect on individuals depends, in part, on the meaning a society ascribes to it. Recognizing this, gerontologists have come to differentiate between *chronological age* and *functional age*. Chronological age refers to the number of years a person has lived. Functional age, by comparison, characterizes individuals by the extent to which they demonstrate physical or mental signs of aging. Chronological age is only one factor contributing to functional age. Others may include an individual's occupation, lifestyle, access to health care, and genetic composition.

As a result of the meaning that society attributes to chronological age, chronological age itself may prompt individuals to accept new roles or reject old ones. *Ageism*—stereotyping and discriminating against a particular age group—may contribute to this phenomenon. Behavior that may be considered acceptable or desirable at one age may be considered undesirable or even pathological at another.

The prevalence and impact of different types of social changes associated with aging vary by how old the person is. The oldest of the old tend to have accumulated the most losses, both in their family and in their social supports. Especially when confined with physical and cognitive declines, this can result in increased isolation and decreased happiness relative to the younger elderly.

One factor that appears to mediate the effect of these types of social changes on older adults is an individual's perceived sense of control over him or herself and over life events. A greater sense of control is associated with a strong, positive impact on their physical and psychological well-being, and a number of studies have provided evidence that it can even increase longevity. Factors affecting one's sense of control include the availability of choice. Individuals who feel they have options, even if those options are related to seemingly unimportant tasks, tend to feel a greater sense of control. Feeling dependent on other people, by contrast, correlates with decreased physical and emotional well-being.

Another factor that appears to mediate the extent and effect of social changes later in life is experiences in younger life. Patterns developed in earlier life, and circumstances faced when younger, can significantly affect the aging experience. Sociologists refer to the concept of *cumulative advantage* to explain how privileges and benefits experienced when younger can lead to increased resilience to changes later in life. Similarly, sociologists refer to the concept of *cumulative disadvantage* to explain how deprivations experienced when younger may undermine an individual's ability to engage in successful aging.

Despite these changes, older adults do maintain patterns of behavior and beliefs. Moreover, even older adults with significant dementia often maintain a meaningful sense of self and retain core values and preferences. Particularly in the early stages of dementia, long-term memory is not as commonly or severely involved as short-term memory. Therefore it is not uncommon for people with dementia to not remember recent events such as what they ate for breakfast, but to still be able to recall even the smallest details of important events during their lifetimes. Thus, to understand aging, gerontologists frequently take a life span approach that emphasizes how people evolve and age over the course of their lives.

QUESTIONS

1. Why might it matter to an attorney how old a client is? For example, how might representing someone in his or her 80s be different from representing someone in his or her 30s?

2. Older persons are often categorized as vulnerable. What does it mean to be vulnerable? Are older people more vulnerable than other populations? In what ways? *See* Martha Fineman, *"Elderly as Vulnerable": Rethinking the Nature of Individual and Societal Responsibility,* 20 ELDER L.J. 101 (2012) (discussing both the universality of vulnerability and implications of the older adults' vulnerability as a group).

3. Suppose you were employed by the National Organization for Women (NOW). Your supervising attorney comes to you and says that NOW is planning a new initiative aimed to protect the civil rights of the elderly. Your supervisor is very annoyed. She says that she joined NOW to fight for women's rights, not for those of old people. How might you respond? Is it fair to say that aging issues are women's issues?

4. Suppose you decided to start an elder law practice. How might you design your office space and structure office procedures to accommodate the needs of your clients? *See* Rebecca Morgan, *The Practical Aspects of Practicing Elder Law: Creating an Elder-Friendly Office,* 38 FAM. L.Q. 269 (2004) (discussing how attorneys can make offices accessible and inviting to older adults).

5. Suppose you were designing an "elder-friendly" courtroom. What might it look like? Why? *See* Rebecca Morgan, *From the Elder-Friendly Law Office to the Elder-Friendly Courtroom—Providing the Same Access and Justice for All,* 2 NAELA J. 325 (Fall 2006) (describing accessibility issues in courtrooms and a model elder-friendly courtroom).

3. Social Services Available to Older Adults

The Older Americans Act of 1965 (OAA), as amended, establishes a national framework of agencies that design and provide services for older adults. *See* 42 U.S.C. §§3021-3030 (2006). The entities that fall within this framework are often called the "aging network." They include *State Units on Aging* (state-run entities responsible for administering and managing benefits, programs, and services for older adults and their families), *Area Agencies on Aging* (state-designated entities that administer services for older adults in a region or locality), and thousands of community organizations providing services to older adults, among them legal service provider organizations.

Area Agencies on Aging (AAAs) are a key resource and point of contact for older adults and those providing care for older adults. While the exact combination of services offered varies from one AAA to the next, AAAs generally coordinate a broad range of services and provide counseling about older adults' options, including counseling about Medicare and Medicaid eligibility and other forms of health insurance, counseling about retirement planning, and counseling focused on assessing individuals' needs to determine what services might help them meet those needs. Other services offered by many AAAs include case management services, caregiver support services, assistance with finding employment, and programming related to preventing and ameliorating elder abuse. In addition, many AAAs run programs such as senior centers and congregate meal sites, adult day care services, or meals on wheels. They can also serve as a source of referrals, and potentially administer payment, for services such as legal assistance, in-home care and assistance, or senior housing.

Until 2012, the aging network was led by the Administration on Aging, an agency within the U.S. Department of Health and Human Services. In 2012, the Administration on Aging merged with the Administration on Developmental Disabilities and the Office of Disabilities to create the new Administration for Community Living (ACL). The ACL is responsible for, among other things, 56 state units on aging and 620 area agencies. The ACL is designed to help reduce the segmentation of services for older people and persons with disabilities that has historically occurred despite the significant overlap in the needs of the two populations.

Understanding the aging network, and especially how it functions at the local level, is a critical component of an elder law attorney's knowledge base. Elder law attorneys with a sophisticated understanding of the aging network resources available in their area are in a better position not only to refer clients to valuable services but also to work collaboratively with social service providers to meet their clients' needs.

CHAPTER 2

Elder Law Practice

A. INTRODUCTION

Elder law attorneys work in a variety of practice contexts. Most commonly, elder law attorneys work in private law firms in which they represent older adults and their family members on a variety of issues related to later-in-life planning. Elder law attorneys also provide traditional representation in non-profit settings as well. Lawyers in legal aid offices, for example, provide assistance to lower income older adults on a variety of planning and public benefits issues. Still other attorneys working in the field of elder law are employed by governmental bodies. Most such work is civil in nature, but there are also opportunities to practice aspects of elder law in a criminal justice setting. For example, a growing number of communities employ prosecutors who specialize in the prosecution of elder abuse, a subject discussed in depth in Chapter 8 of this text.

This chapter explores different approaches that elder law attorneys take to representing clients, and some of the key practical and ethical challenges that elder law attorneys encounter during the course of such representations.

B. MODELS OF ELDER LAW PRACTICE

Elder law attorneys engaged in direct client representation—whether it be in a private law firm or non-profit setting—do so in a variety of ways.

1. Traditional Client Representation

As in other practice areas, the traditional approach to attorney-client relationships in elder law practices is that an attorney represents a single client (typically an older adult planning for his or her future) or a married or otherwise committed couple. Even within this traditional model in which a single lawyer represents a single client or couple with undivided loyalty, however, there is some variation. For example, some elder law attorneys see themselves as exclusively or primarily representing older adults; others take a more fluid approach and are equally amenable to representing either older adults or their family members, depending on the case and situation.

2. Family Representation

In some cases, an elder law attorney may choose to move beyond the traditional model of client representation and represent a family or group. Professor Teresa Stanton Collett has identified four models of representation that might be used by an attorney working with elderly clients seeking estate-planning advice: (1) individual representation, in which the lawyer represents only one individual in a family; (2) representation as intermediary, in which the lawyer serves as an intermediary among multiple family members, all of whom the lawyer considers to be his or her clients, with the aim of furthering the clients' mutual interests and resolving conflicts among them; (3) joint representation, in which the lawyer represents multiple family members to advance their interests against a third party or parties; and (4) family representation, in which the lawyer treats the family—not its members—as the client and works to further the family's interest as a unit. *See* Teresa Stanton Collett, *The Ethics of Intergenerational Representation*, 62 FORDHAM L. REV. 1453 (1994). Although Collett focuses on how the models might function with regard to estate planning, the four models can also be used to describe elder law attorneys' differing approaches to representation on matters other than estate planning.

There is considerable debate over the wisdom and ethics of alternatives to the individual representation model. Professor Russell Pearce has advocated in favor of "optional family representation"—that is, allowing families to choose to be represented as a unit by a single attorney—on the grounds that it "allows families, and not the legal profession, to decide how to represent them. In so doing, it respects the choices of a family as a community and minimizes the legal profession's intrusion into the family." Professor Pearce also argues that family representation is advantageous because it is more affordable, encourages the lawyer to seek solutions that are best for the family as a whole rather than adversarial approaches that only maximize individuals' positions, and increases the likelihood that the lawyer will obtain information relevant to the representation because the lawyer receives information from all family members rather than from a single client. *See* Russell G. Pearce, *Family Values and Legal Ethics: Competing Approaches to Conflicts in Representing Spouses*, 62 FORDHAM L. REV. 1253, 1299-1301 (1994).

By comparison, Professor Janet Dolgin argues that an individual representation approach is preferable—and that family representation should be limited to rare cases. She argues that individual representation is best able to protect individual family members and is consistent with society's modern recognition that family members are autonomous individuals. *See* Janet L. Dolgin, *The Morality of Choice: Estate Planning and the Client Who Chooses Not to Choose*, 22 SEATTLE U. L. REV. 31, 52-53 (1998). Professor Debra Lyn Bassett takes the argument in favor of individual representation one step further, arguing that joint representation should be abolished. Bassett argues that joint representation is inappropriate because "[i]t is impossible for a lawyer to provide his or her utmost loyalty to one client while simultaneously representing another client in the same matter, to whom the lawyer also owes the same duty of utmost loyalty." She is also skeptical of the purported cost savings of joint representations, contending that such savings are "overshadowed by the burden that will fall on the clients if the attorney is subsequently required to withdraw. In exchange for the possibility of reduced costs, the clients face the possibility of finding new counsel, perhaps on short notice. The clients likely will have to pay new counsel to research some of the same issues the first lawyer was paid to do, and may suffer tactical disadvantages during the time the new attorneys are getting up to speed." *See* Debra Lyn Bassett, *Three's a Crowd: A Proposal to Abolish Joint Representation*, 32 RUTGERS L.J. 387, 437-48, 450 (2001).

3. Multi-Disciplinary Practice

As described earlier, the field of elder law is characterized, in part, by its holistic approach to lawyering, which recognizes that clients' legal needs relate to and interact with their medical, social, and financial needs. In addition, many of the issues on which elder law attorneys provide representation have a social work or health care component. Recognizing this, some elder law attorneys hire social workers, nurses, or other health care professionals to work with them to assess clients' needs and help coordinate services.

Such multi-disciplinary collaborations can take a number of different forms. In some cases, they may involve a single employee performing discrete tasks, such as an assessment of a client's needs or cognitive capacity. In other cases, they may be much more holistic in nature. Elder law attorney Timothy Takacs has described his approach to such collaboration as follows:

> In my office, I have five employees, none of whom is a lawyer. One is a Medicare and health insurance specialist, who has almost 20 years of experience in the field (including working for Medicare), and two are "geriatric care managers," both of whom have extensive health-care backgrounds. One of my geriatric care managers is a registered nurse. I hired my geriatric care managers specifically to address the residential options, quality of care, and quality of life issues that my clients and their families face everyday. Our practice is centered around developing and helping implement the "life care plan" for our clients and their families.

> Besides the elder law attorney, members of the Life Care Plan Team may include a geriatric care manager, nurse, social worker, investment adviser, trust administrator, legal assistant, accountant, and insurance agent.

Timothy L. Takacs, *The Life Care Plan: Integrating a Healthcare-Focused Approach to Meeting the Needs of Your Clients and Families into Your Elder Law Practice*, 16 NAELA Q. 2, 6 (2003).

Elder law attorneys wishing to integrate other professionals into their practice are constrained by the ethical rules governing attorneys. As a general matter, under the American Bar Association's Model Rules of Professional Conduct (MRPC), attorneys may not share legal fees with non-attorneys (*see* MRPC 5.4) and must supervise non-attorney members of a practice (*see* MPRC 5.3). There are continuing efforts underway in the states to permit more collaborative models of interdisciplinary legal practice. Nevertheless, as of the date of publication, the District of Columbia was the only jurisdiction that allowed lawyers to enter into partnerships and fee-sharing relationships with non-lawyers, and the American Bar Association continued to take a position opposing such arrangements.

Elder law attorneys working with professionals from other disciplines also need to be aware of, and sensitive to, how those professionals' ethical codes differ from the ethical codes to which the attorneys are themselves bound. For example, both attorneys' and social workers' ethical codes emphasize the importance of confidentiality, but what triggers a duty to maintain confidentiality, their conceptions of who the client is, and acceptable bases for violating client confidentiality can differ. Moreover, as Professor Paula Galowitz has explained, "There is an inherent tension between a lawyer's and a social worker's ethical responsibilities. The lawyer's responsibility is to advocate zealously for the client's wishes, while the social worker's is to safeguard the client's best interest." Paula Galowitz, *Collaboration Between Lawyers and Social Workers: Re-Examining the Nature and Potential of the Relationship*, 67 FORDHAM L. REV. 2123, 2140 (1999). In addition, in some states social workers are required to report suspected elder abuse to government authorities but attorneys are not. In such states, a social worker's compliance with reporting duties may come at the cost of the attorney's duty of confidentiality, as well as the attorney-client privilege if the social worker and attorney are working together.

4. Elder Mediation

A growing number of elder law attorneys offer "elder mediation" services. Mediation is a form of alternative dispute resolution in which a neutral third party helps individuals or groups come together to address a conflict. The aim is typically to achieve a mutually agreeable resolution to the problem, but mediation may also be viewed as a "success" when it increases mutual understanding even in the absence of a resolution. Elder mediation is a sub-specialty within the field of mediation focused on resolving conflict and problem-solving around aging concerns.

Elder mediation is typically employed in situations in which there is a conflict about an issue of critical importance to an older adult and his or her lifestyle. A common situation in which elder mediation is employed is to bring family members together to work on issues surrounding caregiving and the allocation of caregiving responsibilities for an older family member.

The excerpted article that follows explores some of the concerns that have been raised about elder mediation and the rationale for it.

Jennifer L. Wright, Practical Concerns in Elder Law Mediation

The Hennepin Lawyer (Apr. 2011)

Elder law mediation . . . involves disputes about where an elder lives, what kind of health care and assistance in daily living the elder receives, who makes important decisions for the elder, how the elder's financial resources are managed, and with whom the elder maintains important human contacts. The specific kinds of disputes that may be addressed by elder law mediation include disputes with and among care providers and health care professionals over the type and level of care the elder will receive, disputes about whether the elder will remain at home or enter a nursing home or other long-term care facility, disputes between family members over who will assist the elder with managing finances, disputes over how to address possible financial exploitation of the elder, and disputes over whether a guardianship and/or conservatorship is needed to protect the elder's well-being.

Elder law mediation so defined presents several important concerns that are far less salient in other mediation contexts. First, there are multiple potential barriers to full and equal participation by the elder in the mediation process. For one, there is an imbalance of power inherent in the fact that the stakes for the elder are so uniquely high. The elder is in a situation where the very shape of her life and her ability to determine her own future are at issue. The elder has so much more at stake in the elder law mediation that she may find it difficult to enter into discussion on an equal basis with other participants.

Another characteristic of elder mediation is that the mental capacity of the elder to participate fully in the mediation is virtually always potentially at issue. Concern about the elder's ability to satisfactorily make independent decisions and manage his own life is one of the defining characteristics of elder law mediation. Thus, the mediator in an elder law mediation must be sensitive to both the perception and the reality of diminished cognitive capacity on the part of the elder.

In some situations, the elder may not be able to understand and participate in the mediation process. In those cases, the elder law mediator must have the training and skill to identify the problem and to determine how to deal with it. Will supported decision making be possible, and if so, who can provide such support? Or, is it impossible for the case to be mediated because of the inability of a key party to participate? For this reason, among others, many leaders in the elder law mediation field have insisted that best practice standards require that the elder must be represented in elder law mediation, to ensure that she is able to participate equally.

In addition to concerns about the cognitive ability of elders to participate in elder law mediation, serious attention must be given to the accommodation of physical disabilities. Most mediators are aware, in theory, of the need to accommodate physically disabled parties. However, many mediators are not truly prepared and equipped to fully carry out such accommodation. The odds that a profoundly deaf party will find himself unintentionally excluded from some of the rapid back-and-forth discussions that often develop in a multi-party mediation are high. It takes unceasing care to ensure that elders with communication-related disabilities are fully included in all phases of mediation. In addition, elder law mediators need to be aware of the effects of fatigue, chronic health conditions, and medications on the alertness and participation of elders. Elder law mediations may need to be scheduled based on the elder's periods of maximum energy and alertness at times of day that are not necessarily convenient for other participants. Elder law mediations may need to be scheduled in the elder's home or care facility, rather than in the mediator's office or other "neutral setting." Elder law mediations may require several shorter sessions, rather than one long session. The total time from beginning to end of mediation may therefore be substantially greater. As a result of all these considerations, elder law mediation may often involve more caucused discussions, rather than getting all the parties into one room for big mediation sessions.

Family dynamics may also inhibit full participation by the elder. Elders may be dependent on family members for needed care or financial support. They may be embedded in long-standing patterns of family relationships that make it difficult to speak freely and openly about highly personal matters with their adult children or grandchildren. They may have been raised with cultural expectations that they should not directly assert their own concerns and desires in opposition to those of their family. Sadly, elder maltreatment is most often committed by family members. Elder law mediators must also be alert to the signs and consequences of potential abuse or financial exploitation of a vulnerable adult and must determine and disclose their policies regarding how maltreatment will be handled, including whether it will be reported to adult protection.

The opinions of medical and social service providers generally carry great weight in our society and in elder law mediation. Medical and social service providers are primarily motivated to protect elders from risk. In many cases, professional care providers believe that they can make better decisions for an elder than she can make for herself, particularly when the elder is making decisions that the professionals consider "dangerous," such as an elder at risk of falls choosing to stay in her own home. The right to take risks is a central part of human dignity and autonomy. We allow younger people to take extreme risks just for the thrill of the experience (skydiving, bungee jumping, etc.). Psychological research into the well-being of elders indicates that autonomy and the ability to make one's own decisions is a crucial component of well-being, even for those with diminished cognitive capacity. While medical professionals have specialized knowledge and expertise that give their opinions great weight in determining the risks and benefits of different treatment options, they do not have similar expertise when it comes to deciding what relative value should be given to safety versus autonomy in the life of a particular individual. There is a risk in elder law mediation that the opinions of professional care providers will be given undue weight in limiting the range of an elder's choice.

In addition to serious concerns about the ability of elders to participate fully in the elder law mediation process, there are other concerns that arise in elder law mediation. Any resolution involving elders' health care or finances may have significant consequences for elders' eligibility for public benefits or insurance to pay for health care needs. Mediated agreements may have nonobvious, but very serious, unintended consequences. Medicaid rules in particular are extremely complex and nonintuitive and change frequently. Any resolution that results in the elder's assets, or control over the elder's assets, being transferred to someone else creates the possibility of a "disqualifying transfer," which would make the elder ineligible for medical assistance benefits to pay for long-term care for some period. Since this medical assistance is the long-term care insurer of last resort for middle-class as well as low-income seniors, such ineligibility can have extremely serious consequences for a wide range of elders. Any mediated agreement affecting the assets and care of an elder must be carefully vetted by an elder law expert to avoid such problems.

* * *

Some have concluded that the challenges described above make elder law mediation an option to be avoided. . . .

The potential positive benefits of elder law mediation are also great. The difficult discussions that an elder law mediator can facilitate help elders and their family members face up to some of the unpalatable realities of aging in a supportive environment. Elder law mediation can help to preserve important relationships that may be destroyed by conflict and litigation. Research indicates that maintaining strong social connections is a very important predictor of well-being in old age. Elder law mediation can help to resolve conflicts between elders and care providers, enabling caregiving to continue within a structure that is acceptable to both. Elder law mediation can help people in important relationships improve their ongoing ability to communicate with each other about difficult issues. It can give meaningful voice and participation to elders, to their family members, and to their caregivers.

Through elder law mediation, parties may be able to discuss concerns about an elder's living situation before these concerns grow into a serious emergency. Crisis decision making is often seriously destructive of elders' values and goals for life in old age. Elder law mediation can be a means of connecting to valuable community services and resources available to elders, of which they and their family members may be unaware. Elder law mediation encourages creative problem solving that takes into account the needs of all parties rather than one-size-fits-all solutions through the courts. It provides greater protection of privacy for elders and their families. Elder law mediation can reduce financial costs both to participants and to the court system. . . .

QUESTIONS

1. Imagine you are opening a new elder law practice. What model or models of representation would you adopt? Why? *Cf.* Thomas Caffrey & Mary Wander-Polo, *A Brave New World Awaits: The Elder and Special Needs Practice of the Future*, 9 NAELA J. 115, 129 (2013) (suggesting that elder law firms can increase their market share by providing "multidisciplinary services, including financial and health care management" because "clients perceive value from a one-stop solution to their legal, financial, and life care management").

2. Not all professionals specializing in elder mediation are attorneys. Should they be? What are the advantages or disadvantages of lawyers serving as elder mediators?

C. ETHICAL CHALLENGES OF ELDER LAW PRACTICE

Like other attorneys, elder law practitioners are bound by their state's code of ethics. In almost all states, this code is modeled on the American Bar Association's Model Rules of Professional Conduct (MRPC), which cover a vast range of ethical issues facing attorneys, from conflicts of interest, to contact with unrepresented parties, to political contributions. Some provisions in the Model Rules are *permissive* in that they state what a lawyer may do. Others are *mandatory*, stating what a lawyer must do. Each of the Model Rules is subject to interpretation. Accordingly, each is accompanied by comments that aim to provide guidance to those trying to interpret the rules and apply them in specific situations.

All attorneys need to understand the ethical rules constraining and guiding the practice of law. Lawyers who fail to comply with their state's ethical rules may be subject to discipline, including possible suspension of their licenses or disbarment. Elder law attorneys, however, need to be especially aware of the ethical rules governing their practice. This is because the practice of elder law typically involves an unusually demanding and complex set of ethical challenges. Chief among these are ethical challenges that arise when an attorney interacts with multiple members of a family and those that arise when a client is experiencing—or is suspected of experiencing—dementia or another form of diminished cognitive capacity.

This section therefore focuses on three rules that are of particular importance in the context of an elder law practice: MRPC 1.6, which addresses confidentiality; MRPC 1.7, which addresses conflicts of interest; and MRPC 1.14, which addresses the ethical challenges of working with clients who have diminished cognitive capacity.

1. Maintaining Confidentiality and Avoiding Conflicts of Interest

One of the first concerns of any attorney is to identify his or her client. This is important for many reasons, but two stand out. First, an attorney must clearly identify his or her client because an attorney is ethically bound to maintain certain client confidences. Second, an attorney must clearly identify his or her client because an attorney is ethically and professionally bound to take direction from the client. Therefore, until the attorney knows who the client is, the attorney is largely unable to act.

Elder law attorneys, however, can find this seemingly simple task of identifying the client challenging because they frequently interact with multiple members of a family. Among other reasons, multiple interactions can occur because a family member of the older adult initiates or encourages the older adult to seek legal advice, because a family member of the older adult wants advice as to how to meet the needs of the older adult, or because the older adult is being assisted by a family member.

To address the potential conflict of interest concerns that arise when a family member brings or accompanies an elderly individual to an attorney meeting, the National Academy of Elder Law Attorneys (NAELA) recommends that:

> [T]he attorney should carefully explain why a confidential meeting [with the older adult] is important. Ideally, the attorney should meet with the client or prospective client in private at the earliest possible stage. The attorney should take steps to ensure that the client's wishes are identified and respected. If the client objects to a private meeting, the attorney should explain that such a meeting is necessary because the attorney only represents the client and must have the client's input unencumbered and uninfluenced by others. This is especially true when the family member bringing the client to the meeting is gaining any advantage over other similarly situated family members or when asset transfers are being considered. In the private consultation, the attorney should seek to ensure the absence of direct or indirect pressure on the client to make particular decisions.

NAELA, Aspirational Standards for the Practice of Elder Law with Commentaries (2005), *available at* www.naela.org. NAELA's aspirational standards for elder law attorneys, however, do not require elder law attorneys to always insist on private meetings with clients. Rather, the aspirational standards state that "[i]f the attorney determines that it is clearly not in the client's best interest to meet privately with the attorney, the attorney may allow non-clients (including children) to be present at the initial meeting or throughout the representation." *Id.*

In determining how to appropriately maintain confidences and address potential conflicts of interest when confronted with the challenges that arise from interacting with multiple family members, elder law attorneys are guided by their jurisdiction's code of ethics. While the specific code provisions vary from state to state, many follow the basic approach set forth in the Model Rules.

Below are two of the key model rules guiding attorney behavior in such situations. MRPC 1.6 discusses the duty of confidentiality. MRPC 1.7 addresses conflicts of interest with current clients.

Model Rules of Professional Conduct
Rule 1.6: Confidentiality of Information

(a) A lawyer shall not reveal information relating to the representation of a client unless the client gives informed consent, the disclosure is impliedly authorized in order to carry out the representation or the disclosure is permitted by paragraph (b).

(b) A lawyer may reveal information relating to the representation of a client to the extent the lawyer reasonably believes necessary:

(1) to prevent reasonably certain death or substantial bodily harm;

(2) to prevent the client from committing a crime or fraud that is reasonably certain to result in substantial injury to the financial interests or property of another and in furtherance of which the client has used or is using the lawyer's services;

(3) to prevent, mitigate or rectify substantial injury to the financial interests or property of another that is reasonably certain to result or has resulted from the client's commission of a crime or fraud in furtherance of which the client has used the lawyer's services;

(4) to secure legal advice about the lawyer's compliance with these Rules;

(5) to establish a claim or defense on behalf of the lawyer in a controversy between the lawyer and the client, to establish a defense to a criminal charge or civil claim against the lawyer based upon conduct in which the client was involved, or to respond to allegations in any proceeding concerning the lawyer's representation of the client; or

(6) to comply with other law or a court order.

Model Rules of Professional Conduct
Rule 1.7: Conflict of Interest: Current Clients

(a) Except as provided in paragraph (b), a lawyer shall not represent a client if the representation involves a concurrent conflict of interest. A concurrent conflict of interest exists if:

(1) the representation of one client will be directly adverse to another client; or

(2) there is a significant risk that the representation of one or more clients will be materially limited by the lawyer's responsibilities to another client, a former client or a third person or by a personal interest of the lawyer.

(b) Notwithstanding the existence of a concurrent conflict of interest under paragraph (a), a lawyer may represent a client if:
(1) the lawyer reasonably believes that the lawyer will be able to provide competent and diligent representation to each affected client;
(2) the representation is not prohibited by law;
(3) the representation does not involve the assertion of a claim by one client against another client represented by the lawyer in the same litigation or other proceeding before a tribunal; and
(4) each affected client gives informed consent, confirmed in writing.

Selected comments to Rule 1.7

Interest of Person Paying for a Lawyer's Service
[13] A lawyer may be paid from a source other than the client, including a co-client, if the client is informed of that fact and consents and the arrangement does not compromise the lawyer's duty of loyalty or independent judgment to the client. If acceptance of the payment from any other source presents a significant risk that the lawyer's representation of the client will be materially limited by the lawyer's own interest in accommodating the person paying the lawyer's fee or by the lawyer's responsibilities to a payer who is also a co-client, then the lawyer must comply with the requirements of paragraph (b) before accepting the representation, including determining whether the conflict is consentable and, if so, that the client has adequate information about the material risks of the representation.

Informed Consent
[18] Informed consent requires that each affected client be aware of the relevant circumstances and of the material and reasonably foreseeable ways that the conflict could have adverse effects on the interests of that client.... The information required depends on the nature of the conflict and the nature of the risks involved. When representation of multiple clients in a single matter is undertaken, the information must include the implications of the common representation, including possible effects on loyalty, confidentiality and the attorney-client privilege and the advantages and risks involved. ...

Special Considerations in Common Representation
[29] In considering whether to represent multiple clients in the same matter, a lawyer should be mindful that if the common representation fails because the potentially adverse interests cannot be reconciled, the result can be additional cost, embarrassment and recrimination. Ordinarily, the lawyer will be forced to withdraw from representing all of the clients if the common representation fails. ...

NOTE

Other Model Rules addressing conflicts of interest. In addition to MRPC 1.6 and 1.7, a number of other Model Rules address conflicts of interest. MRPC Rule 1.8 provides specific rules for certain types of potential conflicts (e.g., entering into business transactions with a client, receiving gifts or bequests from a client, providing a client with financial assistance, and engaging in sexual relations with a client). MRPC 1.9 addresses conflicts of interest in relation to former clients, an issue particularly likely to arise for elder law attorneys who have previously represented another member of a prospective client's family. MRPC 1.10 limits the ability of different members of a single law firm to represent parties who have conflicting interests. MRPC 1.11 addresses conflicts of interest for former or current government employees and officers.

QUESTIONS

1. As noted above, NAELA's aspirational standards state that attorneys may allow non-clients to be present during client meetings when they determine that meeting privately is "clearly not in the client's best interest." Under what circumstances might private meetings not be in a client's best interest? Can an attorney determine whether or not a private meeting is in the client's interest without first meeting privately with the client?

2. What are the relative advantages and disadvantages of each of the models of representation described by Professor Collett?

3. To what extent does MRPC 1.7 permit or limit each of the models of representation described by Professor Collett?

4. Professor Bassett argues that the Model Rules do not adequately address the problems raised by joint representation because:

> *The current rules require the attorney to ascertain whether the conflict is consentable, and if so, to obtain informed consent from both clients. . . . In theory, client consent empowers clients to make informed choices. However, client consent is based on erroneous underlying assumptions, which renders consent illusory. Waiver in the joint representation context suffers from three flaws: client understanding, possible coercion, and lawyer self-interest.*
>
> *As an initial matter, most individuals simply do not understand the legal significance of conflicts of interest. . . . Next, . . . [o]ne of life's realities, frequently overlooked by proponents of joint representation, is the potential for consent based on a sliding scale of persuasion. The wife (or husband) who agrees to joint representation at the request of a spouse; the employee who agrees to joint representation at the request of an employer; the criminal defendant who agrees to joint representation at the request of a codefendant—any of these scenarios may involve pressure ranging from subtle understandings to active persuasion to threats of retaliation. Such psychological coercion obviously impacts on a client's free will in consenting to joint representation. Economic coercion is also a factor*

impacting on client consent. Cost is often a powerful motivator regardless of a client's actual financial resources. The opportunity to have legal fees paid by, or shared with, another party may result in a decision in favor of joint representation solely due to financial considerations. Finally, the lawyer's self-interest in representing both clients provides an incentive for the lawyer to encourage clients to waive any conflict. If the lawyer declines the representation, the lawyer may have lost income both from that matter and from any future matters for those clients. Thus, the lawyer will be motivated to explain the situation in such a manner that the clients will waive the conflict and consent to joint representation.

Debra Lyn Bassett, *Three's a Crowd: A Proposal to Abolish Joint Representation*, 32 RUTGERS L.J. 387, 440-41 (2001) (internal formatting omitted). Do you share Bassett's concerns? Why or why not?

PROBLEMS

1. Anne and her husband Tim, both 72, have made an appointment with you at your law office. Anne has just been diagnosed with Stage 3 breast cancer. She and Tim are both concerned about whether Tim will be able to afford to remain in their home if she dies. They want you to advise them about what rights Tim has with regard to Anne's pension and Social Security benefits. They also want you to help them write new wills. What ethical concerns does this situation raise for you? How would you proceed? Why?

2. After his wife of over 50 years died two years ago, Fred, 82, sold his home and moved in with his daughter, Darla, Darla's husband Henry, and Darla's two children. Darla brings Fred to your law office, and explains that Fred wants to write a new will. Fred's previous will split his estate equally among his three children. Darla tells you that Fred has changed his mind and wants to leave the vast majority of his estate to Darla and Henry. How would you proceed? Why?

3. According to your administrative assistant, your next appointment is with Betty Jackson, a potential new client. When you open your office door to greet Betty, you see two women sitting in the waiting area. When you ask which one is Betty, the younger of the two rises, holds out her hand, and says: "Hi, I'm Susan. This is my mother, Betty." She smiles and warmly gestures to the older woman. How would you proceed? What specific language would you use?

4. Melinda is a 79-year-old woman who was widowed three years ago after 55 years of marriage. She is increasingly lonely living alone in the four-bedroom colonial home in which she raised her children. In addition, although she does not wish to move, she is finding it difficult to maintain the house on her own. She also is finding the layout of the house problematic; her bedroom is on the second floor and climbing the stairs up to it is sometimes painful due to a hip injury.

Melinda has three children: (1) a daughter named Laura who is a successful management consultant living in a city 500 miles away; (2) a son named Steve from whom she is estranged; and (3) a younger daughter named Helen. Helen was a stay-at-home mother until her divorce ten years ago. Since the divorce, she has worked part time as a teacher's aide but has had trouble making ends meet. Melinda, Laura, and Helen have been talking about how to address Melinda's living situation. They have agreed that it makes sense for Helen to move in with Melinda—that way, Helen would be able to save the money she has been paying to rent a condo nearby, and Melinda would have company and assistance. Thankful that her sister will be providing Melinda with care, Laura has offered to pay to renovate the house in order to turn a downstairs den into a new bedroom for Melinda so that she will no longer have to deal with the stairs on a daily basis. Helen and Laura, however, want to be sure that they inherit the house when Melinda eventually dies. They feel that Steve has shirked his responsibilities as a son and doesn't deserve to inherit. Melinda has said that this seems fair since Helen and Laura are both involved in her life, and Steve will not even return her phone calls.

Laura calls you to set up an appointment to discuss the situation, and to obtain your assistance in making the "necessary legal arrangements." She arrives at the appointment with her mother and sister.

a. What are the initial challenges this situation might present?

b. What form or forms of representation would be appropriate? Ethical?

2. Representing Clients with Actual or Suspected Capacity Concerns

As discussed earlier in this chapter, an individual's *cognitive capacity* is his or her physical ability to think and reason. Because the rate and severity of cognitive declines and disabilities increase as older adults age, elder law attorneys frequently find themselves representing individuals who either have diminished cognitive capacity or who are suspected of having diminished cognitive capacity. This can create significant practical and ethical challenges. Thus, elder law attorneys can find themselves asking a number of critically important questions, including:

▪ Does my client have the capacity to hire me?

▪ Does my client have the capacity to provide me with direction?

▪ Does my client have the capacity to do specific tasks (e.g., execute a will, sign a deed, marry)?

▪ When can or should I act to protect my clients if they cannot or will not do so themselves?

▪ What kinds of protective action can I take?

Such concerns, of course, are not exclusive to attorneys practicing elder law—clients of all ages can have cognitive deficits. Nor is this a problem raised in most elder law representations. While the incidence of cognitive disability does increase with age, the majority of people in the United States with cognitive disabilities (57%) are under the age of 65. That said, as described earlier in this chapter, the incidence of dementia and other cognitive impairments does increase with age. Thus, elder law attorneys frequently encounter such concerns and need to be well prepared to handle them.

a. The Challenge of Assessing Capacity

Elder law attorneys quickly learn that, despite the fact that lawyers typically do not see themselves as being in the business of assessing capacity, doing so is an unavoidable part of the practice of law. First and foremost, a lawyer must determine whether a prospective client has the capacity to retain an attorney. This assessment is rarely explicit or acknowledged. Yet every time a lawyer ethically agrees to represent a new client, the attorney has made a judgment that the client can agree to the representation (i.e., a judgment that the client has the capacity to enter into a lawyer-client relationship). Moreover, when working with a client on a particular matter, the attorney must make a judgment that the client has the capacity to make whatever decisions are being made with regards to that matter. For example, an attorney who has drafted a client's will and is now helping the client to execute that will, must make a judgment that the client has testamentary capacity (i.e., the capacity to execute a will).

Once attorneys recognize that they cannot avoid assessing their clients' cognitive capacities, the question becomes how to do so. Determining whether a client has capacity can be difficult because an individual's decision-making capacity may depend on the context in which the decision is being made. Capacity may vary based on temporal factors such as an individual's temporary medical condition, the individual's setting (some clients may be less confused in more familiar settings), or even the time of day. It may also vary based on domain—that is, the type of decision to be made. Through statutory provisions and common law rulings, states have developed different capacity requirements for different transactions. For example, states generally require a higher level of capacity to enter into more complex transactions; therefore, in many states, the capacity required to enter into a valid contract is higher than that required to execute a will. Where a particular capacity threshold is not specified, the default question tends to be: "Does the individual understand the nature and consequences of the decision he or she is making?"

It is advisable for elder law attorneys to have a system in place for assessing client capacity that is both dependable and consistently applied. However, there is no single, agreed-upon approach to capacity assessment of clients. The National Academy of Elder Law Attorneys (NAELA) has recognized this, and its "Aspirational Standards" for elder law attorneys state simply that an elder law attorney should: "Develop[] and utilize[] appropriate skills and processes for making and documenting preliminary assessments of client capacity to undertake the specific legal matters at hand" and "adapt[] the interview environment, timing of meetings, communications and decision-making processes to maximize the client's capacities."

The most common technique attorneys use when assessing capacity is to simply make a holistic judgment based on their personal experience, knowledge, and "gut" impression. In recent years, however, there has been a proliferation of interest both in the United States and abroad in the development of measurement instruments that lawyers and other professionals working with older clients with diminished capacity can use to assess the capacity of their clients. This has led to the development of assessment guides and tools for attorneys. Administering a cognitive assessment tool with clients, however, creates some significant concerns. Applying the tool to all clients is likely to be tiresome, intrusive, and unwelcome. Yet when the tool is applied selectively, the tool itself may later come to be used as evidence that capacity was questionable if a third party tries to challenge a decision or document (e.g., a will or a contract) that the client made. In addition, standardized cognitive screens and instruments are unlikely to be tailored to the particular type of capacity at issue, the capacity standard in the jurisdiction, and the client (who may have particular physical, psychological, or cultural characteristics which make him or her ill-suited to such evaluation).

An alternative approach is for attorneys to work in an interdisciplinary manner with medical professionals trained in capacity assessment. For example, suppose a client asks an attorney to help them rewrite a will. The attorney, following his or her normal procedure, questions the client about his or her family, whom he or she wants to inherit, and why. The client gives a variety of answers, some of which appear internally inconsistent to the attorney. The attorney might involve a medical professional to assess the capacity of the client before determining how to proceed. Because legal capacity is domain specific (i.e., it depends on the type of decision to be made), attorneys who take this approach need to be sure to provide the clinician with a clear definition of the level or type of capacity they are concerned with (e.g., does my client have the capacity to execute a will in a state which requires X, Y, and Z to execute a will?).

Attorneys who call on other professionals to assist with capacity assessment need to appreciate—and to explain to those colleagues—the difference between legal conceptions of capacity and clinical ones. In assessing capacity, clinicians often speak of a spectrum of cognitive capacity, from more to less capable. Legal capacity, by comparison, is an all-or-nothing construct: either an individual does or does not have the capacity to enter into a legally binding decision at a particular time under particular circumstances.

NOTES

1. *Distinguishing capacity challenges from communication challenges.* The elder law practitioner must be careful not to assume that a client lacks capacity to make a decision simply because he or she has difficulty communicating that decision. *Cf.* Gerry Beyer, *The Communicationally Challenged Testator*, Est. Plan. Dev. for Tex. Prof. (Apr. 2009) (discussing how attorneys can work with communicationally impaired testators to avoid subsequent will challenges).

2. *Consequences of focusing on capacity.* Professor Howard Eglit warns that by focusing on questions of cognitive capacity, the literature addressing the relationship between lawyers and their elderly clients may mistakenly lead lawyers to think that capacity is a more frequent concern than it actually is. *See* Howard Eglit, Elders on Trial: Age and Ageism in the American Legal System 98 (2004).

3. *Mini-Mental State Examination.* The Folstein Mini-Mental State Examination (MMSE) is a short, 30-point test commonly employed to screen for diminished cognitive capacity, especially dementia. Among other things, the MMSE asks subjects to identify the place and day, count backwards by sevens, recall three words, follow directions, and draw a figure. Subjects are given a score based on the accuracy of their answers. The lower the score, the greater the likelihood of diminished cognitive capacity, and the greater the likely severity of the impairment. Although the MMSE can be a useful screening tool, it is not a substitute for a thorough capacity assessment by a trained professional, and there has been much concern raised about over-reliance on MMSE scores.

QUESTIONS

1. States require different thresholds of capacity for different decisions. For example, in New York, "A person has capacity to make health care decisions if he or she has the ability to understand and appreciate the nature and consequences of health care decisions." N.Y. Pub. Health Law §2980 (2013). Individuals can have a guardian appointed to make decisions for them, including health care decisions, if they are "unable to provide for personal needs and/or property management," and "cannot adequately understand and appreciate the nature and consequences of such inability." N.Y. Mental Hygiene Law §81.02 (2013). Why might New York have different capacity standards for these two related issues? Should it?

2. As noted above, it is often said that the default standard for capacity is: "Does the individual understand the nature and consequences of the decision he or she is making." Suppose your client comes to you and says he wants you to represent him in selling his share of the family farm to his brother. What specifically do you think he would need to understand in order to have legal capacity to enter into that transaction? Why?

> ## EXERCISE 2.1
>
> Consider the Capacity Worksheet for Lawyers found on pages 23-26 of a guide for attorneys published by the American Bar Association Commission on Law and Aging and the American Psychological Association (the guide can be found at www.apa.org/pi/aging/resources/guides/diminished-capacity.pdf).
>
> If you were working as an elder law attorney, would you use this tool as part of your practice? Why or why not? What if you were working as a personal injury attorney?

b. The Challenge of Working with Clients with Limited Capacity

As a general matter, as set forth in MRPC 1.2, an attorney is required to take direction from his or her client and abide by the client's decisions. As set forth in MRPC 1.4, an attorney must also, as a general matter, communicate and consult with the client so that the client can make informed decisions about matters on which the client is being represented. Elder law attorneys, however, frequently work with clients who have difficulty providing such direction and difficulty making informed decisions because they have some level of diminished cognitive capacity.

As a practical matter, therefore, the elder law attorney should be alert to the possibility of diminished capacity and prepared to work with clients to maximize their capacity. Since (as discussed in the previous sub-section) a client's capacity to make and articulate decisions may be influenced by a variety of factors such as the time of day, the physical setting he or she is in, whether he or she is well rested, and his or her chronic or temporary medical conditions, altering such factors can have the effect of reducing or increasing the client's capacity. Thus, attorneys may be able to overcome a client's decision-making challenges by taking affirmative steps to maximize the client's capacity.

One way the attorney may be able to maximize the client's capacity is by structuring client meetings in a place and at a time where the client is at his or her highest functional level. For example, if the client is most alert and focused in the morning, the attorney may choose to schedule client meetings exclusively at that time of day. Similarly, if the client functions at his or her highest level at home, the attorney may arrange to meet with the client at the client's place of residence.

Another way the attorney can maximize the client's capacity is by minimizing factors that unnecessarily tax the client's cognitive capacity. For example, speaking slowly, reducing background noise, providing well-lit meeting spaces, and preparing documents in large fonts can reduce distractions and frustrations for clients with visual or auditory challenges. Thus, by accommodating clients' physical needs, the attorney may help maximize clients' cognitive abilities.

Even with such efforts, however, sometimes an attorney will reach the conclusion (perhaps as the result of a formal capacity assessment) that his or her client's capacity is sufficiently diminished such that the client can no longer provide the level of direction or informed consent typically required of a client. The attorney may reach this conclusion at the onset of his or her representation, or during the course of the representation as elder law attorneys frequently work with clients whose capacity is readily declining. The question then becomes how to proceed. Should the attorney continue to consult with the client and follow the client's instructions? Should the attorney act independently to protect the client or his or her interests? Can the attorney do either? The answers to these questions are guided by MRPC 1.14. As of 2012, all but two states had adopted MRPC 1.14.

What follows is the full text of MRPC 1.14, key comments to that rule, and a Washington state case considering whether an attorney's behavior with regard to his elderly client was permissible under Rule 1.14.

MODEL RULES OF PROFESSIONAL CONDUCT
RULE 1.14: CLIENT WITH DIMINISHED CAPACITY

(a) When a client's capacity to make adequately considered decisions in connection with a representation is diminished, whether because of minority, mental impairment or for some other reason, the lawyer shall, as far as reasonably possible, maintain a normal client-lawyer relationship with the client.

(b) When the lawyer reasonably believes that the client has diminished capacity, is at risk of substantial physical, financial or other harm unless action is taken and cannot adequately act in the client's own interest, the lawyer may take reasonably necessary protective action, including consulting with individuals or entities that have the ability to take action to protect the client and, in appropriate cases, seeking the appointment of a guardian ad litem, conservator or guardian.

(c) Information relating to the representation of a client with diminished capacity is protected by Rule 1.6. When taking protective action pursuant to paragraph (b), the lawyer is impliedly authorized under Rule 1.6(a) to reveal information about the client, but only to the extent reasonably necessary to protect the client's interests.

Selected Comments to Rule 1.14

Taking Protective Action
[5] If a lawyer reasonably believes that a client is at risk of substantial physical, financial or other harm unless action is taken, and that a normal client-lawyer relationship cannot be maintained as provided in paragraph (a) because the client lacks sufficient capacity to communicate or to make

adequately considered decisions in connection with the representation, then paragraph (b) permits the lawyer to take protective measures deemed necessary. Such measures could include: consulting with family members, using a reconsideration period to permit clarification or improvement of circumstances, using voluntary surrogate decisionmaking tools such as durable powers of attorney or consulting with support groups, professional services, adult-protective agencies or other individuals or entities that have the ability to protect the client. In taking any protective action, the lawyer should be guided by such factors as the wishes and values of the client to the extent known, the client's best interests and the goals of intruding into the client's decisionmaking autonomy to the least extent feasible, maximizing client capacities and respecting the client's family and social connections.

[6] In determining the extent of the client's diminished capacity, the lawyer should consider and balance such factors as: the client's ability to articulate reasoning leading to a decision, variability of state of mind and ability to appreciate consequences of a decision; the substantive fairness of a decision; and the consistency of a decision with the known long-term commitments and values of the client. In appropriate circumstances, the lawyer may seek guidance from an appropriate diagnostician.

[7] If a legal representative has not been appointed, the lawyer should consider whether appointment of a guardian ad litem, conservator or guardian is necessary to protect the client's interests. Thus, if a client with diminished capacity has substantial property that should be sold for the client's benefit, effective completion of the transaction may require appointment of a legal representative. . . . In many circumstances, however, appointment of a legal representative may be more expensive or traumatic for the client than circumstances in fact require. . . .

Disclosure of the Client's Condition

[8] Disclosure of the client's diminished capacity could adversely affect the client's interests. For example, raising the question of diminished capacity could, in some circumstances, lead to proceedings for involuntary commitment. Information relating to the representation is protected by Rule 1.6. Therefore, unless authorized to do so, the lawyer may not disclose such information. When taking protective action pursuant to paragraph (b), the lawyer is impliedly authorized to make the necessary disclosures, even when the client directs the lawyer to the contrary. Nevertheless, given the risks of disclosure, paragraph (c) limits what the lawyer may disclose in consulting with other individuals or entities or seeking the appointment of a legal representative. At the very least, the lawyer should determine whether it is likely that the person or entity consulted with will act adversely to the client's interests before discussing matters related to the client. The lawyer's position in such cases is an unavoidably difficult one.

Emergency Legal Assistance

[9] In an emergency where the health, safety or a financial interest of a person with seriously diminished capacity is threatened with imminent and irreparable harm, a lawyer may take legal action on behalf of such a person even though the person is unable to establish a client-lawyer relationship or to make or express considered judgments about the matter, when the person or another acting in good faith on that person's behalf has consulted with the lawyer. Even in such an emergency, however, the lawyer should not act unless the lawyer reasonably believes that the person has no other lawyer, agent or other representative available. The lawyer should take legal action on behalf of the person only to the extent reasonably necessary to maintain the status quo or otherwise avoid imminent and irreparable harm. A lawyer who undertakes to represent a person in such an exigent situation has the same duties under these Rules as the lawyer would with respect to a client.

[10] A lawyer who acts on behalf of a person with seriously diminished capacity in an emergency should keep the confidences of the person as if dealing with a client, disclosing them only to the extent necessary to accomplish the intended protective action. The lawyer should disclose to any tribunal involved and to any other counsel involved the nature of his or her relationship with the person. The lawyer should take steps to regularize the relationship or implement other protective solutions as soon as possible. Normally, a lawyer would not seek compensation for such emergency actions taken.

In re Disciplinary Proceeding Against Eugster

209 P.3d 435 (Wash. 2009)

CHAMBERS, J.

Stephen K. Eugster practiced law for 34 years without a history of discipline. Then the Washington State Bar Association (WSBA) charged Eugster with nine counts of attorney misconduct based on Eugster's filing a guardianship petition against his former client without any investigation as to her alleged incompetency and failing to abide by the objectives of the representation. The hearing officer and Disciplinary Board of the Washington State Bar Association (Board) concluded Eugster violated eight current and former Rules of Professional Conduct (RPC). The hearing officer recommended disbarment. A unanimous Board agreed but amended several of the hearing officer's findings of fact.

Eugster challenges 12 findings of fact. He also argues the Board erred in recommending disbarment because his actions were defensible under former RPC 1.13 (1985) and because the Board ignored mitigating factors that would lessen his sanction. The WSBA argues the court should affirm the findings of fact and conclusions of law and disbar Eugster. We conclude that Eugster's misconduct does not merit disbarment but suspend him for 18 months and impose additional conditions.

FACTS

Due to the way this case has been framed, we find it necessary to discuss the facts in some detail in order to properly resolve the issues presented. Marion Stead hired Eugster in June 2004. When Mrs. Stead contacted Eugster, she was 87 and had recently moved into the Parkview Assisted Living Facility after the death of her husband, John. This was not the first time Eugster worked for the Stead family. In the early 1990s, Eugster represented Mrs. Stead's only child, Roger Samuels in the dissolution of his marriage. According to the evidence submitted by the WSBA, Mrs. Stead's objective in contacting Eugster in June 2004 was to remove Roger from his position of control over her affairs and to assist her with estate planning.

In 2003, before John's death, the Steads had executed new wills drafted by attorney David Hellenthal. Under the Hellenthal wills, Roger would inherit the Stead home and his daughter, Emilie, would be the beneficiary of a residual trust. The Hellenthal wills also created a supplemental needs trust for the surviving spouse and named Roger as trustee. As trustee of the supplemental needs trust, Roger had discretion to make or withhold payments so long as it did not disqualify Mrs. Stead from any other assistance. The wills specified the trust was irrevocable and could not, absent a court order, be changed.

In late 2003, dissatisfied with the Hellenthal wills, Mrs. Stead contacted attorney Summer Stahl. Stahl changed the beneficiary of a life insurance policy from Roger back to Mrs. Stead but performed no other services. When Roger discovered that Mrs. Stead had hired Stahl, he became "very upset." Roger saw his mother's consultations with Stahl as a betrayal of family trust and questioned her competence. In January 2004, Roger had Dr. Duane Green, a psychologist, examine his mother for testamentary capacity. Dr. Green noted an "'interpersonal issue between Ms. Stead and her son'" and generally observed that she seemed "'desperate,' as she had no access to funds." Dr. Green concluded Mrs. Stead was upset over the illness of her husband but had testamentary capacity.

Upon John's death in February 2004, Roger became the personal representative of John's estate and acted as trustee of the supplemental needs trust for the benefit of Mrs. Stead. Roger also assumed control over the payment of bills because he did not believe his mother was capable of doing so. During this time the relationship between Roger and his mother continued to deteriorate. From the record it appears that Mrs. Stead felt Roger was manipulating her estate and denying her adequate funds so that he could preserve more for himself and his daughter after her death. In particular, Mrs. Stead felt that she had an adequate estate and did not like the idea of being forced to receive Medicaid benefits and not being permitted to have sufficient spending money. Mrs. Stead and her son's relationship became even more strained as Roger continued to refuse her requests for money. Mrs. Stead hoped removing her son from authority over her affairs would help mend their relationship.

In June 2004, Mrs. Stead hired Eugster to "short circuit" Roger's control over her affairs and also to retrieve certain items of personal property from Roger. Eugster had Mrs. Stead revise her estate planning scheme by creating a revocable living trust for her and recommending that she be her own trustee. On June 30, 2004, Eugster wrote to Mrs. Stead saying, "It would be my recommendation that if you like the estate plan which I have drafted for you, that you continue as the trustee of your estate with perhaps help and direction from me." Mrs. Stead was named the trustee with Eugster serving as successor trustee and Roger as secondary successor trustee. To protect Mrs. Stead consistent with the existing testamentary trust and consistent with her desire that Roger not control her finances, Eugster was given power of attorney both generally and for health care. Eugster contends he reluctantly agreed to so serve as representative and successor trustee after expressing concerns in a letter to Mrs. Stead. Roger served as successor to Eugster in both roles. Eugster testified that installing Roger as second successor trustee enabled Eugster to monitor Roger and prevent him from doing anything untoward against Mrs. Stead's estate without going through Eugster.

In July 2004, Eugster met with Roger to discuss the supplemental needs trust created by John's will. He also consulted with Mrs. Stead's financial planner regarding her suspicion that the supplemental needs trust was overfunded. Eugster made preparations to sell the Stead family home. As to recovering Mrs. Stead's personal property, Eugster located the items she requested but assured her by letter that Roger was keeping them safe. In August, Eugster wrote Mrs. Stead to assure her of Roger's good intentions toward her and recommended Roger resume control over her affairs:

> Roger has been a good and dutiful son to you. I have to be honest about this. You can be proud of Roger. He is not acting to protect himself or to take things from you. He has been acting to ensure that you are taken care of, your bills are paid, your assets are protected, and that you do not have to have unwanted concerns for your welfare as you grow older.
>
> Frankly, you should be very proud of Roger.
>
> . . . .
>
> But, I think you should give serious thought to making Roger the successor trustee to your Trust and the person holding your power of attorney.

In September 2004, Mrs. Stead received another letter from Eugster, suggesting the two of them meet and include Roger. Although Mrs. Stead did not communicate her displeasure to Eugster, it is clear from the record that she was not happy with his response. She responded by seeking the counsel of another attorney, Andrew Braff, who testified that Mrs. Stead wanted to know whether Eugster was representing her or Roger. On September 9, 2004, Braff wrote Eugster notifying him that Braff now represented Mrs. Stead and explicitly revoking Eugster's power of attorney. Eugster responded on September 13, 2004, by letter stating:

> I do not believe that Marion R. Stead is competent. A guardianship should be established for her person and her estate or at least her es[t]ate. Please be advised that I do not recognize that you have been retained to represent her or that the revocation of power of attorney is effective.

Braff then sent a letter dated September 17, 2004, informing Eugster that his "services as Marion Stead's attorney are terminated, and Mrs. Stead wants her files forwarded to this office." In addition, the letter stated "Marion Stead fully expects any and all communications with you to remain confidential and not to be passed on to Roger Samuels." Braff also asked Eugster to advise him of any changes in Marion's competence since the execution of her trust in July where witnesses testified she was of sound mind. Around the same time, Mrs. Stead removed Eugster as successor trustee of her trust and named Stephen Trefts, doing business as Northwest Trustee and Management Services instead.

Eugster states that he believed Mrs. Stead to be a vulnerable senior and that he decided to take action when he learned that Mrs. Stead had hired Trefts. Under the durable general power of attorney prepared by Braff, Northwest Trustee and Management Services was entitled to reimbursement for all costs and expenses and "shall be entitled to receive at least annually, without court approval, reasonable compensation for services performed on the principal's behalf." On October 8, 2004, Trefts informed Roger that Mrs. Stead had resigned as trustee and had named Trefts as successor. Braff and Trefts also attempted to get Roger, as trustee of John Stead's Testamentary trust, to pay $2,000 per month to them for "one-half of her support." Eugster deemed the requested payment improper under the special needs trust.

On September 27, 2004, Eugster petitioned the court to appoint a guardian for Mrs. Stead. Eugster filed the guardianship action pursuant to former RPC 1.13, which provided in part: "(b) When the lawyer reasonably believes that the client cannot adequately act in the client's own interest, a lawyer may seek the appointment of a guardian or take other protective action with respect to a client." Eugster signed his name on the line marked "Petitioner/Attorney" and represented that he was the current attorney for Mrs. Stead. Roger served as copetitioner at the behest of Eugster, and Roger provided some of the information for the petition. Eugster disclosed to Roger his belief that Mrs. Stead lacked competence. Roger eventually hired an attorney to represent him in the guardianship proceeding.

The petition listed Mrs. Stead's personal and financial information, and characterized Mrs. Stead as unable to manage her person and estate and that she had difficulty monitoring her medications, investments, and expenses. It also described Mrs. Stead as "delusional" because she believed "her son Roger Samuels is somehow out to take advantage of her when this is certainly not the case." In the petition, Roger was nominated to act as Mrs. Stead's guardian. The petition for appointment of a guardian was served on Mrs. Stead in the common room of Parkview, which humiliated her.

Eugster filed the petition based upon his personal judgment without conducting any formal investigation into Mrs. Stead's medical or psychological state. There is no evidence Eugster consulted Mrs. Stead's healthcare providers or talked with people in the Parkview community. Eugster testified that Mrs. Stead had told him she had seen a doctor in the last six months for a "sanity test" and was aware that she had been examined by Dr. Green before his representation began. Three months before he filed the petition for appointment of a guardian for Mrs. Stead, Eugster had Mrs. Stead sign a new trust, powers of attorney, and a will he had prepared, indicating he had no concerns about her testamentary capacity at that point. The last date that either Eugster or Roger personally talked to Mrs. Stead was on August 3, 2004, nearly two months before filing the petition.

Eugster offered evidence to support his contention that he at all times was motivated to act on behalf of his client's best interest and not to control her trust. According to Eugster, he believed that his client was elderly, vulnerable, and unable to understand her financial affairs, and perhaps being taken advantage of. He tells us he felt an obligation as her attorney to protect her. She was nearly 88 years old when she contacted Eugster. She was confused about her rights under a complex estate plan, and she did not like the plan created by Hellenthal. Eugster sought to develop a plan to address her concerns, including determining whether there was a legitimate basis for those concerns. Eugster argues Mrs. Stead's desire to contest her late husband's will, her frequent and repetitive inconsequential communications with Eugster's office, and her continued lack of understanding of how her bills were being paid under the irrevocable special needs trust all support his contention.

Eugster appeared before a judge seeking appointment of a guardian on October 19, 2004. He assured the court he had reviewed the ethical issues involved with him seeking to appoint a guardian. He told the court he believed his actions were ethically viable, and the court asked Eugster to brief the issue. Eugster did not supply a brief but instead, two days later, declined his power of attorney.

By letter dated October 21, 2004, Eugster purported to decline his service as successor trustee over Mrs. Stead's trust and as attorney in fact. Trefts replied, stating Eugster's declination was unnecessary given that Mrs. Stead had terminated Eugster's services and amended the trust to appoint Trefts as successor trustee.

On October 26, 2004, the guardian ad litem (GAL) appointed to evaluate Mrs. Stead concluded she was not suffering from any incapacity and was capable of handling her own affairs. He noted Mrs. Stead's strained relationship and distrust of Roger. The GAL concluded Mrs. Stead did not need a guardian but, if the court did appoint one, the guardian should not be Roger.

On November 17, 2004, Eugster withdrew his signature from the guardianship petition. By stipulation of the parties, the court dismissed the guardianship petition on February 1, 2005. Mrs. Stead paid $13,500 to defend herself in the guardianship action.

* * *

CHALLENGES TO FINDINGS

Eugster challenges . . . the original and amended findings of fact as "confusing, incomplete, misleading or erroneous," and as speculative and not supported by substantial evidence. . . .

Many challenges focus on Eugster's view of Mrs. Stead's objective in retaining him. For example, Eugster argues that it was not contrary to Mrs. Stead's objectives to name Roger as her guardian as she had nominated him as such under her previous will. . . . Eugster also challenges several findings based upon his view that he was motivated to file the guardianship petition out of his concern about the potential exploitation of a vulnerable adult client. . . . However, we note that neither do the findings conclude, nor does the WSBA contend, that Eugster did not subjectively believe that Mrs. Stead was incompetent. They conclude only that Eugster failed to make a reasonable investigation into Mrs. Stead's competency before filing the guardianship petition and that Eugster acted with knowledge and intent to control the estate. . . .

Additionally, Eugster contends that he did not disclose Mrs. Stead's confidential communications but rather based his statements in the guardianship petition on his general observations—observations he believes should have been obvious to anyone. However, the guardianship petition prepared and signed by Eugster did contain personal information about Mrs. Stead including her address, date of birth, a generalized description of her health and medications, and a list of her assets and the approximate value of those assets. It is unlikely Eugster would have such personal information unless she had provided it to him in connection with his activities as her lawyer.

While the evidence may have well supported Eugster's interpretations, the hearing officer and the Board arrived at different conclusions. Those conclusions are supported by substantial evidence. . . .

SANCTIONS

* * *

. . . Eugster's misconduct was serious. Eugster's most serious act of misconduct was to file a petition for the appointment of a guardian alleging that Mrs. Stead was incompetent with virtually no investigation. He acted almost entirely upon his own subjective judgment. As appropriately described by the hearing officer:

> Ms. Stead wrote in a sworn statement in the guardianship she believed
> Mr. Eugster was taking the action for his financial gain. Mr. Eugster

proffered a finding of fact that he took the actions because he knew best. This lack of understanding of the lawyer client relationship is telling. A lawyer is hired to help people avoid or solve problems, they serve at the pleasure of those who employ them. We are servants, not masters. We can cajole, wheedle, debate, and try to persuade, [but] we shall not substitute our judgment for the client's. . . .

In filing the petition for guardianship, Eugster breached his duty to maintain his client's confidences, used confidences to take action directly contrary to his client's interests, and created a nightmare for his client who had to spend $13,500 defending a petition to declare her incompetent brought by her former lawyer in whom she had placed her trust. However, Eugster's misconduct was the first in a long career. It involved only one client in one legal proceeding and lasted for approximately two months before he took steps to mitigate his actions. Looking at his misconduct in context, the duties breached, his state of mind and the harm or potential harm to his client and the legal profession [and aggravating and mitigating factors], we find the appropriate . . . sanction to be suspension.

* * *

SUSPENSION

Generally, when we apply the sanction of suspension, we start with a minimum of six months. However, given the seriousness of Eugster's misconduct, the duties breached, the findings that he acted with knowledge and intent, the seriousness of the injury or potential injury, and four aggravating factors and only one mitigating factor, we conclude a suspension for 18 months is the appropriate sanction. Eugster should also pay restitution to Mrs. Stead's estate in the amount of $13,500.

While not condoning Eugster's actions in any way, we are concerned that this matter might send the wrong message to lawyers who represent the elderly—whether they specialize in elder law or are general practitioners who have represented a family or a client for many years. Issues of a client's competency arise in many forms. However, one scenario which is regrettably not uncommon is for a person of advanced years to fall under the influence of a friend, neighbor, or distant family member. It may come to the attention of a lawyer that an impaired client has fallen under such influence. Often, the friend or distant family member has taken the client to his or her own lawyer who has prepared a new will cutting out other family members and frustrating careful estate planning. Under such circumstances, if the lawyer reasonably believes that her client is suffering diminished capacity and is under undue influence, the lawyer may take protective action under RPC 1.14 without fear of provoking charges of ethical misconduct by the WSBA seeking disbarment. A lawyer's decision to have her client declared incompetent is a serious act that should be taken only after an appropriate investigation and careful, thoughtful deliberation.

We emphasize that Eugster's actions are distinguishable. First, Eugster failed to make any reasonable inquiry into Mrs. Stead's competency. Second, he knew or had information available to him to suggest Mrs. Stead had a "sanity" or mental status exam and was determined to be competent within six months of filing the guardianship petition. Third, it seems uncontroverted that Eugster believed Mrs. Stead was competent just months before he filed the guardianship petition, when she signed the estate planning documents Eugster prepared for her. Finally, Eugster fails to explain why his epiphany that his client was incompetent seems to have occurred on the very day he discovered that she had retained new counsel and wanted to discharge him. Lawyers who act reasonably under RPC 1.14 are not subject to discipline. Eugster did not.

CONCLUSION

Eugster acted knowingly and with intent with respect to the consequences when he refused to turn over his client's files and important papers as requested and when he filed a guardianship petition to have his client or former client declared incompetent. In so doing he violated seven ethical duties causing actual and potential harm to his client and the profession for which he is suspended from the practice of law for 18 months and ordered to pay restitution to the estate of Mrs. Stead in the sum of $13,500....

FAIRHURST, J. (dissenting).
    ... The majority's analysis ignores that Stephen K. Eugster failed to abide by Mrs. Marion Stead's objectives and filed a guardianship petition that he knew lacked any factual or legal basis against Mrs. Stead, a vulnerable victim. If successful, the guardianship petition would have financially benefited Eugster through attorney fees, but instead, it ended up costing Mrs. Stead $13,500 and her relationship with her son.... The only conclusion that can be drawn from our well-settled sanction analysis and precedent is Eugster should be disbarred. I dissent....

NOTES

1. *Relationship to Model Rules.* Washington Rule 1.14, discussed in *Eugster*, is identical to MRPC 1.14.

2. *Overview of guardianship.* As described in the preceding opinion, attorney Eugster filed a petition for guardianship over Mrs. Stead. As discussed at length in Chapter 4, guardianship is a process by which a court appoints a third party to make decisions for a person who is partially or fully incapacitated. It is generally agreed that guardianship should be considered a procedure of last resort because imposition of guardianship strips an individual of the legal right to make decisions for him or herself.

QUESTIONS

1. As the above excerpts indicate, the touchstone of Rule 1.14 is that the attorney is to maintain, to the extent reasonably possible, "a normal client-lawyer relationship." What is a normal client-lawyer relationship?

2. Under what conditions would it have been permissible for attorney Eugster to petition for guardianship over Mrs. Stead?

PROBLEMS

1. Carla, 89, lives alone in a two-story home on the outskirts of town. You have been Carla's attorney for nearly ten years, helping her with a variety of real estate issues. Last week, Carla came to your office and told you that she thinks she signed some papers a week earlier and wondered if you had them. You tell her that the last time you saw her was nine months ago and that no papers were signed then. You inquire about the "papers." She says, "I think they gave away my house." You inquire further, but she is unable to say why she thinks they gave away her house, why she signed them, or with whom she might have been when she signed them. You notice that she is looking very thin and having trouble walking. You inquire about her health, and she tells you that getting older is good because she isn't hungry anymore and that she hasn't eaten anything for a day or so. She proudly tells you that her favorite pair of pants from 35 years ago finally fits again.

    How should you proceed?

2. Your client Edward is 91 years old. He has lived in the same apartment for the past 16 years. The apartment complex was recently sold to a new owner, who initiated eviction proceedings against Edward on the grounds that Edward is too disabled to safely live in the apartment. Edward came to you and asked you to help him avoid eviction. Upon reviewing the matter, you determined that the landlord's actions are illegal under the federal Fair Housing Act, which bars certain forms of discrimination in housing (see Chapter 8). With Edward's knowledge, you therefore prepared an Answer and Counterclaim asserting that the eviction is barred under federal law. The deadline for filing is tomorrow. You go to Edward's house to explain it, and find him very agitated. He says that the landlord is right, he is too sick to live at home; in fact, he is too sick to live at all. He says he would be better off dead. He tells you to tear up the paper and leave him alone.

    How would you proceed? Why?

3. Suppose that your state is considering adopting the following rule of professional conduct:

    When the lawyer reasonably believes that: (1) a client has diminished capacity due to cognitive impairment or old age, and (2) that client is at risk of physical, financial or other harm unless action is taken, and

(3) the client cannot adequately act in the client's own interest, then the lawyer must take reasonably necessary protective action. Reasonably necessary protective action may include consulting with anyone who might be able to help the client, seeking the appointment of a guardian for the client, or taking any other action that the lawyer reasonably believes is in the client's best interest.

Would you recommend the state adopt this rule? Why or why not?

4. A caretaker asked an attorney to prepare and draft a will for an elderly widower. The caretaker told the lawyer that the widower was dying and wanted to leave his estate to the caretaker. The attorney drafted the will, and explained to the caretaker the procedure for executing it. In addition, the attorney prepared a certificate to be signed by the widower's physician stating that the widower was competent and instructed the caretaker to have it signed. At no point did the attorney speak to the client about the will. *See Ex parte Alabama State Bar*, 3 So. 3d 178 (Ala. 2008).

   What ethical rules did the lawyer violate? How should he have handled the situation instead?

5. Consider the facts of *In the Matter of Keen Brantley*, 260 Kan. 605 (Kan. 1996), laid out below (quoted remarks are from the court's recitation of the facts). The case involved a seasoned attorney who was found to have violated a multitude of ethical rules during his representation of an elderly widow. Many of the violations arose from his decision to initiate an action for *conservatorship* over her. As discussed in Chapter 4, a conservatorship proceeding is a type of guardianship proceeding in which the court is asked to appoint a third party (called a "conservator") to make financial decisions on behalf of an incapacitated individual (called a "ward"). As you read the facts, ask yourself what attorney Brantley did wrong and what he should have done differently.

   In 1977, Mary Storm's husband, R.E. Pfenninger, died leaving his entire estate (valued at $77,000) to her. In accordance with his will, any property remaining upon her death would be divided among his children from a previous marriage and her only son, Wayne Hendrix, also of a previous marriage. In 1985, Mary's brother, Leo Scott McCormick, died leaving his entire estate (valued at approximately $193,000) to her.

   The following year, Mary wrote a letter to Wayne and his wife Delores stating her intention to leave him most of her brother's estate. Consistent with this letter, in 1986 and 1987, large sums of money totaling $191,425 were transferred from Mary's account (presumably by Mary) to an account that Wayne and Delores had opened at Security State Bank in Scott City, Kansas. Also during this period, Mary—at least in part with the assistance of Keen Brantley, who had been her attorney since 1983—added Wayne as a joint tenant on several certificates of deposit and on several parcels of real estate.

Neither Wayne nor Delores exercised any ownership rights over the certificates or real estate, although they did transfer $85,000 from the Scott City account to one in Alaska, their state of residence.

In December 1986, Mary—who had previously lived in her own home and been self-sufficient—fractured her hip, resulting in a hospitalization followed by a lengthy nursing home stay. In July 1989, her stepson, Ralph Pfenninger, visited Mary at the nursing home and was incorrectly told by the facility's administrator that Mary was "giving all of her money away and would soon have nothing to live on" despite the fact that Mary had a "comfortable income" and liquid assets exceeding $100,000. Ralph also met with Louise Wendler, an officer of the Security State Bank of Scott City, who reported that Mary had transferred significant funds to Wayne.

Ralph then met with attorney Brantley. Ralph "expressed his concerns relative to the feared dissipation of Mary Storm's assets. Respondent Brantley was informed that the Security State Bank of Scott City had indicated a willingness to serve as conservator, and he thereupon conferred with Louise Wendler . . . who further confirmed to him confidential information that Wayne and Delores Hendrix had made transfers from their Kansas account to their Alaska account totaling $85,000. Ms. Wendler further volunteered that, in her opinion, Mary Storm's deposits into the Hendrixes' account could not possibly be gifts due to their large amount. She admitted, however, that she had never consulted Mary Storm about this assumption."

Brantley then called Mary at her nursing home and asked her "if she was aware that Wayne Hendrix was in town withdrawing large amounts from her bank accounts. Understandably, Mary Storm replied that she knew nothing about any recent withdrawals from her accounts. Bank records in evidence reflect that she was correct in her reply." Then, without further conversation or investigation, Brantley prepared a petition for a voluntary conservatorship, which he sent to Mary's nursing home for signature and she presumably then signed. As a result, the Security State Bank was appointed conservator in July 1989. During this process, Brantley viewed himself as simultaneously representing Mary, Ralph, and the Security State Bank in the proceeding.

In September 1989, Brantley filed a petition for the sale of Mary's property at public auction on behalf of Security State Bank and a petition for a guardian ad litem for Mary, both without consulting her. The petition for the sale stated that it was necessary to sell the property to pay taxes and expenses, which was untrue. Mary's grandson, Richard Hendrix, learned of the auction one week before it was to occur and contacted attorney Paul Oller.

Mary hired Oller to represent her in halting the sale and terminating the conservatorship. At a September 29, 1989 hearing he successfully did both. However, later that day, purportedly acting as

Mary's attorney and without giving notice to either Mary or Oller, "Brantley presented to the magistrate judge, ex parte, a Temporary Order restraining the disposition of the estate of the 'conservatee' until the 'petition' could be heard and further orders issued." Then, three days later, he filed an Involuntary Petition for Appointment of Conservator on behalf of Ralph, in which he stated that Mary "was 'completely disoriented as to person, place and time as noted in the letter of Daniel R. Dunn, M.D. marked Exhibit A attached hereto and made a part hereof.' In fact, there was no Exhibit A attached to the petition, there was not in existence any letter from Dr. Dunn, Respondent Brantley never contacted Dr. Dunn to request such a letter, and Respondent Brantley candidly admitted that he made up the language supposedly 'noted in the letter.' At no time during any of the conservatorship proceedings did the Respondent ever meet personally with Mary Storm to determine for himself her state of mind or knowledge of her financial affairs, and his false statements contained in said petition have never been corrected."

A few days later, Brantley obtained Preliminary Orders, which he had prepared on behalf of Ralph. Oller, on behalf of Mary, filed an answer that objected to Brantley acting in a manner adverse to Mary, alleged numerous ethical violations, requested an accounting by the conservator, and requested that Brantley be disqualified and the court-appointed attorney for Mary be discharged. Brantley neither filed a response nor withdrew from the representation of Ralph.

The magistrate judge, acting in a manner which the Kansas Supreme Court described as shocking, interviewed Mary in her nursing home without notice to her family or to Oller on several occasions (including once the day following major surgery). He then, apparently relying on his assessment of Mary, ordered Oller discharged and denied Oller's motions. Oller subsequently filed a renewed answer on Mary's behalf, to no immediate effect.

Finally, a court hearing was held in November 1989, at which Brantley, Wendler, Oller, and Mary's court-appointed attorney all appeared and agreed to the imposition of a partial conservatorship over Mary's assets and the appointment of a new conservator to manage it. After the hearing, Brantley, this time representing the discharged conservator, prepared an order for the discharged conservator to pay various claims, including $575 to Brantley. Brantley neither gave notice of this order or a copy of the bill to either Mary or Oller. Nevertheless, the magistrate approved it and Mary therefore paid for Brantley to represent both the discharged conservator and Ralph for actions taken contrary to her express wishes.

Mary moved back into her home in November 1989 and resided there "with minimal outside assistance" until 1993 when she moved to Alaska to be with Wayne and Delores. Shortly thereafter, she sought to terminate the conservatorship and transfer her assets to Alaska; in *the alternative, she requested that the conservatorship be transferred to Alaska. At the hearing held on this request, Brantley appeared on behalf of Ralph to oppose the request. Over this objection, the conservatorship was eventually transferred. Even after the transfer, however, Brantley sought both to monitor it and obtain confidential information related to it.*

Brantley justified the conservatorship, both in ex parte meetings with the magistrate and in scheduled hearings, on the grounds that Wayne was an alcoholic, was "financially irresponsible," and had stolen $85,000 from Mary. However, "he did not have evidence to support such claims and had not made a reasonable investigation in such regard."

a. What errors did Keen Brantley make in the course of the representation described above? What rules of professional conduct did he violate by doing so?

b. Starting at the point where Ralph Pfenninger came to Brantley and reported his concerns, how should Brantley have proceeded? Why do you think he did not do so?

CHAPTER 3

The Legal Status of Old Age and Age Discrimination

A. INTRODUCTION

This chapter examines the role that age plays in determining a person's legal rights and entitlements. It opens with a discussion of the constitutional permissibility of age-based classifications and then explores how the law employs age-based classifications in a variety of contexts, including health care, safety, and employment. It concludes with a discussion of the debate on a proposed international Convention on the Rights of Older Persons.

The cases and statutes discussed in this chapter represent different forms of age discrimination. The term "age discrimination" is often used in a pejorative sense to connote unfair treatment of older adults. The term conjures up images of older workers being denied employment, older patients being denied health care, and older family members being denied respect. However, social policies that discriminate on the basis of age are diverse, and such discrimination often benefits older adults. For example, most individuals are only eligible for Medicare or Social Security benefits when they reach a qualifying age. Similarly, persons age 65 and older are currently entitled to take a larger standard deduction on their tax returns than are younger persons.

Just as there are many forms of "age discrimination," there are many reasons why laws and policies employ age-based criteria. Discrimination in favor of older adults may also serve to compensate for indignities, ageism, and other disadvantages older adults experience. It can also be a way for society to express appreciation for the contributions that older adults have made over the course of their lives. In addition, programs that provide a social safety net in older age, such as Medicare and Social Security, may make the prospect of aging less daunting to both older and younger adults.

Perhaps the most common reason why age is used to determine legal rights and entitlements is because age is believed to be a convenient indicator of individuals' needs and abilities. Age can be an indicator of health and well-being, mental capacity, and vulnerability. Old age is associated with increased health problems, reduced ability to engage in gainful employment, and declines in certain forms of mental functioning. Older individuals are not only more likely to experience dementia and other organic brain disorders, but they also tend to experience predictable declines in certain problem-solving abilities and reaction times.

While age is a convenient proxy for well-being, it is an imperfect one. As discussed in Chapter 1, gerontologists recognize that *chronological age* is only one factor contributing to functional age (i.e., the extent to which one demonstrates the physical or mental signs of aging). The crude relationship between chronological age and need, combined with the increasing costs associated with certain age-based social policies, has led some to question the wisdom of such policies.

As you analyze the cases, statutes, and problems in this chapter, ask yourself what role chronological age is playing in them, what role chronological age should play, and why. These are important questions to ask in order to understand the current state of the law and how laws may or should change. In the next few decades, demographic, economic, and political pressures will force policymakers to rethink many of the basic age-based entitlements upon which seniors rely. As will be discussed in subsequent chapters, the aging of the population, as well as rising health care costs, are increasing the public cost of age-based entitlement programs such as Social Security and Medicare. At the same time, improvements in health care and access to health care are allowing many older individuals to remain active and employed later in life. The two trends have led critics of Social Security, for example, to question the justifications for the program.

B. THE CONSTITUTIONAL STATUS OF AGE-BASED CLASSIFICATIONS

The Equal Protection Clause of the Fourteenth Amendment to the U.S. Constitution prohibits states from denying any person within their jurisdiction "equal protection of the laws." The clause has been interpreted as limiting the ability of the government to discriminate against different classes of people. The extent of the limitation depends on the nature of the class facing discrimination. Over the years, the Supreme Court has described three broad types of classes: *suspect classes* (including those based on race, national origin, and religion), *quasi-suspect classes* (notably, gender), and *non-suspect classes*. As a general matter, courts apply "strict scrutiny" to discrimination on the basis of a suspect classification, with the result that the classification is permitted only if it is narrowly tailored to a compelling state interest. By contrast, discrimination on the basis of a quasi-suspect classification is given "intermediate scrutiny" and is thus said to be permitted where the classification is substantially related to an important state interest. Finally, discrimination on the basis of non-suspect classification is subject only to "rational basis scrutiny" and is thus said to be permitted so long as the classification is rationally related to a legitimate state interest. *See Plyler v. Doe*, 457 U.S. 202, 216-18 (1982) (summarizing this approach).

In 1976, the Supreme Court considered the question of whether employers may constitutionally discriminate against older workers in the landmark case of *Massachusetts Board of Retirement v. Murgia*. As the decision that follows shows, consistent with the court's prior equal protection jurisprudence, doing so required the court to determine into what type of class the older workers at issue fell.

Massachusetts Board of Retirement v. Murgia

427 U.S. 307 (1976)

PER CURIAM.

This case presents the question whether the provision of Mass. Gen. Laws Ann. c. 32, §26(3)(a) (1969), that a uniformed state police officer "shall be retired . . . upon his attaining age fifty," denies appellee police officer equal protection of the laws in violation of the Fourteenth Amendment.

Appellee Robert Murgia was an officer in the Uniformed Branch of the Massachusetts State Police. The Massachusetts Board of Retirement retired him upon his 50th birthday. Appellee brought this civil action in the United States District Court for the District of Massachusetts, alleging that the operation of §26(3)(a) denied him equal protection of the laws. . . . Upon a record consisting of depositions, affidavits, and other documentary material submitted by the parties, [a three-judge panel of the district court, acting pursuant to orders from the First Circuit Court of appeals] filed an opinion that declared §26(3)(a) unconstitutional on the ground that "a classification based on age 50 alone lacks a rational basis in furthering any substantial state interest," and enjoined enforcement of the statute. We . . . now reverse.

The primary function of the Uniformed Branch of the Massachusetts State Police is to protect persons and property and maintain law and order. Specifically, uniformed officers participate in controlling prison and civil disorders, respond to emergencies and natural disasters, patrol highways in marked cruisers, investigate crime, apprehend criminal suspects, and provide backup support for local law enforcement personnel. As the District Court observed, . . . "even (appellee's) experts concede that there is a general relationship between advancing age and decreasing physical ability to respond to the demands of the job."

These considerations prompt the requirement that uniformed state officers pass a comprehensive physical examination biennially until age 40. After that, until mandatory retirement at age 50, uniformed officers must pass annually a more rigorous examination, including an electrocardiogram and tests for gastro-intestinal bleeding. Appellee Murgia had passed such an examination four months before he was retired, and there is no dispute that, when he retired, his excellent physical and mental health still rendered him capable of performing the duties of a uniformed officer.

The record includes the testimony of three physicians: that of the State Police Surgeon, who testified to the physiological and psychological demands involved in the performance of uniformed police functions; that of an associate professor of medicine, who testified generally to the relationship between aging and the ability to perform under stress; and that of a surgeon, who also testified to aging and the ability safely to perform police functions. The testimony clearly established that the risk of physical failure, particularly in the cardiovascular system, increases with age, and that the number of individuals in a given age group incapable of performing stress functions increases with the age of the group. The testimony also recognized that particular individuals over 50 could be capable of safely performing the functions of uniformed officers. The associate professor of medicine, who was a witness for the appellee, further testified that evaluating the risk of cardiovascular failure in a given individual would require a number of detailed studies.

In assessing appellee's equal protection claim, the District Court found it unnecessary to apply a strict-scrutiny test, for it determined that the age classification established by the Massachusetts statutory scheme could not in any event withstand a test of rationality. Since there had been no showing that reaching age 50 forecasts even "imminent change" in an officer's physical condition, the District Court held that compulsory retirement at age 50 was irrational under a scheme that assessed the capabilities of officers individually by means of comprehensive annual physical examinations. We agree that rationality is the proper standard by which to test whether compulsory retirement at age 50 violates equal protection. We disagree, however, with the District Court's determination that the age 50 classification is not rationally related to furthering a legitimate state interest.

I

We need state only briefly our reasons for agreeing that strict scrutiny is not the proper test for determining whether the mandatory retirement provision denies appellee equal protection. *San Antonio School District v. Rodriguez*, 411 U.S. 1 (1973), reaffirmed that equal protection analysis requires strict scrutiny of a legislative classification only when the classification impermissibly interferes with the exercise of a fundamental right or operates to the peculiar disadvantage of a suspect class. ... Mandatory retirement at age 50 under the Massachusetts statute involves neither situation.

This Court's decisions give no support to the proposition that a right of governmental employment per se is fundamental. ... Nor does the class of uniformed state police officers over 50 constitute a suspect class for purposes of equal protection analysis. *Rodriguez, supra,* 411 U.S. at 28, observed that a suspect class is one "saddled with such disabilities, or subjected to such a history of purposeful unequal treatment, or relegated to such a position of political powerlessness as to command extraordinary protection from the majoritarian political process." While the treatment of the aged in this Nation has not been wholly free of discrimination, such persons, unlike, say, those who have been discriminated against on the basis of race or national origin, have not experienced a "history of purposeful unequal treatment" or been subjected to unique disabilities on the basis of stereotyped characteristics not truly indicative of their abilities. The class subject to the compulsory retirement feature of the Massachusetts statute consists of uniformed state police officers over the age of 50. It cannot be said to discriminate only against the elderly. Rather, it draws the line at a certain age in middle life. But even old age does not define a "discrete and insular" group, *United States v. Carolene Products Co.,* 304 U.S. 144, 152-153 n.4 (1938), in need of "extraordinary protection from the majoritarian political process." Instead, it marks a stage that each of us will reach if we live out our normal span. Even if the statute could be said to impose a penalty upon a class defined as the aged, it would not impose a distinction sufficiently akin to those classifications that we have found suspect to call for strict judicial scrutiny.

Under the circumstances, it is unnecessary to subject the State's resolution of competing interests in this case to the degree of critical examination that our cases under the Equal Protection Clause recently have characterized as "strict judicial scrutiny."

II

We turn then to examine this state classification under the rational-basis standard. This inquiry employs a relatively relaxed standard reflecting the Court's awareness that the drawing of lines that create distinctions is peculiarly a legislative task and an unavoidable one. Perfection in making the necessary classifications is neither possible nor necessary. Such action by a legislature is presumed to be valid.

In this case, the Massachusetts statute clearly meets the requirements of the Equal Protection Clause, for the State's classification rationally furthers the purpose identified by the State: Through mandatory retirement at age 50, the legislature seeks to protect the public by assuring physical preparedness of its uniformed police. Since physical ability generally declines with age, mandatory retirement at 50 serves to remove from police service those whose fitness for uniformed work presumptively has diminished with age. This clearly is rationally related to the State's objective. There is no indication that §26(3)(a) has the effect of excluding from service so few officers who are in fact unqualified as to render age 50 a criterion wholly unrelated to the objective of the statute.

That the State chooses not to determine fitness more precisely through individualized testing after age 50 is not to say that the objective of assuring physical fitness is not rationally furthered by a maximum-age limitation . . . .

We do not make light of the substantial economic and psychological effects premature and compulsory retirement can have on an individual; nor do we denigrate the ability of elderly citizens to continue to contribute to society. The problems of retirement have been well documented and are beyond serious dispute. . . . We decide only that the system enacted by the Massachusetts Legislature does not deny appellee equal protection of the laws.

The judgment is reversed.

[Dissent of Justice Marshall omitted.]

NOTES

1. *Murgia's progeny.* Since *Murgia*, the Supreme Court has consistently refused to subject age-based classifications to heightened scrutiny. For example, in *Gregory v. Ashcroft*, 501 U.S. 452 (1991), the Supreme Court held that a Missouri constitutional provision setting a mandatory retirement age for judges did not violate equal protection guarantees. The Court explained that:

> *The Missouri people rationally could conclude that the threat of deterioration at age 70 is sufficiently great, and the alternatives for removal from office sufficiently inadequate, that they will require all judges to step aside at that age. Because it is an unfortunate fact of life that physical and mental capacity sometimes diminish with age, the people may wish to replace some older judges in order to satisfy the legitimate, indeed compelling, public interest in maintaining a judiciary fully capable of performing judges' demanding tasks. Although most judges probably do not suffer significant deterioration at age 70, the people could reasonably conceive the basis for the classification to be true. Voluntary retirement will not always be sufficient to serve acceptably the goal of a fully functioning judiciary, nor may impeachment, with its public humiliation and elaborate procedural machinery. The election process may also be inadequate, since most voters never observe judges in action nor read their opinions; since state judges serve longer terms than other officials, making them—deliberately—less dependent on the people's will; and since infrequent retention elections may not serve as an adequate check on judges whose performance is deficient. That other state officials are not subject to mandatory retirement is rationally explained by the facts that their performance is subject to greater public scrutiny, that they are subject to more standard elections, that deterioration in their performance is more readily discernible, and that they are more easily removed than judges.*

Id. at 453-54. Similarly, in *Vance v. Bradley*, 440 U.S. 93 (1979), the Court upheld a federal statute setting a mandatory retirement age for federal employees covered by the Foreign Service Retirement and Disability System against an equal protection challenge because the plaintiffs failed to show the statute to be irrational. *See also Kimel v. Fla. Bd. of Regents*, 528 U.S. 62, 83 (2000) ("States may discriminate on the basis of age without offending the Fourteenth Amendment if the age classification in question is rationally related to a legitimate state interest. The rationality commanded by the Equal Protection Clause does not require States to match age distinctions and the legitimate interests they serve with razorlike precision.").

2. *A competing view.* For an argument that, despite *Murgia* and its progeny, certain forms of age discrimination might still be found unconstitutional on equal protection grounds, *see* Nina A. Kohn, *Rethinking the Constitutionality of Age Discrimination: A Challenge to a Decades-Old Consensus*, 44 U.C. Davis L. Rev. 213 (2010).

QUESTION

Constitutional concerns aside, was the Massachusetts law at issue in *Murgia* good policy? How else might the state have achieved its stated goals other than by instituting a mandatory retirement age? Why do you think policymakers in Massachusetts adopted this policy instead of possible alternatives?

C. MEDICAL CARE

Chronological age plays a significant role in people's access to health care. It affects eligibility for certain forms of health insurance. For example, with only a few exceptions discussed in Chapter 6, individuals are typically only eligible for Medicare coverage if they are at least 65 years of age. It also affects the cost of buying health insurance. Private insurance companies typically charge higher premiums for older persons than younger ones, and, under the Patient Protection and Affordable Care Act (PPACA) (commonly called the *Affordable Care Act* or *Obamacare*), premiums bought through state insurance exchanges are allowed to vary by age within certain limits. In addition, chronological age may—although generally not explicitly—affect the type and quality of care an individual receives from health care providers. For example, health care workers' beliefs and attitudes about age may result in older adults' treatment wishes being less likely to be respected and older adults receiving less treatment than their younger counterparts.

As a legal matter, the question is the extent to which treating people differently on the basis of age is, and should be, legally permissible in the context of health care. The next case considers this question in the context of Medicaid. Medicaid, which is discussed at length in Chapter 5, is a public health insurance program supported with both federal and state funds and administered by the states in accordance with federal rules and oversight.

Salgado v. Kirschner

878 P.2d 659 (Ariz. 1994)

MARTONE, Justice.

The question before us is whether federal law allows Arizona to deny life-sustaining transplant coverage to an otherwise eligible Medicaid recipient solely because she is over 21 years of age. We hold that it does not.

I. BACKGROUND

Arizona chose to participate in Medicaid, 42 U.S.C. §§1396-1396v, a joint state-federal funding program for medical care for the needy. . . . Arizona's program is called the Arizona Health Care Cost Containment System (AHCCCS), A.R.S. §§36-2901 to -2975.

Elizabeth Salgado (Salgado), an eligible member of AHCCCS, suffered from primary biliary cirrhosis (PBC), a fatal liver disease affecting mostly middle-aged women. Arising from an altered immunity in the patient, PBC destroys the bile ducts in the liver until it ultimately causes cirrhosis. Because it is idiopathic, there is no connection between PBC and lifestyle abuses like alcohol consumption. Its victims, therefore, have no ability to control its onset and rapid progression. At this time, the only effective medical treatment is liver transplantation.

Salgado was first diagnosed with PBC in 1986 when she was 41 years old. In January 1988, her physicians concluded that a liver transplant was her only hope for survival. She applied for coverage through AHCCCS. As she waited for approval, her condition rapidly deteriorated. AHCCCS did not respond to her request until the late summer of 1989. Although University Famli-Care, Salgado's AHCCCS provider, initially approved funding on August 1, 1989, it later denied coverage under A.R.S. §36-2907(A)(12), which limited coverage for liver transplants to persons under 18.[1]

Because her life was at stake, Salgado, her family, and her physician petitioned the Pima County Board of Supervisors for help. In the meantime, she challenged AHCCCS' denial and exhausted her administrative remedies. Happily for her, Pima County granted her request and funded the transplant. Salgado and Pima County then filed an action in the superior court against the director of AHCCCS, the state, and University Famli-Care, seeking review of administrative agency denial, declaratory relief and special action relief. The trial court granted the defendants' motion to dismiss. Salgado and Pima County appealed to the court of appeals, arguing that the statutory age classification violated the federal Medicaid statute and the equal protection clauses of the United States and Arizona Constitutions. The court of appeals affirmed.

---

1. Now 21 [due to a legislative amendment].

We first granted review to consider the federal and state equal protection claims. But subsequent developments in Medicaid law in the United States Court of Appeals caused us to later grant review of Salgado's and Pima County's statutory claim as well. . . .

II. ANALYSIS

We first address the statutory question so that we may avoid the resolution of constitutional issues if we can. The federal Medicaid statute is long on detail, but short on answers to fundamental questions. For example, as the court of appeals properly noted, it remains uncertain to this day whether Medicaid requires the funding of medically necessary treatment. A state plan for medical assistance must, at a minimum, include . . . (1) in-patient hospital services, (2) out-patient hospital services, (3) laboratory and x-ray services, (4) nursing facility services, early and periodic screening, diagnostic, and treatment services (EPSDT) and family planning services, (5) physicians' services, (6) midwife services, and (7) nurse practitioner services.

* * *

We need not decide whether the broad service categories include all medically necessary treatment because Arizona has chosen to fund organ transplants. We therefore do not have to decide whether Arizona must fund organ transplants but only whether the line it has drawn is consistent with the federal Medicaid statute.

Salgado and Pima County rely upon 42 U.S.C. §1396b(i), which provides in relevant part that federal payment to the states shall not be made

(1) for organ transplant procedures unless the State plan provides for written standards respecting the coverage of such procedures and unless such standards provide that—
   (A) similarly situated individuals are treated alike; . . .

Salgado argues that dividing eligible recipients into age categories fails to comply with the "similarly situated" statutory language.

* * *

We agree with the Ninth Circuit that "similarly situated" means "all patients who can be treated effectively by the same organ transplant procedure." *Dexter* [*v. Kirschner*, 972 F.2d 1113, (9th Cir. 1992),] at 1120. Salgado is within the class of all patients who can be treated effectively by a liver transplant. Thus, to the extent that A.R.S. §36-2907(A)(11) excludes persons from coverage solely because they are over 21, it is in violation of 42 U.S.C. §1396b(i). . . . [A]lthough a state may choose not to participate in Medicaid, once it does so, it must comply with federal Medicaid statutes.

* * *

AHCCCS argues that excluding persons from coverage solely because they are over 21 is reasonable because the federal Medicaid statute itself makes categories of services mandatory for children that are optional for adults. But the special treatment §1396d(r) accords to persons under 21 are for services directly related to their status as young persons: basically well-baby and adolescent care. It includes such things as immunizations, periodic dental checkups, eye glasses, child health maintenance, and early diagnosis.

It is reasonable to expand service categories for age-appropriate care to young persons. But it is unreasonable to allocate treatment within a service category solely on the basis of age. Congress specifically recognized that medically relevant factors, and not solely age, should determine coverage for liver transplants. It acknowledged that there is "no scientific basis for limiting liver transplants to children under 18 years of age," and that "liver transplantation is no longer an experimental procedure for individuals over 18." Comprehensive Omnibus Budget Reconciliation Act, Pub. L. No. 99-272, §9217, 100 Stat. 82, 180-81 (1987).

This is not to say that the state may not use age, if it is medically relevant, as one of the factors in drawing distinctions with respect to medical care. With respect to certain treatment, age may well be one of the factors that is medically relevant. But §36-2907(A)(11) makes age the only factor. As noted in *Dexter*, once a state adopts a policy to cover a category of organ transplants, it may not arbitrarily or unreasonably deny services to an otherwise eligible Medicaid recipient. In terms of life expectancy, no medical evidence has been shown to link youth with a greater response to liver transplant. What has been shown is that other factors, especially the underlying disease, correlate more specifically with survival rates after transplantation.

Thus it is medically irrational to make every person under 21 eligible for a transplant no matter what the chance of survival, and make every person over 21 ineligible, no matter what other medical factors affect the patient's candidacy for a transplant. To illustrate the arbitrariness of an exclusion based solely on age, a terminally ill 20 year old whose chances for success are small even with a liver transplant would have coverage, but a robust 21 year old whose chances for success are great with a liver transplant would not have coverage. The selection of age, as the sole criterion, without regard to other medical factors, is wholly unrelated to the medical decision at hand. Therefore §36-2907(A)(11) fails the reasonableness test under *Dexter*.

III. CONCLUSION

Having concluded that the age limitation of A.R.S. §36-2907(A)(11) fails the reasonableness test and the similarly situated test under the federal Medicaid statute, we need not reach Salgado's and Pima County's claims under the equal protection clause of the United States Constitution and the privileges and immunities clause of the Arizona Constitution.

We vacate the opinion of the court of appeals, reverse the judgment of the superior court and remand for entry of judgment in favor of Salgado and Pima County on their claims for relief.

NOTE

Further reading on age discrimination in health care. For further discussion of how age discrimination impacts the health care that older adults receive, *see* Marshall B. Kapp, *Health Care Rationing Affecting Older Persons: Rejected in Principle but Implemented in Fact*, 14 J. AGING & SOC. POL'Y 27 (2002) (describing the "de facto" age discrimination in health care systems); Mary Crossley, *Infected Judgment: Legal Responses to Physician Bias*, 48 VILL. L. REV. 195, 231-33 (2003) (describing research indicating advanced aged leads to less aggressive medical treatment); and Phoebe Weaver Williams, *Age Discrimination in the Delivery of Health Care Services to Our Elders*, 11 MARQ. ELDER'S ADVISOR 1, 3-4 (2009) (discussing age discrimination in health care).

QUESTIONS

1. Do you agree with the *Salgado* court that the Arizona statute was unreasonable?

2. Suppose you were in charge of developing the policy priorities of the United Network for Organ Sharing (UNOS), the nonprofit organization that, through a contract with the U.S. Department of Health and Human Services (HHS), administers the national organ procurement and transplantation network. Who do you think should be given priority for organ transplants? Should the age of the transplant recipient be considered?

3. The *Salgado* court failed to reach the plaintiff's equal protection claims. Suppose the *Murgia* court considered those issues in *Salgado*. Would the *Murgia* court have found the Medicaid rule at issue in *Salgado* to be constitutional?

D. SAFETY STATUTES

States also use chronological age criteria in laws governing public health and safety. In this context, chronological age is typically used as a proxy for heightened risk of some harm—either to the individual, others, or both. This section examines such criteria in two different types of statutes: those governing the licensure of drivers, and those designed to respond to the problem of elder abuse and neglect. As you read the sample statutes, consider the role that age plays in them, whether it is a proper role, and whether other criteria might be superior.

1. Driving

Driving is both a symbolic and practical means of maintaining independence. The ability and right to drive are especially important for older adults in suburban and rural communities that lack strong public transportation infrastructures. Yet elderly drivers can pose a danger to both themselves and to others. Common problems associated with aging, such as visual or auditory deterioration and reduced reaction times, can make it difficult for older adults to maintain safe driving skills.

Concerns about the safety of older drivers have led a number of states to require testing of older drivers that is not required of younger ones. Compare the following sample statutes:

Fla. Stat. Ann. §322.18(5) (2013)

(a) A licensee who is otherwise eligible for renewal and who is at least 80 years of age:

    1. Must submit to and pass a vision test administered at any driver's license office; or

    2. If the licensee applies for renewal using a convenience service as provided in subsection (8), he or she must submit to a vision test administered by a physician licensed under chapter 458 or 459, an optometrist licensed under chapter 463, or a licensed physician at a federally established veterans' hospital; must send the results of that test to the department on a form obtained from the department and signed by such health care practitioner, and must meet vision standards that are equivalent to the standards for passing the departmental vision test. The physician or optometrist may submit the results of a vision test by a department-approved electronic means.

(b) A licensee who is at least 80 years of age may not submit an application for renewal under subsection (8) by a convenience service unless the results of a vision test have been electronically submitted in advance by the physician or optometrist.

N.D. Cent. Code §39-06-13, 39-06-19 (2013)

Examination of Applications

1. Unless otherwise provided in this chapter, the director shall examine every applicant for an operator's license. The examination must include a test of the applicant's eyesight; ability to read and understand highway signs regulating, warning, and directing traffic; and knowledge of the traffic laws of this state. . . .

2. The examination must include an actual demonstration of ability to exercise ordinary and reasonable control in the operation of a motor vehicle unless waived for an applicant who has successfully passed an actual ability test in this or another state. . . .

3. In lieu of an eyesight test, the applicant may provide a statement of examination from a licensed physician or an optometrist stating the corrected

and uncorrected vision of the applicant, if the examination was within six months of the application.

4. The director may require any other physical or mental examination.

Expiration of License—Renewal

* * *

7. An applicant for renewal of an operator's license must provide a certificate of examination from the driver licensing or examining authorities or a statement as to the corrected and uncorrected vision of the applicant from a licensed physician or an optometrist. . . .

NOTES

1. *Other limitations on driving.* A number of states have shortened renewal periods for older drivers, require additional testing for older drivers, or both. In addition, some states require doctors to report impairments that undermine driving ability to the state's department of motor vehicles.

2. *Civil rights implications of driving restrictions.* Several student notes have considered the civil rights implications that laws regulating drivers' licenses have for older adults. *See* David Rosenfeld, Note, *From California to Illinois to Florida, Oh My!: The Need for a More Uniform Driver's License Policy*, 12 ELDER L.J. 449 (2004) (examining age as a criterion for regulating drivers' license renewals and considering both equal protection and due process arguments); Vasiliki L. Tripodis, Note, *Licensing Policies for Older Drivers: Balancing Public Safety with Individual Mobility*, 38 B.C. L. REV. 1051 (1997) (examining age-based drivers' license renewal policies in light of equal protection and due process guarantees); John C. Bodnar, Note, *Are Older Americans Dangerously Driving Into the Sunset?*, 72 WASH. U. L.Q. 1709 (Winter 1994) (predicting constitutional challenges by older Americans in states that enact age-based drivers' license renewal requirements and concluding that such statutes could withstand constitutional scrutiny).

QUESTIONS

1. From a cost-benefit point of view, which of the above statutes is preferable? How might you re-conceptualize the "costs" associated with each statute in order to reach the opposite result?

2. In California, persons age 55 or older who take a "mature driver improvement course" that meets the requirements set forth in state law are entitled to a discount on their automobile insurance. *See* CAL. VEH. CODE §1675 (2006), CAL. INS. CODE §11628.3 (2006). Is this a good alternative to either of the above statutory approaches? A good addition?

2. Elder Abuse

As discussed in depth in Chapter 8, states are increasingly attempting to address concerns about elder abuse and neglect by passing statutes designed to protect older adults from mistreatment. In order to target these statutes to the population they aim to assist, such statutes frequently use age as a legal criterion for special treatment. The Oregon statute that follows is one such example.

OR. REV. STAT. §124 (2013)

124.050. Definitions

As used in ORS 124.050 to 124.095:

(1) "Abuse" means one or more of the following:

(a) Any physical injury to an elderly person caused by other than accidental means, or which appears to be at variance with the explanation given of the injury.

(b) Neglect.

(c) Abandonment, including desertion or willful forsaking of an elderly person or the withdrawal or neglect of duties and obligations owed an elderly person by a caretaker or other person.

(d) Willful infliction of physical pain or injury upon an elderly person.

(e) An act that constitutes a crime under ORS 163.375, 163.405, 163.411, 163.415, 163.425, 163.427, 163.465 or 163.467. [The references are to various sexual offenses in Oregon's criminal law.—ED.].

(f) Verbal abuse.

(g) Financial exploitation.

(h) Sexual abuse.

(i) Involuntary seclusion of an elderly person for the convenience of a caregiver or to discipline the person.

(j) A wrongful use of a physical or chemical restraint of an elderly person, excluding an act of restraint prescribed by a physician licensed under ORS Chapter 677 and any treatment activities that are consistent with an approved treatment plan or in connection with a court order.

(2) "Elderly person" means any person 65 years of age or older who is not subject to the provisions of ORS 441.640 to 441.665. [These provisions pertain to reports of abuse in long-term care facilities.—ED.]

* * *

(9) "Public or private official" means:

(a) Physician or physician assistant licensed under ORS Chapter 677, naturopathic physician, or chiropractor, including any intern or resident.

(b) Licensed practical nurse, registered nurse, nurse practitioner, nurse's aide, home health aide or employee of an in-home health service.

(c) Employee of the Department of Human Services or community developmental disabilities program.

(d) Employee of the Oregon Health Authority, county health department or community mental health program.

(e) Peace officer.

(f) Member of the clergy.

(g) Regulated social worker.

(h) Physical, speech or occupational therapist.

(i) Senior center employee.

(j) Information and referral or outreach worker.

(k) Licensed professional counselor or licensed marriage and family therapist.

(l) Any public official who comes in contact with elderly persons in the performance of the official's official duties.

(m) Firefighter or emergency medical services provider.

(n) Psychologist.

(o) Provider of adult foster care or an employee of the provider.

(p) Audiologist.

(q) Speech-language pathologist.

* * *

124.055. Policy

The Legislative Assembly finds that for the purpose of preventing abuse, safeguarding and enhancing the welfare of elderly persons, it is necessary and in the public interest to require mandatory reports and investigations of allegedly abused elderly persons.

124.060. Duty of officials to report

Any public or private official having reasonable cause to believe that any person 65 years of age or older with whom the official comes in contact, while acting in an official capacity, has suffered abuse, or that any person with whom the official comes in contact while acting in an official capacity has abused a person 65 years of age or older shall report or cause a report to be made in the manner required in ORS 124.065. Nothing contained in ORS 40.225 to 40.295 affects the duty to report imposed by this section, except that a psychiatrist or psychologist is not required to report such information communicated by a person if the communication is privileged under ORS 40.225 to 40.295. [The references are to sections of the Oregon Evidence Code that protect various privileges, including attorney-client privilege.—ED.].

NOTE

Overview of elder abuse reporting laws. Almost all states require at least certain categories of persons to report elder mistreatment regardless of residential setting. In some states, the requirement to report applies to all victims of the triggering age, regardless of their mental or physical limitations or other vulnerabilities. In other states, age is one of two or more variables triggering a duty to report. In yet other states, age is indirectly a factor triggering reporting duties. While age is not itself a factor, "infirmities" or "impairment" "associated with age" are treated as a basis. Finally, some states avoid making age a factor that triggers, either directly or indirectly, a duty to report. Such states tend to look only at "vulnerability" in general. These approaches are discussed further in Chapter 8.

QUESTIONS

1. What constitutional rights are implicated by Oregon's mandatory reporting law?

2. Compare the age-based trigger in Oregon's elder abuse reporting statute with the age-based trigger in Florida's driving licensing statutes. What are the state interests advanced by each? To what extent do these interests justify limiting individuals' rights based on their age?

E. EMPLOYMENT

Although the Supreme Court has consistently refused to subject age-based employment classifications to heightened scrutiny, Congress has acted to protect older workers from age-based discrimination. Most significantly, in 1967, Congress passed the Age Discrimination in Employment Act (ADEA). The ADEA, as amended, protects employees age 40 and older from a wide range of employment-related discrimination including discrimination in hiring and discharge, in the conditions of employment, and in employee benefits.

The ADEA, however, has a number of exceptions. First, not all employers are covered. To fall under the ADEA, the employer must have at least 20 employees. In addition, although state and local governments are covered employers, only some federal entities are subject to the provisions of the ADEA. Second, not all types of employees are fully covered by the ADEA's protections. For example, the ADEA permits mandatory retirement ages for certain employees who are "bona fide executives" or in "high policymaking positions," as well as for mandatory retirement ages and hiring age limitations for firefighters and law enforcement officers. Third, not all types of discrimination are covered. As discussed later in this section, the ADEA only protects employees from discrimination that amounts to a materially adverse employment action—not mere inconveniences or minor changes in the terms of employment. Similarly, where providing a benefit to older workers costs more than providing that benefit to younger workers (as is commonly the case with life insurance and health insurance), the ADEA permits the employer to offer a reduced benefit to older workers so long as the benefits paid to older workers cost at least as much as those offered to younger workers. Fourth, the ADEA permits age discrimination where age is a *bona fide occupational qualification* (BFOQ) or where a practice that disadvantages older workers is based on a *reasonable factor other than age* (RFOA).

This section begins with statutory excerpts from the ADEA that highlight who it protects and from what types of behavior. It then explores what an individual alleging a violation of the ADEA must do to successfully bring a claim under the statute.

1. Statutory Excerpts

AGE DISCRIMINATION IN EMPLOYMENT ACT
29 U.S.C. §§621 ET SEQ. (2013)

§621. Congressional statement of findings and purpose

(a) The Congress hereby finds and declares that—

(1) in the face of rising productivity and affluence, older workers find themselves disadvantaged in their efforts to retain employment, and especially to regain employment when displaced from jobs;

(2) the setting of arbitrary age limits regardless of potential for job performance has become a common practice, and certain otherwise desirable practices may work to the disadvantage of older persons;

(3) the incidence of unemployment, especially long-term unemployment with resultant deterioration of skill, morale, and employer acceptability is, relative to the younger ages, high among older workers; their numbers are great and growing; and their employment problems grave;

(4) the existence in industries affecting commerce, of arbitrary discrimination in employment because of age, burdens commerce and the free flow of goods in commerce.

(b) It is therefore the purpose of this chapter to promote employment of older persons based on their ability rather than age; to prohibit arbitrary age discrimination in employment; to help employers and workers find ways of meeting problems arising from the impact of age on employment.

§623. Prohibition of age discrimination

(a) **Employer practices.** It shall be unlawful for an employer—

(1) to fail or refuse to hire or to discharge any individual or otherwise discriminate against any individual with respect to his compensation, terms, conditions, or privileges of employment, because of such individual's age;

(2) to limit, segregate, or classify his employees in any way which would deprive or tend to deprive any individual of employment opportunities or otherwise adversely affect his status as an employee, because of such individual's age; or

(3) to reduce the wage rate of any employee in order to comply with this chapter.

* * *

(e) **Printing or publication of notice or advertisement indicating preference, limitation, etc.** It shall be unlawful for an employer, labor organization, or employment agency to print or publish, or cause to be printed or published, any notice or advertisement relating to employment by such an employer or membership in or any classification or referral for employment by such a labor organization, or relating to any classification or referral for employment by such an employment agency, indicating any preference, limitation, specification, or discrimination, based on age.

(f) **Lawful practices; age an occupational qualification; other reasonable factors; laws of foreign workplace; seniority system; employee benefit plans; discharge or discipline for good cause.** It shall not be unlawful for an employer, employment agency, or labor organization—

(1) to take any action otherwise prohibited under subsections (a), (b), (c), or (e) of this section where age is a bona fide occupational qualification reasonably necessary to the normal operation of the particular business, or where the differentiation is based on reasonable factors other than age, or where such practices involve an employee in a workplace in a foreign country, and compliance with such subsections would cause such employer, or a corporation controlled by such employer, to violate the laws of the country in which such workplace is located;

(2) to take any action otherwise prohibited under subsection (a), (b), (c), or (e) of this section—

(A) to observe the terms of a bona fide seniority system that is not intended to evade the purposes of this chapter, except that no such seniority system shall require or permit the involuntary retirement of any individual specified by section 631(a) of this title because of the age of such individual; or

(B) to observe the terms of a bona fide employee benefit plan—

(i) where, for each benefit or benefit package, the actual amount of payment made or cost incurred on behalf of an older worker is no less than that made or incurred on behalf of a younger worker . . . ; or

(ii) that is a voluntary early retirement incentive plan consistent with the relevant purpose or purposes of this chapter . . . ; or

(3) to discharge or otherwise discipline an individual for good cause.

* * *

(j) Employment as firefighter or law enforcement officer. It shall not be unlawful for an employer which is a State, a political subdivision of a State, an agency or instrumentality of a State or a political subdivision of a State, or an interstate agency to fail or refuse to hire or to discharge any individual because of such individual's age if such action is taken—

(1) with respect to the employment of an individual as a firefighter or as a law enforcement officer . . . , and the individual has attained—
(A) the age of hiring or retirement, respectively, in effect under applicable State or local law on March 3, 1983; or
(B)(i) if the individual was not hired, the age of hiring in effect on the date of such failure or refusal to hire under applicable State or local law enacted after September 30, 1996; or
(ii) if applicable State or local law was enacted after September 30, 1996, and the individual was discharged, the higher of—
(I) the age of retirement in effect on the date of such discharge under such law; and
(II) age 55; and
(2) pursuant to a bona fide hiring or retirement plan that is not a subterfuge to evade the purposes of this chapter.

* * *

(l) Lawful practices; minimum age as condition of eligibility for retirement benefits; deductions from severance pay; reduction of long-term disability benefits. Notwithstanding clause (i) or (ii) of subsection (f)(2)(B) of this section—

(1)(A) It shall not be a violation of subsection (a), (b), (c), or (e) of this section solely because—
(i) an employee pension benefit plan . . . provides for the attainment of a minimum age as a condition of eligibility for normal or early retirement benefits; or
(ii) a defined benefit plan provides for—
(I) payments that constitute the subsidized portion of an early retirement benefit; or
(II) social security supplements for plan participants that commence before the age and terminate at the age (specified by the plan) when participants are eligible to receive reduced or unreduced old-age insurance benefits under title II of the Social Security Act (42 U.S.C. 401 et seq.), and that do not exceed such old-age insurance benefits.

(m) Voluntary retirement incentive plans. Notwithstanding subsection (f)(2)(B) of this section, it shall not be a violation of subsection (a), (b), (c), or (e) of this section solely because a plan of an institution of higher education . . . offers employees who are serving under a contract of unlimited tenure (or similar arrangement providing for unlimited tenure) supplemental benefits upon voluntary retirement that are reduced or eliminated on the basis of age. . . .

[Limitations omitted.—ED.]

§631. Age limits

(a) Individuals at least 40 years of age

The prohibitions in this chapter shall be limited to individuals who are at least 40 years of age.

* * *

(c) Bona fide executives or high policymakers

(1) Nothing in this chapter shall be construed to prohibit compulsory retirement of any employee who has attained 65 years of age and who, for the 2-year period immediately before retirement, is employed in a bona fide executive or a high policymaking position, if such employee is entitled to an immediate nonforfeitable annual retirement benefit from a pension, profit-sharing, savings, or deferred compensation plan, or any combination of such plans, of the employer of such employee, which equals, in the aggregate, at least $44,000. . . .

NOTE

Reverse discrimination within the protected class. The Supreme Court has held that the ADEA does not prohibit discrimination against individuals who are 40 and older based on their age if that discrimination is done in favor of individuals who are even older. *See Gen. Dynamics Land Sys. v. Cline,* 540 U.S. 581, 600 (2004) ("We see the text, structure, purpose, and history of the ADEA, along with its relationship to other federal statutes, as showing that the statute does not mean to stop an employer from favoring an older employee over a younger one.").

QUESTIONS

1. What is the justification for limiting the ADEA's protections to those age 40 and older? Should the ADEA be expanded to bar age discrimination in employment across the lifespan?

2. Prior to being amended, the ADEA only barred discrimination against those aged 40 to 65. Congress initially amended the ADEA to extend the age cap to 70, before eliminating it altogether. If you had been a member of Congress at the time the age cap was lifted, would you have supported that change? Why or why not?

PROBLEMS

1. After working as a server for ten years at a trendy restaurant, Wendy, a 36-year-old mother of two, is fired. When she asks her restaurant owner why she was fired, he tells her that the firing is nothing personal: she is just too old. He tells her that he prefers to hire waitresses in their early 20s and says that employing waitresses over the age of 35 is inconsistent with the image he is trying to project. Did the restaurant owner violate the ADEA? Why or why not?

2. Larry, a 66-year-old employee of a local manufacturing company, enjoys his work and the income it brings in; therefore, he has decided not to retire. Until his 65th birthday, his employer put the equivalent of 9 percent of his income into a defined contribution pension plan. Under the employer's policy, however, such contributions are only made until age 65. The employer's rationale is that 65 is the standard retirement age and that persons who have additional income from employment after the age of 65 do not also need additional pension monies. Does the employer's policy violate the ADEA?

3. In 1999, the law firm of Sidley Austin Brown & Wood demoted 32 of its lawyers, most of whom were over the age of 50, from the position of equity partner to counsel or senior counsel. If you represented the law firm, what is the best argument you could make that the demotion did not violate the ADEA? *See E.E.O.C. v. Sidley Austin Brown & Wood*, 315 F.3d 696 (7th Cir. 2002).

2. Types of ADEA Claims

There are two types of claims that a plaintiff may bring under the ADEA alleging that he or she was unlawfully discriminated against on the basis of age: a *disparate treatment* claim and a *disparate impact* claim. A disparate treatment claim is a claim that someone was intentionally discriminated against because of a prohibited factor. In age discrimination cases, therefore, a disparate treatment claim is a claim that someone has been intentionally treated differently because of his or her age. A disparate impact claim is a claim that—regardless of intent—a policy or practice is unlawful because it has a disproportionately negative impact on a particular class of people. In the context of the ADEA, a disparate impact claim is a claim that a policy or practice violates the ADEA because it has the effect of disadvantaging older workers.

The cases that follow address what a plaintiff must show in order to state each type of claim. Before either type of claim may be pursued in court, however, the employee must first file a complaint with the U.S. Equal Employment Opportunity Commission (EEOC), the federal agency charged with enforcing the ADEA. In most cases, the employee must file the complaint with the EEOC within 180 days of the allegedly discriminatory act.

a. Disparate Treatment

Disparate treatment claims can take several different forms. Plaintiffs may allege that they were not hired because of their age, were terminated because of their age, or that their working conditions or benefits were made less favorable because of their age. As you read the Supreme Court's 2009 decision in *Gross v. FBL Financial Services, Inc.*, which is excerpted below, ask yourself what it requires a plaintiff to show to prevail on a disparate treatment claim under the ADEA.

Gross v. FBL Financial Services, Inc.

557 U.S. 167 (2009)

Justice THOMAS delivered the opinion of the Court.

The question presented by the petitioner in this case is whether a plaintiff must present direct evidence of age discrimination in order to obtain a mixed-motives jury instruction in a suit brought under the Age Discrimination in Employment Act of 1967 (ADEA). Because we hold that such a jury instruction is never proper in an ADEA case, we vacate the decision below.

I

Petitioner Jack Gross began working for respondent FBL Financial Group, Inc. (FBL), in 1971. As of 2001, Gross held the position of claims administration director. But in 2003, when he was 54 years old, Gross was reassigned to the position of claims project coordinator. At that same time, FBL transferred many of Gross' job responsibilities to a newly created position—claims administration manager. That position was given to Lisa Kneeskern who had previously been supervised by Gross and who was then in her early forties. . . .

In April 2004, Gross filed suit in District Court, alleging that his reassignment to the position of claims project coordinator violated the ADEA, which makes it unlawful for an employer to take adverse action against an employee "because of such individual's age." 29 U.S.C. §623(a). The case proceeded to trial, where Gross introduced evidence suggesting that his reassignment was based at least in part on his age. FBL defended its decision on the grounds that Gross' reassignment was part of a corporate restructuring and that Gross' new position was better suited to his skills.

At the close of trial, and over FBL's objections, the District Court instructed the jury that it must return a verdict for Gross if he proved, by a preponderance of the evidence, that FBL "demoted [him] to claims projec[t] coordinator" and that his "age was a motivating factor" in FBL's decision to demote him. The jury was further instructed that Gross' age would qualify as a "'motivating factor,' if [it] played a part or a role in [FBL]'s decision to demote [him]." The jury was also instructed regarding FBL's burden of proof. According to the District Court, the "verdict must be for [FBL] . . . if it has been proved by the preponderance of the evidence that [FBL] would have demoted [Gross] regardless of his age." The jury returned a verdict for Gross, awarding him $46,945 in lost compensation.

FBL challenged the jury instructions on appeal. The United States Court of Appeals for the Eighth Circuit reversed and remanded for a new trial, holding that the jury had been incorrectly instructed. . . .

II

The parties have asked us to decide whether a plaintiff must "present direct evidence of discrimination in order to obtain a mixed-motive instruction in a non-Title VII discrimination case." Before reaching this question, however, we must first determine whether the burden of persuasion ever shifts to the party defending an alleged mixed-motives discrimination claim brought under the ADEA. We hold that it does not.

A

Petitioner relies on this Court's decisions construing Title VII for his interpretation of the ADEA. Because Title VII is materially different with respect to the relevant burden of persuasion, however, these decisions do not control our construction of the ADEA.

In *Price Waterhouse* [*v. Hopkins,* 490 U.S. 228 (1989)] a plurality of the Court and two Justices concurring in the judgment determined that once a "plaintiff in a Title VII case proves that [the plaintiff's membership in a protected class] played a motivating part in an employment decision, the defendant may avoid a finding of liability only by proving by a preponderance of the evidence that it would have made the same decision even if it had not taken [that factor] into account." But as we explained in *Desert Palace Inc. v. Costa,* 539 U.S. 90, 94-95 (2003), Congress has since amended Title VII by explicitly authorizing discrimination claims in which an improper consideration was "a motivating factor" for an adverse employment decision.

This Court has never held that this burden-shifting framework applies to ADEA claims. And, we decline to do so now. . . . Unlike Title VII, the ADEA's text does not provide that a plaintiff may establish discrimination by showing that age was simply a motivating factor. Moreover, Congress neglected to add such a provision to the ADEA when it amended Title VII . . . , even though it contemporaneously amended the ADEA in several ways.

We cannot ignore Congress' decision to amend Title VII's relevant provisions but not make similar changes to the ADEA. When Congress amends one statutory provision but not another, it is presumed to have acted intentionally. Furthermore, as the Court has explained, "negative implications raised by disparate provisions are strongest" when the provisions were "considered simultaneously when the language raising the implication was inserted." As a result, the Court's interpretation of the ADEA is not governed by Title VII decisions such as *Desert Palace* and *Price Waterhouse*.

B

Our inquiry therefore must focus on the text of the ADEA to decide whether it authorizes a mixed-motives age discrimination claim. It does not. ... The ADEA provides, in relevant part, that "[i]t shall be unlawful for an employer ... to fail or refuse to hire or to discharge any individual or otherwise discriminate against any individual with respect to his compensation, terms, conditions, or privileges of employment, *because of* such individual's age." 29 U.S.C. §623(a)(1) (emphasis added).

The words "because of" mean "by reason of: on account of." 1 Webster's Third New International Dictionary 194 (1966). ...

It follows, then, that under §623(a)(1), the plaintiff retains the burden of persuasion to establish that age was the "but-for" cause of the employer's adverse action. ... And nothing in the statute's text indicates that Congress has carved out an exception to that rule for a subset of ADEA cases. Where the statutory text is "silent on the allocation of the burden of persuasion," we "begin with the ordinary default rule that plaintiffs bear the risk of failing to prove their claims." ...

Hence, the burden of persuasion necessary to establish employer liability is the same in alleged mixed-motives cases as in any other ADEA disparate-treatment action. A plaintiff must prove by a preponderance of the evidence (which may be direct or circumstantial), that age was the "but-for" cause of the challenged employer decision. ...

IV

We hold that a plaintiff bringing a disparate-treatment claim pursuant to the ADEA must prove, by a preponderance of the evidence, that age was the "but-for" cause of the challenged adverse employment action. The burden of persuasion does not shift to the employer to show that it would have taken the action regardless of age, even when a plaintiff has produced some evidence that age was one motivating factor in that decision. Accordingly, we vacate the judgment of the Court of Appeals and remand the case for further proceedings consistent with this opinion.

It is so ordered.

[Justice Stevens dissented, explaining that "I would simply answer the question presented by the certiorari petition and hold that a plaintiff need not present direct evidence of age discrimination to obtain a mixed-motives instruction." He was joined by Justices Souter, Ginsburg, and Breyer.—Ed.]

Justice BREYER, with whom Justice SOUTER and Justice GINSBURG join, dissenting.

I agree with Justice Stevens that mixed-motive instructions are appropriate in the Age Discrimination in Employment Act context. And I join his opinion. The Court rejects this conclusion on the ground that the words "because of" require a plaintiff to prove that age was the "but-for" cause of his employer's adverse employment action. But the majority does not explain why this is so. The words "because of" do not inherently require a showing of "but-for" causation, and I see no reason to read them to require such a showing.

It is one thing to require a typical tort plaintiff to show "but-for" causation. In that context, reasonably objective scientific or commonsense theories of physical causation make the concept of "but-for" causation comparatively easy to understand and relatively easy to apply. But it is an entirely different matter to determine a "but-for" relation when we consider, not physical forces, but the mind-related characterizations that constitute motive. Sometimes we speak of determining or discovering motives, but more often we ascribe motives, after an event, to an individual in light of the individual's thoughts and other circumstances present at the time of decision. In a case where we characterize an employer's actions as having been taken out of multiple motives, say, both because the employee was old and because he wore loud clothing, to apply "but-for" causation is to engage in a hypothetical inquiry about what would have happened if the employer's thoughts and other circumstances had been different. The answer to this hypothetical inquiry will often be far from obvious, and, since the employee likely knows less than does the employer about what the employer was thinking at the time, the employer will often be in a stronger position than the employee to provide the answer.

All that a plaintiff can know for certain in such a context is that the forbidden motive did play a role in the employer's decision. And the fact that a jury has found that age did play a role in the decision justifies the use of the word "because," i.e., the employer dismissed the employee because of his age (and other things). I therefore would see nothing wrong in concluding that the plaintiff has established a violation of the statute.

But the law need not automatically assess liability in these circumstances. In *Price Waterhouse*, the plurality recognized an affirmative defense where the defendant could show that the employee would have been dismissed regardless. The law permits the employer this defense, not because the forbidden motive, age, had no role in the actual decision, but because the employer can show that he would have dismissed the employee anyway in the hypothetical circumstance in which his age-related motive was absent. And it makes sense that this would be an affirmative defense, rather than part of the showing of a violation, precisely because the defendant is in a better position than the plaintiff to establish how he would have acted in this hypothetical situation. . . .

NOTE

Practical impact of Gross. *Gross* is widely regarded as making it far more difficult for plaintiffs to prevail in an age discrimination case. *See, e.g.*, Michael Foreman, Gross v. FBL Financial Services—*Oh So Gross*, 40 U. Mem. L. Rev. 681 (2010) (concluding that *Gross* "makes it significantly more difficult to bring an age discrimination claim and requires employees who are victims of age discrimination to meet a higher burden of proof than someone alleging discrimination based on race, color, religion, sex, or national origin under Title VII").

▪ ▪ ▪

As the *Gross* case discusses, proving the existence of an ADEA violation is difficult in part because much of the evidence is within the control of the employer. To help ease plaintiffs' evidentiary burden, the courts historically applied the burden-shifting *McDonnell Douglas* test. This test was first articulated in *McDonnell Douglas Corp. v. Green*, 411 U.S. 792 (1973), a case brought under Title VII of the Civil Rights Act of 1964, in which a black former employee argued that his discharge from employment was racially motivated. The *McDonnell Douglas* test, in generalized form, requires that: (1) the plaintiff is part of the protected class; (2) the plaintiff is otherwise qualified for the employment benefit or position at issue; (3) the plaintiff suffers a qualifying adverse action; and (4) the qualifying adverse action occurs under circumstances giving rise to an inference of discrimination. If the plaintiff can show that the four conditions are met, the plaintiff will be able to establish a prima facie case of unlawful discrimination without a direct showing of intent. For cases brought under the ADEA, using the *McDonnell Douglas* approach means the plaintiff can establish a prima facie case of age discrimination by showing that she was at least 40 years of age, otherwise qualified for the position or benefit she had been denied, that the denial was of something sufficiently significant to be considered an adverse employment action, and that the circumstances under which that denial occurred were sufficient to allow a reasonable person to believe the denial was the result of age-based discrimination. The burden of production then shifts to the defendant to show that there is a legitimate non-discriminatory rationale for the complained-of employment action. If the defendant meets this burden, the burden then shifts back to the plaintiff to show that the defendant's proffered reason is merely pretext for the true motive behind the adverse action.

Following *Gross* there was much debate about whether courts should continue to employ the *McDonnell Douglas* test in ADEA cases. The courts that have considered this question have generally held that the test survives *Gross*. For example, in *Jones v. Oklahoma City Public Schools*, 617 F.3d 1273 (10th Cir. 2010), the Tenth Circuit considered a claim brought by a public employee who alleged that she was demoted from Executive Director of Curriculum and Instruction to elementary school principal in violation of the ADEA. The plaintiff produced evidence showing, among other things, that although her former position was eliminated, a very similar position was created shortly thereafter and was filled by a substantially younger individual. In reversing the district court's grant of summary judgment to the defendant, the Tenth Circuit interpreted *Gross*'s "but-for" language as merely clarifying that an ADEA plaintiff must, according to the court, "prove by a preponderance of the evidence that her employer would not have taken the challenged action but for the plaintiff's age." The Court rejected the defendant's alternative interpretation: that *Gross* "established that 'age must have been the only factor' in the employer's decision-making process." The Court then noted that *Gross* expressly declined to say whether the *McDonnell-Douglas* framework should be applied in ADEA cases, and applied the framework on the grounds that doing so was consistent with prior precedent.

PROBLEM

Sheila, 60, is an administrative assistant at a large law firm. She shares a workspace with two other secretaries: Kim, 25, and Pam, 24. Sheila, Kim, and Pam, according to their job descriptions, are to work together to complete the tasks for the six attorneys they assist. Because Sheila has a great deal of experience, she feels Kim and Pam should defer to her judgment and frequently instructs them how best to do their jobs. This infuriates them and they complain loudly to the senior partner about "the old hag." The partner talks to Sheila and asks her to "play nice," but she continues to "advise" Kim and Pam, much to their displeasure. After a few months, the senior partner informs Sheila that she is being fired. She comes to your law office and asks you to be her lawyer. She says she wants to pursue an age discrimination claim and asserts that Kim and Pam "just couldn't handle" an older co-worker. Does Sheila have a viable ADEA claim?

b. Disparate Impact

While it has always been recognized that the ADEA allows plaintiffs to bring a disparate treatment claim, until the U.S. Supreme Court's decision in *Smith v. City of Jackson, Miss.*, 544 U.S. 228 (2005), the federal circuit courts were split on the question of whether a plaintiff may bring a disparate impact claim under the ADEA. As you read *Smith*, try to determine what a plaintiff must show in order to state a viable disparate impact claim under the ADEA.

Smith v. City of Jackson, Mississippi

544 U.S. 228 (2005)

Justice STEVENS announced the judgment of the Court and delivered the opinion of the Court with respect to Parts I, II, and IV, and an opinion with respect to Part III, in which Justice SOUTER, Justice GINSBURG, and Justice BREYER join.

Petitioners, police and public safety officers employed by the city of Jackson, Mississippi (hereinafter City), contend that salary increases received in 1999 violated the Age Discrimination in Employment Act of 1967 (ADEA) because they were less generous to officers over the age of 40 than to younger officers. Their suit raises the question whether the "disparate-impact" theory of recovery announced in *Griggs v. Duke Power Co.*, 401 U.S. 424 (1971), for cases brought under Title VII of the Civil Rights Act of 1964, is cognizable under the ADEA. Despite the age of the ADEA, it is a question that we have not yet addressed.

I

On October 1, 1998, the City adopted a pay plan granting raises to all City employees. The stated purpose of the plan was to "attract and retain qualified people, provide incentive for performance, maintain competitiveness with other public sector agencies and ensure equitable compensation to all employees regardless of age, sex, race and/or disability." On May 1, 1999, a revision of the plan, which was motivated, at least in part, by the City's desire to bring the starting salaries of police officers up to the regional average, granted raises to all police officers and police dispatchers. Those who had less than five years of tenure received proportionately greater raises when compared to their former pay than those with more seniority. Although some officers over the age of 40 had less than five years of service, most of the older officers had more.

Petitioners are a group of older officers who filed suit under the ADEA claiming both that the City deliberately discriminated against them because of their age (the "disparate-treatment" claim) and that they were "adversely affected" by the plan because of their age (the "disparate-impact" claim). The District Court granted summary judgment to the City on both claims. The Court of Appeals held that the ruling on the former claim was premature because petitioners were entitled to further discovery on the issue of intent, but it affirmed the dismissal of the disparate-impact claim. Over one judge's dissent, the majority concluded that disparate-impact claims are categorically unavailable under the ADEA. Both the majority and the dissent assumed that the facts alleged by petitioners would entitle them to relief under the reasoning of *Griggs*.

We granted the officers' petition for certiorari and now hold that the ADEA does authorize recovery in "disparate-impact" cases comparable to *Griggs*. Because, however, we conclude that petitioners have not set forth a valid disparate-impact claim, we affirm.

II

During the deliberations that preceded the enactment of the Civil Rights Act of 1964, Congress considered and rejected proposed amendments that would have included older workers among the classes protected from employment discrimination. Congress did, however, request the Secretary of Labor to "make a full and complete study of the factors which might tend to result in discrimination in employment because of age and of the consequences of such discrimination on the economy and individuals affected." §715, 78 Stat. 265. The Secretary's report, submitted in response to Congress' request, noted that there was little discrimination arising from dislike or intolerance of older people, but that "arbitrary" discrimination did result from certain age limits. Report of the Secretary of Labor, The Older American Worker: Age Discrimination in Employment 5 (June 1965) (hereinafter Wirtz Report). Moreover, the report observed that discriminatory effects resulted from "[i]nstitutional arrangements that indirectly restrict the employment of older workers." *Id.*, at 15.

In response to that report Congress directed the Secretary to propose remedial legislation, and then acted favorably on his proposal. As enacted in 1967, §4(a)(2) of the ADEA, now codified as 29 U.S.C. §623(a)(2), provided that it shall be unlawful for an employer "to limit, segregate, or classify his employees in any way which would deprive or tend to deprive any individual of employment opportunities or otherwise adversely affect his status as an employee, because of such individual's age. . . ." 81 Stat. 603. Except for substitution of the word "age" for the words "race, color, religion, sex, or national origin," the language of that provision in the ADEA is identical to that found in §703(a)(2) of the Civil Rights Act of 1964 (Title VII). Other provisions of the ADEA also parallel the earlier statute. . . . Unlike Title VII, however, §4(f)(1) of the ADEA, 81 Stat. 603, contains language that significantly narrows its coverage by permitting any "otherwise prohibited" action "where the differentiation is based on reasonable factors other than age" (hereinafter RFOA provision).

III

In determining whether the ADEA authorizes disparate-impact claims, we begin with the premise that when Congress uses the same language in two statutes having similar purposes, particularly when one is enacted shortly after the other, it is appropriate to presume that Congress intended that text to have the same meaning in both statutes. . . . Our unanimous interpretation of §703(A)(2) of Title VII in *Griggs* is therefore a precedent of compelling importance.

In *Griggs*, a case decided four years after the enactment of the ADEA, we considered whether §703 of Title VII prohibited an employer "from requiring a high school education or passing of a standardized general intelligence test as a condition of employment in or transfer to jobs when (a) neither standard is shown to be significantly related to successful job performance, (b) both requirements operate to disqualify Negroes at a substantially higher rate than white applicants, and (c) the jobs in question formerly had been filled only by white employees as part of a longstanding practice of giving preference to whites." 401 U.S., at 425-426. Accepting the Court of Appeals' conclusion that the employer had adopted the diploma and test requirements without any intent to discriminate, we held that good faith "does not redeem employment procedures or testing mechanisms that operate as 'built-in headwinds' for minority groups and are unrelated to measuring job capability." *Id.*, at 432.

We explained that Congress had "directed the thrust of the Act to the *consequences* of employment practices, not simply the motivation." *Ibid.* . . . And we noted that the Equal Employment Opportunity Commission (EEOC), which had enforcement responsibility, had issued guidelines that accorded with our view. We thus squarely held that §703(a)(2) of Title VII did not require a showing of discriminatory intent.

While our opinion in *Griggs* relied primarily on the purposes of the Act, buttressed by the fact that the EEOC had endorsed the same view, we have subsequently noted that our holding represented the better reading of the statutory text as well. Neither §703(a)(2) nor the comparable language in the ADEA simply prohibits actions that "limit, segregate, or classify" persons; rather the language prohibits such actions that "deprive any individual of employment opportunities or *otherwise adversely affect* his status as an employee, because of such individual's" race or age. . . . Thus the text focuses on the *effects* of the action on the employee rather than the motivation for the action of the employer.

Griggs, which interpreted the identical text at issue here, thus strongly suggests that a disparate-impact theory should be cognizable under the ADEA. . . .

The RFOA provision provides that it shall not be unlawful for an employer "to take any action otherwise prohibited under subsectio[n] (a) . . . where the differentiation is based on reasonable factors other than age discrimination. . . ." 81 Stat. 603. In most disparate-treatment cases, if an employer in fact acted on a factor other than age, the action would not be prohibited under subsection (a) in the first place. . . .

In disparate-impact cases, however, the allegedly "otherwise prohibited" activity is not based on age. It is, accordingly, in cases involving disparate-impact claims that the RFOA provision plays its principal role by precluding liability if the adverse impact was attributable to a nonage factor that was "reasonable." Rather than support an argument that disparate impact is unavailable under the ADEA, the RFOA provision actually supports the contrary conclusion.

Finally, we note that both the Department of Labor, which initially drafted the legislation, and the EEOC, which is the agency charged by Congress with responsibility for implementing the statute, 29 U.S.C. §628, have consistently interpreted the ADEA to authorize relief on a disparate-impact theory. . . .

The text of the statute, as interpreted in *Griggs*, the RFOA provision, and the EEOC regulations all support petitioners' view. We therefore conclude that it was error for the Court of Appeals to hold that the disparate-impact theory of liability is categorically unavailable under the ADEA.

IV

Two textual differences between the ADEA and Title VII make it clear that even though both statutes authorize recovery on a disparate-impact theory, the scope of disparate-impact liability under ADEA is narrower than under Title VII. The first is the RFOA provision, which we have already identified. The second is the amendment to Title VII contained in the Civil Rights Act of 1991, 105 Stat. 1071. One of the purposes of that amendment was to modify the Court's holding in *Wards Cove Packing Co. v. Atonio*, 490 U.S. 642 (1989), a case in which we narrowly construed the employer's exposure to liability on a disparate-impact theory. While the relevant 1991 amendments expanded the coverage of Title VII, they did not amend the ADEA or speak to the subject of age discrimination. Hence, *Wards Cove*'s pre-1991 interpretation of Title VII's identical language remains applicable to the ADEA.

Congress' decision to limit the coverage of the ADEA by including the RFOA provision is consistent with the fact that age, unlike race or other classifications protected by Title VII, not uncommonly has relevance to an individual's capacity to engage in certain types of employment. To be sure, Congress recognized that this is not always the case, and that society may perceive those differences to be larger or more consequential than they are in fact. However, as Secretary Wirtz noted in his report, "certain circumstances . . . unquestionably affect older workers more strongly, as a group, than they do younger workers." Thus, it is not surprising that certain employment criteria that are routinely used may be reasonable despite their adverse impact on older workers as a group. Moreover, intentional discrimination on the basis of age has not occurred at the same levels as discrimination against those protected by Title VII. While the ADEA reflects Congress' intent to give older workers employment opportunities whenever possible, the RFOA provision reflects this historical difference.

Turning to the case before us, we initially note that petitioners have done little more than point out that the pay plan at issue is relatively less generous to older workers than to younger workers. They have not identified any specific test, requirement, or practice within the pay plan that has an adverse impact on older workers. As we held in *Wards Cove*, it is not enough to simply allege that there is a disparate impact on workers, or point to a generalized policy that leads to such an impact. Rather, the employee is " 'responsible for isolating and identifying the *specific* employment practices that are allegedly responsible for any observed statistical disparities.' " 490 U.S., at 656 (emphasis added). Petitioners have failed to do so. Their failure to identify the specific practice being challenged is the sort of omission that could "result in employers being potentially liable for 'the myriad of innocent causes that may lead to statistical imbalances. . . .' " 490 U.S., at 657. In this case not only did petitioners thus err by failing to identify the relevant practice, but it is also clear from the record that the City's plan was based on reasonable factors other than age.

The plan divided each of five basic positions—police officer, master police officer, police sergeant, police lieutenant, and deputy police chief—into a series of steps and half-steps. The wage for each range was based on a survey of comparable communities in the Southeast. Employees were then assigned a step (or half-step) within their position that corresponded to the lowest step that would still give the individual a 2% raise. Most of the officers were in the three lowest ranks; in each of those ranks there were officers under age 40 and officers over 40. In none did their age affect their compensation. The few officers in the two highest ranks are all over 40. Their raises, though higher in dollar amount than the raises given to junior officers, represented a smaller percentage of their salaries, which of course are higher than the salaries paid to their juniors. They are members of the class complaining of the "disparate impact" of the award.

Petitioners' evidence established two principal facts: First, almost two-thirds (66.2%) of the officers under 40 received raises of more than 10% while less than half (45.3%) of those over 40 did. Second, the average percentage increase for the entire class of officers with less than five years of tenure was somewhat higher than the percentage for those with more seniority. . . . Because older officers tended to occupy more senior positions, on average they received smaller increases when measured as a percentage of their salary. The basic explanation for the differential was the City's perceived need to raise the salaries of junior officers to make them competitive with comparable positions in the market.

Thus, the disparate impact is attributable to the City's decision to give raises based on seniority and position. Reliance on seniority and rank is unquestionably reasonable given the City's goal of raising employees' salaries to match those in surrounding communities. In sum, we hold that the City's decision to grant a larger raise to lower echelon employees for the purpose of bringing salaries in line with that of surrounding police forces was a decision based on a "reasonable factor other than age" that responded to the City's legitimate goal of retaining police officers.

While there may have been other reasonable ways for the City to achieve its goals, the one selected was not unreasonable. Unlike the business necessity test, which asks whether there are other ways for the employer to achieve its goals that do not result in a disparate impact on a protected class, the reasonableness inquiry includes no such requirement.

Accordingly, while we do not agree with the Court of Appeals' holding that the disparate-impact theory of recovery is never available under the ADEA, we affirm its judgment.

It is so ordered.

THE CHIEF JUSTICE took no part in the decision of this case.

[Opinion of Justice Scalia, concurring in part and in the judgment, omitted.]

Justice O'CONNOR, with whom Justice KENNEDY and Justice THOMAS join, concurring in the judgment.

* * *

The legislative history of the ADEA confirms what its text plainly indicates—that Congress never intended the statute to authorize disparate impact claims. The drafters of the ADEA and the Congress that enacted it understood that age discrimination was qualitatively different from the kinds of discrimination addressed by Title VII, and that many legitimate employment practices would have a disparate impact on older workers. Accordingly, Congress determined that the disparate impact problem would best be addressed through noncoercive measures, and that the ADEA's prohibitory provisions should be reserved for combating intentional age-based discrimination.

* * *

Congress' decision not to authorize disparate impact claims is understandable in light of the questionable utility of such claims in the age-discrimination context. No one would argue that older workers have suffered disadvantages as a result of entrenched historical patterns of discrimination, like racial minorities have. . . . Accordingly, disparate impact liability under the ADEA cannot be justified, and is not necessary, as a means of redressing the cumulative results of past discrimination.

Moreover, the Wirtz Report correctly concluded that—unlike the classifications protected by Title VII—there often *is* a correlation between an individual's age and her ability to perform a job. That is to be expected, for "physical ability generally declines with age," [*Mass. Bd. of Retirement v. Murgia*, 427 U.S. 307, 315 (1976)], and in some cases, so does mental capacity, see *Gregory v. Ashcroft*, 501 U.S. 452, 472 (1991). Perhaps more importantly, advances in technology and increasing access to formal education often leave older workers at a competitive disadvantage vis-à-vis younger workers. Beyond these performance-affecting factors, there is also the fact that many employment benefits, such as salary, vacation time, and so forth, increase as an employee gains experience and seniority. Accordingly, many employer decisions that are intended to cut costs or respond to market forces will likely have a disproportionate effect on older workers. Given the myriad ways in which legitimate business practices can have a disparate impact on older workers, it is hardly surprising that Congress declined to subject employers to civil liability based solely on such effects.

* * *

The language of the ADEA's prohibitory provisions was modeled on, and is nearly identical to, parallel provisions in Title VII. . . .

To be sure, where two statutes use similar language we generally take this as "a strong indication that [they] should be interpreted *pari passu*." But this is not a rigid or absolute rule, and it "'readily yields'" to other indicia of congressional intent. . . . Accordingly, we have not hesitated to give a different reading to the same language—whether appearing in separate statutes or in separate provisions of the same statute—if there is strong evidence that Congress did not intend the language to be used uniformly. . . . Such is the case here.

First, there are significant textual differences between Title VII and the ADEA that indicate differences in congressional intent. Most importantly, whereas the ADEA's RFOA provision protects employers from liability for any actions not motivated by age, Title VII lacks any similar provision. In addition, the ADEA's structure demonstrates Congress' intent to combat intentional discrimination through §4's prohibitions while addressing employment practices having a disparate impact on older workers through independent noncoercive mechanisms. . . . There is no analogy in the structure of Title VII. Furthermore, as the Congresses that adopted *both* Title VII *and* the ADEA clearly recognized, the two statutes were intended to address qualitatively different kinds of discrimination. Disparate impact liability may have a legitimate role in combating the types of discrimination addressed by Title VII, but the nature of aging and of age discrimination makes such liability inappropriate for the ADEA.

Finally, nothing in the Court's decision in *Griggs* itself provides any reason to extend its holding to the ADEA. As the plurality tacitly acknowledges, the decision in *Griggs* was not based on any analysis of Title VII's actual language. Rather . . . the Court in *Griggs* reasoned that disparate impact liability was necessary to achieve Title VII's ostensible goal of eliminating the cumulative effects of historical racial discrimination. However, that rationale finds no parallel in the ADEA context and it therefore should not control our decision here. Even venerable canons of construction must bow, in an appropriate case, to compelling evidence of congressional intent. In my judgment, the significant differences between Title VII and the ADEA are more than sufficient to overcome the default presumption that similar language is to be read similarly. . . .

NOTES

1. *Effect of* Smith. After *Smith*, it is clear that both disparate treatment and disparate impact claims are cognizable under the ADEA, but that disparate impact claims are narrowly construed such that they are only allowed where the decision factor that causes a disparate impact can be said to be unreasonable.

2. *Unreasonable factors.* There is scant precedent as to what constitutes an unreasonable factor. However, in *Slattery v. Douglas County, Neb.*, No. 10-CV-319, 2012 WL 893143 (D. Neb. Mar. 15, 2012), female nurses alleged that they were paid less than younger, male nurses in violation of the ADEA. The defendant employer alleged that the pay differences were attributable to the defendant's use of a wage study to determine the appropriate salaries for the nurses' respective positions. In denying the defendant's motion for summary judgment, the court explained that the defendant's credibility was suspect, in part because the wage study was not uniformly applied, and therefore there were "genuine issues of fact with respect to the reasonableness of the defendant's reliance on the studies."

3. *Burden of showing reasonableness.* In *Meacham v. Knolls Atomic Power Laboratory*, 554 U.S. 84 (2008), the Supreme Court clarified that the employer has both the burden of production and the burden of persuasion in showing

that the practice causing a disparate impact was reasonable. The Court explained that the RFOA exemption is an affirmative defense, and thus the burden should lie with the defendant employer.

QUESTIONS

1. Was *Smith* a win for employers or employees?

2. As a normative matter, should the same rules apply to race discrimination claims and age discrimination claims?

3. What might constitute an "unreasonable" factor other than age? Would relying on seniority ever be unreasonable?

4. You have now examined legal issues related to three different types of age discrimination: age discrimination in health care, age discrimination in statutes designed to protect the public, and age discrimination in employment. What justification might you offer for the state barring certain forms of age discrimination while embracing other forms of age discrimination?

PROBLEMS

1. Charles Cheney, 60, works in the warehouse of a local casino. For ten years, his job has been to track inventory. His days are spent either at his desk tracking and ordering inventory, or on the floor of the warehouse inspecting inventory. He works closely with three employees in their 30s whose primary task is to unload, store, and move inventory around the warehouse and deliver it to where it is needed in the casino. To complete these tasks, his co-workers must routinely lift heavy objects. About six months ago, Charles's supervisor started referring to Charles as "our senior statesman" and "the old master" and mentioned that Charles must be looking forward to retirement. Charles responded that he had no plans to retire. Two weeks ago, the supervisor announced a new policy: to protect the health and safety of employees, all warehouse employees must be able to safely lift 50 pounds. When Charles told the supervisor it was against his doctor's orders for him to do so—as he had had back surgery two years earlier—the supervisor informed Charles that he would be discharged and gave him a month's notice.

    Does Charles have a viable claim or claims under the ADEA? Why or why not?

2. Sammy Salesman is a successful used car salesman. Sammy, 58, has been working at Henry Huge's car lot since 1984. In recent years, Huge has been seeking to expand sales by attracting a younger clientele to the dealership. Huge has hired a number of "young guns" to sell to the 20-something crowd and has brought in a number of 20-something-friendly models. Huge's new advertising campaign—"Huge's is Hip"—features ads exclusively showing salespeople in their 20s and 30s. Several months ago, Huge

told Sammy that he "needed to dress hip" and that "youth is where the action is." He also complained about Sammy's failure to adopt email as a way to communicate with potential clients. Last week, Sammy was told he was being let go and was asked to train his new replacement, Ned Newbie, a smart-dressing 29-year-old.

Can Sammy establish a prima facie case of unlawful discrimination in violation of the ADEA? If Sammy succeeds in establishing a prima facie case, how should Huge respond?

3. In a 2005 law review article, Ethan Burger and Douglas Richmond argued that by favoring applicants for faculty positions who publish in academic forums over those who publish in practitioner-oriented journals, law schools tend to disfavor applicants with many years of experience as practicing lawyers. Richmond and Burger argued that law schools might be violating the ADEA because of this practice. *See* Ethan S. Burger & Douglas R. Richmond, *The Future of Law School Faculty Hiring in Light of Smith v. City of Jackson*, 13 VA. J. SOC. POL'Y & L. 1 (2005).

Suppose Jim James, after being turned down for a position at South Eastern School of Law, decided to sue the law school on the grounds that it violated the ADEA. To support his candidacy, James pointed out that he had 14 years of experience as an attorney, had held a variety of different and interesting legal jobs, had published numerous editorials in newspapers and legal periodicals, and had published a number of short articles in periodicals for practicing attorneys. In making his case, he pointed to the individual who had been hired instead: a 30-year-old male with three years of experience in a corporate law practice in New York City who had published only a handful of articles—all of them, however, lengthy academic pieces published in well-respected law reviews.

If you were a lawyer specializing in labor-side employment law, would you take James's case? Why or why not?

4. Suppose that a 56-year-old client comes to you and tells you that his employer has offered him an early retirement package and that he is wondering whether to accept it. What would you want to know in order to be able to adequately counsel him?

3. Adverse Employment Action Requirement

In order to succeed in an ADEA claim, a plaintiff must not only show that he or she was discriminated against on the basis of age, but also that he or she experienced a materially adverse employment action as a result of that discrimination. If the employer's behavior merely amounts to an inconvenience or minor change in the terms of employment, it is insufficient to give rise to a claim under the ADEA. Examples of materially adverse employment actions include being fired or experiencing a significant demotion (e.g., one accompanied by a decrease in wages, less distinguished title, or significantly reduced responsibilities).

A common fact pattern in ADEA claims is for an employee to argue that he or she was forced to resign due to age-based discrimination in the workplace. In such situations, the employee will allege that he or she experienced a "constructive discharge." A constructive discharge is a form of adverse employment action that occurs when an employee resigns as a result of an employer creating conditions of employment that are so intolerable that a reasonable person in the employee's position would believe that he or she has no reasonable option other than to quit.

Another common fact pattern is for an employee to claim that he or she was subject to an adverse employment action because he or she experienced a hostile work environment. This type of claim is considered below in *Dediol v. Best Chevrolet.*

Dediol v. Best Chevrolet, Inc.

655 F.3d 435 (5th Cir. 2011)

Plaintiff-Appellant Milan Dediol ("Dediol") appeals the district court's grant of summary judgment for his former employer, Defendant-Appellee Best Chevrolet, Incorporated ("Best Chevrolet"), on his claims of hostile work environment and for constructive discharge. Because we find genuine issues of material fact, we REVERSE AND REMAND.

I.

Dediol was employed at Best Chevrolet from June 1, 2007, until August 30, 2007. During his tenure, he worked directly under Donald Clay ("Clay"), Best Chevrolet's Used Car Sales Manager. Dediol was 65 years old during his employment with Best Chevrolet, and he was also a practicing born-again Christian. Dediol alleges that, on July 3, 2007, friction surfaced between him and Clay when he requested permission to take off from work for the next morning—July 4, 2007—to volunteer at a church event. Dediol received permission from Clay's assistant manager, Tommy Melady ("Melady"), but Clay overruled Melady in derogatory terms. Dediol alleges that Clay told him, "You old mother* * * * * *, you are not going over there tomorrow" and "if you go over there, [I'll] fire your f* * * * *g ass."

Dediol claims that after his request to take off from work for the morning of July 4th, Clay never again referred to him by his given name, instead calling him names like "old mother* * * * * *," "old man," and "pops." Clay would employ these terms for Dediol up to a half-dozen times a day from on or around July 3, 2007, until the end of his employment. Dediol also claims that

"[Clay] stole a couple of deals from me[,]" and directed them towards younger salespersons.

* * *

Clay also allegedly provoked fights with Dediol. On many occasions, there were incidents of physical intimidation and/or violence between Clay and Dediol. According to Dediol, Clay would threaten him in a variety of ways, including threats that Clay was going to "kick [Dediol's] ass." On one occasion, Clay took off his shirt, and stated to Dediol, "You don't know who you are talking to. See these scars. I was shot and was in jail."

Much of the complained-of conduct occurred in front of Melady. According to Dediol, by the end of July 2007, he requested permission from the acting General Manager (and New Car Manager), John Oliver ("Oliver"), to move to the New Car Department. To wit, Dediol also repeated the offending language in front of Oliver in the days leading up to, and when he made his request to change departments. Dediol avers that his request was precipitated by Clay's conduct. This request was preliminarily approved by Melady. Yet, when Clay learned of Dediol's request, Clay denied Dediol's transfer and stated, "Get your old f* * * * *g ass over here. You are not going to work with new cars."

Tensions escalated and reached a climax at an office meeting on August 29, 2007. During an increasingly volatile exchange, Clay proclaimed, "I am going to beat the 'F' out of you," and "charged" toward Dediol in the presence of nine to ten employees. Dediol continued working the balance of that day and the next. Allegedly, the next day, Dediol grew tired of his employment at Best Chevrolet and working under Clay. In a subsequent meeting with managers, Dediol stated, "I cannot work under these conditions—you are good people, but I cannot work under these conditions. It's getting too much for me." Dediol stopped coming to work after August 30, 2007, after which he was terminated for abandoning his job. Dediol filed a complaint with the Equal Employment Opportunity Commission ("EEOC") and he received his Right-To-Sue letter from the EEOC on July 8, 2008.

On August 22, 2008, Dediol filed suit in the Eastern District of Louisiana alleging [that he was subject to a] hostile work environment based on age. . . . Best Chevrolet and Clay filed a motion for summary judgment, which the district court granted on July 20, 2010. Dediol timely appealed.

II.

* * *

. . . A plaintiff advances [a hostile work environment claim under the ADEA] by establishing that (1) he was over the age of 40; (2) the employee was subjected to harassment, either through words or actions, based on age; (3) the nature of the harassment was such that it created an objectively intimidating, hostile, or offensive work environment; and (4) there exists some basis for liability on the part of the employer.

In order to satisfy the third element of a prima facie case of hostile work environment, a plaintiff must demonstrate that the harassment was objectively unreasonable. A workplace environment is hostile when it is "permeated with discriminatory intimidation, ridicule, and insult, that is sufficiently pervasive to alter the conditions of the victim's employment." *Alaniz v. Zamora-Quezada*, 591 F.3d 761, 771 (5th Cir. 2009). Moreover, the complained-of conduct must be both objectively and subjectively offensive. *EEOC v. WC&M Enters.*, 496 F.3d 393, 399 (5th Cir. 2007). This means that not only must a plaintiff perceive the environment to be hostile, but it must appear hostile or abusive to a reasonable person. To determine whether conduct is objectively offensive, the totality of the circumstances is considered, including: "(1) the frequency of the discriminatory conduct; (2) its severity; (3) whether it is physically threatening or humiliating, or merely an offensive utterance; and (4) whether it interferes with an employee's work performance." *Id.*

* * *

Here, Dediol's age satisfies the first prong of the ADEA/hostile work environment framework. Similarly, Dediol satisfies the second prong of the analysis. Dediol asserts various incidents, many of which were witnessed by Melady, which he claims were harassment. He was called names like "old mother* * * * * *," "old man," and "pops." He also claims that after his request for time off on July 4, Clay never used Dediol's given name to refer to him but instead only called him by these insults. These allegations satisfy the second element. Moreover, as stated above, the record indicates that Dediol was called these names a half-dozen times daily from early July until the conclusion of his tenure at Best Chevrolet.

Here, the third factor is critical. In order to successfully challenge the district court's summary judgment against him, Dediol must establish a genuine issue of material fact that the conduct was both objectively and subjectively offensive. Here, the comments were subjectively offensive, as evidenced by Dediol's reaction in the workplace and ultimately by his leaving the car dealership.

* * *

The district court and the Appellees cite *Moody v. United States Sec'y of Army*, 72 Fed. Appx. 235, 239 (5th Cir. 2003), in support of the grant of summary judgment against Dediol. Moody is not dispositive of the instant appeal. In that case, Pearl Moody, aged 62, alleged that her supervisor harassed her for several years based on her age; refused to give her a promotion or reevaluate her job; and, that he refused to upgrade her pay scale to reflect the work she was actually doing.

In a nonprecedential opinion, a panel of this court . . . considered her assertions that between August 1997 and September 1998, Moody's supervisor uttered the following statements: "Granny, have you not got anything to do?"; "See that old woman and she will take care of you"; "Old woman, when are you going to retire and go home so someone younger can have a job?";

and, "Granny, when are you going to retire and let someone younger have a job?"

This court held that Moody failed to show that these remarks were proximate in time to any employment action, and that the remarks did not evince a hostile work environment under governing law. In contrast, the summary judgment record before us is quite distinct from that presented to the court in *Moody*. Here, Clay's repeated profane references to Dediol, and the strident age-related comments about Dediol used by Clay on almost a daily basis within the work setting, are sufficient to create a genuine issue of material fact concerning Dediol's ADEA-based claim for hostile work environment discrimination.

Dediol also presented evidence indicating that workplace conduct was physically threatening or humiliating. Here, the record is replete with incidents of physically threatening behavior by Clay towards Dediol. First, Clay "charged" at Dediol at a staff meeting on August 29, 2007. Second, Clay would often threaten to "kick [Dediol's] ass." Next, Clay allegedly removed his shirt, and stated to Dediol, "You don't know who you are talking to. See these scars. I was shot and was in jail." The tenor of these comments and physical actions support the inference that the conduct was physically threatening.

The last prong of the WC&M objectively offensive analysis requires the court to consider whether the harassment interfered with Dediol's work performance. Dediol claims that because of his age, Clay steered certain deals away from him and towards younger salespersons. On this issue, the facts are conflicting, and better suited for resolution by a trier of fact.

While hostile work environment jurisprudence is not designed to "prohibit all verbal or physical harassment in the workplace," *Oncale v. Sundowner Offshore Servs., Inc.*, 523 U.S. 75 (1998), the record supports Dediol's assertion that he endured a pattern of name-calling of a half-dozen times daily and that it may have interfered with his pecuniary interests. Moreover, Clay's behavior in threatening to beat up Dediol, "charging" at Dediol on August 29, removing his shirt, and stating to Dediol "You don't know who you are talking to. See these scars. I was shot and was in jail," underscore our conclusion that at the very least, there is a genuine issue of material fact on this claim. These allegations are for the trier of fact to resolve and summary judgment was granted in error on Dediol's claim of hostile work environment based on age. . . .

QUESTIONS

1. Could Dediol have prevailed in defeating the motion for summary judgment had Clay not engaged in physically threatening behavior?

2. Dediol, a practicing born-again Christian, also alleged that the hostile work environment that he experienced was the result of discrimination on the basis of religion in violation of Title VII. As the court explained,

According to Dediol, Clay also began to make comments related to Dediol's religion. Examples of these comments include "go to your God and [God] would save your job;" "God would not put food on your plate;" and "[G]o to your f* * * *ng God and see if he can save your job." Clay disparaged Dediol's religion approximately twelve times over the two months leading up to Clay's departure from Best Chevrolet. At one point, Clay instructed Dediol to go out to the lot to make sales by saying, "Get your ass out on the floor." Dediol responded to this instruction by stating he was busy reading the Bible. To this, Clay responded "Get outside and catch a customer. I don't have anybody in the lot. Go get outside."

After *Gross*, how might this religious discrimination claim complicate Dediol's ADEA claim?

PROBLEM

Consider the facts of *DeWalt v. Meredith Corp.*, 484 F. Supp. 2d 1188 (D. Kan. 2007):

> *Plaintiff Stephen M. DeWalt was formerly a television news photographer for defendant Meredith Corporation d/b/a KCTV-5. . . . Mr. DeWalt resigned following what he contends was an approximately two-year period of age discrimination and harassment that began around the time KCTV-5 implemented a new management regime and news program format entitled "Live. Late-Breaking. Investigative." . . .*
>
> *. . . Mr. DeWalt worked for KCTV-5 for thirty-one years from 1973 until February 8, 2004. From 1975 on, he worked as a television news photographer. . . .*
>
> *Beginning in the spring or early summer of 2002, KCTV-5 management decided to adopt a new format, or "brand," for its local news programming. This new format was called "Live. Late-Breaking. Investigative." According to Regent Ducas, News Director at the station, this meant urgent news, i.e., "[t]hat it's a very urgent sense of the day's news." He further described the news as follows: "No matter what it is, we're going to be there and we're going to have it and [be] investigative in nature." Terry Kurtright, Operations Manager, stated that with the new format "the pressure was enormous on all of us. It had to be right now."*
>
> *At the time the station adopted this format, Mr. DeWalt was (as he had been for years) assigned to the day shift. According to Mr. Kurtright, with the new format Mr. DeWalt could not handle the afternoon news because of the editing required. One of Mr. DeWalt's complaints in this case is that he was denied training on the AVID video editing system, a new technology integral to the new branding "Live. Late-Breaking. Investigative." . . . Mr. DeWalt also contends that he was denied needed training on a new "live truck" that differed in operation from the others. . . .*
>
> *On October 11, 2002, Mr. DeWalt received from Mr. Ducas what Mr. DeWalt regarded to be his first "write-up" in nearly three decades of service. The write-up stated that his work performance did not meet expectations and standards for a news photographer at KCTV-5 because of two incidents that had occurred within the week prior to the write-up. It concluded that*

his ability to get along with others was exemplary and that the station appreciated his efforts, but that he must pay closer attention to details and focus on his day-to-day assignments.

. . .

In November of 2002, Mr. DeWalt was assigned to the overnight shift which ran from 10:00 P.M. to 6:00 A.M. Within months, his shift was adjusted slightly to midnight to 8:00 A.M. Photographers and reporters typically worked in pairs, and the change allowed his shift to coincide with the shift of the reporter with whom he worked at the time. The overnight shift was considered an entry-level position that typically did not lead to high visibility projects or awards. The reason the station reassigned Mr. DeWalt to the overnight shift is highly controverted. Defendant contends that Mr. DeWalt was better suited to the overnight shift because he did not perform as well as other photographers in the stressful, time-sensitive situations (presumably meaning the day shift) whereas the overnight shift involved the production of only a single morning newscast. . . . Contrary to defendant's contention that there was less pressure on the overnight shift, plaintiff believed there was more pressure on the overnight shift than the day shift. He and his on-air reporter would come in and drive all over the city a minimum of a hundred miles a night. Then at 4:00 A.M. they would have to be back to set up a live shot to "hype" something. The evidence Mr. DeWalt has submitted establishes that, at a bare minimum, he was at least an above-average photographer at the station and that defendant's asserted justification for the shift transfer morphed over time and is filled with contradictions. Although Mr. DeWalt characterized the shift change as a demotion, his title, benefits, and responsibilities remained the same. His pay did not change, although he points out that his pay was dictated by union contract and was not subject to change. . . .

Plaintiff contends that the station engaged in a pattern of age-based harassment that permeated the work environment with hostility. He explained as follows:

> *people that had any length of time with Meredith and were over 40 years old were pretty much rounded up, herded out the door. A lot of people were harassed, demoted. There was at least one firing that I know of. And these were all people that had been with that company a long time and had excellent work records.*

> *. . . .*

> *. . . they're just trying to get rid of any older worker that was around there and anybody that had any vacations, seniority, and I think it all stemmed from Mr. O'Brien, his feeling that the workers at Channel 5 were lousy, and just his buzzword for anybody that had any length of time with that company.*

Older employees were demoted and replaced by younger employees. Mr. DeWalt has submitted affidavits from five of his former co-workers which generally support Mr. DeWalt's perceptions of the station's culture. Those affidavits indicate that some of those other individuals were also the victims of arbitrary discipline.

Mr. DeWalt testified in his deposition that the harassment and abusive work environment resulted from KCTV-5 management's belief that they "owned you." He admitted that this attitude applied to all employees, regardless of their age. Throughout the course of his deposition, he described other harassing conduct directed at older employees. He testified that members of management made ageist comments. Alvie Cater, a producer, stated that he believed that the photographers on the overnight shift were assigned there because they were old. Mark Berryhill, who was in charge of news operations for Meredith, instructed Mr. Ducas to "fire all the old reporters." During the first videoconference with Kevin O'Brien, who took over broadcasting at KCTV-5 in June of 2002, Mr. O'Brien "called us dinosaurs over at Channel 5" and "referred once to Old Meredith," which Mr. DeWalt understood to mean "the older employees." Plaintiff has submitted his own affidavit as well as affidavits from four other fifty- and sixty-something former KCTV-5 employees which generally evidence that younger employees were treated more favorably than older employees.

In January of 2004, Mr. DeWalt received a verbal reprimand from Mr. Ducas for allegedly failing to return a call requesting that Mr. DeWalt come in on his day off in order to prepare for coverage of an expected snowstorm. Plaintiff, however, testified in his deposition that he did not receive the call. . . .

* * *

On February 8, 2004, Mr. DeWalt resigned from KCTV-5, effective immediately. . . . Mr. DeWalt testified in his deposition that he resigned due to the helplessness he felt as he watched older employees being harassed and herded out the door.

* * *

During the time Mr. DeWalt was employed by KCTV-5, he never lost pay as a result of any disciplinary action taken against him, never lost a pay grade, and was never suspended.

Based on the above facts, should Mr. DeWalt have prevailed on his claim? Why or why not? Would your answer have been different prior to the *Gross* decision? Why or why not?

F. THE INTERNATIONAL FRAMEWORK

In recent years, there has been a growing interest in developing an international framework on the rights of older persons. Building on the success of the Convention on the Rights of Persons with Disabilities, there are increasing calls for a Convention on the Rights of Older Persons. A new convention is promoted as a way to address discrimination against older adults.

Israel Doron & Itai Apter, The Debate Around the Need for an International Convention on the Rights of Older Persons

50 Gerontologist 586 (2010)

INTRODUCTION

In recent years, there has been a growing interest and debate around the question [of] whether there is a need for an international convention on the rights of older persons. There is no one single reason that can fully explain this new international policy initiative. Probably, a combination of several factors, including the increased awareness of the legal consequences of global aging, the successful completion of the International Convention on the Rights of Person with Disabilities (2007) that opened the door for the "next group" in human rights conventions, or grassroots initiatives from international Non-Governmental Organization[s] . . . looking to advance more internationally binding instruments that can be used on the local/national [level].

Among these different reasons, one can also identify the contribution of empirical-legal studies that exposed an international normative gap in the field of the rights of older persons. For example, Rodriguez-Pinzon and Martin (2003) conducted a broad review of the existing international mechanism regarding the rights of older persons and concluded that

> A strategy to have a comprehensive legal instrument on elderly rights is missing at the international level in both universal and regional system. There are very few provisions in international law that directly address elderly rights. There are isolated efforts by certain international bodies to systematically refer to the rights of the elderly when interpreting their corresponding conventions. . . .
>
> However, there is no specific international body with the mandate to focus on the rights of the elderly. Nor is there an elderly rights convention in place. It is in fact the only vulnerable population that does not have a comprehensive and/or binding international instrument addressing their rights specifically. . . .

It is clear . . . that the debate around the future development of an international convention for the rights of older persons is far from simple or consensual. Although there are strong voices in favor, there are also strong arguments against. . . .

THE CASE FOR

Those who support the international convention for the rights of older persons anchor their position on two premises: One—the existing international law situation is not good enough and two—the international convention is an important and effective legal tool to promote and advance the social position of older persons in the future.

The most powerful argument in support of a new international convention for the rights of older persons is that simple fact that there is no binding international instrument that addresses the rights of older persons. . . .

It is not surprising then that all the supporters of an international convention argue that such a convention can make a real life difference. As described by (Tang & Lee, 2006):

> Overall, the convention would define older people's rights as human rights and demonstrate that the abrogation of human rights is not acceptable. It would stipulate positive obligations on nations to realize equality and the

enjoyment of rights by older people. The treaty would considerably expand the concept of human rights protection for older people, since it would not be only about refraining from doing harm or placing negative obligations on the participating states, but would also lay down norms in order to assist older people to attain a status comparable with that of the rest of the population. To achieve these goals, national governments would be required to ensure that the rights set forth in the convention were reflected in their national legislation.

If one takes into account the existing success of international conventions, such as the International Convention on the Elimination of all forms of Discrimination Against Women (CEDAW) or the Convention on the Rights of the Child (CRC), one can realize the potential importance of an international convention for the rights of the older population.

For example, the CRC globally transformed children's rights. At least normatively, the CRC changed international instruments and discourse about children's rights, as reflected in the resulting worldwide domestic legislation. Some even argue that the CRC created a global consensus on children's rights, turning it into customary international law, which is internationally binding in and by itself.

Specific human rights treaties have also created new legal dimensions that did not exist in some domestic laws. For example, CEDAW attempted to eradicate "private" discrimination (i.e., conducted by private entities) against women at times when most countries recognized only "public" discrimination. . . .

International treaties are also powerful advocacy and empowerment tools. Although CEDAW has not revolutionized women's rights legislation in some member states, it has provided NGOs with an important tool for advocacy and empowerment of women's rights, also due to NGO participation in the drafting process. . . .

The success of existing international human rights conventions is dependent on relatively effective enforcement mechanisms. One of these mechanisms is mandatory country reporting, enhancing monitoring of compliance and internal discussion in member states, and individual complaint mechanisms. . . .

International treaties are also helpful tools in litigation in domestic and international tribunals. Although the use of human rights treaties in international tribunals is natural, the use of such instruments in the domestic realm is much more recent and can be utilized for criminal prosecutions, administrative proceedings, and civil suits for reparations. In reality, there are good examples of parties and NGOs that were engaged in strategic litigation while relying on international human rights treaties and were successful in eventually reaching legal prominence, truly affecting women's lives for example.

It is interesting to note that international human rights conventions affect not only member but also nonmember states. For example, although the

United States is not a CEDAW or CRC member, both have become relevant in the United States. American courts use the treaties for interpretation, resulting in actual real (de facto) effectiveness. Gaps in enforcement can thus be resolved by using the treaty as a platform for making domestic legal claims or by states wishing to protect administrative decisions arising from international obligation (Bruch, 2006).

The importance and advantage of international conventions can be found not only in legal terms as they are also important public education tools. The conventions are tools to educate people—lay and professionals—and to raise awareness about the plight of the targeted groups. They are documents that pronounce clear moral values that can shift public attitudes and biases. This would be true even if at the pre-ratification stage if international players use the proposed treaty when discussing the rights of the targeted groups.

Finally, it should be taken into consideration that an international convention for the rights of older persons could serve as an important "anti-ageist" global policy. . . . Deciding not to support [the] convention can be interpreted as yet another symbolic discriminatory behavior ignoring the unique situation of older persons. Establishing such a treaty on the other hand would potentially be a strong anti-ageism, anti-discriminatory, and mainstreaming legal tool.

THE CASE AGAINST

. . . Those who oppose the international convention for the rights of older persons anchor their position in two arguments: One—from past experience, international conventions do not make a real difference and sometimes even make things worse and two—specifically in the field of older persons' rights, there is no need for an international convention in light of the wealth of existing international documents.

The Convention Will Make No Difference or Even Make Things Worse

Past experience shows that international conventions for human rights create "superficial" legal rights rather than true social change. It is not uncommon on the international arena for countries with the worse human rights record[s] to be the first to sign international human rights conventions. This allows them to argue that they respect human rights, although in fact continue to infringe these rights on the ground.

Past experience also showed that the international and political process of establishing the convention ignores authentic voices of the population it intends to protect. For example, the lack of emphasis on women's participation in CEDAW implementation resulted in superficial equality as no "true" equality could be achieved without consulting the targeted group. . . .

International human rights conventions do not only create "artificial" equality, they are also some times blind to multiculturalism. They ignore specific traditions and sets of beliefs and may ignore long established unique social norms. For example, the imposition of Western values, via the CEDAW, has eroded [the] local traditions better suited to protect women in traditional societies. . . .

Moreover, the international process of enacting any legally binding convention embeds paying a "price" in political compromise in substantive rights. Hence, drafting choices can prove fatal to any human right treaty, and the international political process has proved to be crucial in this field.

* * *

Past experience also shows that there is an "implementation gap" that is exhibited in an actual failure to enforce international conventions. Accountability systems to monitor human rights compliance are weak and overburdened especially at the international level, with no accompanying effective sanctions attached to them, which can be dangerous. For example, the CRC wished to create standards for children's rights, enhancing their international status. Research on CRC's effectiveness, concerning for example Ugandan child soldiers, proved that the failure to enforce it against warring parties legitimized child soldier recruitment. If violations of international rules go unpunished—as is the case with CRC—this sends a message that the illegal actions are permissible and that international conventions are worthless.

In sum, the objectors to a new international convention argue that existing international experience with international human rights conventions, such as CEDAW or CRC, show that despite good intentions, these international legal instruments inhibited women's and children's rights rather than advanced them due to political compromises and defective implementation. These arguments could be written off as the usual cynicism about international law, but they should be construed as genuine concerns resulting from past experiences of international human rights law, which as detailed previously, can sometimes, fail to avoid inherent pitfalls and cause much more harm than good.

The Strength of "Soft Law" and Existing "Hard Law"

Those who oppose a new convention for the rights of older persons argue that the supporters of this legal instrument ignore a unique key element that is specific to the case of older persons: Unlike the case for women, children, or people with disabilities, older persons already have a strong "soft law" solution under international instruments, which makes the establishment of yet another international document redundant. Although other social group[s] did have some soft law at hand prior to their unique rights convention, it was far behind the scope of international documents that are already in force today for the older population.

Starting from the Vienna International Plan of Action on Ageing (1983), moving to the United Nations Principles for Older Persons and Proclamation on Aging (1992), through the Madrid Plan of Action on Ageing (2002) and its implementation documents and reports (2007), there is almost no sphere of social interest concerning the older population that is not covered by very detailed existing international documents.

Specifically ... [a]n intergenerational policy approach that pays attention to all age groups with the objective of creating a society for all ages and a shift from developing policies for older persons toward the inclusion of older persons in the policymaking process were major outcomes of the Madrid Assembly. If indeed the Madrid Plan of Action is taken seriously and implemented properly, there will be no need for any new international convention. However, if the Madrid Plan of Action is not taken seriously, there is no real reason why another international document will be treated any differently.

Moreover, conceptually speaking, soft law—although not binding on the formal level—has been proven to play an important role in the making of customary international law. Through its specificity, soft international law can act as an extremely useful guide for policy matters. Especially on the international level, where flexibility and diversity are needed, soft law in the form of detailed yet unbinding legal formula stands a better chance to be adopted in local policies. For example, the work of [the] United Nations High Commissioner for Refugees in setting standards for the treatment of older refugees—although having no formally binding status—has effectively captured the vulnerability of persons in emergencies as well as provided useful guidance on how to respond best to the needs of older persons in crisis situations.

Soft law is also a powerful tool in constructing existing universal international human rights hard law. Universal international human rights instruments such as [the] International Covenant of Civil and Political Rights or [the] International Covenant on Economic, Social and Cultural Rights (ICESCR) provide sufficient legal ground to protect the rights of older persons. A good example in this context was set by the UN Committee on Economic, Social and Cultural Rights in its "General Comment No. 6" (1995). This legal document while referring to soft law provided an in-depth legal interpretation of ICESCR as it should apply specifically to older persons. This legal construction was made despite the fact that ICESCR does not contain any explicit reference to the rights of older persons.

Therefore, the opponents of the convention argue, specifically in the field of rights of older persons, that there is no real need for yet another international convention. The real need is to implement existing international plans, utilize existing human rights conventions, and respect resolutions and declarations, such as the UN Principles for Older Persons. The action, power, and force should focus on implementing the Madrid Plan of Action on Aging and not ... lose focus on the political struggles for yet another diluted political compromise in the framework of a binding international rights convention. ...

QUESTIONS

1. After setting forth the arguments for and against a Convention on the Rights of Older Persons, Doron and Apter set forth a series of recommendations. As part of these recommendations, they stress the need to address ageism, writing:

   > One of the fears from a convention aimed solely at older persons is such a convention will fall into an "ageist trap." Or, in other words, that such future convention will place much emphasis on issues such as elder abuse and neglect or issues of mental incapacity, legal guardianship, or on institutional long-term care. These issues—which are very important and central to the rights of older persons—paint old age in an ageist perspective. It portrays older persons as weak, incapable, and dependent and incorporates "needs-based" discourse instead of "rights-based discourse."

   Do you share this concern? Is it a sufficient reason for advocates for older adults not to pursue such a convention? What do you think Doron and Apter mean when they distinguish "needs-based" discourses from "rights-based" discourses?

2. Do you think the United Nations should adopt a Convention on the Rights of Older Persons? If so, what should be the content of such a Convention?

3. If the United Nations adopts a Convention on the Rights of Older Persons, should the United States be a signatory? Why or why not?

CHAPTER 4

Surrogate Decision-Making

A. INTRODUCTION

Surrogate decision-making is one of the central concerns of elder law practice and theory. As individuals age, cognitive impairments can make it difficult for them to independently make and execute decisions. The onset of physical disabilities may also make it more difficult for individuals to implement their own decisions. For example, people may know what they want to buy at the store but have physical difficulty shopping without assistance.

There are a myriad of informal arrangements that older adults enter into in order to compensate for the loss of cognitive or physical abilities—giving a key to a neighbor, having a friend buy groceries, asking a daughter to balance the check book, or giving a credit card to a grandchild to run errands. These informal arrangements, while often useful, are rarely sufficient to meet the needs of someone with significant cognitive impairments. Informal assistants' powers are limited because they lack legal authority to act on behalf of the older person. Moreover, the informality of such relationships often makes it difficult to hold helpers accountable for bad behavior.

This chapter explores different mechanisms for creating legally recognized surrogates to act on behalf of persons in need. Some can be executed directly by older adults who, anticipating a potentially imminent decline in their well-being, wish to appoint someone else to make financial or medical decisions on their behalf. Others require the involvement of a third party. Most notable of these is "guardianship," a process by which a court appoints one person to act on behalf of another, incapacitated person.

B. DURABLE POWERS OF ATTORNEY

A *durable power of attorney* (DPOA) is a document in which one person (the *principal*) authorizes another person (the *agent* or *attorney-in-fact*) to make legal or financial decisions on his or her behalf. It is called durable because—unlike a traditional, common law power-of-attorney—it continues to be effective even if the principal subsequently loses the capacity to make decisions for him or herself.

DPOAs are popular planning tools for older adults. This popularity stems in part from their utility. The DPOA allows older adults to select virtually any person of their choosing—most commonly a spouse or an adult child—to act on their behalf. By executing a DPOA, an older adult thus creates a mechanism by which others can help him or her and decreases the likelihood that he or she will require a court-appointed guardian or find him- or herself without assistance. Moreover, unlike a guardianship (which is discussed in Section E of this chapter), a DPOA in no way limits the principal's authority to act on his or her own behalf and can be revoked by the principal at any time at which he or she has the capacity to do so. No court involvement or other form of third-party approval is needed.

1. Types of DPOAs

There are two major types of DPOAs. An *immediately effective DPOA* is effective at the time it is signed. A *springing* DPOA (sometimes called a *standby DPOA*), by contrast, is only effective if a certain event occurs. Typically, *springing DPOAs* specify that they are only effective if the principal becomes cognitively incapacitated. Both types of DPOAs can be *general DPOAs*, which grant the agent the authority to act to the full extent authorized under state law, or *narrow DPOAs*, which limit the agent's authority to a particular set of actions.

Elder law attorneys typically advise their older clients to execute broad, immediately effective DPOAs so that the attorney-in-fact has the flexibility to respond to a variety of situations, many of which may not have been anticipated by the principal. Springing powers of attorney, by contrast, are typically disfavored on the grounds that they are more cumbersome for the attorney-in-fact, who must provide third parties with proof that the triggering event has occured.

Some attorneys attempt to create a hybrid of a springing DPOA and an immediately effective one by having clients execute immediately effective DPOAs that the attorney then retains for safekeeping. The attorney and the client agree that the attorney will release the document to the attorney-in-fact upon the client's request or upon another agreed-upon event, such as the principal becoming incapacitated. Attorneys entering into such agreements, however, may face a variety of ethical and practical problems.

For example, such arrangements may create a future conflict of interest between the attorney and an allegedly incapacitated client. In addition, attorneys may face liability if they improperly release a DPOA.

2. DPOA Execution Requirements and Considerations

DPOAs are relatively easy to execute. They typically require very few formalities. Indeed, in many states they need not even be notarized, although notarization is generally advisable.

In many states an individual executing a DPOA can opt to use a *statutory short form*, a standardized, state-approved DPOA form. Statutory short forms have several advantages. They are generally easy to execute and require minimal assistance to do so. Moreover, use of a statutory short form may facilitate acceptance of the DPOA by third parties as the form is easily recognized by financial institutions, health care facilities, and others accustomed to DPOA arrangements. Some attorneys, however, prefer not to use their state's statutory short form with clients, instead choosing to draft DPOAs that they feel are better tailored to their clients' needs.

In addition to deciding whether to execute an immediately effective or springing power of attorney, principals have a number of important choices to make when executing a DPOA.

First, they must select an agent or agents as well as, potentially, a back-up agent. Selecting an agent can be difficult. Typically, older adults appoint their spouse or adult child to serve as their agent. Above all else, it is important that the agent be someone who is trustworthy. A DPOA typically gives the agent access to all of the principal's resources and very broad authority over those resources. Other considerations include whether the individual being considered for selection is amenable to the role, has the time available to serve, and has the knowledge or skills that would allow him or her to perform well in the role. Principals often give preference as well to someone who lives nearby and may be able to meet with them regularly or attend to affairs at a local financial institution. This consideration, however, has become less important due to the emergence of new forms of communication technology and the widespread use of internet banking.

When a principal is also executing a health care proxy (discussed in Section D of this chapter), the principal should consider appointing the same person as agent under both documents. Otherwise, there may be questions as to whether a particular type of decision falls under the authority of the agent acting pursuant to the DPOA or the agent acting pursuant to the health care proxy.

A second important choice is what powers to give the agent. The broader the powers granted, the more flexibility the agent will have to act in the interest of the principal. On the other hand, broader powers may also increase the risk that the agent will be able to misuse the power of attorney and make decisions contrary to the wishes of the principal. A common concern is whether or not to give the agent the power to give gifts of the principal's property to the agent or other persons. Such gift-giving may be beneficial for a number of reasons, including that it allows the agent to give gifts that the principal would want to give and it allows the agent to engage in estate planning and Medicaid planning (a topic discussed in Chapter 6) on behalf of the principal.

A third choice is whether or not to implement any mechanisms for monitoring the agent. For example, individuals may wish to grant a third party the right to demand an accounting from the agent. For example, a mother might appoint her daughter to be her agent, and grant her son the right to demand records of any actions the daughter takes using the DPOA.

Yet another choice is whether to compensate the agent for his or her work. Historically, agents have typically not been compensated for performing their fiduciary duties, but principals can choose to allow for compensation.

NOTES

1. *Joint bank accounts.* A technique sometimes used in lieu of, or in addition to, a DPOA is to create a joint bank account. In order to enable another person to help manage funds, the owner of those funds may add that person to the account. This approach, while even easier than executing a DPOA, can create significant problems. While the account owner may have only added the name for convenience, the act of adding the other person to the account typically gives that person an ownership interest—or at least a presumed ownership interest—in the account. It also exposes the assets in the account to potential attachment by the third party's creditors. Nevertheless, joint accounts are frequently used for money management purposes, not only because of their simplicity but also because they allow for money to pass at death to the account's joint tenant without the need to go through the probate process.

2. *Burden on the agent.* Serving as an agent under a DPOA can be a time-consuming and conflict-laden task. Writing from the perspective of an elder law attorney and caregiver, Professor Debra Kroll warns that becoming an attorney-in-fact "can put the agent on the road to being blamed unjustly by other family members for unduly influencing or forcing the elderly principal to create the legal document in the first place. It places great scrutiny upon the agent, who in turn has agreed to assume a tremendous burden." Debra Kroll, *To Care or Not to Care: The Ultimate Decision for Adult Caregivers in a Rapidly Aging Society*, 21 TEMP. POL. & CIV. RTS. L. REV. 403, 414 (2012). Kroll therefore recommends that a caregiver "consider carefully" before agreeing to serve as an attorney-in-fact. *Id.*

3. Sample DPOA

In 2008, the Commissioners on Uniform State Laws adopted the Uniform Power of Attorney Act (UPOAA). What follows is the Act's recommended State Statutory Short Form Power of Attorney.

STATUTORY FORM POWER OF ATTORNEY
[AS SET FORTH IN THE UNIFORM POWER OF ATTORNEY ACT]

IMPORTANT INFORMATION

This power of attorney authorizes another person (your agent) to make decisions concerning your property for you (the principal). Your agent will be able to make decisions and act with respect to your property (including your money) whether or not you are able to act for yourself. The meaning of authority over subjects listed on this form is explained in the Uniform Power of Attorney Act.

This power of attorney does not authorize the agent to make health-care decisions for you.

You should select someone you trust to serve as your agent. Unless you specify otherwise, generally the agent's authority will continue until you die or revoke the power of attorney or the agent resigns or is unable to act for you.

Your agent is entitled to reasonable compensation unless you state otherwise in the Special Instructions.

This form provides for designation of one agent. If you wish to name more than one agent you may name a coagent in the Special Instructions. Coagents are not required to act together unless you include that requirement in the Special Instructions.

If your agent is unable or unwilling to act for you, your power of attorney will end unless you have named a successor agent. You may also name a second successor agent.

This power of attorney becomes effective immediately unless you state otherwise in the Special Instructions.

If you have questions about the power of attorney or the authority you are granting to your agent, you should seek legal advice before signing this form.

DESIGNATION OF AGENT

I _____ name the following person as my agent:
      (Name of Principal)
Name of Agent: _____
Agent's Address: _____
Agent's Telephone Number: _____

DESIGNATION OF SUCCESSOR AGENT(S) (OPTIONAL)

If my agent is unable or unwilling to act for me, I name as my successor agent:
Name of Successor Agent: _____

Successor Agent's Address: _____

Successor Agent's Telephone Number: _____

If my successor agent is unable or unwilling to act for me, I name as my second successor agent:

Name of Second Successor Agent: _____

Second Successor Agent's Address: _____

Second Successor Agent's Telephone Number: _____

GRANT OF GENERAL AUTHORITY

I grant my agent and any successor agent general authority to act for me with respect to the following subjects as defined in the Uniform Power of Attorney Act [insert citation]:

(INITIAL each subject you want to include in the agent's general authority. If you wish to grant general authority over all of the subjects you may initial "All Preceding Subjects" instead of initialing each subject.)

(_____) Real Property
(_____) Tangible Personal Property
(_____) Stocks and Bonds
(_____) Commodities and Options
(_____) Banks and Other Financial Institutions
(_____) Operation of Entity or Business
(_____) Insurance and Annuities
(_____) Estates, Trusts, and Other Beneficial Interests
(_____) Claims and Litigation
(_____) Personal and Family Maintenance
(_____) Benefits from Governmental Programs or Civil or Military Service
(_____) Retirement Plans
(_____) Taxes
(_____) All Preceding Subjects

GRANT OF SPECIFIC AUTHORITY (OPTIONAL)

My agent MAY NOT do any of the following specific acts for me UNLESS I have INITIALED the specific authority listed below:

(CAUTION: Granting any of the following will give your agent the authority to take actions that could significantly reduce your property or change how your property is distributed at your death. INITIAL ONLY the specific authority you WANT to give your agent.)

(_____) Create, amend, revoke, or terminate an inter vivos trust

(____) Make a gift, subject to the limitations of the Uniform Power of Attorney Act [insert citation to Section 217 of the act] and any special instructions in this power of attorney

(____) Create or change rights of survivorship

(____) Create or change a beneficiary designation

(____) Authorize another person to exercise the authority granted under this power of attorney

(____) Waive the principal's right to be a beneficiary of a joint and survivor annuity, including a survivor benefit under a retirement plan

(____) Exercise fiduciary powers that the principal has authority to delegate

[(____) Disclaim or refuse an interest in property, including a power of appointment]

LIMITATION ON AGENT'S AUTHORITY

An agent that is not my ancestor, spouse, or descendant MAY NOT use my property to benefit the agent or a person to whom the agent owes an obligation of support unless I have included that authority in the Special Instructions.

SPECIAL INSTRUCTIONS (OPTIONAL)

You may give special instructions on the following lines:

_____

_____

_____

_____

_____

_____

EFFECTIVE DATE

This power of attorney is effective immediately unless I have stated otherwise in the Special Instructions.

NOMINATION OF [CONSERVATOR OR GUARDIAN] (OPTIONAL)

If it becomes necessary for a court to appoint a [conservator or guardian] of my estate or [guardian] of my person, I nominate the following person(s) for appointment:

Name of Nominee for [conservator or guardian] of my estate:_____
Nominee's Address:_____
Nominee's Telephone Number:_____

Name of Nominee for [guardian] of my person:_____
Nominee's Address:_____
Nominee's Telephone Number:_____

RELIANCE ON THIS POWER OF ATTORNEY

Any person, including my agent, may rely upon the validity of this power of attorney or a copy of it unless that person knows it has terminated or is invalid.

SIGNATURE AND ACKNOWLEDGMENT

_____   _____
Your Signature   *Date*

_____
Your Name Printed

_____
Your Address

_____
Your Telephone Number

*State of*_____
*[County] of*_____

*This document was acknowledged before me on*_____,
                                                          (Date)

*by*_____.
         (Name of Principal)

_____   *(Seal, if any)*
Signature of Notary

*My commission expires:*_____

[This document prepared by:

_____
_____ *]*

IMPORTANT INFORMATION FOR AGENT

Agent's Duties

When you accept the authority granted under this power of attorney, a special legal relationship is created between you and the principal. This relationship imposes upon you legal duties that continue until you resign or the power of attorney is terminated or revoked. You must:

(1) do what you know the principal reasonably expects you to do with the principal's property or, if you do not know the principal's expectations, act in the principal's best interest;

(2) act in good faith;

(3) do nothing beyond the authority granted in this power of attorney; and

(4) disclose your identity as an agent whenever you act for the principal by writing or printing the name of the principal and signing your own name as "agent" in the following manner: (Principal's Name) by (Your Signature) as Agent.

Unless the Special Instructions in this power of attorney state otherwise, you must also:

(1) act loyally for the principal's benefit;

(2) avoid conflicts that would impair your ability to act in the principal's best interest;

(3) act with care, competence, and diligence;

(4) keep a record of all receipts, disbursements, and transactions made on behalf of the principal;

(5) cooperate with any person that has authority to make health-care decisions for the principal to do what you know the principal reasonably expects or, if you do not know the principal's expectations, to act in the principal's best interest; and

(6) attempt to preserve the principal's estate plan if you know the plan and preserving the plan is consistent with the principal's best interest.

Termination of Agent's Authority

You must stop acting on behalf of the principal if you learn of any event that terminates this power of attorney or your authority under this power of attorney. Events that terminate a power of attorney or your authority to act under a power of attorney include:

(1) death of the principal;

(2) the principal's revocation of the power of attorney or your authority;

(3) the occurrence of a termination event stated in the power of attorney;

(4) the purpose of the power of attorney is fully accomplished; or

(5) if you are married to the principal, a legal action is filed with a court to end your marriage, or for your legal separation, unless the Special Instructions in this power of attorney state that such an action will not terminate your authority.

Liability of Agent

The meaning of the authority granted to you is defined in the Uniform Power of Attorney Act. If you violate the Uniform Power of Attorney Act or act outside the authority granted, you may be liable for any damages caused by your violation.

If there is anything about this document or your duties that you do not understand, you should seek legal advice.

NOTE

Durability. States differ on whether a DPOA must explicitly say that it is durable to be so. As you can see from the above statutory short form, the UPOAA takes the position that a power of attorney is durable unless it states that it is not. This reflects the fact that because of the popularity of DPOAs the term "power of attorney" has become synonymous in common parlance with "durable power of attorney."

EXERCISE 4.1

Imagine you are 79 years old. You have just been diagnosed with early Alzheimer's disease. Several years ago, you fell and broke your hip. You have had a hip replacement but, nevertheless, have somewhat limited mobility. You find it difficult to travel outside of your home without assistance, especially when there is bad weather (e.g., heavy rain or snow, or ice). You anticipate that, given your physical impairments and your new diagnosis, you are going to increasingly need help with managing your finances. You have two children: (1) a daughter who is a professional artist living 20 miles from you and who frequently helps you with your shopping and doctors' appointments, and (2) a son who is an accountant living in a neighboring state, approximately four hours away. You also have a spouse, age 80, who has similar physical limitations but no apparent cognitive impairments. As a successful attorney, you have been able to accumulate a home valued at $500,000 and other property worth approximately $950,000. Your attorney has suggested that you execute a durable power of attorney. If you do so, whom will you appoint to act as your agent? What powers do you think your agent should have? Why? Now try filling out the Uniform Power of Attorney Act's model statutory short form based on your thoughts. To what extent does the resulting document reflect your wishes?

4. DPOA Abuse

An attorney-in-fact has a *fiduciary* duty to the principal. As discussed further in Section F of this chapter (see page 187), this means that the attorney-in-fact must act with care and maintain loyalty to the principal when acting pursuant to a DPOA. Unfortunately, a subset of attorneys-in-fact violate their fiduciary duties by engaging in self-dealing, by acting in a way that is inconsistent with the principal's wishes, or by otherwise acting outside the scope of their authority. In addition, an attorney-in-fact may engage in abusive behavior by unduly pressuring a principal to give him or her powers under a DPOA.

Although it is simply not known how many people are victims of DPOA abuse each year, anecdotal reports suggest that misuse is common. The American Bar Association's Commission on Law and Aging has identified six key factors that facilitate DPOA abuse. They include:

- The breadth of the decision-making authority granted,
- Lack of monitoring,
- Unclear standards for agent conduct,
- Principals' lack of awareness of the risk of abuse,

- Delay in detecting abuse, and
- Difficulty in holding abusers accountable.

See Lori A. Stiegel & Ellen VanCleave Klem, ABA Commission on Law & Aging, AARP Public Policy Institute, Power of Attorney Abuse: What States Can Do About It 5-6 (2008). *See also* Linda S. Whitton, *The Uniform Power of Attorney Act: Striking a Balance Between Autonomy & Protection*, 1 Phoenix L. Rev. 343, 355 (2008) (discussing different forms of DPOA abuse).

Some of these risks are inherent—for example, a DPOA is generally only an effective planning tool if it gives the agent broad authority. Fortunately, as suggested in the previous discussion of different types of DPOAs and considerations when executing them, there are a variety of precautionary measures that can be employed to decrease the risk of misuse. One approach is to try to educate agents about their duties and the potential consequences of violating them. This can be done by meeting with the agent or by inserting language alerting the attorney-in-fact of his or her duties into the document itself. The UPOAA, for example, states that the agent's duties should be clearly laid out in the instrument. The agent may even be asked to sign the document acknowledging his or her duties. Another approach is to limit the agent's ability to engage in certain, suspect transactions. For example, the UPOAA only permits the agent to engage in certain types of transactions (e.g., gift giving) where the principal has expressly authorized those transactions. Yet another approach is for principals to empower a third party to monitor the agent's actions. Still another way some attorneys try to prevent improper use of a DPOA is by retaining the client's fully executed, immediately effective DPOA; the attorney and client agree that the attorney will release the DPOA to the agent at the request of the principal or upon another event, such as the attorney determining that the client is incapacitated. As discussed in the previous subsection, however, such arrangements potentially expose attorneys to liability for improperly releasing the DPOA and may promote future conflicts of interest between the attorney and client.

The next two cases examine key issues surrounding the potentially improper use of DPOAs. *Mowrer* examines a situation in which attorneys-in-fact used a DPOA to self-deal and the extent to which such self-dealing can be undone. *Gupta* examines a similar situation, but asks what effect such self-dealing has on third parties who rely on the DPOA.

Mowrer v. Eddie

979 P.2d 156 (Mont. 1999)

Honorable John Warner . . . District Judge, delivered the Opinion of the Court.

This is an appeal from a judgment of the District Court of the Eleventh Judicial District, Flathead County, entered July 24, 1998, in favor of Clara Mowrer and against Maurice Eddie and Peggy Eddie, in the amount of

$807,582.44, imposing a trust on certain of Eddies' property, and dismissing their petition to be appointed guardians and conservators of Mowrer. We affirm . . . .

BACKGROUND

Clara Mowrer was born September 13, 1894. She lived in Kansas until August of 1995, when she was brought to Montana by her niece, Peggy Eddie, and her niece's husband, Maurice Eddie. She has remained in Montana and now lives at a care facility in Kalispell.

Mowrer fell and broke her hip in June of 1995. She was hospitalized for about two months. The day before she was released from the hospital, Peggy Eddie arrived in Kansas. Maurice Eddie arrived in Kansas shortly thereafter. Mowrer was released from the hospital in late July 1995 and returned home. The Eddies stayed with her in her home.

On August 5, 1995, Mowrer executed a durable power of attorney to the Eddies at her attorney's office in Kansas. That same day, several of Mowrer's bank accounts were closed, and the funds transferred to the Eddies. Other assets, including cash and certificates of deposit, were also transferred to the Eddies.

The Eddies brought Mowrer to Montana in late August of 1995. Before the end of that year, $594,715.00 of Mowrer's assets had been transferred to Peggy and Maurice Eddie by means of the power of attorney and upon Mowrer's signature. In addition, in September of 1995, Maurice Eddie received cashier's checks in the amount of $99,950.00, from certificates of deposit that had been owned by Mowrer.

In the fall of 1995, the Eddies took stock certificates with a value in excess of $300,000.00 from Mowrer's safety deposit box in Kansas, brought them to Montana, and made arrangements with a broker for the transfer of such stock to themselves on the death of Mowrer.

In October of 1995, Maurice Eddie consulted attorney James Johnson, a partner of Gary Christiansen, concerning Mowrer making a new will and filing a gift tax return. Near the end of this meeting Johnson and Maurice Eddie also discussed a possible estate plan for the Eddies. An appointment was made to return to Johnson's office with Mowrer. That appointment was not kept. Later, the Eddies took Mowrer to an attorney in Kalispell who had previously represented them and their family. This attorney prepared, and Mowrer signed, a new will that left all of her property to the Eddies. This new will excluded her other nieces, nephews, long-time friends, and charitable organizations to which she had bequeathed property in prior wills.

The Eddies used their power of attorney to spend Mowrer's money on living expenses and to acquire land, remodel their home, travel, and make gifts to their son and grandson. They also spent some of Mowrer's funds that are not accounted for.

During 1995, 1996 and until February, 1997, Mowrer lived with the Eddies. She then moved to the BeeHive care facility in Kalispell, where she still lives. On May 16, 1997, Mowrer revoked the power of attorney to the Eddies. Her counsel, Gary Christiansen, wrote the Eddies a letter demanding an accounting.

On June 19, 1997, Eddies filed a petition to be appointed guardians and conservators of Mowrer. She responded by resisting the appointment of either a guardian or conservator, and counterclaimed for an accounting. Substantial discovery was undertaken. The trial took seven different days between December 22, 1997, and March 10, 1998. On July 27, 1998, the District Court entered its Findings of Fact, Conclusions of Law and Judgment. The court found that Mowrer was competent, did not need a guardian or conservator, had not made gifts to the Eddies and that the transfers to the Eddies had been the result of duress and undue influence. The court ordered the Eddies to repay $807,582.44 to Mowrer, and imposed a trust on certain real property owned by Eddies to secure the judgment. Eddies' motion for new trial was denied September 22, 1998, and they appeal from such denial.

DISCUSSION

Issue 1.

Did the District Court abuse its discretion when it denied appellants Maurice Eddie and Peggy Eddie's motion to disqualify respondent's counsel, grant a mistrial, and order new discovery?

Eddies first claim that Mowrer's counsel, Gary R. Christiansen, must be disqualified, the case be remanded for a new trial, and any discovery or other proceedings in which Christiansen participated be declared a nullity, stricken, and not used for any purpose. They assert because Maurice Eddie consulted with Christiansen's partner James Johnson in October of 1995 about a possible estate plan for themselves, as well as Mowrer's estate plan and gifts she had made to them, Christiansen had a conflict of interest. . . .

The record shows Maurice Eddie consulted Johnson on behalf of Mowrer. During such single conference they discussed Mowrer's assets, her previous actions, and what she purportedly wanted Johnson to do for her. At Johnson's insistence, an appointment was made for him to consult personally with Mowrer. Under such circumstances, Eddies could not reasonably believe that Johnson represented them. Nor could they reasonably believe that such lawyer would not be free to relate the contents of such discussions to Mowrer or her representatives. Eddies could not reasonably believe they could prevent Johnson from divulging the details of such discussion, should Mowrer desire to do so. . . .

We hold that the District Court did not abuse its discretion in denying the motions for mistrial and to disqualify Christiansen.

Issue 2.

Does Montana or Kansas law apply in determining if transfers of property made in Kansas from Mowrer to the Eddies were the result of undue influence?

[The challenged] transactions, along with the execution of a power of attorney from Mowrer to Eddies, took place in Kansas when Mowrer was a Kansas resident. Eddies claim that, as the District Court did not apply Kansas law in reaching its conclusions of law and Kansas law conflicts with that of Montana, the judgment must be reversed.

* * *

This Court has not had occasion to clearly set out the applicable considerations in making a choice of law in cases where Montana law conflicts with that of sister states. It is not necessary to do so in this instance. The laws of Montana and Kansas relating to the questions presented are substantially the same and would produce the same results. Thus, what may be termed a "false" conflict of laws is presented. In such instances the law of the forum state, here Montana, is applied.

* * *

In Montana, undue influence is defined as:

(1) the use by one in whom a confidence is reposed by another who holds a real or apparent authority over him of such confidence or authority for the purpose of obtaining an unfair advantage over him;
(2) taking an unfair advantage of another's weakness of mind; or
(3) taking a grossly oppressive and unfair advantage of another's necessities or distress.

To determine if gifts were the result of undue influence, Montana courts examine: (1) any confidential relationship of the person alleged to be attempting to influence the donor; (2) the physical condition of the donor as it may affect the ability to withstand influence; (3) the mental condition of the donor as it may affect the ability to withstand influence; (4) the unnaturalness of the disposition as it relates to showing an unbalanced mind or a mind easily susceptible to influence; and (5) the demands and importunities as they may affect a particular donor taking into consideration the time, place and surrounding circumstances.

As a part of these criteria, Montana courts examine the surrounding circumstances and the special facts of each case. Any gift must be made by the exercise of the free will of the donor and when the gift is the result of fraud, duress, or undue influence, it may be set aside. Consideration is given to the nature of the relationship between the donor and the donee, the donor's susceptibility to undue influence, and the reasonableness of the transfers in light of the existing circumstances.

* * *

Issue 3.

Is the evidence sufficient to sustain the judgment that Mowrer was acting under undue influence exerted upon her by the Eddies when she transferred property to them?

Eddies argue that the District Court's findings of fact were not sufficient under Kansas law to set aside Mowrer's transfers of property to them based on coercion or undue influence. As we have determined that Kansas law is similar to Montana law, and that Montana law was correctly applied, we have reviewed the record to determine if the evidence supports the judgment . . . .

Conflicting evidence was presented concerning whether the gifts and other transfers from Mowrer to the Eddies were freely made. Much of the evidence presented at trial consisted of witness testimony. The District Court heard all of the evidence, considered the circumstances, and found that Mowrer and those witnesses presented by her were credible. The court did not find the Eddies' version of the facts to be true.

After hearing the evidence, the trial court made detailed findings of fact. It found that Mowrer was physically weak when the Eddies arrived at her home in Kansas. They moved into her home and immediately secured several hundred thousand dollars of her money. The Eddies then moved Mowrer to Montana, far from her other family and long-time friends, and kept her isolated in their home. The Eddies changed their phone number, and the new number was unlisted. Visitors wishing to see Mowrer were discouraged, and when they did see her, they were allowed to visit only in the presence of Maurice or Peggy Eddie. Caregivers were instructed not to discuss Mowrer's assets with her and were instructed not to allow her to have visitors. During the time Mowrer was isolated the Eddies continued to have her assets transferred to themselves, their children and their grandchildren. The District Court, after hearing the witnesses testify, specifically found that while Clara Mowrer was mentally competent, she was under the absolute and inappropriate control of the Eddies, that she was susceptible to undue influence because of advanced age and physical infirmity, and that Eddies took advantage of her weakness and their control over her to secure an unnatural disposition of essentially all of her property to them. The record supports each of these findings. In making a determination whether undue influence was exercised in a case where the credibility of witnesses is of prime importance, the determination of the weight given to the testimony is the primary function of the trial judge. . . . Viewing the evidence in the light most favorable to the prevailing party, Mowrer, it is substantial and sufficient to sustain the judgment.

Affirmed.

Gupta v. Lincoln National Life Insurance Co.

2005 WL 3304019 (Ohio Ct. App. 2005)

McGRATH, J.

Plaintiff-appellant, Uma Gupta, M.D. ("appellant"), appeals from the judgment of the Franklin County Court of Common Pleas granting summary judgment in favor of defendant-appellee, Lincoln National Life Insurance Company ("appellee").

Appellant and her husband were married in 1974. On April 10, 1987, appellant executed a general power of attorney authorizing her husband to act on her behalf. The power of attorney provided that appellant's husband was appellant's "true and lawful attorney for herself and in her name, place and stead," and conferred upon him:

> [F]ull power and authority to do and perform all and every act and thing whatsoever, requisite, necessary or proper to be done in and about the premises, as fully to all intents and purposes, with the same validity, as She might or could do if personally present, hereby ratifying all that her said Attorney shall lawfully do by virtue hereof. This power of attorney shall not be affected by the disability of the principal.

It is undisputed that appellant signed the power of attorney and recognized her husband as her appointed agent. It is also undisputed that at no time did appellant ever rescind or revoke the power of attorney.

Due to some domestic problems, appellant filed a complaint for separation from her husband on July 9, 2001. However, appellant and her husband continued to reside together until his death in November 2001.

Appellee received a letter requesting a withdrawal of funds in the amount of $50,000 from contract no. 96-9483584, a retirement account belonging to appellant. In response, appellee sent out a loan application. Appellant's husband completed, and returned the loan application to appellee on July 9, 2001. Because the signature on the loan application did not match the signature on file at appellee's business, appellee contacted the Gupta residence via telephone. Appellant's husband informed appellee that he had completed the loan application, and that he had the authority to do so pursuant to the power of attorney executed by appellant. Appellant's husband then faxed a copy of the power of attorney to appellee. Thereafter, on July 12, 2001, appellee processed the loan application, and on July 16, 2001, tendered a check made payable to appellant. Appellee mailed the check to the address listed on the loan application.

Appellant learned of the withdrawal of funds from her account in August 2001 when she came across a paper "that said $50,000 from the Lincoln account."[1] Insisting that she did not authorize the $50,000 transaction, and was not aware of her husband's actions, appellant requested that appellee restore the funds to her account. Appellee refused, and sought repayment of the loan from appellant in accordance with the loan agreement.

---

1. Appellant became aware of this transaction in August 2001. However, appellant was aware of her husband's mismanagement of money beginning in 2000, including "over-the-limit charging," bills not being paid, and her husband's unauthorized use of her credit card, all of which led appellant to open her own checking account and change her credit card. (Depo. 27, 52, 56-57.)

Appellant filed a complaint in the Franklin County Court of Common Pleas seeking a declaratory judgment as to the "meaning, construction and validity of the use of the alleged Power of Attorney by [appellant's] deceased husband [and to] declare the rights and duties of the parties as to the funds released by [appellee] to [appellant's] now deceased husband and for costs incurred herein."

Appellee filed a motion for summary judgment contending that it was justified in processing the loan request because in so doing it relied on a valid and enforceable power of attorney executed by appellant. The trial court granted appellee's motion for summary judgment, and this appeal followed.

* * *

In her first assignment of error, appellant argues that it was error for the trial court to grant summary judgment in favor of appellee, and thereby permit the use of a power of attorney by a "self-dealing attorney-in-fact in an unauthorized loan transaction to create an obligation to a lender without ratification by the principal."

It is a fundamental principal of law that the holder of a power of attorney has a fiduciary relationship with his or her principal. The holder of a power of attorney owes the "utmost loyalty and honesty to his principal." Further, we agree with appellant's contention that a general, durable power of attorney does not authorize the holder of a power of attorney to self-deal, or transfer assets to oneself, unless the power of attorney explicitly confers that power to the holder of the power of attorney. While the law sets forth that the conduct of a holder of a power of attorney who engages in self dealing transactions without authority or ratification of the principal is actionable, the law does not set forth that the conduct of a third-party is actionable when the conduct was undertaken upon reliance of a valid power of attorney.

It is undisputed that in the case before us the power of attorney did not authorize appellant's husband to engage in self-dealing. It is also undisputed that appellant in no way ratified the actions of her husband. However, while the court can empathize with appellant's frustration and disappointment resulting from her husband's actions, we cannot find that the trial court erred in granting summary judgment to appellee. The trial court did not, as appellant suggests, "permit" the actions of appellant's husband. Rather, the trial court held that appellee, under the circumstances of this case, could not be held liable for the acts of appellant's husband.

Appellee relied upon a general power of attorney executed, and never revoked, by appellant. It is undisputed that the general power of attorney, despite being signed in 1987, was in fact valid when used by appellant's husband. We find that appellant has failed to provide any evidence to establish a genuine issue of material fact on this issue. Accordingly, appellant's first assignment of error is overruled.

In her second assignment of error, appellant argues that summary judgment in favor of appellee was not appropriate because appellee failed to verify appellant's ratification of her husband's use of the power of attorney to create the loan obligation. While we agree with appellant that there is no evidence that she in any way ratified her husband's actions, we do not agree with her contention that appellee had a duty to verify such.

Appellant cites no authority in support of her position that a financial institution has a duty to determine that the holder of a valid power of attorney is not engaging in self-dealing before honoring a request for a withdrawal of funds in the name of the principal. We conclude that no such duty exists. To impose such an onerous requirement on financial institutions would not only be impracticable, but would essentially eliminate the power of attorney as a useful tool in the transaction of business of any elderly, disabled, absent, or otherwise incapacitated individual.

Appellant argues that appellee should have been aware of the "suspicious circumstances" underlying the transaction. When the signatures did not match, appellee called the Gupta residence, and appellant's husband informed appellee that he was in fact the one who signed the loan application, and that he had the authority to do so pursuant to the power of attorney. He then faxed a copy of the power of attorney to appellee, and appellee acted in accordance with the loan application. Appellee had no reason to know that appellant had filed for a separation from her husband, or that he had previously engaged in unauthorized financial transactions regarding appellant's finances, which were not related to the retirement account held by appellee. . . .

In the case sub judice, appellee was presented with a valid power of attorney, which was undisputedly signed by appellant. Appellant's husband was properly identified as being the designated holder of the power of attorney. Appellee had the right to assume that appellant's husband was acting lawfully in the performance of his duties as appellant's agent. Further, appellee had a duty to honor the agent's request because it was made pursuant to a valid power of attorney. Appellee had no knowledge that appellant would not cash the check that was tendered to her at her agent's request. Absent an act amounting to participation in wrongdoing, we cannot impose liability on appellee for failing to verify the principal's ratification, or lack thereof, of the agent's actions. As stated previously, to impose such a requirement would effectively eliminate the power, and frustrate the purpose, of the power of attorney, for which the legislature has provided to facilitate the public policy of being able to authorize an individual to act on one's behalf. As such, we find that the trial court did not err in granting summary judgment in favor of appellee. Accordingly, appellant's second assignment of error is overruled. . . .

Judgment affirmed.

NOTES

1. *Revocation.* Once misuse has occurred, the first step is typically to revoke the DPOA to prevent further misuse. Revocation, however, is only possible if the principal has sufficient mental capacity to do so.

2. *Sanctions for misuse.* An agent who has misused a DPOA may be both civilly and criminally liable. Civil approaches include bringing suit to seek rescission of actions taken pursuant to a DPOA or bringing an action in tort for conversion of the principal's assets. Criminal approaches may include prosecuting the agent for crimes such as fraud, theft, or larceny, and, in some states, for specialized crimes such as elder abuse or exploitation of a vulnerable adult. For further discussion of such approaches, see Section C of Chapter 8.

QUESTION

If you were revising your state's durable power of attorney statute, would you protect banks from liability in situations like that described in *Gupta*? Why or why not?

C. LIVING TRUSTS

Living trusts or *inter vivos trusts* are sometimes used as an asset management tool in lieu of, or in addition to, a DPOA. A trust is an arrangement where property is held by one party (the *trustee*) for the benefit of another (the *beneficiary*). In a living trust that is designed for money management purposes, the person creating the trust (the *settlor* or *grantor*) is also the beneficiary, the trust is managed for his or her benefit during his or her lifetime, and the funds in the trust (the *trust corpus*) pass to one or more named beneficiaries when the settlor dies. As with other types of trusts, the trustee has a fiduciary relationship to the beneficiary and can either be a natural person or an entity such as a corporation.

There are different types of living trusts. Some living trusts are *revocable*, meaning that they can be changed or revoked by the settlor so long as he or she has the cognitive capacity to do so. Other trusts are *irrevocable*, meaning that they are not subject to alteration by the settlor. Which type of trust is appropriate for an individual depends on the individual's needs and the purpose for which he or she is creating the trust. The chief advantage of revocable trusts relative to irrevocable ones is that they provide settlors with greater control over the trust corpus. By contrast, the chief advantage of irrevocable trusts relative to revocable ones is that they provide significant protection from creditors, a characteristic that can make them an attractive tool for individuals engaging in Medicaid planning, a topic discussed in Chapter 6.

Trusts also vary based on whether or not they are immediately funded. For individuals who are not yet ready to have a trustee manage their assets, *standby living trusts* are an option. Such trusts are only funded when a particular event occurs (e.g., the principal becomes ill or incapacitated).

Managing assets through a trust instead of through an agent acting pursuant to a DPOA has some advantages. One is that it can provide the settlor with greater control. When establishing a trust, the settlor can set clear rules for the trustee's behavior with which the trustee must comply. Another is that trustees are often professional individuals or entities and thus may provide more professional and better quality management. In addition, living trusts have potential tax benefits and can be successfully employed to avoid probate because assets titled in the trust's name do not pass under a will.

On the other hand, managing assets through living trusts is both more complex and more expensive than doing so through a DPOA arrangement. Individuals establishing a living trust generally incur substantial attorney fees, and ongoing fees are to be expected where the trustee is a professional individual or agency. In addition, a trust is more limited in its abilities in that it can only manage assets within the trust corpus. Thus, a living trust should generally not be considered to be an alternative to a DPOA, but rather as an additional tool for managing resources.

D. ADVANCE DIRECTIVES

Unlike DPOAs and trusts, which provide for the management of property, *advance directives* are tools for managing health care decisions. Specifically, advance directives are various types of documents that an individual can execute in order to state his or her wishes with regard to future medical treatment or to appoint a surrogate to make decisions on his or her behalf in the event of incapacity. This section explores each of these types of advance directives, problems that can arise in their use, and how medical decisions are to be made for patients who lack advance directives.

1. Types of Advance Directives

A *health care proxy*, also known as a *power of attorney for health care*, is a document by which one person appoints another person to make health care decisions for him or her in the event that he or she becomes unable to do so. A health care proxy only goes into effect when a qualified medical care provider finds that a patient lacks capacity to make medical decisions for him or herself.

The procedure for executing a health care proxy differs by state, as such documents are authorized by state statutory law. States differ, for example, in (1) the scope of powers conferred upon health care agents, (2) whether or not an agent can agree to or refuse certain types of treatment if the principal has not specifically stated his or her preferences regarding such care (e.g., the preference not to receive life sustaining treatment in the event of a terminal illness), (3) the process for determining if the principal lacks capacity, and (4) the process for resolving disputes between health care providers and agents over the use of a proxy. In addition, states differ on what they call health care proxies, with many using the term "power of attorney for health care" instead.

A health care proxy is only one of several types of advance directives for health care. There are several other types of documents that state preferences or instructions for health care but which do not involve the appointment of a surrogate. One is a *living will.* A living will states instructions for providing or withholding life-sustaining care in the event of a terminal illness (i.e., an incurable, lethal medical condition). Living wills can also be used to provide instructions in the event that an individual lapses into permanent unconsciousness (referred to as a *persistent vegetative state* or PVS) or has such irreversible brain damage that they will be permanently unable to make or express preferences. Living wills are typically used to indicate a preference for withholding or withdrawing life-sustaining treatment in such situations. However, a living will can also be used to indicate a preference in favor of the provision and continuation of life-sustaining treatment in such conditions. States differ in their treatment of living wills. Some states treat living wills as binding documents. Other states treat them merely as evidence of a patient's wishes that can be used to guide future decision-making.

Another type of advance directive for health care that does not appoint a surrogate decision-maker is a *Do Not Resuscitate Order* (DNR). A DNR is a document that instructs health care providers not to resuscitate a patient in the event he or she stops breathing. Commonly, this means no *cardiopulmonary resuscitation* (CPR) in the case of a heart attack. DNRs are typically used only with patients who are seriously or terminally ill, and, in particular, in situations in which CPR is unlikely to work or is likely to leave the patient brain damaged or physically worse off than before the heart stopped. Unlike a health care proxy or living will, a DNR is a doctor's order and thus cannot be completed without the involvement of an individual's medical provider. While a DNR does not require the appointment of a surrogate, an individual can provide instructions in a health care proxy to instruct the agent as to the conditions under which the agent should consent to a DNR.

A more recent addition to the ranks of advance directives is the *psychiatric advance directive* (PAD), which is also known as a *mental health advance directive.* A PAD states treatment preferences for mental health care and/or names a surrogate decision-maker to make mental health care decisions. A PAD becomes effective in the event that the principal loses decision-making capacity due to acute mental illness. While all states have statutes enabling the use of standard advance directives for health care, only approximately half have adopted statutes to make PADs legally binding. The PAD was designed to be used by persons living with mental illness (e.g., schizophrenia or bipolar disorder) who wish to plan for periods of acute illness. *But see* Lisa Brodoff, *Planning for Alzheimer's Disease with a Mental Health Advance Directives*, 17 ELDER L.J. 239 (2010) (arguing that mental health advance directives may also be valuable planning tools for persons who have been diagnosed with Alzheimer's disease).

It is important to note that advance directives do not necessarily provide the authority to make all possible health-related decisions, such as decisions about who may visit a patient in a hospital or to whom a deceased individual may be released for burial. Instead, such rights are typically afforded to "family members." Individuals whose primary supporters and loved ones are not related by blood may, therefore, benefit from additional advance planning. In particular, since many older lesbian, gay, bisexual, and transgender (LGBT) persons have formed families and networks that work outside of blood lines and marriage, additional advance planning is often particularly important for them. As Professor Nancy Knauer has explained:

> Health care powers of attorney and advance directives have particular relevance for LGBT elders, but they typically do not address a number of important decisions that are customarily left to "family," such as hospital visitation orders and funeral or burial instructions. For this reason, LGBT elders should supplement the traditional trio of estate planning documents—will, durable power of attorney, and advance directive—with clear written instructions delineating their wishes with respect to hospital visitation, burial, and anything else they feel strongly about, such as the care of their pets or organ donation. In many instances, the actual legal force of these documents may be unclear, but, at the very least, they provide some indicia of what the elder would have wanted had the elder been able to express his or her wishes. These supplemental documents also provide some protection against the potentially conflicting wishes and values of next of kin who may not have been close to the elder and who may disapprove of the elder's chosen family.

* * *

> A hospital visitation authorization form is another type of document that has become a common feature of gay and lesbian estate planning. Necessitated by hospital policies that restrict visitors to "family members," it had long been unclear whether these documents carry any legal force. In response to a 2010 Presidential Memorandum, the Department of Health and Human Services (HHS) issued regulations "to ensure that hospitals that participate in Medicare or Medicaid respect the rights of patients to designate visitors." The Memorandum was prompted by a heartbreaking case in Florida where a same-sex partner was denied access to her dying partner despite the fact that she held her partner's power of attorney. It directs that "participating hospitals may not deny visitation privileges on the basis of race, color, national origin, religion, sex, sexual orientation, gender identity, or disability." The new regulatory measures were later extended to apply to long-term care facilities, but much remains to be seen regarding implementation and the extent to which facilities can impose restrictions based on medical necessity.

Nancy Knauer, *"Gen Silent": Advocating for LGBT Elders*, 19 ELDER L.J. 289, 329-30, 332 (2012).

Partially in recognition of the fact that advance directives fail to capture all of a patient's preferences, many states now authorize *Physician Orders for Life Sustaining Treatment* (POLST) (also known as *Medical Orders for Life Sustaining Treatment* or MOLST) as supplements to advance directives. The POLST is a standardized, highly visible (typically hot pink or another bright color) form on which a health care provider can document the treatment preferences of a seriously ill individual as communicated to the provider either by the patient or by his or her surrogate decision-maker. Unlike advance directives, which are executed in contemplation of future care needs, POLST forms are designed to address a patient's current needs and wishes and, like DNRs, are doctors' orders meant to be used in medical settings. Advocates of POLST describe it as a way to encourage substantive discussion with health care providers about patient's treatment wishes. The POLST approach is seen as advantageous because it transforms a patient's advance directives and other instructions into a medical order upon which health care providers can act. Thus, POLST forms are not a substitute for advance directives but rather supplement them.

NOTES

1. *A workbook approach to advance planning.* In recent years, several non-profit organizations have developed and popularized advance planning tools that provide individuals with an opportunity to work through a series of questions or problems to create a comprehensive statement of their preferences for future care. For example, the non-profit Aging with Dignity has created Five Wishes, a propriety multi-section form that explains a variety of end-of-life issues and provides individuals with a chance to select a proxy, state medical treatment preferences, state specific preferences with regard to comfort care and interpersonal interactions, and craft a message to their loved ones. Similarly, the American Bar Association's Commission on Law and Aging has created the Consumer Tool Kit, which is designed to help people understand their own treatment preferences and to communicate those preferences to potential surrogates. Such documents are not necessarily a substitute for other forms of advance directives. For example, the Consumer Tool Kit cannot be used to directly create a formal advance directive, and the Five Wishes document does not meet the legal requirements to be treated as a legally binding advance directive in all states (although it appears to satisfy the requirements of most states). For further discussion of such alternative forms, see Dorothy Nachman, *Living Wills: Is it Time to Pull the Plug?*, 18 ELDER L.J. 289, 328-31 (2011) (concluding that such documents promote important conversations).

2. *Advance directive registries.* A number of states have created state registries for health care proxies. For example, North Dakota authorized its secretary of state to create a web-accessible advance directive registry. Individuals can register health care proxies for a "reasonable" fee, and registered proxies can

be accessed by entering a file number and password on the state website. The file number and password may only be disclosed to the principal and his or her agent; the state itself, however, can also provide a registered proxy to the principal, his or her agent, and his or her health care provider. *See* NDCC, 23-06.5-19. By comparison, Oklahoma has also created a state registry that grants access to a registered proxy not only to the principal and his or her named agents, but also to persons related within the fourth degree of consanguinity or affinity to the principal and to all healthcare providers caring for the principal. *See* 63 OKLA. STAT. ANN. §§3102.1 et seq. (2013).

3. *Authority to consent to nursing home admission.* One of the most fundamental decisions an agent may be called upon to make on behalf of a principal is whether to consent to the principal's admission to a nursing home. If a principal appoints two different people to serve as attorney-in-fact and health care agent, it may be unclear which agent has the authority to admit the principal to a nursing home. This is because the decision to reside in a nursing home is a hybrid of a health care decision and a financial decision: It has significant consequences for an individual's healthcare as well as the individual's finances and legal rights. Unfortunately, many states' statutes enabling DPOAs and health care proxies are unclear as to whether such agents have the authority to consent to nursing home admission. For example, many states' statutes simply indicate that health care agents have authority to consent to "health care decisions" and attorneys-in-fact have authority to consent to "financial decisions," but do not fully define what types of decisions constitute "health care decisions" or "financial decisions." A number of states with ambiguous statutory language, however, have adopted state statutory short forms for appointing health care agents that state that agents appointed under them have the authority to admit the principal to a nursing home. This suggests that the nursing home admission decisions fall within the purview of health care agents in those states, although arguably only if the health care agent is specifically authorized to consent to admission.

The few states that do clarify which agent has authority to consent to nursing home admission appear to differ in whether they assign that authority to the health care agent or the attorney-in-fact. *Compare* CAL. PROB. CODE §4123 (2013) ("with regard to personal care, a power of attorney may grant authority to make decisions relating to the personal care of the principal, including, but not limited to, determining where the principal will live"); KAN. STAT. ANN. §58-629(a) (2013) ("a durable power of attorney for healthcare decisions may convey to the agent the authority to . . . make all necessary arrangements for the principal at any hospital, psychiatric hospital or psychiatric treatment facility, hospice, nursing home or similar institution"). Notably, Wisconsin takes an unusual approach to this issue: It statutorily grants health care agents the authority to place a principal in a nursing home, but only temporarily. Longer placements must be explicitly authorized by the principal's power of attorney for health care decisions. *See* WIS. STAT. ANN. §155.20 (2013).

As a practical matter, who has authority to consent to nursing home admission primarily becomes an issue in two situations: (1) when the attorney-in-fact and health care agent disagree as to whether nursing home placement is appropriate, and (2) when the principal or his or her agent is arguing that a provision in a nursing home admission contract is not enforceable because the person signing the contract lacked authority to do so.

4. *Scope of authority with regards to nursing home admission.* Case law in some states suggests that even if a health care agent is empowered to admit a person to a nursing home, he or she does not necessarily have the authority to bind the person to all admission contract provisions (e.g., to a binding arbitration clause). See Chapter 7 (page 425) for a discussion of the effect of binding arbitration clauses in nursing home contracts.

QUESTIONS

1. Although health care proxies are important planning tools, especially for older adults who are experiencing or anticipating a serious decline in their health, the majority of Americans have not executed them. Individuals with lower socioeconomic status and racial minorities are particularly unlikely to have done so. Why might this be the case? Should something be done to change this situation? If so, what?

2. What are the principal advantages and disadvantages of the registry systems discussed in Note 2 on pages 119-120? If you were drafting a bill to create a health care proxy registry for your state, what provisions would you want to include? Why?

PROBLEM

An older man with severe dementia previously appointed his son as his agent under his DPOA and his daughter as his agent under his health care proxy. The daughter believes her father should be cared for at home with the assistance of paid caregivers. The son believes that such care is unnecessarily expensive and refuses to pay for it. He plans to sell the father's house and arrange to have his father admitted to a local nursing home with a good reputation for caring for persons with dementia. Does he have the authority to do so? If the son and daughter continue to disagree as to their father's care, should a court intervene and appoint a guardian?

2. Advance Directive Execution Requirements and Considerations

Execution requirements for advance directives vary depending on the state. The Uniform Health Care Decisions Act takes the position that a health care proxy must be signed to be effective, but does not need to be witnessed or acknowledged. Some states have more significant execution requirements. For example, it is common for states to require that health care proxies be witnessed.

Regardless of the state in which a person executes a health care proxy, however, he or she has several important choices to make. First, he or she must decide whom he or she wishes to appoint as surrogate and whether to appoint a back-up surrogate in the event the first surrogate is unable or unwilling to serve.

The choice of the surrogate is an important one as not all surrogates are equally equipped to effectuate a patient's wishes. Conventional wisdom is that surrogates should be chosen based on their willingness and availability to serve (which may be affected in part by their proximity to the principal), their trustworthiness, and their willingness to respect and comply with the principal's wishes. Some research suggests, however, that another important consideration is the surrogate's own values and preferences. Although individuals are generally counseled that they should discuss their values and treatment preferences with their surrogates so that their surrogates will be able to make decisions that are consistent with the principal's wishes, the empirical literature on surrogate decision-making suggests that such conversations do not significantly increase the likelihood that a surrogate will make the decisions the patient would have made if able. Specifically, studies suggest that surrogates are likely to make the treatment choice a patient would have made only slightly over two-thirds of the time, and that—despite conventional wisdom to the contrary—discussions do little to improve accuracy. A better predictor that the surrogate will make the decisions that the patient would want made is that the surrogate would make those same decisions for him- or herself under the circumstances. *See* Nina A. Kohn & Jeremy A. Blumenthal, *Designating Health Care Decisionmakers for Patients without Advance Directives: A Psychological Critique*, 42 GA. L. REV. 979, 1003 (2008) (reviewing the empirical literature). Accordingly, attorneys should consider advising clients to not only discuss their own preferences with potential surrogates but also the potential surrogate's own preferences, and to consider favoring surrogates with similar values and preferences.

A second critical choice that a principal must make in executing an advance directive is whether or not to include specific instructions about how the surrogate should go about making health care decisions. As discussed in depth in Chapter 9, many states do not allow surrogate decision-makers to refuse life sustaining treatment unless there is clear and convincing evidence that the patient would have refused it if able to do so. Accordingly, clients who wish not to be kept alive by artificial means (at least under certain circumstances) are generally well-advised to include language to that effect in their advance directives. As a practical matter, this means that attorneys should be familiar with different forms of end-of-life care and life-sustaining treatment so that they can advise as to the substance of such instructions.

A third choice—and one often overlooked—is whether to revise an existing advance directive. Research shows that individuals' treatment preferences evolve over time, and that individuals are limited in the ability to predict their future preferences. In order to increase the likelihood that advance directives reflect an individual's current wishes, it is therefore commonly recommended that they be revisited every few years.

3. Sample Advance Directives

HEALTH CARE PROXY

(1)   I, **Jane Doe**, of 100 Mountainview Road, Ithaca, New York, 14850, hereby appoint **John Doe**, also of 100 Mountainview Road, Ithaca, New York, 14850, cell phone number 607-555-0100, **as my health care agent to make any and all health care decisions** for me, except to the extent that I state otherwise. This proxy shall take effect only when and if I become unable to make my own health care decisions.

(2)   **First Alternate Agent:** If the person I appoint is unable, unwilling, or unavailable to act as my health care agent, I hereby appoint **Mary Frank**, of 241 Sunny Meadow Road, Hinesburg, Vermont 05461, home telephone 802-555-0199, as my health care agent to make any and all health care decisions for me, except to the extent that I state otherwise.

(3)   Unless I revoke it or state an expiration date or circumstances under which it will expire, this proxy shall remain in effect indefinitely.

(4)   I direct my health care agent to make health care decisions according to my wishes and limitations, as he or she knows and as stated below:

In the event that I am in a coma or unconscious with no hope of recovery or have brain damage or disease that renders me unable to recognize people or communicate with people with no hope of recovery, I direct my agent to withhold or withdraw treatment that merely prolongs my life. In particular, if I am in such a condition, I do not want to receive any of the following if they are designed merely to prolong my life: artificial nutrition, artificial hydration, mechanical respiration, surgery, blood or blood products that would replace lost blood, invasive diagnostic tests, kidney dialysis, or cardiopulmonary resuscitation (CPR). This does not preclude the administration of medication designed to alleviate pain or any other treatments designed to alleviate pain or increase comfort.

(5)   The persons named as my health care agent and alternate health care agent above shall also be considered my personal representatives for purposes of the disclosure of personally identifiable health information pursuant to the Health Insurance Portability and Accountability Act of 1996 (HIPAA) as implemented by 42 C.F.R. §164.502.

(6)   **My Identification**
      My Name: Jane Doe
      My Signature: _____   Date:_____
      My Address: 100 Mountainview Road, Ithaca, New York, 14850

(7)   **Statement by Witnesses**
      I declare that the person who signed this document is personally known to me and appears to be of sound mind and acting of his or her own free will. He or she signed (or asked another to sign for him or her) this document in my presence.
      Date_____   Date_____
      Name_____   Name_____
      Signature_____   Signature_____
      Address_____   Address_____

QUESTIONS

1. What would be the effect of the instructions that Jane Doe included in the above health care proxy?

2. What are the advantages or disadvantages of providing such detailed instructions?

3. If you were writing a health care proxy for yourself, what choices would you make? How might it differ from Jane Doe's health care proxy?

4. To what extent does Jane Doe's health care proxy convey her wishes to her agent? Can you think of any circumstances under which the agent might be unsure of how to act because Jane Doe's preferences are unclear?

UNIFORM HEALTH CARE DECISIONS ACT
ADVANCE HEALTH-CARE DIRECTIVE FORM

Explanation

You have the right to give instructions about your own health care. You also have the right to name someone else to make health-care decisions for you. This form lets you do either or both of these things. It also lets you express your wishes regarding donation of organs and the designation of your primary physician. If you use this form, you may complete or modify all or any part of it. You are free to use a different form.

Part 1 of this form is a power of attorney for health care. Part 1 lets you name another individual as agent to make health-care decisions for you if you become incapable of making your own decisions or if you want someone else to make those decisions for you now even though you are still capable. You may also name an alternate agent to act for you if your first choice is not willing, able, or reasonably available to make decisions for you. Unless related to you, your agent may not be an owner, operator, or employee of [a residential long-term health-care institution] at which you are receiving care.

Unless the form you sign limits the authority of your agent, your agent may make all health-care decisions for you. This form has a place for you to limit the authority of your agent. You need not limit the authority of your agent if you wish to rely on your agent for all health-care decisions that may have to be made. If you choose not to limit the authority of your agent, your agent will have the right to:

(a) consent or refuse consent to any care, treatment, service, or procedure to maintain, diagnose, or otherwise affect a physical or mental condition;

(b) select or discharge health-care providers and institutions;

(c) approve or disapprove diagnostic tests, surgical procedures, programs of medication, and orders not to resuscitate; and

(d) direct the provision, withholding, or withdrawal of artificial nutrition and hydration and all other forms of health care.

Part 2 of this form lets you give specific instructions about any aspect of your health care. Choices are provided for you to express your wishes regarding the provision, withholding, or withdrawal of treatment to keep you alive, including the provision of artificial nutrition and hydration, as well as the provision of pain relief. Space is also provided for you to add to the choices you have made or for you to write out any additional wishes.

Part 3 of this form lets you express an intention to donate your bodily organs and tissues following your death.

Part 4 of this form lets you designate a physician to have primary responsibility for your health care.

After completing this form, sign and date the form at the end. It is recommended but not required that you request two other individuals to sign as witnesses. Give a copy of the signed and completed form to your physician, to any other health-care providers you may have, to any health-care institution at which you are receiving care, and to any health-care agents you have named. You should talk to the person you have named as agent to make sure that he or she understands your wishes and is willing to take the responsibility.

You have the right to revoke this advance health-care directive or replace this form at any time.

* *

PART 1

POWER OF ATTORNEY FOR HEALTH CARE

(1) DESIGNATION OF AGENT: I designate the following individual as my agent to make health-care decisions for me:

_____

(name of individual you choose as agent)

_____

(address) (city) (state) (zip code)

_____

(home phone) (work phone)

OPTIONAL: If I revoke my agent's authority or if my agent is not willing, able, or reasonably available to make a health-care decision for me, I designate as my first alternate agent:

_____

(name of individual you choose as first alternate agent)

_____

(address) (city) (state) (zip code)

_____

(home phone) (work phone)

OPTIONAL: If I revoke the authority of my agent and first alternate agent or if neither is willing, able, or reasonably available to make a health-care decision for me, I designate as my second alternate agent:

_____

(name of individual you choose as second alternate agent)

_____

(address) (city) (state) (zip code)

_____

(home phone) (work phone)

(2) AGENT'S AUTHORITY: My agent is authorized to make all health-care decisions for me, including decisions to provide, withhold, or withdraw artificial nutrition and hydration and all other forms of health care to keep me alive, except as I state here:

_____

_____

_____

(Add additional sheets if needed.)

(3) WHEN AGENT'S AUTHORITY BECOMES EFFECTIVE: My agent's authority becomes effective when my primary physician determines that I am unable to make my own health-care decisions unless I mark the following box. If I mark this box [ ], my agent's authority to make health-care decisions for me takes effect immediately.

(4) AGENT'S OBLIGATION: My agent shall make health-care decisions for me in accordance with this power of attorney for health care, any instructions I give in Part 2 of this form, and my other wishes to the extent known to my agent. To the extent my wishes are unknown, my agent shall make health-care decisions for me in accordance with what my agent determines to be in my best interest. In determining my best interest, my agent shall consider my personal values to the extent known to my agent.

(5) NOMINATION OF GUARDIAN: If a guardian of my person needs to be appointed for me by a court, I nominate the agent designated in this form. If that agent is not willing, able, or reasonably available to act as guardian, I nominate the alternate agents whom I have named, in the order designated.

PART 2

INSTRUCTIONS FOR HEALTH CARE

If you are satisfied to allow your agent to determine what is best for you in making end-of-life decisions, you need not fill out this part of the form. If you do fill out this part of the form, you may strike any wording you do not want.

(6) END-OF-LIFE DECISIONS: I direct that my health-care providers and others involved in my care provide, withhold, or withdraw treatment in accordance with the choice I have marked below:

[   ] (a) Choice Not To Prolong Life

I do not want my life to be prolonged if (i) I have an incurable and irreversible condition that will result in my death within a relatively short time, (ii) I become unconscious and, to a reasonable degree of medical certainty, I will not regain consciousness, or (iii) the likely risks and burdens of treatment would outweigh the expected benefits, OR

[   ] (b) Choice To Prolong Life

I want my life to be prolonged as long as possible within the limits of generally accepted health-care standards.

(7) ARTIFICIAL NUTRITION AND HYDRATION: Artificial nutrition and hydration must be provided, withheld, or withdrawn in accordance with the choice I have made in paragraph (6) unless I mark the following box. If I mark this box [   ], artificial nutrition and hydration must be provided regardless of my condition and regardless of the choice I have made in paragraph (6).

(8) RELIEF FROM PAIN: Except as I state in the following space, I direct that treatment for alleviation of pain or discomfort be provided at all times, even if it hastens my death:

_____

_____

(9) OTHER WISHES: (If you do not agree with any of the optional choices above and wish to write your own, or if you wish to add to the instructions you have given above, you may do so here.) I direct that:

_____

_____

(Add additional sheets if needed.)

PART 3

DONATION OF ORGANS AT DEATH
(OPTIONAL)

(10) Upon my death (mark applicable box)
[   ] (a) I give any needed organs, tissues, or parts, OR
[   ] (b) I give the following organs, tissues, or parts only

(c) My gift is for the following purposes (strike any of the following you do not want)
   (i) Transplant
   (ii) Therapy
   (iii) Research
   (iv) Education

PART 4

PRIMARY PHYSICIAN

(OPTIONAL)

(11) I designate the following physician as my primary physician:

_____
(name of physician)

_____
(address) (city) (state) (zip code)

_____
(phone)

OPTIONAL: If the physician I have designated above is not willing, able, or reasonably available to act as my primary physician, I designate the following physician as my primary physician:

_____
(name of physician)

_____
(address) (city) (state) (zip code)

_____
(phone)

(12) EFFECT OF COPY: A copy of this form has the same effect as the original.

(13) SIGNATURES: Sign and date the form here:

_____   _____
(date)   (sign your name)

_____   _____
(address)   (print your name)

_____
(city) (state)

(Optional) SIGNATURES OF WITNESSES:

First witness   Second witness

_____   _____
(print name)   (print name)

_____   _____

(address)	(address)
(city) (state)	(city) (state)
(signature of witness)	(signature of witness)
(date)	(date)

4. Interpreting Ambiguous Instructions

Unfortunately, advance directives may include language that is ambiguous or arguably ambiguous. This can lead to disputes about whether or not the agent is complying with the patient's instructions. As the next case illustrates, when disputes arise, courts may look to the patient's past expressions and evidence of the patient's values to determine the proper construction of the language.

S.I. & F.H v. R.S. & South Nassau Communities Hospital

877 N.Y.S.2d 860 (N.Y. Sup. Ct. 2009)

[Petitioners (F.H. and S.I.) sought to have F.H. appointed as guardian for their brother (S.S.) and to void the appointment of the brother's wife (R.S.) as his health care agent pursuant to a health care proxy he had executed in January 2009.—Ed.]

* * *

The matter sub judice pits a patient's siblings against his wife. Not only are their differing positions based upon their relationship with the patient, religion and other beliefs, the very intent of the principal is at issue. Herein the principal, while verbally expressing a wish to live his way and on his terms without being dependent upon machines, in response to being advised by his doctor that his future may well be dependent upon the use of a respirator, created a health care proxy stating "I wish to live." This Court is charged with trying to reconcile those seemingly incongruent and impossible desires to determine the principal's wishes and whether the agent is acting in accordance with those wishes.

The principal and patient S.S. was described by witnesses as a magnetic, loud, colorful, outspoken, "in your face kind of guy" who loved to work, loved the Yankees and loved life. He suffered from obesity, which impacted on his ability to breathe. Despite having his stomach banded several years ago, S.S. still loved to eat and continued to battle his weight and the adverse effects it had on his health. Approximately two and one half years ago in November 2006, S.S. was rushed to the emergency room and during that hospitalization, due to elevated carbon dioxide (CO_2) levels, had to have a tracheotomy.

Dr. A., S.S.'s treating Pulmonologist, who has treated S.S. since that hospitalization testified. Dr. A. is both a friend and doctor to S.S. and he began treating S.S. for abdominal distress and breathing difficulties after seeing him in the emergency room in November 2006. S.S. had an extended stay in ICU at that time. S.S. was able to be weaned off the respirator and was sent for rehabilitation upon his release from the hospital. After a brief re-hospitalization, S.S. returned home and while frustrated by limitations pertaining to the trache, for example his inability to swim, he resumed working and went about his activities of daily living.

After S.S. fell ill on January 5, 2009 R.S. took him to see Dr. A. Petitioner F.H. followed them to the doctor's office in her own car and waited in the waiting room while R.S. and S.S. met with Dr. A. At that visit, Dr. A discussed S.S.'s condition and treatment alternatives going forward, including antibiotics, a stomach scope and a respirator. S.S. said he did not want a mechanical ventilator or artificial nutrition. According to Dr. A. and R.S., S.S. often complained about the trache and repeatedly tried to have it removed because "This is no way to live."

S.S. spoke about the people he saw while he was in ICU and "rehab," dependent on tubes to live and was very animated and emphatic that he was willing to die rather than live like that. This was so, despite having already benefitted from the type of devices he was now rejecting, i.e., the NG (nasogastric feeding) tube and respirator during the November 2006 hospitalization.

In light of that, Dr. A. brought up the subject of a Health Care Proxy and provided the form, which meets the statutory criteria, to S.S. and encouraged him to fill it out. R.S. actually completed the form for S.S.'s signature. At S.S.'s direction, R.S., in paragraph "2. Optional Instructions" wrote: "I wish to live." Dr. A. acknowledged never having seen anyone write such a statement on a health care proxy, but explained that S.S. did not want the doctor to give up on him, he wanted the trache out "in the worst way," so that he could go to the beach club, and wanted to live on his terms, not in a nursing home. The doctor said that S.S. spoke to him on a number of occasions about the value S.S. placed on the quality of life. S.S. was very emphatic, very clear about how he wanted to live, and spoke often on the subject, including his desire to go to Yankee games and the beach club.

Although Dr. A. did not recall F.H. being in the waiting room on that visit, he acknowledged speaking to her about S.S. on other occasions. S.S. did not list an alternate health care agent. S.S.'s siblings, the Petitioners herein, while interested in S.S.'s care, were not chosen by S.S. to be his health care agents, nor did he advise Dr. A. that he would like to discuss his care and treatment or the health care proxy with them prior to signing it.

Petitioners are Orthodox Jews and while S.S. was brought up in an Orthodox household, he has not been observant for decades. S.S. clearly respected his family's observances but he did not belong to a temple, he worked on the

Sabbath, including during the year of mourning following his father's death, and did not keep a Kosher home or attend religious services on a regular basis. The strongly held views of Petitioners were not S.S.'s. . . .

F.H., upon learning at Dr. A.s' [sic] office that the doctor told S.S. that he must lose weight or he would be on a respirator and that S.S. had signed a health care proxy stating that he "wished to live" never discussed with S.S. what he meant by that, or what S.S.'s wishes were, nor did she inquire as to why she was not an alternate agent. Indeed, she acknowledged that S.S. was not an Orthodox Jew, and while her position, based upon her religious beliefs, is to prolong life no matter what the circumstance, the evidence did not establish that S.S. shared her religious views. F.H. also denied ever having a specific conversation with S.S. regarding the use of a ventilator or artificial nutrition and hydration, but stated that they talked about his funeral arrangements.

Petitioners allege that Respondent R.S. is acting contrary to S.S.'s religious beliefs; not in his best interests in that she has not agreed to the insertion of a PEG tube, for optimum care to replace the NG tube; and further that she is acting in bad faith in that she is motivated by fear of the financial ramifications of S.S.'s health care. No evidence was presented to establish that S.S.'s insurance would not be continued or that financial circumstances were dire or that R.S.'s decisions are being made for financial reasons. While the Petitioners testified that S.S. honored his father's wishes and joined in his siblings' decision not to withhold life sustaining treatment from his dying father four years ago, there was no evidence that S.S. sought the same treatment for himself . . . .

. . . The agent's unfortunate use of punctuation (!!!) after writing S.S.'s "I wish to live!!!" statement was not at S.S.'s direction and the Court credits R.S.'s explanation of her "habit" of adding exclamation points and does not share Petitioners' contention that the punctuation was significant or meaningful to S.S. The Court notes that at the time R.S. unilaterally added the exclamation points, S.S. was walking, talking and while not in robust health, was on his way home from an office visit and not *in extremis.*

The Petitioners did not produce any witnesses who claimed to have discussed S.S.'s wishes regarding health care. The only evidence presented at the hearing regarding S.S.'s expressed wishes with respect to his health care and treatment was adduced through the testimony of Dr. A. and R.S. Both individuals had numerous conversations with S.S., wherein he indicated his desire to live life to the fullest, but that he did not want to be on a respirator. Indeed, he did not even want the trache, a less burdensome form of treatment. R.S. testified that she and S.S. discussed the Terri Schiavo case when it was being reported in the news and how he did not want to live like that. She also recalled that while S.S. was in rehab, each day she wheeled him by the room next to his, he would look at the young girl, laying all but lifeless in her bed, hooked up to machines and tubes and would say that he would not want to live like that.

The testimony supports a finding that S.S. wanted to live life to the fullest, not to merely exist, unable to communicate and interact with his family and friends. The evidence established S.S. expressly entrusted his wife to be his health care agent and to carry out his wishes, as expressed again to R.S. and to Dr. A., just days before suffering a heart attack and severe neurological damage to his brain.

I find that the Health Care Proxy executed by S.S. on January 5, 2009 is valid and meets the statutory criteria set forth in Public Health Law §2981. While this proceeding was properly commenced by the principal's siblings, the Petitioners have failed to establish any ground upon which the agent should be removed, they have not established that the agent is acting in bad faith; nor have they proffered any proof that would warrant overriding the agent's decision on the grounds that the decision was made in bad faith or that it was not in accordance with PHL §2982(1) or (2). Mere speculation or hope, regardless of how heartfelt, can not override the agent's decisions, which have priority over other surrogates.

Having determined that the Health Care Proxy is valid, there is no need for a guardian of the person or property of S.S. . . .

Accordingly, the Petition is dismissed.

5. Factors Triggering the Use of Advance Directives

Unlike a DPOA, which is typically effective once signed, advance directives are only effective when the principal lacks capacity. If the principal has capacity to do so, health care providers should instead look to the principal to directly make decisions or his or her own behalf. Thus, a health care agent acting pursuant to a health care proxy is only entitled to make decisions on behalf of a principal if the principal lacks capacity to make those decisions for him- or herself. Similarly, a health care provider should only take direction from a surrogate decision-maker when the patient is not presently able to make his or her own health care decisions.

The next case explores how a determination of such incapacity should—and should not—be made.

Payne v. Marion General Hospital

549 N.E.2d 1043 (Ind. Ct. App. 1990)

BUCHANAN, Judge.

CASE SUMMARY

Counter-plaintiff-appellant, the Estate of Cloyd Payne (Estate), appeals from the entry of summary judgment in favor of the counter-defendants-appellees

Miles W. Donaldson, M.D. (Dr. Donaldson), Marion General Hospital, Inc. (Hospital) and Marion Family Practice, Inc. (Practice), claiming the trial court erred when it determined there was no genuine issue of material fact.

We reverse in part and affirm in part.

FACTS

The facts most favorable to the non-moving party (the Estate) reveal that Cloyd Payne (Payne) was admitted to the Hospital on June 6, 1983. Payne was suffering from a variety of maladies, including malnutrition, uremia, hypertensive cardiovascular disease, chronic obstructive lung disease, non-union of a previously fractured left humerus, and congenital levoscoliosis of the lumbar spine. Payne was a 65-year-old alcoholic who had allowed his condition to deteriorate to the point he required hospitalization.

Throughout his stay in the Hospital, Payne was subjected to various tests, which confirmed the admitting diagnosis of malnutrition and uremia. By June 10 his condition was deteriorating. He ate poorly and his respirations became labored. On the morning of June 11, Dr. Donaldson examined Payne but made no modifications in Payne's treatment. Payne ate poorly and was visited by family. At approximately 7:00 P.M., Payne's condition worsened as his temperature rose and his respirations became more frequent and labored. Payne appeared to be awake and alert.

At approximately 9:25 P.M., Payne became congested and mucus was aspirated from his lungs. Shortly thereafter, the nurses attempted to reach Payne's nephew, but were unable to contact him. The nurses did contact Payne's sister and she arrived at the Hospital a short time later. The nurses also contacted Dr. Donaldson and related Payne's condition. Dr. Donaldson then ordered some minor adjustments in Payne's treatment.

After observing Payne for several minutes, his sister informed the nurse she did not want Payne resuscitated if he began to die. The nurse contacted Dr. Donaldson and informed him of Payne's condition and of his sister's request. After consulting with the nurse and talking to Payne's sister, Dr. Donaldson then authorized the entry of a "no code" on Payne's chart, after verifying his order with another nurse pursuant to the Hospital's policy. A "no code" is a designation on a patient's chart that no cardiopulmonary resuscitation is to be given in the event the patient begins to expire. The "no code" was entered by the nurse attending Payne, and no efforts to give Payne cardio-pulmonary resuscitation were attempted.

Supportive care was continued, including the suctioning of mucus from Payne's lungs. Occasionally, Payne was awake and alert, and he made eye contact with the nurses attending him. Payne was conscious and capable of communicating with the nurses until moments before his death. His condition continued to worsen, and at 12:55 A.M. on June 12, 1983, Payne died, and no cardio-pulmonary resuscitation was attempted.

Dr. Donaldson later sued the Estate for compensation, and the Estate counter-claimed, alleging Dr. Donaldson committed malpractice when he issued the "no code." The counter-claim averred that Dr. Donaldson was acting as an agent of the Practice, and joined the Practice as a party. The counter-claim also included a claim of negligence against the Hospital for failing to provide the proper procedural safeguards when doctors issue "no codes." Dr. Donaldson, the Practice and the Hospital moved for summary judgment and introduced the medical review panel's opinion, issued in accordance with the requirements of the medical malpractice law, which determined the defendants were not negligent. The motions were granted and summary judgment was entered in favor of Dr. Donaldson, the Practice and the Hospital.

* * *

DECISION

* * *

This is a case of first impression, in which a doctor is sought to be held liable for issuing a "do not resuscitate" order, commonly referred to as a "no code." While numerous courts have considered similar issues, such as a patient's right to refuse medical treatment and the consent needed to effectuate that right for incompetent patients, no court has considered the physician's liability after having entered a "no code."

Our focus is different. The Estate's claim is that Payne was competent at the time the "no code" was issued and that Dr. Donaldson failed to obtain Payne's informed consent before he issued the "no code." The Estate appeals from the grant of a motion for summary judgment in favor of Dr. Donaldson and the Practice.

* * *

In Indiana, the tort of medical malpractice has the same elements of other negligence torts. The elements are: (1) a duty on the part of the defendant in relation to the plaintiff; (2) a failure on the part of the defendant to conform his conduct to the requisite standard of care required by the relationship; and (3) an injury to the plaintiff resulting from that failure.

The duty owed to Payne by Dr. Donaldson is well established as a matter of law. A physician has the duty to make reasonable disclosure of material facts relevant to the care of a patient. The patient's right of self-determination is the *sine qua non* of the physician's duty to obtain informed consent. ... Dr. Donaldson's first response is that Payne was an incompetent, terminally ill patient, and therefore he owed Payne no duty to obtain his consent for the entering of the "no-code," and that his sister's consent was sufficient.

Whether Payne was competent and terminally ill, however, are questions of fact. An examination of the record reveals that genuine issues of fact exists as to whether Payne was competent and terminally ill, precluding the entry of summary judgment in favor of Dr. Donaldson and the Practice.

There is evidence in the depositions of the nurses who attended Payne during the last day of his life from which a jury could conclude Payne was conscious, alert, and able to communicate when the "no code" was entered, and that he remained competent until shortly before his death.

Shirley Lyons, a licensed practical nurse who attended Payne in the morning and early afternoon on the day of his death, testified as follows:

"Q Did you have occasion during his confinement to speak with him at all?
A Yes.
Q What would the nature of your speech have been?
A As to how he felt and what I could do for him to assist him.
Q Do you recall whether or not he was capable of verbal response?
A Yes.
Q I assume that means you can recall, will you tell me whether or not he was verbal in his responses?
A I did not have a lengthy conversation with him.
Q But he did speak to you?
A Yes.
Q Did he speak in words or phrases that you could understand?
A Yes.
Q Did his answers appear to be responsive to your questions?
A Yes.
Q Did he appear capable of communicating meaningful thoughts to you?
A Meaning what?
Q Did he give you the information that you sought in your questions?
A Yes.
Q Did you respond on the basis of his answers?
A Yes.
Q And care for him in response to his own expressions?
A Yes.
Q Would it be fair to say that you gave credence to his answers?
A I don't understand.
Q You considered them in the course of your conduct as a licensed practical nurse?
A Yes.
Q Took what he said at face value?
A Yes.

. . . .

Q Do you recall whether on that day, the 11th of June, 1983, you addressed him in conversation?
A No.
Q You don't recall?
A You said on that date? I recall, as I said before, talking to him and answering questions as far as what I could do for him but not in a long conversation.
Q Would the brief exchanges that you have just described taken place on the 11th?
A Yes."

Edna Cardwell, a registered nurse who received Dr. Donaldson's order issuing the "no code," attended Payne during the afternoon and evening on the day he died. She testified:

"Q Do you have any reason to suspect that on the 11th of June, 1983, Mr. Payne was unable to speak?

A   Well, it would be the same as he would respond to conversation. If you would talk to him he would look at your [sic] and appeared to understand but he verbally did not respond to me.

Q Do you have any reason to suspect that he was not capable of responding verbally?

A   How do you mean not capable?

Q Not physically able to speak words?

A   He was quite short of breath but I would not say that he wasn't capable.

Q *I believe in your prior answer you indicated that on the 11th of June, 1983, he appeared to understand what was being said to him, is that what you said?*

A   *Yes.* Because he looked up at you, when you would speak to him he would look at you. He did not respond to me but you would know that he could hear you.

Q Is there a method that nurses in general or you, in particular, use to communicate with patients who are in that type of condition? Do you ask yes or no questions?

A   Yes. Sometimes we ask a patient and they shake their head.

Q Is there sometimes some signal that you devise, moving a finger or blinking an eye for affirmative or negative answers?

A   Well, that always don't hold true, blinking an eye, everyone blinks an eye so you aren't positive whether they can understand you or not.

Q But are there methods that are utilized by nurses to communicate with patients who may have difficulty in verbal communication?

A   I really don't understand what you mean.

Q *There are methods that you can use to communicate with a person who has a mental faculty but is unable to speak?*

A   *Yes.*

Q *Did there come a time on the 11th of June where in your opinion Mr. Payne lost the ability to communicate entirely?*

A   *No, not on my tour of duty.*

Q Which would have been ending at 11:00?

A   Yes.

Q Is there anything in your notes to indicate that Mr. Payne was other than conscious during your shift on the 11th?

A   Well, I've noted at 7:00 P.M., 'responds when spoken to,' which would be by expression of his eyes or movement of his head.

Q You have said, Mrs. Cardwell, that you as charge nurse would make note of any significant change in condition. Would that hold true of the loss of consciousness? Would you as charge nurse normally make an entry when a patient losses [sic] his ability to comprehend?

A   Yes.

Q And there is no such entry in Mr. Payne's case?

A   No.

Q *So is it fair to assume that to the end of your shift he maintained consciousness?*

A   *Yes.*

Q And the last time that he actually responded to you was 7:00, did you say?

A   That's the first entry I made that p.m.

Q *And it was never reported to you by any of your nursing staff that Mr. Payne had lost consciousness at any time during the night?*
A *No."*

Bonnie Jean Cunningham, a licensed practical nurse who attended Payne during the last hours of his life, testified:

"Q *Do you have reason to believe that he was aware of your presence?*
A *Yes.*
Q Do you have reason to believe that he was aware of his condition and surroundings and where he was?
A In my mind I thought so.
Q In your mind was he oriented as to time and place?
A I doubt that he was oriented as to the time.
Q In your impression did he know that he was at Marion General Hospital?
A I would think so.
Q And that you were nurses on the staff?
A Yes.
Q And that you were treating him for a medical condition of some sort?
A Yes.
Q Do you have reason to believe he was aware of the presence of his sister?
A Yes.
Q Were you making any effort to keep him informed of what you were doing or was it patently obvious what you were doing?
A I guess it was patently obvious what we were doing. We were working very hard to keep him comfortable, suctioning him, trying to keep the oxygen as much as possible. His skin color was a little dusky looking. He was not getting enough oxygen to keep himself going. That's why we suctioned so frequently.
Q Do you know or do the records indicate to you when Mr. Payne died?
A 12:55.
Q That would be the end of this hour that we are discussing?
A Yes.
Q *Was there a point prior to his death that you feel he lost consciousness?*
A *Maybe right before 12:55.* How do you describe it. As he filled up more we suctioned more but we can't possible (sic) go that far down, with this dark blood stuff coming up and I would say probably—I don't know an exact time.
Q Would it have been within minutes of his death?
A Yes.
Q Prior to that period of minutes before his death, was his condition as you have previously described it in our conversation today?
A Increasingly serious as the hour went on.
Q *But it would have been within moments of his death that he was unable to, in your opinion, comprehend his condition, what was happening to him?*
A *True.*
Q Mr. Payne, at the time that we are discussing, the hour between 12:00 midnight and 12:55 on the 12th of June, 1983, was what is referred to as a no code, is that correct?
A Yes.

. . . .

Q   In situations where patients are weak physically or for one reason or another unable to communicate in words, do members of your profession devise ways of communicating and answering the questions with the movement of a body part?

A   I think eye contact has a lot to do with it.

Q   *In your opinion was this method of communication possible with Mr. Payne during the hours of 11:00 P.M. on the 11th to shortly before he died?*

A   *Yes.*

Q   *Do you feel that he would have had the capacity to hear and understand what you were saying to him?*

A   *Yes, part of the time.*

Q   Do you feel that he would have had the ability to process that information and give you a response?

A   I don't know about a verbal response.

Q   How about eye contact or whatever?

Q   His eye contact—yes. He looked into your eyes a lot."

This evidence unmistakably establishes a genuine issue of fact exists as to whether Payne was competent when the "no code" was issued. Therefore, viewing the evidence in the light most favorable to the nonmovant, we must conclude Payne was competent when Dr. Donaldson issued the "no code."

As to whether Payne was terminally ill, the Estate points to the fact that in March of 1982, Payne was treated by Dr. Donaldson for precisely the same conditions he was suffering from when he was admitted into the Hospital on June 6, 1983.

Dr. Donaldson's responses to the Estate's interrogatories included the following:

"1. Did you have occasion to treat Cloyd A. Payne during a hospital stay in March of 1982?
RESPONSE: Yes.
2. What were you treating the patient for at that time?
RESPONSE:
Malnutrition; uremia; hypertensive cardiovascular disease; chronic obstructive lung disease; non-union of old fractured left humerus; and congenital levoscoliosis of the lumbar spine.
3. Did you have occasion to treat Cloyd A Payne during June of 1983?
RESPONSE: Yes.
4. If so, state:
a. What did you determine the patient was suffering from during June of 1983?
b. What services did you render to the patient during June of 1983?
RESPONSE:
a. *Malnutrition; uremia; hypertensive cardiovascular disease; chronic obstructive lung disease; non-union of old fractured left humerus; and congenital levoscoliosis of the lumbar spine.*
b. Supportive treatment."

As Payne had previously survived the identical conditions from which he suffered at the time of his admission in June of 1983, whether Payne was terminally ill cannot be resolved by reference to undisputed facts. Because this evidence has *some* probative value, we must conclude a genuine issue of fact exists as to whether Payne was terminally ill. . . . Because the evidence could support a conclusion that Payne was competent and not terminally ill at the time the "no code" was issued, we cannot accept Dr. Donaldson's and the Practice's claim that no duty to obtain his consent was owed to Payne.

In the alternative, Dr. Donaldson and the Practice argue that the Estate's lack of expert medical testimony as to the standard of care required by Dr. Donaldson's relationship with Payne, to rebut the medical review panel's opinion Dr. Donaldson and the Practice were not negligent, is fatal to its cause of action. . . . [N]ot every medical malpractice case needs expert medical testimony to survive summary judgment. . . .

We believe that this is a situation within the realm of the ordinary laymen's comprehension. No disclosure whatsoever was made. Further, the evidence establishes that Dr. Donaldson made *no* effort to determine if Payne was competent. The "no code" was issued over the phone and Dr. Donaldson had not seen Payne for several hours when he issued the "no code." If a jury concludes that Payne was competent at the time the "no code" was issued, it could conclude that the fact Dr. Donaldson made *no* effort to obtain Payne's consent and that he made *no* effort to determine whether Payne was competent was a breach of his duty to obtain Payne's consent. A jury would not weigh a disclosure to determine if it met the requisite standard of care, as is typically the task undertaken by the jury in informed consent cases.

Whether Payne was damaged by Dr. Donaldson's failure to obtain his informed consent is a question of fact for the jury to determine. The record demonstrates that, had the "no code" not been issued, efforts to resuscitate Payne would have been undertaken, including cardio-pulmonary resuscitation. Even Dr. Donaldson and the Practice admit that resuscitation efforts offer *some* chance for the patient to keep body and soul together. As a jury could conclude Payne was not terminally ill, it could determine some damage was sustained due to Dr. Donaldson's failure to obtain Payne's informed consent, and therefore summary judgment was inappropriate.

To recapitulate, genuine issues of material fact exist as to whether Payne was competent and as to whether he was terminally ill when Dr. Donaldson issued the "no code." Because of the existence of these issues, the trial court erred by granting summary judgment in favor of Dr. Donaldson and the Practice.

[The court then considered the second issue: whether the trial court erred in granting summary judgment to the hospital. The court concluded that there was no error because the estate had failed to show that the hospital's alleged negligence—failing to have a written policy concerning "no codes"—fell below the requisite standard of care.—ED.]

6. Removing a Health Care Agent

Typically, the basis for removing a health care agent is that the agent has breached his or her fiduciary duty to the patient. A key question is whether there are other acceptable reasons for removing the agent. In the case of *In re Guardianship of Mason*, 669 N.E.2d 1081, 1085 (Mass. App. Ct. 1996), the Massachusetts Appeals Court found that appointment of a guardian was appropriate where the principal's son, Joseph, who was allegedly appointed her agent pursuant to a health care proxy, was unfit to be her agent. In describing why the son was unfit, the court explained that:

> As reported by the guardian ad litem, interviews with various health care providers who had worked with Elma [the principal] and Joseph [the son] over the past five years revealed that they found Joseph to be of the view that he is the only person capable of implementing a suitable treatment program for his mother, he is "articulate, but is not a good listener," he is "hostile toward" his mother's caretakers and often behaves in a "belligerent or inappropriate manner toward them," his decisions concerning his mother, although well-motivated, are not always sound, health care providers have declined to take on the mother as a client or patient because of Joseph's behavior, he argues with health care providers, and attempts "to micromanage every aspect of his mother's life and care," he "has difficulty accepting the change in his mother's health status and is experiencing a lot of denial about the deterioration in his mother the past year," he is too "combative" to work with, and he does not have the "objectivity necessary to be the substitute decision maker for his mother."
>
> The guardian ad litem also spoke with Joseph. He described him as demanding and "display[ing] signs of distrustfulness and paranoia." He carries a portable tape recorder into which he dictates throughout the day, noting dates, times, and observations about his immediate surroundings, and he advised the guardian [ad litem] that he intended to hire a private investigator to delve into the guardian [ad litem]'s relationship with counsel for [the hospital of which Elma was a ward].

Removal of an agent can be a way to resolve an intractable disagreement between agent and the patient's health care providers. A health care provider may seek to have a court remove an agent (and potentially appoint a guardian instead) when the agent is making decisions that the provider believes not to be in the best interest of the patient. For example, when an agent is demanding care that a health care provider believes to be futile, the health care provider may seek the agent's removal on the grounds that the agent's insistence on futile care is inconsistent with the agent's fiduciary duties.

QUESTION

Should an agent's inability to get along with health care providers be a basis for removing the agent? Why or why not?

7. Default Surrogate Statutes: An Alternative to Health Care Proxies?

Most states have adopted statutes that authorize surrogate decision-making for health care for people who lack a valid health care proxy. Typically, these *default surrogate statutes* establish a "priority list" indicating who should act as the patient's surrogate in the absence of an advance directive. This priority list generally consists of members of the patient's immediate family, beginning with his or her spouse. For example, under the Uniform Health-Care Decisions Act (UHCDA), Section 5, if the patient has not designated a surrogate or the patient's designee is not "reasonably available," a health care provider should take direction from the following individuals, listed in order of priority:

(1) the spouse, unless legally separated;
(2) an adult child;
(3) a parent; or
(4) an adult brother or sister.

If none of these are reasonably available, any other adult "who has exhibited special care and concern for the patient, who is familiar with the patient's personal values, and who is reasonably available" may serve as the surrogate. Under the UHCDA, if more than one member of a class assume the decision-making authority in accordance with the priority list, the patient's supervising health care provider is instructed to comply with the wishes of the majority.

Most states require health care providers to adhere to their state's priority list when identifying default surrogate decision-makers for incapacitated patients. Colorado and Hawaii, however, allow specified "interested persons" to decide amongst themselves who should serve as the surrogate based on who is close to the patient and likely to be familiar with the patient's wishes. Tennessee also deviates from the rigid priority list approach. In Tennessee, the priority list is merely a "consideration" when selecting a surrogate.

While the UHCDA does not do so, some states recognize non-traditional families by including close friends or domestic partners in their priority lists. A number of states also authorize physicians to make decisions for patients if no other surrogate is available.

QUESTIONS

1. Should default surrogate statutes be considered an alternative to health care proxies? Why or why not?

2. Assuming your state has a default surrogate law, why might you nevertheless urge a client to execute a health care proxy?

3. Should states require doctors to adhere to a rigid priority list in selecting a default surrogate decision-maker, or should doctors have some flexibility in the selection? Why?

4. If you favor flexibility, under what circumstances should a doctor be permitted to depart from the priority list. Why?

EXERCISE 4.2

You are a staff attorney with the Office of Legislative Council of the State of South Illinois. The State of South Illinois does not currently have a default surrogate statute. The majority leader of the South Illinois House of Representatives would like to introduce legislation authorizing default surrogate decision-makers and has asked your office to draft a proposed default surrogate statute for her consideration. You have been assigned the task. Working alone or with a partner, draft a statute that provides a comprehensive set of rules establishing who has authority to make medical decisions for an incapacitated person who has not appointed a surrogate decision-maker or whose surrogate decision-maker is unwilling or unable to serve.

E. GUARDIANSHIP

It is generally presumed that all adults have the capacity and right to make their own decisions. Sometimes, however, adults lack the capacity to make reasoned decisions on their own behalf. In such situations, using its inherent *parens patriae* ("parent of the country") power, the state can intervene to protect the individual. The common way the state does this is through a statutorily defined *guardianship* system. In a guardianship proceeding, a court is asked to determine whether a person lacks capacity, and, if the court finds that the person lacks capacity, to appoint a third party to manage some or all of that person's affairs. A third party appointed in this manner is called a *guardian,* and the incapacitated person is often referred to as a *ward.*

Guardianship can often be avoided through advance planning. Indeed, one of the primary goals of the type of comprehensive later-in-life planning that is the hallmark of elder law practice is to avoid guardianship. By authorizing surrogate decision-makers through the use of durable powers of attorney and advance directives for health care, often in combination with the creation of trusts for the management of property, older adults can generally avoid the need for a court-appointed guardian.

The desire to avoid guardianship reflects the fact that the process of obtaining a guardianship is not only costly and time-intensive (as discussed in the next subsection), but also that imposition of guardianship is a drastic remedy: It can strip adults of even their most fundamental civil rights. Accordingly, it is generally agreed that it should be employed only as a last resort and that less restrictive options should be pursued where possible. This approach is often called the *least restrictive alternative doctrine.*

Despite the significance of guardianship, it is unknown how many people are subject to guardianship. Estimates suggest that approximately 1.5 million people in the United States may be subject to adult guardianship at any given time, but the actual number is unknown in part because many states do not maintain the types of records necessary for a national assessment.

1. Overview of the Process of Obtaining a Guardianship

The guardianship process is governed by state law and, accordingly, procedural requirements vary significantly from state to state. Indeed, even the terminology used in guardianship proceedings varies from state to state. The Uniform Guardianship and Protective Proceedings Act and many states use the term *conservator* to refer to a guardian appointed to make financial decisions on behalf of a ward and use the term *guardian* to refer to someone appointed to make personal and health care decisions for a ward. Others use the term guardian to refer to both, as does this textbook. A few states, such as California and Connecticut, use the term "conservator" to refer to someone appointed to make both financial and personal decisions. Louisiana, reflecting its civil law tradition, uses an altogether different term: *interdiction. See* La. Civ. Code Ann. art. 389 (2000).

In general, the first step in any guardianship proceeding is for an interested party to file a *petition* with the appropriate court. The petition alleges that the subject of the petition, referred to as the *respondent* or the *alleged incapacitated person* (AIP), is incapable of making all or some decisions on his or her own behalf and that, therefore, the state should appoint a *guardian* for that person.

States commonly allow any person with an interest in the AIP to file a petition. Typically, petitions are filed by relatives of the AIP, but petitions are also frequently filed by friends, nursing homes, hospitals, and social service agencies. In some states, an AIP may file the petition on his or her own behalf. Where the AIP does so, the proceeding is called a *voluntary guardianship* proceeding. At first blush, voluntary guardianship may seem paradoxical: If the AIP has sufficient capacity to petition for a guardianship, it would seem that she likely has too much capacity to warrant a guardianship. However, a voluntary guardianship may be appropriate where the AIP has sufficient capacity to understand that she needs assistance and the oversight provided by the court, but lacks the capacity to make some other types of decisions for which a guardian could be appointed.

The requirements for the content of a guardianship petition vary from state to state. Common requirements include:

- The name and address of the AIP,
- An allegation of incapacity,
- A statement of the cause and extent of that incapacity,
- An explanation of why the petitioner believes a guardianship is necessary, and
- The name and address of any proposed guardian.

All states require that the AIP be given notice of the petition, generally by personal service, and that his or her family, creditors, and heirs receive notice as well. The amount of notice required varies, but it is usually at least one or two weeks. The Uniform Guardianship and Protective Proceedings Act (UGPPA), which is incorporated into Uniform Probate Code (UPC), encourages states to adopt broad notice requirements. The UGPPA requires notice be given to all persons listed in the petition for guardianship. Under the UGPPA, the guardianship petition must list, to the extent known, the name and address of any person responsible for the care or custody of the AIP, any legal representative of the AIP, and any person the AIP has nominated to serve as guardian. Notice must also be given to the AIP's spouse; if the AIP does not have a spouse, then notice is to be given instead to "an adult with whom the respondent has resided for more than six months before the filing of the petition." Finally, notice must be given to the AIP's adult children; if the AIP does not have any adult children, notice is to be given instead to "the respondent's parents and adult brothers and sisters, or if the respondent has none, at least one of the adults nearest in kinship to the respondent who can be found." UNIFORM PROBATE CODE §§5-304 & 5-309.

The filing of the petition triggers a court process for determining whether a guardianship should be imposed on the AIP, and, if so, what type of guardianship and who should serve as guardian. A notable feature of a guardianship proceeding is that, unlike most other court proceedings in the United States, the court is empowered to independently seek information about a party to the proceeding. Specifically, in a guardianship proceeding, the court may independently appoint a disinterested person (alternatively called an *investigator, examiner, guardian ad litem,* or *court visitor*) to investigate the AIP's physical, mental, and social conditions and make a report about them to the court. The court will also typically require a clinical evaluation by a physician, social worker, psychologist, or other professional with expertise in assessing cognitive capacity.

A judicial hearing is required before a guardianship may be imposed. All states allow the AIP to be present at the hearing. However, only a minority *require* the AIP's presence, and guardianship proceedings routinely occur in the absence of the AIP. While many states permit the AIP to request a jury trial instead of a hearing before a judge, jury trials are very rare. AIPs are also entitled to be represented by counsel in the proceeding—indeed, in many states, representation is required, and an attorney may be appointed for an AIP who is unable to afford one.

Once the court has decided that appointment of a guardian is appropriate, the question becomes whom to appoint. Typically, states require that the guardianship petition nominate an individual or entity to serve as guardian. Courts are not obligated to select that nominee, but they often do so. Most state statutes require the court to consider a hierarchy of persons, beginning with any individual or entity nominated by the individual, followed by the spouse, adult child, parent, other relatives or friends. However, the court has discretion to act in the person's best interest in making an appointment. A guardian can be a family member or other individual, a guardianship professional (including a lawyer who serves as part of his or her practice), a non-profit agency, or a for-profit agency. A guardian of property can be a bank or other financial institution. If there is no one to serve, a court may appoint a public agency, including a specifically designated *public guardianship agency*. In addition to the primary appointment, a court may choose to appoint a *standby guardian*, one who can take over in the event that the guardian dies or is otherwise unable to serve.

Once established, a guardianship can only be terminated by the death of the ward or by a court with jurisdiction to do so.

Overall, the guardianship process is typically a costly one for both the petitioner and the AIP. Many of the costs are monetary. These include the cost to the AIP of retaining counsel, the cost of a professional evaluation of the AIP, and the cost to the petitioner of hiring an attorney to help file and support the petition, which, although a petitioner is entitled to proceed *pro se*, is generally recommended. In addition, a guardian is usually entitled to reasonable compensation for his or her services, which is paid out of the ward's resources unless the ward is indigent. Thus, expenses may continue to be incurred after a guardian is appointed.

Other costs are intangible. The guardianship process is, by design, an adversarial one. This can cause or exacerbate conflict between the AIP, the petitioner, and other family members or associates. It can also be highly stigmatizing due to the nature of the allegations made about the AIP. Finally, the decision to grant a guardianship petition comes at the cost of at least certain of the ward's civil rights.

NOTES

1. *Jurisdiction.* A guardianship petition should generally be filed in the county in which the AIP resides. In some situations, there may be a question as to where jurisdiction and venue for a guardianship proceeding lie. Examples of such situations include those where the AIP has dual residences or where the AIP has relocated to seek care and it is unclear or disputed whether relocation is temporary or permanent. The Uniform Adult Guardianship and Protective Proceedings Jurisdiction Act (UAGPPJA), which was promulgated in 2007 and which is rapidly being adopted by the states, is expected

to help clarify interstate disputes over guardianship jurisdiction by ensuring that only one state has jurisdiction over a guardianship proceeding at a given time. The UAGPPJA creates guidelines specifying when a court has jurisdiction to appoint a guardian, establishes a mechanism for prioritizing state claims to jurisdiction, and provides that, once a court has jurisdiction over a guardianship proceeding, it retains that jurisdiction until the proceeding is terminated or transferred.

2. *Spousal preference.* Courts tend to favor appointing an incapacitated person's spouse as his or her guardian. This is not necessarily the case for an incapacitated person's domestic partner, which may pose particular problems for same-sex couples.

3. *Competing views of the importance of the presence of the AIP.* Requiring the AIP be present at the guardianship hearing is seen by some as essential to protecting the AIP's due process rights. Yet few states truly require the AIP to be present, in part because doing so is seen as costly. For example, Professor Lawrence Frolik has written that, "Requiring mentally incapacitated or severely physically impaired individuals to be brought into court resulted in delays in scheduling hearings, significant costs in bringing the individual to the courtroom, and embarrassment to individuals who would have preferred not to appear at their guardianship petition. Some court hearings were held at the side of hospital beds, expensive in judicial time and public money." Lawrence A. Frolik, *Guardianship Reform: When the Best Is the Enemy of the Good*, 9 STAN. L. & POL'Y REV. 347, 348 (1998).

QUESTIONS

1. Who should be entitled to notice of a petition for guardianship? Do you support the broad approach of the UGPPA? Are there any people to whom the UGPPA would require notice be given that you do not believe should be entitled to such notice? Are there additional other individuals or entities that should be entitled to notice?

2. Should states require that the AIP be present at the guardianship hearing?

3. The UGPPA only requires a court to obtain a professional evaluation of the AIP if the AIP requests one. Should such evaluations be required even if the AIP fails to make such a request? Should it be considered sufficient for the court to simply obtain a clinical statement from a physician who has treated the AIP?

PROBLEM

Wendy, 90, has been found to be incapacitated and in need of a guardian. She has been separated from her husband, Peter, for 30 years. Although Wendy and Peter separated by mutual agreement and remain cordial to one another, they have not spoken in over two years and Peter now lives with his girlfriend,

Bella. Wendy has a daughter, Darla, who adores Wendy and visits her regularly, but who suffers from an addiction to prescription pain killers that is increasingly interfering with her management of her own affairs. Wendy also has a son, Sam, who has a tense relationship with his mother and rarely calls her. Other than her husband and children, Wendy's only close relative is her brother, John. John is 80 years old. He has his full mental faculties, but is increasingly having difficulty driving and uses a cane to get around. For the past five years, Wendy's neighbor, Nancy, has been an active part of Wendy's life, coming by several times a week to check in on her. Nancy is a 45-year-old single mother with limited income who works two jobs to make ends meet for her family.

a. How should the judge decide whom to appoint as Wendy's guardian?
b. Should the judge forgo appointing all of the above-named individuals in favor of a professional guardian?

2. The Role of Counsel for the AIP

An attorney for an AIP is typically expected to maintain a normal attorney-client relationship and thus to follow the AIP's direction and to keep the AIP's confidences. Therefore, unless the AIP is willing to acquiesce to imposition of a guardianship, the AIP's counsel will typically argue against imposition of guardianship. Even if the AIP does not object to a guardianship, the AIP may object to the scope of the proposed guardianship or to the proposed guardian and, therefore, desire representation on those issues.

However, some states' guardianship schemes require that, when counsel is appointed for an AIP, the lawyer serve both as the AIP's "defense counsel" (whose job is to be a vigorous advocate) and his or her guardian ad litem (whose job it is to advise the court on what is in the AIP's best interest). This approach has been criticized on the grounds that it creates confusing and frustrating dual roles for the attorney. *See* A. Frank Johns, *Three Rights Make Strong Advocacy for the Elderly in Guardianship: Right to Counsel, Right to Plan, and Right to Die*, 45 S.D. L. Rev. 492, 494 (2000) (offering this critique). Similarly, attorneys Susan G. Haines and John J. Campbell have argued that an attorney cannot ethically serve as both counsel for the AIP and the AIP's guardian ad litem. They write:

> A guardian ad litem is a special fiduciary whose primary obligation is to make informed decisions for the incapacitated person, while the attorney must counsel and represent the incapacitated person's legal interests. An attorney who also accepts an appointment as guardian ad litem for the same incapacitated person deprives that person of an effective advocate.
>
> In a traditional attorney-client relationship, the attorney must preserve the client's confidentiality and may not disclose confidential information without the client's consent. The Model Rules of Professional Conduct also require an attorney to maintain that relationship to the extent possible when the client is incapacitated. When the attorney assumes the role of

guardian ad litem, the reporting requirement might force him or her to breach the client's confidentiality.

Confidentiality is not the only concern. The Model Rules of Professional Conduct provide that a lawyer may seek appointment of a guardian or take other protective action only when the lawyer "reasonably believes that the client cannot adequately act in the client's own interest." A guardian ad litem, on the other hand, must recommend to the court whether a guardian should be appointed. In doing so, the guardian ad litem must disclose the extent and nature of the client's disability, a disclosure that may adversely affect the incapacitated person's interests. This creates a severe conflict for an attorney who attempts to play both roles.

* * *

If an attorney representing an incapacitated person cannot ethically act as guardian ad litem, then what should a guardian ad litem who is not acting as an advocate do? The guardian ad litem's function is objectively and independently to recommend a course of action that is in the ward's best interest. This may mean that the guardian ad litem must oppose the ward's attorney, if the ward has an attorney, and protect the interests of a ward who may be unaware of the extent to which he needs protection or supervision.

Susan G. Haines & John J. Campbell, *Defects, Due Process, and Protective Proceedings: Are Our Probate Codes Unconstitutional?*, 14 QUINNIPIAC PROB. L.J. 57, 94-97 (1999).

Even where counsel for the AIP is not simultaneously serving as guardian ad litem, however, the role can be fraught with controversy, as the below case illustrates.

In re Guardianship of Herke

93 Wash. App. 1054 (Wash. Ct. App. 1999)

KATO.

This family tragedy began with a man's petition for guardianship of his wife, evolved into a dissolution action, went to mediation and unsuccessfully to binding arbitration, and then came to an end a week before the man died. The only issue left to resolve the one the court is required to address here is a dispute over attorney fees. We affirm the superior court's fee award.

Carl Herke filed a petition for appointment of a guardian for his 78-year-old wife, Helen Herke, in February 1993. Attorney Robert W. Inouye was appointed Mrs. Herke's guardian ad litem. With Mr. Inouye's approval, Mr. Herke's attorney obtained an order restraining Mr. Herke and the couple's five children from discussing the guardianship with Mrs. Herke, causing or attempting to cause Mrs. Herke to transfer property, or interfering with Mrs. Herke's medical care.

Mrs. Herke, who vehemently opposed appointment of a guardian, retained as her attorney Gary L. Sandersen of Halverson & Applegate, P.S.

Mr. Sandersen's retainer letter warned Mrs. Herke the case would be "lengthy and expensive. We cannot even begin to estimate the attorney's fees, but between both sides, the attorney's fees will be very large." Mr. Sandersen informed Mr. Inouye that Mrs. Herke intended to "fight the guardianship to the bitter end." Mr. Sandersen noted that if a guardian were to be appointed, Mrs. Herke's first preference would be her daughter, Joyce Johnson, and her second preference would be Mrs. Herke's brother or sisters.

* * *

[After several years of significant legal wrangling and much conflict between the parties and their children, the court appointed Mrs. Herke's sister, Julia Decoto, as her guardian with "some oversight" by Mrs. Herke's daughter, Mary Jane Craigen. A week after the resolution, Mr. Herke died.—ED.]

In January 1997, Halverson & Applegate filed a claim against Mr. Herke's estate for $84,490 in attorney fees and costs. In March 1997, the firm petitioned for payment of attorney fees from Mrs. Herke's guardianship estate. Mrs. Herke's guardian, Mrs. Decoto, submitted an affidavit stating she was satisfied with Halverson & Applegate's representation and recommended payment of $90,000. Ms. Craigen, now personal representative of Mr. Herke's estate, opposed the fees.

The court consolidated the two attorney fee requests for hearing in June 1997. The court also ordered the guardian ad litem, Mr. Inouye, to prepare a written report on the fees. Mr. Inouye's report concluded a reasonable fee for representing Mrs. Herke in the guardianship would be $25,000. The report continued:

> The fees presently being requested by Mrs. Herke's attorneys are more than four times my $25,000 estimate. I believe this is primarily due to a difference in philosophy, regarding the proper role of an Alleged Incapacitated Person's attorney. Clearly the AIP's attorney is obligated to represent his client, and to assist the client in pursuing her own subjective goals. (This is different from the guardian ad litem's role, which looks more directly to the best interests of the AIP.) That being said, there are still two discrete modes which the AIP's attorney can choose between:
>
> > 1. The AIP's attorney can choose to latch on to the AIP's stated goals, march resolutely in that direction, defend staunchly against all perceived resistance, view all opponents with a healthy dose of skepticism, and generally encourage the client to stick to her guns while supporting her vociferously with good technical legal skills.
>
> This approach is a traditional and successful one for some types of litigation.
>
> > 2. The AIP's attorney can choose to educate the client, offer a balanced external perspective to the beleaguered client, keep an eye on the broader family context, make recommendations consonant with long-term goals and realistic options, and encourage the client towards a resolution which minimizes unnecessary conflict.

This approach is better suited for some situations.

> Depending on the strengths, weaknesses and circumstances of a specific AIP, either mode might be the appropriate one. In my observation, the legal representation given to Mrs. Herke initially set the pattern for this case based on the first mode. However, I believe that the second mode would have been better suited to her particular circumstances and needs, and would have arrived at the same outcome by a less circuitous route.

A hearing was held in superior court on June 16-18, 1997. Halverson & Applegate presented the opinion of its expert, attorney J. Eric Gustafson, who concluded a fee of $75,000 to $80,000 would be warranted in this case. Ms. Craigen, who was allowed to give her opinion as personal representative of her father's estate, testified a reasonable fee would be $5,000. After the hearing, the superior court . . . awarded judgment to Halverson & Applegate of $55,006.75 (taking into account amounts previously paid), to be paid from the guardianship estate. Half of that amount was to be reimbursed to the guardianship estate by the estate of Carl Herke.

* * *

[As part of her argument objecting to the fee award,] Ms. Craigen . . . contends . . . that Mr. Sandersen's "scorched earth" approach polarized the family and prevented an early settlement of the dispute. She relies on RPC 2.1, which provides:

> In representing a client, a lawyer shall exercise independent professional judgment and render candid advice. In rendering advice, a lawyer may refer not only to law but to other considerations such as moral, economic, social and political factors, that may be relevant to the client's situation.

Ms. Craigen argues Halverson & Applegate's attorneys should have performed their duties as lawyers essentially by substituting their own professional judgment for Mrs. Herke's, or at least by candidly advising her of the folly of the course she chose. She contends the eventual result could have been achieved much earlier if Mr. Sandersen had not adopted his initial adversarial approach. This argument is both legally unjustified and factually unsupported.

RCW 11.88.045(1)(b) provides:

> Counsel for an alleged incapacitated individual shall act as an advocate for the client and shall not substitute counsel's own judgment for that of the client on the subject of what may be in the client's best interests. Counsel's role shall be distinct from that of the guardian ad litem, who is expected to promote the best interest of the alleged incapacitated individual, rather than the alleged incapacitated individual's expressed preferences.

Halverson & Applegate's attorneys thus were statutorily forbidden to work for what they may have believed to be Mrs. Herke's best interests. That was Mr. Inouye's duty as guardian ad litem. Mrs. Herke's attorneys had the statutory duty to promote her expressed interests. . . . Mrs. Herke's attorneys were required to promote her expressed interests while exercising their own professional judgment and giving her candid advice.

The record indicates the Halverson & Applegate attorneys promoted their client's expressed interests while appropriately exercising their own professional judgment. Mrs. Herke opposed appointment of a guardian, but if one were to be appointed she preferred her daughter, Joyce Johnson, or her sister, Julia Decoto. Mr. Sandersen made this position clear shortly after he was appointed as Mrs. Herke's attorney. The fact it took more than three years to reach a negotiated settlement consistent with this position cannot be attributed directly to Mr. Sandersen's approach. In fact, the difficulties in reaching an agreement are at least as likely to be the result of the family's deep rift, which predated Mr. Sandersen's involvement and continued through the next several years.

* * *

Implicit in Ms. Craigen's argument is her belief that Mrs. Herke was incapable of rationally expressing her interests. The difficulty with this argument is that, whatever the state of Mrs. Herke's mental health at the time, she had not been declared incapacitated pursuant to RCW 11.88. Moreover, her attorneys found her fully capable of articulating her interests and participating in her representation. Eccentricity alone is not a justification for finding a person incapacitated. Even when a guardian was appointed at the end of this exhaustive process, Mrs. Herke retained the right to vote and (with supervision) to maintain a bank account in her name. Although in a hypothetical case a person's incapacity may be so severe as to require a lawyer to exercise his or her independent professional judgment in contradiction of the client's expressed interests, this is not such a case.

Nothing in the record suggests Mr. Sandersen or any other Halverson & Applegate attorney failed to exercise independent professional judgment or to offer their candid advice to Mrs. Herke. There is no factual basis for further reduction of the firm's fees on this ground. The superior court's decision is within the range of acceptable choices, is supported by the record, and is based on the correct legal standard. The superior court's discretion therefore was not manifestly unreasonable, exercised on untenable grounds or for untenable reasons. There was no abuse of discretion.

* * *

Affirmed. . . .

QUESTIONS

1. Should states require that the AIP be represented by counsel? What benefits might representation provide? What concerns arise if the AIP is unrepresented?

2. How should counsel for the AIP proceed if the attorney cannot meaningfully communicate with the AIP?

3. Determination of Incapacity

The central question in a guardianship proceeding is whether the AIP is actually incapacitated and, if so, in what way or ways. The answer should determine both whether a guardian is appointed and the extent of the guardian's powers.

a. Standard for Incapacity

Different states have different definitions of what constitutes "incapacity" for the purpose of guardianship. Historically, courts frequently relied on medical diagnoses to determine capacity for the purposes of guardianship. The modern approach, however, is to use a *functional definition* of capacity instead of, or in combination with, a medical definition.

A functional definition of capacity defines capacity based on the individual's ability to function within his or her environment, as opposed to the individual's underlying medical condition. For example, New York takes a functional approach to defining capacity. In general, New York permits a court to appoint a guardian for the AIP only if the court determines that (1) doing so "is necessary to provide for the personal needs of that person, including food, clothing, shelter, health care, or safety and/or to manage the property and financial affairs of that person," and (2) the AIP either agrees to the appointment or the court finds, based on clear and convincing evidence, that the AIP is likely to suffer harm because he or she is "unable to provide for personal needs and/or property management . . . and . . . cannot adequately understand and appreciate the nature and consequences of such inability." N.Y. MENTAL HYG. LAW §81.02.

Similarly, the Uniform Guardianship and Protective Proceedings Act (UGPPA) creates a two-part functional standard for incapacity. Under the UGPPA, a guardian may be appointed where the court determines: (1) by clear and convincing evidence that the AIP "is unable to manage property and business affairs because of an impairment in the ability to receive and evaluate information or make decisions, even with the use of appropriate technological assistance . . . ," or because the individual is missing, detained, or unable to return to the United States; and (2) by a preponderance of evidence, that the AIP "has property that will be wasted or dissipated unless management is provided or money is needed for the support, care, education, health, and welfare of the individual or of individuals who are entitled to the individual's support and that protection is necessary or desirable to obtain or provide money." UNIFORM PROBATE CODE §5-401(2).

The cases that follow explore how a court should analyze evidence of capacity or incapacity in order to determine whether a particular individual should be considered incapacitated for the purposes of imposing a guardianship.

Matter of Maher

207 A.D.2d 133 (N.Y. App. Div. 1994)

FRIEDMANN, J.

On this appeal . . . we are asked to consider the propriety of a determination by the Supreme Court, Kings County (Leone, J.), embodied in a judgment entered October 8, 1993, that the respondent, Francis E. Maher, was not incapacitated as that term is defined in the recently enacted Mental Hygiene Law article 81. Based upon this determination, the court dismissed, with prejudice, the petition for a guardian for the respondent's property which had been brought by Francis E. Maher, Jr., the respondent's son. Since the court properly applied the standards and carried out the legislative intent of Mental Hygiene Law article 81, we now affirm.

On December 11, 1992, the respondent, attorney Francis E. Maher, suffered a stroke which left him with right-sided hemiplegia and aphasia. He was admitted to St. Luke's-Roosevelt Hospital where, on December 12, he underwent surgery, inter alia, to evacuate a hematoma from the frontal portion of his brain. For some time after the operation, the respondent remained partially paralyzed and aphasic, although occasionally he was able to speak a few words and to move a bit on his right side.

* * *

At the hearing, testimony was taken from the respondent's sister, Betty Maher, two of his sons, George and the appellant, his speech pathologist, Susan Sachs, and Dr. Valerie Lanyi, a rehabilitation specialist who had treated the respondent at the Rusk Institute, and who had seen him in consultation as recently as June 10, 1993. Testifying for the respondent were the respondent himself, and his wife, Mrs. Helen Kelly Maher. At the conclusion of the hearing, the court found that the appellant had not carried his burden of proving by the requisite clear and convincing evidence that (1) the respondent was incapacitated, and (2) a guardian was necessary to manage his property and financial affairs.

* * *

Contrary to the appellant's contention, the clear and convincing evidence in the hearing record establishes only that the respondent suffers from certain functional limitations in speaking and writing, but not that he is likely to suffer harm because he is unable to provide for the management of his property, or that he is incapable of adequately understanding and appreciating the nature and consequences of his disabilities. Indeed, by granting a power of attorney to Irwin Simon, and by adding his wife as a signatory on certain of his bank accounts, the respondent evidenced that he appreciated his own handicaps to the extent that he effectuated a plan for assistance in managing his financial affairs without the need for a guardian.

Several witnesses testified to the respondent's ability to understand what he was told and to make his wishes known demonstratively. For example, the respondent's sister testified that she believed that her brother understood her when she provided him with information about the office. The appellant himself conceded that he routinely discussed collection and related business matters with the respondent, and that the respondent had regularly indicated his satisfaction with the appellant's management of his law firm's affairs. Dr. Lanyi, the physician in charge of the respondent's rehabilitation, expressed her doubt that at the time of his discharge from the Rusk Institute in mid-March 1993, the respondent could have managed his checkbook as he had formerly done, but opined that he was nonetheless, even at that time, aware of the magnitude of the sums he was spending. Moreover, according to Dr. Lanyi, when she last saw the respondent on June 10, 1993, her patient appeared to understand everything she said to him or asked of him, noting that on that occasion he had consistently responded to her remarks and inquiries in a prompt, calm manner, with appropriate words or gestures. The respondent's speech therapist, too, documented a steady improvement in her patient's ability to comprehend and respond to the tests she administered. Generally, the consensus among all witnesses was that the respondent had made, and was continuing to make, dramatic progress in his ability to comprehend information and to express himself-as well as in his mobility, which seemed essentially restored to normal-since the initial cerebrovascular episode.

Moreover, the court, which was in the best position to observe the respondent throughout the hearing, remarked that he reacted fittingly to the proceedings—even to the point of making it clear to his attorney and the court when he felt that certain questions or answers were objectionable. The court was further persuaded that the respondent knew the correct responses to the questions put to him on the stand, although he was not able verbally to express them.

* * *

Although [there is a] . . . very substantial estate involved here, we do not find the size of the property involved, standing alone, to be dispositive. Rather, in the matter before us, there has been no showing that the respondent has lost the ability to appreciate his financial circumstances, or that others have taken control of his affairs without his comprehension or rational supervision. There has further been no demonstration of any waste, real or imminent, of the respondent's assets. There is an absence of proof that the respondent's chosen attorney and his wife (who is also an attorney) are incapable of managing the property at issue in accordance with the respondent's wishes. Under such circumstances, the appellant has failed to demonstrate the need for a guardian under the standards enunciated in Mental Hygiene Law article 81.

The court did not err in excluding from evidence certain "tests" or "demonstrations" of the respondent's inability to expatiate on the meaning of a complicated legal text, to write checks in differing amounts to different payees, to separate and count diverse kinds of currency, and to explain his execution of two successive powers of attorney. The court was already well aware of the respondent's difficulty—due to his expressive aphasia and apraxia—in verbally communicating his understanding of the questions posed to him, and in writing or counting numbers clearly—although he could make himself understood to those to whom he could demonstrate non-verbally. Therefore, such "tests" would not have served to inform the court about the material issue before it—namely, whether the respondent appreciated the nature and consequences of his alleged inability personally to manage his property, and that he could suffer harm as a result. As the evidence sought to be elicited would merely have distracted the court from the main point at issue, the court properly exercised its discretion in denying the admission of that evidence.

* * *

Therefore, the judgment is affirmed insofar as appealed from.

Smith v. Smith

917 So. 2d 400 (Fla. Dist. Ct. App. 2005)

GRIFFIN, J.

Ann Smith a/k/a Annie May Smith ["Smith"] appeals an order finding her incompetent and appointing a limited guardian of her person and property.

The petitioner below, Nathan Smith ["Nathan"], is Smith's sixty-four-year-old stepson. On September 17, 2004, Nathan filed a petition seeking to be appointed plenary guardian over Smith's person and property. The petition alleged that Smith was incapacitated due to her "doctor's diagnosis of dementia of an Alzheimer's type." It asserted that Smith was seventy-nine years old and had assets valued in excess of $191,250.18. When the petition was filed, Smith was apparently residing with her step-granddaughter, Cassandra Dinkins (who is Nathan's niece), in a home Smith owns in Apopka. Nathan, who had been handling Smith's finances under a power of attorney from Smith, filed the petition after learning that Smith had purchased a van for her step-granddaughter at a cost of more than $11,000. Nathan also filed a petition seeking to be appointed emergency temporary guardian on the same grounds.

After counsel was appointed to represent Smith, the court appointed a three-member examining committee to determine Smith's competency. All three members of the committee had filed written reports with the court by October 18, 2004, in which they recommended appointment of a plenary guardian for Smith. At a hearing on October 20, 2004, the court appointed a professional guardian, Teresa Barton ["Barton"], to serve as temporary guardian and determined to appoint yet another doctor to examine Smith. The fourth member appointed to the examining committee submitted his report to the court on November 4, 2004. Like the other members of the committee, he recommended appointment of a plenary guardian for Smith.

The court held a hearing on the petition on January 7, 2005. All four members of the examining committee testified at the hearing, and their reports were entered into evidence. All four members testified that Smith suffered from dementia, and all recommended guardianship.

Smith was called to the stand and questioned by the attorney for the temporary guardian. She exhibited some confusion during direct examination, for example, that the current date was February of 1936 or 1938 and was unsure of her lawyer's name. She said she got in touch with her lawyer after her husband died in 1960 or 1969, even though her husband had died in 1999. Smith said she was good at math and was asked to do some simple mathematical calculations. When asked to subtract nineteen from thirty-six, she came up with 725. When Smith was asked if she had given any money to her attorney in connection with the hearing, she said she did not know how much.

Smith called a psychologist, Dr. Charles English, who spent approximately four hours examining her, to testify. Dr. English is a licensed mental health therapist. He prepared a written report in which he concluded that Smith was perfectly capable of doing such things as entering into contracts, managing her property, and consenting to medical treatment. He thought that her responses were normal for "an African American woman of her age and status in life." He saw no need for treatment or intervention unless she chose to obtain assistance with her affairs. He testified that he saw no problems with Smith's short-term memory and thought she was capable of making her own decisions. Dr. English felt that the others who had examined Smith were "talking to another person" and he disagreed "wholeheartedly" with how they evaluated her. He said that she had confided that she was never really pleased with Nathan's behavior, while she was comfortable with her step-granddaughter, Cassandra. Dr. English said that if Smith found that she was unable to handle her own financial affairs, she could hire someone she trusts to do that for her. He said that the testing he had done was designed to identify major mental disorders, personality disorders, psychoses, and things of that sort. It is not really geared toward dementia. However, his assessment was sufficient to determine that she was not suffering from dementia.

Milton Collins ["Collins"], a licensed psychotherapist and social worker, worked in nursing homes for over ten years, specializing in mental health treatment and support services for the elderly. He saw Smith on two occasions and performed a geriatric assessment on her. He submitted his own report in which he determined that Smith was competent to manage all of her own affairs. Among other things, he stated in the report that she was "medically stable," as well as "alert, cooperative, [and] oriented," and said he thought she demonstrated "a great deal of common sense, given her age and limited education." He stated that he was "confident" of her ability to "mentally and intellectually recognize who can best assist her in her daily living skills and to assist her in making sound common sense decisions that our (sic) in her best interest." He noted that she was unhappy with her stepson's behavior and felt comfortable that her step-granddaughter was looking after her interests. At the hearing, Collins explained he had seen Smith on two occasions. He found that she was "fairly" oriented to time and place and very much oriented to person. He thought she may have been misdiagnosed with dementia or Alzheimers because of the failure to take into account various psycho-social and cultural factors, such as her fourth grade education. In his opinion, she was normal.

The court executed a written order determining that Smith was incapacitated and finding that a limited guardian of Smith's person and property should be appointed. The order determined that Smith was incapable of making virtually all decisions about her person and property, except that it found she had the ability to determine her residence, to vote, and to regulate her social environment and other social aspects of her life. Barton was appointed to serve as Smith's limited guardian.

Smith contends on appeal that the evidence presented in this case was insufficient to support a finding of incapacity by "clear and convincing evidence." See In re Bryan, 550 So. 2d 447 (Fla. 1989). She acknowledges that all four members of the examining committee found that she was incompetent to proceed, but notes that the reports contain certain internal inconsistencies, such as statements that she was "oriented to person and place," her speech was "organized," she did not appear to be suffering from psychosis, and she had good long-term memory. She further notes that both experts hired by the defense found her competent to proceed, and there was no medical evidence to support a finding of incompetency. Where, as here, the experts reach such contradictory results, she argues that as a matter of law the evidence should be deemed insufficient to establish incompetency by clear and convincing evidence.

Although the two experts hired by the defense disagreed with the conclusions drawn by the examining committee, this conflict in the evidence does not preclude a finding that the evidence of incompetency was clear and convincing. Nor would conflicts in the evidence require the court to find a lack of clear and convincing evidence.

* * *

AFFIRMED.

NOTE

Standard for terminating a guardianship. A guardianship may only be terminated by a court. As noted above, under the Uniform Guardianship and Protective Proceedings Act, incapacity must be established by clear and convincing evidence before a guardian may be appointed. However, under the same Act, the standard to restore legal capacity—that is to terminate a guardianship—is simply "prima facie evidence." This distinction reflects the Commissioners' position that there should be a higher standard of proof to take away individual rights than to restore them.

QUESTIONS

1. Do you think the *Maher* court would have reached the same result as the *Smith* court had it been considering the facts of that case?

2. In both *Maher* and *Smith*, the courts applied a "clear and convincing evidence" standard of proof. If you were drafting your state's guardianship law, is this the standard you would recommend? Why or why not?

b. Extent of Incapacity

In addition to determining *whether* an AIP is incapacitated, a court must determine the *extent* of any incapacity in order to determine what type of guardianship should be imposed. In a *plenary guardianship*, the guardian possesses the full legal rights of the ward, and the ward is completely stripped of legal decision making capacity. In a *limited guardianship*, the ward retains the right to make certain types of decisions that the judge has not found the person to be incapable of making. Thus, limited guardianship recognizes that capacity is not a "all or nothing" phenomenon. Almost all states allow for the use of limited guardianship where appropriate, and some explicitly state that a court must appoint a limited guardian in appropriate situations.

The next case explores the conditions under which a limited guardianship should be granted in lieu of a plenary guardianship.

In re Guardianship of Inez B. Way

901 P.2d 349 (Wash. Ct. App. 1995)

GROSSE, Judge.

* * *

The Department of Social and Health Services (DSHS) filed a guardianship petition as to Way on August 31, 1992. The court appointed a guardian ad litem, and Way requested a jury trial pursuant to RCW 11.88.045(3)....

The jury found Way incapacitated both as to her person and her estate. A full guardianship was imposed as to Way's estate and all her rights with respect thereto were restricted.... A limited guardianship was imposed as to Way's person. In a special verdict form, the jury was asked to determine which rights Way would retain as to her person under the limited guardianship. Notwithstanding its finding of incapacity, the jury determined that Way should retain all the rights set forth in the special verdict form as to her person. Those rights were: the right to give informed consent to medical treatment; the right to determine where she will live; the right to marry or divorce; the right to vote or hold an elected office; the right to decide who shall provide care and assistance; and the right to make decisions regarding social aspects of her life.

DSHS brought a motion for reconsideration, motion to vacate, and motion for judgment notwithstanding the verdict. The court denied the motion for reconsideration, and denied the motion to vacate and the motion for judgment notwithstanding the verdict in all respects except that the court restricted Way's right to decide who shall provide for care and assistance.

In the spring of 1992, after receiving referrals from numerous concerned citizens, a DSHS caseworker visited Way's residence. The caseworker and other social workers and medical personnel who visited the residence testified as to the deplorable living conditions they encountered. The caseworker who initially visited the house found Way, who at the time was in her upper 70's, lying naked in a bed soaked with urine and feces. Her skin was red and excoriated. A geriatric nurse practitioner examined Way and found her skin red and sore in her perineal area and blood evident around her bottom. Way was in need of bathing. Her hair was so dirty and matted that it was necessary to cut most of it off.

Windows and doors were broken in the house and the heating system did not work. The roof needed repair, as did the ceilings, floors, and walls inside the house. The interior of the house was filled with clutter and junk. Rats and rat droppings were found throughout the house. Plastic bags of human waste were found in the house, and the plumbing was inoperable.

For the past 20 to 25 years, Way lived with Al Soper, who was in his 80's at the time of the proceedings. Soper was Way's sole caretaker. Because Way was bedridden, she completely depended upon him for her every need. Soper wore a pacemaker and suffered from heart trouble. He did not have a driver's license and was unable to drive to grocery stores to bring Way food and supplies. Soper and Way depended upon transients who frequently lived in the house to bring them supplies from convenience stores. These transients sometimes stole money and other items from the house. Soper was characterized as having an obsessive-compulsive disorder that caused him to overload the house with collectibles so that navigation through the house was limited to narrow pathways carved through the clutter. He was experiencing early dementia, memory lapses, and mild Alzheimer's disease. Soper testified that he wanted a "fairy godmother" to come and help him take care of Way.

* * *

DSHS . . . contends [that] the trial court erred by not granting its motion for judgment notwithstanding the verdict in its entirety so as to impose a more restricted guardianship as to Way's person. We disagree.

* * *

Preliminarily, DSHS contends that in connection with our review of the trial court's order, we are precluded from considering evidence which was not before the trial court regarding events which occurred subsequent to the entry of the limited guardianship order. DSHS cites the general rule that "a record on appeal may not be supplemented by material which has not been included in the trial court record." (Footnote omitted.) *Snedigar v. Hoddersen*, 114 Wash. 2d 153, 164, 786 P.2d 781 (1990). Pursuant to this general rule DSHS argues that we should not consider that within 6 months of entry of the limited guardianship order, Way was moved to a convalescent center which provides all of her personal care needs. At the facility, Way has undergone physical therapy treatment. She has also received hospital care for upper respiratory problems. DSHS would also have us ignore the fact that the trial court has authorized the sale of Way's real and personal property. DSHS claims we must review the trial court's actions in light of the circumstances as they existed at the time the limited guardianship order was entered, circumstances that are quite different from present circumstances.

We fail to see the wisdom, or the justice, in reviewing the issues presented in an outdated context. Situations such as those involving dependent children or incapacitated persons are fluid and ever changing. Unfortunately due to the nature of the judicial system within which we operate, immediate review of a dependency order or a guardianship order is not always available. In order to ensure the relief we afford is in the best interests of the parties, particularly the dependent child or the incapacitated person, we must have before us the most complete and up-to-date record possible, even if that means considering evidence or circumstances which were not before the trier of fact. Consequently, we hold that in guardianship proceedings, the general rule precluding supplementation of the record with material not in the trial court record will normally be deemed waived and the record supplemented with information so as to apprise the reviewing court of the most current set of circumstances. We add the caveat that if any supplemental information is contested by the parties a referral to the trial court will normally be required.

In light of the events occurring since the limited guardianship order was entered in the present case, we decline to disturb the trial court's ruling. The statutes require that only such specific limitations and restrictions be placed on an incapacitated person as are necessary for such person's protection and assistance. . . . The evidence shows that with the limitations placed on Way as a result of the court's order, Way has been provided adequate protection and assistance. She is receiving the medical attention she needs, she has been removed from the deplorable conditions existing at her residence, and she is living in a facility wherein her personal care needs are satisfied. This living situation in which Way was placed after the guardianship order was entered adequately provides for her health and safety. Present circumstances do not support DSHS's contention that a more restricted guardianship is needed. Moreover, should circumstances change, there is nothing to prevent DSHS from requesting additional relief of the trial court.

For the foregoing reasons, the decision of the trial court is affirmed.

4. Guardians' Authority and Responsibilities

In general, a guardian has a wide range of powers. However, states may require specific authorization for certain types of decisions. Thus, depending on the state, a guardian may be required to seek the court's approval before making certain potentially harmful decisions, such as the decision to make gifts of the ward's resources, disclaim an inheritance, make changes in estate-planning documents, or terminate life-sustaining treatment.

A guardian's duties may also vary based on whether the ward has previously appointed an agent pursuant to a durable power of attorney (discussed in Section B of this chapter) or an advance directive for health care (discussed in Section D of this chapter). In some states, such documents remain in effect even after the appointment of a guardian, in which case the guardian may need to defer to the decisions of the previously appointed agent when he or she is making decisions pursuant to the authorizing document.

As a general matter, a guardian's duties are shaped by the fact that a guardian stands in a *fiduciary* relationship to the ward. As discussed further in Section F (see page 187), this means that the guardian must act with a high degree of care and loyalty toward the ward. What specific actions are required to fulfill these duties, however, is the subject of some disagreement, both among the states and among lawyers and scholars. Key questions include:

- How active should the guardian be in overseeing and managing the ward's daily affairs?
- How frequently should the guardian be in contact with the ward?
- To what extent should the guardian consult with the ward about decisions made on the ward's behalf?
- To what extent should the guardian's actions be guided by the ward's previously or currently expressed preferences?

In an attempt to ensure that guardians are fulfilling their duties, states require that courts engage in certain forms of monitoring. Most commonly, guardians are required to file periodic accounting and personal status reports with the court. To protect against the possibility that a guardian will fail to comply with his or her duties, states typically allow the court appointing the guardian to require that the guardian be bonded; that is, they require that the guardian secure a bond that guarantees that the ward will be reimbursed for funds lost as a result of the guardian breaching his or her fiduciary duty. Unfortunately, it is widely agreed that current monitoring efforts are generally inadequate to protect wards' interests.

The next case considers the scope of guardians' authority, as well as the value of court review in ensuring that guardians comply with their fiduciary duties.

Karbin v. Karbin

977 N.E.2d 154 (Ill. 2012)

Justice FREEMAN delivered the judgment of the court, with opinion.

In this case we consider whether we should overrule *In re Marriage of Drews*, 115 Ill. 2d 201, 104 Ill. Dec. 782, 503 N.E.2d 339 (1986), which held that a plenary guardian lacks standing to institute dissolution of marriage proceedings on behalf of the ward. For the reasons that follow, we believe a guardian has the authority to seek permission from the court to file a dissolution petition on behalf of the ward if such petition is found to be in the ward's best interests.

BACKGROUND

Jan and Marcia Karbin were married on June 2, 1984. At that time, Marcia had one daughter, Kara, whom Jan adopted. . . .

After a serious car accident in 1997, Marcia suffered brain damage and became totally disabled, requiring full-time care. Jan was appointed plenary guardian of Marcia's person and estate. For the next seven years, Jan provided for Marcia's needs in their home. Jan also established an annuity for Marcia's lifetime care out of the proceeds of a large personal injury settlement award resulting from the car accident.

By 2004, however, Jan could no longer care for Marcia due to his own Parkinson's disease, and transferred his plenary guardianship of Marcia to Kara. . . .

On November 9, 2007, after living apart for nearly three years, Jan petitioned the circuit court of Cook County for dissolution of his marriage. The petition alleged noncohabitation and irreconcilable differences. On May 19, 2008, Marcia, through Kara, filed a verified counterpetition, alleging the same bases as Jan.

Discovery ensued. In 2009, Marcia filed a motion to compel discovery and petitioned the court for interim attorney fees and costs. Soon after, Jan moved for voluntary dismissal of his petition for dissolution. Jan alleged he had filed the petition at Kara's request, with the understanding that "each party would retain the assets and liabilities in their own name." Jan further claimed it was never his wish to divorce Marcia, but he had been willing to accommodate Kara's wishes as Marcia's guardian.

* * *

Jan thereafter moved to dismiss Marcia's counterpetition, maintaining that pursuant to this court's decision in *In re Marriage of Drews*, 115 Ill. 2d 201, 503 N.E.2d 339 (1986), Kara, as Marcia's plenary guardian, had no authority to pursue a dissolution proceeding on Marcia's behalf. Marcia responded by alleging that Jan's motives for requesting dismissal of her counterpetition were "purely financial in nature, as Jan would stand to inherit from Marcia's estate in the event of her death."

On January 5, 2010, the probate court held that Kara had no standing to file a petition for dissolution of marriage on Marcia's behalf. Thereafter, on April 30, 2010, the judge in the domestic relations case ruled that under *Drews*, "a guardian does not have the authority to litigate a dissolution of marriage action as a petitioner" and granted Jan's motion to dismiss Marcia's counterpetition.

Marcia appealed. A majority of the appellate court panel affirmed, holding that *Drews* controlled. In dissent, Justice Cahill believed *Drews* to be factually distinguishable.

* * *

ANALYSIS

... *In re Marriage of Drews* ... we held that a plenary guardian of a disabled adult does not have standing to initiate an action for the dissolution of a ward's marriage. That case involved a mother who was named as plenary guardian for her son after he had suffered a head injury. After the son was abandoned by his wife, his guardian petitioned for dissolution of marriage, which the son's wife opposed.

In ruling against the guardian, the court noted that a strong "majority rule" existed which held that "absent statutory authorization, a guardian cannot institute an action, on behalf of a ward, for the dissolution of the ward's marriage." *Id.* at 205.

The court looked to whether the General Assembly explicitly authorized the guardian of a person to so act. Section 11a-17 of the Probate Act states that such a guardian's duties include providing for the ward's "support, care, comfort, health, education and maintenance, and professional services as are appropriate." The provision also directs the guardian to assist the ward in "the development of maximum self-reliance and independence." The court concluded that nothing in section 11a-17 provided the explicit authorization required under the traditional rule for a guardian to commence dissolution proceedings.

The court also looked to section 11a-18, which specifies the duties of the guardian of the estate, including "the care, management and investment of the estate." The court also found no explicit authorization in that provision. Indeed, the court concluded that when read together, both sections 11a-17 and 11a-18 "grant only limited standing related solely to matters directly bearing on the management of the ward's estate."

Marcia argues that soon after *Drews* was decided, this court abandoned the strict construction of sections 11a-17 and 11a-18 that had been embraced in that decision. . . .

As noted, *Drews* held that the guardianship provisions of the Probate Act "grant only limited standing related solely to matters directly bearing on the management of the ward's estate." Nevertheless, this court some three years later abandoned the notion that decisions which fall outside this limited area must be expressly authorized by the legislature. In *In re Estate of Longeway*, 133 Ill. 2d 33, 45-46, 139 Ill. Dec. 780, 549 N.E.2d 292 (1989), this court read section 11a-17 expansively to authorize a plenary guardian to make the decision on behalf of the ward regarding the use of life-sustaining measures. . . . The court thus relied on the notion of "implied authority" rather than requiring only explicit authority in determining the power of a guardian to act under the Probate Act.

This court's next opportunity to interpret these same guardianship provisions of the Probate Act came in *In re Marriage of Burgess*, 189 Ill. 2d 270, 244 Ill. Dec. 379, 725 N.E.2d 1266 (2000). There, after the husband had filed a petition for dissolution, he was adjudicated to be disabled, and his sister was appointed his plenary guardian. The wife then moved to dismiss the dissolution action pursuant to *Drews*. By way of a certified question, the appellate court, relying on *Drews*, held that the guardian could not maintain the husband's action.

This court, however, found *Drews* factually distinguishable on the basis that in that case the guardian petitioned to institute the dissolution action on the ward's behalf, whereas in *Burgess* the guardian merely continued a dissolution action previously begun by a ward prior to incapacity. Notwithstanding the factual distinction, the court's analysis did not end there, but went further. Commenting on the broad powers given to a guardian under sections 11a-17 and 11a-18 of the Probate Act, the court construed these provisions in a manner opposite the construction afforded the identical provisions in *Drews*. Rather than accepting *Drews'* interpretation of the powers conferred to guardians under the Probate Act as being exclusive or limiting, the court interpreted those powers broadly, concluding that, although not specifically stated in the statute, a guardian's authority to maintain a dissolution action on behalf of a ward "may be implied" from these provisions. With respect to section 11a-17(a), the court determined that the statute provided a "broad description of a guardian's powers," from which the authority of a guardian to continue a dissolution action on behalf of a ward may be implied. In direct contrast to *Drews*, the court acknowledged that "[t]he status of a ward's marriage impacts the ward's support, care, comfort, and development of self-reliance and independence," which we held were "areas in which a guardian may be empowered to act under [section 11a-17](a)." . . .

Since *Burgess*, our appellate court has also applied the "implied authority" construction of the guardianship statute rather than *Drews*' narrow construction. For example, in *In re Estate of K.E.J.*, 382 Ill. App. 3d 401, 320 Ill. Dec. 560, 887 N.E.2d 704 (2008), the court held that under the provisions of section 11a-17(a) of the Probate Act, a guardian may seek to have a ward undergo involuntary sterilization.

This review of the case law concerning the construction of these provisions of the Probate Act confirms that the court has moved away from requiring explicit grants of statutory authority in order for a guardian to act, instead allowing "implied authority" to suffice. . . .

Jan concedes that the case law interpreting the guardian's powers relating to decisions of a personal nature is inconsistent. He asserts, however, there are legitimate reasons that support maintaining the traditional rule that a plenary guardian may not bring dissolution proceedings on behalf of the ward. He argues that a guardian can never be sure that divorce conforms to the disabled spouse's true wishes and it is for this reason alone that *Drews* should be reaffirmed.

Although *Drews* cited to Illinois' recognition of the "majority rule," the court did not speak to the rule's origin or the rationale underpinning it. Rather, the court cited with approval several decisions from other states, two of which best express the rule's rationale. In *Wood v. Beard*, 107 So. 2d 198 (Fla. Dist. Ct. App. 1958), the court explained that the majority rule "is deeply embedded in the concept that a marriage relationship is exclusively personal and that it may be dissolved only by the voluntary consent and the comprehending exercise of the will of an *injured* spouse." (Emphasis added.) . . .

Similarly, in *Mohrmann v. Kob*, 291 N.Y. 181, 51 N.E.2d 921 (1943), the New York Court of Appeals explained that the majority rule was grounded in the volition of the parties to end the marriage. . . . Accordingly, where the injured spouse is incompetent and cannot intelligently make that choice, the rule provides that no other person—including a guardian—can exercise that option.

Thus, because the decision to divorce was viewed as a uniquely personal matter, oftentimes involving religious and moral precepts, courts were reluctant to have others speak for an incompetent adult in such situations. The rule reflected the view that "marriage is sacred and that only the most serious of marital offenses should be grounds for divorce." Kurt X. Metzmeier, *Note, The Power of an Incompetent Adult to Petition for Divorce Through a Guardian or Next Friend*, 33 U. LOUISVILLE J. FAM. L. 949, 951-52 (1995). This view also went hand-in-hand with the policy that ending a marriage required a legal injury in which the court would assign blame or fault to a specific spouse. The rule, therefore, comported with those states in which the sole grounds for divorce laws were predicated upon concepts of fault and injury, as was the case in Illinois prior to the enactment of the no-fault provisions of the Illinois Marriage and Dissolution of Marriage Act. In such states, only the injured spouse could seek a divorce.

* * *

With the concept of "injury" removed from divorce in Illinois, it is difficult for us to accept the view that the decision to divorce is qualitatively different from any other deeply personal decision, such as the decision to refuse life-support treatment or the decision to undergo involuntary sterilization. Each of these latter decisions can rarely be undone. The same cannot be said for the decision to divorce—if the disabled adult regains competency and disagrees with the guardian's decision, remarriage to the former spouse may be possible. Thus, there is no reason why the guardian should not be allowed to use the substituted-judgment provisions found in section 11a-17(e) of the Probate Act to make all types of uniquely personal decisions that are in the wards's best interests, including the decision to seek a dissolution of marriage. . . .

In light of the above, we cannot agree with Jan that policy considerations regarding divorce compel our reaffirmation of *Drews*. As is apparent, the traditional rule espoused in *Drews* is no longer consistent with current Illinois policy on divorce as reflected in the Illinois Marriage and Dissolution of Marriage Act.

We also note that the continued application of the traditional rule results in an inequity to disabled spouses that conflicts with the policy underlying our Probate Act. Under the traditional rule, a disabled spouse under a guardianship "is helpless to change the situation if his or her competent spouse does not want a divorce. The incompetent, vulnerable spouse is trapped in an unwanted, potentially abusive, marriage." [Mark Schwarz, *Note, The Marriage Trap: How Guardianship Divorce Bans Abet Spousal Abuse*, 13 J.L. & Fam. Stud. 187, 188.] As another commentator has observed: "To provide a mentally competent spouse with [the power to bring a divorce action against an incompetent spouse] in the absence of a corresponding power to the incompetent to seek divorce (through a guardian) is to grant the competent spouse 'absolute, final control over the marriage,' leaving 'an incompetent spouse completely at the mercy of a competent spouse' to the marriage contract. Principles of equity demand equal treatment and equal access to the courts for all individuals. . . ." [Diane Snow Mills, Comment, *"But I Love What's–His–Name": Inherent Dangers in the Changing Role of the Guardian in Divorce Actions on Behalf of Incompetents*, 16 J. Am. Acad. Matrimonial Law, 527, 548-49.]

Accordingly, if we were to agree with Jan and reaffirm *Drews*, we would be allowing the law to unfairly treat incompetent spouses, leaving them at the complete mercy of the competent spouse without consideration of their best interests. . . .

* * *

. . . To do otherwise would mean that a guardian would be prevented from seeking permission from the court to bring an action for dissolution on behalf of an incompetent ward, even if the ward was in danger as a result of being in the marriage. Given that the purpose of the Probate Act is to protect the ward, we would contravene that purpose if we were to prohibit the exercise of the guardian's power in the best interest of the ward while endorsing a power imbalance against the incompetent spouse which could result in physical or emotional abuse, financial exploitation, or neglect of the incompetent spouse by the "competent" partner. By construing the Probate Act to prohibit a guardian from being able to seek permission from the court to bring a dissolution action on behalf of the ward, we would be improperly carving an exception to the broad powers of a guardian set forth by the General Assembly in the Probate Act. In our view, it is only by giving these provisions their full meaning that we can accomplish the legislature's intent to protect the vulnerable members of our society and to ensure their safety.

Whether a guardian is initiating, responding to, or continuing a dissolution action, the interests of the ward that may require protection remain constant, regardless of the procedural posture of the case. Because under the Probate Act the guardian must always act in the best interests of the ward, when a guardian decides that those best interests require that the marriage be dissolved, the guardian must have the power to take appropriate legal action to accomplish that end. We therefore find no compelling reason to treat a guardian's decision to seek court permission to institute a dissolution action on behalf of a ward any differently from the multitude of other innately personal decisions which may be made by guardians on behalf of their wards, including undergoing involuntary sterilization or ending life-support measures. All of these decisions made by guardians without knowing a ward's wishes are just as personal—if not more so—than the decision to seek a divorce. All also may implicate the ward's moral and religious beliefs. The provisions of our Probate Act cannot be so arbitrary as to empower a plenary guardian to make decisions with respect to all these matters except for the decision to end a marriage. Either the guardian can act in the best interests of the ward for all personal matters, or for none at all.

This ensures that the most vulnerable members of our society are afforded fundamental fairness, equal protection of the laws and equal access to the courts. Therefore, *In re Marriage of Drews* is hereby overruled.

* * *

We therefore reverse the judgments of both the circuit and appellate courts and hold that Marcia's petition should be allowed to be filed. On remand, we direct the circuit court to hold a "best interests" hearing in order to determine whether it is in Marcia's best interests to seek the dissolution of her marriage. . . .

In our view, the circuit court's assessment of the petition for dissolution filed by a guardian on behalf of a ward pursuant to the standards set forth in section 11a-17(e) provides the needed procedural and substantive safeguards to ensure that the best interests of the ward are achieved while preventing a guardian from pursuing a dissolution of marriage for his or her own financial benefit, or because of the guardian's personal antipathy toward the ward's spouse. To further safeguard the interests of all parties involved, we agree with Marcia that the guardian must satisfy a clear and convincing burden of proof that the dissolution is in the ward's best interests. . . .

CONCLUSION

For the foregoing reasons, we reverse the judgments of the appellate and circuit courts. This cause is remanded to the circuit court for further proceedings consistent with this opinion.

Judgments reversed.

NOTES

1. *Guardians' authority regarding divorce.* There is significant disagreement among the states as to whether a guardian has authority to petition for divorce on behalf of a ward. As in *Karbin,* some states see this as within the scope of the guardian's authority. *See, e.g., Broach v. Broach,* 895 N.E.2d 640 (Ct. App. Ohio 2008) (finding that petitioning for divorce on behalf of a ward is within the scope of a guardian's authority); *Houghton ex rel. Johnson v. Keller,* 662 N.W.2d 854 (Mich. App. 2003) (same); *Kronberg v. Kronberg,* 623 A.2d 806 (N.J. Super. 1993) (same). Others disagree, typically reasoning that the decision to marry or divorce is a uniquely personal one. *See, e.g., Luster v. Luster,* 17 A.3d 1068 (Conn. 2011) (holding that a conservator could not bring a civil action for dissolution of marriage on behalf of a ward); *Brockman ex rel. Jennings v. Young,* 2011 WL 5419713 (Ky. Ct. App. 2011) (dismissing guardian's petition for dissolution of ward's marriage on the grounds that the guardian lacked authority to file the petition).

2. *Debate over the proper breadth of surrogate's authority.* For an argument in favor of allowing surrogates—including guardians—broad authority to make intimate decisions, *see* Alexander Boni-Saenz, *Personal Delegations,* BROOK. L. REV. 1231 (2013).

3. *Research on guardianship abuse and monitoring.* In response to concerns about abuse of wards by guardians, advocates have pushed for increased monitoring of guardians. For further research about mistreatment of wards by guardians, see U.S. GOV'T ACCOUNTABILITY OFFICE, GAO-10-1046, CASES OF FINANCIAL EXPLOITATION, NEGLECT, AND ABUSE OF SENIORS (2010) (identifying "hundreds of allegations" of abuse of seniors under guardianship as well as confirming cases). For a studies of court oversight and its potential to address such mistreatment, see Naomi Karp & Erica F. Wood, *Guardianship Monitoring: A National Survey of Court Practices,* 37 STETSON L. REV. 143 (2007), and NAOMI KARP & ERICA F. WOOD, AARP PUBLIC POLICY INSTITUTE, GUARDING THE GUARDIANS: PROMISING PRACTICE FOR COURT OVERSIGHT (Dec. 2007).

4. *Guardianship standards.* To help guide guardians in performing their duties, a number of state and national organizations have come together to develop guardianship standards. For an overview of the standards developed as part of the Third National Guardianship Summit, see *Third National Guardianship Summit Standards and Recommendations*, 2012 UTAH L. REV. 1191 (2012).

QUESTIONS

1. Should a guardian be allowed to commence a divorce proceeding on behalf of a ward? Change a will? Decide who may visit the ward? Vote on the ward's behalf?

2. Do you agree with the *Karbin* court that requiring the lower court to find by clear and convincing evidence that divorce is in Marcia's best interest provides sufficient procedural and substantive safeguards? Why or why not?

3. Who should be allowed to demand an accounting or report from a guardian? Should a ward have such a right?

5. Critiques of Guardianship

The guardianship system, both in the United States and abroad, has been subject to extensive criticism. One concern is that guardianship is harmful to wards because it isolates and stigmatizes them. Another concern is that it violates individuals' human rights. For example, some in the disability rights community have argued that the concept of guardianship—or at least the concept of plenary guardianship—is inconsistent with Article 12 of the United Nations Convention on the Rights of Persons with Disabilities (CRPD), which states that "persons with disabilities enjoy legal capacity on an equal basis with others in all aspects of life" and that governments that are parties to the CRPD "shall take appropriate measures to provide access by persons with disabilities to the support they may require in exercising their legal capacity." (As of the date of publication, the United States was a signatory to the CRPD but had not ratified it.)

The most common critique of guardianship, however, is a more pragmatic one: that the courts routinely fail to properly apply state law because they are too quick to appoint guardians, and then fail to properly oversee them. Specifically, the concern is that the courts fail to treat guardianship as a last resort and instead routinely appoint plenary guardians without adequately assessing the AIP's capacity or investigating alternative ways to meet the AIP's needs such as with a limited guardianship. This concern is well-founded. In some cases, disability itself—as opposed to functional ability—appears to be used as the justification for guardianship. In many cases, very little time is devoted to assessing the allegedly incapacitated person's abilities and condition. Indeed, a study in the mid-1990s found that most guardianship hearings last less than 15 minutes. *See* LAUREN BARRITT LISI ET AL., CENTER FOR SOCIAL GERONTOLOGY, NATIONAL STUDY OF GUARDIANSHIP SYSTEMS: FINDINGS AND RECOMMENDATIONS (1994).

Over the past several decades, states have attempted to reform their guardianship systems to reduce the overuse of plenary guardianship by encouraging the use of limited guardianships instead. Not only have states added limited guardianship as an option, but some states have explicitly added language to their statutes requiring courts to consider alternative approaches before imposing a guardianship. For example, Florida requires that:

> When an order determines that a person is incapable of exercising delegable rights, the court must consider and find whether there is an alternative to guardianship that will sufficiently address the problems of the incapacitated person. A guardian must be appointed to exercise the incapacitated person's delegable rights unless the court finds there is an alternative. A guardian may not be appointed if the court finds there is an alternative to guardianship which will sufficiently address the problems of the incapacitated person.

FLA. STAT. §744.331(6)(b) (2007). In addition, Florida explicitly requires that:

> The order appointing a guardian . . . must be the least restrictive appropriate alternative, and must reserve to the incapacitated person the right to make decisions in all matters commensurate with the person's ability to do so.

FLA. STAT. §744.344(2) (2007).

Nevertheless, such reforms appear to have done little to change courts' behavior. As Professor Lawrence Frolik has explained:

> It seems that as long as the law permits plenary guardianship, courts will prefer to use it. But not all guardianships are so clearly candidates for plenary guardianship. Surely, there exist some individuals who, though in need of a guardian, still have the ability to handle some of their affairs. In these cases, the failure to use limited guardianship may reflect the belief that despite the plenary guardianship, the guardian will permit the ward to control his or her life to the greatest extent possible. For example, a guardian might give the ward small amounts of spending money for discretionary spending. More likely, judges may not use limited guardianship because they do not understand its value nor do they appreciate the gain to the ward in limiting the power of the guardian. Rather, judges know all too well the financial costs of additional court appearances as guardians with insufficient authority to deal with the needs of their wards ask the courts to expand the limits of the guardianships.

Lawrence A. Frolik, *Guardianship Reform: When the Best is the Enemy of the Good*, 9 STAN. L. & POL'Y REV. 347, 354 (1998). Frolik has therefore urged those seeking to reform guardianship to "focus their efforts on persuading judges to adopt the doctrine of the least restrictive alternative and to use limited guardianships more frequently." *Id.* at 355.

In part in response to courts' continued reliance on plenary guardianship, some critics of guardianship have argued for replacing it, or supplementing it, with *supported decision-making*. Supported decision-making is described as a process in which an individual with cognitive challenges retains decision-making authority and control but is assisted in decision-making by one or more people who explain issues and, if necessary, interpret the individual's behavior and words to determine the individual's wishes. The most frequently cited model of supported decision-making is British Columbia's Representation Agreement, a document which can be used to authorize a third party to act on another's behalf for a wide swath of personal decisions and many financial decisions as well. Persons may execute a Representation Agreement even if they are incapable of executing a contract or managing their affairs and do not relinquish their right to make decisions on their own behalf by doing so.

NOTES

1. *Effect of total incapacity.* Even a finding of total incapacity does not necessarily support a conclusion that a plenary guardianship should be imposed. In *In re Guardianship of Fuqua*, 646 So. 2d 795 (Fla. Dist. Ct. App. 1994), a quadriplegic appealed an order finding him totally incapacitated and appointing a plenary guardian. The court agreed that the ward was totally incapacitated but nevertheless remanded the case for reconsideration on the grounds that the record did not indicate that the lower court had considered less restrictive alternatives to plenary guardianship.

2. *Further reading on supported decision-making.* For further discussion of supported decision-making practices, and their potential impacts, see Nina A. Kohn, Jeremy A. Blumenthal & Amy Campbell, *Supported Decision-Making: A Viable Alternative to Guardianship?*, 117 Penn St. L. Rev. 1111 (2013) (summarizing the existing empirical research on supported decision-making and outlining a research agenda for further evaluation); Terry Carney & Fleur Beaupert, *Public & Private Bricolage—Challenges Balancing Law, Services and Civil Society in Advancing CRPD Supported Decision-Making*, 36 Univ. New S. Wales L.J. 174 (2013) (describing supported decision-making as "conceptually ill-defined," noting that it "has been interpreted as spanning everything from targeted legal powers and authorities through to facilitation of the normal interactions of daily family or social intercourse," and calling for research evaluating supported decision-making approaches because "the right to equality of participation on the part of people with cognitive and psychosocial disabilities is too fragile to be entrusted to experimental law-making or well-intentioned but ultimately mistaken application of normative principles"); Robert D. Dinerstein, *Implementing Legal Capacity Under Article 12 of the UN Convention on the Rights of Persons with Disabilities: The Difficult Road from Guardianship to Supported Decision-Making*, 19 Hum. Rts. Brief 8 (2012) (describing how countries are moving toward

supported decision-making approaches in response to Article 12 of the CRPD); and Leslie Salzman, *Guardianship for Persons with Mental Illness—A Legal & Appropriate Alternative?*, 4 St. Louis U. J. Health L. & Pol'y 279, 306 (2011) (describing supported decision-making and its potential to divert potential wards away from the guardianship system, and suggesting that without such an alternative the guardianship system will never truly be a last resort).

QUESTIONS

1. No guardianship system will be perfect. In close cases, should guardianship systems err on the side of granting petitions for guardianship or on the side of denying petitions for guardianship?

2. Is supported decision-making a viable alternative to guardianship? What would you want to know in order to decide?

PROBLEM

Ned has been appointed as guardian for his great-aunt Adele, who has severe dementia and congestive heart failure. Adele, 86, was devastated when she first learned that she was developing dementia. She was deeply troubled at the thought of living an "undignified" life, and once remarked to Ned that she hoped that "the Lord would be kind and make this go quick." Despite her current condition, however, Adele appears content and at ease when Ned visits her in the nursing home in which she now resides. Several days ago, Adele was admitted to the hospital with pneumonia. Adele's treating physician believes that a DNR order would be appropriate for Adele. Should Ned be entitled to consent to a DNR order directly, or should he be required to obtain court approval to do so? If state law requires court approval, how should the court determine whether or not grant it?

6. Guardianship Diversion and Mediation

Guardianship diversion is a process whereby, instead of having a guardian appointed, an individual agrees to services or other arrangements that render a guardian unnecessary. Increasingly, court systems are creating guardianship diversion systems that can serve to increase awareness of and encourage alternatives to guardianship. Guardianship diversion is seen as a way of actualizing the doctrine of the least restrictive alternative because it provides a mechanism for petitioners and AIPs to work together to find alternative ways to address the AIPs' needs.

Guardianship diversion programs are not, however, without risks. One concern about guardianship diversion is that it may become unduly coercive, pressuring the AIP to relinquish much of his or her independence. On the other hand, guardianship diversion may allow an AIP to avoid the more significant deprivation of liberty that would result from imposition of guardianship.

In cases in which a guardianship petition is triggered at least in part by a family conflict, *guardianship mediation* may be one option for avoiding guardianship. Guardianship mediation is a process by which a neutral third party mediator works with the AIP, his or her family, and other interested persons to try to find a mutually agreeable way to meet the AIP's needs. With the mediator's facilitation, the individuals may reach an agreement on such matters as where the AIP will live or how the AIP's financial resources will be managed, thus avoiding the need or perceived need for a guardianship. Guardianship mediation can occur either before or after a petition for guardianship has been filed and can also be incorporated into a guardianship diversion program. Additionally, it may be a way to address disputes that arise after the appointment of a guardian.

Unlike a guardianship proceeding, guardianship mediation allows private individuals—not a judge—to function as the primary decision-makers. As outlined by Professor Mary Radford, other differences include that:

> A court proceeding is usually public and its outcome a matter of public record, while a mediation is held in private and the proceedings are meant to remain confidential. A court proceeding is often adversarial and typically results in a victory by only one party. It is governed by rigid procedural rules and its outcome is limited to a few strict legal alternatives. Mediation is designed for cooperative decision-making, uses a flexible and open procedure, and is designed to encourage the parties to reach resolutions that meet their needs without necessarily adhering to strict legal principles. Because the restrictive rules of evidence do not apply in a mediation, the parties are more free to discuss underlying motivations and tensions. This flexibility is viewed by many as one of the advantages mediation has over more formalized procedures. The nonadversarial nature of mediation is another perceived advantage, in that parties to a mediation may be less prone to the shattering of relationships that often accompanies a protracted adversarial proceeding. Finally, mediation typically is viewed as being less costly and more efficient than a formal court proceeding.

Mary F. Radford, *Is the Use of Mediation Appropriate in Adult Guardianship Cases?*, 31 Stetson L. Rev. 611, 618 (2002).

Guardianship mediation, like other forms of elder mediation discussed in Section A.4 of Chapter 2, can take different forms. The two archetypes of mediation are *evaluative* mediation and *facilitative* mediation. In an evaluative mediation, the mediator assesses the participants' situation and may share that assessment with participants and encourage them to reach certain outcomes. By contrast, in facilitative mediation, the mediator's role is limited to helping the parties understand their own and one another's situations and empowering the parties to reach their own resolution. In reality, mediation falls along a continuum, however, with different mediators displaying different degrees of facilitative and evaluative behavior, and some mediators varying the extent to which they employ one method or the other depending on the case they are mediating.

Guardianship mediation raises several important questions. First and foremost, does it empower or disempower older adults? One of the potential advantages of guardianship mediation is that it allows for the active involvement of individuals who would not have standing in a guardianship proceeding. This may allow for more creative, community-focused approaches to meeting an individual's needs. On the other hand, it may thrust the AIP into a situation in which people with no pre-existing legal right to do so are treated as if they are entitled to have a role in determining the AIP's future and living conditions. Moreover, because the focus of mediation tends to be reaching an agreement, the AIP may feel pressure—either consciously or subconsciously—to consent to guardianship or otherwise relinquish rights in order to "go along," maintain peace, or otherwise appear reasonable. A related question is whether the privacy afforded by mediation benefits or harms AIPs. On one hand, mediation may help the AIP avoid the stigma associated with a public proceeding and the airing of "dirty laundry" in court. On the other hand, that same privacy may shield from public scrutiny those who seek to pressure the AIP to accept certain arrangements.

The next case explores the potential for undue influence and coercion when petitioners and AIPs negotiate in the shadow of a guardianship petition.

In re Guardianship of Macak

871 A.2d 767 (N.J. Super. Ct. App. Div. 2005)

S.L. REISNER, J.A.D.

Walter J. Macak appeals from an order of the trial court granting summary judgment. The trial court dismissed a 2003 application in which Mr. Macak asked the court to set aside a 2002 judgment declaring him incapacitated and to restore him to legal capacity. . . . We reverse and remand for a plenary hearing.

I

In 2002, Mr. Macak's daughter filed a complaint . . . seeking the appointment of a guardian for her father based on her contention that he was incapacitated. The complaint was supported by affidavits from two doctors. The impetus for the complaint was her concern that Mr. Macak had Alzheimer's disease, was unable to manage his finances, and was falling prey to financial "scam artists." Further, he was living alone in a large house cluttered with debris. Mr. Macak directed his attorney to oppose the guardianship application and specifically indicated his opposition to having his daughter appointed as his guardian, if he was declared incapacitated.

Instead of opposing the guardianship or advocating for Mr. Macak's choice of guardian, his attorney negotiated a "settlement" under which she signed a consent order on Mr. Macak's behalf. The consent order, which the trial court signed without holding a hearing or making findings of fact and conclusions of law, declared Mr. Macak to be incapacitated and appointed an attorney, LaDonna Burton, as his guardian. Ms. Burton was to serve without bond, although, at the time, Mr. Macak's estate was worth approximately one million dollars. The consent order also provided that the guardian would continue Mr. Macak's "gifting program" of giving his daughter $18,000 per year. Mr. Macak also signed a separate written agreement with Ms. Burton, in which he agreed to move out of his house into an assisted living facility within five days of the date of the agreement and she agreed to permit him to visit his house on a regular basis.

On this appeal, the parties stipulated that Mr. Macak entered into the 2002 agreement because his attorney and Ms. Burton convinced him that if he were declared incapacitated, absent the agreement, the court would appoint his daughter as his guardian against his wishes.

In 2003, Mr. Macak persuaded a friend to help him retain an attorney to assist him in re-opening the guardianship. Mr. Macak's attorney filed a complaint contending that Ms. Burton had prevented Mr. Macak from visiting his house, that he had signed the guardianship "agreement" under duress, and that he was not incapacitated but only needed assistance in managing his finances. He therefore asked the court to set aside the guardianship, restore him to legal capacity, and appoint a conservator for him.

Following some limited discovery, both sides filed reports from doctors who had examined Mr. Macak, and reports from a geriatric specialist concerning whether he could resume living in his house. Mr. Macak's doctor, Dr. Paul Rosenberg, opined that he suffered from mild dementia, but was not incapacitated. The doctor retained by the guardian, as well as the court-appointed doctor, disagreed with Dr. Rosenberg. Anthony J. Serra, Esq., a guardian ad litem appointed by the court, issued a fifty page report cogently detailing the errors in the prior guardianship proceeding and advocating that the court consider allowing Mr. Macak to resume living in his house.

The court declined to hold an evidentiary hearing. Instead, the court granted the guardian's motion for summary judgment, concluding that Dr. Rosenberg's opinion was in the "vast minority."

II

After reviewing the record, including all of the medical reports and the report of the guardian ad litem, we conclude that the initial guardianship proceeding in 2002 was fraught with error, mandating that the matter be remanded for a hearing on the issue of Mr. Macak's capacity. We are also persuaded that the existence of material disputes of fact entitled Mr. Macak to an evidentiary hearing on his 2003 application to re-open the guardianship. Therefore, we remand this matter to the trial court for a hearing on the following issues: whether Mr. Macak is incapacitated such that he requires a guardian; if so, whether the guardianship should be plenary or whether Mr. Macak retains the ability to make certain decisions for himself such that the guardianship should be limited in certain aspects; if Mr. Macak is incapacitated, whether the guardian should continue to be authorized to make gifts to his daughter.

If Mr. Macak is not incapacitated, the court on remand should adjudicate his application for the appointment of a conservator.

An incapacitated person cannot enter into a consent order declaring him to be incapacitated nor can he consent to the appointment of a plenary guardian. An incapacitated person by definition "is unfit and unable to govern himself or herself and to manage his or her affairs," ... and hence cannot "settle" a guardianship action in such a fashion. . . . Further, as this case illustrates, the potential for overreaching and undue influence is unacceptably high. Even if the parties agree that the court can consider the reports of the examining doctors without requiring their testimony, ... and even if the alleged incapacitated person chooses not to testify, the court must still independently consider all of the evidence, including the doctors' reports and the report of the court appointed attorney, and must make findings by clear and convincing evidence as to whether the person is incapacitated.

If the court finds that the person is incapacitated, the court must then independently determine whom to appoint as guardian. In making this determination, the court should consider the recommendations of the court-appointed attorney and the wishes of the incapacitated person, if expressed. A person who is incapacitated may nonetheless still be able to express an intelligent view as to his choice of guardian, which view is entitled to consideration by the court. . . . It is the duty of the court appointed attorney to advocate for the client's choice of guardian as well as to advocate the client's position with respect to the underlying issue of whether the client is incapacitated. . . . If there is a significant issue as to the appropriate choice of guardian, or as to the underlying issue of incapacity, the court may appoint a guardian ad litem to advise the court as to the person's best interests. Under no circumstances should a person in Mr. Macak's situation be coerced into agreeing to a guardianship under the threat that, if he does not do so, the court will appoint a particular person as guardian whom he does not want to serve as his guardian.

* * *

These procedures, essential for the ward's protection, were completely abrogated in this case. Instead, the court merely accepted a "settlement" in which the allegedly incapacitated person agreed to be declared incapacitated, agreed to the appointment of a guardian, and agreed that the guardian could continue to make substantial monetary gifts to his daughter. No hearing was held. The court did not make the required findings, by clear and convincing evidence, concerning whether or not Mr. Macak is incapacitated. The court further failed to make the findings . . . necessary to authorize the guardian to make gifts of Mr. Macak's money to his daughter. This omission was particularly troubling, because Mr. Macak's daughter was also the plaintiff in the guardianship action. Moreover, counsel for the guardian readily concedes that Mr. Macak agreed to this "settlement" in order to avoid the likelihood that, should he insist on a hearing and be declared incapacitated, his daughter would be appointed his guardian.

A person who is not incapacitated may nonetheless be subject to undue influence. Whether or not Mr. Macak was incapacitated at the time of the settlement, the entire scenario presents the possibility of overreaching and undue influence. Even if all concerned had only his best interests at heart, his legal interests were not properly protected.

In addition, for reasons not explained on this record, Ms. Burton was permitted to serve without bond; hence, in this respect also, Mr. Macak's financial interests were not safeguarded. Mr. Macak has assets of over one million dollars. In view of the size of his estate, the court should require an individual appointed as his permanent guardian to post bond. If there are extraordinary reasons justifying the waiver of a bond, that determination should be set forth in a decision supported by appropriate factual findings.

We also agree with Mr. Macak that he was entitled to an evidentiary hearing on his 2003 application to re-open and set aside the guardianship and to appoint a conservator. The Court Rules require a testimonial hearing on an application to restore a person to legal capacity. . . . Even if there had been no deficiencies in the original 2002 guardianship proceedings, Mr. Macak was entitled to a hearing on his 2003 application, because the proofs presented on that application created a material dispute of fact as to his capacity. Ms. Burton contends, in essence, that a hearing would be an expensive waste of time, and she implies that Mr. Macak's current attorneys are taking advantage of him. In support of her motion for summary judgment, she presented what may prove at hearing to be entirely convincing evidence of Mr. Macak's incapacity. On the other hand, Mr. Macak presented a report from Dr. Paul Rosenberg that contradicted the evidence submitted by Ms. Burton. In light of the conflicting evidence, the court should have held a hearing. The fact that, as the trial court stated, Dr. Rosenberg's opinion was in the "vast minority" did not defeat Mr. Macak's right to a hearing. . . .

Consequently, we reverse the grant of summary judgment and remand this matter to the trial court for a hearing.

* * *

In addition to determining whether Mr. Macak is incapacitated, the trial court should determine whether, despite his incapacity, he retains the ability to make some decisions for himself and, therefore, whether the guardianship should be limited in any way. It may be that some or all of the terms included in the "settlement" of the initial guardianship action would be appropriate for inclusion in a court order of limited guardianship. . . . [I]f Mr. Macak is incapacitated, the court must also determine whether to approve any continued gifting of Mr. Macak's assets to his daughter. If the court concludes that Mr. Macak is not incapacitated, the court should then adjudicate his application for the appointment of a conservator. In light of the issues presented, the guardian ad litem should participate in the proceedings on remand. . . .

III

. . . Reversed and remanded.

NOTE

Mediating among potential guardians. Guardianship mediation is commonly assumed to involve a potential ward entering into a discussion with potential guardians or other interested third parties. In such situations, mediation is only possible where the AIP has sufficient capacity to actively participate in the process. Mediation, however, may also have a role to play in the guardianship process where the AIP is unable to participate. Even in this context, a mediator may need to address the existence of unequal balance of power. As Professor Susan Gary has explained:

> In some disputes connected with guardianship, the older person will not be an active disputant. For example, two adult children may be in conflict over treatment for the protected person or may be competing for appointment as guardian. In those cases, unequal power in the mediation will be an issue only if the adult children have unequal negotiating skills or if there is a family history of domination by one sibling over the other. A mediator may be able to manage a power imbalance in those situations.

Susan N. Gary, *Mediation and the Elderly: Using Mediation to Resolve Probate Disputes Over Guardianship & Inheritance*, 32 WAKE FOREST L. REV. 397, 432 (1997).

QUESTIONS

1. Suppose Mr. Macak and his daughter had engaged in mediation with the help of a professional mediator. Do you think they would have reached the same agreement? Why or why not?

2. Does guardianship mediation raise similar concerns to those involved in the "settlement" reached in *Macak*? Why or why not?

3. In discussing guardianship mediation, Professor Mary Radford posed the following question:

   > Guardianship adjudications are designed to offer maximum protection to that individual because he or she may not be capable of protecting himself or herself. Mediation, on the other hand, is grounded in the principle of self-determination and presumes that the parties are capable of participating in the process and bargaining for their own interests. Can these two concepts be reconciled?

   Mary F. Radford, *Is the Use of Mediation Appropriate in Adult Guardianship Cases?*, 31 STETSON L. REV. 611, 639-40 (providing Professor Radford's own analysis of the answer).
   How would you respond? Is the fact that an AIP is able to engage in guardianship mediation proof that he or she does not require a guardian?

7. Sample Statute

Below are key provisions from New York's statute governing most types of guardianship (New York uses a separate, controversial scheme for certain persons with developmental or intellectual disabilities). As you read the selected sections, consider who it protects and how. What provisions are particularly important? Why?

NEW YORK MENTAL HYGIENE LAW
ARTICLE 81 (2013)

§81.02 Power to appoint a guardian of the person and/or property; standard for appointment

(a) The court may appoint a guardian for a person if the court determines:

1. that the appointment is necessary to provide for the personal needs of that person, including food, clothing, shelter, health care, or safety and/or to manage the property and financial affairs of that person; and

2. that the person agrees to the appointment, or that the person is incapacitated as defined in subdivision (b) of this section. In deciding whether the appointment is necessary, the court shall consider the report of the court evaluator, as required in paragraph five of subdivision (c) of section 81.09 of this article, and the sufficiency and reliability of available resources, as defined in subdivision (e) of section 81.03 of this article, to provide for personal needs or property management without the appointment of a guardian. Any guardian appointed under this article shall be granted only those powers which are necessary to provide for personal needs and/or property management of the incapacitated person in such a manner as appropriate to the individual and which shall constitute the least restrictive form of intervention. . . .

(b) The determination of incapacity shall be based on clear and convincing evidence and shall consist of a determination that a person is likely to suffer harm because:

1. the person is unable to provide for personal needs and/or property management; and

2. the person cannot adequately understand and appreciate the nature and consequences of such inability.

(c) In reaching its determination, the court shall give primary consideration to the functional level and functional limitations of the person. Such consideration shall include an assessment of that person's:

1. management of the activities of daily living . . . ;

2. understanding and appreciation of the nature and consequences of any inability to manage the activities of daily living;

3. preferences, wishes, and values with regard to managing the activities of daily living; and

4. the nature and extent of the person's property and financial affairs and his or her ability to manage them.

It shall also include an assessment of (i) the extent of the demands placed on the person by that person's personal needs and by the nature and extent of that person's property and financial affairs; (ii) any physical illness and the prognosis of such illness; (iii) any mental disability, as that term is defined in section 1.03 of this chapter, alcoholism or substance dependence as those terms are defined in section 19.03 of this chapter, and the prognosis of such disability, alcoholism or substance dependence; and (iv) any medications with which the person is being treated and their effect on the person's behavior, cognition and judgment.

(d) In addition, the court shall consider all other relevant facts and circumstances regarding the person's:

1. functional level; and

2. understanding and appreciation of the nature and consequences of his or her functional limitations.

§81.06   Who may commence a proceeding

(a) A proceeding under this article shall be commenced by the filing of the petition with the court by:

1. the person alleged to be incapacitated;

2. a presumptive distributee of the person alleged to be incapacitated . . . ;

3. an executor or administrator of an estate when the alleged incapacitated person is or may be the beneficiary of that estate;

4. a trustee of a trust when the alleged incapacitated person is or may be the grantor or a beneficiary of that trust;

5. the person with whom the person alleged to be incapacitated resides;

6. a person otherwise concerned with the welfare of the person alleged to be incapacitated. For purposes of this section a person otherwise concerned with the welfare of the person alleged to be incapacitated may include a corporation, or a public agency, including the department of social services in the county where the person alleged to be incapacitated resides regardless of whether the person alleged to be incapacitated is a recipient of public assistance;

7. the chief executive officer, or the designee of the chief executive officer, of a facility in which the person alleged to be incapacitated is a patient or resident.

§81.07 Notice

(a) *Proceeding.* A proceeding under this article shall be commenced upon the filing of the petition.

(b) *Order to show cause.* Upon the filing of the petition, the court shall:

1. set the date on which the order to show cause is heard no more than twenty-eight days from the date of the signing of the order to show cause. The court may for good cause shown set a date less than twenty-eight days from the date of the signing of the order to show cause . . . ;

2. include in the order to show cause the name, address, and telephone number of the person appointed as court evaluator . . . ;

3. require the order to show cause to be served together with a copy of the petition and any supporting papers upon the alleged incapacitated

person, the court evaluator, and counsel for the alleged incapacitated person. . . .

(c) *Form of the order to show cause.* The order to show cause shall be written in large type, in plain language, and in a language other than English if necessary to inform the person alleged to be incapacitated of his or her rights, and shall include the following information:

1. date, time, and place of the hearing of the petition;

2. a clear and easily readable statement of the rights of the person alleged to be incapacitated . . . ;

3. the name, address, and telephone number of the person appointed as court evaluator . . . ;

4. the name, address, and telephone number of the attorney if one has been appointed for the person alleged to be incapacitated . . . ; and

5. a list of the powers which the guardian would have the authority to exercise on behalf of the person alleged to be incapacitated if the relief sought in the petition is granted.

(d) *Legend.* The order to show cause shall also include on its face the following legend in twelve point or larger bold face double spaced type:

IMPORTANT

An application has been filed in court by _____ who believes you may be unable to take care of your personal needs or financial affairs. _____ is asking that someone be appointed to make decisions for you. With this paper is a copy of the application to the court showing why _____ believes you may be unable to take care of your personal needs or financial affairs. Before the court makes the appointment of someone to make decisions for you the court holds a hearing at which you are entitled to be present and to tell the judge if you do not want anyone appointed. This paper tells you when the court hearing will take place. If you do not appear in court, your rights may be seriously affected.

You have the right to demand a trial by jury. You must tell the court if you wish to have a trial by jury. If you do not tell the court, the hearing will be conducted without a jury. The name and address, and telephone number of the clerk of the court are: _____.

The court has appointed a court evaluator to explain this proceeding to you and to investigate the claims made in the application. The court may give the court evaluator permission to inspect your medical, psychological, or psychiatric records. You have the right to tell the judge if you do not want the court evaluator to be given that permission. The court evaluator's name, address, and telephone number are: _____.

You are entitled to have a lawyer of your choice represent you. If you want the court to appoint a lawyer to help you and represent you, the court will appoint

a lawyer for you. You will be required to pay that lawyer unless you do not have the money to do so.

(e) *Service of the order to show cause.*

1. The persons entitled to service of the order to show cause shall include:

(i) the person alleged to be incapacitated; and

(ii) the attorney for the person alleged to be incapacitated, if known to the petitioner; and

(iii) the court evaluator.

* * *

(g) *Notice of the proceeding.*

1. Persons entitled to notice of the proceeding shall include:

(i) the following persons, other than the petitioner, who are known to the petitioner or whose existence and address can be ascertained by the petitioner with reasonably diligent efforts: the spouse of the person alleged to be incapacitated, if any; the parents of the person alleged to be incapacitated, if living; the adult children of the person alleged to be incapacitated, if any; the adult siblings of the person alleged to be incapacitated, if any; the person or persons with whom person alleged to be incapacitated resides; and

(ii) in the event no person listed in subparagraph (i) of this paragraph is given notice, then notice shall be given to at least one and not more than three of the living relatives of the person alleged to be incapacitated in the nearest degree of kinship who are known to the petitioner or whose existence and address can be ascertained by the petitioner with reasonably diligent efforts; and

(iii) any person or persons designated by the alleged incapacitated person with authority pursuant to sections 5-1501, 5-1505, and 5-1506 of the general obligations law [provisions governing powers-of-attorney], or ... two thousand nine hundred eighty-one of the public health law [a provision permitting the use of health care proxies], if known to the petitioner; and

(iv) if known to the petitioner, any person, whether or not a relative of the person alleged to be incapacitated, or organization that has demonstrated a genuine interest in promoting the best interests of the person alleged to be incapacitated such as by having a personal relationship with the person, regularly visiting the person, or regularly communicating with the person; and

(v) if it is known to the petitioner that the person alleged to be incapacitated receives public assistance or protective services ... , the local department of social services; and

(vi) if the person alleged to be incapacitated resides in a facility, the chief executive officer in charge of the facility; and

(vii) if the person alleged to be incapacitated resides in a mental hygiene facility, the mental hygiene legal service of the judicial department in which the residence is located; and

(viii) such other persons as the court may direct based on the recommendation of the court evaluator....

2. Notice of the proceeding together with a copy of the order to show cause shall be mailed to the persons identified in paragraph one of this subdivision not less than fourteen days prior to the hearing date in the order to show cause.

3. The court may direct that the notice of proceeding be mailed within a time period less than the period required in paragraph two of this subdivision for good cause shown.

§81.11 Hearing

(a) A determination that the appointment of a guardian is necessary for a person alleged to be incapacitated shall be made only after a hearing.

(b) In a proceeding brought pursuant to this article any party to the proceeding shall have the right to:

1. present evidence;

2. call witnesses, including expert witnesses;

3. cross examine witnesses, including witnesses called by the court;

4. be represented by counsel of his or her choice.

(c) The hearing must be conducted in the presence of the person alleged to be incapacitated, either at the courthouse or where the person alleged to be incapacitated resides, so as to permit the court to obtain its own impression of the person's capacity. If the person alleged to be incapacitated physically cannot come or be brought to the courthouse, the hearing must be conducted where the person alleged to be incapacitated resides unless:

1. the person is not present in the state; or

2. all the information before the court clearly establishes that (i) the person alleged to be incapacitated is completely unable to participate in the hearing or (ii) no meaningful participation will result from the person's presence at the hearing.

* * *

§81.12 Burden and quantum of proof

(a) A determination that a person is incapacitated under the provisions of this article must be based on clear and convincing evidence. The burden of proof shall be on the petitioner.

(b) The court may, for good cause shown, waive the rules of evidence....

§81.16 Dispositional alternatives

(a) *Dismissal of the petition.*

If the person alleged to be incapacitated under this article is found not to be incapacitated, the court shall dismiss the petition.

(b) *Protective arrangements and single transactions.* If the person alleged to be incapacitated is found to be incapacitated, the court without appointing a guardian, may authorize, direct, or ratify any transaction or series of transactions necessary to achieve any security, service, or care arrangement meeting the foreseeable needs of the incapacitated person, or may authorize, direct, or ratify any contract, trust, or other transaction relating to the incapacitated person's property and financial affairs if the court determines that the transaction is necessary as a means of providing for personal needs and/or property management for the alleged incapacitated person. Before approving a protective arrangement or other transaction under this subdivision, the court shall consider the interests of dependents and creditors of the incapacitated person, and in view of the person's functional level, whether the person needs the continuing protection of a guardian. The court may appoint a special guardian to assist in the accomplishment of any protective arrangement or other transaction authorized under this subdivision. The special guardian shall have the authority conferred by the order of appointment, shall report to the court on all matters done pursuant to the order of appointment and shall serve until discharged by order of the court. The court may approve a reasonable compensation for the special guardian. . . .

(c) *Appointing a guardian.*

1. If the person alleged to be incapacitated is found to have agreed to the appointment of a guardian and the court determines that the appointment of a guardian is necessary, the order of the court shall be designed to accomplish the least restrictive form of intervention by appointing a guardian with powers limited to those which the court has found necessary to assist the person in providing for personal needs and/or property management.

2. If the person alleged to be incapacitated is found to be incapacitated and the court determines that the appointment of a guardian is necessary, the order of the court shall be designed to accomplish the least restrictive form of intervention by appointing a guardian with powers limited to those which the court has found necessary to assist the incapacitated person in providing for personal needs and/or property management.

* * *

(f) When a petition is granted, or where the court otherwise deems it appropriate, the court may award reasonable compensation for the attorney for the petitioner, including the attorney general and the attorney for a local department of social services.

§81.19 Eligibility as guardian

(a)   1. Any individual over eighteen years of age, or any parent under eighteen years of age, who is found by the court to be suitable to exercise the powers necessary to assist the incapacitated person may be appointed as guardian, including but not limited to a spouse, adult child, parent, or sibling.

2. A not-for-profit corporation organized to act in such capacity, a social services official, or public agency authorized to act in such capacity which has a concern for the incapacitated person, and [certain] community guardian program[s].

3. A corporation, except that no corporation (other than as provided in paragraph two of this subdivision) may be authorized to exercise the powers necessary to assist the incapacitated person with personal needs.

* * *

(d) In making any appointment under this article the court shall consider:

1. any appointment or delegation made by the person alleged to be incapacitated . . . ;

2. the social relationship between the incapacitated person and the person, if any, proposed as guardian, and the social relationship between the incapacitated person and other persons concerned with the welfare of the incapacitated person;

3. the care and services being provided to the incapacitated person at the time of the proceeding;

4. the powers which the guardian will exercise;

5. the educational, professional and business experience relevant to the nature of the services sought to be provided;

6. the nature of the financial resources involved;

7. the unique requirements of the incapacitated person; and

8. any conflicts of interest between the person proposed as guardian and the incapacitated person.

(e) Unless the court finds that no other person or corporation is available or willing to act as guardian, or to provide needed services for the incapacitated person, the following persons or corporations may not serve as guardian:

1. one whose only interest in the person alleged to be incapacitated is that of a creditor;

2. one, other than a relative, who is a provider, or the employee of a provider, of health care, day care, educational, or residential services to the incapacitated person, whether direct or indirect.

* * *

§81.20 Duties of guardian

(a) *Duties of guardian generally.*

1. a guardian shall exercise only those powers that the guardian is authorized to exercise by court order;

2. a guardian shall exercise the utmost care and diligence when acting on behalf of the incapacitated person;

3. a guardian shall exhibit the utmost degree of trust, loyalty and fidelity in relation to the incapacitated person;

4. a guardian shall file an initial and annual reports in accordance with sections 81.30 and 81.31 of this article;

5. a guardian shall visit the incapacitated person not less than four times a year or more frequently as specified in the court order;

6. a guardian who is given authority with respect to property management for the incapacitated person shall:

(i) afford the incapacitated person the greatest amount of independence and self-determination with respect to property management in light of that person's functional level, understanding and appreciation of his or her functional limitations, and personal wishes, preferences and desires with regard to managing the activities of daily living;

(ii) preserve, protect, and account for such property and financial resources faithfully;

(iii) determine whether the incapacitated person has executed a will, determine the location of any will, and the appropriate persons to be notified in the event of the death of the incapacitated person and, in the event of the death of the incapacitated person, notify those persons;

(iv) use the property and financial resources and income available therefrom to maintain and support the incapacitated person, and to maintain and support those persons dependent upon the incapacitated person;

(v) at the termination of the appointment, deliver such property to the person legally entitled to it;

(vi) file with the recording officer of the county wherein the incapacitated person is possessed of real property, an acknowledged statement to be recorded and indexed under the name of the incapacitated person identifying the real property possessed by the incapacitated person, and the tax map numbers of the property, and stating the date of adjudication of incapacity of the person regarding property management, and the name, address, and telephone number of the guardian and the guardian's surety; and

(vii) perform all other duties required by law.

7. a guardian who is given authority relating to the personal needs of the incapacitated person shall afford the incapacitated person the greatest amount of independence and self-determination with respect to personal needs in light of that person's functional level, understanding and appreciation of that person's functional limitations, and personal wishes, preferences and desires with regard to managing the activities of daily living.

QUESTIONS

1. What are the key protections that New York provides to allegedly incapacitated persons as part of a guardianship proceeding?

2. To what extent are those protections necessary to safeguard the rights and interests of such persons?

F. REPRESENTATIVE PAYEES

In certain situations, the need for a guardianship—or even a durable power of attorney for finances—may be avoided by the use of a *representative payee*, a government-appointed agent to manage public benefits on behalf of a beneficiary unable to manage them for him- or herself. The most common types of representative payees are those appointed by the Social Security Administration to manage Social Security benefits and those appointed by the Veterans' Administration to manage veteran's benefits. The vast majority of representative payees are relatives of the beneficiary.

A representative payee arrangement typically arises after a federal agency providing benefits is notified by a third party that the beneficiary is unable to manage those benefits for him- or herself. The decision to appoint a representative payee is an administrative decision made without a hearing. However, the affected beneficiary has a right to appeal the decision to appoint a representative payee, and the right to object to the appointment of a particular appointee.

The representative payee program is large. In fiscal year 2010, there were approximately 5.6 million representative payees in the United States, who together managed $61 billion in annual benefits for 7.6 million beneficiaries. Slightly over half of these beneficiaries, however, were minor children.

G. DECISION-MAKING STANDARDS

An agent acting as a surrogate—whether they are a guardian, an attorney-in-fact, or a health care agent acting pursuant to an advance directive—is a fiduciary. As a fiduciary, the agent has two clear duties: (1) a duty of loyalty and (2) a duty of care. This means that the agent must act for the benefit of the principal or ward and must take care in doing so. Yet merely knowing that the surrogate is a fiduciary tells us very little about how the agent should go about making a decision on behalf of the principal or ward.

Consider the following situation:

Amy Agent is appointed pursuant to a valid durable power of attorney as the agent for her mother Patty Principal, who still lives in the home where Amy was raised. As Patty's health declines, she becomes increasingly confused and has difficulty communicating her wishes. Patty's doctor has explained that, in order to remain safe, Patty needs either in-home help or to move to a more supervised setting. Given Patty's limited resources, Amy is concerned that Patty will not be able to afford in-home health for very long and thinks it would be best for Patty to sell the home and move into an assisted living community. At the same time she knows that Patty always said that she wanted to die in her family home and that she never wanted to be "put in a home."

What decision should Amy make? What principle or principles should guide that decision? *See* Nina A. Kohn, *Elder Empowerment as a Strategy for Curbing the Hidden Abuses of Durable Powers of Attorney*, 59 RUTGERS L. REV. 1 (2006) (originating this hypothetical and discussing potential answers).

There are two primary types of decision-making rules that Amy could use in this situation. The first is a *substituted judgment* rule. Under this approach, Amy would be charged with making the decision that she thinks Patty would have made if she were able to do so. The second is a *best interests* rule. Under this approach, Amy would make the decision that she thinks is in Patty's best interest.

Neither approach will necessarily be easy to apply. A substituted judgment approach requires the agent to speculate as to what the principal or ward would have done in the situation—something which may be impossible to know with any real certainty even if they have had a conversation about the issue. A best interests approach is complicated by the fact that a single individual has many different types of interests. Thus, even this seemingly simple approach actually encompasses multiple decision-making rules. In a discussion of medical decision-making at the end of life, Professor Leslie Pickering Francis described four primary types of interests that a person with dementia may possess. According to Francis, "experiential interests" are an individual's interest in physical and emotional comfort and pleasure. "Expressed preferences" are the stated or otherwise manifested preferences of the individual at the time a decision is to be made. In addition, a person also has an interest—or "rational desire"—in being treated or acting in a manner consistent with his or her values. Finally, human beings have certain "objective interests," such as an interest in life. *See* Leslie Pickering Francis, *Decisionmaking at the End of Life: Patients with Alzheimer's or Other Dementias*, 35 GA. L. REV. 539, 580-84 (2001).

To some extent, an agent can determine which decision-making standard to use by looking at the underlying state law governing his or her situation. Such laws frequently instruct the agent as to whether to use a substituted judgment or best interests approach. However, sometimes statutes do not spell out which approach to take, and statutes that instruct agents to take a best interests approach typically do not define that approach. Moreover, some statutes may take a hybrid approach. For example, the Uniform Health Care Decisions Act (UHCDA) instructs surrogates to make health care decisions "in accordance with the patient's individual instructions, if any, and other wishes to the extent known to the surrogate. Otherwise, the surrogate shall make the decision in accordance with the surrogate's determination of the patient's best interest." UHCDA, Prefatory Note.

QUESTION

The Uniform Durable Power of Attorney Act instructs attorneys-in-fact, as a general matter, to "carry out the principal's reasonable expectations to the extent actually known by the agent and, otherwise, act in the principal's best interest" and to "attempt to preserve the principal's estate plan, to the extent actually known by the agent, if preserving the plan is consistent with the principal's best interest." The Act places no duty on the attorney-in-fact to determine the principal's wishes.

Do you favor this approach or should an agent have a duty to ascertain the wishes of the principal? Why?

PROBLEM

Consider the hypothetical with Amy Agent and Patty Principal on page 187. If you were Amy, what decision would you make and why? If you were Patty, what decision would you want Amy to make and why?

H. REPRESENTING CLIENTS WITH APPOINTED SURROGATES

Elder law attorneys frequently represent individuals who have an appointed surrogate decision-maker. Typically, this is either a guardian appointed by a court or an agent appointed under DPOA. In such situations, a number of difficult ethical questions can arise.

The first is from whom should the attorney take direction. If the agent is acting on behalf of an entirely incapacitated person, the answer is generally easy: The attorney should take direction from the agent. The tricky questions arise when the principal retains at least some capacity, or there is a question as to whether the principal retains capacity.

A second question is to what extent an attorney should maintain client confidences by limiting the dissemination of confidential information about the client to the client's agent or, alternatively, by limiting dissemination of confidential information about the agent to the principal.

A third question is whether the attorney is under any duty to communicate directly with the principal in order to, for example, determine his or her level of capacity or keep him or her informed of the agent's actions. Complicating this question is how the attorney is to behave if the agent objects to such contact.

A fourth critical question is to what extent must an attorney follow the agent's direction, and how much latitude does the attorney have to question the agent's decisions.

The official comments to Rule 1.14 of the Model Rules of Professional Conduct provide some guidance as to how to proceed, but that guidance is limited. Specifically, the comments state that:

> The fact that a client suffers a disability does not diminish the lawyer's obligation to treat the client with attention and respect. Even if the person has a legal representative, the lawyer should as far as possible accord the represented person the status of client, particularly in maintaining communication.
>
> * * *
>
> If a legal representative has already been appointed for the client, the lawyer should ordinarily look to the representative for decisions on behalf of the client. In matters involving a minor, whether the lawyer should look to the parents as natural guardians may depend on the type of proceeding or matter in which the lawyer is representing the minor. If the lawyer represents the guardian as distinct from the ward, and is aware that the guardian is acting adversely to the ward's interest, the lawyer may have an obligation to prevent or rectify the guardian's misconduct.

ABA, MODEL R. PROF. CONDUCT 1.14, comments 2 & 4.

The American College of Trusts and Estates Counsel (ACTEC) commentary on Rule 1.14 provides further guidance, as does the excerpted ethics opinion which follows it.

ACTEC Commentary on MRPC 1.14

Lawyer Retained by Fiduciary for Person with Diminished Capacity. The lawyer retained by a person seeking appointment as a fiduciary or retained by a fiduciary for a person with diminished capacity, including a guardian, conservator, or attorney-in-fact, stands in a lawyer-client relationship with respect to the prospective or appointed fiduciary. A lawyer who is retained by a fiduciary for a person with diminished capacity, but who did not previously represent the disabled person, represents only the fiduciary. Nevertheless, in such a case the lawyer for the fiduciary owes some duties to the disabled person. *See* ACTEC Commentary on MRPC 1.2 (Scope of Representation and Allocation of Authority Between Client and Lawyer). If the lawyer represents the fiduciary, as distinct from the person with diminished capacity, and is aware that the fiduciary is improperly acting adversely to the person's interests, the lawyer may have an obligation to disclose, to prevent, or to rectify the fiduciary's misconduct. *See* MRPC 1.2(d) (providing that a lawyer shall not counsel a client to engage, or assist a client, in conduct that the lawyer knows is criminal or fraudulent).

As suggested in the Commentary to MRPC 1.2, a lawyer who represents a fiduciary for a person with diminished capacity or who represents a person who is seeking appointment as such, should consider asking the client to agree that, as part of the engagement, the lawyer may disclose fiduciary misconduct to the court, to the person with diminished capacity, or to other interested persons.

Person With Diminished Capacity Who Was a Client Prior to Suffering Diminished Capacity and Prior to the Appointment of a Fiduciary. A lawyer who represented a client before the client suffered diminished capacity may be considered to continue to represent the client after a fiduciary has been appointed for the person. Although incapacity may prevent a person with diminished capacity from entering into a contract or other legal relationship, the lawyer who represented the person with diminished capacity at a time when the person was competent may appropriately continue to meet with and counsel him or her. Whether the person with diminished capacity is characterized as a client or a former client, the lawyer for the fiduciary owes some continuing duties to him or her. . . . If the lawyer represents the person with diminished capacity and not the fiduciary, and is aware that the fiduciary is improperly acting adversely to the person's interests, the lawyer has an obligation to disclose, to prevent, or to rectify the fiduciary's misconduct.

Wishes of Person With Diminished Capacity Who Is Under Guardianship or Conservatorship When the Fiduciary Is the Client. A conflict of interest may arise if the lawyer for the fiduciary is asked by the fiduciary to take action that is contrary either to the previously expressed wishes of the person with diminished capacity or to the best interests of the person, as the lawyer believes those interests to be. The lawyer should give appropriate consideration to the currently or previously expressed wishes of a person with diminished capacity.

Ethics Opinion 353

District of Columbia Bar Assoc. (2010)

. . . A lawyer has requested guidance for resolving the following dilemma: the lawyer was hired by a durable power of attorney agent (POA agent) to represent an elderly incapacitated individual in a foreclosure suit involving that individual's residence. The client is unable to communicate. The POA agent is the client's granddaughter as well as the client's primary caregiver. The client selected her granddaughter to be her POA agent before the client became incapacitated. The lawyer filed suit on the client's behalf alleging that the mortgage was an unconscionable, predatory home loan. The mortgage company is defending against the suit claiming the mortgage was fair, the family knew about the terms, and the family, including the POA agent, spent the money on themselves. According to the inquirer the family denies the allegations but the allegations have tainted the litigation. To improve the atmospherics and maintain the focus of the litigation on the nature of the loan, the lawyer asked the POA agent to resign in favor of an independent agent to present a "clean" agent to the court. The POA agent refused. The lawyer asks if he can or must withdraw based on the POA agent's alleged bad acts or whether he may pursue a substitute guardianship in spite of the POA agent's refusal to step down.

. . . We think the answer comes from the guidance provided in Rule 1.14 for taking protective action.

In this instance, while the inquirer expressed some concerns about the POA's past conduct, nothing in the inquiry suggests that the POA agent is currently engaged in criminal conduct, intends to engage in criminal conduct, or intends to use the lawyer's services to engage in criminal conduct or perpetrate a fraud on the court. Nor is there any indication that the POA agent is currently failing to provide ongoing care to the client, or failing to pursue any legal recourse to prevent the foreclosure. . . .

Thus, neither the POA agent's interest nor allegations of past bad conduct requires protective action by the lawyer. Instead, the determination of whether protective action is permitted comes down to one of reasoned judgment about the impact of the POA agent's decision not to withdraw and her ongoing presence in the litigation.

If the difference between the lawyer's recommended course of action for withdrawal and the course preferred by the POA agent does not rise to the circumstance that would allow a lawyer to take protective action on behalf of a client if the disagreement was between the lawyer and a client with diminished capacity, then it is not permissible for a lawyer to take action against the directive of the client's surrogate decision-maker. Thus, if the ongoing presence of the POA agent in the litigation does not create a risk of substantial harm, the lawyer cannot seek a new surrogate decision-maker.

On the other hand if, in the lawyer's judgment, the failure to secure a "clean agent" presents a substantial risk that the client will lose her residence, then protective action can be taken. That action should be narrowly fashioned. In the instant case, the information used to pursue a new surrogate should be limited to the allegations made by the defendant and the scope of the substitute guardianship should be limited to the instant litigation.

The inquiry also asked if withdrawing from the matter was required or an available option. According to the inquirer, withdrawal at this stage in the litigation will likely result in the residence being lost. Withdrawal that would harm the client is only permitted in five enumerated circumstances. . . . None of these circumstances are present here. Further, it is difficult to imagine a circumstance under which permissive withdrawal causing substantial harm would be appropriate when representing a client with diminished capacity. Instead, if the client or the POA agent were to engage in the conduct described in Rule 1.16(b) that would ordinarily cause a lawyer to withdraw, that is a circumstance under which the lawyer should take protective action pursuant to Rule 1.14. This could include seeking the appointment of a surrogate decision-maker if the client does not have one, or seeking a substitute surrogate decision-maker where the client does have one.

NOTES

1. *Attorney-client relationship.* When does the attorney hired by an agent acting pursuant to a DPOA have an attorney-client relationship with the principal? In *Estate of Keatinge v. Biddle*, 316 F.3d 7 (1st Cir. 2002), the court considered whether a jury could find that an attorney-client relationship existed between a father and the attorney who had represented his son while the son was acting as attorney-in-fact under the father's DPOA. The court held that such a relationship was a question of fact for the jury. In doing so, the court noted that, under the applicable state law, mere retention of counsel by the son did not create an attorney-client relationship with the father.

2. *Duty to disclose.* When should an attorney for a guardian disclose that the guardian is, or may be, acting contrary to the ward's interests? In *Ethics Opinion 98-2*, the Alaska Bar Association considered whether an attorney for a Trust Company that had been appointed as the conservator for an elderly man (referred to simply as "Elderly") should report the Trust Company's conflict of interest to the man's personal attorney. In finding that he should, the Bar Association explained that "Lawyer Baker has ethical responsibilities to both Trust Company and Elderly. In this situation, however, attorney Baker's principal responsibility is to protect the interests of Elderly. If it appears that Elderly's interests are being compromised by Trust Company, Lawyer Baker is ethically obligated to insure that Elderly's interests are protected. Under this fact situation, disclosure to personal attorney appears to be a satisfactory solution." Alaska Bar Association, *Ethics Opinion No. 87-2*: CONFLICT OF INTEREST RELATING TO REPRESENTATION OF PERSON UNDER DISABILITY (1987).

QUESTION

Was the D.C. Bar's Ethics Committee correct in looking to Rule 1.14 to answer the question presented in Ethics Opinion 353? Do you think it correctly applied Rule 1.14?

PROBLEM

Helen Holmes is a 75-year-old woman with advanced *chronic obstructive pulmonary disease* (COPD). As a result of her disease, she is experiencing significant difficulty breathing, painful morning headaches, and mild weight loss. Her doctor has told her that as the disease progresses, she may become unable to breathe without the assistance of a machine. Helen has explained to her doctor that she wants a "natural death" and does not want to be kept alive by machines, but has also told her doctor that she would be willing to do "absolutely anything" if it meant a cure. For example, she told her doctor that she would be willing to pursue experimental therapies even if her Medicare plan would not cover them. However, her doctor has told her there is absolutely no cure available.

Helen is increasingly having difficulty living independently and therefore is increasingly relying on the assistance of her daughter, Myra, who lives nearby. Myra does Helen's grocery shopping, takes her to the doctor's office and bank, and has arranged for a housekeeper to come into Helen's apartment once a week to do the cleaning. Today, Myra has brought Helen to your office to seek your legal advice.

Myra explains to you that helping Helen has not only been very time-consuming, but that it has been difficult because she does not have any authority to act on Helen's behalf. Until she had Helen add her name to Helen's checking account last week, in order for Myra to even cash a check for Helen she needed to bring Helen with her to the bank. Myra explains that they are looking to draw up legal documents that will enable Myra to act on Helen's behalf whenever Helen needs her to. Myra says that up to this point Helen has not trusted anyone to manage her affairs, but now realizes that she needs help.

Based on what you have learned in Chapters 2 and 4, answer the following two questions:

- a. How would you structure the appointment with Mrs. Holmes and Myra? Why?
- b. What legal documents, if any, would you advise Helen to execute and why? What advice would you give her about the documents you recommend?

CHAPTER 5

Income in Older Age—Sources and Challenges

A. INTRODUCTION

As people age, they face new challenges and opportunities for maintaining an adequate income. For example, many older people retire and therefore experience a decrease in wage income. Typically, older adults can compensate for at least a portion of this loss by drawing on alternative sources of income, such as pensions, Social Security, family support, and other forms of savings.

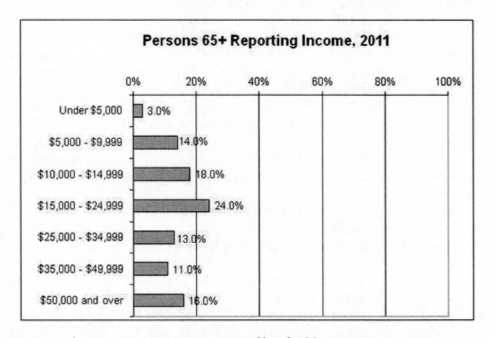

Source: Administration on Aging, A Profile of Older Americans: 2012.

This chapter explores different sources of income in old age and the legal issues that arise in obtaining and maintaining them.

In thinking about income maintenance in later life, it is important to recognize that older adults are an economically diverse group. In 2010, the median household income in households headed by people age 65 and over was $45,763, and the median income for an individual age 65 or older was $18,819. However, older adults differ significantly in the amount of income they have, as suggested by the above chart.

Older adults also differ in their sources of income and the relative importance of those sources to their income profile. According to the Administration on Aging (AOA):

> The major sources of income as reported by older persons in 2010 were Social Security (reported by 86% of older persons), income from assets (reported by 52%), private pensions (reported by 27%), government employee pensions (reported by 15%), and earnings (reported by 26%). In 2010, Social Security benefits accounted for 37% of the aggregate income of the older population. The bulk of the remainder consisted of earnings (30%), asset income (11%), and pensions (18%). Social Security constituted 90% or more of the income received by 36% of beneficiaries (23% of married couples and 46% of non-married beneficiaries).

ADMINISTRATION ON AGING, PROFILE OF OLDER AMERICANS: 2012, *available at* www.aoa.gov.

Although older adults experience somewhat lower rates of poverty than the adult population as a whole, a significant number of older adults are impoverished. Specifically, as of 2011, an estimated 3.6 million elderly persons (8.7%) lived below the poverty line, and another 2.4 million (5.8%) were "near-poor" (meaning that their income fell within 125% of the poverty level). Poverty among the elderly population disproportionately affects persons of color. According to AOA figures, only 6.7 percent of elderly whites had income below the poverty line, compared to 17.3 percent of elderly African Americans, 11.7 percent of elderly Asians, and 18.7 percent of elderly Hispanics. Poverty is also more likely to affect older persons in large cities and those in rural and small towns than those who live in suburban areas or smaller cities. In addition, older women are more likely to live in poverty than older men.

While old age is associated with retirement, and the vast majority of workers will eventually retire, older adults are increasingly delaying retirement. A 2012 survey by the Employee Benefit Research Institute (EBRI) found that 25 percent of workers reported that the age at which they anticipated retiring had increased in the past year. According to the survey, the leading reason given for this change in expectations was a poor economy (cited by more than a third of respondents) followed by a lack of faith in the government or Social Security. Indeed, only 24 percent of workers surveyed in 2012 reported that they planned to retire before age 65, compared to 50 percent surveyed 21 years earlier in 1991. In addition, just over a quarter of workers surveyed in 2012 reported that they did not anticipate retiring before age 70—a nearly three-fold increase from 1991. Moreover, older adults increasingly engage in paid work following their official retirement. The 2012 EBRI survey found that over a quarter of "retired" workers had worked for pay during retirement. Of those, nine out of ten reported that this work was motivated, at least in part, by financial concerns. *See* EMPLOYEE BENEFIT RESEARCH INSTITUTE, 2012 RETIREMENT CONFIDENCE SURVEY, *available at* http://www.ebri.org/pdf/surveys/rcs/2012/EBRI_IB_03-2012_No369_RCS.pdf.

B. SOCIAL SECURITY BENEFITS

1. Overview of OASDI

The Old-Age, Survivors, and Disability Insurance System (OASDI) is the program Americans typically mean when they talk about "Social Security." The program began, in a limited form, as part of President Franklin D. Roosevelt's New Deal response to the Great Depression. The program has evolved significantly to the point where it is the country's most significant form of income in old age, accounting for at least half of the income of two-thirds of U.S. retirees.

Social Security is a combination of an entitlement program, an insurance program, and a welfare program. It is an entitlement program in that persons who qualify for Social Security are entitled to it, regardless of how many other people qualify for its benefits. It is an insurance program in that individual workers pay into the system to qualify for benefits, and those who pay more receive more. At the same time, it is a welfare system in that it is redistributive in nature. Workers who contribute less to the system receive proportionately more than those who contribute more. Moreover, since most beneficiaries receive significantly more in benefits than they paid into the system, Social Security is a mechanism for redistributing resources between generations— with younger persons paying to support older ones.

OASDI is funded by the Federal Insurance Contributions Act (FICA) tax levied on earned income. Non-earned income, such as rents, capital gains, dividends, and interest, is exempt. The FICA tax funds both the Social Security system and the Medicare system (discussed in Chapter 6). Historically, the Social Security portion of the FICA tax has consisted of a 6.2 percent tax levied on workers' wage and salary income up to an annual cap ($113,700 in 2013); employers have been required to contribute a matching 6.2 percent up to the same annual cap. For 2011 and 2012, however, the Social Security portion of the FICA tax was reduced to 4.2 percent for employees. This payroll tax "holiday" ended in 2013.

Although self-employed individuals are not subject to the FICA tax, they are subjected to a parallel tax on their self-employment income up to an annual cap identical to that for the FICA tax ($113,700 in 2013). The rate of taxation on self-employment income, however, has historically been 12.4 percent—double that imposed on an employee under FICA. The rationale for this larger tax is that no employer is making a contribution on self-employment earnings. For 2011 and 2012, the rate temporarily dropped by 2 percent to 10.4 percent of self-employment income, before returning to 12.4 percent in 2013.

PROBLEM

After law school, you decide to become a contract attorney providing freelance services to other lawyers. You move to the shores of Maine and set up your home office from your dream house with views over the Atlantic. To supplement your income, you rent a small cottage on your property to summer vacationers. Do you have to pay Social Security (FICA) tax on all of your income? Do you have to pay more or less than you would have to pay if you were employed by a law firm? Why?

2. Eligibility for OASDI

a. Becoming Insured

To qualify for Social Security benefits an individual must first become "fully insured" under the program. Most, but not all, jobs are eligible for Social Security. Examples of persons not covered by OASDI include certain state and local employees whose state has not opted into the OASDI program, most federal workers hired before 1984, and students working for the educational institution that they attend. Once a worker has become fully insured, his or her spouse also becomes covered by the OASDI program.

A worker can become fully insured by obtaining at least 40 "quarters of coverage." The term "quarters of coverage" refers to the four quarters of a calendar year, but an individual is not actually required to work four quarters of the year in order to be credited for four quarters of coverage. Although a person cannot earn more than four quarters of coverage in a year, a person will be credited with four quarters if he or she earns four times the minimum amount in a single quarter. The dollar amount required for a quarter of coverage is adjusted annually for inflation. In 2013, the amount was $1,160. Quarters of coverage need not be earned sequentially, but, rather, can be earned sporadically throughout an individual's life.

The fact that an individual is fully insured for Social Security benefits does not, however, mean that he or she is currently entitled to receive such benefits. He or she will only be able to do so once he or she reaches early retirement age or experiences a qualifying disability.

b. Age-Based Eligibility

A fully insured worker can apply to begin collecting Social Security as soon as he or she reaches early retirement age, which is currently set at 62. Beginning to collect benefits at early retirement age, however, reduces the amount of an individual's monthly Social Security benefits. To receive the standard Social Security benefit to which he or she is entitled, an individual must wait until he or she reaches full retirement age. When this is depends on the year in which the individual was born. Full retirement age is in the process of increasing from 65 for those born before 1938 to 67 for those born in 1960 or later. The chart below shows the full retirement age for those who are currently reaching it or who will do so in the future.

Birth Year	Full Retirement Age
1943-1954	66 years
1955	66 years, 2 months
1956	66 years, 4 months
1957	66 years, 6 months
1958	66 years, 8 months
1959	66 years, 10 months
1960 or later	67

An individual may also choose to delay benefits in order to increase the amount of his or her monthly Social Security benefits. The factors that should be considered in deciding when to take Social Security benefits will be discussed later in this chapter.

c. Disability-Based Eligibility

Even if he or she has not obtained 40 quarters of coverage, a worker may be eligible to receive disability benefits if the worker is experiencing a disability that prevents him or her from performing "any substantial gainful activity by reason of any medically determinable physical or mental impairment." 42 U.S.C. §416(i)(1)(A). This is a high bar for most workers, as it is by no means sufficient to show that the individual is no longer able to perform his or her former job. Instead of showing a requisite number of quarters of work, a worker seeking disability benefits must meet a recent work test and a duration of work test. The precise tests vary according to the worker's age at onset of disability. A worker claiming onset at age 60, for example, would need to have worked at least 9.5 years and five out of the past ten years. By contrast, a worker claiming onset at age 50 would only need to have worked seven years and five out of the past ten years.

d. Derivative Eligibility

The Social Security system provides benefits not only to those who directly pay into the system, but also to their families. Specifically, the spouse, former spouse, and minor children of a worker can be eligible for "derivative" benefits—that is, benefits based on the worker's earning record.

In order to collect benefits on a spouse's earnings record (i.e., "spouse's") benefits), an individual must generally: (1) have been married to a fully insured worker for at least one year (less time may be permitted under certain conditions), (2) be in a marriage that is recognized as valid by the federal government; and (3) be married to a worker who has already filed an application for Social Security benefits. In addition, the spouse who is seeking derivative benefits must have reached at least early retirement age *or* be caring for the worker's child who is under 16 years of age.

When his or her spouse is deceased, the surviving spouse of a federally recognized marriage may be entitled to "widow's" or "widower's" benefits. To be eligible for such benefits, the surviving spouse must: (1) be unmarried *or* have remarried after the age of 60 (unless the surviving spouse is disabled, in which case the remarriage can have occurred after age 50), *and* (2) be at least age 60 years old *or* caring for the deceased spouse's minor child.

An individual may be able to collect on the earnings of a former spouse despite having divorced him or her. Individuals who were in a federally recognized marriage to a fully insured worker, but who are now divorced from that worker, are eligible for Social Security benefits on the worker's account if: (1) they were married to the worker for at least ten years; (2) they are at least 60 years old; (3) they have not remarried unless the remarriage occurred after the age of 60 or, if the beneficiary is disabled, the remarriage occurred after the age of 50; and (4) the worker on whose account they are collecting is at least 62 years old. Notably, the ex-spouse need not have elected to begin collecting Social Security benefits.

Children of an individual receiving Social Security are also eligible for benefits in certain situations. The child must be under 18 years old, or under 19 years old and attending a primary or secondary school, or be mentally or physically disabled prior to reaching age 22.

Finally, some older adults are eligible for "parent's" benefits. Among other requirements, in order to receive parent's benefits, the older adult must have been the dependent of a deceased, fully insured worker.

Thomas v. Sullivan

922 F.2d 132 (2d Cir. 1990)

KEARSE, Circuit Judge:

Plaintiff Gertrude Thomas appeals from a final judgment of the United States District Court for the Southern District of New York, Leonard B. Sand, *Judge*, dismissing her complaint for review of a decision of the Secretary of Health and Human Services ("Secretary"), which denied her application for widow's insurance benefits ("widow's benefits") under §216(h)(1)(B) of the Social Security Act (the "Act"), 42 U.S.C. §416(h)(1)(B) (1988), on the ground that her marriage was invalid and she had not gone through a marriage ceremony. The complaint contended that the distinction drawn in §416(h)(1)(B) between invalid ceremonial and invalid common-law marriages violates the equal protection component of the Due Process Clause of the Fifth Amendment. The district court dismissed the complaint on the ground that the distinction drawn in §416(h)(1)(B) has a rational basis. . . .

I. BACKGROUND

Gertrude Thomas ("Gertrude") lived with Joseph Thomas ("Joseph") for 47 years, from 1938 until his death in 1985, and they had 10 children together. They lived together in Atlanta, Georgia, for many years until they moved to New York. Georgia law recognizes common-law marriages; though New York law does not, it gives full faith and credit to such marriages that are valid under the laws of other states.

In October 1978, Gertrude applied for wife's insurance benefits ("wife's benefits") under §202(b) of the Act, 42 U.S.C. §402(b) (1988), stating that she and Joseph had married on January 25, 1943. In support of that application, Joseph submitted a signed statement to the Social Security Administration ("SSA"), identifying Gertrude as his wife, certifying that they had been married by a "[c]lergyman or authorized public official," and stating that his previous marriage to one "Janie Mills" had ended with Janie's death in 1940. Thereafter, Gertrude received wife's benefits; these were converted to widow's benefits when Joseph died in May 1985.

In July 1985, a woman identifying herself as Janie Thomas ("Janie") applied for benefits as the widow of Joseph Thomas. In support of her application she submitted a marriage certificate showing that she and Joseph had married in September 1918. Janie stated in her application that although she and Joseph had separated in 1933, they had never been divorced and she had never been notified of any attempt by Joseph to obtain a divorce. SSA notified Gertrude that her widow's benefits might be terminated as a result of Janie's claim and gave her an opportunity to present evidence to prove her own entitlement.

A search by SSA turned up no record of a divorce in any of the places where Joseph or Janie had lived since 1933. As a result, SSA determined that Janie was Joseph's lawful widow and that Gertrude's marriage to Joseph was not valid. It notified Gertrude that she would no longer receive widow's benefits. Gertrude promptly requested reconsideration, contending that she was entitled to those benefits, having been told by Joseph that he was divorced and having gone through a marriage ceremony with him. In support of her request for reconsideration, she submitted a statement that in October 1942 she had obtained a marriage license in Decatur, Georgia, and that, shortly thereafter, she and Joseph had been married by a minister in Atlanta. She also stated, "[m]y husband had told me that he was previously married and divorced. But, he never gave me any details about the first marriage." Gertrude submitted a second statement in which she described having met Joseph's first wife:

In fact, when Mr. Thomas and I first married, we lived together in Atlanta, Ga. with his mother, his first wife Janie Thomas would come to the house to visit Joseph's mother and she knew Joseph and I married [*sic*]. She never once expressed the fact that she and Joseph never divorced. I never discussed with Joseph where the divorce was taken out or who took out the divorce. He never wanted to discuss anything about his first marriage.

In a March 1986 "Reconsideration Determination," SSA indicated that it had searched the marriage records of Decatur and had found no record of a marriage of Gertrude and Joseph, and that it had separately searched for any record of issuance to them of a marriage license, also without success. As a result, SSA concluded that "[s]ince Gertrude Thomas was not validly married to Mr. Thomas," and since "no evidence of a ceremonial marriage has been submitted or located," Gertrude was not eligible for widow's benefits.

Gertrude timely requested and received a hearing before an Administrative Law Judge ("ALJ"). At the hearing, she testified that she had obtained a marriage license and she and Joseph had been married by a minister in 1938. She said the only witnesses to the wedding had been members of the minister's family, whom she did not know. Her own family was informed of the wedding a few days thereafter; none of the family was still alive at the time of the hearing. Gertrude testified that after the ceremony, the minister "told us that he was going to mail the license in so it could be recorded, and mail us our marriage certificate, which he never did." She explained that her failure to verify that the marriage had been recorded was a result of her youthful trust in Joseph:

> [Gertrude]: I didn't follow up as I should have, because I was quite young at the time and I just took what he said to be true, and at the time I was 21 and he was 45, so I can see now where I could have been very much easy to lead, to be led by what he said and I was in love with him and I just accepted what he told me, thinking everything was okay.
> ALJ: It happens when you are in love.
> [Gertrude]: Oh, yes Sir. But I can see my mistake now. It's just too late.

After giving Gertrude more time to attempt to produce additional evidence, the ALJ found that because Joseph had remained married to Janie until his death, he "was under a legal impediment preventing him from entering into a valid marriage with Gertrude" and that Gertrude "has not supplied any evidence of a ceremonial marriage with Joseph Thomas and therefore cannot be considered as a deemed widow" within the meaning of §416(h)(1)(B). . . .

Gertrude timely sought review of the ALJ's decision by the SSA Appeals Council. While conceding that she was "unable to prove her assertion that she and the wage earner were ceremonially married," she contended that the Secretary's refusal to grant benefits to her in light of her good-faith belief in the validity of her common-law marriage violated her right to equal protection. Gertrude's request for review was denied, and she brought the present action for review of that denial.

The district court rejected Gertrude's constitutional challenge to §416(h)(1)(B), finding that there was a rational basis for the statute's distinction between invalid ceremonial marriages and invalid common-law marriages. . . .

II. DISCUSSION

Section 216(h)(1)(A) of the Act provides that for purposes of deciding an application for, *inter alia*, widow's benefits, the Secretary will recognize as valid a marriage that would be recognized as valid by the courts of the state in which the wage earner was domiciled. Where there is no valid marriage, §216(h)(1)(B) of the Act requires the Secretary to "deem[ ]" the applicant for benefits to be a widow in certain cases where she has in good faith gone through a marriage ceremony. . . .

For the reasons below, we conclude that this provision does not violate principles of equal protection.

There is no fundamental right to the receipt of benefits from the government. In deciding an equal protection challenge to a statute that classifies persons for the purpose of receiving such benefits, we are required, so long as the classifications are not suspect or quasi-suspect and do not infringe fundamental constitutional rights, to uphold the legislation if it bears a rational relationship to a legitimate governmental objective. . . . We will uphold the legislation if we can ascertain that the classifications Congress has created can be explained on the basis of factors relevant to the administration and purposes of the particular benefit program, and are not "merely an unthinking response to stereotyped generalizations" about the excluded group. . . .

Congress may have modeled §416(h)(1)(B) after the civil-law doctrine of "putative marriages." Under this doctrine, some states recognize an invalid marriage as valid when one or both parties have a good faith belief in the validity of a marriage and were ignorant of the legal impediment that makes the marriage invalid. Traditionally, this recognition was not given unless the participants had gone through a ceremonial marriage, a requirement imposed to demand proof of their good faith, albeit mistaken, belief in the validity of their marriage. . . .

Though Congress gave no explanation in the legislative history for its decision to limit the deeming rule of §416(h)(1)(B) to applicants who have gone through ceremonial marriages, it is inferable that the decision to continue to deny benefits to invalidly married persons who had not gone through such ceremonies had two purposes. First, Congress may have sought a means of reducing the incidence of fraudulent claims. In these modern times, many couples, with or without uncertainty as to the dissolution of a prior marriage, decide to cohabit without marrying. Congress may have envisioned the possibility that an unlimited deeming provision would invite fraudulent claims from such persons. Further, Congress may have adopted the more traditional view that a willingness to go through a formal marriage ceremony constitutes some objective evidence of a good-faith belief in the dissolution of any prior marriages. It could rationally have believed that persons who have doubts about whether a prior marriage has been validly ended will be more reluctant to go through a marriage ceremony than they will to enter into an informal cohabitational relationship, perhaps from fear of public criticism, or from fear of having word get back to the prior spouse, or from fear of violating laws against bigamy.

Second, since §416(h)(1)(B) requires the applicant to show that but for the unknown impediment there would have been a valid marriage, Congress may have sought to establish a criterion that is entirely objective and normally susceptible to documentary proof in order to limit the administrative cost of determining whether that prerequisite is met. If the deeming rule had been made applicable to invalid common-law marriages, the applicant would have to show that all of the prerequisites to common-law marriage were met. Traditionally, the two fundamental requirements for a common-law marriage imposed by the states that have recognized such marriages were (1) the parties' express agreement to be husband and wife, and (2) their holding themselves out to the world as married. The first requirement has been eroded somewhat by rulings that have allowed the existence of the required agreement to be inferred from the fact that the couple has lived together "for all intents and purposes" as husband and wife. Whichever test is applied, however, the focus is on the parties' intent. Thus, establishment of a purported common-law marriage would generally require proof of an element that is ultimately subjective.

A ceremonial marriage, on the other hand, is an objectively observable event occurring at a defined place and time. Proof of such a marriage will normally be available through documentary evidence such as the original marriage certificate, a certified copy of a public record of marriage, or a certified copy of a church or synagogue record of marriage. Such documentary evidence is normally accepted by the Secretary as conclusive proof that there was a marriage ceremony. By extending benefits only to those invalidly married persons who can prove that they went through such a ceremony, Congress has made it possible for the Secretary to make a determination in part on the basis of one objective, rather than subjective, criterion, and on the basis of documentary, rather than testimonial, proof.

To be sure, the marriage ceremony requirement in the deeming rule does not relieve the Secretary of all need to assess subjective factors or testimonial evidence. . . .

Nonetheless, in most instances, the ceremonial marriage requirement does lessen the Secretary's administrative burden by eliminating the need to receive and assess testimonial evidence on one element, and it is therefore rationally related to the goal of reducing administrative costs. In these circumstances, the fact that the line drawn does not lessen the burden in all instances is unimportant.

In sum, though the result of the deeming rule structured by Congress may seem harsh in the present case, we conclude that it is rationally related to legitimate governmental objectives and may not be overturned.

CONCLUSION

For the foregoing reasons, we affirm the judgment dismissing the complaint.

[Concurring opinion omitted.]

QUESTIONS

1. Suppose Janie had obtained a divorce from Joseph, would she have been able to collect benefits on his accounts? Why or why not? What is the policy rationale behind this result?

2. What policy goals are advanced by recognizing ceremonial marriages but not Gertrude's marriage?

PROBLEM

Sally, a woman with a mop of grey hair and a well-wrinkled face, has come to your law office to seek your help. She is very upset because she is not receiving Social Security benefits, and she is sure she is entitled to them. She asks for your help in figuring out why she has yet to receive benefits. What questions should you ask to determine why Sally has not received benefits?

3. The Amount of OASDI Benefits

a. Calculating the Basic Entitlement

In 2013, the maximum monthly Social Security benefit for a worker at full retirement age was $2,533. The average Social Security monthly benefit, however, is significantly lower than the maximum benefit. In 2012, for example, the average monthly benefit was approximately $1,230, roughly half of the maximum benefit that year. To calculate the amount of monthly benefits to which a Social Security beneficiary is entitled, the SSA begins by calculating the beneficiary's *Average Indexed Monthly Earnings* (AIME). To calculate the AIME, the SSA determines the amount of wages subject to the Social Security tax that the beneficiary earned during each of his or her working years. Each year's countable wages are then adjusted to account for wage growth. Next, the SSA takes the sum of the 35 highest earning years (after the adjustment). This number is then divided by 420 (representing the number of months in a 35-year period) to calculate the AIME. If the beneficiary has worked less than 35 years, the AIME is still calculated based on 35 years; the result is that the beneficiary's AIME will be reduced as a result of averaging in years in which the beneficiary had no earnings.

Using the AIME, the SSA then calculates the beneficiary's *Primary Insurance Amount* (PIA). The PIA is calculated in a progressive manner such that the beneficiary's PIA consists of 90 percent of the AIME up to a certain amount ($791 in 2013), plus 32 percent of the AIME up to another amount (the next $3,377 in 2013), plus 15 percent of the remaining AIME (that over $4,768 in 2013). The result is that lower wage earners have a disproportionately high PIA relative to higher wage earners. This is consistent with the redistributive nature of the OASDI system, as discussed earlier in this chapter.

The PIA represents the amount of benefits that a Social Security beneficiary receives per month upon reaching full retirement age. In subsequent years, the PIA will be adjusted upwards to reflect the effects of inflation.

b. Timing the Taking of Benefits

To begin receiving benefits, an individual must apply for those benefits. The amount of benefits received will depend in part on the age at which the individual applies.

A beneficiary can elect to take Social Security benefits as early as age 62; however, electing to take early benefits results in a permanent reduction in benefits. Specifically, for each month before the beneficiary reaches 65, benefits will be reduced by five-ninths of 1 percent; for each month after age 65 but before the beneficiary reaches full retirement age, benefits will be reduced by five-twelfths of 1 percent. As such, a worker whose full retirement age is 67 would experience a 30 percent reduction in monthly benefits if he or she elected to take benefits as soon as he or she reached age 62.

Just as a beneficiary can decrease his or her monthly payments by taking Social Security before full retirement age, he or she can increase his or her monthly payment by choosing to delay taking benefits beyond full retirement age. For every year up to age 70 that a beneficiary delays receiving Social Security benefits, his or her PIA will be increased by a certain percent. For persons born in 1942 or later, the increase is 8 percent a year.

c. Electing and Timing Derivative Benefits

A person who is qualified to collect benefits based on a spouse or an ex-spouse's earnings record can claim either his or her own benefits or 50 percent of the spouse or ex-spouse's benefits. If the spouse of a currently married beneficiary dies, moreover, the widow or widower is entitled to collect 100 percent of the deceased spouse's benefits. This increase reflects, in part, the fact that it is generally more economical to live as a couple than to live alone.

The result is that whether a beneficiary takes his or her benefits early, at full retirement age, or after full retirement age affects not only that beneficiary's benefits, but also the widow's or widower's benefits that his or her spouse may collect in the future.

As discussed earlier in this chapter in Section B.2.d, beneficiaries cannot receive OASDI benefits on their spouses' earnings records until (1) they reach at least early retirement age (62); and (2) their spouse is eligible for, and has applied for OASDI benefits. As a practical matter, this means that both members of the married couple must be at least 62 years of age before the spouse can receive derivative benefits. By contrast, an individual can begin receiving benefits on the record of a former spouse (either one they have divorced or one who is deceased) at age 60, or even earlier if they have a qualifying disability or are caring for a qualifying minor child.

To see the implications of the rule that one cannot collect spousal benefits until the other spouse has filed for their own benefits, consider the following hypothetical couple: Adele and Miguel. Adele is 66 and wishes to begin collecting Social Security benefits. Miguel, by contrast, is only 60. Over the years, Miguel has earned significantly more money than Adele and, as a result, his benefit at full retirement age will be more than twice Adele's benefit on her own earnings record. Accordingly, Adele would prefer to collect on Miguel's record instead of her own. However, Adele cannot do so at this time because Miguel is not eligible to apply for his own benefit. Adele can, however, begin collecting on her own record. Once Miguel is eligible for and applies for Social Security, she can then switch to collecting on his benefit. If Miguel applies before his full retirement age, however, not only will his benefit be reduced, but her spousal benefit on his record will be reduced as well.

Now suppose that Adele began collecting on her own record at the age of 62, and Miguel has just turned 66 and applied for OASDI benefits. Adele can still switch to collecting on Miguel's earnings record. However, because Adele started receiving Social Security before she attained full retirement age, she will receive a reduced spousal benefit and not a full 50 percent of Miguel's benefit.

As these examples suggest, couples wishing to maximize their total Social Security benefits may engage in strategic behavior around the timing of election. In addition to the more obvious strategies for doing so, there are two somewhat more convoluted strategies that beneficiaries are increasingly using.

The first strategy is called "file and suspend" and it can benefit married couples where one spouse has earned significantly more than the other over the course of their careers. As a general matter, in order for a spouse to begin receiving derivative benefits, the spouse on whose earning records benefits are being obtained must have begun receiving benefits. Using the file and suspend strategy, the higher earning spouse applies for benefits, thereby triggering his or her spouse's eligibility to receive derivative benefits. The higher earning spouse then suspends his or her own benefits and delays collecting so as to increase the size of his or her eventual benefit. The strategy is especially appealing where the lower earning spouse is expected to outlive the higher earning spouse for some significant period of time. This is because, as a widow or widower, the lower earning spouse will be entitled to receive the full amount that the deceased spouse received—which has been increased due to the delay in collecting benefits. Notably, however, the file and suspend strategy is only of value where the benefits that the lower earning spouse would receive on his or her own earning record are less than half of the benefits that the higher earning spouse would receive on his or her record. Otherwise, derivative benefits will be less desirable than benefits obtained on one's own record.

The second, also somewhat convoluted, strategy that can benefit married couples is called a "restricted application." Using this approach, a married individual files for benefits and explicitly requests to only receive benefits on the record of his or her spouse. In this way, the individual "restricts" his or her application to an application for the spousal benefit. By not collecting on his or her own account, the benefit that the individual will be entitled to on his or her own record increases to reflect the delay in collection. When the individual reaches age 70, he or she then switches from collecting the spousal benefit to collecting on his or her own record. To be eligible to make a restricted application, the individual filing the restricted application must be full retirement age, have not filed on his or her own earnings record, and have a spouse who has filed for benefits on his or her own record.

As a general matter, restricted applications typically do not make sense unless the lower earning spouse has a Social Security retirement benefit that is at least half as much as that of the higher earning spouse. If the lower earning spouse's benefit is less than half of that of the higher earning spouse, "file and suspend" will likely be a more profitable strategy.

To see how these strategies might be employed, consider the following hypothetical couple: Betsy (age 66) and John (age 67). John has had a relatively successful career as an architect. Betsy raised the couple's three children and then returned to the workforce part-time as a substitute teacher. As a result, Betsy's PIA is $800, whereas John's PIA is $2,400. The couple decides that it would be best for John to delay receiving his OASDI benefit so that when John dies, Betsy (who has a life expectancy that significantly exceeds that of John) will receive a higher widow's benefit. They also, however, would prefer to have Betsy collect on John's earning record as opposed to her own because half of his PIA is greater than her entire PIA on her own earnings record. John therefore files for Social Security and immediately suspends payment of his own benefits. Betsy can begin collecting $1,200 per month in Social Security on John's record. When John elects to receive benefits, he will collect an increased amount that reflects his deferred benefit credits. If Betsy survives John, she will then collect the amount he would have collected and thus will also benefit from the deferral.

Alternatively, the couple could pursue the restricted application strategy with the same result. Using this approach, Betsy could elect to collect on her own record and John could file a restricted application on Betsy's record. The couple would still have combined Social Security benefits of $1,200 and John could earn deferred benefit credits by waiting to collect on his own record. When he reaches 70, however, he begins collecting on his own record.

Now suppose that Betsy and John have more similar earnings records. Betsy's PIA is $1,400 and John's PIA is $1,600. Here it would matter which strategy they use. If they employ the file and suspend strategy, the household will have current Social Security benefits totaling $800 (i.e., half of John's PIA). If they use the restricted application strategy, the household will have current Social Security benefits totaling $2,100 (i.e., 150% of Betsy's PIA).

To see the opposite incentive, suppose Betsy and John have more disparate earnings records. Betsy's PIA is $700 and John's PIA is $2,400. Here again it would matter which strategy they use. If they employ the file and suspend strategy, the household will have current Social Security benefits totaling $1,200. By contrast, if they employ the restricted application strategy, the household will have current Social Security benefits totaling $1,050.

QUESTIONS

1. What are some of the incentives and disincentives created by the Social Security system's manner of computing and awarding derivative benefits?

2. The spousal benefit has been criticized as rewarding traditional, single bread-winner, married families at the expense of two-earner households and non-traditional families. However, simply eliminating the benefit would severely undermine the retirement security of spouses who opt to provide unpaid labor (e.g., by raising children or caring for elderly relatives) instead of participating in the paid labor force or whose participation in the paid labor force is reduced because of their unpaid labor contribution. With this concern in mind, some scholars have proposed an "earning sharing" model approach as an alternative to the spousal benefit. As described by Professors Karen C. Burke and Grayson M.P. McCouch:

> Drawing on community property concepts, the earnings sharing model would treat each spouse as earning one-half of the couple's total wages earned during marriage, for purposes of determining social security benefits. Since each spouse would be directly entitled to primary benefits based on one-half of the couple's aggregate earnings, a spouse who did not participate in the workforce would no longer be treated as a "dependent." Spousal benefits would be eliminated, and each spouse's share of the couple's earnings record would be fully portable in case of divorce. Moreover, earnings sharing would eliminate existing disparities between one-earner and two-earner married couples, so that couples with identical total wages would receive the same benefits.

Karen C. Burke & Grayson M.P. McCouch, *Women, Fairness, and Social Security*, 82 Iowa L. Rev. 1209, 1232 (1997).

Should the United States eliminate the spousal benefit in favor of an earning sharing approach? What would be the distributional effects of such a change?

3. Concerned by the fact that women tend to receive lower Social Security benefits in part because they engage in a disproportionate amount of unpaid care work, Madonna Harrington Meyer and Pamela Herd have proposed that parents caring for children have the option of receiving "care credit" on their Social Security earnings records in the amount of one-half of the median wage for up to five years for caring for one child and up to nine years for caring for more than one child. *See* Madonna Harrington Meyer & Pamela Herd, Market Friendly or Family Friendly? The State of Gender Inequality in Old Age (2007).

Would you support such a care credit? Should a similar credit be extended to those who provide unpaid care for aging relatives?

PROBLEM

Roger and Miriam are a married couple. Roger has had a successful career as an attorney. Miriam has earned far less income as an artist. Her Social Security benefits are smaller than Roger's benefits. Roger is 66, Miriam is 63.

a. For what benefits is Roger eligible?

b. For what benefits is Miriam eligible?

c. If Roger dies, to what benefits will Miriam be entitled?

d. How might Roger and Miriam maximize the total amount of Social Security benefits they receive as a couple? What factors should they take into consideration when deciding what approach to take?

d. Effect of Earnings on OASDI Benefits

For beneficiaries below full retirement age, Social Security payments are reduced when their earnings exceed a certain level. How much benefits are reduced depends on (1) the individual's age, and (2) the amount the individual earned. In the portion of the calendar year that individuals will reach full retirement age but have yet to do so, their benefits will be reduced by $1 for every $3 they earn over a specified amount. In 2013, for example, the specified amount for these individuals was $3,340 per month. For all other beneficiaries, their benefits will be reduced by $1 for every $2 they earn over a specified limit. In 2013, for example, that limit was $15,120 per year for all other beneficiaries receiving early Social Security benefits.

By contrast, there is no earnings test for Social Security beneficiaries once they reach full retirement age. Therefore, at full retirement age and beyond, individuals can earn an unlimited amount of money without seeing any reduction in their Social Security benefits.

QUESTION

Previously, there was an earnings test for beneficiaries even after they reached full retirement age. In your opinion, was elimination of the earnings test for beneficiaries who have reached full retirement age a change for the better or a change for the worse?

PROBLEMS

1. Frank just turned 62 years old. Last week, he was fired from his job as a night manager of a local restaurant after giving the restaurant owner an overly frank assessment of the owner's personal flaws. He is pessimistic about his ability to find a new job. He wants to know whether he should apply for Social Security benefits now.

   a. Is Frank eligible for Social Security? Why or why not?
   b. Would you advise him to apply for Social Security? Why or why not?

2. Paul, 63, is employed as a janitor at a local high school where he has worked for the past decade. His wife, age 61, has just been diagnosed with cancer. As a result, she has stopped working, and the couple has begun to incur significant medical expenses. Paul does not know how they will make ends meet, and the couple has already begun falling behind on their monthly mortgage payments. He asks you whether he should apply for Social Security.

   a. Is Paul eligible for Social Security? Why or why not?
   b. Would you advise Paul to apply for Social Security? Why or why not?

3. Michelle just reached full retirement age, but she doesn't feel ready to retire. She's been working as a pastry chef for over 30 years, and she likes her work. She wonders if she should start collecting Social Security now or whether she should wait. What would you tell her? What information would you want to know in order to provide the best possible advice?

4. Special Protections for OASDI Benefits

Unlike most other forms of income, Social Security benefits have special protection from the claims of creditors. Specifically, they are not subject to "execution, levy, attachment, garnishment, or other legal process, or to the operation of any bankruptcy or insolvency law" by creditors other than the federal government. 42 U.S.C.A. §407(a). Many beneficiaries, however, are unaware of this protection. Moreover, it is not uncommon for creditors to access Social Security funds to which they are not entitled and for banks to freeze accounts containing Social Security funds.

The U.S. Treasury Department requires banks to determine whether Social Security funds have been electronically deposited in an account in the past two months before freezing an account; if so, the bank cannot deny the beneficiary those Social Security funds. This rule, however, does not protect funds deposited more than two months prior to a creditor's claim, nor does it protect funds that were not directly deposited into the account. Accordingly, beneficiaries will generally need to look to state consumer protection laws to enforce their right not to have their Social Security benefits seized by a creditor. These protections are sometimes weaker where the beneficiary has deposited his or her benefits in a bank account along with non-protected money. Therefore, if the beneficiary has reason to be concerned about a creditor's claims, it is generally advisable for him or her to place Social Security benefits in a bank account that does not include other assets.

Notably, these same protections apply to *Supplemental Security Income* (SSI) benefits, which are covered in Section F of this chapter.

5. Appealing SSA Determinations

Beneficiaries who have received an adverse Social Security determination are entitled to appeal that determination. The first step is for the beneficiary to request "reconsideration"—that is, to request that a SSA employee other than the one who made the original determination review the original claim as well as any new evidence. Assuming that reconsideration does not yield a favorable result, the second step is for the beneficiary to request an administrative hearing in front of an *administrative law judge* (ALJ). New evidence may be presented at the hearing stage, including witness testimony. While traditionally administrative hearings were conducted in person, today they are frequently conducted via video conference technology which—although promoted by the SSA as being convenient for beneficiaries—is sometimes perceived as a frustrating, alienating experience.

Should the ALJ determination also be unfavorable, the third step in challenging the decision is to request review by the SSA's Appeals Council. While beneficiaries are required to request Appeals Council review prior to initiating an action in federal court, the Appeals Council is not actually required to review challenged determinations. It can either do so, or it can decline to engage in such review. If the beneficiary has exhausted these administrative procedures and is still faced with an adverse determination, he or she may choose to bring a challenge in federal court. The next case illustrates this process in greater detail.

Hermes v. Secretary of Health & Human Services

926 F.2d 789 (9th Cir. 1991)

SNEED, Circuit Judge:

Plaintiff seeks an order reversing the final decision of the Secretary of Health and Human Services (Secretary) denying his claim for social security retirement insurance benefits under Title II of the Social Security Act. Appellant's sole contention is that the administrative law judge (ALJ) wrongly concluded that his date of birth was November 21, 1928 rather than May 25, 1925. The district court upheld the Secretary's finding. We affirm.

The decision of a district judge granting summary judgment is reviewed de novo. The panel's review is governed by the same standard used by the trial court. The Secretary's decision should only be disturbed "if it is not supported by substantial evidence or it is based on legal error." *Green v. Heckler*, 803 F.2d 528, 529 (9th Cir. 1986). When the evidence as a whole can support either outcome, the court may not substitute its judgment for that of the ALJ's. . . .

Appellant filed an application for social security retirement insurance benefits on November 30, 1987. The Social Security Administration (SSA) denied appellant's claim initially, and again after reconsideration, on the ground that appellant was born on November 21, 1928 and at the time of application had not yet reached the age of 62. Plaintiff appealed the denial and the ALJ heard the case de novo. Appellant testified before the ALJ on January 1, 1989. On March 21, 1989, the ALJ issued her decision and concluded that appellant was born on November 21, 1928. This determination became the "final decision" of the Secretary when the Appeals Council denied appellant's request for review of the ALJ's decision on August 10, 1989.

Appellant filed this action in district court on September 28, 1989. On April 2, 1990, upon cross-motions for summary judgment, the district court, as already indicated, ruled in favor of the Secretary after concluding that appellant's date of birth was November 21, 1928.

The appellant produced an entire series of documents indicating numerous birth dates between 1925 and 1930. A table detailing the various records, the birth dates they indicate, and the time they were recorded, can be found below. Appellant admitted in his hearing before the ALJ that he had listed the various birth dates. He testified that he never intended to defraud anyone but that he simply wanted to appear younger.

Table of Possible Birth Dates for Fred J. Hermes

Document	Date Established	Age or Date of Birth Recorded
SSA Record	December 1953	May 14, 1927
College Record	Feb. 1954	Nov. 21, 1928
Marriage Certificate	Jan. 25, 1960	Age 31/DOB 1928
SSA Record	Jan. 1961	Nov. 21, 1928
Divorce Action Questionnaire	July 5, 1962	Age 32/DOB 1929-30
Law School Record	Sept. 24, 1962	Nov. 21, 1929
Certificate of Naturalization	Oct. 19, 1965	Nov. 21, 1928
State Bar Application	1966	Nov. 21, 1930
Life Insurance Application	Aug. 20, 1967	Nov. 21, 1930
Certificate of Birth	Feb. 16, 1981	May 25, 1925
Driver's License	Oct. 10, 1985	Nov. 21, 1929
Insurance Card	Prior to Oct.1987	May 1925
Personnel Document	Feb. 17, 1988	May 21, 1925
Kanon Affidavit (distant relative & friend)	March 23, 1988	Early 1920s
Hermes Declaration	Jan. 26, 1989	May 1925

Appellant argued that he was born in 1925. He placed great emphasis on his religious birth record obtained from Iraq in 1981. This record shows a baptismal date of November 21, 1925 and a birth date of May 21, 1925. The document was recorded on February 16, 1981. Normally, a birth record is classified as "preferred evidence." The regulations on preferred evidence provide that:

> The best evidence of your age, if you can obtain it, is either: a birth certificate or hospital birth record recorded before age 5; or a religious record which shows your date of birth and was recorded before age 5.

20 C.F.R. §404.716(a) (1990). If a birth record meets these criteria, it is generally considered convincing. The ALJ and district court both concluded that the Iraqi birth record was not preferred evidence. We agree. The birth record was not recorded within five years of appellant's birth. Moreover, §00307.540 of the Social Security Administration's Operations Manual System (POMS) cautions against the use of religious records from Iraq.

> Religious records from all sources within Iraq are highly suspect. This includes religious records secured by or through churches in the U.S. from religious authorities in Iraq. Many Iraqi churches do not have records for older persons, or where such records do exist, they are in such poor condition as to be unusable. Experience has shown that religious authorities have issued certificates for events which occurred in other parishes or countries, for events for which there are no records, based on the statements of interested parties even where they conflicted with existing records, or because the individual appeared old and/or in need.[1]

The ALJ and district court, doubting the reliability of this record, were entitled to examine the additional evidence. *See* 20 C.F.R. §404.709 (1990).

The ALJ carefully reviewed the other evidence. The court concluded that the oldest evidence of the appellant's age or date of birth, which could be corroborated, would have the greatest probative value. In determining the probative value of documents submitted as proof of age "consideration will be given to when such other documents were established or recorded, and the circumstances attending their establishment or recordation." 20 C.F.R. §416.803 (1990).

The oldest evidence, the SSA record of December 1953, contained a birth date that could not be corroborated. The court turned to the next oldest piece of evidence, the claimant's college record, which indicated a birth date of November 21, 1928. Finding that this was further corroborated by the claimant's marriage certificate, a later SSA record, and his certificate of naturalization, the ALJ properly concluded that the claimant's birth date was November 21, 1928.

---

1. POMS is a policy manual and, therefore, does not have the force and effect of law. It is, nevertheless, persuasive.

The five pieces of evidence that support a birth date in 1925 were recorded just previous to, or after, appellant filed his application for benefits. This is too recent to overcome the force of the older evidence. The ALJ and the Secretary clearly were entitled to accord greater weight to the documentation that was recorded many years earlier.

Although the evidence supports several possible birth dates, an examination of this evidence in its entirety demonstrates that the Secretary's decision was supported by substantial evidence and was free of legal error. Where there is substantial evidence to support the decision made by the ALJ, as well as evidence to support a contrary determination, this court will not substitute its judgment for that of the ALJ.

AFFIRMED.

6. The Effect of SSA Overpayments

Sometimes, the SSA pays a beneficiary a greater amount than that to which he or she was entitled. Overpayments can occur for a variety of reasons. For example, a SSI beneficiary may be overpaid if he or she receives SSI payments in a month in which he or she was over the resource limit (resource limitations for SSI are discussed in Section F of this chapter).

In general, overpayments, regardless of whether they are the fault of the beneficiary or of the SSA, must be repaid. However, a beneficiary is entitled to request waiver of repayment. Such a waiver will be granted only if the beneficiary is able to show that the beneficiary was without fault and that recovery would either:

- Defeat the purpose of the program involved, or
- Be against equity and good conscience, or
- If the beneficiary is an SSI recipient, would impede efficient or effective administration of the program because of the small amount of money involved.

The next case illustrates the difficulty of obtaining such a waiver.

Johnson v. Barnhart

2006 WL 2329400 (W.D. Tex. 2006)

FRED BIERY, J.

The Court has considered the action filed by plaintiff Leonard Johnson regarding the determination of the Social Security Administration (SSA) that plaintiff is not entitled to be re-paid recovered overpaid social security payments made by the SSA in error. Plaintiff appeals the Appeals Council's July 22, 2005 decision finding that plaintiff is not without fault in accepting the overpayment of old-age insurance benefits of $8,618.00 for January 1996 through February 2000, and that plaintiff is not entitled to waiver of recovery of the overpayment. . . .

[T]his Court is limited to a determination of whether the decision is supported by substantial evidence and whether the Commissioner applied the proper legal standards in evaluating the evidence. . . .

Plaintiff objects to the finding by the Magistrate Judge that substantial evidence supports the Commissioner's finding. Plaintiff maintains the Social Security system is not reliable because the mistake in his monthly payment amount was unnoticed for "some four (4) years," and the mistake was not his but that of the Social Security Administration because he made the Administration aware of his pension but no adjustments were made. Plaintiff maintains and believes he is "not at fault."

. . . Mr. Johnson bears the burden of proof that he was without fault. For purposes of recouping an overpayment of benefits, fault "applies only to the individual." The fact the Social Security Administration "was at fault in making any overpayment does not relieve the overpaid individual from liability if such individual was also at fault." "Fault will be found if the incorrect payment resulted from," as found in this case, "acceptance of an overpayment which the individual knew or could be expected to know was incorrect." In making the fault determination, the Administration is to consider "all relevant circumstances, including age, intelligence, and any physical, mental, educational or linguistic limitations of the individual."

In evaluating the evidence in this case, the ALJ noted:

> There is no question that the claimant has been frustrated throughout the appeal process due to his requests for action not being properly addressed or the claimant not being given understandable explanations for what was going on. Then once he finally was granted a hearing and received a hearing decision that quoted conflicting amounts of his overpayment, he had to go through the additional frustration of his case file being lost and the time expended to reconstruct it. Certainly the claimant has been put through the proverbial wringer in pursuing his case and this is really regrettable. The appeal process can be frustrating enough for a claimant, but the obstacles faced by this claimant have understandably been a source of extreme consternation. Having dealt with thousands of Social Security cases, the undersigned recognizes that the problems experience [sic] by this claimant are more the exception than the rule, but that certainly is no consolation to him in his battle to protect his due process rights.

In evaluating whether the plaintiff was without fault, the ALJ explained:

> When the claimant filed his application for retirement benefits he stated that he was working for USPS and would be due a pension upon retirement from that entity. He also said that he recognized that when that occurred, his Social Security benefits would need to be recalculated because of the windfall provision of federal law concerning eligibility for two or more government pension programs. The letter to the claimant of December 24, 1999 states

that SSA had just become aware of the claimant receiving Social Security retirement benefits and a pension from USPS. However, there is in evidence a copy of SSA-795 signed by the claimant on February 29, 1996 informing SSA that he would be retiring from USPS on March 1, 1996. This appears to be another failure of SSA to properly process information provided by claimant.

The initial question to be address [sic] as to waiver of recovery of the overpayment is whether the claimant was without fault in causing the overpayment. In this case, the claimant was not given erroneous information by a SSA employee, but instead did not have information filed by him with SSA process expeditiously. Numerous errors were committed by SSA in this case, but the claimant is not entirely without blame. His statements show that he was aware that his Social Security retirement benefits would be negatively affected when he began receiving the pension from USPS. However, there is no evidence that he ever contacted SSA to question why he was continuing to receive the same amount of monthly Social Security retirement benefits after he began receiving the USPS pension. The fact that he advised SSA that he would be entitled to USPS pension beginning March 1996 does not completely absolve him of the responsibility to question the receipt of benefits that he has reason to believe he is not due.

The ALJ concluded plaintiff "was overpaid SSA retirement benefits in the amount of $8,618; that he was partially at fault in causing the overpayment; that such amount has already been recovered by SSA; and that there is no longer an overpayment to be waived."

Plaintiff appealed this decision to the Appeals Council who revised the ALJ's decision finding the plaintiff "is not without fault in accepting the overpayment of old-age insurance benefits of $8,618 for January 1996 through February 2000." In reaching this conclusion, the Council explained:

The claimant has submitted voluminous material in support of his case which demonstrates that he is not limited in understanding his rights and responsibilities in regard to the benefits he receives because of his age or intelligence, or any physical, mental, education, or linguistic limitations (including any lack of facility with the English language). The claimant initially indicated that he understood his benefits would be reduced when he started to receive his civil service annuity. The claimant notified the Social Security Administration shortly before he began receiving his civil service annuity. The claimant continued to accept benefits which did not reflect the expected reduction. The claimant had reason to know that the payments he was receiving were not correct, but he did not inquire as to why the payments had not decreased. The Appeals Council finds that the claimant accepted payments which he either knew or could have been expected to know were incorrect. Therefore, the claimant is not without fault in accepting the overpayments.

Given that this Court cannot re-weigh the evidence, try the issue de novo, or substitute its judgment for the Commission, the Court ... finds substantial evidence does support the Commissioner's decision finding plaintiff was not without fault in accepting the overpayment of old-age insurance benefits and that plaintiff is not entitled to waiver of recovery of the overpayment.

Therefore . . . the decision of the Commissioner should be affirmed and plaintiff's motions or requests for relief, including a jury trial and appointed counsel, should be denied. . . .

NOTE

Overpayments and SSI. Although *Johnson v. Barnhart* deals with overpayment in the context of retirement benefits, the same issue arises with overpayments of Supplemental Security Income (SSI), which is discussed in Section F of this chapter. Indeed, SSI beneficiaries are particularly prone to over-payment because SSI is a means-tested program. If the beneficiary's income or assets exceed the permitted threshold and the beneficiary fails to report this change to the SSA, it can result in an overpayment.

7. Controversies over OASDI

In recent years, there has been intense political attention paid to the future of the OASDI system. Much of this attention has focused on concerns about the solvency of the system. The Social Security system relies on the contributions of current workers to help pay for the benefits paid to today's retirees. As the numbers of retirees increases as a result of the retirement of the Baby Boomers and increased longevity, the Social Security system will not be able to continue to pay benefits at current levels unless it increases revenues. There is currently a surplus of money available to pay benefits (a surplus that is often misleadingly referred to as the "Social Security trust fund"). However, the OASDI surplus is expected to be depleted in 2033, according to the 2013 Report of the Board of Trustees of the OASDI and DI trust funds. When that occurs, either the system will need to reduce benefits, change eligibility requirements, increase revenue, or do some combination of the three.

As Professor Kathryn Moore has explained:

> There is no magic rabbit or costless way to resolve Social Security's long-term deficit. . . . Restoring Social Security's solvency requires that the system's revenues be increased, benefits reduced, or some combination of increased revenues and reduced benefits.
>
> Revenue increases could take a variety of forms. For example, the taxable wage base could be increased. . . . The maximum taxable wage base could gradually be increased until it reaches eighty-seven percent or ninety percent of taxable payroll as some commentators have suggested. In the alternative, the taxable wage base could simply be increased to a higher amount, such as $250,000, or totally eliminated and all wages could be subject to the payroll tax.
>
> Another way to increase revenues is to increase the payroll tax rate. . . .
>
> Revenues could also be increased by extending coverage to state and local employees. Currently, the Social Security system only covers about

seventy-five percent of all state and local employees; about four million state and local government employees are not covered by the Social Security system. A number of analysts and advisory groups have recommended that coverage be extended to include newly hired state and local employees.

Another way to increase Social Security's revenues is to transfer general revenues to the system or earmark other taxes for Social Security. For example, [former commissioner of the Social Security program] Robert Ball has proposed earmarking the estate tax for Social Security. . . .

Just as revenues may be increased in a variety of ways, there are a multitude of ways to decrease benefits. Perhaps the most straightforward, though not necessarily best, method of reducing benefits would be to impose an across-the-board reduction in benefits. For example, benefits could be reduced by three percent or five percent for all new beneficiaries beginning in 2010.

Benefits could also be reduced by increasing the normal retirement age. Under current law, a retired worker is entitled to receive "full" benefits at her normal retirement age (NRA). The NRA is sixty-five for workers who reached sixty-two before 2000 and is scheduled to increase gradually to sixty-seven by 2022. If a worker retires before the NRA, her benefits are actuarially reduced to reflect the earlier collection of benefits. Thus, increasing the NRA is almost economically identical to an across-the-board reduction in benefits for retirees. In recent years, a number of policymakers and commentators have recommended that the currently scheduled increase in the NRA be accelerated and/or that the NRA be increased further.

Another way to reduce benefits is to change the benefit formula. For workers reaching age sixty-two in 2008, the Social Security benefit formula replaces ninety percent of the first $711 of AIME, plus thirty-two percent of AIME between $711 and $4,288, plus fifteen percent of AIME above $4,288. Benefits could be reduced by reducing one or more of these factors. For example, all of the factors could be reduced by twenty percent, or the top two factors could be reduced from thirty-two percent to twenty percent and from fifteen percent to ten percent, respectively, or the top factor could be reduced from fifteen to ten percent.

A third method of reducing benefits is to change Social Security's cost of living adjustments. Under current law, once initial Social Security benefits are calculated, they are then adjusted for increases in the cost of living. Benefits could be reduced by reducing the annual cost-of-living increase by some set amount, such as one percentage point or by a half a percentage point. In the alternative, a new cost of living measure could be used. Currently, benefits are indexed to changes in the Consumer Price Index (CPI) for Urban Wage Earners and Clerical Workers (CPI-W). Some analysts have argued that this measure should be replaced with a new "chained" CPI that takes into account the fact that individuals substitute purchases and change their spending habits as prices rise. Cost-of-living adjustments are expected to be slightly lower under the chained CPI than under the current CPI-W.

Kathryn Moore, *The Future of Social Security: Principles to Guide Reform,* 41 J. MARSHALL L. REV. 1061, 1078-81 (2008). For a more detailed discussion of key proposals for change, see Kathryn Moore, *Social Security Reform: Fundamental Restructuring or Incremental Change,* 11 LEWIS & CLARK L. REV. 341 (2007).

Each of these approaches has been the subject of extensive debate. For a sense of the complexity of this issues, consider the debate over raising the retirement age. Those who advocate for raising either the *Full Retirement Age* (FRA), *Early Eligibility Age* (EEA), or both frequently point out that (on average) persons in the United States live longer and in better health today than they did when the FRA was initially set at age 65, that a smaller percentage of workers are employed in positions requiring physically taxing labor than in previous eras, and that raising the retirement age would encourage a number of workers to stay in the work force longer (thus reducing their need for a social safety net and generating additional tax revenue). Those opposed to raising either age, by contrast, tend to focus on the disproportionate effect that doing so would have on already disadvantaged populations, especially persons of color and manual laborers. For example, Eric Kingson and Nancy Altman write that:

> [R]aising the FRA is arguably a blunt and distributively perverse policy tool. Many older workers with health problem have little or no alternative to claiming permanently reduced benefits at early age. Twenty-seven percent of all workers aged 60 to 61 report "work-limiting health conditions," with higher percentages reported for minority workers—36.5 percent of African Americans and 31.5 percent of Latinos. Moreover, 45 percent of workers aged 58 and older work in jobs that are either physically demanding or have difficult working conditions. These workers are likely to suffer the most by having to postpone retirement and/or accept cuts in benefits. Workers, primarily women, who become primary caregivers for family members who become chronically ill are also disadvantaged. Moreover, raising the FRA disadvantages lower wage workers who, on average, have seen little or no increase in life expectancy.

Eric Kingson & Nancy Altman, *The Social Security Retirement Age(s) Debate: Perspectives and Consequences*, 21 PUB. POL'Y & AGING REP. 1 (2011).

Raising the early retirement age is perhaps particularly controversial. While raising the early eligibility age would likely encourage many workers to remain in the workforce longer (and potentially do so much more effectively than raising the FRA would), it would also eliminate the critical social safety net that early eligibility Social Security provides for many who cannot find sufficient employment to meet their needs but who do not qualify for other disability-based anti-poverty programs (e.g., are not sufficiently disabled to qualify for SSI or SSDI). Those advocating for raising the early retirement age typically focus on the fiscal benefits it would provide to the Social Security system (e.g., by increasing revenue through payroll and income taxes and by reducing benefit payments). By contrast, Professor Benjamin Templin has argued in favor of raising the early eligibility age on the grounds that it would protect people from making bad decisions. Specifically, Templin has argued that:

> At age sixty-two, the decision of whether to retire is a complex one involving the state of finances, health, employment, and other factors. Given that most

workers at age sixty-two have been working since their early twenties, it is likely a decision fueled by emotional content. The appearance of an instant benefit—especially to lower income workers—may be too difficult to resist.

Raising the EEA as a paternalistic response to dysfunctional economic behavior will force workers to stay in the labor force longer than anticipated. . . . The upside is significant in that workers reduce their longevity risk (the risk of outliving one's savings and benefits) because their Social Security benefits will increase, and they will have additional years in the workforce for an opportunity to save and reduce the span upon which they will draw upon their resources. . . .

Opponents principally argue that some workers will slip into poverty—a likely possibility. Unfortunately, when dealing with large populations and crafting general rules that apply to all, there are some subpopulations that may suffer. These harms can be mitigated by expanding disability under SSDI and using means-based programs, such as SSI, to compensate for lost wages. To the extent that means-based programs do not suffice, many innovative ideas that leverage the Social Security system have been suggested.

One idea is an elastic EEA that would allow early eligibility for groups with short life expectancies. . . .

Another possibility is establishing a low level adjudication process that allows an exception for poor health or financial exigency so that certain low income workers can begin to receive the same level of benefits that they would have received had the EEA not been increased.

Benjamin Templin, *Social Security Reform: Should the Retirement Age Be Increased?*, 89 Or. L. Rev. 1179, 1247-49 (2011).

QUESTIONS

1. There are two fundamentally different ways to change the Social Security system to close the gap between its resources and its promised benefits: 1) increase revenues, or 2) decrease benefits. Which approach is preferable? Why? Should both be pursued simultaneously?

2. Should the full retirement age, early eligibility age, or both be increased? If so, what should be the timeframe for the increase?

C. PRIVATE PENSIONS

Private pensions are an important component of income security in later life. They are, however, a relatively recent invention. The first U.S. pension plan was a relatively meager plan developed in 1875 by American Express Corporation, which was then in the railroad business. It was not until the 1910s and 1920s that pensions became common, and even then they were far from universal in their coverage. It was not until the 1950s that employer-sponsored pension plans became a key source of income security for a wide swath of American workers.

1. Incentives that Encourage Private Pensions

Unlike the Social Security system, in which federal law requires employers to participate, employers are not required to offer pension programs. By providing tax-favorable treatment to qualified plans, however, the government incentivizes employers to provide such benefits. This favorable tax status allows employers to deduct contributions to plans at the time they are made, allows employees not to count such contributions in their income, allows earnings on contributions to be tax-exempt until benefits are paid, and allows participants who receive a lump-sum distribution from their pension plan to roll this money over into an *individual retirement account* (IRA) or other account to further defer tax payments. The effect is that the pension plan or account receives a tax-free loan from the government in the amount of the deferred taxes.

To qualify for this favorable treatment, plans must, among other things: (1) cover a certain, minimum number of employees to ensure that the plan does not just benefit a few, high-level employees; (2) not engage in discriminatory contributions or benefits; (3) vest benefits within the time periods required by federal law as described below; and (4) meet minimal funding standards designed to ensure that employers can actually pay promised benefits. *See* 26 U.S.C. §§401, 411, 412, 415.

2. Types of Pension Plans

There are two major types of pension plans: *defined benefit plans* and *defined contribution plans.*

A defined benefit plan promises employees a specific monthly benefit at retirement. This benefit may be a precise dollar figure or an amount calculated based on a set of factors such as length of employment and salary.

A defined contribution plan, by contrast, does not promise an employee a certain benefit. Rather, the employer, employee, or both contribute an annual amount to the plan. Typically, employer contributions are made at a set rate, often representing a particular percentage of the employee's annual salary. These contributions are then invested on behalf of the employee, who may be given choices about how the contributions are invested. Common examples of defined contribution plans are 401(k) plans and 403(b) plans (which are roughly equivalent to 401(k) plans but are only available to employees of tax-exempt organizations).

There is currently a strong trend among employers away from offering defined benefit plans and toward offering defined contribution plans instead. According to the Employee Benefit Research Institute, as of 2010, 66 percent of medium and large private employers offered retirement plans to employees—but only 30 percent offered defined benefit plans whereas 54 percent offered defined contribution plans. By comparison, only 35 percent of small private employers offered retirement plans—and then only 9 percent offered defined benefit plans whereas 31 percent offered defined contribution plans. Defined benefit plans, by contrast, are more common among public sector employers. In part, this reflects the fact that defined benefit plans are most common in heavily unionized employment sectors. Overall, according to the Bureau of Labor Statistics, as of March 2012, 68 percent of all workers have access to employer-sponsored retirement plans (either defined benefit or defined contribution), but only 65 percent of those employed in the private sector had such a plan.

The rise of defined contribution plans means that employees face greater responsibility and risk related to their retirement savings. These responsibilities do not end, moreover, with retirement. Rather, retirement triggers the need to make important decisions about how to receive accrued pension benefits. When the employee retires, he or she may choose to take either a lump sum payment or to receive a series of payments over an extended period of time by using the accrued benefits to purchase an annuity (see Section D of this chapter for a discussion of annuities). If he or she chooses a lump sum distribution, he or she will then have a variety of options with what to do with that sum. A common approach is to "roll over" the funds, tax-free, into an IRA. This allows the funds to continue to grow tax-free.

As Professor Lawrence Frolik writes, regardless of whether retirees with 401(k) plans roll over their plan, "they face two formidable financial planning problems that will continue for the rest of their lives." Frolik explains that:

> First, they must successfully invest the accounts for what is likely to be 20 or more years of their remaining lives. To maintain the value of their retirement funds they must successfully invest them—not lose capital—with the hope that the investment return will at least equal the rate of inflation. As the financial collapse of the markets in 2008 . . . demonstrated, however, even the modest goal of creating earnings equal to the rise in the cost of living may be difficult to achieve. Second, they must spend their retirement funds at a rate that will not exhaust them before they die, yet at an amount sufficient so that they will have enough on which to live. This is even trickier than being a successful investor. Although the two goals, investment returns that at a minimum keep pace with inflation and taking distributions at a rate that neither exhausts the fund nor leaves the retiree in poverty, can support each other—good investing means more to spend while tempered withdrawals maintain capital—the two goals are also in conflict. The more the retiree withdraws to live on, the less there is to invest and so the smaller the investment return.

Lawrence A. Frolik, *Protecting Our Aging Retirees: Converting 401(k) Accounts into Federally Guaranteed Lifetime Annuities*, 47 SAN DIEGO L. REV. 277, 285-86 (2010).

In making decisions about their 401(k) plans, participants are both guided by and constrained by federal law governing the withdrawal of funds from 401(k) plans. With a few exceptions (e.g., for a qualifying disability or for the death of a participant), a plan participant cannot withdraw money from a 401(k) plan until age 59½ without facing an additional 10 percent tax on the funds withdrawn. Conversely, an employee must begin taking distributions no later than April 1st of the year after the participant reaches age 70½ or the year in which the participant retires, whichever is later.

QUESTIONS

1. As an employee, would you prefer to be enrolled in a defined benefit or defined contribution plan? Why?

2. As an employer, would you prefer to offer a defined benefit plan or a defined contribution plan? Why?

3. As a taxpayer, which type of plan would you prefer that employers offer? Why?

3. Federal Protections for Pension Beneficiaries

The Employee Retirement Income Security Act (ERISA) is the federal law that governs employer-sponsored pensions. It preempts state regulation of such plans, which means that the law governing employer-provided benefits is one of the few areas of elder law governed almost exclusively by federal law.

A full discussion of ERISA and its implications is well beyond the scope of this book. However, it is important to recognize that ERISA provides a number of key protections for pension plan beneficiaries.

First, ERISA requires defined benefit plans to allow participants to claim full retirement benefits by either age 65, after ten years of service to the employer, or upon termination of employment.

Second, ERISA places limits on how long employers may wait until their employer-provided pension benefits are guaranteed (or "vested") even if beneficiaries' employment is terminated or they quit. Under ERISA, an employer-sponsored defined benefit plan can require employees to wait up to five years for their benefits to vest. If the plan chooses to require such a long wait, however, the benefits must fully vest after five years. Alternatively, employers can opt for a graduated vesting scheme under which they can require employees to work as many as seven years to become fully vested in the benefits, but must provide for at least 20 percent vesting after three years, 40 percent vesting after five years, and 50 percent vesting after six years. By contrast, an employer-sponsored defined contribution plan cannot require an employee to wait more than three years to vest, and if the employee is required to wait three years, he or she must fully vest at the end of those three years. Alternatively, the employer can opt for a graduated vesting plan under which an employee must be at least 20 percent vested after two years, 40 percent vested after three years, 60 percent vested after four years, 80 percent vested after five years, and 100 percent vested after six years.

Third, ERISA requires defined benefit pension plans to provide spousal benefits. Specifically, under ERISA, a plan must provide a surviving spouse (who had been married to the participant for at least one year) with an annuity worth at least half of the participant's pension. However, if both spouses waive the right to this survivor benefit, the plan need not provide it. One reason spouses might choose to waive this right is because it could increase the amount of pension benefits paid during the participant's lifetime.

Fourth, ERISA sets minimum amounts of money that defined benefit pension sponsors must put toward promised pension benefits. This is important not only to protect beneficiaries, but also to protect the government coffers. This is because qualified private pension plans are guaranteed by the Pension Benefit Guaranty Corporation (PBGC), which insures such plans up to a certain amount per month (the cap depends on the age of the beneficiary—in no case is it more than about $4,000 a month).

QUESTIONS

1. Why might employers wish to delay vesting of employee pension benefits?

2. Why does the government have an interest in incentivizing retirement savings? What is the extent of that interest?

D. SAVINGS

After retirement, many older adults rely on private savings to supplement their income flow. Such savings are not only an asset to be liquidated, but also a source of interest income—although such interest income is typically modest.

The extent to which savings contribute to the income and wealth of older adults varies significantly by socioeconomic status. Older adults with higher socioeconomic status rely much more heavily on savings than do older adults with lower socioeconomic status. Lower income individuals, women, and single persons are particularly likely to experience a gap between their actual savings and the savings they need in older age.

There are many reasons why people do not save as much as experts would recommend. Common ones include a lack of understanding of the value of accumulated savings, a failure to predict or appreciate future needs, other demands on resources, and being confused or overwhelmed by different savings options. According to the National Endowment for Financial Education:

> Even though pension and Social Security wealth account for about half of total wealth for the median household in the United States, many workers know little about their pensions. According to recent data . . . , half of older workers do not know which type of pension they have and fewer know about their pension wealth. Many workers could not even venture a guess about

their Social Security wealth. Despite many years of annual mailings of individual benefit statements from the Social Security Administration, less than twenty percent of workers in the population knew the correct age at which they were entitled to full Social Security benefits.

NATIONAL ENDOWMENT FOR FINANCIAL EDUCATION, INCREASING THE EFFECTIVENESS OF RETIREMENT SAVINGS FOR FEMALES AND LOW-INCOME EMPLOYEES: A MARKETING APPROACH (2009), *available at* http://www.nefe.org.

The federal government incentivizes saving for retirement by providing for tax-favored retirement savings accounts. The two basic types of such accounts are *Traditional Individual Retirement Accounts* (traditional IRAs) and *Roth Individual Retirement Accounts* (Roth IRAs).

Contributions to traditional IRAs are tax deductible, which means that contributing to a traditional IRA generally lowers the total amount of federal income taxes that an individual pays. The individual does not have to pay tax on these accumulated IRA savings until they are distributed. Individuals under the age of 70½ can contribute up to a certain amount annually to a traditional IRA. In 2013, the limit was $5,000 for individuals under the age of 50, and $6,000 for persons age 50 and older, with two caveats. First, individuals cannot contribute more than the amount of their annual compensation. Second, income limitations apply for individuals who are covered by an employer-sponsored retirement plan or whose spouses are covered by such a plan. For these individuals, the deduction decreases as their income rises, such that above a certain amount it is entirely eliminated.

A Roth IRA, by contrast, is a retirement investment vehicle to which an individual contributes after-tax dollars. Since the contributions are after-tax, when the individual later withdraws the funds, they are not subject to income tax. They are therefore attractive to individuals who anticipate that they will be taxed at a higher rate during retirement than at the present time.

As with a traditional IRA, there are limits on how much an individual can contribute annually to a Roth IRA. In 2013, the limits were $5,000 for individuals under the age of 50, and $6,000 for persons age 50 and older. The amount is reduced and eventually eliminated as income rises for single individuals, married individuals living apart from their spouse earning more than $112,000 annually, and married cohabitating individuals earning more than $178,000 annually.

For both types of IRAs, there is generally a 10 percent tax penalty for withdrawing funds prior to age 59½. A number of exceptions, however, apply. These include exceptions for individuals with qualifying disabilities, individuals with significant unreimbursed medical expenses, individuals using the funds for qualified higher education expenses, and individuals using the funds to purchase their first home.

Annuities are another important savings tool. As a general matter, an annuity is a financial product in which the purchaser pays a bank or other financial institution a set sum in return for future payments. Annuities vary in a variety of important ways. First, they vary by period of time over which they make payments. "Fixed term" annuities pay the buyer only for a predetermined period of time; "life" annuities pay the buyer for the remainder of his or her life. Second, annuities vary based on whether they provide a guaranteed payment amount ("fixed annuity") or whether the amount they pay depends on the performance of some underlying investment ("variable annuity"). Third, annuities differ by when they commence payments. "Immediate" annuities commence directly after they are purchased; "deferred" annuities do not start paying benefits until a predetermined period of time has passed. Fourth, annuities vary based on how the funds in them are invested. Individuals with variable annuities may play an active role in determining the nature of that investment. Fifth, different annuities have different fees associated with them. A final important difference is that annuities vary by whether or not they will pay benefits to a third party if the purchaser dies. Some annuities end if the primary purchaser dies. Others continue to pay out to a survivor, either for the survivor's life or for a set period of time.

Annuities are attractive investment tools for a variety of reasons. One reason is that deferred annuities are tax-favored because contributions are not taxed, and thus the investment interest compounds untaxed. Taxes are instead deferred until payments are made. Where payment is made in retirement, the tax rate of the beneficiary may be lower than the beneficiary's tax rate while employed.

Annuities, however, are also associated with significant costs, including broker commissions, penalties for early withdrawal, and annual management fees. In addition, withdrawals made before the beneficiary reaches age 59½ are subject to an additional 10 percent penalty. Similarly, federal law imposes a tax penalty on most annuity holders who do not begin to receive minimum required distributions by 70½ years of age.

QUESTIONS

1. In what ways does the government encourage individuals to save?

2. How active should the government be in promoting private savings? What is the government's interest in doing so?

3. Should lawyers encourage their clients to save? Is this consistent with their professional role?

E. FAMILY SUPPORT

Family support—both in the form of cash and in-kind services—is an important part of the income of many older adults. Many family members make out-of-pocket expenditures to help support ill or elderly family members. When researchers attempt to place a monetary value on the care that older adults receive, the resulting figures can seem staggering. For example, the

AARP Public Policy Institute estimated that unpaid "informal" adult caregivers' contributions to other adults totaled $450 billion of annual economic value in 2009. *See* Lynn Feinberg et al., AARP Public Policy Institute, Valuing the Invaluable: 2011 update (2011).

Family support is typically voluntary in nature and is motivated not by the law, but by human emotions such as affection or a sense of duty. However, under certain circumstances, family members may be legally required to provide support for their elderly relatives. Legal rules requiring parental support have existed for thousands of years. Early Roman law, as well as Jewish and Christian scripture, clearly articulated this duty, and even the philosopher Aristotle discussed it.

A majority of U.S. states currently have laws requiring adult children to support their aged parents in certain situations. Of these, only about half explicitly condition this requirement on financial ability to pay, and approximately one-third make failure to provide such support a criminal act. Such laws, however, are generally only enforced sporadically.

The next two cases consider challenges to attempts to enforce filial responsibility laws.

Swoap v. Superior Court of Sacramento County

516 P.2d 840 (Cal. 1973)

Sullivan, Justice.

We are again called upon to determine whether an adult child of a recipient of aid to the aged under the Old Age Security Law (Welf. & Inst. Code, div. 9, pt. 3, ch. 3, §12000 et seq.) may constitutionally be required to reimburse the state. . . .

Two recipients of aid to the aged, Ila Huntley and Bieuky Dykstra, and their adult children, Howard Huntley and Julius Dykstra, brought a class action seeking to enjoin state officials from requiring adult children to reimburse the state, pursuant to sections 12100 and 12101, for aid to the aged extended to their parents.

Plaintiff Howard Huntley is the 60-year-old son of 88-year-old widow Ila Huntley, who is the recipient of aid to the aged. Huntley alleges in the complaint that he and his 67-year-old wife had a net monthly income of $656.25; that they are trying to save money for their imminent retirement; that the San Joaquin County Welfare Department ordered him, effective October 1, 1971, to pay the department $70 per month for the support of his mother; and that he could not provide for his own family and at the same time pay such a large sum.

Plaintiff Julius Dykstra is the son of 78-year-old widow, Bieuky Dykstra, who is the recipient of aid to the aged. Dykstra alleges that the same welfare department demanded that he pay $75 per month for the support of his mother; that he works as a truck driver and does not have $75 per month left after paying his own family bills, including $180 a month for child support and $145 a month for rent.

On October 14, 1971 the Superior Court of Sacramento County issued a statewide temporary restraining order, enjoining defendants from "(e)nforcing against plaintiffs Julius Dykstra and Howard Huntley, and the class of persons similarly situated, and plaintiffs Bieuky Dykstra and Ila Huntley, and the class of persons similarly situated, the provisions of W & I Code, §§12100 and 12101, as amended, and Civil Code, $206, as amended." Defendants seek a writ of prohibition to prevent the Sacramento Superior Court from enforcing its restraining order on the ground that, since sections 12100[2] and 12101,[3] and Civil Code section 206[4] are valid, the court had no jurisdiction to enjoin defendants from administering these statutes.

Under the Old Age Security Law public assistance is extended to aged needy persons. Pursuant to section 12101 the adult children of such recipients are required to contribute to the recipient's support according to a fixed schedule. . . .

. . . [T]he real question . . . in the instant case is whether the class of adult children in general are otherwise under a duty to support needy or poor parents which duty provides a rational basis for upholding the relatives' responsibility created by sections 12100 and 12101 against the challenge that such statutes are impermissibly discriminating. We answer this question in the affirmative.

It is abundantly clear that children have generally been subject to a duty to support poor parents for a very long time, indeed. It is true . . . that there was no such duty at common law. Nevertheless, the duty is deep rooted and of venerable ancestry; it can be traced back over almost four centuries to the year 1601, when it emerged as part and parcel of the Elizabethan Poor Law. . . .

This duty, codified in California in 1872 as section 206 of the Civil Code in language remarkably similar to the Elizabethan Poor Law, has existed unchanged until the recent 1971 amendment. The purpose of such legislation is identical to that underlying the Elizabethan Poor Law: ". . . to protect the public from the burden of supporting people who have children able to support them."

---

2. Section 12100 provides: 'If an adult child living within this state fails to contribute to the support of his parent as required by Section 12101, the county granting aid under this chapter may proceed against such child . . . to recover that portion of the aid granted as it is determined that the child is liable to pay, and to secure an order requiring payment of any sums which may become due in the future. . . .'

3. [Section 12101 sets forth how the amount of a relatives' required contribution is to be determined.—ED.] [According to Section 12101,] [r]egulations of the [welfare] department shall prescribe the criteria, methods of investigation and test check procedures relating to the determination of the maximum amount any adult child may be held liable to contribute toward the support of a parent to the end that the required contribution does not impose an undue hardship upon the adult child and administrative time and effort are not expended on non-productive investigative activities. . . .

4. . . . Section 206 prior to its 1971 amendment read in pertinent part as follows: 'It is the duty of the father, the mother, and the children of any Poor person who is unable to maintain himself by work, to maintain such person to the extent of their ability.'

In 1930 the state undertook to support needy aged by inaugurating the present state-county old age assistance program. Aged persons, however, who had children able to support them and responsible under the law for their support were specifically excluded from the system. . . . Apparently the Legislature determined that aged persons who had children were adequately protected by the existing provision in Civil Code section 206.

In 1937 the Legislature slightly modified the statutory scheme. Only aged persons who were actually receiving support from responsible relatives, including children, were disqualified from receiving aid. Aged persons not receiving such support but having responsible relatives, including children, who were able and legally responsible to provide support, were unconditionally entitled to receive aid. However, the county granting aid was allowed to recover from "a spouse or adult child pecuniarily able to support" a person receiving aid "such portion of the aid granted as said relative is able to pay." This statutory scheme continues today in substantially the same form.

It is thus abundantly clear that a long tradition of law, not to mention a measureless history of societal customs, has singled out adult children to bear the burden of supporting their poor parents. This duty existed prior to, and independent of, any duties arising out of the state assistance to the aged. Subsequent statutes imposing liability upon the adult children of persons receiving aid to the aged merely selected a class of relatives who were otherwise legally responsible for the support of their parents. . . .

Plaintiffs, apparently recognizing that these sections do not touch on or affect a "fundamental interest," argue that the statute creates a suspect classification on two separate theories: (1) by distinguishing between people on the basis of wealth; and (2) by distinguishing between people on the basis of ancestry.

While it is indisputable that "careful examination on our part is especially warranted where lines are drawn on the basis of wealth" it is equally clear that these sections do not draw lines on the basis of wealth. They apply to all adult children of parents in need. They draw no distinction between such children and do not single out either wealthy children or poor children for special treatment, except to provide that parent and children shall bear the duty to support "to the extent of their ability." (Civ. Code, §206.)

Plaintiffs claim, however, that these sections discriminate between adult children on the basis of their Parents' wealth, since only adult children of "parents in need" are required to support their parents. While this argument has a surface plausibility and appears to establish that these sections create a suspect classification based on wealth, a closer examination exposes the argument as pure sophistry.

The class "parents in need" is the only class in which the state has an interest or to which it owes a duty. . . . The state interest advanced, namely to offset the cost of public assistance to the needy comes into play only when the needy are involved and therefore focuses only on a class of needy people. However, insofar as the state acts toward this class of needy people, it is conferring a benefit upon them either by directly granting aid under the Old Age Security Law or by providing them with the remedy to secure support from their adult children under Civil Code section 206. Plaintiffs do not contend that the state acts improperly in conferring such a benefit only upon "parents in need." Insofar as the state imposes a correlative liability upon the adult children of "parents in need," it does so without discriminating between such children on the basis of wealth. The state selects the children to bear the burden not on the basis of wealth, but on the basis of parentage. Since these sections do not discriminate on the basis of wealth, it creates no suspect classification based on wealth.

Plaintiffs urge that ancestry is a suspect classification calling for application of the "strict scrutiny" test. . . . [I]f classifications based on the general fact of descent, as opposed to racial classification, were viewed as suspect, established areas of the law, as for example the statutes of succession, would be undermined.

Since these sections do not touch upon a fundamental interest and do not create any suspect classifications, their constitutionality is to be determined by the normal "rational relationship" test, namely by "'requiring merely that distinctions drawn by a challenged statute bear some rational relationship to a conceivably legitimate state purpose.'"

. . . [T]he state purpose of the relatives' responsibility statutes is to "relieve the public treasury of part of the burden cast upon it by the public assumption of responsibility to maintain the destitute." It is uncontested that this is a legitimate state purpose. . . . The sole question therefore is whether placing the burden for this support upon the adult children bears some rational relationship to the accomplishment of the state purpose of relieving the public treasury.

It seems eminently clear that the selection of the adult children is rational on the ground that the parents, who are now in need, supported and cared for their children during their minority and that such children should in return now support their parents to the extent to which they are capable. Since these children received special benefits from the class of "parents in need," it is entirely rational that the children bear a special burden with respect to that class.[15]

Plaintiffs argue, however, that the only support obligations which are rational are those arising out of a relationship voluntarily entered into, as for example marriage and parental relationship, because there the prospective husband or parent knows of the obligations attendant upon entering the relationship and voluntarily consents thereto. On the contrary, so the argument runs, since children do not themselves voluntarily enter into the relationship with their parents, it is arbitrary to force upon them the obligations of such relationship.

---

15. In apparent recognition of this rationale, section 12104 provides that adult children who were abandoned for two years during their minority are exempt from the reimbursement duty.

Assuming that normally a child has no choice in the creation of a relationship with his parents, this fact does not per se establish that the classification is arbitrary as to children. Indeed, as we have explained, the existence of special benefits for the class arising out of the relationship provides an adequate basis for imposing upon it a duty to support parents. . . .

We therefore arrive at these final conclusions. The provisions of the Old Age Security Law (§§12100 and 12101) requiring adult children to contribute to the support of their parents do not thereby arbitrarily charge to one class in society the cost of public assistance to the aged who are poor or in need. A rational basis for such classification is found in, and provided by, Civil Code section 206, which itself rests soundly on our Anglo-American legal tradition. Accordingly the liability imposed by the Old Age Security Law on responsible relatives does not deny them the equal protection of the laws. Since these provisions pass constitutional muster, . . . they are entitled to enforcement and respondent court acts in excess of its jurisdiction in restraining and enjoining petitioner from enforcing them against real parties in interest and the class or classes of persons they purport to represent.

We are not unmindful that these provisions may involve harsh results in certain instances and we are indeed sympathetic with the plight of such persons. However, the amelioration of any harsh results must rest in the hands of the administering authorities, since these provisions are constitutional.

Let a peremptory writ of prohibition issue as prayed for.

WRIGHT, C.J., and McCOMB and BURKE, JJ., concur.

* * *

TOBRINER, Justice.

I dissent.

The majority propose, by the instant opinion, to establish a new constitutional standard for determining when the state may compel some of its citizens to pay for benefits which the state, in its wisdom, decides to provide to other citizens. Under the test proposed by the majority, a state can charge one class of citizens with the costs of providing public programs to another class whenever there is simply some "rational relationship" between the group of benefited individuals and those who must pay the bill. Applying this "minimal rationality" test in the instant case, the majority hold that since the class of children have generally benefited from parents, the state can require those children whose parents happen to be poor to reimburse the state for the cost of public old age assistance, regardless of whether a particular child is otherwise legally obligated to provide such support to his parent.

. . . [U]nder our state constitutional guarantee of equal protection of the laws . . . the state may seek reimbursement for the costs of public programs from a relative of a benefited person. Only when the relative would have been legally responsible for providing such service even if the state had not undertaken its public program. By the instant opinion, the majority have discarded the legal analysis which has guided California courts in this field for the past decade.

Moreover, the rationale underlying the majority opinion represents not only a sharp break with precedent but, more fundamentally, a dangerous inroad into basic principles of individual freedom and minority rights which have long flourished in this state. The majority opinion greatly expands the power of the state to foist general expenses onto the shoulders of small classes of citizens, permitting the majority, by a unilateral decision to provide certain benefits to some of its citizens, to require a designated minority to bear expenses for which they would otherwise not be responsible. As the few examples described below illustrate, acceptance of the majority's new constitutional analysis would open the door to a wide abuse of majoritarian power.

Instead of adopting this unprecedented approach, I believe the court should continue to apply the standard that has been established by California cases to date. Under this test, the state may properly seek reimbursement for expenses of a public program from a class of individuals who do not directly receive the benefit of the program only when such individuals bear a legal duty to provide such services which duty exists independently of the state's decision to initiate its program. As discussed below, applying this test to the "relative responsibility" provisions at issue in the instant case, I conclude that the challenged provisions are invalid, both because an adult child's legal duty to support poor parents is not "independent" of the state's decision to provide welfare benefits and because the section works an invidious discrimination against poor families as a class. I therefore believe that the decision of the superior court, granting a temporary injunction to restrain the enforcement of the challenged provisions, should be affirmed.

* * *

Under the majority's newly propounded "rationality" test, a government intent on reducing the general tax burden could single out insulated minority classes to bear a disproportionate share of the tax burden of a whole range of public services. Thus, for example, the "mere rationality" standard would permit the state not only to charge adult children with the costs of old age benefits but would authorize public savings by charging such children for the costs of subsidized housing projects, medical care, recreational centers, reduced public transportation fares and the various other social programs the state decides to make available to its senior citizens. Although the children of the recipients of such benefits may have had no preexisting obligation to pay for such services, the majority's constitutional test would presumably sanction such charges on the ground that children as a whole have benefited from parents. Moreover, since the circumstances of the individual case are assertedly irrelevant, the state presumably could require even a child who had been abandoned by his parents to pay the costs of these varied public programs.

A further example may provide an even sharper illustration of the potential dangers loosed by the majority's constitutional approach. Assume the state decided to initiate bilingual educational programs to improve the educational opportunities offered to children from non-English-speaking households. Could the state, to reduce public costs, require the parents to such children to finance this entire public program? ...

Moreover, nothing in the mere "rationality" test proposed by the majority would limit the state's power to obtain reimbursement to Relatives of recipients of public benefits. Many diverse groups of people receive "benefits" from persons who in turn are beneficiaries of government programs. Under the majority approach, for example, homeowners whose houses are saved from destruction by local firemen could presumably be required to finance the fire department's retirement benefit program; citizens who seek the assistance of police could be made responsible for widow's benefits paid in the event of a policeman's death. ...

Under established constitutional principles, sections 12100 and 12101 are invalid both because the duty of support imposed upon adult children by section 206 is not "independent" of the state's reimbursement scheme and because the sections invidiously discriminate against poor families.

The validity of sections 12100 and 12101, I submit, must be judged by the constitutional criteria developed in our prior cases. Under these precedents, the relevant question in the instant case is whether adult children bear a "preexisting" or "independent" duty to support their needy parents which the state discharges by its grant of old age benefits, or, in other words, whether such adult children would be obligated to support their parents even if the state had not decided to provide such aid. When this question is faced directly, I believe it becomes clear that no such "independent" duty is present.

Defendants, of course, rely upon Civil Code section 206 as providing the "independent" duty of adult children to support their needy parents which purportedly rationalizes the relative responsibility provisions at issue here. In one sense, section 206 as amended does provide a duty "independent" of sections 12100 and 12101, for under its terms an adult child may be responsible for supporting his poor parent whether or not the state actually provides the parent with old age benefits. But such a narrow interpretation of the "independent legal duty" requirement loses sight of the fundamental purpose served by this requirement.

... Defendants do not contest that the newly amended provisions of section 206 were enacted as an integral part of the challenged relative responsibility scheme. Under these circumstances, the new portion of section 206, placing a duty on adult children to support parents "in need," can in no sense be said to establish an "independent" legal duty as that term has been used in our prior cases.

Moreover, even the long established provisions of section 206 which preceded the 1971 amendments cannot properly be said to establish an "independent duty" of adult children to support their poor parents. As the majority recognize, the duty to support embodied by section 206 did not exist at common law but was first established as part of the Elizabethan Poor Law. As this court has pointed out on numerous occasions in the past, and as the majority concede, from its very inception this provision "'was designed to indemnify the public and to minimize its costs in relieving the poor' ... 'It has been stated that the main purpose of the statute seems to be to protect the public from the burden of supporting people who have children able to support them.'"

* * *

Furthermore, even if section 206 could be said to create an "independent" duty on adult children under our prior decisions, I still believe the challenged provisions are invalid as an invidious discrimination against the children of poor parents.

As noted earlier, the majority uphold the rationality of the provisions at issue by observing that since children as a class have benefited from the support of their parents, it is reasonable to require children to support their parents. The fallacy with this reasoning as applied to the instant case, however, is that the state has not chosen to charge all children with the cost of supporting parents but instead it has singled out children of poor or needy parents to bear this burden. The fact that such children of poor parents in general have benefited from the support of their parents does not distinguish this class from the large class of "adult children" who are not required to assume the contested financial burden; these other adult children, whose parents either have sufficient resources of their own or have already died, presumably also benefited from parental support during their youth but they are not required to make financial contributions under the challenged provisions. Instead, it is only the adult children whose parents continue to live and happen to be poor who are compelled to shoulder the financial burden. In my view, the singling out of this group for such a burden denies them the equal protection of the laws.

The majority's response to this contention is apparently that the state is not required to grant aid to parents with sufficient financial resources and since it has chosen to give aid only to poor parents it is proper to seek reimbursement only from the children of such poor parents. No one, of course, contends that the state should give aid to financially secure persons. But the permissibility of limiting aid to the needy aged does not answer the question of how the adult children of such persons can rationally be distinguished from other adult children who are similarly situated with respect to prior parental benefits. The fact of the matter is that the challenged provisions attach serious financial consequences to the frequently fortuitous circumstances of whether one's parents are alive and in need.

Moreover, the classification scheme created by the relative responsibility provision is doubly invidious because, as a practical matter, in the great majority of cases the adult children of "parents in need" themselves command only very modest incomes. Technically, of course, it is true that, as the majority point out, the challenged provisions apply to all children of poor parents, whether the children be rich or poor. We blind ourselves to reality, however, if we do not recognize that by and large poor parents have less-than-wealthy adult children, adult children who, more often than not, are beginning to raise their own families and attempting to improve their economic condition. It is this class of citizens that the challenged provisions single out to bear an additional burden, a burden which is imposed not because of any personal failing of the adult child, but simply because his parent happens to be poor. Thus, in addition to all the disadvantages poverty may earlier have cast on this class of citizens, these adult children are required once again to bear an increased burden simply because their family is poor.

* * *

It might be possible to understand the reasons for the majority's uprooting of a consistent line of precedent and creation of a novel constitutional ruling if the legislation challenged in the instant case offered the promise of unquestionably beneficial social consequences; under such circumstances one might expect to find the court questioning past decisions that impeded the salutary result. The statutes in question here, however, offer no such beneficent social consequences.

On the contrary, almost all observers agree that the social effects of the challenged relative responsibility provisions are harsh and self-defeating. "[A] large body of social work opinion [has long maintained] that liability of relatives creates and increases family dissension and controversy, weakens and destroys family ties at the very time and in the very circumstances when they are most needed, imposes an undue burden upon the poor . . . and is therefore socially undesirable, financially unproductive, and administratively infeasible." . . .

Jenny Baxter, a 75-year-old California receiving Old Age Security benefits, eloquently summarized the true effect of the relative responsibility laws: "No one is born into this world with a debt to their parents for their birth and contributions until their maturity. That is the parents' contribution to life and society. When the child reaches maturity, he starts a new separate unit and in turn makes his contribution to life and society as did his parents, carrying on the generation cycle on through eternity. The children should not be saddled with unjust demands that keep them at or near poverty level with no hope to escape it, just because a parent still breathes. And aged parents should not have to live their remaining lives facing the heartbreaking experience of being such a burden to this children. . . ."

* * *

I would affirm the superior court judgment invalidating the challenged provisions as a denial of equal protection of the laws.

Mosk, J., concurs.

Health Care & Retirement Corp. of America v. Pittas

46 A.3d 719 (Pa. Super. 2012)

Appellant, John Pittas, appeals from the judgment entered April 13, 2011, in favor of Appellee, Health Care and Retirement Corporation of America ("HCR"). We affirm.

The record reflects the relevant factual and procedural background of this matter as follows:

On or about September 24, 2007, after completing rehabilitation for injuries sustained in a car accident, Appellant's mother was transferred to an HCR facility for skilled nursing care and treatment. Appellant's mother resided in the facility and was treated by HCR until March of 2008. In March of 2008 Appellant's mother withdrew from the HCR facility and relocated to Greece.

A large portion of the bills incurred by Appellant's mother due and owing to HCR went unpaid. As a result, on or about May 12, 2008, HCR instituted a filial support action against Appellant. Pursuant to 23 Pa. C.S.A. §4603, entitled "Relatives' liability," HCR sought to hold Appellant liable for the outstanding debt incurred as a result of his mother's treatment and care. The parties submitted the case to arbitration, whereupon a three-member arbitration panel found in favor of Appellant. HCR appealed the arbitration award to the trial court. The trial court held a three-day non-jury trial, after which it entered a verdict in favor of HCR in the amount of $92,943.41. Appellant filed post-trial motions, which the trial court denied on January 13, 2011. This timely appeal followed.

Appellant presents three issues on appeal:

Did the trial court commit reversible error or abuse its discretion in determining the burden of proof was on the [Appellant] to prove his inability to support his "indigent" mother?

Did the trial court commit reversible error or abuse its discretion in not considering alternate sources of income to satisfy the alleged support obligation?

Did the trial court commit reversible error or abuse its discretion in deciding [Appellant's mother] was indigent, without competent evidence to do so?

* * *

Appellant's first issue on appeal challenges the trial court's application of 23 Pa. C.S.A. §4603. Pursuant to that statute:

(a) Liability.—

(1) Except as set forth in paragraph (2), all of the following individuals have the responsibility to care for and maintain or financially assist an indigent person, regardless of whether the indigent person is a public charge:

(i) The spouse of the indigent person.

(ii) A child of the indigent person.

(iii) A parent of the indigent person.

(2) Paragraph (1) does not apply in any of the following cases:

(i) If an individual does not have sufficient financial ability to support the indigent person.

(ii) A child shall not be liable for the support of a parent who abandoned the child and persisted in the abandonment for a period of ten years during the child's minority.

Considering the above-quoted statutory language, the trial court made the following finding:

> We further find that [Appellant] has a sufficient financial ability to support [his mother], the indigent person. Specifically, the Act indicates at Section (a)(1)(ii) that the Child of the indigent person has a responsibility to care for and maintain or financially assist an indigent person. Section (a)(2)(i) indicates that the first paragraph does not apply if an individual does not have sufficient financial ability to support the indigent person. Set forth in this fashion, the Act appears to place the burden on the individual to establish that [he does] not have sufficient financial ability to support the indigent person. [Appellant] has not done that. His testimony was very general and he provided insufficient documentation. For example, he did not provide a specific statement as to all of his finances, income, expenses, assets, liabilities and things of this nature. This, together with his very general responses to questioning, causes the [trial court] to find him of low credibility and, therefore, we find none of his testimony to be truthful.

Based upon the above finding, Appellant argues that in construing Section 4603, the trial court improperly placed the burden upon him to affirmatively prove his inability to financially support his mother. Rather, Appellant argues that, pursuant to a plain reading of Section 4603, it was HCR's burden to prove that Appellant has the ability to pay for his indigent mother, not his burden to prove his inability to pay. . . .

HCR does not dispute that pursuant to Section 4603, it was obligated to establish Appellant's ability to pay for his indigent mother's expenses. . . . HCR maintains, however, that even accepting that burden, the record establishes that it provided sufficient evidence to establish Appellant's ability to support his indigent mother.

We agree with both parties that pursuant to the plain language of Section 4603, HCR, as movant, had the burden to establish Appellant's "financial ability to support" his indigent mother. . . .

As a result, we next consider HCR's claim that, even accepting that it had the burden to prove Appellant's financial ability to support his mother, HCR presented sufficient evidence to meet that burden. In support of this claim, HCR points out that it presented Appellant's 2005, 2006, 2007, and 2008 individual and "S" corporation joint tax returns, and bank account statements. In addition, HCR elicited testimony from Appellant that his net income was in excess of $85,000.00, and that he had recently paid-off a tax lien by making monthly payments of $1,100.00.

Considering all of the above, we hold that HCR fulfilled its burden to present sufficient evidence that Appellant has "sufficient financial ability to support [his] indigent [mother]." See 23 Pa. C.S.A. §4603. Indeed, at trial Appellant did not dispute the above evidence, but instead testified that he could not financially support his mother because of other bills. Appellant, however, failed to substantiate those other bills, and ultimately the trial court found his testimony lacked credibility. Considering that credibility determinations are for the discretion of the finder of fact (in this case the trial court), we do not find fault in the trial court's acceptance of HCR's evidence over that of Appellant's. Consequently, though Appellant is correct that it was HCR's burden to establish his ability to support his mother, we hold that HCR met its burden. As a result, Appellant's first request for a new trial is without merit.

Appellant's second issue on appeal claims that the trial court abused its discretion in refusing to consider alternative sources of income available to his mother before finding Appellant liable to HCR. According to Appellant, before finding him liable, the trial court was obligated to consider income sources such as his mother's husband, her two other grown children, and her application for medical assistance that was pending on appeal at the time. Failure to consider those other sources of income, Appellant argues, resulted in an abuse of discretion. Additionally, Appellant argues that, at the very least, determination of this filial matter was premature and should have been stayed pending disposition of his mother's appeal for medical assistance.

Appellant's argument, however, disregards the plain language of Section 4603. Nothing in that statute requires a movant or a court to consider other sources of income or to stay its determination pending the resolution of a claim for medical assistance. Consequently, we decline to read such requirements into the plain language or legislative intent for the statute. Indeed, while sympathetic with Appellant's obligation to support his mother without the assistance of his mother's husband or her other children, we note that if Appellant had desired to share his support-burden, he was permitted to do so by joining those individuals in this case. However, Appellant took no such action. Furthermore, Appellant admits that if his mother were to win her appeal and receive medical assistance, those funds will be used to relieve him of liability. Consequently, Appellant suffers no prejudice by the resolution of this issue prior to the conclusion of the medical assistance appeal. Therefore, we hold that Appellant's second issue is without merit.

Appellant's final issue on appeal claims that HCR presented insufficient evidence for the trial court to find that his mother is "indigent." What it means to be "indigent" is not defined within the applicable statute. Therefore, in applying Section 4603, our Courts have applied the common-law definition of indigence. In so doing, we have held that:

> the indigent person need not be helpless and in extreme want, so completely destitute of property, as to require assistance from the public. Indigent persons are those who do not have sufficient means to pay for their own care and maintenance. "Indigent" includes, but is not limited to, those who are completely destitute and helpless. It also encompasses those persons who have some limited means, but whose means are not sufficient to adequately provide for their maintenance and support.

Savoy v. Savoy, 433 Pa. Super. 549, 641 A.2d 596, 599-600 (1994).

In this matter, Appellant argues that the only evidence presented to the trial court regarding his mother's financial status was her bank statement and admission sheet when she entered the HCR facility. Such evidence, Appellant argues, did not provide the trial court with sufficient information to conclude that his mother is indigent. Consequently, Appellant seeks a reversal of the trial court's determination.

HCR disputes Appellant's challenge, arguing that his mother's bank statement established her social security income and her share of her husband's Veteran's Administration benefit. The combination of those incomes, HCR explains, results in a monthly income of only $1,000 a month, an insufficient amount to adequately provide for her maintenance and support. Furthermore, based upon her admission sheet, HCR argues that it is aware of no other income or assets available to Appellant's mother. Consequently, HCR maintains that it sufficiently established Appellant's mother's indigent status.

We agree. Considering the common law definition of indigent, and the evidence within the certified record, we do not believe that the trial court abused its discretion in finding Appellant's mother "indigent" within the meaning of Section 4603. The trial court considered Appellant's mother's sources of income and accurately determined that those sources of income are insufficient to adequately provide for her maintenance and support. Furthermore, while Appellant argues that HCR needed to present "more" evidence of his mother's indigence, we note that Appellant failed to establish that any such evidence exists; if his mother only has one bank statement, what more would Appellant like HCR to present? Indeed, Appellant presents sheer speculation, but no evidence to counter HCR's claims. Consequently, Appellant's argument in opposition does not overcome the evidence presented by HCR. As a result, Appellant's third issue is without merit.

Judgment affirmed.

NOTES

1. *Intra-family inequality.* One potential problem with filial responsibility statutes is that they may not be applied fairly either within or between families. The *Pittas* case illustrates the potential problem. After incurring the nursing home bill at issue, John Pittas's mother, Maryann, moved to Greece, where her other two children and husband also resided. John was the only immediate family member remaining in the country, and hence the target of the state's collection efforts. *See* Susanna Kim, *Pennsylvania Man Appeals to Court to Avoid Paying Mom's $93,000 Nursing Home Bill,* ABC News (May 23, 2012), *available at* http://abcnews.go.com/Business/pennsylvania-son-stuck-moms-93000-nursing-home-bill/story?id=16405807.

2. *Scope of filial responsibility laws.* In *State v. Flontek,* 693 N.E.2d 767 (Ohio 1998), the Supreme Court of Ohio considered whether an involuntary murder charge could be predicated on Ohio's filial responsibility statute. The case concerned a daughter who was found guilty of non-support of a dependent and involuntary manslaughter after her elderly mother, with whom she resided, died as a result of what the coroner concluded was

"gross physical neglect." The court found that the "support obligation" in Ohio's filial responsibility law was limited to financial support and thus the daughter, who had provided financial support, could not be held criminally liable under the statute for failing to provide non-financial support. In reaching this conclusion, the court reasoned that:

> [A]n expansive interpretation of [the state's filial responsibility law] . . . could result in continued unwarranted prosecutions of adult children who have elderly parents who may be in need of medical attention or care but have refused to seek treatment for their conditions. The problem is even further compounded if the adult child is separated geographically from his or her elderly parent. Hence, we can only presume that the General Assembly . . . was aware of the endless problems that could possibly arise if the term "support" was intended to include nonfinancial factors. . . . Indeed, we do not believe that the General Assembly intended to place adult children in such untenable situations and create fertile grounds for unreasonable and excessive prosecutions. . . . Absent further guidance by the General Assembly in this area, an adult child's duty in these types of cases rests upon a moral obligation, not an obligation enforceable by law.

Id. at 771.

3. *Other forms of support.* In *Swoap* and *Pittas*, the courts considered the duty of adult children to support their parents financially. The duty to provide financial support should not be confused with a duty to provide in-kind support such as personal services or emotional support. Duties to provide non-financial support, to the extent that they exist, are typically limited to the duty of caregivers not to neglect individuals for whom they have assumed responsibility. These duties are discussed further in Chapter 8, which addresses elder abuse and neglect.

4. *Frequency of enforcement.* Professor Katherine Pearson's research on state filial responsibility laws suggests that, except in Pennsylvania and South Dakota, such laws are rarely enforced. She predicts, however, that enforcement actions may increase as the aging of the Baby Boom generation leads to further increases in the costs associated with health care and long-term care. *See* Katherine C. Pearson, *Filial Support Laws: A Comparison*, 20 ELDER L.J. 269 (2013). *See also* Seymour Moskowitz, *Filial Responsibility Statutes: Legal & Policy Considerations*, 9 J.L. & POL'Y 709, 716-18 (2001) (providing an overview of filial responsibility laws in the United States and noting that their enforcement is sporadic).

5. *China's expansive approach to filial support.* In 2013, media around the world reported, with some incredulity, that China had passed a law requiring children to visit and care for their parents. The reports were prompted by China's decision to amend its Law of Protection of Rights and Interests of the Elderly to require children of parents age 60 and over to visit their parents "frequently." At the time the law was amended, it already required adult children to provide financial support and care for their parents age 60

and older, and allowed such parents to seek "alimony" from children who failed to satisfy their duties.

EXERCISE 5.1

After law school, you take a job as chief policy advisor to the Health and Human Services committee of the State of Northern Virginia. Currently, the State of Northern Virginia does not have a filial responsibility law. The Committee is considering adopting such a law.

a. Please advise the Committee as to whether or not they should adopt a filial support law and why.

b. After (and perhaps despite of) considering your advice, the Chair of the Committee has decided that she wishes to propose a bill creating a filial support law for the State of Northern Virginia. She has asked you to draft the new law. Please draft an ideal filial responsibility law for the Chair.

F. OTHER SOURCES OF INCOME

1. Supplemental Security Income (SSI)

Supplemental Security Income (SSI) is a public benefit administered by the Social Security Administration. Approximately 2 million Americans age 65 and older receive SSI and many more are eligible for SSI but do not receive it because they have failed to apply for it.

Younger adults are only eligible for SSI if they are injured or disabled. Persons age 65 and older, however, can be eligible for SSI simply because they are impoverished. Specifically, to qualify for SSI, an older adult must meet both an income test and a resource test.

In order to be eligible for SSI in 2013, an individual living alone could have a countable monthly income of less than $710, and a couple could have a countable monthly income of less than $1,066. Most forms of income are considered "countable." This includes earned income (e.g., wages, self-employment earnings, and royalties), unearned income (e.g., OASDI benefits, pensions, interest income, cash gifts), and in-kind income (e.g., food or shelter provided for less than fair market value). However, there are a number of types of income that are not considered countable income. They include, among other things:

- The first $20 of most income received in a month;
- The first $65 of earnings and one-half of earnings over $65 received in a month;

- Supplemental Nutrition Assistance Program (SNAP) benefits (commonly called "food stamps");
- Income tax refunds;
- Home energy assistance;
- Need-based assistance funded by a state or local government;
- Small amounts of income received irregularly or infrequently;
- Food or shelter based on need provided by nonprofit agencies;
- Loans that require repayment; and
- Third-party payments of expenses for items other than food or shelter.

To meet the resource test, an individual must have no more than $2,000 in countable resources, and a couple must have no more than $3,000 in countable resources. The cap for the resource test has remained stagnant for some time; despite inflation, it has not been raised in a number of years. It is important to distinguish between countable and exempt resources. A number of resources are exempt for SSI purposes. They include:

- A person's home and the land it is located on;
- Household goods and personal effects;
- Wedding and engagement rings;
- Burial plots for a beneficiary and his or her immediate family;
- A burial fund of up to $1,500 per spouse;
- Life insurance policies with a combined value of $1,500 or less;
- A vehicle, regardless of its value, if used for necessary transportation; and
- Retroactive SSI or OASDI benefits for up to nine months after they are received.

Qualifying for SSI is important for many older adults not simply because doing so provides them with extra income, but also because qualifying for SSI can lead to eligibility for other important benefits. For example, in most states, a person who becomes eligible for SSI will automatically become eligible for Medicaid and food stamps.

PROBLEM

Mr. and Mrs. Brown, both 70, live together in their fully owned home. Their adult daughter, Shelly, lives with them and pays them $80 a month in rent. Both Mr. and Mrs. Brown are retired. Mrs. Brown, however, occasionally babysits for her neighbor's seven-year-old. On average, she earns about $50 a month from such babysitting. The Browns own a 2006 Ford Escort, which they use primarily for trips to the grocery store and to their doctors' offices. They also own a 2002 GM mini-van, which they use only when family comes to visit. They have $2,700 in the bank, and generally keep about $50 cash on hand. Are Mr. and Mrs. Brown eligible for SSI? If so, how could Mr. and Mrs. Brown maximize their SSI benefits?

2. Military Retirement Benefits and Veterans' Pensions

The military maintains a complex system of retirement benefits for its members. As part of that system, service members are entitled to regular retirement benefits after completing 20 years of active service or after being retired for medical reasons.

In addition, pension benefits are available to low-income veterans who have served during a war time period. Specifically, pensions are available through the Veteran's Administration to low-income veterans who served during a war time period if they are (1) 65 years of age and older or (2) permanently and totally disabled. To qualify as a "veteran," the individual must not have been dishonorably discharged and must have served for a sufficient period of time (90 days or, for veterans who entered active duty after September 7, 1980, generally either 24 months or the full period they were called to active duty). Income eligibility thresholds vary depending on both the number of dependents that the veteran has and the veteran's disability status.

CHAPTER 6

Financing Health Care

A. INTRODUCTION

Health care is a concern for people of all ages. It is a special concern for older people, however, because they tend to utilize greater amounts of health care services. This means that they also tend to incur larger health care expenses, as illustrated by the below chart based on figures from the U.S. Bureau of Labor Statistics.

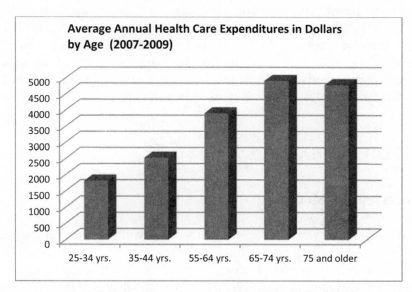

Source: Figures taken from U.S. Census Data: Statistical Abstract of the U.S. (2012 report), Table 143.

As a result of this increase in utilization, access to health care and access to sources of payment to cover health care expenses are important concerns for older adults.

While those with higher income and greater levels of education tend to use more health care than those with lower incomes and lower levels of education, health care costs are typically especially burdensome for those at the lower end of the income spectrum because those costs represent a significantly larger portion of their total income. A 2010 report by the Urban Institute found that though the bottom quintile of persons age 65 and older spend 21 percent of their income on health care, the middle quintile spend 12 percent while the top quintile spends only 5 percent; the Report predicted that this disparity will increase significantly in future decades. *See* RICHARD W. JOHNSON & CORINA MOMMAERTS, URBAN INSTITUTE, WILL HEALTH CARE COSTS BANKRUPT AGING BOOMERS? (2010).

Given the centrality of health care concerns later in life, it is important that elder law attorneys understand health care benefit issues and how to help clients achieve eligibility for various types of health care benefits. This is especially true for elder law attorneys who represent poor people and clients of modest means. This chapter therefore explores the two primary public systems that provide health care coverage for older adults: Medicare and Medicaid. Although Medicare and Medicaid are both administered by the Centers for Medicare and Medicaid Services (CMS), which is part of the U.S. Department of Health and Human Services (HHS), they are very different programs. Medicare is available to older adults regardless of their financial status, whereas Medicaid is a means-tested program intended as part of the government's "safety net" for poor people. Moreover, Medicare is a primarily age-based program, whereas Medicaid is not an age-based program and older beneficiaries constitute only a minority of Medicaid enrollees.

This chapter explores how one obtains eligibility for Medicare and Medicaid, what the programs provide and under what conditions, and how one can appeal adverse decisions. It also discusses other sources of health care payment, including employer-based health care plans.

B. MEDICARE

1. Overview of Medicare

Medicare is the primary source of health care insurance for persons age 65 and older. Indeed, over 45 million Americans are covered by Medicare. While Medicare is a central feature of the U.S. health care system, it did not come into existence until 1966, a year after it was signed into law as part of the Social Security Amendments of 1965. Consistent with this history, the statutory basis for Medicare is found in Title XVIII of the Social Security Act.

It is important to recognize that Medicare does not pay all health care costs for beneficiaries. Medicare beneficiaries are typically responsible for a variety of co-payments and deductibles. In addition, some forms of care are simply not covered. These include experimental treatments, treatments that the Medicare program determines are not reasonable and necessary, and long-term care.

2. The Four Parts of Medicare

Medicare in its current form consists of four separate components: Medicare Part A (commonly called *hospital insurance*), Medicare Part B (commonly called *medical insurance, supplemental medical insurance*, or SMI), Medicare Part C (a managed care option currently called *Medicare Advantage*), and Medicare Part D (the *prescription drug benefit*).

Medicare is financed by a combination of a dedicated tax and beneficiary premiums. Medicare Parts B and D are financed from general tax revenues as well as premiums from the majority of beneficiaries. Medicare Part A is financed by a dedicated tax and premiums contributed by beneficiaries who would not otherwise qualify for Part A coverage. Employed individuals generally pay a 1.45 percent tax on wages and salaries, and employers contribute a matching 1.45 percent tax. Self-employed individuals, by contrast, generally pay 2.9 percent of net self-employment income. Starting in 2013, however, the employee's share increased by 0.9 percent to 2.35 percent on income in excess of $200,000 per year for single individuals, $250,000 for married couples who file joint tax returns, or $125,000 for married taxpayers who file separate tax returns. In addition, although the dedicated tax has historically applied only to earned income, starting in 2013, persons with modified adjusted gross income in excess of the above amounts were subject to a tax on net investment income.

Although an understanding of how the different components of Medicare are financed is critical to understanding the Medicare system, elder law attorneys representing clients on Medicare-related issues typically are concerned not with whether their clients have established eligibility for Medicare, but rather with whether their clients have been improperly denied Medicare coverage for a particular service. Accordingly, this section focuses on the eligibility criteria for each part of Medicare and the benefits provided by each. Special attention is paid to the home health benefit as it is of critical importance to many beneficiaries.

a. Medicare Part A

To be eligible for Medicare Part A, an individual must either:

■ Be at least 65 years old and have paid for Medicare Part A either by (a) previously paying for 40 quarters of coverage through earlier employment taxes; (b) previously "paying" for 40 quarters of coverage through a spouse's employment taxes or an ex-spouse's employment taxes (if the marriage lasted at least 10 years); or (c) currently paying a monthly premium for Part A coverage;

- ▪ Be afflicted with end-stage renal disease and in need of dialysis or kidney transplant; or
- ▪ Be disabled within the meaning of the Social Security Act for at least 24 months.

For those who obtain eligibility through a combination of age and premium payments, the amount of the payments depends on the number of quarters that they are deficient. Those who have more covered quarters pay lower premiums.

Medicare Part A provides coverage for a wide range of services including:

- ▪ Inpatient care in a hospital or religious, nonmedical health care institution. This includes coverage for a semi-private room, meals, general nursing care, drugs provided in the course of inpatient care, and other hospital services and supplies.
- ▪ Inpatient rehabilitative care in a skilled nursing facility for up to 100 days. To qualify for this coverage, a beneficiary must first have a qualifying three-day hospital stay within 30 days of the admission to the nursing facility and receive care in the nursing facility for a condition that was treated during that hospital stay. Coverage includes a semi-private room, meals, skilled nursing and rehabilitative services (e.g., physical therapy and occupational therapy services), and other services and supplies. It does not, by contrast, include long-term or custodial nursing home care.
- ▪ Certain home health care services (discussed later in this chapter).
- ▪ Hospice services (discussed in Chapter 9).
- ▪ Blood as medically necessary.

To offset some of the costs of the Medicare program, Medicare Part A has a significant cost-sharing element. Specifically, beneficiaries are expected to engage in two forms of cost-sharing. First, benefits are subject to a deductible ($1,184 in 2013) for each "spell of illness." Second, beneficiaries have *co-insurance payments* (sometimes simply referred to as "co-pays") due for certain services. The most significant co-pays are those for skilled nursing care and those for inpatient hospital care. In 2013, the co-pay for skilled nursing care was $148 per day for days 21-100 of a qualifying stay (with no co-pay for the first 20 days). In 2013, the co-pay for inpatient hospital care was:

- ▪ A total of $1,184 for a hospital stay of 1-60 days.
- ▪ $296 per day for days 61-90 of a hospital stay.
- ▪ $592 per day for days 91-150 of a hospital stay.
- ▪ All costs for each day beyond 150 days.

Notably, days 91-150 are *lifetime reserve days*. This means they can only be used once. Thus, if Mrs. Longstay's first Medicare-covered hospital stay lasts 120 days, she will only have 30 remaining lifetime reserve days. These may be used during a single stay or divided among multiple stays.

NOTE

Observation status. Patients typically assume that if they stay overnight in a hospital, they have been admitted to the hospital and are an inpatient. However, CMS permits hospitals to classify some patients as "observation status" patients and not as inpatients. Moreover, even if a patient has been admitted to a hospital, that hospital is permitted (under certain circumstances) to retroactively reclassify the stay as providing merely observation services. In recent years, hospitals have increasingly been classifying patients who are Medicare beneficiaries as "observation status" because hospitals face financial penalties if they admit Medicare beneficiaries whose care could have been provided in an outpatient setting. Being classified as "observation status" (and not as a hospital inpatient) has significant, negative consequences for Medicare beneficiaries. It means that they may be ineligible for Medicare coverage for subsequent care at a nursing home, and that the services they are provided in the hospital are subject to coverage under Medicare Part B and not Medicare Part A (resulting in higher costs for home health benefits and potentially no coverage for certain other services such as prescription drugs provided in the hospital). As of the time of publication, the Center for Medicare Advocacy was challenging CMS's current observation status rule in court, and CMS had proposed a new rule limiting the use of observation status. Even under the proposed rule, however, hospitals would not be required to notify patients when they are placed on observation status.

b. Medicare Part B

To be eligible for Medicare Part B, an individual must generally pay a monthly premium. Most beneficiaries pay a standard premium, the amount of which increases annually. In 2013, the standard premium was $104.90 per month. High income individuals, however, are required to pay an enhanced premium. In 2013, enhanced premiums applied to beneficiaries who filed an individual tax return with annual income above $85,000, and beneficiaries who filed a joint tax return with annual income above $170,000. Enhanced premiums in 2013 ranged from $146.90 to $335.70, depending on income level. The highest premium level only applied to individual tax return filers with annual income above $214,000, and joint tax return filers with annual income above $428,000. Notably, the premium requirements are in addition to a small annual deductible ($147 in 2013).

In addition to paying a premium, to be eligible for Medicare Part B, the individual must:

- Be age 65 or older; or
- Be afflicted with end-stage renal disease and in need of dialysis treatment or kidney transplant; or
- Be disabled within the meaning of the Social Security Act for at least 24 months.

Part B covers a wide range of services including physicians' services (whether they are provided while a beneficiary is hospitalized or outpatient), other outpatient care, and certain home health services. Each benefit has its own set of eligibility criteria. In addition, care is only covered to the extent deemed reasonable and necessary by the Secretary of HHS.

Medicare beneficiaries are expected to make co-payments for most services they receive under Medicare Part B. The amount of the co-payment will depend, in part, on whether the beneficiary's provider has chosen to "participate" in the Medicare program. A participating provider is one who has elected to accept a specific fee schedule for all Medicare claims. A participating physician is said to "accept assignment." If the beneficiary obtains services from a participating physician, Medicare will directly pay the physician 80 percent of the "scheduled" or standard fee, and the beneficiary will be expected to pay the remaining 20 percent of that fee. If the physician is not a participating physician, he or she is entitled to charge the patient up to 115 percent of Medicare's approved fee for the service. Medicare will send 80 percent of the scheduled fee to the beneficiary, who will be billed directly by the physician for both Medicare's share and the remaining sum.

A physician is only allowed to charge a Medicare beneficiary more than 115 percent of the Medicare approved fee if he or she satisfies the provisions set forth in 42 U.S.C. §1395a (provisions referred to as the *Kyl Amendment* of 1997). Under the Kyl Amendment, a physician may privately contract with a Medicare beneficiary to charge an amount in excess of the Medicare approved rate only if the two enter into a written contract prior to the provision of the service, the contract specifies the patient's responsibilities and explicitly informs the patient that Medicare's fee limits will not apply, and the contract is not entered into when the beneficiary is "facing an emergency or urgent health care situation." *See* 42 U.S.C. §1395a. A physician who opts to engage in the type of private contracting permitted by the Kyl Amendment agrees not to accept any Medicare money for two years.

PROBLEMS

1. Mrs. Smith is a Medicare beneficiary who is enrolled in both Medicare Part A and Medicare Part B. Identify which part, if either, covers the following:

   a. Mrs. Smith goes to the primary care physician for her semi-annual check-up.

   b. Mrs. Smith suffers a stroke and is hospitalized. Her bill includes costs for:

      i. Room and board in the hospital,

      ii. Lab work in hospital,

      iii. Medications in the hospital,

      iv. Being seen by her doctor while in the hospital, and

      v. A walker that she is given to use in the hospital.

c. Mrs. Smith returns home after her hospital stay. There, she receives the following services:

  i. In-home physical therapy to help her regain her ability to walk, and

  ii. A four-pronged cane to assist her while walking.

d. Mrs. Smith falls in her house. She is rushed to the emergency room and receives five stitches. She returns home the same day.

e. Mrs. Smith goes to her optometrist. Her bill includes costs for:

  i. Her eye exam, and

  ii. A new pair of prescription glasses.

f. Mrs. Smith goes to her dentist. Her bill includes costs for:

  i. Her regular dental cleaning, and

  ii. A root canal.

2. Why does it matter whether Mrs. Smith's care in the above problem is covered under Part A or Part B. Why might she prefer coverage under one or the other?

c. Medicare Part C

Medicare Part C, currently called Medicare Advantage, is a managed care option. Beneficiaries who elect to use this option select a plan from a non-governmental health care insurance provider. This provider then assumes responsibility for providing the type of benefits offered under Medicare Parts A and B, and, if the beneficiary chooses, under Medicare Part D.

Beneficiaries may opt for a Medicare Advantage plan over traditional Medicare for any number of reasons, but the most common reasons are that the Medicare Advantage plan offers benefits or services (e.g., fitness services, coverage for eyeglasses) that traditional Medicare does not, or that the plan has lower deductibles or co-payment requirements.

There are a broad range of different types of Medicare Advantage plans. They include:

- **Medicare Health Maintenance Organizations (HMOs):** Beneficiaries are generally required to use only doctors, hospitals, and other providers that are part of the HMO's network, although some HMOs may cover out-of-network care at a reduced benefit rate.

- **Medicare Preferred Provider Organizations (PPOs):** Medicare PPOs are very similar to Medicare HMOs, with two key exceptions: (1) they cover some of the cost of out-of-network care, and (2) they generally do not require the beneficiary to see a primary care physician prior to seeing a specialist.

- **Private Fee-for-Service (PFFS) Plans:** Beneficiaries who enroll in these plans can obtain coverage for the services of any physician or health care provider who participates in the plan. These plans differ from Medicare HMOs and Medicare PPOs in that they do not have their own formal networks, but instead rely on providers who decide to participate with them.

■ **Medicare Special Needs Plans (SNPs):** Beneficiaries with special needs—such as nursing home residents or those with serious chronic conditions—may opt to enroll in a Medicare Special Needs Plan.

■ **Medicare Medical Savings Account (MSAs):** Beneficiaries have the option of managing their health care dollars directly by enrolling in a Medicare Medical Savings Account. Beneficiaries who enroll in this option will have two mechanisms for paying for their health care: (1) a high-deductible health insurance plan, and (2) a savings account into which the plan deposits a set amount that the beneficiary can use to pay for qualified health care expenses (including their deductible). Monies remaining in the account at the end of the calendar year may be "rolled over" to cover future health care costs. MSAs do not cover Medicare Part D benefits, although a beneficiary can enroll in both a MSA and a Part D plan.

For decades, the Medicare program has contracted with private health plans wishing to offer Medicare beneficiaries a Medicare managed care option. This option was redesigned in 2003 and, at that time, renamed "Medicare Advantage." In order to encourage enrollment in Medicare Advantage plans, Congress offered generous reimbursement rates to those who offered them. This resulted in such plans being paid, on average, more per beneficiary than Medicare spent for its non-managed care beneficiaries. This, in turn, allowed Medicare Advantage programs to offer benefits that have attracted growing numbers of beneficiaries. According to the Kaiser Family Foundation, in 2013, there were 14.4 million Medicare beneficiaries (or 28% of the Medicare population) enrolled in Medicare Advantage plans, an increase of 30% from 2010. Enrollments vary significantly among states (ranging from 49 percent in 2013 in Minnesota to less than 1 percent in 2013 in Alaska) and among counties. Enrollment also varies by community type, with higher enrollment in urban settings than in rural ones. *See* Kaiser Family Foundation, *Medicare Advantage 2013 Spotlight: Enrollment Market Updates* (June 2013), *available at*: http://kff.org/medicare/issue-brief/medicare-advantage-2013-spotlight-enrollment-market-update/.

The high reimbursement rates for Medicare Advantage led to significant criticism of the program. Consider, for example, Professor Timothy McBride's 2007 critique of the illusory nature of Medicare Advantage's promised cost savings:

> Although the M[edicare] A[dvantage] [(MA)] plans were designed to reduce Medicare spending, especially the growth in Medicare spending, evidence emerged in 2007 showing that, on average, MA plans were paid 112% of the mean costs of covering a traditional Medicare recipient. [Private Fee-for-Service Plans (PFFS)] were the most overpaid, receiving payments

equal to 119% of traditional Medicare [Fee-for-Service (FFS)] costs. In addition, the Congressional Budget Office (CBO) estimates that if MA plans were paid at 100% of FFS costs, then Medicare spending would be reduced by "$54 billion over the 2009-2012 period and $149 billion over the 2009-2017 period." . . .

Medicare's private plans were expected originally to lower Medicare costs because, at the time they were introduced, the costs of managed care plans were lower than the costs of traditional FFS plans. This expectation was based on the theory established when Congress created the Medicare risk contract program, namely to pay Medicare HMOs at 95% of the adjusted average per capita cost (AAPCC). Thus, the expectation was that these plans would cost 5% less than traditional Medicare FFS. However, the current payment rate, 112% of traditional Medicare FFS, indicates that managed care is not leading to 5% savings but, instead, to 12% higher costs. The Medicare Trustees also confirm that shifting Medicare beneficiaries to MA plans does not lead to considerable savings, since they currently are assuming that shifting beneficiaries from traditional Medicare FFS to MA plans will save just 0.03% annually in the long run.

Timothy D. McBride, *Medicare Advantage: What Are We Trying to Achieve Anyway?*, 1 St. Louis U. J. Health L. & Pol'y 405, 418-19 (2007).

In 2010, Congress addressed these financial concerns by making changes to Medicare Part C as part of its broader health reform efforts. Specifically, Congress changed the methodology that CMS uses to determine how much Medicare Advantage programs are paid. Under the new system, Medicare Advantage program's payments vary based, in part, on whether they meet quality targets. These changes were anticipated to significantly reduce projected spending on Medicare Part C. Some early research on the effects of the changes suggests that reducing overpayment to Medicare Advantage plans has led to a reduction in the number of plans available to Medicare beneficiaries (primarily in regions with higher per-enrollee costs prior to the changes), but has not resulted in fewer beneficiaries enrolling in Medicare Advantage plans. *See* Christopher C. Afendulis et al., *The Impact of the Affordable Care Act on Medicare Advantage Plan Availability and Enrollment*, 47 Health Serv. Res. J. 2339 (2012).

d. Medicare Part D

Traditionally, Medicare did not provide coverage for prescription drugs outside of inpatient care settings. The Medicare Modernization Act of 2003 changed that by introducing Medicare Part D, which provides prescription drug coverage to Medicare beneficiaries. The controversial act was promoted as a way of reducing older adults' out-of-pocket prescription drug costs, thereby reducing the likelihood that they would fail to take—or skip doses of—medically necessary drugs.

Like Medicare Part C, Medicare Part D is a market-based program through which CMS contracts with private entities to provide benefits and services to Medicare beneficiaries. A Medicare beneficiary can obtain Part D coverage either through a Medicare Advantage Plan or by selecting an independent *prescription drug plan* (PDP). Plans have significant flexibility in structuring the benefit that they offer. They can elect to provide either a standard benefit set by the federal government, or they can provide (subject to CMS approval) a benefit that is the actuarial equivalent of the standard benefit.

Consistent with this privatized approach, Medicare Part D plans differ in a number of ways, including:

- *Premiums:* Does the plan require a monthly premium? If so, what is the cost?
- *Co-payment requirements:* What are the co-payment requirements and how do they differ between different classes of drugs?
- *Deductibles:* Does the plan have a deductible? If so, how does the deductible work?
- *Coverage gaps:* Is coverage suspended after the beneficiary has incurred a certain amount of annual expenses, and, if so, at what level of spending does coverage resume?
- *Formularies:* What medications does the plan cover?
- *Step therapy requirements:* Does the plan require a beneficiary to try lower-cost drugs before receiving higher-cost ones? If so, under what conditions?
- *Procedures:* If the beneficiary needs a drug that is normally not covered by the plan, or normally is not covered without step therapy, what is the process for requesting an exception to the plan's standard policy?

Because of the significant variance among plans, choosing a Medicare Part D plan can be a time-consuming process for beneficiaries.

Each Part D plan must, under certain conditions, grant a beneficiary an exception to certain plan rules. For example, each plan can create its own *formulary*, or list of drugs that it will cover; however, a plan must cover a drug that is not within its formulary when the requested drug is "medically necessary" and "would be covered but for the fact that it is an off-formulary drug." 42 C.F.R. §423.578(b) (2009). Similarly, plans are required to have a process to allow exceptions to step therapy requirements. Such exceptions, however, may only be made if a prescribing physician or other prescriber states that the requested drug would be more effective, or have a less adverse effect, than the drug preferred by the Part D plan for the patient's condition.

PROBLEM

Mr. Dahl enrolled in a Medicare Part D plan offered by Excellment, a private company.

When he went to refill his prescriptions, he found he could not get one because it is not on the plan's formulary, he could not get another medication because he is required to try a less expensive drug first, and he could not get a third because he is required to obtain prior authorization. What, if anything, can and should Mr. Dahl do about these problems?

EXERCISE 6.1

To facilitate the process of selecting a PDP, CMS has created an online tool that allows beneficiaries to compare plans based on their individual needs. The tool is available at www.medicare.gov. Suppose you are a Medicare beneficiary trying to select a Medicare Part D plan. You currently take one baby aspirin every night, a tablet of Aricept before bed, one small Ativan pill four times a day, and one 20 mg pill of Lipitor once a day. Using Medicare's prescription drug plan finder application, try to determine which of the plans available to persons living in your county is the best for you. What challenges do you face in doing so?

3. Paying for Out-of-Pocket Costs

As should be apparent from the above subsections, Medicare does not pay all of its beneficiaries' medical expenses.

Beneficiaries may therefore wish to purchase private insurance to cover some of the expenses that Medicare does not. Medicare Supplement Insurance, commonly called *Medigap*, is insurance that covers the "gaps" in traditional Medicare by paying for some costs that Medicare beneficiaries not enrolled in a Medicare Advantage plan would otherwise have to pay out-of-pocket. Medigap is sometimes called *wraparound* insurance, reflecting the fact that it is used in conjunction with Medicare. Unlike insurance options under Medicare Part C or Part D, Medigap insurance plans are standardized by law. In most states (Massachusetts, Minnesota, and Wisconsin have a different structure for their Medigap plans), beneficiaries can select from one of 11 plans. All of the standard plans cover the hospital co-insurance payments under Medicare Part A. All also pay for all or some Medicare Part B co-insurance payments, out-of-pocket blood costs, and hospice co-payments. Depending on the plan, Medigap insurance may also cover such costs as skilled nursing facility co-payments, Part A or Part B deductibles, and emergency care outside of the United States.

Low-income Medicare beneficiaries may qualify for a *Medicare Savings Program*—a type of federal program that can help them pay for some or all of the out-of-pocket expenses associated with Medicare Parts A and B. There are three types of Medicare Savings Programs: (1) the *Qualified Medicare Beneficiary* program (QMB), (2) the *Specified Low-Income Medicare Beneficiary* program (SLMB), and (3) the *Qualified Individual* program (QI). All are designed to help lower-income beneficiaries afford Medicare's cost-sharing requirements. Each has its own income guidelines, which change annually. Depending on the state in which the beneficiary resides, such benefits may be limited to people with assets below a set amount. To obtain assistance through the QMB, SLMB, or QI programs, beneficiaries should apply through their local department of social services.

The most generous Medicare Savings Program, the QMB program, pays for Medicare Part A premiums for those who owe them, the Medicare Part B premium, the Medicare Part B annual deductible, and co-payments and deductibles for services under both Medicare Parts A and B. The SLMB program, by contrast, only covers Part B premiums. Beneficiaries can qualify for the SLMB program if they have income between 100 percent and 120 percent of the federal poverty level. The QI program expands the benefits of the SLMB program—that is, coverage of Part B premiums—to persons whose income is between 120 percent and 135 percent of the federal poverty level.

Subsidies are also available to help pay for Medicare Part D expenses. Persons who are eligible for both Medicare and Medicaid (called *dual eligibles*) are eligible for Part D coverage without paying premiums or deductibles, and have only limited co-payments. In addition, individuals who are not Medicaid eligible, but who nevertheless have limited income and resources, may be eligible for the federal government's *Extra Help* program, under which the government helps pay for Part D premiums, deductibles, and co-payments.

Medigap insurance, the Medicare Savings Program, dual eligibility for the Medicaid program, and the Extra Help program all reduce the effect of Medicare's cost-sharing mechanisms on beneficiaries. The result is that beneficiaries will tend to be less price-sensitive than they would be without these programs. Whether or not reduced price sensitivity is desirable is the subject of significant debate. On one hand, research suggests that programs that help Medicare beneficiaries pay for out-of-pocket costs increase the rate at which beneficiaries utilize health care. This is because those without supplemental insurance are more hesitant to seek medical care than those with such insurance. The concern is that these higher rates of utilization will increase health care costs, including costs for unnecessary health care services. On the other hand, supplemental insurance programs appear to reduce certain costs by encouraging beneficiaries to seek basic care and early interventions, which help them to avoid more costly interventions later on. For example, supplemental insurance programs appear to make it easier for those with chronic conditions to better manage those conditions, thus reducing the likelihood that they will develop more acute and serious problems. Therefore, especially for low-income beneficiaries, increasing cost-sharing appears to promote the utilization of fewer, but more expensive, health care interventions.

4. Medicare Appeals Process

The Centers for Medicare and Medicaid Services (CMS), the agency within the U.S. Department of Health and Human Services that is responsible for administering the Medicare program, enters into agreements with private contractors who directly administer much of the program. These contractors—often called fiscal intermediaries—are typically insurance companies. They are responsible for making initial claim determinations as to whether a given service is covered under Medicare Part A or Medicare Part B.

If a beneficiary disagrees with an intermediary's decision, he or she has 120 days to initiate an appeals process by requesting a *redetermination* by the intermediary. If the beneficiary is unsatisfied by the resulting redetermination, within the next 180 days, he or she can seek a subsequent redetermination from a *qualified independent contractor* (QIC). If the beneficiary wishes to appeal the QIC determination, and the amount in controversy exceeds a minimum threshold ($140 in 2013), the beneficiary may request a hearing before an *Administrative Law Judge* (ALJ). The request for an ALJ hearing must generally be made within 60 days of the QIC determination. An ALJ hearing provides the beneficiary the opportunity to present new evidence and to conduct discovery if the intermediary elects to participate in the hearing process. The ALJ's determination, in turn, can be appealed to the Medicare Appeals Council (MAC) so long as the appeal is made within 60 days of the ALJ decision. Only after the MAC has issued a decision or declined review, and only if the amount in controversy exceeds a minimum threshold ($1,400 in 2013), may the beneficiary seek review in federal court.

The redetermination and appeals processes are typically slow. However, a beneficiary is entitled to an expedited appeal process when the beneficiary faces a discontinuation of certain types of services for lack of—or believed lack of—Medicare coverage. Specifically, a beneficiary may challenge termination of Medicare-covered services from a hospital, skilled nursing facility, home health agency, rehabilitation facility, or hospice by requesting review by a *Quality Improvement Organization* (QIO). QIOs are organizations that specifically contract with CMS to provide expedited determinations for beneficiaries challenging such terminations.

When a beneficiary timely requests QIO review of termination of services, the beneficiary is entitled to a review within 72 hours and, if that review is unfavorable, a QIC redetermination review within another 72 hours. Such requests for review commonly arise where a Medicare beneficiary is challenging his or her discharge from a hospital on the grounds that (contrary to the hospital's position) the beneficiary still needs hospital-level care. The beneficiary cannot be charged for the disputed care during the time the QIO is reviewing the case. However, should the beneficiary lose the appeal, he or she may be required to pay for the cost of care received after the services were scheduled to end.

A truncated review process is also available where the beneficiary is challenging a denial of Medicare coverage on constitutional grounds. If the challenge is based on such grounds, the beneficiary can skip both the ALJ and MAC stages of review.

Notably, although ALJ decisions reversing those made at the QIC level are common, the MAC rarely reverses ALJ decisions. According to the Center for Medicare Advocacy:

> Suggesting the MACs have a rubber stamp denial rate is hardly an exaggeration. In fact, of the 2,045 redetermination decisions received by the Center last quarter for skilled nursing facility and home health care, the Medicare Contractors granted coverage in only 3 cases. Yet, our general experience is that

at least half of cases that are brought to the Administrative Law Judge (ALJ) level in fact receive coverage. This cannot possibly reflect a full and fair review of the facts of each case in light of Medicare coverage criteria. Adding insult to injury, in some instances, the MACs actually take back coverage that was previously granted. This occurs, for example, in situations where some, but not all, of the services during a home health episode were previously covered by Medicare. In such cases, the MAC may not only deny an appeal for the rest of the episode, but also retract coverage that was previously provided.

Comments Submitted to the Senate Finance Committee re: Medicare Fraud, CENTER FOR MEDICARE ADVOCACY (June 2012), *available at* http://www.medicare advocacy.org/october-2012-updates-on-medicare-appeals-and-complaints/.

Beneficiaries enrolled in a Medicare Advantage plan, as well as those challenging decisions made by a Part D plan, face a slightly different appeals process. Initial coverage decisions for Medicare Advantage and Part D are made by the beneficiary's plan. If the beneficiary is dissatisfied with the determination, he or she can request reconsideration by the plan. If the beneficiary is still dissatisfied, he or she may request reconsideration by an *Independent Review Entity* (IRE), an organization contracted by CMS that provides a parallel service to that provided by QICs for Part A and Part B appeals. Only after this step may the beneficiary appeal to an ALJ. From the ALJ stage onwards, the process parallels that for appeals under Medicare Parts A and B.

The below graphic, provided by the Office of Medicare Hearings and Appeals (www.hhs.gov/omha), provides a visual overview of the Medicare appeals process.

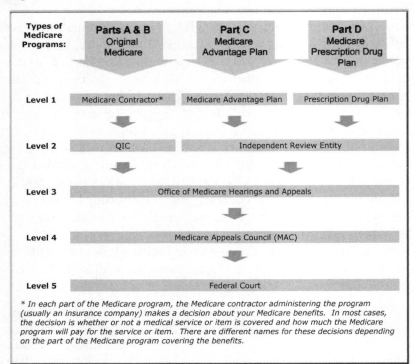

5. Limitations on Coverage

As a general matter, Medicare will only pay for care provided by Medicare-eligible providers and care that the Secretary of HHS deems "reasonable and necessary." Medicare Advantage beneficiaries also face additional limitations on their coverage as a result of their care management. In addition, there are specific eligibility criteria for various Medicare services such as hospice care (as discussed in Chapter 9) and home health care (as is discussed in Section B.6 of this chapter).

a. Traditional Medicare Limitations

Smith v. Thompson

210 F. Supp. 2d 994 (N.D. Ill. 2002)

ORDER ADOPTING REPORT AND RECOMMENDATION

GOTTSCHALL, District Judge.

Neither party filed timely objections to Magistrate Judge Ashman's report and recommendation. . . . Final judgment in favor of defendant is entered.

REPORT AND RECOMMENDATION

ASHMAN, United States Magistrate Judge.

Fred Smith seeks judicial review of the Secretary's decision to deny Medicare coverage of claims concerning a surgical procedure known as cryosurgical ablation of the prostate. The Administrative Law Judge (the "ALJ") denied the claims because cryosurgery was "not reasonable and necessary" for the treatment of Smith's prostate cancer. Smith maintains that cryosurgery was in fact reasonable and necessary for the treatment of his prostate cancer considering that the procedure was safe and effective, was generally accepted by the medical community, was his only option, and was a complete success. For the following reasons, this Court recommends that Smith's motion be denied.

I. PROCEDURAL BACKGROUND

Dr. Charles McKiel, Smith's physician, and Rush-Presbyterian-St. Luke's Medical Center, the hospital where Smith's surgery was performed, submitted claims to Health Care Service Corporation ("HCSC"), the Medicare Part A and Part B carrier for Illinois. . . . HCSC denied both claims initially and on reconsideration because it concluded that cryosurgery was not reasonable and necessary for the treatment of Smith's prostate cancer as the procedure was experimental and investigational. Smith requested review of the Part B decision . . . by a HCSC hearing officer. On February 26, 1996, the hearing officer issued an on-the-record decision denying the Part B claim.

Smith elected to have an in-person hearing on April 15, 1996, before a different hearing officer but with respect to the same Part B claim.

The hearing officer affirmed the previous Part B denial, noting that HCSC had issued a Local Medical Review Policy stating that "Medicare would not approve claims for cryosurgery of the prostate," and noting that Smith was aware of the policy prior to surgery. A final on-the-record decision was issued by a hearing officer on November 24, 1997. The hearing officer denied the Part B claim because cryosurgery of the prostate "has not yet been established as an effective treatment for prostate cancer." On May 14, 1996, Smith requested review of the hearing officers' decisions before an administrative law judge. On December 2, 1997, Smith requested review of HCSC's denial of the Part A claim before an administrative law judge, too.

The ALJ upheld HCSC's denials of payment under Medicare Part A and Part B on April 10, 1998, because cryosurgery was not reasonable and necessary for the treatment of Smith's prostate cancer as the procedure was experimental and investigational. Smith timely appealed the ALJ's decision to the Medicare Appeals Council, which subsequently denied Smith's request for review and adopted the ALJ's decision as the final decision of the Secretary. Smith now seeks review of the ALJ's decision pursuant to 42 U.S.C. §1395ff(b).

II. FACTUAL BACKGROUND

On September 14, 1994, Smith learned that he had an elevated Prostate Specific Antigen serum level of 80 mg/ml, indicating that he could have cancer of the prostate. Smith's physicians, Drs. Nader Sadoughi and John Saran, ordered a biopsy, which confirmed the diagnosis of carcinoma of the prostate. After consultation, Smith elected to have a radical surgical prostatectomy.

On November 3, 1994, Dr. Sadoughi initiated the prostatectomy, but he had to abort the procedure because of the size and location of Smith's tumor. Dr. Sadoughi informed Smith that he was not a candidate for radiation therapy because his PSA level was above 15 mg/ml. Instead, Dr. Sadoughi recommended that Smith consider cryosurgery of the prostate, an experimental and investigational procedure that involved destroying cancerous tissue with extremely cold temperatures. Smith accepted Dr. Sadoughi's recommendation, despite being aware of the experimental and investigational nature of the procedure, and despite being aware that Medicare likely would not pay for the procedure.

On November 22, 1994, Smith signed a document tendered by Dr. McKiel that stated: "I have been notified by Affiliated Urologists that they believe that Medicare is likely to deny payment for [cryosurgery of the prostate] [because the procedure is not a reasonable and necessary procedure under Medicare law]. If Medicare denies payment, I agree to be personally and fully responsible for payment." On March 27, 1995, Smith acknowledged receipt of a document prepared by Rush-Presbyterian that stated: "[Y]our observation stay for [cryosurgery of the prostate] will not be covered by [Medicare] because the planned procedure is considered investigational. . . . If you decide to be admitted to an observation bed at [Rush-Presbyterian] for this procedure, you will be financially responsible for all customary charges for services rendered. . . ."

Dr. McKiel performed cryosurgery on Smith on March 27, 1995. The surgery was successful as per subsequent biopsies and other laboratory tests.

* * *

IV. DISCUSSION

A. Standard of Review

Judicial review of the Secretary's decision to deny a Part A or Part B claim encompasses an assessment of the factual basis and legal basis of that decision. With regard the ALJ's factual findings, the court's role is limited: if the ALJ's findings are supported by substantial evidence, then the court must affirm the ALJ's decision. . . . In determining whether substantial evidence exists, the court cannot reevaluate the facts, reweigh the evidence, or substitute its own judgment for that of the ALJ.

The court reviews the ALJ's application of law without deference and without regard to the volume of evidence that supports the ALJ's findings. . . .

B. The Reasonableness and Necessity of Cryosurgery of the Prostate

Smith's sole argument on appeal is that the ALJ's decision was arbitrary and capricious. . . . Smith indicates that he presented evidence to the ALJ to overwhelmingly demonstrate that cryosurgery of the prostate was safe and effective, that the medical community generally accepted the procedure as safe and effective, that the procedure was the only option available to Smith, and that the procedure was and continues to be a complete success in Smith's particular case. The argument goes that, to deny the claims in light of this evidence, the ALJ acted arbitrarily and capriciously.

Clearly though such a charge does not square with the ALJ's treatment of this case. The ALJ made not a single legal error. He identified the pertinent rules and regulations. . . .

HCSC's policy in 1995 that cryosurgery of the prostate was not covered by Medicare Part B because the procedure was experimental and investigational evinces that cryosurgery of the prostate was indeed experimental and investigational on March 27, 1995. The American Urological Association's description of cryosurgery of the prostate in 1995 as "experimental and investigational" also evinces that cryosurgery of the prostate was indeed experimental and investigational on March 27, 1995. Lastly, the 1997 National Coverage Determination that "cryosurgery of the prostate cannot be considered reasonable and necessary under [42 U.S.C. §1395y(a)(1)(A)]" due to the lack of proof demonstrating the effectiveness of the procedure evinces that cryosurgery of the prostate was indeed experimental and investigational on March 27, 1995. All of this evidence was expressly relied on by the ALJ to make his decision. After reviewing the entire record, we find that this collection of evidence constitutes substantial evidence to support the ALJ's decision.

... The reality that cryosurgery of the prostate was safe, effective, and necessary in Smith's particular case, a point that no one has ever contested in this litigation, does not compel the conclusion that the procedure was a reasonable and necessary form of treatment for Smith's prostate cancer on March 27, 1995, under Medicare law. A form of treatment may be necessary and completely successful in a particular case yet still be per se unreasonable and unnecessary under 42 U.S.C. §1395y(a)(1)(A) if the treatment is properly deemed experimental and investigational as a general rule by someone with the authority to do so.

* * *

V. CONCLUSION

For the reasons stated, this Court recommends that Smith's motion be denied.

NOTE

Elimination of the Improvement Standard. Until 2012, the Medicare program limited coverage for skilled home health care or rehabilitative care to beneficiaries whose condition would improve as a result of those services. As a result of litigation brought by public interest advocates, however, CMS has agreed to also cover skilled nursing and rehabilitative services that are necessary to maintain beneficiaries' health.

QUESTIONS

1. What additional procedural step would Mr. Smith need to take today?

2. What standard of review does the court use in *Smith v. Thompson*? Why is it important?

PROBLEM

David, a Medicare beneficiary, has severe osteoarthritis of the hip that makes it painful to walk. His doctor originally advised a hip replacement, but changed his mind after learning that David's body had reacted poorly to the prosthetic used when David had a knee replacement several years ago. Unsure how to proceed, David's doctor referred him to Dr. Grand, a leading surgeon specializing in hip problems. Dr. Grand has recommended that David undergo a "hip resurfacing" procedure. Resurfacing is a surgical alternative to total hip replacement that has been used for some years in younger adults, but is just beginning to be expanded to the older adult population. If David seeks Medicare coverage for the resurfacing procedure, what problem might he encounter? Can David expect that the procedure will be covered by Medicare so long as Dr. Grand certifies that it is reasonable and necessary?

b. Managed Care Limitations

Shah v. Secretary of Health & Human Services

2010 WL 1489984 (D. Ariz. 2010)

G. Murray Snow, District Judge.

Pending before the Court is the appeal of Petitioner Rajumati Shah ("Ms. Shah"), which challenges the decision of the Department of Health and Human Services denying reimbursement of health-related expenses that Ms. Shah incurred while visiting India. For the reasons set forth below, the Court affirms that decision.

BACKGROUND

Ms. Shah is a seventy-seven year old Medicare beneficiary who receives health-care benefits through a program known as "Medicare Advantage." Under the "Medicare Advantage" program, eligible individuals, such as Ms. Shah, can elect to receive Medicare benefits by enrolling in a privately-managed care plan whereby the beneficiary agrees to use pre-selected service providers. [42] U.S.C. §1395w-22(d)(1). Additionally, an enrollee in a Medicare Advantage program may only obtain reimbursement for out-of-network services under limited circumstances. *Id.* at §1395w-22(d)(1)(C)-(E). An enrollee, however, is entitled to reimbursement for out-of-network expenses under the following exceptions: (1) where "the services were medically necessary and immediately required" but "it was not reasonable given the circumstances to obtain the services through the organization;" and (2) where services are needed to evaluate or stabilize an "emergency" medical condition. See *id.*

In January 2007, Ms. Shah was enrolled in a Medicare Advantage program administered by Health Net of Arizona ("Health Net") when she traveled with her husband to India to visit family. According to her agreement with Health Net, Ms. Shah was entitled to reimbursement for out-of-network services under the following circumstances:

> If you need care when you are outside the service area, your coverage is limited. The only services we cover when you are outside your service area are care for a medical emergency, urgently needed care, renal dialysis, and care that Health Net of Arizona or a plan provider has approved in advance.

And, as explained in further detail in the Discussion Section of this Order, the agreement further provides definitions of "medical emergency" and "urgently needed care" that closely track the statutory language found in §1395w-22(d)(1)(C)-(E).

Upon arrival in India, on January 11, 2007, Ms. Shah's left knee "locked up," and she began experiencing severe pain. As a result of the pain and inability to move her knee, Ms. Shah visited an out-of-network physician by the name of Bharat S. Mody ("Dr. Mody"), who recommended knee replacement surgery. Due to Ms. Shah's history of diabetes, high cholesterol, high blood pressure, anxiety, and aortic valve disorder, however, Dr. Mody indicated that he could not perform the procedure until he reviewed Ms. Shah's medical records. These records, which were located in the United States, arrived in India more than a week later on January 19, 2007. In the interim, Dr. Mody prescribed pain killers to help alleviate Ms. Shah's discomfort. On January 21, after Dr. Mody reviewed her medical history, Ms. Shah was admitted to the Center for Knee Surgery in India. The following day, she underwent a total knee replacement. Upon discharge from the Center on January 27, 2007, Ms. Shah checked into a nearby hospital where she remained for two months while she received physiotherapy. The total cost of her treatment was $6,801.01.

In April of 2007, Ms. Shah filed a claim with Health Net, seeking reimbursement for the expenses related to her knee replacement. Health Net, however, denied the claim in its entirely on the ground that the "[p]rovider [was] not within [her] assigned network of providers and the service [was] not considered emergent." After Ms. Shah sought reconsideration, Health Net referred the matter to an independent review body, Maximus Federal Services, Inc. ("Maximus") for further review. Maximus determined that Ms. Shah's visit with Dr. Mody on January 12, 2007 met Medicare guidelines for urgently needed care, but found that the remainder of the services did not meet the guidelines for emergency or urgently needed services.

Ms. Shah next sought review by an administrative law judge . . . on May 15, 2008. During the hearing, Ms. Shah presented a letter from Dr. Mody explaining that the knee surgery was appropriate because "the alternative of moving [Ms. Shah] to [the] USA with a locked knee, considering her age . . . anxiety, poor physical stamina, and the considerable strain involved in a long air journey in economy class, was not feasible." Ms. Shah also presented testimony at the hearing in which she explained that she could not have tolerated a flight back to the United States for treatment from an in-network provider because she was experiencing excruciating pain. Ms. Shah's husband then added that his wife was in extreme pain and that they decided to go forward with the procedure based on the advice of the Indian doctors. He also testified that he attempted to obtain preauthorization for the surgery from Health Net, but that he was unable to do so due to time zone and telephone difficulties.

After Ms. Shah presented her case, a representative from Health Net, Renne DeStafano, testified [that] Ms. Shah could not have endured a ten-day wait if the situation had truly been urgent or an emergency. The final witness to testify at the hearing was Debra Brown ("Dr. Brown"), an expert retained by Health Net. Dr. Brown testified that, given Ms. Shah's initial diagnosis of osteoarthritis, a total knee replacement was not urgently required or emergent. . . . Dr. Brown also testified that "if this was truly an emergency," Ms. Shah should "have been evaluated on an emergency basis, gotten cardiac clearance and a surgical intervention" immediately rather than waiting for ten days.

The ALJ rejected Ms. Shah's claim in a July 7, 2008 decision . . . Ms. Shah, appearing pro se, then filed the instant appeal.

* * *

DISCUSSION

The issue before the Court is whether the ALJ and MAC erred when they concluded that Health Net of Arizona is not required to reimburse Ms. Shah's out-of-network total knee replacement, impatient [sic] hospital stay, and associated expenses related to her surgery. This question turns on whether there is substantial evidence supporting the ALJ's conclusion that Ms. Shah's knee surgery was neither emergent nor urgently needed. Though the Court sympathizes with Ms. Shah's situation, the Court concludes that the ALJ's determination is supported by substantial evidence.

First, there is substantial evidence that Ms. Shah's knee replacement surgery was not a "medical emergency." Under the statute authorizing Medicare Advantage programs, "an emergency medical condition" is defined

> as a medical condition manifesting itself by acute symptoms of sufficient severity (including severe pain) such that a prudent layperson, who possesses an average knowledge of health and medicine, could reasonably expect the absence of immediate medical attention to result in—(i) placing the health of the individual (or, with respect to a pregnant woman, the health of the woman or her unborn child) in serious jeopardy, (ii) serious impairment to bodily functions, or (iii) serious dysfunction of any bodily organ or part.

42 U.S.C. §1395w-22(d)(3)(B). Similarly, Health Net's coverage agreement defines "medical emergency" as "when you reasonably believe your health is in serious danger when every second counts. A medical emergency includes severe pain, a bad injury, a serious illness, or a medical condition that is quickly getting much worse." Here, the ALJ based his determination that Ms. Shah's condition was not a medical emergency on the fact that the doctors in India waited ten days after Ms. Shah's initial consultation to perform the knee replacement surgery. Dr. Brown further testified that the delay undermined any claim of an emergency, and the ALJ credited this opinion. And though Ms. Shah believed that she required emergency medical services, her subjective belief is insufficient to require Health Net to reimburse her medical expenses as both the statutory definition of an emergency medical condition and Health Net's definition indicate that the individual's belief must be reasonable....

There is also substantial evidence that the total knee replacement was not urgently needed. Under §1395w-22(d), urgently needed care is defined as "[care that involves non-emergency services that are] medically necessary and immediately required because of an unforeseen illness, injury, or condition, and [that occurs under circumstances where] it was not reasonable given the circumstances to obtain the services through the organization[.]" §1395w-22(d)(1)(C)(i).

... Here, the ALJ was presented with conflicting evidence concerning whether it was reasonable for Ms. Shah to undergo a total knee replacement before returning to the United States. While her treating physician, Dr. Mody, offered evidence that it was not "feasible" for Ms. Shah to return to the United States, Dr. Brown testified that a total knee replacement is a drastic, last-step option and that performing such surgery before pursuing other treatment options deviates from the standard of care.

The ALJ was persuaded by Dr. Brown's opinions, finding that the ten-day delay corroborated Dr. Brown's determination that a total knee replacement was not medically necessary and immediately required. Additionally, given that there was no evidence that Dr. Mody considered any alternative treatment options, the ALJ relied on Dr. Brown's undisputed testimony that much less drastic treatment could have been done for Ms. Shah to enable her to return to the United States for evaluation by an in-network provider. Accordingly, the ALJ's decision is supported by substantial evidence from the administrative record.

IT IS THEREFORE ORDERED that the decision of the Medicare Appeals Council is AFFIRMED. . . .

6. The Medicare Home Health Benefit

Medicare will pay for home health care provided to "homebound" individuals in situations where the care is (1) medically necessary, (2) intermittent, (3) skilled (e.g., skilled nursing care, physical therapy, occupational therapy, and speech-language pathology), (4) ordered by a doctor, and (5) provided by a Medicare-certified home health agency.

The cost of such home care benefits to the beneficiary depends on whether the benefits are covered under Medicare Part A or Medicare Part B. Medicare Part A will pay for benefits if, in addition to meeting the basic requirements for home health coverage, the beneficiary has had a qualifying three-day hospital stay (or rehabilitative care in a skilled nursing facility following a hospitalization) no more than 14 days before home health services commence. Part A coverage is limited to no more than 100 home health visits per spell of illness. If an individual qualifies for home health coverage under Part A, there are no co-payments required for the home health services. Part B coverage, by contrast, does not require a preceding hospital or nursing facility stay. However, co-payments of 20 percent of the permitted cost are required.

The next case explores how the "homebound" requirement is interpreted and applied.

Russell v. Sebelius

686 F. Supp. 2d 386 (D. Vt. 2010)

[The below opinion is that of John M. Conroy, U.S. Magistrate Judge. The Recommendation and Report was subsequently approved and adopted by the U.S. District Court for the District of Vermont, and an order consistent with the Magistrate's recommendation was entered.—ED.]

BACKGROUND

I. Procedural History

Russell received home health services from the Visiting Nurse Association of Chittenden and Grand Isle Counties from June 26, 2004 through December 6, 2004 (hereafter "the service period"). . . . Russell filed claims with Medicare's contracted fiscal intermediary, Associated Hospital Service ("AHS"), for reimbursement for the services provided, which claims were denied initially and upon reconsideration. Thereafter, Maximus Federal Services, a Medicare qualified independent contractor, also issued unfavorable determinations.

Russell timely requested a hearing before an Administrative Law Judge ("ALJ"), which occurred via video teleconference on July 18, 2007. On July 30, 2007, ALJ Brenda Etheridge Seman issued a decision denying Russell's consolidated claim on the grounds that Russell was not "home confined," within the meaning of the Medicare Act, during the service periods. Russell requested review of the ALJ decision, and on February 15, 2008, the Medicare Appeals Council ("MAC") adopted the decision.

On June 10, 2008, having exhausted all administrative remedies, Russell filed a Complaint against the Secretary, initiating this action.

II. Medical History

During the service period, Russell was approximately 67 years old, and was receiving home health services primarily for care of a non-healing surgical wound that resulted from hernia repair surgery which occurred on January 20, 2004. Russell's major health issues following the surgery were as follows: she had a large, non-healing wound which ultimately required a skin graft almost one year after the initial surgery; she fatigued easily, to the point of needing a blood transfusion; and she experienced nausea, abdominal pain and swelling, and arthritic hip pain after ambulating. Additionally, Russell suffered from hypertension "affecting daily functioning" and requiring "ongoing monitoring," pure hypercholesterolemia, and esophageal reflux. As a result of her pain, Russell was prescribed the painkiller Vioxx, before switching to the painkillers Celebrex and Bextra in October 2004.

The bulk of Russell's medical care during the service period consisted of daily nurse visits for management and evaluation of Russell's wound, including assessment and documentation of the wound's size, color, granulation, odor, and drainage in "Wound Assessment Flow Sheets." . . .

Russell and her sister, Joyce Hojohn, submitted Affidavits to the ALJ. Therein, they state that, from June 2004 through the end of the service period, Hojohn visited Russell three to four times each day to check on Russell, complete household chores at Russell's home, and care for Russell's dog. Hojohn's residence was located approximately 50 feet from Russell's, "across the backyard and through a gate." Russell and Hojohn further state in their respective Affidavits that, during the relevant time period, Hojohn took Russell grocery shopping at Shaw's once or twice a month and to Big Lots to buy discounted canned goods once a month, for about 20 to 60 minutes per trip, with Hojohn doing all the driving, lifting, and carrying. In her Affidavit, Russell states that after these trips, she would come home feeling exhausted and needing to lay down and rest. Finally, Russell and Hojohn state in their respective Affidavits that, beginning in July 2004, when the weather was nice, Russell would walk with Hojohn while Hojohn walked Russell's dog for a distance of approximately 50 feet. According to Russell and Hojohn, these short dog walks, as well as the 20- to 60-minute trips to the supermarket and to Big Lots a couple of times a month, were the only trips Russell took outside her home during the service period, other than when Hojohn or Russell's son took Russell to medical appointments. There is no evidence in the record that Russell attended any religious services or social engagements, or visited any stores other than the supermarket and Big Lots, during the service period.

* * *

ALJ DECISION

In this case, as noted above, the ALJ determined that Russell was "not home confined" on the dates of service. . . . [T]he ALJ stated: "In sum, the status of [Russell's] wound site was such that it did not significantly impair her ability to leave the home."

Next, the ALJ considered Russell's "general condition" during the service period, . . . [and] concluded that Russell was "capable of leaving the home for extended periods of time for nonmedically related activities, such as shopping." The ALJ further concluded that Russell's level of functionality and ability to travel without an assistive device "suggests that leaving the home did not require a considerable and taxing effort." Thus, the ALJ determined that the home health services provided to Russell during the service period were not covered by Medicare Part A.

ANALYSIS

Reimbursement for home health services is contingent upon a showing that the claimant is confined to the home, under the care of a physician, in need of skilled services, and under a plan of care. 42 C.F.R. §§409.42(a)-(d). In relevant part, the regulations state as follows:

> To qualify for Medicare coverage of home health services, a beneficiary must meet each of the following requirements:
>
> (a) Confined to the home. The beneficiary must be confined to the home or in an institution that is not a hospital, SNF or nursing facility. . . .
>
> (b) Under the care of a physician. The beneficiary must be under the care of a physician who establishes the plan of care. . . .
>
> (c) In need of skilled services. The beneficiary must need at least one of the following skilled services as certified by a physician in accordance with the physician certification and recertification requirements for home health services under §424.22 of this chapter.
>
> . . .

(d) Under a plan of care. The beneficiary must be under a plan of care
   that meets the requirements for plans of care specified in §409.43.

The only disputed issue in this case is whether Russell was confined to her
home, as defined in the Medicare Act, during the service period. Under the
Medicare Act, an individual is considered to be "confined to [her] home" if
she has a condition "that restricts [her] ability . . . to leave . . . her home
except with the assistance of another individual or the aid of a supportive
device (such as crutches, a cane, a wheelchair, or a walker), or if the individual
has a condition such that leaving . . . her home is medically contraindicated."
42 U.S.C. §1395f(a). The claimant "does not have to be bedridden to be
considered 'confined to home,'" but she should have a "normal inability
to leave home," and leaving home should require "a considerable and taxing
effort." *Id.* Absences from the home for medical purposes, including the
receipt of health care or therapeutic treatment, do not disqualify a claimant
from being considered "confined to home." *Id.* Moreover, non-medical
absences which are "infrequent or of relatively short duration" do not
disqualify a claimant from being considered "confined to home." *Id.*

* * *

Russell argues that she met the legal standard of being "confined to
home" during the service period, and that the record lacks substantial
evidence to support the ALJ's determination to the contrary. Specifically, Russell contends that she required the assistance of another person to leave her
home, and that leaving the home required considerable and taxing effort due
to her nausea, abdominal pain, hip pain, anemia, and fatigue. Russell further
contends that her non-medical absences from the home were infrequent and
of relatively short duration, and that the ALJ's failure to make a finding on
this issue was legal error. The Secretary counters that clinical evidence, including nurse notes stating that Russell was able to leave the home "independently," demonstrates that Russell was not confined to her home[,] and
that the ALJ used the proper standards in making this determination.

Having considered both parties' arguments and the evidence as a whole, I
find that the ALJ neglected to resolve conflicts in the evidence, ignored probative evidence, and misapplied the law. Taken individually, each of these
errors could be considered harmless; but taken together, they are significant.
Therefore, for the reasons discussed below, I recommend remanding for a re-
weighing of the evidence and a new decision.

I. The ALJ Failed to Weigh the Evidence and Make Credibility Determinations.

A. Conflicting Nurse Notes

Despite the Secretary's detailed analysis in her Motion, the ALJ decision
does not include a weighing and balancing of conflicting and probative nurse
notes. Instead, the decision merely states: "[T]he assessment expressly indicates that the patient was not homebound." The decision fails to note that,
although it is true that there are assessments in the record which state that

Russell was able to leave her home "independently," there are also assessments in the record which state that Russell was "homebound."

* * *

... The conflicts among nurse notes regarding Russell's ability to leave the home during the service period, reflect that either: (a) different nurses had different opinions as to Russell's capabilities and actions during the service period, with respect to leaving her home; or (b) each nurse had her own unique definition of the terms "homebound," "housebound," and/or "independent," which definition may have differed from that prescribed in the Medicare Act. ... A review of the evidence as a whole demonstrates that the latter option is likely.

* * *

... It is not for the court to engage in this credibility analysis in the first instance; the ALJ should have weighed the credibility of this important and probative evidence, and made findings as to which nurse notes were more credible and why. ...

B. Affidavits of Russell and Hojohn

As described above, the Affidavits of Russell and her sister, Joyce Hojohn, unambiguously state that during each of Russell's non-medical trips outside the home during the service period, she was accompanied (and assisted) by her sister. ...

The only evidence that Russell left home for any other purpose, excluding medical appointments, is Nurse Shepard's statements in her assessments that Russell left home for "visiting friends," for "visiting" generally, and for "visiting family." ... Perhaps Nurse Shepard's recording of Russell's "visits" with family and friends referred to Russell and Hojohn's trips to the supermarket or 50-foot dog walks. Alternatively, Nurse Shepard could have been referring to visits she believed Russell was having with her sister at her sister's home, which was located across the backyard and approximately 50 feet from Russell's home. But there is no other evidence that such visits at Hojohn's home occurred during the service period. Moreover, if the ALJ had concluded that Russell had visited Hojohn at Hojohn's home during the service period, she necessarily would have had to find that the Affidavits of Russell and Hojohn, which specifically refute the existence of such visits, lacked credibility. The ALJ did not make this finding in her decision; in fact, the decision makes no reference at all to the Affidavits.

* * *

If the ALJ disbelieved Russell's and Hojohn's testimony ... she should have said so and explained why. The ALJ's failure to mention [the affidavits] her decision "could lead to a conclusion that [s]he neglected to consider [them] at all." *Baerga v. Richardson*, 500 F.2d 309, 312 (3d Cir. 1974). ...

II. The ALJ Applied an Erroneous Legal Standard in Assessing Whether Russell Was Able to Leave Her Home Without Assistance.

The ALJ erred in finding that Russell was not confined to her home, in part, because "[s]he could ambulate without an assistive device," and she was "able to go shopping with minimal assistance." First, it appears from this and other statements in the ALJ's decision that the ALJ improperly neglected to consider whether, even assuming Russell was able to leave the home without an assistive device, she could leave the home without the assistance of another individual. Such consideration is required under 42 U.S.C. §1395f(a). . . .

Moreover, the ALJ's statement that Russell was able to go shopping "with minimal assistance" reveals the ALJ's application of an erroneous legal standard. The standard is not whether a claimant is able to leave the home with minimal assistance; it is whether the claimant is able to leave the home with no assistance. . . .

III. The ALJ Neglected to Make a Finding Regarding the Frequency and Duration of Russell's Trips Outside the Home.

In determining whether a claimant was "confined to home" during the relevant service period(s), the Medicare Act requires the ALJ to consider the frequency and duration of the claimant's non-medical absences from his or her home during the service period. Here, although the ALJ stated in her decision that Russell was "capable of leaving the home for extended periods of time for nonmedically related activities, such as shopping," the ALJ made no findings as to the frequency or duration of Russell's actual trips outside the home during the service period.

In fact, there is no evidence in the record which demonstrates that Russell left her home frequently or for a long duration during the service period. . . .

In prior opinions, this Court has discussed and decided what types of absences are considered "infrequent" and of "relatively short duration," for Medicare purposes. In *Dennis v. Shalala*, No. 5:92-CV-210, 1994 WL 708166, at **4-5 (D. Vt. Mar. 4, 1994), for example, the Court found that the claimant was "homebound," despite taking nine trips to the grocery store during the seven-month service period. The Court explained:

> . . . Congress considered the "confined to home" designation to include claimants who had to leave home for medical purposes, as well as those who could . . . leave home for such nonmedical purposes as an infrequent family dinner, an occasional drive or walk around the block, or a church service. The obvious thrust is that the definition of "confined to home" should not serve to imprison the elderly by creating a penalty of loss of Medicare benefits for heroic attempts to live a normal life. [The claimant] shopped at the grocery store only nine times during the seven-month period at issue in this case; she should not lose her benefits merely because she has made an "heroic attempt" to engage in the activities of daily living.

Additionally, proposed federal regulations provide that one non-medical outing per week is an insufficient basis on which to deny an individual homebound status. . . .

In *Labossiere v. Sec'y of Health and Human Servs.*, No. 90-CV-150, 1991 WL 531922, at **3, 6 (D. Vt. July 25, 1991), on the other hand, the Court found that the claimant's shopping trips and attendance at an adult day care three to four days a week for up to eight hours at a time were frequent and regular. Likewise, in *Richardson v. Shalala*, No. 2:93-CV-387, 1995 WL 441956, at *3 (D. Vt. Jan. 27, 1995), where the claimant visited an adult day care three times a week for six hours at a time, the Court found that the claimant was not homebound. Finally, in *Pope v. Sec'y of Health and Human Servs.*, No. 89-CV-256, 1991 WL 236173, at *4 (D. Vt. Aug. 28, 1991), the Court affirmed the ALJ's determination that the claimant was not homebound, "based in part on her ability to leave home for periods of 1-4 hours at least once a week to shop, visit friends, attend church, and run errands."

In this case, unlike in *Labossiere, Richardson*, and *Pope*, the ALJ made no specific findings as to the duration and frequency of the trips Russell took outside the home during the service period. Moreover, Russell's trips outside the home—which consisted of less than 2.5 hours per month spent food shopping for no longer than one hour per trip and 50-foot dog walks in nice weather—do not rise to the same frequency and duration as those involved in *Labossiere, Richardson*, and *Pope*, but rather, bear a more similar resemblance to the trips at issue in *Dennis*, where the claimant was found to be confined to the home.

IV. The ALJ's Determination that Russell's Trips Outside the Home Did Not Require "Considerable and Taxing Effort" is Not Supported by the Evidence.

Finally, the ALJ erred in determining that Russell's trips outside the home "did not require a considerable and taxing effort," without even mentioning (or ostensibly considering) the medical evidence stating that Russell was exhausted after her brief and infrequent trips to the supermarket and her 50-foot dog walks with Hojohn. . . .

CONCLUSION

Findings of fact made by the ALJ "are conclusive when supported by substantial evidence . . . , but are not conclusive when derived by ignoring evidence [or] misapplying the law. . . ." *Nguyen v. Chater*, 172 F.3d 31, 35 (1st Cir. 1999). In this case, as discussed above, the ALJ ignored probative evidence and misapplied the applicable law. Therefore, I recommend that Russell's Motion to reverse be GRANTED, and the Secretary's Motion to affirm be DENIED. Because this case involves conflicting evidence, and resolution of conflicts in the evidence is for the ALJ and not the courts, I recommend REMANDING for further proceedings, if necessary, a re-weighing of the evidence, and another decision, consistent with this Report and Recommendation.

NOTE

Privileged absences. As a matter of law, absences "attributable to the need to receive health care treatment" or for the purpose of attending a "religious service" may not disqualify a Medicare beneficiary from being considered confined to the home for the purpose of receiving home health benefits. See 42 U.S.C. §1395f(a)(8).

PROBLEMS

1. Mr. Simpson is very unstable on his feet. He only leaves his house to walk down his short driveway to get his mail or when his daughter picks him up to take him grocery shopping or to a doctor's appointment. Is Mr. Simpson homebound for Medicare purposes?

2. Suppose that instead of having his daughter take him grocery shopping and to his doctor, Mr. Simpson drives to both on his own. However, his doctor has told him that this practice is unsafe and is threatening to write to his state's department of motor vehicles to have Mr. Simpson's license revoked. The doctor is concerned, in part, because Mr. Simpson has fallen several times in the last three months when walking independently. Is Mr. Simpson homebound for Medicare purposes?

7. The Future and Financial Status of Medicare

Medicare expenditures are growing rapidly. The following chart shows how Medicare expenses are projected to grow relative to *Gross Domestic Product* (GDP) and expenses for the Social Security system. Specifically, the below chart shows *Old-Age and Survivors Insurance* (OASI) and *Disability Insurance* (DI) and *Health Insurance* (HI—or Medicare Part A) and *Supplemental Medical Insurance* (SMI—Medicare Parts B and D) as a percentage of GDP.

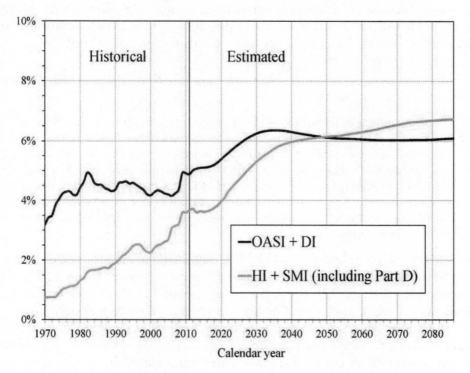

Source: Trustees of Social Security & Medicare, Summary of the 2012 Annual Reports, available at *www.ssa.gov/OACT/TRSUM/index.html.*

As the chart shows, costs of both Social Security and Medicare are projected to increase sharply between 2015 and 2030. This steep increase reflects the fact that more people are expected to be receiving OASDI benefits and Medicare benefits as the Baby Boom generation retires.

Although the costs of both programs are expected to increase, Medicare's costs are increasing more rapidly because of the increasing cost of health care (reflecting only, in part, anticipated increases in the "complexity" of health care services). The result is that Medicare represents not only an increasing portion of GDP, but also a rapidly growing portion of the federal budget. Notably, however, Medicare spending is projected to grow less rapidly than private health insurance spending in the next decade.

In an effort to control Medicare costs, the Affordable Care Act (ACA), often referred to as *Health Care Reform* or *Obamacare*, created the Independent Payment Advisory Board (IPAB). Under the ACA, IPAB is to consist of 15 members appointed by the President and subject to confirmation by the U.S. Senate. If the growth of Medicare expenditures exceeds annual cost-per-beneficiary growth targets, IPAB must propose spending reductions to bring spending down to the targeted rate. The Secretary of Health and Human Services is then required to implement IPAB's proposal unless Congress adopts an alternative proposal. While IPAB is thus a powerful entity, its powers are tightly constrained by the ACA, which limits both the types and total amount of spending reductions IPAB can propose. Among other limitations, IPAB may not propose reductions that "ration" care, raise revenues, increase premiums or cost-sharing, or alter eligibility criteria. Moreover, IPAB will not be implemented until 2015, and it may be a number of years after that until Medicare actually exceeds the spending limits triggering its duty to propose cuts.

As Professors Ann Marie Marciarille and J. Bradford DeLong explain, IPAB is a policy experiment:

> The functioning of the IPAB will be an experiment by Congress in binding itself to the mast, as Odysseus did when confronted by the Sirens. In the past Congress has exercised its discretion to reject—or, rather, to fail to act on—proposals to reform Medicare reimbursement rates put forward by entities Congress created to advise it. The belief is that the IPAB process, which removes much of Congress's discretionary authority not to act over recommendations on rates, will lead to Medicare payment decisions that are closer to the social optimum.

Ann Marie Marciarille & J. Bradford DeLong, *Bending the Health Cost Curve: The Promise & Peril of the Independent Payment Advisory Board*, 22 HEALTH MATRIX 75, 79-80 (2012) (describing the role of the IPAB, acknowledging challenges it faces, and providing an "optimistic" view of its potential).

IPAB is highly controversial. Supporters argue that Congress is too political to be able to adopt sound policies to reduce Medicare spending and that an executive branch entity is less likely to be influenced by special interests. Detractors, including many health care providers, describe IPAB as anti-democratic and worry that (especially since it cannot ration care or change eligibility criteria) IPAB will cut payments to health care providers. This in turn could lead some health care providers to refuse to accept Medicare, thereby reducing beneficiaries' options.

While the effect of IPAB is not yet known, even with this cost containment measure, Medicare expenditures are expected to continue to grow, reflecting both an increase in health care costs overall and an increase in the number of Medicare beneficiaries. Nevertheless, despite concerns about Medicare's financial stability, in the excerpted article that follows Professor Richard Kaplan calls the notion that Medicare is going bankrupt one of the ten top "myths" about Medicare.

Richard Kaplan, Top Ten Myths of Medicare

20 Elder L.J. 1 (2012)

One of the most frequently propounded contentions, usually with an air of absolute certainty, is that the Medicare program is going bankrupt, will soon run out of money, or some similar formulation of complete financial exhaustion. . . . Medicare consists of several distinct components with differing methodologies of financing their costs. In particular, Medicare Parts B and D utilize premiums paid by current-year enrollees and general tax revenues. These components of Medicare make no pretense of pre-funding and rely on funds that are generated in the current fiscal year. In other words, Medicare Parts B and D are funded on a current-year basis and as a result cannot "go bankrupt" in any customary sense of that phrase. As long as the federal government receives tax revenues from any source and there are any enrollees in Medicare Parts B and D, those specific programs can be funded.

To be sure, general tax revenues are always subject to competing demands, whether for national defense or for other fundamental functions of government such as law enforcement and the judicial system. In addition, funding challenges may arise in the future as a result of financial demands caused by unparalleled natural disasters like Hurricane Katrina in 2005 or unanticipated fiscal crises like the global financial meltdown of 2008. Consequently, future Congresses may choose not to fund Medicare Parts B and D to the same extent that present and past Congresses have done. Those future Congresses might adjust the applicable funding formula to make those programs more reliant on enrollee premiums and less reliant on general tax revenues. The bottom line, however, is that Medicare Parts B and D can be financed indefinitely if they are deemed appropriate uses of federal funds.

Medicare Part A is essentially in the same position, but it presents an additional complication in that the payroll taxes imposed for this component are directed to a dedicated "trust fund" to pay for its expenditures. In the normal course of trust fund accounting, if this fund lacks sufficient monies to pay the program's costs, those costs cannot be paid. A trust fund operated by a national government with the power to create money, however, does not necessarily play by the same rules that apply to trust funds generally. Much like the equally mythological and equally confusing trust fund that pays Social

Security benefits, such benefit payments are not realistically restricted to the monies that are "available" in the fabled trust fund. Tax revenues go into the federal government, and that same government can choose to spend whatever sums it wants on whatever programs it deems worthy of funding.

After all, there is not now, nor has there ever been, a Department of Defense "trust fund" or any similar account for the Department of Homeland Security. The absence of such a dedicated funding source, however, has not presented any impediment to financing protracted and unusually expensive wars in Iraq, Afghanistan, or anywhere else. Notwithstanding the wisdom or inefficacy of those military engagements, no objection was ever raised that funds were not available to pay for these engagements.

In similar fashion, if Congress finds that the reported balance in the "trust fund" designated for Medicare Part A is insufficient, it can appropriate funds to cover the resulting "deficiency" just as it does for Medicare Parts B and D. Thus, Medicare cannot "go bankrupt." It may, to be sure, become a serious and exploding drain on the federal government's budget, but if future Congresses prioritize this program over other competing demands, Medicare can continue to pay its bills in full and on time.

QUESTIONS

1. Is IPAB a sensible approach to reducing Medicare costs? Why or why not?

2. What might be an alternative approach or approaches to reducing Medicare costs?

C. MEDICAID

1. Overview of Medicaid Coverage

Medicaid is a federal-state partnership program that provides health care coverage to financially needy individuals. Unlike Medicare, Medicaid covers long-term custodial care. Today, it is the primary payer for nursing home care in the United States.

Because Medicaid is jointly administered by the states and the federal government, there are significant differences between states in the program's coverage, eligibility requirements, and other administrative rules and processes. Although there are extensive federal regulations governing Medicaid, many of these regulations give states "options" in how they administer the program. These options range from whether they cover particular types of individuals, to whether they cover particular services, to how they determine eligibility for services. In addition, states can apply for waivers of certain federal requirements. Such waivers allow them to divert federal Medicaid dollars from otherwise required programs to target needs not otherwise met by the program. For example, through a "1915(c)" waiver, a state can divert resources to provide home and community-based care to individuals who would otherwise require nursing home care. Moreover, states differ in their interpretations of Medicaid statutes and regulations.

In short, states have tremendous discretion in how they implement Medicaid. Indeed, states even have discretion in what they call their Medicaid programs. While most states refer to their programs as Medicaid, some have adopted names unique to the state, specifically: Arizona Health Care Cost Containment System (Arizona), Medi-Cal (California), Kansas Medical Assistance Program (Kansas), MaineCare (Maine), MassHealth (Massachusetts; Medicaid is absorbed into the state's broader "MassHealth" program), Medical Assistance (Minnesota), Oregon Health Plan (Oregon), Sooner Care (Oklahoma); Medical Assistance (Pennsylvania), TennCare (Tennessee), and ForwardHealth (Wisconsin; Medicaid is one portion of the ForwardHealth program).

2. Eligibility for Basic Medicaid Coverage

Medicaid is only available to persons with limited income and resources. There are two types of tests that an individual can satisfy to qualify for Medicaid: the *categorically needy* test and the *medically needy* test.

An individual will be deemed categorically needy if he or she is eligible for SSI. Since SSI is only available to people with limited income and assets who are also blind, disabled, or at least 65 years old, the effect is that elderly individuals are far more likely to qualify for Medicaid than are their younger counterparts. As discussed in Chapter 5 (see page 242), there are strict income and assets limits for SSI eligibility. In 2013, in order to be eligible for SSI, an individual was limited to countable monthly income of less than $710 for an individual or $1,066 for a couple, and countable resources of no more than $2,000 for an individual or $3,000 for a couple.

It is important to recognize that not all income and resources are counted in determining whether a person is eligible for Medicaid. As a general matter, countable income for Medicaid eligibility purposes is determined the same way it is determined for SSI purposes (see Chapter 5, page 242). Thus, countable income is any cash or in-kind income that can be used to meet an individual's need for food or shelter. Similarly, countable resources for Medicaid purposes are generally determined in the same way as countable resources for SSI purposes. Thus, non-countable resources include an automobile used for transportation, a burial plot worth up to $1,500, and a primary residence in which the beneficiary's equity does not exceed a certain level. In 2013, the equity limit was $536,000 (or as much as $802,000 if the state elected to grant a higher exemption). Another form of non-countable asset is a qualified *Special* or *Supplemental Needs Trust* (SNT), discussed at length in Section C.4.b of this chapter (see page 319).

If the person seeking Medicaid is institutionalized, however, whether or not their home is a countable asset depends on several factors, including whether the beneficiary intends to return home. If the beneficiary does, then the home is not a countable asset so long as the individual's equity in the home is below the permissible amount. The beneficiary's intent to return home need not be objectively reasonable: A subjective intent to return home is sufficient.

To be deemed medically needy, by contrast, an individual must meet the same income and asset requirements as those who are categorically needy *after* the monthly cost of their qualified, out-of-pocket health care expenses are taken into account. Suppose, for example, that Mrs. Arthur (a widow who lives alone) meets the resource limits for eligibility for Medicaid, but her income is $1,000 a month, and the income level to qualify as categorically needy for Medicaid is $710 for a single individual. However, Mrs. Arthur has $500 a month in out-of-pocket medical costs. She is medically needy because her monthly income—after subtracting her monthly medical costs—is below the Medicaid income limit. After she "spends down" for the month by paying $300 toward her medical expenses, the remaining $190 in medical expenses will be eligible for Medicaid coverage.

Some states limit those who can qualify for the medically needy category to persons below a certain income level. Typically, these states do not allow someone whose income is above 300 percent of the SSI level to be deemed medically needy for Medicaid purposes. The effect is the creation of a *Medicaid gap group*, a group consisting of persons who are ineligible for Medicaid but whose medical expenses nevertheless impoverish them. Individuals who fall into the gap group, however, may avoid ineligibility by creating a *Miller Trust* (also known as a *Income Only Trust*). If all income in excess of 300 percent of the SSI level is placed in the trust and the state is then named the beneficiary of the trust for up to the amount of Medicaid paid to the beneficiary, the individual can be deemed Medicaid eligible. *See* 42 U.S.C. §1396P(d)(4)(B).

PROBLEM

Suppose a would-be Medicaid recipient is in possession of an IOU from her niece promising to pay back a loan in the amount of $5,000. Is this a countable asset? Upon what might it depend?

3. Eligibility for Medicaid Coverage for Long-Term Care

Additional rules apply to determining eligibility for Medicaid coverage of nursing home care or care provided under a *home and community-based services* (HCBS) waiver. A HCBS waiver is a waiver granted by the federal government to a state that allows that state to provide long-term care services that would traditionally be provided in a nursing home in a less restrictive setting instead. Applying for a HCBS waiver is optional, but almost all states and the District of Columbia have applied for at least one HCBS waiver. Provisions in the Affordable Care Act provide financial incentives for states to continue to expand Medicaid coverage for home and community-based services.

One key difference when an individual is seeking coverage for nursing home or HCBS services is that a house may be considered as a countable asset if the beneficiary is residing in an institution and does not intend to return home. A second key difference is that states are required to penalize Medicaid applicants seeking Medicaid coverage for nursing home care or care provided through a HCBS for making certain types of transfers. A third key difference is how a spouse's income and resources are treated. The rules governing these later differences are discussed in the next two subsections.

a. Effect of Transfers for Less Than Fair Market Value

Under the rules set forth in the Deficit Reduction Act of 2005, when an individual applies for Medicaid for nursing home care or care provided through a HCBS waiver, the government will "look back" to see if that individual made any transfers for less than *fair market value* (FMV) for the purpose of establishing Medicaid or SSI eligibility during the past five years. If he or she did, he or she will generally face a *penalty period* that renders him or her ineligible for Medicaid coverage for a set period of time. Providing the documentation to show that no such transfer was made is often a time-intensive and difficult process, especially when the would-be beneficiary has not kept clear records of his or her financial transactions.

A wide variety of actions and inactions are deemed to constitute a transfer for less than FMV. These include:

- A transfer of income or resources made without consideration.
- A transfer of income or resources in exchange for something worth less than the income or resources transferred.
- A refusal to accept resources (e.g., a decision to disclaim an inheritance, a failure to elect an elective share).
- A purchase of a life estate in a home unless the purchaser lives in that home for a minimum of one year following the purchase.
- Purchasing certain types of annuities. While there are some exceptions, in order not to be considered transfers for less than fair market value, annuities must generally be irrevocable, non-assignable, actuarially sound, and make payments in equal amounts during the term of the annuity (e.g., no balloon payments). In addition, the state must be named as the remainder beneficiary of the annuity for at least the amount of Medicaid paid. An exception is made where the spouse or minor of disabled child is named as the remainder beneficiary.

However, there are exceptions. A penalty period will not be imposed if:

- The transfer was made for a purpose unrelated to Medicaid.
- The transferred resources are returned to the Medicaid applicant.
- The transferred resources were transferred into a *special needs trust* by a transferor who was under 65 years of age at the time and who had a qualifying disability.

■ The resources were transferred to a qualifying family member. An exception is made for all transfers for less than FMV to the applicant's spouse and/or the applicant's blind or disabled child. In addition, if the transfer is of the applicant's residence, an exception is also made if the transfer was to 1) the applicant's sibling who has an equity interest in the home and who lived in it for at least a year before the beneficiary's institutionalization, 2) the applicant's adult child who lived in the home for at least two years before the beneficiary's institutionalization and who provided care to the beneficiary during that period, or 3) the applicant's minor child.

■ Applying the penalty period would cause undue hardship. The Deficit Reduction Act of 2005 specified that undue hardship must be found when applying the transfer penalty would deprive the Medicaid applicant "of medical care such that the individual's health or life would be endangered" or "of food, clothing, shelter, or other necessities of life." *See* Pub. L. 109-171, title VI, §6011(d), Feb. 8, 2006.

In addition, since the look-back period is five years, no penalty will be imposed for transfers made more than five years before the Medicaid application at issue.

The penalty period is a length of time during which an individual will be ineligible for long-term care Medicaid benefits. It is designed to deny coverage for roughly the length of time that the transferred assets could have covered the applicant's nursing care had they not been transferred. The penalty period is calculated by dividing the dollar value of the transfer by the average monthly cost of nursing home care in the would-be beneficiary's region. The resulting number is the number of months that the individual will be ineligible for Medicaid. For example, suppose Mr. Dickens gives his daughter $80,000 three years before applying for Medicaid, and the average cost of a month of nursing home care in the region where Mr. Dickens lives is $8,000. Mr. Dickens will be subject to a ten-month-long penalty period. The penalty period begins on the first day of the month after the transfer, or on the first day of the month the institutionalized individual is receiving nursing facility services for which Medicaid would otherwise pay, whichever comes later. Thus, Mr. Dickens's ten-month penalty period will not begin until Mr. Dickens would otherwise be eligible for Medicaid.

Under current law, it is presumed that a transfer made for less than FMV was made for the purpose of establishing SSI or Medicaid eligibility. However, this presumption can be rebutted if there is "convincing evidence that the resource was transferred exclusively for some other reason." 20 C.F.R. §416.1246(e). According to the relevant regulation:

Convincing evidence may be pertinent documentary or non-documentary evidence which shows, for example, that the transfer was ordered by a court, or that at the time of transfer the individual could not have anticipated becoming eligible due to the existence of other circumstances which would have precluded eligibility. The burden of rebutting the presumption that a resource was transferred to establish SSI or Medicaid eligibility rests with the individual (or eligible spouse).

Id. Accordingly, in *Longhi v. Department of Health & Rehabilitative Servs.*, 691 So. 2d 583 (Fla. Dist. Ct. App. 1997), money transferred to a Medicaid applicant's daughter to help the daughter pay off a mortgage was deemed not to be a transfer for the purpose of establishing Medicaid eligibility where the money was transferred prior to the applicant incurring the injury that led to her nursing home placement.

In general, where the transferor is of an advanced age and sickly, attorneys should anticipate that it will be harder to rebut the presumption that a transfer for less than FMV during the look-back period was done for the purpose of establishing Medicaid eligibility. *Cf. Matter of Loiacono v. Demarzo*, 72 A.D.3d 969 (N.Y. App. Div. 2d Dep't 2010) (treating the petitioner's age and medical condition as relevant to the question of whether the petitioner had rebutted the presumption that transfers to her son were made for the purpose of establishing Medicaid eligibility).

The next case represents one beneficiary's attempt to rebut the presumption that a transfer was made for the purpose of establishing eligibility.

Godown v. Department of Public Welfare

813 A.2d 954 (Pa. 2002)

Opinion by Judge LEADBETTER.

Albert Godown petitions this court to review the order of the Department of Public Welfare (Department) that affirmed a hearing officer's decision that Godown is ineligible for nursing home benefits because Godown and his wife transferred their residence to their children for a nominal amount approximately fifteen months before Godown applied for medical assistance (MA). The issue before this court is whether the Department erred in concluding that Godown transferred his property in order to qualify for MA. We affirm.

In March of 2000, Godown and his wife transferred ownership of their residence and commercial property to their children for consideration in the amount of one dollar. At that time, Godown, who was approximately 77 years old, needed a walker and used a motorized cart to traverse his property. Following the transfer, Godown and his wife resided in an apartment on the property and their children resided in the main residence. On July 12, 2001, Godown suffered a stroke, which rendered him unable to care for himself. Godown's wife was also unable to care for Godown because she was legally blind and suffered from diabetes, peripheral neuropathy, and heart disease. Godown did not attempt to sell the property. Rather, in August of 2001, he applied for MA. Godown's application for benefits indicated that the property had been transferred the year before, and at the time of the transfer, the property had a fair market value of $500,000.

When the County Assistance Office (CAO) learned of the transfer, it gave Godown's children the opportunity to transfer the property back to their parents. The children refused, however, because they had obtained a $100,000 mortgage on the property. The CAO then denied Godown MA on the basis that he had transferred property valued at $500,000 for less than fair consideration. Godown appealed and a hearing followed. Of note, the evidence of record demonstrated that the Godowns' property consisted of approximately 10 acres upon which the main residence was situated, along with a commercial greenhouse with an apartment below it. Mrs. Godown testified that she had been gravely ill prior to the transfer of the property and that the property was transferred to the children so that it could remain in the family. According to Mrs. Godown, she was declared legally blind in 1999. She also testified that since 1997, Godown had used a walker and was able to do some work in the greenhouse prior to his stroke.

Based upon the record and the applicable regulations, the hearing officer concluded that Godown was ineligible for MA due to the transfer of the property for less than fair consideration. Specifically, the hearing officer opined:

> While [Godown] argues that the transfer of property occurred to keep the property within the family, [Godown] certainly should have anticipated a need for nursing home care considering his age and deteriorating condition. At the time of the transfer of property, [Godown] was 77 years old and required the assistance of a walker and motorized cart to move about the property. Because [Godown's] disability was not unexpected, [Godown] failed to rebut the presumption that the property was disposed of to qualify for medical assistance.

The Department affirmed and the present appeal followed.

* * *

The Department's regulations provide that if an applicant disposes of assets for less than fair market value within . . . the "look-back period" . . . the applicant will be temporarily ineligible for MA. . . . An applicant who transferred assets for less than fair market value will not be ineligible for MA if the applicant can demonstrate, inter alia, that he/she intended to dispose of the assets for fair market value or other valuable consideration, that the transferred assets have been returned to the applicant, or that the assets were transferred exclusively for a purpose other than to qualify for MA.

It is important to note that under the applicable statute, regulations and caselaw, the MA applicant bears the burden of demonstrating eligibility for MA; this includes the burden to demonstrate that transfers of assets during the look-back period were made for fair market value or exclusively for a purpose other than to qualify for MA. Moreover, when reviewing an application for MA, the Department is entitled to presume that assets disposed of for less than fair market value during the look-back period were transferred in order to qualify for MA. The applicant bears the burden of rebutting the presumption, with evidence pertaining to: (1) the purpose of the transfer; (2) any attempts to dispose of the asset for fair market value; (3) the reason for accepting less than fair market value of the asset; (4) the plans for self-support following transfer of the asset; and (5) the applicant's relationship to the individual to whom the asset was transferred. If the applicant fails to rebut the presumption that the assets were transferred to qualify for MA, the applicant will be disqualified from receiving MA for the appropriate period of time.

On appeal, Godown argues that the Department erred in concluding that he transferred his property to his children in order to qualify for MA. . . . Godown contends that he is entitled to MA pursuant to the exception in §1396p(c)(2)(C) because he demonstrated that the transfer of the property was not connected to his application for MA as he transferred the property when he was still able to travel around his home and property, tend to items in the greenhouse and was not in need of institutional medical care. While we sympathize with Godown's predicament, we are unpersuaded by his arguments.

Here, at the time the Godowns transferred the property to their children, both Mr. and Mrs. Godown suffered from ailments that could eventually render them in need of institutionalized care. In addition, the transfer of the property left Mr. Godown virtually penniless, without any obvious means of paying for nursing home care if needed. The only explanation offered for transferring the property to the children without receiving any consideration in return was the desire to keep the property in the family. In light of the Godown's circumstances, it was reasonable for the hearing officer to interpret this explanation to mean precisely that the assets were transferred so that they would not be eroded by medical expenses. Because MA would instead provide for the medical care, the property could remain in the family. Far from rebutting the presumption, this explanation confirms it. Even if Mrs. Godown's testimony were construed otherwise, the hearing officer, as the fact-finder, is charged with the responsibility of resolving conflicts in testimony and may reject the testimony of any witness. Therefore, we conclude that substantial evidence of record supports the Department's conclusion that Godown gave the property to his children in order to qualify for MA.

Based upon the foregoing, the Department's order is affirmed.

NOTES

1. *Demonstrating undue hardship.* States are required to establish processes for allowing Medicaid applicants to prove undue hardship. In *Howell v. Ohio Dep't of Job & Family Servs.*, 2009 Ohio 1510 (Ohio Ct. App., Belmont County Mar. 27, 2009), an appellate court found that a trial court had abused its discretion in applying the hardship exemption despite a lack of evidence that "a good faith effort was made to recover or make the transferred resources available" or that the applicant "had exhausted all legal remedies and appeals to challenge the planned discharge from the nursing home facility." The court found that applying the exemption under such circumstances was inconsistent with Ohio's regulations governing the undue hardship exemption.

2. *Scope of transfer penalties.* States are required under federal law to impose penalties for transfers for less than fair market value when a would-be Medicaid beneficiary seeks coverage for nursing home care or for services provided pursuant to a HCBS waiver. States may choose to also extend the penalty to other long-term care services such as home health services.

3. *Rounding.* In determining the length of the penalty period, states have the option of rounding up fractional months of ineligibility. They may not round them down.

4. *The nature of the undue hardship exception.* As noted in 1-7 LONG-TERM CARE ADVOCACY §7.12 (Matthew Bender 2011): "It might seem that a period of ineligibility assessed against a nursing facility resident always would create undue hardship—the resident would need nursing facility care but be unable to pay for it. However, because such reasoning essentially would allow all transfer penalties to be waived, neither Medicaid agencies nor courts have followed this line of reasoning."

PROBLEMS

1. Ms. Williams is currently a resident of Sunny View Nursing Home. She has applied for Medicaid. Her income is $1,200 per month. She has $25,000 in life-time savings. Aside from household furnishings and personal effects, her only other belongings are her home (valued at $510,000) and her car (which she has no intention of ever using again). She hopes to be able to return home, although her physician does not think that will ever be possible. She has never married and lives alone. Is she eligible for Medicaid to cover her nursing home care?

2. Mr. Gonzales gave $45,000 to his daughter in March of 2010. In June of 2013, he moved to a skilled nursing facility. At that time, he had $35,000 in countable resources and a monthly income of $1,500. By October, his countable resources were reduced to under $2,000 and he applied for Medicaid. His nursing home is in Rochester. Suppose that the monthly regional rate for Rochester is $9,000. How does the transfer affect his eligibility for Medicaid?

b. Spousal Impoverishment Protections

In 1988, Congress adopted legislation aimed at protecting spouses from becoming impoverished in the event that their husbands or wives are institutionalized in a nursing home. The effect of the resulting *spousal impoverishment protections* is to allow an individual who would not otherwise qualify for Medicaid coverage to do so by changing the way eligibility is determined for individuals in federally recognized marriages.

Spousal impoverishment protections have historically only applied to spouses of nursing home residents, although states had the option of extending those protections to spouses of persons receiving long-term care services through a HCBS waiver program. As of January 2014, however, states are required to extend spousal protections to such spouses (although the requirement will expire after five years unless renewed).

Historically, an additional limitation on the spousal impoverishment protections was that, as a result of the federal Defense of Marriage Act (DOMA), none of the protections directly applied to same-sex spouses. In a 2011 letter to state Medicaid directors, however, CMS invited states to use the undue hardship exemption to waive penalties resulting from the transfer of assets from a same-sex spouse or domestic partner. CMS also advised states that they had the option of not placing a lien on the home of a Medicaid beneficiary if the beneficiary's same-sex spouse or domestic partner resided in that home. Finally, CMS invited states to use the undue hardship exception to estate recovery to not recover from an estate where there was a surviving same-sex spouse or domestic partner. Subsequently, in *United States v. Windsor*, 133 S. Ct. 2675 (2013), the Supreme Court held Section 3 of DOMA (which excluded same-sex married couples from receiving federal benefits and protections reserved for married persons) to be unconstitutional, and today such protections should be considered to apply equally to all married couples whose marriage is recognized in the state in which they live. As of the date of publication, however, it is not entirely clear that states must provide spousal impoverishment protections to same-sex couples who enter into a valid marriage in one state but then move to a state that does not recognize their marriage.

i. Calculating Standard Spousal Impoverishment Protections

As a result of the spousal impoverishment protections, the non-institution-alized spouse (called the *community spouse*) is entitled to keep all of the income that is in his or her own name. In addition, if the community spouse's own income falls below a certain minimum amount, referred to as the *Minimum Monthly Maintenance Needs Allowance* (MMMNA), the community spouse is also entitled to the portion of the institutionalized spouse's income needed to reach the MMMNA level. The portion of the institutionalized spouse's income that the community spouse keeps is called the *Community Spouse Monthly Income Allowance* (CSMIA). States have flexibility in setting the amount of the MMMNA. In 2013, states were allowed to set the MMMNA anywhere between $1,892 and $2,898.

The community spouse is also entitled to retain the couple's home and certain other exempt resources such as a vehicle used for transportation by the community spouse. In addition, the community spouse is entitled to keep a certain amount of the couple's otherwise countable assets called the *Community Spouse Resource Allowance* (CSRA). In determining the amount of the CSRA, all assets are treated as if they are jointly owned, regardless of whose name they are in. Thus, the couple cannot protect assets simply by transferring them to the community spouse. As with the MMMNA, states have considerable flexibility in setting the amount of the CSRA. In 2013, states were allowed to set the CSRA anywhere between $23,184 and $115,920.

The next case describes the process by which a state determines eligibility for Medicaid when there is an institutionalized spouse. It also shows the potential limitations of the spousal impoverishment protections.

Poindexter v. Illinois

890 N.E.2d 410 (Ill. 2008)

Justice FITZGERALD delivered the judgment of the court, with opinion:

This appeal arises out of the state's administrative efforts to recover from plaintiffs costs of their respective spouses' nursing home care. . . . The circuit court found in favor of plaintiffs and enjoined the state from seeking spousal support. The appellate court reversed over a dissent. We granted plaintiffs leave to appeal and affirm the appellate court.

BACKGROUND

We first discuss the federal provision at issue, then the state provision that is allegedly in conflict with it, and then the specific procedural facts of this case.

A. Medicare Catastrophic Coverage Act

Medicaid is a cooperative federal-state program authorized under Title XIX of the Social Security Amendments of 1965 (42 U.S.C. §1396 et seq.). It provides medical services to both the categorically needy and the medically needy. Under prior law, a couple needed to deplete nearly all of their assets before either one could satisfy Medicaid eligibility requirements, leaving the spouse who remained in the community in a financially precarious position. In 1988, Congress attempted to fix the Medicaid system to prevent "spousal impoverishment." 42 U.S.C. §1396r-5 (2000). The MCCA provided a formula for allowing the institutionalization of one spouse, while keeping the spouse remaining in the community some distance from the poverty line.

Another goal of the MCCA was "preventing financially secure couples from obtaining Medicaid assistance." *Wisconsin Department of Health & Family Services v. Blumer*, 534 U.S. 473, 480 (2002). The MCCA prevented an "institutionalized spouse" from qualifying for Medicaid by transferring his or her interest in assets to the "community spouse." Therefore, the MCCA tried to balance two goals: "preventing impoverishment of the community spouse and ensuring that no one avoided contributing his or her fair amount to medical care." *Thomas v. Commissioner of the Division of Medical Assistance*, 425 Mass. 738, 740, 682 N.E.2d 874, 876 (1997).

To determine eligibility under these provisions, the state agency takes a "snapshot" of the couple's total current and forecasted resources and income as of the beginning of the first continuous period of institutionalization. Based on this snapshot, the agency attributes the couple's resources and income into spousal shares by a process of "deeming" and "diversion."

The MCCA's provisions consider both income and resources in determining an applicant's eligibility. Under the income category, the institutionalized spouse's income cannot exceed the maximum level set by the state. However, the community spouse's income may not be "deemed available" to the institutionalized spouse in determining eligibility. This is often called the "name-on-the-check" rule. Under this rule, a community husband's income that he retains for himself will not, under state law, be counted against (or "deemed available" to) his institutionalized spouse at the eligibility phase of the Medicaid process.

Next, the eligibility rules look at a couple's total resources. The state agency evaluates a couple's assets collectively, regardless of ownership. This collective evaluation of the couple's assets closed the loophole that allowed the couple to shelter resources solely in the name of the community spouse. A couple's total resources must be below a certain statutorily pre-scribed level called the "Community Spouse Resource Allowance" (CSRA) before the institutionalized spouse will be eligible. If the total resources are above this limit, the couple must "spend down" to gain eligibility.

The CSRA also diverts some of the institutionalized spouse's resources where the community spouse has little of his or her own resources. This may occur in the common case of a spouse who spent his or her entire career working in the home. To avoid having to "spend down" the entirety of a couple's assets to qualify the institutionalized spouse for Medicaid and thus impoverish himself or herself in the process, the community spouse is allowed to keep the CSRA. In other words, the state agency diverts some of the institutionalized spouse's assets to the community spouse to prevent spousal impoverishment. Conversely, if the community spouse retains most of the wealth, then his or her assets must be "spent down" only to the point of the CSRA.

The MCCA also provides diversion procedures regarding the couple's income to prevent spousal impoverishment. Once eligibility is reached, the state agency reexamines the ailing spouse's income to determine how much must be contributed toward nursing home costs and whether any of it should be left available to the community spouse. The institutionalized spouse is permitted to divert a portion of monthly income to the community spouse. This deduction from the institutionalized spouse's monthly income is known as the "community spouse monthly income allowance" (CSMIA). If the community spouse's income falls below the "minimum monthly maintenance needs allowance" (MMMNA), the agency allocates a portion of the institutionalized spouse's income to the community spouse. . . . Thus, if the name-on-the-check rule does not provide the community spouse with this measure of sufficient income, the agency must look to the institutionalized spouse's income to bring the community spouse's income up to the MMMNA.

Finally, the MCCA provides a "fair hearing" procedure through which a couple may challenge the results of the state agency's "snapshot." At the fair hearing, also known as an "(e)(2)(C) hearing," the state agency can address any dissatisfaction with the CSRA and the MMMNA. For example, "[i]f the couple succeeds in obtaining a higher CSRA, the institutionalized spouse may reserve additional resources for posteligibility transfer to the community spouse. The enhanced CSRA will reduce the resources the statute deems available for the payment of medical expenses; accordingly, the institutionalized spouse will become eligible for Medicaid sooner." *Blumer*, 534 U.S. at 483-84.

B. Spousal-Support Provisions

After the institutionalized spouse has received benefits, a state agency may seek recovery of nursing home costs from the community spouse. Other states refer to this as a "pay and chase" system. The State of Illinois' spousal support provisions are found in article X of the Illinois Public Aid Code (305 ILCS 5/10-1 through 10-28 (West 2006)). When one spouse receives Public Aid, the other spouse is liable to the agency providing the benefits. Section 10-11 of the Code provides that if the appropriate state agency determines that a spouse owes support, the collections unit of that agency may issue an administrative order reflecting the amount owed to the state as reimbursement.

The regulations promulgated by the state provide that the Illinois Department of Human Services "shall seek to obtain support for recipients from legally responsible individuals and shall seek the enforcement of support obligations." 89 ILL. ADM. CODE §103.10. However, "the Department shall not seek to obtain support for residents of long term care facilities if income of the spouse in the community is less than or equal to the" MMMNA. 89 ILL. ADM. CODE §103.10. In other words, the state may only recover from a community spouse whatever monies that spouse may have in addition to the MMMNA. Above that limit, 1% per month of the community spouse's gross annual income earned above $7,000 will be assessed as responsible-relative liability. . . .

C. Procedural History

* * *

Plaintiffs alleged that each plaintiff was the "community spouse" of an "institutionalized spouse" receiving medical assistance under the Medicaid program administered by the State of Illinois. Plaintiffs claimed that article X and its implementing regulations conflicted with the MCCA, and thus were preempted pursuant to the supremacy clause of the United States Constitution (U.S. CONST., art. VI, cl. 2). The MCCA, according to plaintiffs, prohibited the collection of income from the community spouse after the eligibility determination. They principally cited section 1396r-5(b)(1), which provides as follows: "During any month in which an institutionalized spouse is in the institution, except as provided in paragraph (2), no income of the community spouse shall be deemed available to the institutionalized spouse." 42 U.S.C. §1396r-5(b)(1) (2000). According to plaintiffs, this section prohibits the state from seeking a contribution for the nursing home costs from the community spouse as long as the institutionalized spouse remained in the institution. Therefore, plaintiffs sought a declaration that Illinois' spousal support provisions, article X and its companion regulations, conflict with the MCCA and thus are preempted under the supremacy clause. . . .

ANALYSIS

[After rejecting Defendants argument that plaintiffs' action was barred because plaintiffs had failed to exhaust administrative remedies, the Court addressed the preemption issue.—ED.]

The supremacy clause of the United States Constitution provides that "[t]his Constitution, and the Laws of the United States . . . shall be the supreme Law of the Land . . . any Thing in the Constitution or Laws of any State to the Contrary notwithstanding." U.S. CONST., art. VI, cl. 2. "State law is preempted under the supremacy clause in three circumstances: (1) when the express language of a federal statute indicates an intent to preempt state law; (2) when the scope of a federal regulation is so pervasive that it implies an intent to occupy a field exclusively; and (3) when state law actually conflicts with federal law." *Village of Mundelein v. Wisconsin Central R.R.*, 227 Ill. 2d 281, 288, 317 Ill. Dec. 664, 882 N.E.2d 544 (2008), citing *English v. General Electric Co.*, 496 U.S. 72, 78-79 (1990). The determination of whether state law is preempted turns on the intent of Congress.

Here, . . . plaintiffs' argument centers on the third circumstance of preemption, whether the state law actually conflicts with federal law. Plaintiffs contend that MCCA section 1396r-5(b)(1) prohibits defendants from collecting spousal support under article X. Defendants argue that section 1396r-5(b)(1) applies only to eligibility determinations. They emphasize eligibility language throughout the MCCA, and also point out that the "deemed eligible" language contained in subsection (b)(1) applies only to eligibility determinations. We agree with defendants.

A careful review of the language of the MCCA reveals an absence of consideration of the spousal support laws of which plaintiffs complain. Rather, it sets out a mechanism of deeming and diversion to implement the MCCA's twin goals of ameliorating spousal impoverishment and "preventing financially secure couples from obtaining Medicaid assistance." *Blumer*, 534 U.S. at 480. To achieve this, Congress directed that the state agency, in making its eligibility determination, take a "snapshot" of the couple's current and future resources to determine what income needed to be deemed to the institutionalized spouse and what income needed to be diverted to the community spouse. . . . [T]he MCCA . . . makes no further provisions for the income of a community spouse which may be above the MMMNA, except to the extent that a community spouse may request a "fair hearing" to raise the MMMNA or CSRA.

Thus, the community spouse's income becomes an issue only when he or she does not receive sufficient income to cover the basic costs of living. In that case, he or she may seek, through a "fair hearing," a portion of the institutionalized spouse's income to help defray necessary costs. . . . This accords with the purposes of the Act: to prevent impoverishment of the community spouse and to prevent financially secure couples from receiving benefits. . . . Accordingly, while the MCCA addresses the posteligibility income of a potentially impoverished spouse, it says nothing about the state's ability to seek reimbursement from an otherwise financially secure community spouse.

The plaintiffs further argue the appellate court improperly limited the MCCA to the first eligibility determination, pointing out that eligibility is an ongoing, monthly proposition. But the court did not do so; it merely stated that the eligibility determination does not include issues of ongoing spousal support owed to the state. Nevertheless, although an institutionalized spouse's Medicaid eligibility may be redetermined each month, this is irrelevant to the community spouse's state-law obligation to pay spousal support when their community-spouse income exceeds the MMMNA.

We therefore find that the MCCA does not preempt article X of the Public Aid Code. Accordingly, the appellate court correctly reversed the trial court's grant of declaratory, injunctive, and other relief to the plaintiffs. . . .

QUESTIONS

1. *Poindexter* provides a good illustration of the latitude states have in crafting their Medicaid laws. Should states have so much discretion? What are the advantages and disadvantages of giving states such broad latitude?

2. Suppose that the state of North Virginia sets its MMMNA at the lowest permissible level ($1,892 in 2013). Could it choose to seek to recover the cost of providing Medicaid to an institutionalized spouse from a community spouse so long as the community spouse has income above that level? Could it choose to seek to recover the cost of providing Medicaid to an institutionalized spouse from a community spouse with income below that level? Would the result be different if the state had set its MMMNA allowance at the highest permissible level ($2,898 in 2013)?

3. Spousal impoverishment protections have historically only applied where one spouse is a nursing home resident. What incentives does such a restriction create?

PROBLEMS

1. Mr. Sherry lives with his wife, Iris, in a home that they own and that is worth $250,000. His income consists of a pension of $1,200 per month and Social Security income of $1,000 per month. Her income consists of $500 in Social Security income. They have savings valued at $54,000. If Mr. Sherry becomes a nursing home resident and applies for Medicaid, what income and resources can Iris keep? For the purpose of answering this question, assume that the state they live in adopts the most generous spousal impoverishment protections allowed under federal law.

2. Lynn and Pat Burbank, a married couple, live together. Lynn is 80 and recently had a stroke. After a month in rehabilitative care, Lynn returned home. Pat, 65, has been trying to provide Lynn with the in-home care Lynn needs, but is having difficulty doing so. In part this is because Lynn needs a great deal of care; in part, it is because Pat also has a part-time job to try to make ends meet. Lynn's income is $1,200 per month; Pat's income is $2,000 per month. They jointly own a home worth $256,000, a car, and have $141,000 in savings. Assuming that there are no changes to their finances and Lynn requires nursing home care, what will be the financial effect on Pat? For the purpose of answering this question, assume that the state they live in adopts the most generous spousal impoverishment protections allowed under federal law.

ii. Retaining Additional Assets and Income

Under limited circumstances, a community spouse may retain income above the MMMNA or resources above the CSRA.

Either spouse may seek a fair hearing to increase the MMMNA. To succeed, the petitioner must show that additional income is needed because of "exceptional circumstances resulting in significant financial duress." *See* 42 U.S.C.A. §1396r-5(e)(2)(B).

Either spouse may similarly seek a fair hearing to increase the CSRA. An increase is permitted where the community spouse's income, including the CSMIA, falls below the MMMNA. In such situations, the community spouse is entitled to an increase in the CSRA in an amount sufficient to generate income to bring the community spouse's income up to the MMMNA. The next case explores the state's discretion in determining the extent of that increase.

Johnson v. Lodge

673 F. Supp. 2d 613 (M.D. Tenn. 2009)

ALETA A. TRAUGER, District Judge.

BACKGROUND

In both of these consolidated cases, the plaintiffs were denied Medicaid benefits by the state of Tennessee. The defendant, Gina Lodge, is the Commissioner of the Tennessee Department of Human Services, which administers the state's Medicaid program.

Medicaid provides medical assistance to financially needy persons. A patient in a skilled nursing facility or an intermediate care facility is eligible to receive Medicaid benefits if he or she meets certain income and resource requirements. Specifically, nursing home patients are eligible if they have assets of $2,000 or less, excluding certain types of exempt property. *See* 20 C.F.R. §416.1205 (2009). Previously, federal law required both spouses of a married couple to spend down their assets to this level if one spouse applied for benefits. But in 1988, Congress passed the Medicare Catastrophic Coverage Act ("MCCA"), 42 U.S.C. §1396r-5, to prevent "spousal impoverishment"—that is, to allow the non-institutionalized spouse to retain a certain level of assets and income. The states are responsible for administering the MCCA's requirements.

When applying for Medicaid nursing home benefits, a married couple must list all of their jointly and individually owned assets.[2] The state then calculates the community spouse resource allowance ("CSRA"), which is essentially the amount of assets that the non-institutionalized spouse (also called the "community spouse") can retain. The CSRA is one-half of the couple's non-exempt assets, provided that this amount is above the statutory floor of $20,880 and below the cap of $104,400.[3] The couple is required to spend down the rest of their assets, until they have only $2,000 in non-exempt assets remaining (excluding the CSRA), before the institutionalized spouse can receive Medicaid benefits.

The MCCA also allows the community spouse to receive a certain level of income, called the minimum monthly maintenance needs allowance ("MMMNA"). If the community spouse's income is below this level, he or she can receive part or all of the institutionalized spouse's income. If the couple's combined income is still below the MMMNA, the state may increase the CSRA to an amount that generates enough income to meet the MMMNA. This CSRA adjustment occurs when the applicant and his or her spouse appeal an initial denial of benefits and participate in a "fair hearing" before a hearing officer.

Plaintiff Benjamin Johnson is an 83-year-old nursing home resident. His wife, Wilma Johnson, is 84. When the Johnsons applied for Tennessee Medicaid benefits, the state determined that they had combined, non-exempt assets of $164,694. Wilma's CSRA was one-half of this, or $82,347. The couple's combined monthly income was approximately $1,358, which fell short of the MMMNA by $432 per month.

Because the Johnsons had not sufficiently spent down their assets, the state refused to provide Medicaid benefits. The Johnsons appealed, arguing that Wilma's CSRA should be raised to account for the MMMNA income shortfall. They argued that the new CSRA should be $172,800—effectively allowing Wilma to keep all of the couple's assets—because $172,800 is enough principal, at a 3% interest rate, to provide $432 of income per month. The hearing officer denied the Johnsons' appeal.

Plaintiffs John and Julia Crips faced a substantially identical situation. Julia is an 85-year-old nursing home resident, and John is her 81-year-old husband. The couple's non-exempt assets totaled $256,415.44. One-half of that amount exceeds the $104,400 maximum, so John's CSRA was set at

---

2. Certain property is exempt, including the couple's home and personal property. 42 U.S.C. §1396r-5(c)(5).

3. These figures were effective during the 2008 calendar year, the time period relevant to this case. They are regularly adjusted for inflation.

$104,400. The couple's income fell short of the MMMNA by $409.50. After their application for benefits was denied, they argued on appeal that the CSRA should be raised to $280,800, which at a 1.75% interest rate would provide $409.50 per month in income. The hearing officer's ruling affirmed the denial of benefits without directly discussing the monthly income issue and kept the CSRA at $104,400.

ANALYSIS

The plaintiffs claim that by refusing to increase their CSRA amounts, the state has ignored the statutory requirements of the MCCA and violated 42 U.S.C. §1983. They seek an injunction ordering the state to increase their CSRAs. The plaintiffs and the defendant have filed cross-motions for judgment on the pleadings pursuant to Federal Rule of Civil Procedure 12(c).

I. Motion for Judgment on the Pleadings Standard

The court approaches a Rule 12(c) motion for judgment on the pleadings the same way it approaches a Rule 12(b)(6) motion to dismiss. Thus, the court will "construe the complaint in the light most favorable to the plaintiff, accept its allegations as true, and draw all reasonable inferences in favor of the plaintiff." . . .

II. The MCCA's Statutory Requirements

The plaintiffs' sole argument is that if a married couple's income does not meet the MMMNA, 42 U.S.C. §1396r-5 requires the state to increase the CSRA to an amount that can generate interest income sufficient to cover the shortfall. They seek an order forcing the defendant to increase their CSRA amounts "as required by application of the formula set forth in 42 U.S.C. §1396r-5(e)(2)(C)."

* * *

The relevant provision of the MCCA states:

> Revision of community spouse resource allowance. If either such spouse establishes that the community spouse resource allowance (in relation to the amount of income generated by such an allowance) is inadequate to raise the community spouse's income to the minimum monthly maintenance needs allowance, there shall be substituted, for the community spouse resource allowance under subsection (f)(2), an amount adequate to provide such a minimum monthly maintenance needs allowance.

42 U.S.C. §1396r-5(e)(2)(C). Thus, if a couple's monthly income is less than the MMMNA, and the "amount of income generated" by the standard CSRA does not cover the shortfall, the statute requires states to "substitute[ ]" a new CSRA amount that is "adequate to provide [the MMMNA]."

The plaintiffs argue that the only permissible method for increasing the CSRA is to set it at an amount that would provide enough interest income to make up the MMMNA shortfall. . . . This argument, however, runs afoul of the text and purpose of the statute, the relevant regulatory interpretation, and the relevant case law.

A. *Statutory Text*

First, despite the plaintiffs' allegations to the contrary, the text of the statute does not set out an "arithmetical formula" for adjusting the CSRA. . . . The statute simply requires that states set the CSRA at an amount where "the income generated" by the CSRA is "adequate to provide [the MMMNA]." Certainly, one way of doing this is to set the CSRA high enough that the assets would, if placed in an interest-bearing account, produce sufficient interest income. The court will refer to this as the "interest-income method." But the statute does not foreclose other methods.

The defendant argues that states may comply by setting the CSRA at an amount sufficient to purchase a single premium immediate annuity that covers the income shortfall.[7] The court will refer to this as the "annuity method" of determining CSRA increases. . . . If, for example, the income shortfall is $500 per month, and the community spouse is able to buy a $500 per month annuity for $60,000, a CSRA of $60,000 would be enough to meet the requirements of subsection (e)(2)(C).

The court finds that this annuity method is allowed under the plain language of the statute. If a person uses assets to purchase an annuity, it is entirely proper to say that the monthly annuity payments are "income generated" by those assets. A CSRA that is equal to or higher than the cost of a sufficient annuity is thus "[ ]adequate to raise the community spouse's income to the [MMMNA]," 42 U.S.C. §1396r-5(e)(2)(C); there is no requirement that the state increase such a CSRA.

Applied to the plaintiffs' cases, the annuity method does not require CSRA increases. Wilma Johnson's MMMNA shortfall was $432 per month, and her CSRA was $82,347. An 84-year-old woman living in Tennessee can purchase an annuity that pays $432 per month for $37,073. Thus, Ms. Johnson can easily raise her monthly income to the statutory minimum by buying an annuity. Similarly, John Crips' MMMNA shortfall was $409.50 per month, and his CSRA was $104,400; an 81-year-old man in Tennessee can purchase an annuity that pays $410 per month for $37,766. Even if both plaintiffs had purchased annuities with their CSRA assets, they still would have been left with more than $20,880, which was the CSRA floor in 2008.

* * *

---

7. A single premium immediate annuity is an insurance product. The purchaser pays an initial sum of cash in exchange for regular monthly payments from the insurance company for the rest of that person's lifetime. Typically, when the person dies, the insurance company keeps the remaining principal, if any. . . .

The plaintiffs' claim fails because they have misinterpreted the plain, unambiguous text of the statute. Nevertheless, the court will further examine the persuasive authority offered by the parties.

B. Statutory Purpose

The annuity method is consistent with the purpose of the MCCA, which is to "protect community spouses from 'pauperization' while preventing financially secure couples from obtaining Medicaid assistance." *Blumer*, 534 U.S. [473, 480 (2002)]. . . . The annuity method achieves the MCCA's purpose by providing a relatively high monthly income from a relatively small capital investment. Obviously, Medicaid applicants will prefer the plaintiffs' interest-income method, because it results in a higher CSRA and ultimately allows applicants to pass more assets on to their heirs. But this preference is at odds with the welfare-program nature of Medicaid. "Congress designed a program to benefit welfare recipients, not persons seeking to benefit their heirs at the expense of other taxpayers." *Ford* [*v. Iowa Dep't of Hum. Svcs.*, 500 N.W.2d 26, 31 (Iowa 1993)].

The plaintiffs argue that the annuity method fails to prevent spousal impoverishment because (1) the community spouse's monthly needs might eventually increase and exceed the MMMNA, and (2) the community spouse might lose the institutionalized spouse's income when the institutionalized spouse dies. But these problems are inherent in any method of increasing the CSRA to cover an income shortfall. The plaintiffs' argument highlights potential shortcomings of the concept of a fixed MMMNA and the practice of attributing the institutionalized spouse's income to the community spouse—not shortcomings of the annuity method.

Furthermore, in certain cases, the plaintiffs' interpretation of the statute would lead to absurd results. If a married couple had millions of dollars in assets but no monthly income, the plaintiffs' interest-income method would require that the community spouse be allowed to retain a huge amount of assets. Using the plaintiffs' preferred 1.75% interest rate, a community spouse with no income would be given a CSRA of $1.2 million, which is enough to generate $1,750 per month in interest income. In contrast, a community spouse receiving a $1,750 per month pension could be given a CSRA as low as $20,880. This is an illogical and inequitable result, and an elderly couple with over $1 million in assets is certainly one of the "financially secure" couples that Congress sought to exclude from the Medicaid program. Using the annuity method, the CSRA of the asset-rich community spouse would be much lower—for example, a 75-year-old woman in Tennessee can purchase an annuity that pays $1,750 per month for just over $227,000. This comports better with the purpose of the MCCA.

C. Regulatory Interpretation

In addition, the federal agency charged with interpreting Medicaid statutes has explicitly approved the annuity approach. In a July 27, 2006 letter sent to state Medicaid directors, the Centers for Medicare and Medicaid Services ("CMS"), an agency within the Department of Health and Human Services, gave guidance on spousal impoverishment guidelines. ... CMS said:

> If ... there is [some MMMNA] "shortfall" remaining for the community spouse, determine the amount of increased resources needed to generate that amount of income for the community spouse. In making this calculation, States may use any reasonable method for determining the amount of resources necessary to generate adequate income, including adjusting the CSRA to the amount a person would have to invest in a single premium annuity to generate the needed income, attributing a rate of return based on a presumed available rate of interest, or other methods.

Although the CMS letter is not entitled to *Chevron* deference, ... [f]ederal appellate courts have consistently found CMS' guidance to be informative in similar circumstances. ... Here, the deference that CMS is due supports the court's reading of the statute.

D. Relevant Case Law

Finally, although there is little on-point case law, the courts that have interpreted subsection (e)(2)(C) agree that the statute permits the annuity method. As indicated above, the Iowa Supreme Court has found that the annuity method serves the overall purpose of the MCCA. *Ford*, 500 N.W.2d at 31-32. Similarly, the New York trial court in *Lynch v. Commissioner of the New York State Department of Health*, No. 5871-07, 18 Misc. 3d 1113(A), 2008 WL 80611, at *3-4, 2008 N.Y. Misc. LEXIS 21, at *4 (N.Y. Sup. Ct. Jan. 9, 2008), held that subsection (e)(2)(C) does not "manifest[ ] an intent on the part of Congress to require that community spouses be able to meet the MMMNA from interest only, without touching the [CSRA] principal portion."[13] ...

CONCLUSION

If a community spouse's income does not meet the MMMNA, that person can purchase a single premium immediate annuity to make up the shortfall. Under the plain terms of 42 U.S.C. §1396r-5(e)(2)(C), a state is not required to increase a CSRA if the CSRA already exceeds the cost of such an annuity.

---

13. The *Lynch* court went on, however, to draw a distinction between the "base CSRA, which reflects a legislative judgment as to the level of 'necessary, but not excessive, ... assets' that a community spouse should be permitted to retain," and the "additional resource allowance ... represent[ing] assets that are only 'necessary' for the limited purpose of providing the community spouse with the MMMNA." 2008 WL 80611, at *4, 2008 N.Y. Misc. LEXIS 21, at *5. This distinction is not supported by the text of the statute, which ... clearly contemplates that sometimes, the standard CSRA will be adequate to raise the community spouse's income to the MMMNA level. The court thus declines to follow *Lynch* on this point.

Accordingly, the defendant's motion will be granted, and the plaintiffs' motion will be denied. The two consolidated cases will be dismissed. . . .

NOTE

State-specificity. Note that the *Johnson* court describes a particular method for calculating the amount of the MMMNA and the CSRA, but does not acknowledge that this method can differ depending on the state nor that the amounts in question change annually. Such omissions are, unfortunately, common in descriptions of the spousal impoverishment protections.

QUESTION

Could Tennessee have used the interest approach advocated by the plaintiffs if the state had wished to do so?

c. Medicaid Liens and Estate Recovery

The federal government requires all states to adopt *estate recovery programs* (ERPs) designed to partially recoup state Medicaid expenditures from the estates of beneficiaries. States have significant discretion in how to structure their ERP.

The most significant impact of state ERPs is the effect they have on the treatment of beneficiaries' homes. Note that, as previously discussed, the home is a non-countable asset for the purpose of establishing Medicaid eligibility unless the beneficiary has equity in the house above the state's limit. Moreover, a beneficiary who is receiving care in a nursing home is entitled to retain their home—as opposed to selling it to generate funds to pay for their care—so long as they intend to return home.

State ERPs, however, allow states to put a lien on the home owned by a Medicaid beneficiary. The result is that, although the home was not counted as an asset for the purpose of determining Medicaid eligibility, it is not necessarily protected from the state. However, estate recovery is not permitted during the lifetime of a surviving spouse (no matter where he or she lives). Estate recovery is also not permitted from a surviving child who is under age 21, or who is blind or permanently disabled. Moreover, no lien may be enforced against the home if it is lived in by a sibling of the beneficiary who 1) has an equity interest in the home, 2) lives in the home for at least a year before the beneficiary was institutionalized, and 3) has continuously lived in the home since. Similarly, no lien may be enforced against the home if it is lived in by an adult child for at least two years before the beneficiary was institutionalized, the adult child has lived there continuously since, and the adult child provided care that may have delayed institutionalization to the beneficiary while the two resided together.

The next case helps to illustrate the discretion afforded to the states in designing their ERPs, and the variability among ERPs that can result from that discretion.

In re Estate of Darby

68 So. 3d 702 (Miss. App. 2011)

EN BANC.
KING, C.J., for the Court:

The DeSoto County Chancery Court granted summary judgment in favor of Linda Darby Stinson, executrix of the estate of Arlyn Darby, denying the Division of Medicaid's claim against the estate. The chancellor determined that the estate was composed of exempt property, which descended outside of the probate estate, free and clear of any debts and claims of the Division of Medicaid or any other creditor. Medicaid raises three issues: (1) whether Medicaid is entitled to reimbursement from Darby's estate, (2) whether exempt property is included within Darby's estate for purposes of the Medicaid estate recovery program, and (3) whether Darby's execution of the contract for Medicaid benefits waived his right to claim exemptions.

We find no error and affirm.

FACTS

Arlyn E. Darby was a resident of the Sardis Community Nursing Home at the time of his death on May 20, 2009. Darby had been receiving Medicaid benefits while he was a resident of the nursing home. At the time of his death, Darby owned his house and a small amount of personal property. The value of his homestead did not exceed $75,000 and the value of his personal property did not exceed $10,000. The property was devised to his children and one grandchild.

The Division of Medicaid filed a probate claim against the estate pursuant to the provisions of Title 42 of the United States Code section 1396p(b) (2006) and Mississippi Code Annotated section 43-13-317 (Rev. 2009). The claim of $123,716.13, represented the total amount Medicaid expended for Darby's medical care after he reached the age of fifty-five.

Linda Darby Stinson, Darby's daughter and executrix of the estate, filed an objection to the probated claim asserting that the property Darby owned was exempt property and not subject to Medicaid's claim. Stinson relied on Mississippi's homestead exemption statute to support her objection. The relevant portion of the statute reads "a householder shall be entitled to hold exempt from seizure or sale, under execution or attachment, the land and buildings owned and occupied as a residence." MISS. CODE ANN. §85-3-21 (Rev. 1999). Medicaid responded to the objection arguing that the real property was not exempt property because none of Darby's heirs were living in the home and declaring it as their homestead.

Stinson filed a motion for summary judgment requesting the court to determine that Medicaid's claim was not valid against Darby's property. Stinson alleged that because the property was exempt, it passed outside of the estate and therefore, was not subject to Medicaid's claim. In response to Stinson's argument that the property was exempt, Medicaid argued that even if the property were exempt, Stinson contractually waived the exemption when she submitted the application for Medicaid benefits on behalf of Darby. The court granted summary judgment in favor of Stinson. Medicaid then timely filed its notice of appeal.

ANALYSIS

* * *

1. Entitlement to Reimbursement

There is no dispute of Medicaid's right to recover its expenses from the property of a recipient's estate. The Omnibus Budget Reconciliation Act of 1993 included a provision requiring states to seek recovery of nursing home services, home and community-based services and related hospital and prescription drug services from the estate of a deceased Medicaid recipient who was fifty-five years of age or older when the assistance was received. 42 U.S.C. §1396p(b). Effective July 1, 1994, pursuant to Mississippi Code Annotated section 43-13-317, Mississippi implemented its estate recovery program.

The governing statute is as follows:

> (1) The division shall be noticed as an identified creditor against the estate of any deceased Medicaid recipient under Section 91-7-145.
>
> (2) In accordance with applicable federal law and rules and regulations, including those under Title XIX of the federal Social Security Act, the division may seek recovery of payments for nursing facility services, home- and community-based services and related hospital and prescription drug services from the estate of a deceased Medicaid recipient who was fifty-five (55) years of age or older when he or she received the assistance. The claim shall be waived by the division (a) if there is a surviving spouse; or (b) if there is a surviving dependent who is under the age of twenty-one (21) years or who is blind or disabled; or (c) as provided by federal law and regulation, if it is determined by the division or by court order that there is undue hardship.

MISS. CODE ANN. §43-13-317.

2. Exempt Property

Even though it appears that Medicaid has the right to recover from Darby's estate, the more difficult task is determining what property is included within that estate. The Omnibus Budget Reconciliation Act defines the estate as follows: "For purposes of this subsection, the term 'estate,' with respect to a deceased individual—(A) shall include all real and personal property and other assets included within the individual's estate, as defined for purposes of State probate law. . . ." 42 U.S.C. §1396p(b)(4)(A) (emphasis added).

However, the next subsection of the Act grants each state the option of expanding the definition of estate to include,

> "any other real and personal property and other assets in which the individual had any legal title or interest at the time of death (to the extent of such interest), including such assets conveyed to a survivor, heir, or assign of the deceased individual through joint tenancy, tenancy in common, survivorship, life estate, living trust, or other arrangement."

42 U.S.C. §1396p(b)(4)(B).

The federal statute clearly permits each state to specifically define what assets are included within an estate for purposes of Medicaid recovery. The State Medicaid Manual, provided by the Centers for Medicare & Medicaid Services, which is the Medicare and Medicaid governing agency within the United States Department of Health and Human Services, instructs each state to "Specify in your State plan the definition of estate that will apply." State Medicaid Manual, §3810 B.4

A. Definition of Estate

Pursuant to 42 U.S.C. section 1396p(b)(4)(B), a number of states have expanded the definition of estate to allow recovery beyond probate assets. Following the direction of the state medicaid manual, some states have incorporated a broad definition of estate for Medicaid expense recovery programs to include, but not limited to; living trusts, joint property and accounts, life insurance proceeds, non-probate assets, and the entirety of both a beneficiary's and his or her spouse's estates. Not only are states permitted to expand the assets included in a beneficiary's estate, but many states allow liens, authorized by the Tax Equity and Fiscal Responsibility Act of 198210, to be placed on real property even before the death of the Medicaid recipient. Currently, there are very few states that limit estate recovery until after the beneficiary's death while also limiting recovery from assets within the probate estate; Mississippi is a member of this category.

The Mississippi statute permitting estate recovery does not expand the definition of estate and provides that recovery is permitted "[i]n accordance with applicable federal law. . . ." Miss. Code Ann. §43-13-317. The applicable federal statute permits Medicaid to recover from those assets of Darby's that pass through probate according to Mississippi law.

B. Mississippi's Probate Laws

Neither party disputes that Darby's real property qualified as his homestead exemption pursuant to Mississippi Code Annotated section 85-3-21 (Rev. 1999). The Mississippi Supreme Court has held exempt property is not part of the estate to be administered and descends directly by statute;

and this is true whether the estate is solvent or insolvent. The descent of exempt property is governed by Mississippi Code Annotated section 91-1-19 (Rev. 2004), which states, "The property, real and personal, exempted by law from sale under execution or attachment shall, on the death of the husband or wife owning it, descend to the survivor of them and the children and grandchildren of the decedent. . . ." The supreme court has interpreted this statute to allow those entitled, including spouse, children and grandchildren, to inherit the exempt property in fee simple free of the decedent's debts.

Mississippi Code Annotated section 91-1-21 provides that exempt property is not liable for the debt of the decedent if there is a surviving spouse, children or grandchildren. The supreme court has held that the specific language of section 91-1-21 continues a decedent's homestead exemption for a surviving spouse, children or grandchildren. Therefore, Darby's children and grandchild are entitled to inherit the exempt property free of his debts.

Medicaid raises an argument that the broad homestead exemption descent statute coupled with a narrow definition of estate will limit the effectiveness of the estate recovery act. It is true that the Mississippi homestead exemption descent statute places no limitation on the age of the surviving children or grandchildren, nor does it impose occupancy restrictions. However, the statutes concerning the homestead, and its descent, are plain and unambiguous. This Court will not engage in statutory interpretation if a statute is plain and unambiguous.

Darby predeceased his children and a grandchild to whom he devised all of his property. Pursuant to the unambiguous language of the statutes, coupled with case law, the homestead, with its exemption, passed from Darby to his children and grandchildren free of his debts. Thus, Medicaid is not entitled to pursue a claim against the exempted property as it is not a part of the estate. We find this issue without merit.

3. Waiver

Medicaid claims that Stinson waived the exemption when she entered into a contractual relationship with Medicaid on behalf of Darby in order to become eligible for benefits. Medicaid argues that waiver is found in the following language of the contract, which states:

> I (We) understand that upon my/our death, the Division of Medicaid has the legal right to seek recovery from my estate for services paid by Medicaid in the absence of a legal surviving spouse or a legal surviving dependent. Consideration will be made for hardship cases. An estate consists of real & personal property. Estate recovery applies to nursing homes, home and community based waiver clients age 55 or older.

Medicaid suggests that the language "an estate consists of real & personal property," waives Darby's right to claim his homestead exemption. . . .

This Court has further explained the necessary requirements for a valid waiver, saying:

> Under Mississippi law, a "waiver" presupposes a full knowledge of a right existing, and an intentional surrender or relinquishment of that right. It contemplates something done designedly or knowingly, which modifies or changes existing rights, or varies or changes the terms and conditions of a contract. It is the voluntary surrender of a right. To establish a waiver, there must be shown an act or omission on the part of the one charged with the waiver fairly evidencing an intention permanently to surrender the right alleged to have been waived.

Taranto Amusement Co., Inc. v. Mitchell Assocs., Inc., 820 So. 2d 726, 729 (¶13) (Miss. Ct. App. 2002).

A. Knowledge of Waiver

The record does not support the idea that Darby had any knowledge of the benefits a homestead exemption provided, nor that he intentionally waived his right to the benefit of that exemption. The contract does not provide any information pertaining to, or even mention, the significance of any exemption.

The purpose of homestead exemption is to protect families from financial misfortune by preventing creditors from using a family's home to satisfy debts. . . . As valuable as the homestead exemption is, a party must be informed in order to waive the right. Many states have implemented laws governing the procedure in which a waiver of the homestead exemption may be accomplished, and at least two states have implemented laws governing the specific language that must be contained within a contract to effectuate a valid waiver. In this case, there is no substantial evidence to support the suggestion that Darby had any knowledge of the existence or significance of his right to waive his homestead exemption.

B. Intent to Waive Exemption

There is no evidence of Darby's intent to waive any of his rights. In determining a party's intent within a contract, the court must look to the express language of the contract. In this case, the alleged waiver clause merely provides a general definition of "estate." This general definition of estate does nothing to state, or even suggest, that it takes precedence over the homestead exemption statute nor does the language within the contract adopt the specific language of the federal statute to affirmatively include non-probate assets within the estate.

. . . By entering into the contract, Darby merely acknowledged Medicaid as a creditor of his estate. Unfortunately, Darby's estate has no property against which Medicaid may recover. Considering the general presumption against the finding of a waiver coupled with the lack of evidence that Darby knew the significance or intended to waive his right to an exemption, we find this issue without merit.

* * *

IRVING, J., dissenting:

... I believe that the application that Stinson submitted for Medicaid benefits effectively waived Stinson's right to assert a homestead exemption. ... Darby (or Stinson on his behalf) acknowledged that the Division of Medicaid could "seek recovery" from his estate. There was no limitation stated on the recovery other than that "[c]onsideration will be made for hardship cases." In my opinion, a reasonable person reading this statement would understand that he was allowing the Division of Medicaid to recover from his estate, regardless of any existing homestead exemption.

Therefore, I would reverse and render.

[The above opinion has been reformatted to improve readability.—ED.]

QUESTIONS

1. In *Darby*, why can the State of Mississippi only recover from assets that pass through probate?

2. Suppose that, even after *Darby*, the State of Mississippi wished to recover monies paid to deceased Medicaid beneficiaries by making a claim against beneficiaries' former homes (i.e., their "homesteads"). What would the state need to do in order to be able to effectuate such recoveries?

4. Medicaid Planning

Medicaid planning is the process by which an individual structures his or her finances to maximize his or her eligibility for Medicaid. In general, this is done with the aim of obtaining Medicaid coverage for long-term care (e.g., nursing home care). Since Medicaid is a means-tested program designed to serve those who are financially needy, Medicaid planning typically involves engaging in behavior that reduces an individual's financial resources.

The federal government is understandably unenthusiastic about the prospect of individuals self-impoverishing in order to obtain taxpayer-funded benefits. Therefore, the federal government has created a series of rules that aim to prevent people who have self-impoverished from obtaining Medicaid benefits. These rules were significantly strengthened as part of the Deficit Reduction Act of 2005, which limited the ability to engage in Medicaid planning by creating a five-year look-back period for all transfers for less than fair market value (FMV) and changing the date of onset of the penalty period for such transfers. As such, many Medicaid planning techniques that were used prior to 2005 are no longer effective.

a. Ethical Considerations

Medicaid planning is sometimes criticized as unethical or immoral. There are two primary types of ethical and moral criticisms leveled at Medicaid planning.

First, Medicaid planning is criticized on the grounds that it is unethical or immoral because it allows individuals to avoid paying for their own care and to force taxpayers to pay for that care instead. There are several responses that are commonly offered to this critique. One is to point out that most individuals who engage in Medicaid planning are doing so for the purpose of protecting relatively small amounts of assets, not fortunes. Another response is that long-term care should be seen as a community responsibility and that it is ultimately unfair to penalize individuals who are unlucky enough to need significant long-term care by forcing them to pay for that care until they are utterly impoverished. For example, attorneys Timothy Takacs and David McGuffey have argued that one reason Medicaid planning should not be considered immoral is that:

> Whether they are rich or poor, elders are participants in an amoral health care market. . . . For an elder who is "lucky" enough to develop an acute illness, such as myocardial infarction or a stroke, Medicare will pay the bill. For persons who are unlucky and develop a chronic illness such as Alzheimer's disease that requires years of costly long-term care, the American health care market place forces them to "spend down" to Medicaid eligibility. This acute/chronic dichotomy can be explained only as an artifact of the American long-term care financing system. . . . No one intends to get sick. No moral opprobrium should therefore attach to efforts by the sufferer and his family to engage in Medicaid planning to minimize the financial impact chronic illness imposes on them.

Timothy L. Takacs & David L. McGuffey, *Medicaid Planning: Can it be Justified? Legal and Ethical Implications of Medicaid Planning*, 29 WM. MITCHELL L. REV. 111, 152 (2002).

A second type of ethical critique of Medicaid planning is that attorneys or others who assist older adults with Medicaid planning are endangering those they claim to be assisting. Some have even suggested that Medicaid planning should be seen as a form of elder financial exploitation. This line of critique recognizes that when individuals engage in Medicaid planning not only are they potentially placing themselves at the mercy of those to whom they have transferred their assets, but they may be undermining their ability to access high quality health care and, especially, more desirable nursing home facilities. As Professor Richard Kaplan has noted:

> Becoming a Medicaid recipient is, after all, not without its consequences. It is an open secret that many long-term care facilities limit the number of Medicaid recipients that they will accept, and some institutions do not participate in the program at all. Recent trends towards ever-lower Medicaid rates paid by the government reduce further the number of places available to Medicaid recipients. Thus, not only does one's status as a Medicaid recipient limit his

initial choice of nursing facilities, but if the quality of care deteriorates at his facility, being a Medicaid recipient might affect that person's ability to move elsewhere.

In addition, the impoverishment that Medicaid demands can affect relations with an older person's family members. A Medicaid recipient's ability to give money and property to favored relatives or on special occasions is significantly curtailed, and such gifting activity is often an important source of family pride and self-esteem. Furthermore, the prospect of lost inheritances can motivate family members to consider various strategies that typically diminish an elder's financial independence.

Richard L. Kaplan, *Cracking the Conundrum: Toward a Rational Financing of Long-Term Care*, 2004 U. ILL. L. REV. 47, 71-72 (2004). Indeed, the difficulty that Medicaid recipients can face when trying to obtain admission to a nursing home of their choice is not only an "open secret" but one that has been repeatedly documented in the social sciences literature. *See, e.g.*, Madonna Harrington Meyer, *Medicaid Reimbursement Rates and Access to Nursing Homes: Implications for Gender, Race, and Marital Status*, 23 RES. ON AGING 532 (2001) (noting prior research indicating that nursing homes are less willing to admit Medicaid beneficiaries, and finding that fewer Medicaid recipients are admitted to nursing homes where the difference in the private pay rate and the Medicaid rate is large than to homes where the difference is small, thus suggesting that discrimination in admissions increases as the financial incentive to discriminate increases).

One response to the criticism that Medicaid planning endangers clients is simply to note that it is the attorney's ethical duty to represent the client's wishes, not simply the client's best interest. Helping a client engage in Medicaid planning if the client desires to do so is thus fully consistent with the attorney's ethical obligation. A second response is that those who assist with Medicaid planning are helping older adults to preserve resources that third parties can use to provide for the older adult—resources that might soon be readily depleted and unavailable to that person without such planning. For example, attorneys Joseph Karp and Sara Gershbein argued that:

> When one engages in Medicaid planning, protected assets may be used to enhance the quality of the institutionalized person's life. With Medicaid planning, assets frequently wind up in the hands of spouse, children, or grandchildren. Often there is an implicit understanding among the parties that the money will be used to subsidize the institutionalized elder's care. Medicaid provides only the bare minimum, if that. Money in the hands of family can be used to improve the institutionalized elder's quality of care, and hence quality of life, by purchasing additional services such as more personal care through an aide. If Medicaid planning were not used, an individual's money supply would quickly be depleted by the costs of the nursing facility. When one engages in Medicaid planning, the cost of nursing care is subsidized, leaving money that can be spent over time to supplement care. . . .

Joseph S. Karp & Sara I. Gershbein, *Poor on Paper: An Overview of the Ethics & Morality of Medicaid Planning*, FLA. BAR J. (Oct. 2005).

Although much attention has been focused on the ethics of Medicaid planning, the Medicaid program has itself been criticized for creating a structure that forces individuals in need of long-term care to choose whether to pre-emptively self-impoverish or whether to become impoverished by paying the massive costs associated with nursing home care. Professor John Miller, for example, has emphasized the emotional costs such a system imposes on older adults, explaining:

> Voluntary impoverishment conflicts with the core American value of self reliance and, hence, it may feel shameful and opportunistic. Ours is a society that places a high value on material achievement and personal autonomy. People who have spent their whole lives seeking to establish and maintain their financial and personal independence are likely to suffer great loss of self regard after becoming impoverished and being placed in a program explicitly labeled as for "the needy."
>
> . . . [N]ot only does voluntary impoverishment impose high costs in terms of personal security and self-respect, but the spend down alternative may be just as personally destructive. This is because a person who chooses not to engage in voluntary impoverishment may experience a strong feeling that he has been a chump or a sucker. He may feel that only an idiot would choose to spend his life's savings to buy something he can have at substantially lesser cost or, possibly, for free. This sense of having played the fool must be especially bitter for those persons who, as is likely, spend down their assets and end up impoverished, humiliated, and stigmatized anyway. When the choice is between becoming impoverished through spend down and becoming impoverished by gifting to loved ones, the person who chooses to spend down may regard himself as having been stupidly honorable at the expense of those who matter most to him or her. Moreover, by gifting away assets that are destined to be lost anyway, the donor can at least hope to gain the donee's goodwill. By engaging in spend down, however, that opportunity is lost. Thus, the person who chooses to spend down may end up believing that he has deprived both himself and his loved ones out of mere stubborn pride, and his family may feel the same way. The person who engages in spend down pays a heavy price emotionally as well as financially.
>
> Thus, the present structure of the law offers a choice between being a free-loader and an uncaring fool. In both cases, one is likely to approach life's end in circumstances of dire financial peril. This is hardly a desirable state of affairs.

John A. Miller, *Voluntary Impoverishment to Obtain Government Benefits*, 13 CORNELL J.L. & PUB. POL'Y 81, 100-01 (2003) (suggesting that one way to improve the system would be to raise the resource levels for Medicaid eligibility and repeal estate recovery rules so that individuals would not need to self-impoverish to receive long-term care, but would nevertheless remain partially responsible for paying for their long-term care needs). *See also* Kaplan, *Cracking the Conundrum, supra* page 305, at 71-72 (2004) (characterizing the federal government's decision to limit long-term care coverage to those who are Medicaid-eligible as "cruel" in part because it encourages older adults to liquidate their live savings leaving them feeling vulnerable and despondent).

The next two cases explore two different aspects of the debate over the ethics and morality of Medicaid planning. The first considers the constitutionality of a federal law that prohibited assistance with Medicaid planning. The second considers whether a guardian should be permitted to engage in Medicaid planning on behalf of his ward.

New York State Bar Association v. Reno

999 F. Supp. 710 (N.D.N.Y. 1998)

McAVOY, Chief Judge.

Plaintiff, the New York State Bar Association ("NYSBA"), seeks to enjoin the Attorney General of the United States from enforcing section 4734 of the Balanced Budget Act of 1997. . . . Plaintiff asserts that section 4734 violates the First and Fifth Amendments to the United States Constitution.

I. BACKGROUND

A. Statutory Background

Before Congress enacted section 217 of the Health Insurance Portability and Accountability Act of 1996, certain transfers of assets up to 36 months prior to an application for Medicaid benefits and certain transfers to trusts up to 60 months prior to application, could result in a period of ineligibility for Medicaid benefits. 42 U.S.C. §1396p(c). In enacting section 217, Congress left the ineligibility period intact, but added certain criminal penalties. Essentially, section 217 made it a crime to dispose of assets in order to become eligible for Medicaid benefits if the disposition of assets "resulted in the imposition of a period of ineligibility." §1320a-7b(a)(6) (sometimes referred to as the "Granny Goes to Jail Act"). Violators were subject to fines of up to $25,000 or imprisonment for up to 5 years, or both.

A number of organizations lobbied for the repeal of section 217, including the NYSBA. Rather than repeal the Granny Goes to Jail Act, Congress amended section 217 by enacting section 4734 of the Balanced Budget Act of 1997. Section 4734, which became effective August 5, 1997, struck the former language and added a provision making it illegal to counsel or assist an individual to dispose of certain assets to qualify for Medicaid:

> **Criminal penalties for acts involving Federal health care programs** (a) Making or causing to be made false statements or representations Whoever— . . . (6) for a fee knowingly and willfully counsels or assists an individual to dispose of assets (including by any transfer in trust) in order for the individual to become eligible for medical assistance under a State plan under subchapter XIX of this chapter, if disposing of the assets results in the imposition of a period of ineligibility for such assistance under section 1396p(c) of this title, shall . . . (ii) in the case of such a statement, representation, concealment, failure, conversion, or provision of counsel or assistance by any other person, be guilty of a misdemeanor and upon conviction

thereof fined not more than $10,000 or imprisoned for not more than one year, or both. 42 U.S.C. §1320a-7b(a).

While section 4734 was in conference, the Congressional Research Service ("CRS") prepared a memorandum, dated July 11, 1997, analyzing the legal and constitutional issues raised by the proposed language of section 4734. CRS expressed concern that the language would infringe the First Amendment. . . . Congress nevertheless passed the provision without modification, and the President signed section 4734 into law.

B. Procedural Background

Plaintiff filed the instant motion for a preliminary injunction on January 27, 1998. After a number of extensions and adjournments, Defendant now states that it will neither defend the constitutionality of 42 U.S.C. section 1320a-7b(a)(6) nor enforce its criminal provisions. On March 11, 1998, Attorney General Janet Reno notified the United States House of Representatives and the United States Senate that the Department of Justice would not enforce the aforementioned criminal provisions. Not surprisingly, Defendant now argues that a preliminary injunction is no longer needed.

In response, NYSBA filed opposition arguing that its members' free speech rights are still being chilled. Essentially, NYSBA argues that section 4734 is unconstitutional for the following reasons: (1) it violates the First Amendment because it unconstitutionally restricts free speech; (2) it violates the First Amendment because it is overly broad; and (3) it violates the Fifth Amendment because it is vague.

II. DISCUSSION

A. Standing

[The court determined that the NYSBA had standing to pursue the action.—ED.]

B. Preliminary Injunction

In this circuit the standard for obtaining a preliminary injunction is well established. In order to obtain a preliminary injunction the movant must make an affirmative showing of: (1) irreparable harm; and either (2) likelihood of success on the merits; or (3) sufficiently serious questions going to the merits to make them a fair ground for litigation and a balance of hardships tipping decidedly in favor of the movant. However, "where the moving party seeks to stay governmental action taken in the public interest pursuant to a statutory or regulatory scheme, the district court . . . should not grant the injunction unless the moving party establishes, along with irreparable injury, a likelihood that he will succeed on the merits of his claim." *Plaza Health Laboratories, Inc. v. Perales*, 878 F.2d 577, 580 (2d Cir. 1989). . . .

i. Irreparable Harm

* * *

Turning to the first prong of this test, if the government's enforcement of section 4734 will deprive Plaintiff of its First Amendment rights, this constitutes *per se* irreparable injury to Plaintiff. *See Elrod v. Burns*, 427 U.S. 347 (1976). In *Elrod v. Burns*, the Supreme Court instructed that "[t]he loss of First Amendment freedoms, for even minimal periods of time, unquestionably constitutes irreparable injury." 427 U.S. at 373; *see also Paulsen v. County of Nassau*, 925 F.2d 65, 68 (2d Cir. 1991) (stating that even a temporary abridgment of the First Amendment right to free expression constitutes irreparable injury).

* * *

Governmental infringement of the First Amendment does not exist merely in the *imposition* of criminal sanctions. As the Supreme Court noted in *Elrod*, the First Amendment is implicated whenever free speech is "either threatened or in fact being impaired at the time the relief [is] sought." "These freedoms are delicate and vulnerable, as well as supremely precious in our society. The threat of sanctions may deter their exercise almost as potently as the actual application of sanctions." *National Ass'n for Advancement of Colored People v. Button*, 371 U.S. 415 (1963).

Even in the absence of hardship from imminent prosecution or threat of prosecution, however, a "claim might still be ripe under First Amendment jurisprudence if ... First Amendment rights have been restricted or 'chilled.'" ... The reasons for relaxing the ripeness analysis in this context is the chilling effect that unconstitutional burdens on free speech may occasion. ...

The irreparable harm that exists here is the potential for self-censorship among NYSBA members. NYSBA members have an ethical obligation as attorneys to respect and uphold the law. In fact, Plaintiff's affidavits state that section 4734 actually has resulted in NYSBA members refraining from providing certain counsel and assistance to clients. Furthermore, Defendant provides no assurance that NYSBA members will not be prosecuted on some future date or that state Medicaid fraud units will also not enforce section 4734.

Accordingly, inasmuch as section 4734 remains part of the laws of the United States, which NYSBA members are ethically bound to uphold, the limitation on free speech found in section 4734 constitutes irreparable injury to Plaintiff. Thus, Plaintiff has satisfied the first of the two elements required for a preliminary injunction.

ii. Likelihood of Success

The second element requires the Court to determine whether Plaintiff is likely to succeed on the merits of its constitutional challenge. As this Court stated in *Nakatomi Investments* [*v. City of Schenectady*, 949 F. Supp. 988 (N.D.N.Y 1997)], "it has long been axiomatic that once a party shows that a regulation deprives them of a protected First Amendment interest, the burden shifts to the Government to justify the infringement."

At this time, however, it does not appear that the government contests the unconstitutionality of section 4734. Therefore, the Court must find that Plaintiff will likely succeed on the merits of its claims.

III. CONCLUSION

For the foregoing reasons, Plaintiff's Motion for a Preliminary Injunction is GRANTED. It is hereby ORDERED that pending final judgment, the United States, its agents, servants, employees, attorneys, and all persons in active concert and participation with Defendant are enjoined from commencing, maintaining, or otherwise taking action to enforce 42 U.S.C. §1320a-7b(a)(6).

IT IS SO ORDERED.

PROBLEM

Mrs. Smith, a widowed former schoolteacher, anticipates that she may in coming years need long-term care. She wants to be sure her money is inherited by her daughter Cindy, and does not want to spend her life savings paying for nursing home care. In your opinion, is it ethical for you to advise her as to how to structure her finances to enable this to happen? Would you do so?

In the Matter of Mildred Keri

853 A.2d 909 (N.J. 2004)

Chief Justice PORITZ delivered the opinion of the Court.

This case presents the question whether self-sufficient adult children who serve as their incompetent parents' legal guardians may transfer to themselves all or part of their parents' assets in order to hasten their parents' eligibility for Medicaid benefits. We hold that when certain criteria are satisfied, they may, in order to effectuate a decision their parents would have made if competent.

I.

When this litigation commenced two years ago, Mildred Keri (Keri), now ninety years old, lived alone in her New Brunswick home. Since 1995, she had been dependent exclusively on the care of her two sons, Richard Keri (Richard or petitioner) and Charles Keri (Charles). To forestall placing her in a nursing home, both men visited her regularly on alternating days and made numerous arrangements for their mother's care in their absence. Among other things, they arranged for Keri's lunch to be delivered daily at noon by Meals on Wheels, and provided her evening meal themselves when they visited with her.

In the months preceding this litigation, Keri became increasingly difficult to care for, refusing her sons' requests for her to live with them and neglecting to maintain her personal hygiene. After finding her house filled with smoke one day, her sons had the stove disconnected and capped to prevent future harm to their mother. Her condition deteriorated to the point where Richard and Charles finally determined that they could no longer avoid placing her in a nursing home. Keri's treating physicians certified she suffered from an irreversible dementia that had so impaired her cognitive abilities that she could no longer care for herself. They concluded Keri would not experience any significant improvement in the future even with treatment. In their view, her condition would render her vulnerable to abuse, exploitation, and neglect.

Financially, Keri's unencumbered residence was found to constitute the bulk of her net worth (at approximately $170,000 according to appraisals requested by the petitioner), whereas her pension benefits and Social Security provided a monthly income of $1,575.45. Although Keri's will divides her estate equally between her two sons, petitioner is her agent by a general power of attorney executed on November 11, 1996. That instrument allowed petitioner to apply for Medicaid benefits for his mother, but did not authorize him to make gifts on her behalf for any reason.

On May 10, 2002, pursuant to *N.J.S.A.* 3B:12-25, petitioner sought guardianship of his mother and her estate. He also submitted for court approval his proposed Medicaid "spend-down plan." He sought authority to sell his mother's house and transfer a significant portion of the proceeds to himself and his brother in equal shares as a means of "spending down" her assets to accelerate her Medicaid eligibility. Assuming that his mother's monthly nursing home expenses would be $6,500 and that the sale of her house would net $170,000, Richard determined that, after subtracting her monthly income of $1,575.45, Keri would need $4,924.55 per month from her savings to cover her stay. Based on those figures, petitioner sought permission to transfer $92,000 of the proceeds to himself and his brother in equal shares. According to his calculations, the remaining $78,000 would be sufficient to pay his mother's nursing home bills during the sixteen-month period of Medicaid ineligibility triggered by the transfer. In other words, seventeen months after the proposed transfer, Keri would have "spent down" enough of her assets to qualify for Medicaid.

Throughout the trial below, petitioner maintained that, if not so ill, his mother would have approved of and undertaken such an estate planning strategy to preserve a significant portion of her assets for her two sons. His brother, Charles, did not object to the proposal. As required, Keri's court-appointed counsel prepared a Report of a Court Appointed Attorney recommending that the court approve petitioner's estate plan, although he did not offer any evidence or cross-examine Richard.

On June 26, 2002, the trial court granted petitioner's guardianship application and ordered the sale of Keri's residence and her placement in a nursing home. The trial court denied petitioner authority to execute the Medicaid spend-down plan, however, refusing to approve strategies designed to "[pauperize] human beings and citizens in the United States solely to make them [wards] of the taxpayers."

The Appellate Division affirmed in part, reversed in part, and remanded for further proceedings. Because the panel would not presume that a competent and reasonable adult would engage in spend-down Medicaid planning, it held that courts should employ a purely subjective standard "to protect the incompetent's right to self-determination." Under that standard, approval of a spend-down plan proposed by an incompetent's self-sufficient adult children should occur only when the incompetent person has indicated that preference before losing competency. Keri had never expressed a preference, and therefore the Appellate Division found that the trial court properly rejected petitioner's proposal. Further, out of concern for Keri's wishes and best interests, the Appellate Division reversed and remanded the matter for reconsideration whether petitioner should be permitted to sell his mother's house and place her in a nursing facility, and directed the trial court to seek intervention of the Public Guardian on Keri's behalf.

We granted Richard's petition for certification. . . . We now reverse.

II.

A.

* * *

[W]hen managing the estates of incompetent persons, including the exercise of the power to make gifts, our courts must find that the proposed action is in "the best interests of the ward," *N.J.S.A.* 3B:12-50, and that any gifts proposed are such "as the ward might have been expected to make," *N.J.S.A.* 3B:12-58. Together, those statutory provisions incorporate and reconcile the best interests standard with the common law equitable doctrine of substituted judgment. Only when the estate contains the resources necessary for the benefit of the ward (best interests), may the guardian make gifts "in the same manner as the incompetent would if able to function at full capacity" (substituted judgment).

B.

The concepts found in the statutes governing the powers of courts and guardians have long been a part of our law. Prior to the enactment of *N.J.S.A.* 3B:12-36 to -64, our courts relied on the doctrine of *parens patriae* to "intervene in the management and administration of an incompetent's estate in a given case for the benefit of the incompetent or of his estate." *In re Trott*, 118 N.J. Super. 436, 440, 288 A.2d 303 (Ch. Div. 1972). In *Trott*, the court . . . endorsed the principle that in the management of the estate of [an] incompetent, "the guardian should be authorized to act as a reasonable and prudent [person] would act [in the management of his own estate] under the same circumstances, unless there is evidence of any settled intention of the incompetent, formed while sane, to the contrary."

* * *

To answer in a specific case the question whether the guardian should be permitted "to make the gifts proposed," *Trott* requires the guardian to establish five criteria: (1) the mental and physical condition of the incompetent are such that the possibility of her restoration to competency is virtually nonexistent; (2) the assets of the estate of the incompetent remaining after the consummation of the proposed gifts are such that, in the light of her life expectancy and her present condition of health, they are more than adequate to meet all of her needs in the style and comfort in which she now is (and since the onset of her incompetency has been) maintained, giving due consideration to all normal contingencies; (3) the donees constitute the natural objects of the bounty of the incompetent by any standard . . . ; (4) the transfer will benefit and advantage the estate of the incompetent by a reduction of death taxes; (5) there is no substantial evidence that the incompetent, as a reasonably prudent person, would, if competent, not make the gifts proposed in order to effectuate a saving of death taxes.

* * *

The *Trott* criteria, which we now adopt, have been applied by our courts in exercising their statutory authority to determine whether estate-planning proposals offered by guardians are in the wards' best interests and give effect to the wards' wishes had they been able to express them. . . . In effect, *Trott* provides a framework consisting of a set of objective tests (criteria (1), (3) and (4)) for the application of substituted judgment, taking into account the ward's best interests (criterion (2)). Criterion (5), however, introduces a subjective test with a high evidentiary burden to rebut substituted judgment: that "there is no substantial evidence" the ward, "if competent," would not approve a Medicaid spend-down plan.

* * *

C.

The New Jersey cases we have reviewed support the petitioner's claim that when a Medicaid spend-down plan does not interrupt or diminish a ward's care, involves transfers to the natural objects of a ward's bounty, and does not contravene an expressed prior intent or interest, the plan, *a fortiori*, provides for the best interests of the ward and satisfies the law's goal to effectuate decisions an incompetent would make if he or she were able to act. That approach accords with decisions of the New York courts addressing the same issues.

Under N.Y. Mental Hyg. Law §81.21(a) (McKinney 1996), a court may authorize the guardian to exercise those powers necessary and sufficient . . . to transfer a part of the incapacitated person's assets to or for the benefit of another person on the ground that the incapacitated person would have made the transfer if he or she had the capacity to act. . . . When legal guardians have satisfied the statutory requirements, New York permits them to engage in Medicaid planning even when the guardians themselves may be the recipients of transfers from the wards' assets. . . . Indeed, New York has established a presumption in favor of approving Medicaid spend-down proposals on the ground that a reasonable and competent person "'would prefer that the costs of his care be paid by the State, as opposed to his family.'"

We agree with the New York courts. We find, further, that the *Trott* criteria impliedly establish a presumption in favor of spend-down proposals by recognizing the benefit to the ward's estate of increasing the amounts available to beneficiaries by reducing payments to the government out of the estate. Also significant, *Trott* requires "substantial evidence that the incompetent, as a reasonably prudent person, would, if competent, not make the gifts proposed." . . . Thus, under *Trott*, which we have adopted today, the presumption can be overcome only with "substantial evidence," a high threshold that is consonant with the approach in New York.

III.

In this case, we find that petitioner's proposed Medicaid spend-down plan meets the *Trott* criteria and should be approved. It is undisputed that the first criterion of *Trott* is satisfied because Keri suffers from irreversible dementia. "[H]er restoration to competency is virtually nonexistent." Richard's spend-down plan is designed to provide adequate funding for his mother's nursing home care during the triggered period of Medicaid ineligibility and therefore meets the second criterion of *Trott*. The testimony indicates that Keri needs care twenty-four hours a day and that Richard was concerned about locating an appropriate facility for her. The trial court found that placement in a nursing home was necessary. Because both state and federal law prevent a Medicaid approved facility from transferring a patient based on a change in pay status, we should not anticipate that when Medicaid assumes Keri's financial obligations, the quality of her care will suffer. Further, New Jersey statutes do not distinguish nursing homes that participate in Medicaid or Medicare from those that do not. . . .

Federal law is no less demanding; Medicaid funding is conditioned on nursing home compliance with federal standards for dignified care. . . . [5]

The third criterion of *Trott*, that the donees of petitioner's spend-down plan "constitute the natural objects of the bounty of the incompetent," unquestionably is met. . . . Richard and Charles are Keri's sons, and her will leaves her estate in equal parts to them. . . . And, the proposed transfer of assets "will benefit and advantage the estate of the incompetent," as required by the fourth

---

5. We are informed by amicus curiae, New Jersey Chapter of National Academy of Elder Law Attorneys, that New Jersey has 358 nursing homes, 320 of which participate in the Medicaid Program.

Trott criterion. . . . Assuming Keri nets $170,000 from the sale of her house, the plan proposes to preserve $92,000 of those proceeds for her sons to share. If Keri spends the remainder of her life in a nursing home without selling her house, the state would be authorized to impose a lien for Medicaid cost reimbursement and Richard and Charles likely would get nothing. . . . If Keri sold the house without transferring her assets, then her entire financial investment would be paid out in less than three years for nursing home costs, and, again, Richard and Charles likely would get nothing. Under petitioner's plan, Keri could preserve approximately $46,000 from the proceeds of the sale of her home for each of her sons, the beneficiaries of her will.

Finally, the fifth *Trott* criterion is satisfied because there is no evidence in the record indicating that Keri would have disapproved petitioner's proposed spend-down plan. The Appellate Division focused on Keri's preference to stay in her house, a preference that conflicted with petitioner's proposed plan. But, if Keri could not live in her house without twenty-four hour care, as the trial court found, then she would have to pay for around-the-clock nursing. The result is a veritable "Catch-22"—without selling her house, Keri does not have the funds to maintain in-home care for more than a short period. Moreover, because of her dementia Keri had become difficult at best, suggesting that in-home care would not be feasible. The question, then, is whether substantial evidence indicates that Keri would have disapproved petitioner's Medicaid planning proposal in those unfortunate circumstances. There simply is nothing in the record to suggest that disapproval.

We therefore find that petitioner's spend-down plan represents a decision that his mother "might have been expected to make," *N.J.S.A.* 3B:12-58, and satisfies both the applicable statutes and the *Trott* criteria.

IV.

The Public Guardian for the Elderly takes the position that a child-beneficiary who serves as a guardian should not be permitted to propose a Medicaid spend-down plan for his or her ward because to do so would be a clear conflict of interest. He claims that here petitioner "is violating his fiduciary duty to his mother by self-dealing through medicaid planning." The Appellate Division accepted that position, stating:

> Unlike the situation involving spouses, there is a greater likelihood of conflict of interest when the gift-beneficiaries are children. As [a] Florida court observed . . . : "Courts must make room for the possibility that some children may try to pressure vulnerable parents into divesting themselves of assets so that the estate is not depleted by the costs of nursing home care."

There is a fundamental problem with the approach taken by the Public Guardian and the court below. As in this case, the natural objects of a ward's bounty often are the same persons likely to be chosen by the courts as guardians, *i.e.*, children, spouses, close friends or relatives. . . . Disqualifying those individuals from receipt of asset transfers on conflict of interest grounds prevents the use of substituted judgment in the majority of cases because, if not disabled, incompetent persons most likely would transfer their assets to their guardians. . . .

Finally, the Appellate Division's characterization of Medicaid spend-down plans requires a response from this Court. The panel described such plans as follows:

> Putting euphemisms to one side, the plan, if followed by a competent person, is nothing other than self-imposed impoverishment to obtain, at taxpayers' expense, benefits intended for the truly needy. . . .

Yet, the panel also acknowledged:

> Nonetheless, a competent individual may engage in such planning. . . . The question for us to resolve is whether it should be permitted by a guardian for the benefit of an incompetent's self-sufficient, adult children. . . .

As *amicus curiae* Legal Services and the New Jersey State Bar Association point out, Medicaid planning is legally permissible under federal and state Medicaid law. Notwithstanding the Appellate Division's laudable purpose to preserve public monies for those who are in need, Congress has carefully defined and circumscribed Medicaid planning, as has the State of New Jersey. By its actions, Congress has set the public policy for this program and although some might choose a different course, the law has not. Few would suggest that it is improper for taxpayers to maximize their deductions under our tax laws to preserve income for themselves and their families—even though they are, by their actions, reducing the amount of money available to government for its public purposes. So long as the law allows competent persons to engage in Medicaid planning, incompetent persons, through their guardians, should have the same right, subject to the legal constraints laid out herein.

V.

The judgment of the Appellate Division is reversed, and the matter is remanded to the trial court for the entry of an order consistent with this opinion.

NOTE

At the time *Keri* was decided, the look-back period was three years and the penalty period began the month after the date that the transfer for less than FMV was made. It was therefore possible for individuals to use a Medicaid planning strategy referred to as *half-a-loaf* planning in which the would-be beneficiary would give away half of his or her resources and use the other half to pay for nursing home care during the penalty period. It was this strategy that Richard was seeking to use in *Keri*. Since the penalty period now begins at the date the would-be beneficiary is otherwise eligible for Medicaid, the half a loaf strategy is no longer viable.

QUESTIONS

1. To what extent should attorneys assisting clients with Medicaid planning warn those clients of the hazards of self-impoverishment? Consider this explanation offered by attorneys Kenney F. Hegland and Robert B. Fleming in a self-help book about elder law for older adults:

> Medicaid planning entails shedding yourself of the assets and income which would make you ineligible; in other words, making yourself poor. The downside, of course, is that you will be poor.
>
> You'll have to give most of your life savings away. They won't be there for an emergency or, more hopefully, for a totally irresponsible fling. Most people give their assets to their kids, counting on them to bail them out if need be. But even if your kids are more grateful than two of Lear's daughters and drink less than Falstaff, *their* creditors can get what were *your* assets. How's the kids' driving?

KENNEY F. HEGLAND & ROBERT B. FLEMING, NEW TIMES, NEW CHALLENGES: LAW AND ADVICE FOR SAVVY SENIORS AND THEIR FAMILIES 77 (2010).

If you were an elder law attorney, would you offer similar words of caution to your clients before assisting them with Medicaid planning? Why or why not?

2. Does the reason why an individual is engaging in Medicaid planning make an ethical difference? Karp and Gershbein suggested that it should, writing:

> [T]here is less justification for Medicaid planning when it is at the insistence of children who are trying to protect their inheritance.... Medicaid planning is justified only if the goal of bettering the elder's life takes priority over protecting the elder's assets.

Joseph S. Karp & Sara I. Gershbein, *Poor on Paper: An Overview of the Ethics & Morality of Medicaid Planning*, FLA. BAR J. (Oct. 2005).

Do you agree? Why or why not?

3. Is Medicaid planning a form of cheating? Why or why not?

4. Who benefits from Medicaid planning? Who is disadvantaged by it?

5. Does Medicaid planning ever benefit older adults? If not—or if it rarely does—what are the ethical implications (if any) for attorneys?

b. Medicaid Planning Techniques

Even after the Deficit Reduction Act of 2005, there are a wide variety of Medicaid planning techniques utilized by attorneys to maximize their clients' Medicaid eligibility and coverage. These vary greatly both in their complexity and in the likelihood that they will successfully preserve assets. This subsection explores a variety of the more prominent approaches.

Transfer assets to a third party. Perhaps the simplest technique is to transfer assets to a qualifying family member. As described in Section C.3.a of this chapter, a transfer will not trigger a penalty if it is made to the applicant's spouse and/or the applicant's blind or disabled child. In addition, a transfer of a home is an exempt transfer if the home is transferred to 1) the applicant's sibling who has an equity interest in the home and who lived in it for at least a year before the beneficiary's institutionalization, 2) the applicant's adult child who lived in the home for at least two years before the beneficiary's institutionalization and who provided care to the beneficiary during that period, or 3) the applicant's minor child. However, transferring assets to a spouse will only protect a limited amount of assets because, as described on page 285 of this chapter, a married person is generally only eligible for Medicaid where the combined assets of the couple fall below a state-mandated level. Moreover, the technique does not work for many people because the people whom they wish to benefit (e.g., non-disabled children, grandchildren) do not fall within these narrow categories; thus transfers to them must be made more than five years before a Medicaid application in order to avoid a period of ineligibility.

Purchase exempt resources and pre-pay expenses. Especially where relatively small amounts of money are involved, a viable strategy may be for the individual to make improvements to exempt resources (e.g., making repairs to their primary vehicle or a house), to purchase exempt resources (e.g., household goods, a car that can be used for transportation, or a new residence), or to pre-pay expenses (e.g., the year's telephone bill). This allows the individual to use resources for his or her own benefit, while simultaneously accelerating Medicaid eligibility. Such purchases are likely to be particularly valuable where they will be enjoyed by a spouse even if the purchaser moves to a long-term care facility, or where the items purchased can be used the individual even if they live in a long-term care facility.

Transfer assets to a trust. Assets transferred by an individual to an irrevocable trust are generally not deemed to be part of an individual's assets for Medicaid eligibility purposes if the trust principal cannot be paid to that individual or used for the benefit of that individual. However, transfers that occur within five years of an application are generally considered a transfer for less than FMV. Thus, by the time many individuals decide to engage in Medicaid planning, it is likely to be too late to use this technique.

Convert assets to income. Assets can be converted into income by having the client or his or her spouse purchase an annuity. The purchase will not be deemed a transfer for less than FMV if it is actuarially sound, irrevocable, and starts immediately. By purchasing an annuity, a would-be beneficiary converts a resource to an income stream. The resulting income will be deemed available to pay for the individual's care, unless it is counted as part of the spouse's income as discussed in this chapter's earlier discussion of spousal impoverishment protections. Thus, it is particularly likely to be advantageous in situations in which the community spouse would otherwise not have sufficient income to meet the MMMNA. In addition to providing an income stream for the community spouse, the technique can also preserve assets for the beneficiary's family. This is because if the primary beneficiary is a spouse, a minor child, or a disabled child, and that beneficiary survives the Medicaid recipient, he or she may retain the balance of the annuity after the Medicaid recipient's death, so long as the state is named as the remainder beneficiary for at least the value of Medicaid assistance paid (and therefore will get at least a portion of the remaining sums if no such person survives the Medicaid recipient).

Buy a life estate. The would-be Medicaid beneficiary can purchase a life estate in the home of a person they wish to benefit. Such purchases will not be deemed transfers for less than FMV if: (1) the purchaser resides in the home for a continuous period of at least one year after the date of purchase, and (2) the purchase is actuarially sound (i.e., the purchaser did not overpay relative to his or her life expectancy).

Direct funds to a special needs trust. A *Special* or *Supplemental Needs Trust* (SNT) is a trust created for the benefit of a disabled person and which consists of funds that cannot be used to pay for food, shelter, or medical care for which Medicaid would pay. Instead, such trusts pay for supplemental items such as clothing, transportation, technology such as a telephone or computer, supplemental medical care and companionship services, travel, and entertainment. The assets in a valid SNT do not constitute a countable resource for determining Medicaid eligibility. However, to qualify for this favorable treatment, if the SNT is established using the beneficiary's own funds, any money remaining in it upon the death of the beneficiary must be used to pay back the state for the value of the Medicaid benefits paid to the beneficiary.

SNTs are of somewhat limited use for Medicaid planning purposes for two reasons. First, transfers to SNTs may be treated as transfers for less than FMV, triggering a penalty period. Second, persons age 65 and older are limited in their ability to create a SNT. SNTs are commonly set up by parents to provide for the needs of adult children with disabilities, as they allow parents to effectively provide an inheritance to such a child that might render him or her ineligible for critical Medicaid and SSI benefits. By contrast, only certain types of SNTs may be established for older, disabled individuals. A stand-alone SNT cannot be established for an individual who is age 65 or older by either that individual or his or her spouse (although a person over age 65 can be the beneficiary of such a trust if it was established prior to that person reaching age 65). Rather, individuals age of 65 or older (or those with the duty to support them) can only establish a SNT for such individuals if it is a *pooled SNT*. A pooled SNT is a trust managed by a non-profit organization that, among other things: (1) maintains separate accounts for each beneficiary but jointly invests and manages funds for a group of beneficiaries; (2) allows funds to be used only for the benefit of trust beneficiaries; and (3) uses any funds remaining in a beneficiary's account upon his or her death to reimburse the state for public assistance paid to the beneficiary or retains the funds for the benefit of other disabled individuals. Thus, with a pooled SNT, there is no ability to direct funds remaining after death to family, friends, or a chosen charity.

Like individuals under the age of 65, however, a person over the age of 65 may be the beneficiary of a SNT established by a third party who has no legal obligation to support the beneficiary. Thus, a testamentary SNT may be established to allow an older adult to benefit from an inheritance without jeopardizing his or her Medicaid eligibility.

Transfer assets in return for a promissory note. Using this technique, the would-be Medicaid beneficiary transfers a portion (e.g., half) of his or her money as a gift, and an equal portion (e.g., the other half) in return for a promissory note. The gifted portion of the transaction is an obvious transfer for less than FMV. The promissory note portion of the transaction may not, however, be deemed a transfer for less than FMV if the transaction is actuarially sound, repayments are made in equal amounts during the term of the loan (e.g., no deferred payments or balloon payments), and the note is not subject to cancellation on the Medicaid recipient's death. The gifted portion will create a penalty period starting on the date the would-be Medicaid beneficiary would otherwise be eligible for coverage. The idea is that if the promissory note is properly structured, however, the cost of nursing home care during the penalty period can be paid for using the monthly repayments from the promissory note.

The use of promissory notes for Medicaid planning, however, was seriously called into question by the Third Circuit in *Sable v. Velez*, 437 Fed. Appx. 73 (3d Cir. 2011). In *Sable*, the court considered how to treat promissory notes that the plaintiffs, individuals seeking Medicaid coverage for nursing home and HCBS waiver care, had purchased from their adult children. The relevant Medicaid agencies had determined that the promissory notes were to be treated as "trust-like devices" and, as such, their value would be considered a countable resource. The plaintiffs, by contrast, wished to have the promissory notes treated as cash loans whose repayment would create an income stream but whose underlying value would not be considered a countable resource. The Third Circuit upheld the District Court's decision to deny plaintiffs' motion for a preliminary injunction prohibiting the state from considering the notes to be countable resources. In doing so, the court found that the plaintiffs were unlikely to succeed on the merits of their claim because there was a lack of evidence showing the feasibility of the repayment plans for the notes, and because the plaintiffs were unlikely to show that the instruments were made in good faith. The Third Circuit explained that:

> In finding that that the transaction was not in good faith, the District Court considered that (1) the loans were not arms-length transactions, (2) the loans were informal between family members not in the business of lending money, (3) that some of the children had power of attorney over their parents, (4) the loans are not backed by collateral and there was no documentation about the borrowers' ability to repay the loans, (5) the timing of the loans made prior to the filing of the applications was suspicious, and (6) the loans were in the exact amount of excess resources preventing Medicaid eligibility. We agree with the District Court that based on these facts, the plaintiffs have not met their burden of showing a likelihood of success on the

merits as to whether the instruments were bona fide agreements made in good faith—and, thus, cash loans. . . .

Id. at 76-77.

Enter into a personal services contract. Yet another planning technique is for the would-be Medicaid beneficiary to enter into a personal services contract with an individual whom he or she wishes to benefit. Using this technique, the would-be beneficiary agrees to pay another person (e.g., an adult child, a friend) to provide certain caregiving services. This type of arrangement can be used to transfer resources while avoiding a transfer penalty (because the older adult is receiving something of equal value in return). Moreover, it can be used even if the person being paid would otherwise have provided the services for free if the services have monetary value. Even if Medicaid is never sought, moreover, the technique can have advantages because it allows resources to be passed to an heir without probate, gift tax, or estate tax (although this is rarely a concern for those engaging in Medicaid planning given the high exemption levels—$5,250,000 in 2013). To qualify as a transfer for FMV, the terms of the contract must be reasonable in light of the amount of care promised and the older adult's life expectancy. A key disadvantage of such agreements, however, is that the resulting income is subject to income tax, as well as to Social Security and Medicare taxes.

The next two cases, and the note that follows them, explore this technique and its limits.

Reed v. Missouri Department of Social Services, Family Support Division

193 S.W.3d 839 (Mo. Ct. App. 2006)

Sherri B. Sullivan, J.

INTRODUCTION

Missouri Department of Social Services, Family Support Division (the Division) appeals from the judgment of the trial court reversing the decision of the Division that Eileen Reed (Reed) was ineligible for medical assistance vendor benefits for four months. The judgment is affirmed.

FACTUAL AND PROCEDURAL BACKGROUND

On July 25, 2003, Reed entered the Blanchette Place Care Center (the Care Center). On September 30, 2003, Reed and her daughter, Sandra Teson (Teson), entered into a "Personal Care Contract" (the Contract) identifying Reed as the "Care Recipient" and Teson as the "Care Provider." The Contract set out duties of the Care Provider such as preparation of nutritious, appropriate meals, house cleaning and laundry; assistance with grooming, bathing, dressing, and personal shopping, including purchase of clothing, toiletries and other personal items; assistance with purchasing hobby, entertainment or other goods for Reed's use and enjoyment, taking into account Reed's ability to pay for such items; monitoring of Reed's physical and mental condition and nutritional needs in cooperation with health care providers; arranging for transportation to health care providers and to the physician of Reed's choice, as well as arranging for assessment, services and treatment by appropriate health care providers for Reed; assisting Reed in carrying out the instructions and directives of Reed's health care providers; arranging for social services by social service personnel as needed; visiting at least weekly and encouraging social interaction; arranging for outings and walks, if reasonable and feasible for Reed; and interacting with and/or assisting any agent of Reed in interacting with health professionals, long-term care facility administrators, social service personnel, insurance companies, and government workers in order to safeguard Reed's rights, benefits, or other resources as needed.

On October 6, 2003, Teson, as Reed's Conservator, filed the Contract as well as a Petition for Expenses (Petition) with the probate court. That same day, the court approved the Petition, permitting a payment of $11,000.00 to be made to Teson as the Conservator under the Contract. On October 14, 2003, an $11,000.00 check was written to Teson. Two days later, the Division received Reed's Application for Medical Assistance Vendor Benefits (the Application). The Application was submitted with the Petition, the Contract and a copy of the $11,000.00 check.

On October 23, 2003, a request for interpretation of policy was submitted to the Income Maintenance Section, Program and Policy in Jefferson City. The Application and Contract were forwarded for evaluation as to whether or not the $11,000.00 was a transfer of property rendering Reed ineligible for medical assistance vendor coverage. On December 3, 2003, Reed was notified that her Medicaid application was rejected because the $11,000.00 given to Teson was determined to be a transfer of property disqualifying her for vendor coverage until February 2004.

Reed submitted an Application for State Hearing. At the hearing, the hearing officer considered evidence from the Division and Teson on Reed's behalf, and issued a decision affirming the Division's rejection of Reed's application for medical assistance vendor benefits. Reed appealed to the circuit court, which reversed the Division's decision and found in favor of Reed. The Division now appeals.

POINT ON APPEAL

Reed maintains that the Division erred in its decision that the $11,000.00 payment by Reed to Teson was made without consideration because the weight of the competent and substantial evidence established that in exchange for the payment Reed received a binding and enforceable personal care contract to receive personal services for the rest of her life, which is, as a matter of law, fair and valuable consideration.

* * *

DISCUSSION

The Division maintains that it correctly determined that the $11,000.00 payment through the Contract was a transfer of property because the Contract lacked fair and valuable consideration in that the services rendered by Teson were largely duplicative of the services provided by a licensed skilled nursing facility. . . .

We find this conclusion is against the weight of the competent and substantial evidence on the record as a whole for the following reasons. There were substantial services provided by Teson under the Contract that were not duplicative of the nursing home's services, and for which $11,000.00 was fair compensation over an eleven-year plus period.[1] Namely, the Contract provided that Teson would provide a communication link between Reed and her doctors and nurses regarding the status of her health, as well as interact with facility personnel to safeguard Reed's rights and benefits. Reed, as a result of her medical problems which include a stroke, has difficulty with verbal communication and is withdrawn and avoids communication with staff. Teson testified that "My mom doesn't speak well, and she doesn't communicate with a lot of different people, outside of me."

Reed has trouble eating because of her stroke and Parkinson's disease. Specifically, she has trouble bringing utensils to her mouth. The staff is not able to spend lengthy amounts of time with Reed, helping her learn to hold a spoon and feed herself. Teson, on the other hand, does. She devotes time on a constant basis helping Reed to feed herself. Teson asked a nurse what happens when she is not there to help Reed feed herself, and the nurse replied that they give Reed a nutrition shake. The staff states they just do not have time to do otherwise. Teson provides a valuable service to Reed not provided for by the facility staff and medical caregivers.

Teson has also purchased substantial items for Reed out of the payment for her services. Teson stated that the wheelchairs provided by the facility are often the wrong size for Reed, and so Teson just went out and bought one for Reed. Teson also purchased Reed a lounge chair, which somehow got misplaced. Teson spent over a week trying to recover the chair and making phone calls trying to find out where it was. It was finally found in the facility's basement. Teson stated that it was her efforts that recovered this chair, and the staff just does not have time to devote to things like a lost chair. Teson stated that Reed's walker was also lost. For two weeks Reed did not have a walker, so Teson went out and purchased one for her.

---

1. The contract states that Reed has a life expectancy of 11.3 years, which has not been disputed.

Reed went from 110 pounds to 98 pounds after her stroke. In addition to taking time to feed Reed, Teson uses her payment for her services to purchase, prepare and bring Reed outside food, such as mashed potatoes and gravy, Spaghettios, snacks and drinks that Reed especially likes, and takes her out to eat in order to make sure she does not keep losing weight. Teson also purchased Reed all new clothes with the remuneration she gets for her services because her old ones did not fit her anymore. Teson stated also that clothing often gets lost in nursing homes, and thus she frequently takes stock of Reed's wardrobe and buys Reed things she needs, such as shoes, socks, underwear, leggings, housecoats, gowns, and shirts.

Teson makes a special effort to take note of parties or recreational events held by the facility, so that she can make sure Reed attends. Teson stated that one time she visited, the facility was having a sing-along with music, but she discovered Reed in her room, in her bed. Teson said that when she asked the staff why they do not take Reed to these events, they stated that when they ask Reed, she says she is not sure she wants to go. Obviously the staff is not going to force Reed to go if she says she does not want to go. Teson adjusts her schedule around these events, goes to the facility, gets Reed up and takes her to these events, and joins in herself. If Teson did not do this for Reed, Teson maintains Reed would just stay in her room.

Teson stated that on days when it is warm and nice out, she takes Reed on one or two-hour drives around St. Charles, so that Reed can get out of the facility and enjoy rides around town, a service which is not provided by the facility.

One time Teson noticed a pharmacy bill that was for 90 pills for one month, when Teson knew that Reed only took one pill a day. Teson brought this discrepancy to the nursing home's attention, and they rectified the error. Teson maintains that such an error has been made more than once. One time, the morning nurse was giving Reed a pill, and the evening nurse was also giving Reed this pill, when she was only to have one a day. Teson noticed Reed was lethargic, checked into her medications, and they were able to rectify the problem.

Teson drives sixty miles round-trip three to four times per week to perform her services for Reed. Without the remuneration she receives for her services, Teson would not be able to afford the gas, not to mention the time that these trips take.

We find that these services, among others, support Reed's independence, autonomy, well-being and care in ways that the facility's services do not. They enhance Reed's life in ways that the facility does not, and are above and beyond the care provided by the facility. As such, we conclude that the services provided by Teson under the Contract constitute valuable consideration for the $11,000.00 payment made by Reed to Teson.

* * *

The judgment is affirmed.

Estate of Ethel Barnett v. Department of Health & Human Services

2006 WL 1668138 (Me. Super. Ct. 2006)

ROLAND A. COLE, Justice.

This case comes before the Court on the Estate of Ethel Barnett's (the "Estate") 80C appeal challenging a final administrative decision made by the Commissioner of the Department of Health & Human Services (the "Department") holding that certain personal care expenses paid to Ethel Barnett's daughter Amy Barnett were disallowed and assessing a penalty on the transfer of $57,346 between December 2003 and June 2004.

FACTUAL BACKGROUND

Ethel Barnet [*sic*], an elderly resident of the Springbrook Nursing Home, applied for MaineCare benefits on July 26, 2004. The Department granted the application for care beginning December 2004, but denied the application for care prior to December 2004. The Department found that Ethel Barnett had improperly transferred assets in the form of the performance of certain personal care services and a monthly gift.

Amy Barnett, Ethel's daughter and power of attorney, executed a personal care agreement for Ethel by which Amy would provide personal services for Ethel in exchange for compensation while Ethel was in the nursing home. Amy received monthly payments for paying Ethel's bills; filing paperwork; shopping for supplies, medications, clothing, and holiday presents; and taking Ethel to her appointments with her doctor, dentist, and lawyer. During her visits to the nursing home, Amy was also compensated for assisting Ethel with meals, brushing her teeth, giving her manicures, trimming her hair, cleaning her hands and face, and bringing her sister for a visit. Amy kept a log to prove the existence of the personal care services she provided for her mother. The log indicates that Amy provided fourteen hours a week of services.

DISCUSSION

The Estate contends that the Department erred in assessing a penalty for a number of the personal care services she provided. She argues that they were delivered in accordance with the personal care agreement and therefore should be honored. The Estate also disputes the method of calculation of the transfer penalty.

In reviewing an administrative agency decision, the Superior Court, in its intermediate appellate capacity, will uphold the decision unless the agency has abused its discretion, made an error of law, or its findings are not supported by substantial evidence in the record. . . .

a. Personal Care Services

Section 4120.01 of the Maine Medical Assistance Eligibility Manual provides that a transfer of fair market value from a MaineCare applicant to another incurs no penalty if the transfer is in the form of past support for basic necessities and if such support is measurable and verified. Section 4120.01 further provides that relatives may provide past support or basic necessities, which include clothing, transportation, and personal care services only if these services were provided as part of a legally written enforceable agreement.

In the instant case, although the Department was concerned that the client's daughter agreed to pay herself for personal care services from her mother's funds, the Department allowed the transfer of compensation for bill paying, paperwork, shopping for necessities, and appointments without assessing a penalty. However, the Department determined that the services charged for and provided by Amy that were the same services that were provided by the nursing home were impermissible transfers that incurred a penalty, namely assistance with meals, personal hygiene, and visitation. The Department held that these services were not measurable or verifiable.

The Court agrees with the Department in that the payment for personal hygiene services, which are provided by the nursing home, are not measurable. These services, along with visitation, do not fall within the definition of support for basic necessities for which a fair market value can be assessed. Rather, they are the services that any daughter would provide for her ailing mother without charge. Moreover, the record lacks other sources to verify that these services occurred. The only evidence of these personal services is in Amy's log and her employer indicating that she left work to go visit her mother.

If the Court were to sanction personal services such as these in this context, it would essentially be allowing all MaineCare applicants to empty their bank accounts into the accounts of their children under the guise of providing service. This scheme ultimately forces the taxpayers of the State of Maine to cover the costs of caring for ineligible recipients. The Court is not willing to read the Medical Assistance Eligibility Manual so liberally. The rules set out in the Manual are meant to prevent MaineCare applicants from distributing their money to family and friends in order to qualify prematurely for MaineCare. This decision is in line with this purpose. . . .

NOTES

1. *Value of personal care services.* Even when payment pursuant to a personal care contract is found to be a compensated transfer, there may be significant disagreement as to the value of the care provided. For example, in *In the Matter of Kerner v. Monroe County Department of Human Services*, 75 A.D.3d 1085 (N.Y App. Div. 2010), the court considered a situation in which an elderly man paid his son $9,283 a month to provide "room and board; care and supervision; food and food preparation—both meals

and snacks; any daily assistance . . . with showering, dressing, etc; laundry & cleaning; medical office visits and transportation thereof; and any medical care such as changing bandages or assisting with medications. . . ." The county department of human services had subsequently imposed a penalty period of 13 months on the father on the grounds that he had made an uncompensated transfer to the son. The court overturned the county's determination on the grounds that the transfers were not uncompensated because the son actually provided services, and remitted the matter to the county for a determination of the true value of the services. In so doing, it rejected the father's argument that the monthly value of the services could be calculated by looking to the monthly cost of nursing home care. Instead, it held that the value of the services should be determined based on the number of hours the son spent providing services and the fair market value of those services.

2. *Living large as a potential complement or alternative to Medicaid planning.* Where the would-be beneficiary is able to experience pleasure from activities (e.g., attending a play, eating out at a restaurant, going to a baseball game, or having a pedicure) or travel (e.g., a vacation and perhaps including the cost of bringing a care provider along on the vacation), an alternative approach is to spend-down by simply "blowing" the individual's life savings (or a portion of them) on such experiences. This approach does not, of course, preserve assets, but it does allow the assets to be used for the enjoyment of the individual instead of for his or her care.

QUESTIONS

1. Would it matter to the *Reed* or *Barnett* courts whether the applicants' children would have performed the enumerated services without compensation? Should the outcome of these cases turn on whether the residents could have obtained such services without paying for them?

2. Are *Reed* and *Barnett* consistent with one another? With *Kerner*?

3. Would *Barnett* have been decided differently if Amy had been Ethel Barnett's niece? Friend? Son? Should it have been?

4. On page 305, Karp and Gershbein contend that those engaging in Medicaid planning often have an "an implicit understanding" that the money transferred will be used for the benefit of the older adult transferring it. If this is the case, should the courts treat those assets as being held in a constructive trust? If so, are those assets still those of the transferor?

5. As noted earlier, the compensation earned through a personal care contract is subject to income tax as well as Social Security and Medicare taxes. Gifts are not subject to such taxes. What incentives does this create and for whom? *Cf.* Richard Kaplan, *Federal Tax Policy and Family-Provided Care for Older Adults*, 25 VA. TAX REV. 509 (2005) (discussing the taxation of elder care provided by family members).

PROBLEMS

1. Mr. Ulysses is a widower who has $80,000 in countable resources in addition to his home, which is assessed at $220,000. He has two sons, Romulus and Remus. He is close to Romulus and Romulus's wife Helen, who regularly helps him with transportation and household management. Mr. Ulysses has been diagnosed with early-stage Alzheimer's disease and, due to serious problems with his knees, is having trouble walking on his own. He would like to remain at home as long as possible but anticipates that he may need nursing home care in the future. He would like to make sure his needs are met, but he would also like to preserve a sizeable portion of his assets for the benefit of his family. How might he do so?

2. Marnie Medina, age 78, has been living alone. Her daughter, Stephanie, has been urging Ms. Medina to move in with her. Ms. Medina had been resisting doing so because she does not want to give up her independence. However, she is now considering the possibility because (in part due to a recent fall) she no longer feels safe alone and feels that it would be easier for Stephanie to help her if they lived together. She has come to your law office for the purpose of redoing her will so that Stephanie will inherit the bulk of her estate. Her current will divides her moderately sized estate equally among her three children, but Ms. Medina feels that Stephanie should be rewarded for all the help she provides.

   Would you raise the issue of Medicaid planning as part of your conversation with Ms. Medina? If so, what Medicaid planning techniques might you suggest to her? What factors would be relevant in determining which, if any, Medicaid planning techniques would be appropriate for Ms. Medina?

3. Recall Lynn and Pat Burbank, a married couple, from earlier in the chapter (see page 291). Lynn is 80 and recently had a stroke. After a month in rehabilitative care, Lynn returned home. Pat, 65, has been trying to provide Lynn with the in-home care Lynn needs but is having difficulty doing so. In part, this is because Lynn needs a great deal of care; in part, it is because Pat also has a part-time job to try to make ends meet. Lynn's income is $1,200 per month; Pat's income is $2,000 per month. They jointly own a home worth $256,000 and a car, and have $141,000 in savings. How might they structure their finances to maximize Medicaid benefits?

4. Bill and Ted, an unmarried couple, have been together for ten years and currently live in a home owned by Ted. They share a car, a 2013 Honda CRV, which is also in Ted's name. Bill, 60, is a chef who earns $3,500 per month. Ted, 72, is retired and his sole income is $1,600 per month in Social

Security benefits. Two days ago, Ted had a serious stroke and he is currently hospitalized. Bill and Ted are considering getting married. What would be the legal consequences of marriage for Bill and Ted? Would you advise them to marry?

c. Spousal Refusal as a Medicaid Planning Technique

Another way a person may try to protect his or her income and assets from being used to pay for the care of his or her spouse is to engage in *spousal refusal*—that is, to refuse to make his or her income and/or resources available to the state. The next case considers the effect of such a refusal.

Morenz v. Wilson-Coker

415 F.3d 230 (2d Cir. 2005)

CALABRESI, Circuit Judge.

I. INTRODUCTION

This is an appeal from a grant of summary judgment by the United States District Court for the District of Connecticut (Underhill, J.) to plaintiffs-appellees, Robert and Clara Morenz (the "Morenzes"). The Morenzes sued defendant-appellant, Patricia Wilson-Coker, the Commissioner of the Connecticut Department of Social Services ("DSS"), for declaratory and injunctive relief, after the DSS denied Mr. Morenz's application. The DSS rejected the application on the ground that the Morenzes' combined assets exceeded the threshold for Medicaid eligibility. The Morenzes contended that Mr. Morenz could not be deemed ineligible on account of his spouse's assets because he had effected a valid assignment of spousal support rights to the State of Connecticut. The district court ruled in favor of the Morenzes on cross-motions for summary judgment. We affirm.

II. FACTUAL BACKGROUND

Mr. Morenz has lived at the Wilton Meadows nursing home in Wilton, Connecticut, since October 2000. Mrs. Morenz, his spouse, lives at the family home, also in Wilton. For the purposes of the federal Medicaid statutes, therefore, Mr. Morenz is an "institutionalized spouse," and Mrs. Morenz is a "community spouse." 42 U.S.C. §1396r-5(h). A Medicaid application in Mr. Morenz's name was filed in January 2004 with the DSS, the Connecticut agency responsible for administering the state's Medicaid program. As part of Mr. Morenz's application, an Assignment of Spousal Support Rights was submitted by Mr. Morenz, through Mrs. Morenz, who held his power of attorney. The assignment purported to transfer to the State of Connecticut any rights to support that Mr. Morenz had from Mrs. Morenz. In addition, Mrs. Morenz submitted a signed "Spousal Refusal Statement" to the DSS declaring that she "decline[s] to further contribute to the financial support" of Mr. Morenz.

On March 1, 2004, the DSS denied Mr. Morenz's Medicaid application on the ground that the Morenzes' combined resources exceeded the statutory eligibility amount. The countable assets in Mr. Morenz's name fell within the $1,600 personal resource allowance permitted for Medicaid eligibility. With certain enumerated exceptions discussed below, however, a state Medicaid participant must deem a community spouse's resources as available to the institutionalized spouse in determining the institutionalized spouse's initial Medicaid eligibility. 42 U.S.C. §1396r-5(c)(2)(A). Although a community spouse is permitted to retain a sizeable community spouse resource allowance ("CSRA") beyond that permitted to the institutionalized spouse, 42 U.S.C. §1396r-5(c)(2), the assets in Mrs. Morenz's name exceeded this allowance by approximately $157,500.... Under the DSS Uniform Policy Manual ("UPM"), the sole exception to considering the combined assets of both spouses in determining an institutionalized spouse's initial Medicaid eligibility is "when undue hardship exists." UPM §4025.67(B).

The Morenzes concede that, at the time of Mr. Morenz's application, their circumstances did not qualify as "undue hardship" under DSS regulations.... They contend, however, that the DSS is required to honor their assignment of Mr. Morenz's support rights to the state. And they argue that, pursuant to the provisions of the Medicare Catastrophic Coverage Act of 1988 ("MCCA"), 42 U.S.C. §1396r-5(c)(3)(A), such assignment immunizes the community spouse's assets from consideration in calculating the institutionalized spouse's initial Medicaid eligibility.

On February 25, 2004, the Morenzes moved for a temporary restraining order and preliminary injunction to prohibit the DSS from including Mrs. Morenz's assets in determining Mr. Morenz's Medicaid eligibility. The district court denied that motion without prejudice in favor of a summary judgment hearing. Both the Morenzes and Wilson-Coker moved immediately for summary judgment. In an opinion dated June 10, 2004, the district court granted summary judgment to the Morenzes. *Morenz v. Wilson-Coker*, 321 F. Supp. 2d 398 (D. Conn. 2004). The court enjoined Wilson-Coker from denying Mr. Morenz's Medicaid application. Pursuant to the Medicaid statute's retroactive benefits provision, the court also ordered that Mr. Morenz's eligibility become effective three months prior to the court's decision. Wilson-Coker filed a timely notice of appeal.

III. DISCUSSION

* * *

1. MCCA Support Rights Provisions

The MCCA governs the extent to which a community spouse's assets may factor into an institutionalized spouse's initial Medicaid eligibility determination. Paragraph (2) of the MCCA's rules for treatment of a community spouse's resources states that, aside from the CSRA, "all the resources held by either the institutionalized spouse, community spouse, or both, shall be considered to be available to the institutionalized spouse" in calculating the institutionalized spouse's resources at the time of application. See 42 U.S.C. §1396r-5(c)(2). The next paragraph, however, provides that:

> The institutionalized spouse shall not be ineligible by reason of resources determined under paragraph (2) to be available for the cost of care where—
>
> (A) the institutionalized spouse has assigned to the State any rights to support from the community spouse;
>
> (B) the institutionalized spouse lacks the ability to execute an assignment due to physical or mental impairment but the State has the right to bring a support proceeding against a community spouse without such assignment; or
>
> (C) the State determines that denial of eligibility would work an undue hardship.

42 U.S.C. §1396r-5(c)(3). The district court found that, under these provisions, "if Mr. Morenz assigns rights to support from Mrs. Morenz to the State of Connecticut . . . he 'shall not be ineligible' for Medicaid because of excess resources."

We see no reason to disturb this holding. This court has held it to be "a fundamental principle of statutory construction that the starting point must be the language of the statute itself." *Rose v. Long Island R.R. Pension Plan*, 828 F.2d 910, 919 (2d Cir. 1987). . . . Here, as the district court noted, the language of the statute could not be less ambiguous. A community spouse's resources cannot be included in making an institutionalized spouse's initial eligibility determination if the institutionalized spouse has assigned support rights to the state or undue hardship is present.

Wilson-Coker would, in effect, have us read this disjunctive "or" as a conjunctive "and." . . . Wilson-Coker notes that, under federal law, a state Medicaid plan must always condition aid upon the assignment to the state of an applicant's rights to support. 42 U.S.C. §1396k(a)(1)(A). To provide an exemption from the general spousal-contribution requirements for precisely the same assignment of support rights, Wilson-Coker argues, would be bizarre. Even if we were to assume that these two assignment of support rights provisions cannot live comfortably together—which we do not—Wilson-Coker has, at most, demonstrated poor drafting. Without more, textual inconsistency within a complicated federal statute falls short of demonstrating the kind of clearly expressed legislative intention that would lead us not to apply the language of the statute as written.

* * *

2. Connecticut Assignment of Support Rights Statute

Although federal law prohibits a community spouse's assets from preventing an institutionalized spouse from becoming eligible for Medicaid when all support rights are assigned to the State, whether a particular assignment of support rights is valid for purposes of §1396r-5(c)(3)(A) is a question of state law. . . . Connecticut's law governing the assignment of spousal support of an institutionalized Medicaid applicant provides as follows:

> An institutionalized person or person in need of institutional care who applies for Medicaid shall assign to the Commissioner of Social Services the right of support derived from the assets of the spouse of such person, provided the spouse of such person is unwilling or unable to provide the information necessary to determine eligibility for Medicaid. If such applicant lacks the ability to execute an assignment due to physical or mental impairment, the commissioner may bring a support proceeding against such applicant's spouse without such assignment. CONN. GEN. STAT. §17b-285.

Wilson-Coker argues that this provision limits the assignment of support rights to situations in which the community spouse is unwilling or unable to provide the information necessary to determine the institutionalized spouse's eligibility. Any other attempted assignment, Wilson-Coker contends, is not permitted by state law. Since the Morenzes concede that Mrs. Morenz has cooperated in providing the necessary information, Wilson-Coker's argument, if correct, would prevent the Morenzes from availing themselves of the MCCA's exemption based on their attempted assignment of support rights.

As the district court correctly held, however, neither the statute nor DSS's own published regulations support Wilson-Coker's interpretation of the assignment statute. . . . By using the word "shall," the statute constitutes a mandate to institutionalized Medicaid applicants whose spouses have not provided information, but it does not by its terms limit the circumstances under which an institutionalized applicant may assign support rights. . . . Consistent with this interpretation, the DSS's own Uniform Policy Manual states only that "[t]he applicant of Medicaid benefits must assign to the Department rights to support available from the assets of the community spouse when the community spouse is unable to provide the information necessary to complete an assessment of spousal assets." DSS Uniform Policy Manual §7520.07 (emphasis added). It nowhere forbids or invalidates such an assignment in other circumstances.

* * *

IV. CONCLUSION

For the reasons stated above, the judgment of the district court is AFFIRMED.

D. OTHER SOURCES OF HEALTH CARE COVERAGE

1. Long-Term Care Insurance

Long-term care insurance is an insurance product that typically provides coverage for nursing home care, as well as care in assisted living facilities, and potentially even home-based care.

Private long-term care insurance plans differ in the extent of their coverage, as well as in the conditions and processes for triggering that coverage. In selecting a long-term care policy, therefore, a consumer should consider a number of different issues.

First, what is the cost of the policy? In considering cost, the consumer should not only consider the cost of the initial premium, but also related issues such as whether the policy is guaranteed to be renewable, whether there are limits on the extent to which premiums may increase in future years, whether policyholders must continue to pay premiums once they qualify for coverage, whether premiums are partially refundable if the policy is not utilized or only minimally utilized, and whether premiums must continue to be paid annually or if there is a point at which premium payments can stop but coverage will nevertheless continue.

Second, what services will the policy cover? Will the policy only cover skilled nursing facility care, or will it also cover home-based care and care in lower-level facilities such as assisted living facilities? If so, who decides which level of care the policyholder will receive and how?

Third, how much coverage will the policy provide for those services? Some policies set a maximum per-day amount of coverage. These limits may be a percentage of the costs of the covered care or a set dollar figure. Depending on the policy, that figure may be adjusted for inflation, or the consumer may have an option to purchase an inflation protector rider at an additional cost. Policies may also limit the length of time coverage will be provided or the total dollar figure of benefits that will be provided. In addition, they may impose waiting periods such that a policyholder will not become eligible for coverage for a certain length of time (e.g., 30 days) that the policyholder would otherwise be eligible.

Fourth, what conditions will trigger coverage? Does the policy exclude pre-existing conditions, require a prior hospitalization to trigger eligibility, or only provide coverage for care received in certain preferred facilities? And what level of need must the policyholder demonstrate to receive coverage? Typically, policies will cover not only long-term care needs created by certain serious medical conditions, but also needs created as a result of the policyholder's inability to perform a certain number of *activities of daily living* (ADLs). ADLs include performing basic personal hygiene (e.g., bathing, grooming, shaving and oral care), dressing, toileting, feeding oneself, and transferring (e.g., moving from a seated position to a standing one and the reverse, and getting in and out of bed).

To encourage individuals to purchase long-term care insurance, and to thereby avoid Medicaid covering such individuals' long-term care needs instead, many states have established *Long-Term Care Partnership Programs*. Under such programs, if individuals buy a qualifying long-term care insurance policy, but exceed the coverage limitations of such policies (e.g., by needing more long-term care than covered by a plan's three-year maximum coverage period), the state will provide the individual with Medicaid coverage without requiring the individual to spend his or her resources down to normal Medicaid resource limit levels. The precise requirements of and benefits of state partnership programs vary significantly from state to state.

In 2010, as part of the Patient Protection and Affordable Care Act discussed earlier, Congress enacted the federal Community Living Assistance Services and Supports (CLASS) Act. The CLASS Act created a voluntary, publicly run long-term care insurance option. Under the Act, an individual would have been eligible for coverage if they (1) paid premiums for at least 60 months (at least 24 of which are consecutive), (2) worked for at least three calendar years during the first 60 months in which they were enrolled in the program, and (3) earned enough in each of those years to earn "a quarter of coverage" under the OASDI program. The public insurance option created by the CLASS Act had some distinct advantages over private long-term care insurance. Premium levels were expected to be predictable, the program was to be open to all employed persons regardless of their previous medical histories, there was no lifetime limit on coverage, and benefits could be used in a variety of care settings. On the other hand, it was designed to benefit only employed persons, with no coverage for people who do not participate in the paid economy. It was also unclear whether or not benefit levels would be sufficient to meet beneficiaries' long-term care needs.

The CLASS Act was never implemented. In October 2011, the U.S. Department of Health and Human Services (HHS) announced that it would not implement the CLASS Act. HSS explained that the Act was not financially viable because the premiums would be more than consumers would be willing to pay. One reason for high premiums was that the program was expected to face serious problems from adverse selection, as it would have been most attractive to those who have a disability or anticipate having a disability in the near future, and the program was not permitted to screen people for pre-existing medical conditions or charge different premiums to people based on their pre-existing conditions. In addition, the program would have provided lifetime benefits (whereas private insurance typically imposes limits) and the benefit was cash (not services), which might make people more interested in applying to receive the benefit. There was also concern that—because of the desire to accommodate persons with disabilities—the program's work requirements were not sufficiently robust. In sum, it appeared unlikely that the program would be self-sustaining—that is, that it would pay for its benefits using participant premiums—as was statutorily required.

The CLASS Act was ultimately repealed in January 2013. For further discussion of the CLASS Act and its challenges, see Joshua Wiener, *The CLASS Act: Is It Dead or Just Sleeping?*, 24 AGING & SOC. POL'Y 118 (2012) (arguing that the CLASS Act was not financially viable because it did not mandate enrollment, because subsidies for low-income individuals were inconsistent with the self-financing requirement, and because of its weak work requirements, which would have enabled already disabled individuals to enroll).

QUESTIONS

1. If you were an elder law attorney, under what circumstances might you advise your clients to buy long-term care insurance? Why?

2. In a 2011 Policy Brief, the Robert Wood Johnson Foundation proposed a variety of ways that the CLASS Act could be revised to make it financially viable, including: 1) screening out those who are already disabled by increasing the amount of money an individual must earn or the number of hours they must work in order to participate in the program, 2) increasing the number of years that workers would have to pay into the system before becoming eligible for benefits, 3) changing the premium structure to "strongly discourage" late enrollment in the program, 4) creating incentives for employers to enroll their employees in the program, and 5) using tax revenues to cover part of the program's cost. *See* ROBERT WOOD JOHNSON FOUNDATION, HEALTH POLICY BRIEF (May 12, 2011), *available at* http://www.rwjf.org/files/research/72381class201105.pdf.

   Which approach would you have recommended and why? Do you think it would have been enough to save the CLASS Act? What would you need to know in order to determine whether it would have been sufficient?

2. Employer-Provided Health Care Benefits

Even once an individual is eligible for Medicare, they may still benefit from employer-provided health benefits. This is because employer-provided health care plans supplement Medicare coverage for many Medicare beneficiaries. As Professor Susan Cancelosi has noted, by providing health care benefits to Medicare beneficiaries, "employment-based retiree health benefits have consistently plugged many of the glaring coverage gaps in a safety net program riddled with holes." Susan E. Cancelosi, *The Bell is Tolling: Retiree Health Benefits Post-Health Reform*, 19 ELDER L.J. 49, 51 (2011). As a general matter, however, such employer-provided benefits are becoming both less common and less generous. As Cancelosi has explained,

> Despite their importance to covered individuals, retiree health benefits have sharply declined over the past two decades. Struggling to handle rapidly escalating health care costs and preserve active employee insurance, employers often have chosen to terminate retiree coverage. Employers who have retained retiree benefits have tried to manage costs in part by shifting expenses to the retirees themselves through increased premiums, deductibles, co-payments, and coinsurance. Over time, retiree health insurance has come to seem almost a relic of an earlier era when compensation packages were generous and long-term employment relationships were commonplace.

Id.

As employers try to rein in costs, they may seek to change the terms and conditions of benefits provided to their retirees. While there are some constraints on such changes, employers have more freedom to change health benefits than they do to change pension benefits. This is because the Employee Retirement Income Security Act (ERISA), discussed in Chapter 5, provides important protections for workers with employer-sponsored pensions. ERISA, however, does not apply to "welfare" benefits, such as employer-provided health care benefits, as the next case illustrates.

Sprague v. General Motors Corp.

133 F.3d 388 (6th Cir. 1998)

DAVID A. NELSON, Circuit Judge.

This is a purported class action in which the plaintiffs—retired employees of the defendant, General Motors Corporation—allege that GM violated the Employee Retirement Income Security Act of 1974, 29 U.S.C. §§1001 et seq. ("ERISA"), by denying them fully "paid-up" lifetime health care benefits. The district court certified a class of some 50,000 employees who had taken early retirement, but the court declined to grant class status to about 34,000 "general retirees" who had retired in accordance with the company's normal criteria. As to the general retiree plaintiffs, the court held that the benefits in question did not vest under the pertinent plan documents. As to the early retirees, however, the district court held that each of the 50,000 members of the class had entered into a separate contract that called for the benefits in question to be furnished for life at no cost to the recipient. In the alternative, the court ruled that GM was estopped to rely on the terms of the plan documents to defeat the claims of any early retiree.

We shall affirm the judgment of the district court as to the general retirees, but reverse the court's certification of the class of early retirees. Insofar as the merits of the claims asserted by the named plaintiffs are concerned, we conclude that the claims fail as a matter of law.

I

A

In 1961 General Motors began paying part of the cost of health insurance for its salaried retirees and their surviving spouses. Three years later GM assumed the full cost of basic health insurance for its salaried retirees, and in 1968 it extended this benefit to surviving spouses as well. (In the interest of simplicity, further reference to surviving spouses will generally be omitted.)

In addition to basic health insurance, GM offered its salaried retirees supplemental coverage under what was called the Comprehensive Medical Expense Insurance Program. Participants in this optional program were required to pay a share of the premiums, and co-payment was required for certain medical services. There were also annual deductibles.

Prior to 1985 the health care benefits were provided through arrangements with private insurers. The insurers issued each covered person a certificate of insurance describing the terms and conditions of the underlying policy.

GM became fully self-insured in 1985. At that time the company prepared a document, entitled "The General Motors Health Care Insurance Program for Salaried Employees," that set forth the terms and conditions of GM's self-insured health care program. The district court found that this document, together with subsequent documents announcing changes in coverage, comprised GM's health care benefits plan from and after 1985. The new plan gave participants a choice between traditional fee-for-service coverage and enrollment in a managed care organization. GM continued its supplemental coverage program, shortening the name to the Comprehensive Medical Expense Program.

GM has long made it a practice to inform its salaried employees and retirees of their health care coverage by providing them booklets containing summaries of the company's health insurance policies and programs. . . .

A number of the booklets contained language informing plan participants that the health care plan called for GM to pay health insurance costs during retirement:

- "If you retire . . . and are eligible to receive retirement benefits under the provisions of the GM Retirement Program for Salaried Employees, you may keep your basic hospital, surgical and medical expense coverages in effect. . . . GM will pay the full monthly premium or subscription charge for such coverages." The General Motors Insurance Program for Salaried Employees (1968). The 1971 version was nearly identical.

- "Hospital-Medical Coverages: Your basic coverages will be provided at Corporation expense for your lifetime. . . ." Highlights of Your GM Benefits (1974).

- "Your basic health care coverages will be provided at GM's expense for your lifetime. . . ." Your Benefits in Retirement (1977).

- "General Motors pays the full cost of any basic health care coverages that are continued for most retired employees and for eligible surviving spouses and children of deceased retirees." Your Benefits in Retirement (1977).

However, most of the booklets also put plan participants on notice of GM's right to change or terminate the health care plan at any time:

- "General Motors believes wholeheartedly in this Insurance Program for GM men and women, and expects to continue the Program indefinitely. However, GM reserves the right to modify, revoke, suspend, terminate, or change the Program, in whole or in part, at any time. . . ." The General Motors Insurance Program for Salaried Employees (1965, 1968, and 1971).

- "General Motors Corporation reserves the right to amend, change or terminate the Plans and Programs described in this booklet." Your GM Benefits (1985).
- "The Corporation reserves the right to amend, modify, suspend, or terminate its benefit Plans or Programs by action of its Board of Directors." Your Benefits in Retirement (1985).

B

For more than two decades GM has engaged in systematic reductions in the size of its salaried workforce. In this connection the company has launched special early retirement programs designed to induce salaried workers to retire before reaching normal retirement age. The inducements have included, among other things, offers to provide pension benefits to early retirees at levels not reduced to reflect the longer periods over which such benefits can be expected to accrue. . . .

Salaried employees who accepted early retirement were often asked to sign documents evincing their acceptance of the terms of the particular program under which they were retiring. . . .

[The] forms had numerous variants, but all stated in essence that the early retiree had "reviewed the benefits applicable" and "accept[ed] them." In return for such benefits, the early retirees agreed to waive certain causes of action they might have had against GM.

Not all early retirees signed a statement of acceptance. Some merely signed a "statement of intent" to retire, while others apparently signed nothing.

In the course of explaining its special early retirement programs, GM made numerous oral and written representations about the health care benefits available to early retirees. Most of the early retirees participated in exit interviews where a particular early retirement program was described. These interviews were conducted by plant supervisors, members of the benefits staff, and others. Many of the early retirees also received documents summarizing applicable retirement benefits. These summaries often informed retirees that their health insurance would be paid by GM for life. Again, however, such documents sometimes put the retirees on notice of GM's right to change benefits. . . .

Some early retirees received individualized letters about early retirement programs. And a small number of early retirees explicitly asked GM representatives about future changes to health care benefits. The answers given, it seems, were accurate—benefits could be changed in the future.

C

Late in 1987 GM announced that early in the following year significant changes would become effective in health care coverage for both salaried employees and retirees. In the case of plan participants who elected traditional fee-for-service coverage, the changes included an annual deductible of $200 for individuals and $250 for families. Fee-for-service participants were required to make 20% co-payments on medical services, up to an annual maximum co-payment of $500. By reason of these two changes, fee-for-service plan participants could find themselves responsible for paying as much as $700 a year (with individual coverage) or $750 (with family coverage) that would previously have been paid by GM.

These were not the only changes made to the health care plan for salaried employees and retirees. Vision and hearing aid coverages were eliminated, for example, while there were cost-sharing increases for participants in the Comprehensive Medical Insurance Program. At the same time, however, some benefits and coverages were improved.

D

The present lawsuit was commenced in August of 1989 by 114 salaried retirees who challenged the legality of the changes to the health care plan that took effect in 1988. The main thrust of the plaintiffs' complaint was that GM had bound itself to provide salaried retirees and their spouses basic health coverage for life, entirely at GM's expense. The right to such coverage vested upon retirement, according to the plaintiffs, so the coverage could never be changed or revoked.

Seven separate causes of action were pleaded: (1) failure to maintain the written plan documentation required by ERISA; (2) violation of the health care plan; (3) breach of fiduciary duty; (4) breach of contract; (5) equitable or promissory estoppel; (6) failure to supply requested information; and (7) failure to comply with the requirements for summary plan descriptions. The named plaintiffs purported to represent a class of some 84,000 similarly-situated individuals, about 50,000 of whom were early retirees and 34,000 of whom were general retirees.

The district court entered partial summary judgment in favor of GM after making the following rulings:

- the plaintiffs' benefits did not vest under the terms of the welfare plan;
- the summary plan descriptions generally put the plaintiffs on notice of GM's right to amend or terminate the plan; and
- the plaintiffs had no claim for breach of fiduciary duty, GM not having acted in a fiduciary capacity when amending the plan.

After *Sprague I*, the district court allowed the early retirees to proceed on a bilateral contract theory and allowed everyone to proceed on an estoppel theory. The procedural course of the litigation was further shaped by the following pretrial rulings:

- the plaintiffs were not entitled to a jury trial;
- the general retirees could not proceed as a class; and
- the early retirees could proceed as a class pursuant to Rule 23(b)(2), Fed. R. Civ. P.

Following a lengthy bench trial, the district court made these rulings on the merits:

- GM was found to have made a bilateral contract with each early retiree to vest health care benefits at retirement;
- these bilateral contracts were held to be enforceable as ERISA plans or as modifications to the general plan;
- GM was held not to be estopped from changing the health care benefits of the general retirees, to whom it made no promises to vest benefits;
- GM was held to be estopped from changing the health care benefits of the early retirees based on the oral and written representations it made to them; and
- GM was enjoined during this appeal from making further adverse changes to the health care benefits of the prevailing plaintiffs.

In August of 1994 the district court entered a final judgment embodying all of its previous rulings. The plaintiffs and GM perfected timely appeals, and each of the aforementioned rulings was challenged by one side or the other. The appeals were consolidated, and a three-judge panel of this court affirmed the rulings in favor of the early retirees and remanded the case for reconsideration of the issues (except the plaintiffs' jury demand) on which the district court had held for GM. A majority of the active judges of this court subsequently voted to rehear the case en banc, and the panel decision was thereby vacated. . . .

II

In certifying a class of 50,000 early retirees, the district court concluded that the class satisfied the four prerequisites of Rule 23(a), Fed. R. Civ. P. (numerosity, commonality, typicality, and adequacy of representation) and that the action could be maintained under Rule 23(b)(2). . . . GM appeals the certification of the class of early retirees, while the plaintiffs appeal the district court's refusal to certify a class of general retirees.

* * *

We conclude that the district court's refusal to certify a class or sub-class of general retirees was unexceptionable as far as the plaintiffs are concerned. Ironically, perhaps, the general retirees may have been better-suited for class treatment than the early retirees. The general retirees, not having received individualized inducements to retire, base their claims on the plan itself and the summary plan description booklets—documents common to all salaried retirees. But by the time it made a certification decision, the district court had rejected the primary claim of the named general retiree plaintiffs. For reasons we shall explain presently, we believe that the court acted correctly in doing so. The plaintiffs have no basis for complaining of a refusal to certify a proposed class where the representatives of the class cannot prevail on the merits. . . .

A

We turn now to the class that was certified—the early retirees. With regard to Rule 23(a), we shall confine our analysis to the commonality and typicality requirements.

The commonality requirement deals with shared questions of law or fact. . . .

GM's statements to the early retirees were not uniform. Among other things, the statements varied (1) based on the person making the representation, (2) based on the particular special early retirement program that applied, (3) from facility to facility, and (4) from time to time. Given the wide variety of representations made, there must have been variations in the early retirees' subjective understandings of the representations and in their reliance on them. Some retirees might have interpreted GM's statements to mean that their benefits were vested. Others might have understood that their benefits were subject to change. Some early retirees might have relied on GM's statements about health care benefits, while for others the statements might have made no difference at all in the decision to retire early.

Given these myriad variations, it seems to us that the plaintiffs' claims clearly lacked commonality. Because each plaintiff's claim depended upon facts and circumstances peculiar to that plaintiff, class-wide relief was not appropriate.

B

The class of early retirees fails the typicality test of Rule 23(a) as well. . . .

"Typicality determines whether a sufficient relationship exists between the injury to the named plaintiff and the conduct affecting the class, so that the court may properly attribute a collective nature to the challenged conduct. . . . A necessary consequence of the typicality requirement is that the representative's interests will be aligned with those of the represented group, and in pursuing his own claims, the named plaintiff will also advance the interests of the class members."

In pursuing their own claims, the named plaintiffs could not advance the interests of the entire early retiree class. Each claim, after all, depended on each individual's particular interactions with GM—and these, as we have said, varied from person to person. . . .

The claims of the 114 named plaintiffs are still before the court, however, regardless of whether these individuals represent the purported class. We see no reason not to address the merits of the named plaintiffs' claims.

III

A

The plaintiffs' first theory of recovery is that GM committed a breach of the terms of the plan documents when it implemented the changes in 1988.

Under the plan documents, according to the plaintiffs, their health care benefits were vested—and having vested, the benefits could not be altered without the plaintiffs' consent.

The district court rejected this theory, holding that the plan documents, including the summary plan descriptions, effectively reserved a right on GM's part to amend or terminate the plan. The court's holding, in our view, was manifestly correct; we shall affirm the summary judgment that was entered in favor of GM on this issue.

ERISA distinguishes between pension plans and welfare plans. A pension plan "provides retirement income to employees" or "results in a deferral of income by employees for periods extending to the termination of . . . employment or beyond. . . ." 29 U.S.C. §1002(2). Welfare plans, in contrast, include plans "established or . . . maintained for the purpose of providing . . . medical, surgical, or hospital care or benefits. . . ." Id. §1002(1). Because the plan in question here provided health insurance to its participants, it was a welfare plan.

Welfare plans are specifically exempted from vesting requirements to which pension plans are subject. 29 U.S.C. §1051(1). Therefore, employers "are generally free under ERISA, for any reason at any time, to adopt, modify, or terminate welfare plans." Employers may vest welfare benefits if they choose to do so, however.

To vest benefits is to render them forever unalterable. Because vesting of welfare plan benefits is not required by law, an employer's commitment to vest such benefits is not to be inferred lightly; the intent to vest "must be found in the plan documents and must be stated in clear and express language." It is the plaintiffs' burden to prove GM's intent to vest.

The plaintiffs have not seriously disputed that the plan itself permitted GM to amend or terminate benefits. Instead the plaintiffs focus on the plan summaries, which must "be written in a manner calculated to be understood by the average plan participant, and shall be sufficiently accurate and comprehensive to reasonably apprise such participants and beneficiaries of their rights and obligations under the plan." 29 U.S.C. §1022(a)(1).

* * *

Most of the summary plan descriptions unambiguously reserved GM's right to amend or terminate the plan. For example:

- ■ "General Motors Corporation reserves the right to amend, change or terminate the Plans and Programs described in this booklet." Your GM Benefits (1984).
- ■ "The Corporation reserves the right to amend, modify, suspend, or terminate its benefit Plans or Programs by action of its Board of Directors." Your Benefits in Retirement (1985).

The plaintiffs counter by pointing out that these summaries also told them that their health coverage would be paid "at no cost to" them and "for [their] lifetime[s]." Such language, they argue, created an ambiguity within the summaries that must be resolved by extrinsic evidence.

We have rejected this argument in the past, and we reject it again now. We see no ambiguity in a summary plan description that tells participants both that the terms of the current plan entitle them to health insurance at no cost throughout retirement and that the terms of the current plan are subject to change.

* * *

In the first place, . . . [a]n omission from the summary plan description does not, by negative implication, alter the terms of the plan itself. The reason is obvious: by definition, a summary will not include every detail of the thing it summarizes. GM's failure to include in some summaries a notice of its right to change the plan does not trump the clearly-stated right to do so in the plan itself.

In the second place, GM was not required to disclose in the summary plan descriptions that the plaintiffs' benefits were not vested.

ERISA specifies in detail the information that every summary plan description "shall contain." See 29 U.S.C. §1022(b). Among the items a summary must include is "a description of the provisions providing for nonforfeitable pension benefits." Id. Despite having required that summaries inform plan participants about the vesting of benefits under pension plans, Congress did not require such information for welfare plans; neither did the Department of Labor in its ERISA reporting and disclosure regulations. . . .

Neither the GM plan itself nor any of the various summaries of the plan states or even implies that the plaintiffs' benefits were vested. Accordingly, we conclude that the district court acted correctly in granting summary judgment to GM on the plaintiffs' claim that the company violated the terms of its plan.

B

We turn next to the theory that GM bilaterally contracted with each early retiree to vest benefits. All of the early retirees took retirement under one of the special early retirement programs offered by GM between 1974 and 1988. The early retirees argue that, as the district court held, the statements, promises, and representations GM made to them in connection with these programs, and the documents that they signed, created binding bilateral contracts. The alleged contracts, which supposedly provided for vesting of the early retirees' health care benefits, are said to be enforceable either as modifications to the general plan, or as ERISA plans themselves, or as a matter of federal common law.

* * *

Our court has consistently refused to recognize oral modifications to written plan documents.

. . . The plaintiffs may not invoke oral statements by GM personnel in order to modify the terms of the written plan.

Neither can we accept the argument that the plan was modified or superseded either by the written "statements of acceptance" signed by some of the named plaintiffs or by the written representations received by some from GM. . . . None of GM's representations suggested that the plan was being modified. The statements of acceptance, moreover, merely said that the employee "ha[d] reviewed the benefits applicable to [him]" and "accept[ed] them." . . .

For us to sanction informal "plans" or plan "amendments"—whether oral or written—would leave the law of employee benefits in a state of uncertainty and would create disincentives for employers to offer benefits in the first place. Such a result is not in the interests of employees generally, and it is certainly not compatible with the goals of ERISA. . . .

IV

The plaintiffs argue that GM is estopped from enforcing the terms of the written plan against them. After the bench trial, the district court found that GM made no misleading representations to the general retirees. That finding appears unassailable. As to the early retirees, however, the district court ruled that GM was estopped from enforcing the plan because it misrepresented the plan's terms. In this, we believe, the court erred as a matter of law.

We have held that equitable estoppel may be a viable theory in ERISA cases, at least in regard to welfare plans. The elements of an equitable estoppel claim . . . are as follows: (1) there must be conduct or language amounting to a representation of material fact; (2) the party to be estopped must be aware of the true facts; (3) the party to be estopped must intend that the representation be acted on, or the party asserting the estoppel must reasonably believe that the party to be estopped so intends; (4) the party asserting the estoppel must be unaware of the true facts; and (5) the party asserting the estoppel must reasonably or justifiably rely on the representation to his detriment.

Principles of estoppel, however, cannot be applied to vary the terms of unambiguous plan documents; estoppel can only be invoked in the context of ambiguous plan provisions. There are at least two reasons for this. First, as we have seen, estoppel requires reasonable or justifiable reliance by the party asserting the estoppel. That party's reliance can seldom, if ever, be reasonable or justifiable if it is inconsistent with the clear and unambiguous terms of plan documents available to or furnished to the party. Second, to allow estoppel to override the clear terms of plan documents would be to enforce something other than the plan documents themselves. That would not be consistent with ERISA.

In the case at bar, we conclude that the plaintiffs' estoppel claims fail as a matter of law. As we have said, GM's plan and most of the summary plan descriptions issued to the plaintiffs over the years unambiguously reserved to GM the right to amend or terminate the plan. In the face of GM's clearly-stated right to amend—a right contained in the plan to which the plaintiffs had access and in many of the summaries they were given—reliance on statements allegedly suggesting the contrary was not, and could not be, reasonable or justifiable, especially when GM never told the plaintiffs that their benefits were vested or fully paid-up.

V

The last theory of recovery, applicable only to the early retirees, is that GM was in breach of the fiduciary duty it owed such retirees as administrator of their welfare plan. The district court dismissed this claim in its entirety, holding that an employer is not a fiduciary when it amends or terminates a plan.

The court's holding was correct as far as it went. GM did not act as a fiduciary in deciding to change its health insurance policies. The plaintiffs argue, however, that the district court misconstrued the breadth of their fiduciary duty claim. The claim, they say, encompassed all of GM's oral and written representations to them in connection with the special early retirement programs. We agree with this interpretation of the complaint.

* * *

. . . GM may have acted in a fiduciary capacity when it explained its retirement program to the early retirees. As a matter of law, however, we do not believe that GM committed a breach of any applicable fiduciary duty. In the first place, GM never told the early retirees that their health care benefits would be fully paid up or vested upon retirement. What GM told many of them, rather, was that their coverage was to be paid by GM for their lifetimes. This was undeniably true under the terms of GM's then-existing plan.

* * *

GM's failure, if it may properly be called such, amounted to this: the company did not tell the early retirees at every possible opportunity that which it had told them many times before—namely, that the terms of the plan were subject to change. . . .

In the second place, as we have said, GM was not required to disclose in its summary plan descriptions that the plan was subject to amendment or termination. It would be strange indeed if ERISA's fiduciary standards could be used to imply a duty to disclose information that ERISA's detailed disclosure provisions do not require to be disclosed. . . .

Had an early retiree asked about the possibility of the plan changing, and had he received a misleading answer, or had GM on its own initiative provided misleading information about the future of the plan, or had GM been required by ERISA or its implementing regulations to forecast the future, a different case would have been presented. But we do not think that GM's accurate representations of its current program can reasonably be deemed misleading. GM having given out no inaccurate information, there was no breach of fiduciary duty.

* * *

VIII

The certification of the class of early retirees is REVERSED, and the injunction is VACATED. Insofar as it applies to any unnamed member of the plaintiff class, the final judgment of the district court is VACATED. Insofar as it applies to the named plaintiffs, the final judgment is AFFIRMED IN PART and REVERSED IN PART. The parties shall bear their own costs.

LIVELY, Circuit Judge, concurring in part and dissenting in part.

... I concur in the majority opinion to the extent it affirms summary judgment for General Motors on the claims of the general retirees.

I agree with Judge Martin's dissent, however, in its conclusion that the district court correctly certified a class action for the claims of the early retirees and that the early retirees had vested health care benefits for the rest of their lives.

There is a fundamental difference between the claims of the two sets of retirees. The general retirees based their claims solely on plan documents, which reserved the right to change terms of the plan. The early retirees, on the other hand, claimed a new agreement with GM, supported by a new consideration—their agreement to leave their employment early, and as a consequence to save GM significant future costs. I believe the district court correctly found that GM entered into bilateral contracts with the early retirees. Further, I believe that the district court's findings of fact and conclusions of law following the bench trial are entitled to deference by this court, and should be affirmed.

With respect to the class action issue, the district court did not abuse its discretion in certifying a class consisting of the early retirees. The claims of the early retirees were all based on a common contention: that GM created a new condition for them with respect to future health care benefits by entering into new agreements that accorded them vested rights never given to general retirees. Thus, the "commonality" requirement of Rule 23(a) was satisfied.

I believe, further, the "typicality" requirement was met by the district court's creation of four subclasses, defined by the evidence upon which the early retirees relied (long form statement of acceptance, short form statement of acceptance, statement of intent to retire, and oral representations at time of entering into agreement for early retirement). ...

The majority concedes that while welfare plan benefits are not vested by the terms of ERISA, an employer can give up its freedom not to vest such benefits. I believe this is a case where the employer did just that. The district court found that "early retirement was presented ... as a special package deal that included health care, separate and distinct from the regular GM retirement program." *Sprague v. General Motors Corp.*, 843 F. Supp. 266, 271 (E.D. Mich. 1994) (*Sprague II*). This finding is not clearly erroneous; to the contrary, it is supported by substantial evidence. Unlike the general retirees, the early retirees were sought out by GM and offered inducements to leave their employment before reaching the normal retirement age. The general retirees necessarily had to rely only on plan documents that unilaterally created health care benefits. The early retirees, on the other hand, relied on new agreements that modified the welfare benefit plan. Rather than having only the employer's unilateral "gift" of health care coverage, they bargained with the employer for their coverage. I believe under the circumstances of this case the district court properly considered the evidence of the early retirees that went beyond plan documents. The district court's findings, based on this evidence, supported its conclusion that GM was estopped to deny the early retirees lifetime health benefits.

I also believe the majority is in error in concluding that GM did not act in a fiduciary capacity in its dealings with the early retirees. While I agree that an employer does not ordinarily act as a fiduciary in administering a welfare plan, it seems to me that the manner in which GM reached early retirement agreements with these employees necessarily involved a fiduciary relationship. The majority stresses that GM was not required to state, along with its explanation to the retirees that health care coverage was to be provided for their lifetimes at GM's expense, that it also retained the right to change this commitment. I disagree. Given that GM was seeking a new agreement from those employees that changed their previous expectations about the time of their retirement, GM could not in equity remain silent if it intended to reserve a right to change or eliminate this important benefit in the future. It was misleading to tell these employees they would have company-provided health care throughout their lives while at the same time failing to advise them that it was claiming to reserve the right to withdraw the benefit after the employees accepted early retirement. Given the setting in which GM was presenting these employees with a new set of conditions relating to their retirement, GM had a fiduciary obligation to be completely open, with no undisclosed conditions.

. . . This was a situation where silence was misleading. The reservations in the plan and descriptive materials all related to normal retirement. When, at GM's instigation, some employees were induced to retire early, they should have been told that these reservations applied to the new relationship created by early retirement if that was GM's intent. There was a fiduciary duty to inform them, and GM breached that duty.

I respectfully dissent from the majority's denial of all relief to early retirees, both named plaintiffs and putative class members.

* * *

BOYCE F. MARTIN, Chief Judge, with whom Judges MOORE and COLE join, dissenting.

* * *

This is a classic case of corporate shortsightedness. When General Motors was flush with cash and health care costs were low, it was easy to promise employees and retirees lifetime health care. Later, when General Motors was trying to sweeten the pot for early retirees, health care was another incentive to get employees off General Motors's groaning payroll. Of course, many of the executives who promised lifetime health care to early and general retirees are probably long since gone themselves. Rather than pay off those perhaps ill-considered promises, it is easier for the current regime to say those promises never were made. There is the tricky little matter of the paper trail of written assurances of lifetime health care, but General Motors, with the en banc majority's assistance, has managed to escape the ramifications of its now-regretted largesse.

* * *

The plaintiff class's claims for lifetime health care lie in shambles despite General Motors's repeated assurances of just such coverage. As I survey the wreckage of these claims, I am reminded that ERISA's underlying purpose is "to protect . . . the interests of participants in employee benefit plans and their beneficiaries." 29 U.S.C. §1001(b). ERISA is not a cure-all for disputes between companies and employees over welfare and pension plans, but this case provides a role for ERISA. The en banc majority opinion validates General Motors's decision to institute premiums and raise deductibles on retirees' health insurance, but the decision bestows upon General Motors the freedom to eliminate health care coverage completely. Seemingly, any reservation of rights, no matter how weakly worded or unconnected to the grant of rights, will protect a company from having to live up to its obligations in the future. Ultimately, the en banc majority puts a new twist on an old aphorism, and what is good for General Motors is not good for the country but rather is bad for its retirees. I therefore respectfully dissent.

QUESTIONS

1. In *Sprague*, GM changed its plan to make it less favorable to retirees, but did not eliminate benefits entirely. Suppose it had. Would the outcome of the case have been different? From a policy perspective, should the two situations be treated differently?

2. As *Sprague* illustrates, ERISA does not require welfare benefits to vest within a specific time frame. By comparison, as discussed in Chapter 5, such vesting requirements do apply to pension plans. Should welfare plans be subject to the same vesting requirements as pension plans? Why or why not?

CHAPTER 7

Housing and Long-Term Care

A. INTRODUCTION

This chapter explores housing-related issues that occur across a variety of housing settings, ranging from private homes to nursing home facilities. In later life, the level and type of services individuals need frequently determine where they live. As individuals' care needs increase, they may transition to housing that provides a greater array of household and health care services. This transition typically involves moving from a private residence to an institutional setting seen as capable of providing superior services or as providing services in a more affordable manner (e.g., because of economies of scale or because it is eligible for Medicaid coverage).

The different housing settings that this chapter discusses are thus often described as representing a continuum of care—with home-based settings providing the lowest level of services, assisted living facilities providing a higher level of care, nursing homes providing the highest level of care, and *continuing care retirement communities* (CCRCs) providing all three levels. In reality, characterizing these different models as falling along a continuum of care is an over-simplification. For example, given sufficient financial and social resources, nursing home level services can be delivered in a person's home or in other community-based settings. Indeed, as discussed in the final section of this chapter, federal anti-discrimination legislation limits the ability of housing providers to reject potential residents on the basis of their care needs and limits states' ability to restrict public payment for long-term care to that which is provided in institutions.

Because of the close relationship between housing and the provision of care, housing and housing-related concerns are at the core of much of elder law practice. Elder law attorneys engage in a wide variety of legal activities aimed at helping their clients secure, finance, and remain in the housing of the client's choice. Elder law attorneys can also play important roles in helping clients realize their rights in different housing settings—for example, rights to basic care in a nursing home, to have disabilities accommodated in an assisted living facility, or to receive services in a CCRC or at home.

Recognizing that older adults typically wish to remain in the homes they inhabited as younger adults, this chapter begins by exploring older adults' desire to "age in place" and the various techniques and tools that elder law attorneys can use to help clients to do so. It then explores issues specific to certain types of housing that are predominantly inhabited by older adults: nursing homes, assisted living facilities, and CCRCs. Finally, it explores issues related to housing discrimination, and the legal protections that can help older adults stay in the housing of their choice—whether it be a community-based setting or an institutional one—even when experiencing a significant disability.

B. AGING IN PLACE

"Aging in place" is a phenomenon that occurs when older adults are able to remain in the home and community in which they resided when younger while receiving the services and care they require to meet their needs. Older adults across the socioeconomic spectrum indicate a strong desire to age in place, although they differ in what they mean by this. To some, aging in place means staying in their current residence. To others, it means staying in their neighborhood, town, or community more broadly defined.

As individuals care needs and care-related expenditures increase, however, aging in place may be harder and harder to do. There are a variety of techniques that can be employed to enable seniors to age in place in the face of these challenges. This section explores the appeal and value of aging in place, tools and programs that can provide financial resources for aging in place, and legal issues related to hiring in-home help.

1. The Appeal of Aging in Place

Staying in their home is often of paramount importance to older adults. A telephone survey of housing preferences conducted by AARP in 2010 found that 88 percent of people age 65 and older reported that they wished to stay in their current residence "for as long as possible." *See* AARP Research & Strategic Analysis, Home and Community Preferences of the 45+ Population (Nov. 2010).

This preference for aging in place reflects the myriad of ways that housing affects older adults' lives. As Professor Lawrence Frolik has written:

> [H]ousing is much more than shelter . . . in the larger sense housing embodies:
>
> ▪ Security. Not just actual safety, but also a sense of knowing the risks and safety of the community. We feel secure when we understand the relative

risks of our environment, but may feel insecure in a perfectly safe, but unknown environment. Security is knowing whether it is safe to walk down this street after dark or knowing who to turn to for aid and assistance if you should become sick and need [a] ride to the doctor's office.

- A Sense of Place. The feelings that arise from a sense of the past, traditions, memories and rituals. "Every Thanksgiving the extended family gathers for dinner in the [dining] room." or "In this room I watched my daughter take her first steps."

- Community. Not only friends, but the fabric of daily life that is provided by acquaintances, business and service persons: "Jim at the dry cleaners," "Betty, the cashier at the deli," clubs and community associations: "Ryan at the Garden Club," and religious affiliations and activities: "Owen in the Bible Club" or "Rachael and David who accompany me to Temple."

- Recreation. Both formal, such as sporting events and bowling leagues, and informal such as regular coffee groups and walks in the mall with the "regular striders." . . .

- A Sense of Self. For many, elderly housing defines in a profound sense who they are. It expresses the past and reflects their values. It is the "place" at which their life is anchored and from where they metaphorically step-out into the world.

Lawrence A. Frolik, *The Client's Desire to Age in Place: Our Role as Elder Law Attorneys*, 15 NAELA Q. 6, 6 (2002).

While the desire to age in place and to facilitate aging in place is increasingly driving public policy approaches to long-term care as well as private planning, critics caution against over-emphasizing its importance. In the following excerpt, Professor Stephen Golant, a gerontologist and geographer, argues for a more critical approach to aging in place.

Stephen Golant, Commentary: Irrational Exuberance for the Aging in Place of Vulnerable Low-Income Homeowners

20 J. Aging & Soc. Pol'y 379 (2008)

Vulnerable low-income older homeowners can have difficulties aging in place successfully because they confront multiple problems: unmet caregiving needs resulting in poor quality care; financially burdensome housing costs restricting their other expenditures; physically inadequate dwellings in need of substantial maintenance and upgrades; design deficiencies resulting in unsafe or uncomfortable settings; and declining neighborhoods that have become physically and socially inhospitable places to live.

Advocates typically respond by arguing for more resources to address these downsides. At some point, however, we must reasonably ask under what individual and environmental conditions might it be better to recommend that these older homeowners move to other more affordance dwellings and neighborhoods? At what point do we concede that family caregiving is not working well and is endangering the well-being of both older persons and their caregivers and that professionally managed home care is failing to address the full complement of unmet needs? Is there a limit to the government funding we offer these homeowners to pay for their high winter heating expenses, their home repairs and modifications, and their excessive property tax and insurance bills? At what point do we pay attention to studies showing that home modifications that remove home safety hazards may not necessarily reduce the incidence of falling. Should we be encouraging cash-poor older homeowners to take out financially draining reverse mortgages so that they can consume their housing wealth to pay for their long-term care expenses, even as they are living in unaffordable and physically deficient dwellings and potentially retarding the rejuvenation of their physically and social deprived neighborhoods? At what point do we acknowledge that older persons living in places with an inadequate supply of affordable housing are institutionalized more frequently and with fewer dependencies? . . .

Alternatively, we could be more honest about the downsides of aging in place and make it more attractive for older homeowners to relocate to other more appropriate shelter and care settings. Foremost, we must better inform older homeowners about their options:

- Educate these vulnerable older homeowners (and the social workers, care managers and professional service providers who advise them) about the social, psychological, and economic costs and disadvantages of staying put.
- Show them (hand-holding tours) alternative housing and residential care options.
- Counsel them about the specific merits of moving to these housing arrangements.
- Offer them financial scenarios whereby they can use the equity in their dwellings to defray the costs of these housing arrangements.
- Help them cope with the many potential stresses associated with the moving experience.

* * *

Today, we favor public policies and private-sector responses that enable older persons to remain in their owned homes, irrespective of the types or acuity of their health or disability problems or their dwelling conditions. We are in danger, however, of displaying an irrational exuberance for aging in place solutions and failing to recognize that not all housing settings are appropriate fulcrums around which to organize long-term care solutions. Although moving is obviously not appropriate for all or most of these homeowners, neither should we unequivocally endorse one-size-fits-all aging in place solutions. . . .

NOTE

Aging in place for LGBT older adults. Aging in place may be especially challenging for LGBT individuals, both because of family structures and because of concerns about bias in the provision of care. As Professor Nancy Knauer explains:

> [T]he prospect of aging in place presents obvious difficulties for LGBT elders because it often requires assistance from informal caregivers, and LGBT elders are much more likely than their non-LGBT peers to be estranged from their next of kin. Chosen families may also be limited in how much support they can provide as their members age together and require increasing amounts of support. As a result, LGBT elders may be more likely than their non-LGBT peers to require home health care assistance, but they are less likely to use supportive services. If they are unable to age in place, LGBT elders are also less likely to have the financial wherewithal to pay for long-term care, leaving them with Medicaid as their only option.

Nancy Knauer, *"Gen Silent": Advocating for LGBT Elders*, 19 ELDER L.J. 289, 333-34 (2012).

QUESTION

Professor Frolik has argued that "helping clients to age in place must be an essential aspect of elder law planning. For if our legal advice does not support, encourage and ultimately succeed in enabling the client to age in place, or in the vernacular, to stay put, then our planning has fallen short." Lawrence A. Frolik, *The Client's Desire to Age in Place: Our Role as Elder Law Attorneys*, 15 NAELA Q. 6, 6 (2002). Do you agree?

2. Leveraging a Home to Support Aging in Place

For many older adults, their home is their primary resource. When older adults need greater income, they may wish to leverage the equity in the home to generate that income.

a. Sale and Leaseback

One technique for leveraging home equity is to enter into a sale and leaseback arrangement. In such an arrangement, the older adult sells his or her home to a third party (typically an adult child) and then leases it back. This is a way for the third party to provide needed or desired income to the older adult while getting value in return. Sale and leaseback arrangements have significant risks as the older adult is transformed from a homeowner into a renter, decreasing his or her control over the property and potentially risking eviction. Moreover, if the house is sold for less than fair market value, it may create a penalty period for Medicaid coverage of long-term care, as discussed in Chapter 6.

b. Reverse Mortgage

A common technique for leveraging home equity to support aging in place is for the homeowner to obtain a *reverse mortgage*. Reverse mortgages are financial devices that allow homeowners to convert equity in their homes into cash. Unlike a traditional mortgage (sometimes called a *forward mortgage*), in which the lender advances the homeowner money to purchase a home, a lender in a reverse mortgage advances a homeowner money (in the form of a lump sum, monthly payment, or line of credit) in return for an interest in the home. Therefore, unlike with a second mortgage or a home equity loan, homeowners can qualify for a reverse mortgage regardless of their income or credit. Instead, they generally need to own their home outright or with minimal outstanding liens. In addition, federal law requires reverse mortgage borrowers to be at least 62 years old.

A key distinction between different reverse mortgages is when the loan *matures* (i.e., when repayment is due). A *tenure loan* matures when certain life events occur: the borrower dies, sells the home, or does not occupy the home for a year or more. By contrast, a *term loan* matures at a pre-determined date. Either type of loan, however, may become due and payable if a homeowner does not fulfill his or her responsibility to protect the home by, for example, maintaining its condition, paying property taxes, and carrying homeowner's insurance.

Reverse mortgages can be a valuable source of money for older adults. Not only do they allow older adults to take advantage of the equity in their homes, but, since the payments received through a reverse mortgage are loan advances, they are not subject to income tax.

However, in recent years, there has been growing concern about seniors being steered into inappropriate reverse mortgages. A report issued by the National Consumer Law Center in 2009, summarized the concern as follows:

> Certainly, the continuing availability of reverse mortgages is good news for seniors who need to cash out some of their housing wealth to supplement Social Security, to meet unexpected medical costs, or to make needed home repairs. But growth in the reverse mortgage market has unleashed other, more malign forces. . . .
>
> Reverse mortgages are complicated. The opportunities for abuse abound. Seniors, many of whom lack experience with complex financial products, often depend upon lenders and brokers for expertise and guidance. Reverse mortgage lenders, like subprime lenders, emphasize the benefits that they provide to borrowers and often tout their commitment to responsible lending principles. However, such claims are undermined by a growing public record of how subprime lenders—including some now active in the reverse mortgage market—profited from acting irresponsibly during the recent mortgage boom. In addition, reverse mortgage lenders have followed in the footsteps of their subprime counterparts by using financial incentives to reward brokers for arranging deals that boost lenders' profits and raise the costs paid by borrowers. By adjusting reverse mortgage loan terms, such as interest rates, servicing fees, rate adjustment intervals and

distributions, brokers and lenders can maximize their profits at the expense of senior homeowners.

Seniors are also vulnerable to other abuses associated with reverse mortgages. Some seniors have been persuaded to sink proceeds from reverse mortgages into complicated annuity contracts or expensive long-term care insurance products. These products generate large commissions for sellers, but frequently prove financially toxic for senior homeowners. While counseling is required for all borrowers of federally insured reverse mortgages, only a handful of states require counseling for all types of reverse mortgages. And while quality counseling can be helpful to seniors, counseling remains inconsistent and underfunded.

NATIONAL CONSUMER LAW CENTER, SUBPRIME REVISITED: HOW REVERSE MORTGAGES PUT OLDER HOMEOWNERS' EQUITY AT RISK (2009), *available at* www.nclc.org/images/pdf/foreclosure_mortgage/predatory_mortgage_lending/reverse-mortgages-report1009.pdf.

The next case illustrates the potential for reverse mortgage lending to become predatory in nature, and the context in which such predatory lending can occur.

Munoz v. Financial Freedom Senior Funding Corp.

573 F. Supp. 2d 1275 (C.D. Cal. 2008)

CORMAC J. CARNEY, District Judge.

***

Defendant Financial Freedom Senior Funding Corporation ("Financial Freedom") moves to dismiss the second amended class action complaint of Plaintiff Mary P. Munoz. Ms. Munoz, a senior citizen, alleges that Financial Freedom preyed upon her by selling her a reverse mortgage and failing to prohibit her from purchasing a deferred annuity with the proceeds of that reverse mortgage. Financial Freedom moves to dismiss Ms. Munoz's claims on the ground that they are preempted by federal law, which exclusively regulates the activities of federal savings associations. Ms. Munoz opposes Financial Freedom's motion, arguing that her claims are not preempted by federal law because they implicate only a lender's common law obligations in the marketplace, and are not specific to its lending activity. For the following reasons, Financial Freedom's motion is GRANTED WITH PREJUDICE.

BACKGROUND

On June 2, 2008, the Court granted in part and denied in part Financial Freedom's motion for judgment on the pleadings with respect to Ms. Munoz's first amended complaint. The Court held that Ms. Munoz's claims against Financial Freedom predicated upon allegedly deceptive or illegal fees, disclosures and advertising were preempted by the Home Owners Loan Act of 1933 ("HOLA"), 12 U.S.C. §1461 (1933). However, because the Court could not definitively conclude that

Ms. Munoz was unable to allege any non-preempted claims against Financial Freedom, she was afforded leave to amend her complaint.

In her second amended complaint, Ms. Munoz, age seventy-eight, makes new allegations about the reverse mortgage transaction that she claims has caused her financial injury. In September 2004, defendant Kathleen Miller offered financial advisory services to Ms. Munoz. During the course of their relationship, Ms. Miller advised Ms. Munoz that a reverse mortgage would suit her financial needs by giving her ready access to the equity in her home. The reverse mortgage was brokered by defendant Louis Soqui, a broker employed by defendant Carteret Mortgage Corporation. Financial Freedom, the lender, "originated and/or underwrote the reverse mortgage loan entered into by Ms. Munoz." After closing costs and fees, Ms. Munoz received $118,174, and Financial Freedom obtained a mortgage on her property as security. One month later, in October 2004, Ms. Miller sold Ms. Munoz a deferred annuity, claiming that it was a suitable financial vehicle to provide her a steady income for the remainder of her life and to pay off her outstanding debts and expenses. With an initial investment of $60,000 in the deferred annuity, Ms. Munoz received a monthly payment of approximately $200 per month. When this monthly payment proved insufficient to cover her monthly and other expenses, Ms. Munoz was forced to withdraw over $26,000 from the annuity early, incurring significant penalties and fees.

Ms. Munoz seeks to hold Financial Freedom liable for failing to prohibit her from investing the proceeds of her reverse mortgage into a deferred annuity, failing to inform her than an annuity purchase was not required in connection with the reverse mortgage, and failing to advise her that the annuity was "not proper" in connection with the reverse mortgage. She alleges that the practice of selling deferred annuities "concurrently" with reverse mortgages is a prohibited form of elder abuse. To that end, Ms. Munoz alleges that Financial Freedom "is and was fully aware of the estate, tax and financial ploys utilized by Sales Agent Defendants [Ms. Miller, Mr. Soqui and Carteret]. . . ." She claims the lender took "insufficient action to prevent these abusive marketing and sales tactics and has instead ratified these tactics and continued to accept the benefits of these abusive sales practices."

Based on these allegations, Ms. Munoz asserts the following class claims against Financial Freedom: (1) breach of fiduciary duty by selling Ms. Munoz a reverse mortgage and "permitting unsuitable deferred annuities to be sold concurrently with its reverse mortgage loans," (2) aiding and abetting breach of fiduciary duty, (3) fraudulent concealment for failing to disclose the risk of purchasing an annuity with the proceeds of a reverse mortgage, (4) unjust enrichment for retaining fees generated by the reverse mortgage practice, (5) breach of the implied covenant of good faith and fair dealing for "failing to have a policy prohibiting the sale of deferred annuities in conjunction with the purchase of its reverse mortgage," and (6) negligence/negligent misrepresentation for "failing to have a policy that prohibits the sale of deferred annuities[]."

***

ANALYSIS

Financial Freedom has again moved to dismiss Ms. Munoz's complaint because her claims are preempted by federal law. Federal law may preempt state law in three ways, two of which are potentially applicable here:

> First, Congress may preempt state law by so stating in express terms. Second, preemption may be inferred when federal regulation in a particular field is so pervasive as to make reasonable the inference that Congress left no room for the States to supplement it. In such cases of field preemption, the mere volume and complexity of federal regulations demonstrate an implicitly congressional intent to displace all state law.

Bank of Am. v. City & County of S.F., 309 F.3d 551, 558 (9th Cir. 2002) (internal quotation marks and citations omitted). Typically, there is a presumption against federal preemption of state laws. That presumption does not exist, however, "when [a] state regulates in an area where there has been a history of significant federal presence." *United States v. Locke*, 529 U.S. 89, 108 (2000). Banking is one such area in which Congress has created a long-standing federal regulatory framework. . . .

Under the Home Owners' Loan Act of 1933 ("HOLA"), 12 U.S.C. §1461 (1933), and associated regulations, Congress authorized broad authority to promulgate regulations governing savings and loan institutions to the Office of Thrift Supervision ("OTS"). The regulations authored by OTS pursuant to HOLA include a preemption regulation, 12 C.F.R. §560.2, which provides as follows:

> OTS hereby occupies the entire field of lending regulation for federal savings associations. OTS intends to give Federal savings associations maximum flexibility to exercise their lending powers in accordance with a uniform federal scheme of regulation. Accordingly, federal savings associations may extend credit as authorized under federal law, including this part, without regard to state laws purporting to regulate or otherwise affect their credit activities, except to the extent provided in paragraph (c) of this section. . . .

The OTS regulations also contain the framework for analyzing whether a state law is preempted under HOLA. If the state law in question is of a type listed in paragraph (b) of §560.2, "the analysis will end there; the law is preempted." Included in paragraph (b) is a category of state regulation Financial Freedom argues is applicable here. Section 560.2(b)(10) requires preemption of state laws governing "[p]rocessing, origination, servicing, sale or purchase of, or investment or participating in, mortgages."

* * *

In her second amended complaint, Ms. Munoz's asserts the legal theory that Financial Freedom had a duty, either as a fiduciary or by operation of common law, to prohibit her from using the proceeds of her reverse mortgage to purchase a deferred annuity. She bases this proposed duty on a variety of state and federal legislative statements and enactments, as well as reports of consumer watchdog groups which all conclude that the combination of a reverse mortgage and a deferred annuity is predatory and financially risky for senior citizens. Financial Freedom argues that Ms. Munoz's amended claims, like her unfair competition claims in her first amended complaint, are preempted by HOLA. Particularly, Financial Freedom contends that any state law applied to mortgage lenders that obligates them to monitor a borrower's use of reverse mortgage proceeds necessarily implicates how the lender originates, processes or services the mortgage under §560.2(b). It must therefore be preempted.

A state law of general applicability—that is, one which does not purport to directly regulate the conduct of mortgage lenders—may be preempted by HOLA if, "as applied," it is a type of state law that falls within §560.2. Thus, Ms. Munoz's amended claims are preempted by HOLA if her common law claims as applied would regulate the "origination, processing [or] servicing" of mortgages, or if application of the state law would more than incidentally affect lending. *See* §560.2.

* * *

Any law which purports to require a lender to restrict or monitor the use of proceeds generated by a reverse mortgage implicates the origination, servicing or processing of the loan. The language of §560.2(b)(10), in its entirety, evidences an intent on the part of OTS to cover a wide range of activities which occur during the lifetime of the mortgage. A borrower's primary purpose in entering into a reverse mortgage transaction is to secure access to cash for immediate uses, such as living and medical expenses, debts, or housing payments. Thus, an integral aspect of the reverse mortgage process is that the cash generated from the transaction may be used for any of those purposes; it is not limited for purchasing a particular piece of property as would a standard mortgage loan. Were the Court to apply state laws to reverse mortgage activity in such a way as to restrict the use of those funds, the law would be regulating an integral aspect of the reverse mortgage transaction, namely the borrower's freedom to use the proceeds for any purpose. Accordingly, Ms. Munoz's state and common law claims are preempted because, as applied, they relate to integral activities within the life of the loan, including those which occur during the origination, processing, or servicing of the loan.

* * *

The Court further notes another major problem with Ms. Munoz's legal theory. Courts have no authority to impose restrictions on how any individual, whether a senior citizen or otherwise, can use her own money, even if that money comes from a reverse mortgage. Just as Financial Freedom has no obligation or power to prevent senior citizens from using the proceeds of a reverse mortgage at a casino (which is certainly a risky use of capital for a fixed-income senior citizen), it likewise has no obligation or power to require or restrict the investments that its customers make with their reverse mortgage proceeds. Of course, should there be allegations or evidence that Financial Freedom conspired with, instructed, contracted with, or in any other way affirmatively associated with a deferred annuity provider to swindle senior citizens, Ms. Munoz's legal theory would be more viable. However, here she only alleges that Financial Freedom was "fully aware" of the allegedly deceptive business practices of the sales agents. There is no allegation that there was an ongoing business relationship or conspiracy whereby Financial Freedom funded reverse mortgages to facilitate a senior citizen's purchase of a risky deferred annuity. In fact, Ms. Munoz's alleges she purchased her annuity one month after the reverse mortgage, not "concurrently" as would more plausibly create an inference of impropriety on the part of Financial Freedom.

Like her first amended complaint, Ms. Munoz has again asserted claims against Financial Freedom that are preempted by federal law. And, the claims now asserted in the second amended complaint advance a more tenuous legal theory, exposing the deficiencies in her allegations against Financial Freedom. The Court concludes that amendment would be futile and Financial Freedom's motion to dismiss is therefore GRANTED WITH PREJUDICE.

QUESTIONS

1. When might you recommend that a client consider a reverse mortgage?

2. How might pursuing the goal of aging in place conflict with pursuing Medicaid planning? Are there techniques you might employ to help a client with Medicaid planning that might endanger his or her ability to age in place? Are there techniques you might employ to help a client age in place that might be disadvantageous from a Medicaid planning perspective?

c. Home Sharing

In lieu of hiring someone to come into the home to provide assistance, some older adults enter into *home sharing* arrangements. Home sharing is an arrangement by which an older adult provides housing to another person in return for that other person providing some service or services, and sometimes rent in addition. Services range from limited companionship to significant personal care. However, as a general matter, home sharing is more likely to be recommended where the older adult needs only limited assistance, companionship, or the security of the presence of another.

In a number of states, nonprofit organizations facilitate home sharing by helping to match older adults with those in need of housing. Even where such nonprofits provide some level of screening, entering into a home sharing arrangement can pose risks for both parties in the arrangement. Accordingly, individuals entering into home share arrangements would generally be well advised to seek counsel to execute formal contracts in advance of entering into the arrangement.

PROBLEM

HomeShare Vermont, a nonprofit that matches homeowners in need of care or company with prospective home sharers, offers the following "model agreement." Those completing the agreement are advised: "Remember to involve a family member or friend in completing the Homesharing Agreement if you need help. It is important that you be comfortable with your agreement and feel that each section is workable." *A Vermonter's Guide to Homesharing* 16 (2013), *available at* http://www.homesharevermont.org/.

What are the advantages and disadvantages of this approach? What additional or alternative provisions might you suggest if you represented the homeowner? The prospective home sharer?

Sample Homesharing Agreement

We _____ and _____
          Person offering the home   *Person moving in*

agree to participate in the following arrangements to begin on _____.
                                                              Date

I, _____ , **agree to provide the following:**
          Person offering the home

Yes/No
- ☐ ☐ Bedroom (Can it be decorated/painted?) _____
- ☐ ☐ Parking _____
- ☐ ☐ Laundry Facilities _____
- ☐ ☐ Other _____

I, _____ , **agree to provide the following:**
          Person moving in

Yes/No
- ☐ ☐ Rent in the amount of $ _____ due on_____
- ☐ ☐ Share of utilities (heat/electric/internet/cable/phone)?
- ☐ ☐ Exchange of services for _____ hours per week, to include:
- ☐ ☐ Housekeeping _____
- ☐ ☐ Meal preparation/eating together_____
- ☐ ☐ Grocery shopping/errands _____
- ☐ ☐ Transportation _____
- ☐ ☐ Companionship _____
- ☐ ☐ Yard Work _____
- ☐ ☐ Shoveling Snow _____
- ☐ ☐ Laundry_____
- ☐ ☐ Other_____

Clarify the following items:
Use of dishes, pots, etc._____
Food storage _____
Use of common areas _____
Mail _____
Visitors: ☐ Daytime ☐ Nighttime ☐ Notice required? _____
Pets _____
Guns or weapons in the home? _____
Schedule: ☐ Away, notice required? _____
Emergency contacts exchanged? _____

We also agree to the following:
Loans or gifts of money or substantial property are not part of this agreement and are strongly discouraged. Participants may amend their homesharing agreement by mutual agreement.

Each participant agrees to give a written notice of _____ days in the event she or he desires to end the homesharing match.

_____   _____
Signature of person offering the home   *Date*

_____   _____
Signature of person moving in   *Date*

3. Obtaining In-Home Help

In order to remain safely and comfortably in their homes, many older adults require help from another person. Most older adults who receive care in their home are cared for by unpaid family members and friends. Indeed, an estimated 80 percent of recipients of home care rely exclusively on unpaid caregivers, whereas only 8 percent rely exclusively on paid caregivers, with the remainder combining paid and unpaid forms of care. *See* THE CAREGIVING PROJECT FOR OLDER AMERICANS, CAREGIVING IN AMERICA (c. 2006).

As the number of older adults needing care increases, there will be increased demand for both unpaid and paid in-home caregivers. In-home care providers can perform a wide range of services from skilled nursing services, to homemaking services such as cleaning and cooking, to assistance with activities of daily living such as bathing and walking, to companionship and intellectual stimulation.

a. Rights Under the Americans with Disabilities Act

Many older adults who need or desire in-home help cannot afford to pay for it. Fortunately for them, the Medicaid program has the potential to provide financial support for community-based long-term care services. Although Medicaid has covered certain forms of home and community-based long-term care from its inception, government funding of long-term care has historically been biased in favor of care provided in institutional settings. However, in the watershed case *Olmstead v. Zimring*, 527 U.S. 581 (1999), the Supreme Court held that governments may not require individuals to receive care in institutions regardless of the individuals' needs or desires. Such a requirement would, according to the Court in *Olmstead*, constitute discrimination by reason of disability in violation of the Americans with Disabilities Act (ADA). Writing for the majority, Justice Ginsberg explained that:

> Recognition that unjustified institutional isolation of persons with disabilities is a form of discrimination reflects two evident judgments. First, institutional placement of persons who can handle and benefit from community settings perpetuates unwarranted assumptions that persons so isolated are incapable or unworthy of participating in community life. Second, confinement in an institution severely diminishes the everyday life activities of individuals, including family relations, social contacts, work options, economic independence, educational advancement, and cultural enrichment.

Olmstead, 527 U.S. at 600-01. Therefore, to comply with the ADA, states providing long-term care to persons with disabilities must cover care in a community-based setting where such services are appropriate for the individual's condition, not contrary to the wishes of the person with a disability, and can be reasonably accommodated given the state's resources and the needs of others with disabilities. Thus, while *Olmstead* does not prohibit states from supporting care in institutional settings such as nursing homes, it limits the circumstances under which a state may refuse to cover care in a more integrated, community-based setting.

Despite *Olmstead*, demand for home and community-based services continues to exceed supply, and many states continue to rely very heavily on nursing homes to meet citizen's long-term care needs. As Professor Sidney Watson has explained:

> The most recent data shows that, as a result of *Olmstead* and efforts at the federal level to educate and encourage states to redirect their Medicaid funding from nursing home care to home based care, Medicaid funding for community based services has now risen to forty-one percent of all Medicaid long-term care spending. But while national statistics have risen substantially, the gap among the states . . . also widened: Mississippi is still spending only twelve percent on community-based services, while at the top-end, five states are now spending between sixty to seventy-five percent of their Medicaid long-term care dollars on community-based care. At the bottom, almost one third of the states (sixteen) spend less than a third of their long-term care dollars on home and community-based care.
>
> Moreover, demand for Medicaid community-based services far outstrips the supply: thirty-eight states report waiting lists for Section 1915(c) HCB Waiver services with almost 400,000 people waiting for services. Some of this shortfall in waiver services is the result of state legislatures' unwillingness to appropriate state tax dollars to help fund additional HCBW slots. However, even where state appropriations were available, a severe shortage of community care personnel and other resources limit waiver slots.

Sidney D. Watson, *From Almhouses to Nursing Homes and Community Care: Lessons from Medicaid's History*, 26 GA. ST. U. L. REV. 937, 966-67 (2010).

Olmstead, however, calls into serious question the ability of a state to limit the availability of services designed to provide individuals with alternatives to nursing home placement to only a subset of those persons otherwise qualified for them. For example, in *Helen L. v. DiDario*, 46 F.3d 325 (1999), the Third Circuit relied on *Olmstead* to find that Pennsylvania violated the ADA when it placed a paralyzed woman who was otherwise eligible for in-home care services on a waiting list for such services, and would only pay for her to receive needed services if she lived in a nursing home even though home-based services would have cost Pennsylvania considerably less than it was spending on her nursing home services. Courts have been less willing to find a violation where providing home-based services would be equally or more expensive than nursing home services. Since states do not have to provide home-based alternatives where doing so would amount to a "fundamental alteration" in their program, the question in large part is whether the additional cost should be viewed as constituting such an alteration.

NOTES

1. Rodriguez v. City of New York. *Helen L.*, noted above, was an easy case because it was clear that the nursing home care was costing the state considerably more than integrated services. By contrast, in *Rodriguez v. City of New York*, 197 F.3d 611 (1999), the Second Circuit held that New York State did not violate the ADA when it refused to provide Medicaid coverage for safety monitoring services that plaintiffs, beneficiaries with mental disabilities (including Alzheimer's disease), needed to remain safely at home.

2. *Cause of Medicaid's institutional bias.* As part of her discussion of the history of Medicaid coverage for long-term care, Professor Watson explained the reason for the program's institutional bias as follows:

> When Medicaid was originally enacted the nation already had a large nursing home industry ready, willing and eager to accept the new Medicaid funding. The nursing home industry fought to get Medicaid funding and keep Medicaid funding. They lobbied Congress to create new, lower levels of nursing home care . . . thereby creating new kinds of institutions for people with disabilities. No such cadre of community care providers existed in 1965. As the decades have gone by, home and community-based providers have evolved, but there has always been—and continues to be—too few community caregivers for the demand for community-based services. Medicaid's persistent nursing home bias is partly the result of the fact that the statute makes nursing home care a mandatory service. But [intermediate care facilities] and [intermediate care facilities for the persons with intellectual disabilities] are optional services, and states were quick to embrace them because they perceived them to be of benefit to their state tax coffers and (mistakenly) to people with disabilities. Making home and community-based services a mandatory category would certainly push the most laggard states to begin making a serious investment in home and community-based services, but even that is unlikely to be a panacea.

Sidney D. Watson, *From Almhouses to Nursing Homes and Community Care: Lessons from Medicaid's History*, 26 GA. ST. U. L. REV. 937, 938-40 (2010).

b. The Emergence of Consumer Directed Care

Individuals paying for care privately have long had the option of choosing whether to independently hire and supervise their care providers, or whether to work with a home health agency that supplies care providers. By contrast, Medicaid coverage for home-based care has traditionally meant that state Medicaid programs contract with home health care agencies, which in turn employ home health aides to provide direct care to Medicaid beneficiaries. Under this approach, the agency is responsible for hiring (and potentially firing) the aide, training the aide, and setting the terms of the aide's employment.

In recent years—thanks in large part to the disability rights movement and, in particular, the independent living movement—there has been a shift away from the agency model and toward what is termed *consumer directed care*. Consumer directed care aims to empower and respect persons with disabilities by providing them with the opportunity to control the personal care services that they receive. As Professor Andrew Batavia has explained:

> Under this model, individuals receive services in their homes from one or more personal assistants who are not trained as health care workers or supervised by health care professionals. Typically, the consumer advertises for assistants in a local newspaper, interviews them, and informs them of the requirements and benefits of the position. The individual receiving the service is considered an autonomous, self-directed consumer (rather than a patient), who hires, trains, supervises and, if necessary, fires his or her personal assistant(s). This independent living model, which gives consumers substantial control over their personal assistance services, may be contrasted with the medical model and the informal support model in which others often control the timing and manner in which services are provided.

Andrew I. Batavia, *A Right to Personal Assistance Services: "Most Integrated Setting Appropriate" Requirements and the Independent Living Model of Long-Term Care*, 27 Am. J.L. & Med. 17, 18-19 (2001).

Almost all states include some consumer directed services in their Medicaid program. Thus, although the consumer directed care model has developed for use primarily for younger persons with disabilities, older adults with qualifying disabilities can also be eligible for Medicaid coverage for such services. In the article excerpted below, scholar Daniela Kraiem discusses the appeal and growth of consumer directed care, while raising concerns about its impact.

Daniela Kraiem, Consumer Direction in Medicaid Long-Term Care: Autonomy, Commodification of Family Labor, and Community Resilience

19 Am. U. J. Gender Soc. Pol'y & L. 671 (2011)

Agencies that contract to provide Medicaid-funded long term care workers suffer from the severe labor shortage, especially for recipients who live in rural or high crime areas, live in communities with poor public transportation, do not speak English, or need care outside of normal working hours. Agencies suffer from an extremely high rate of aide turnover. The problem is especially acute in federally funded long term care programs, because they cannot rely upon the labor of undocumented immigrants, who provide an unknown but significant portion of the low wage labor in the private long term care market.

* * *

"Consumer directed long term care" is a type of HCBS program designed to mitigate the labor shortage and autonomy concerns associated with agency-based home health care. . . . Instead of having a Medicaid contracting agency organize and oversee long term care services, the beneficiary receives a stipend to purchase his or her own care on the private market. A popularized alternative name for consumer directed long term care is "Cash and Counseling." As this name suggests, the program has two basic components. Essentially, these programs are a cash allocation to elderly persons or persons with disabilities, which the recipient can use to purchase goods or services related to long-term care, coupled with some assistance from the state, or counseling, in managing their services.

* * *

Under consumer direction, the consumer is responsible for locating his or her own long term care workers—freeing the state from this obligation. Importantly, many consumer directed long term care programs explicitly allow participants to hire relatives, even those such as parents or spouses who are already legally obligated to provide support. While there have been a number of state-funded programs that have allowed payment to legally liable family members, in general this has not been the norm and was not allowed under previous Medicaid regulations. States do not have to enact this option, but it appears that many will. This new legally liable caretaker rule represents a major shift in law relating to caretaking and support.

The option to hire a worker without going through an agency has a specific effect: demonstration studies of experimental consumer directed programs show that the majority of beneficiaries hire members of their own families. Consumer direction increases the labor supply by tapping into the labor of friends and family members who are unlikely to work for a home health agency but who may be willing to care for a relative with a disability. It may also bring into the system a small portion of family caretakers who are already providing care without being paid. It is important to note that consumer direction increases the labor supply by tapping into new pools of labor rather than improving wages and working conditions to make the profession more attractive. . . .

Putting aside for the moment concerns about the specific effects on labor force, the commodification of family labor alone is significant, as it is largely unprecedented in American social policy. Organizations representing family caretakers have been advocating for many years to allow family members to receive payment for providing long term care. Some feminist theorists have advocated for the commodification of care work in general, highlighting its significance to the economy and emphasizing that housework and care work are indeed work. The move not only to allow the state to pay family members to provide care, but also to create a system in which this does not require that the family member become an employee of a home health agency, is both welcome and long overdue.

* * *

On the other hand, decreased state control over care is linked in the American legal system with decreased state regulation over all aspects of the caretaker-care receiver relationship. If the state is no longer the employer, it does not bear liability for abuse of the beneficiary or responsibility to monitor quality of care. In the free market, the consumer should simply choose another caretaker if the care offered by one is inadequate.

If the state is no longer the employer, it also sheds its responsibility to protect the worker, in more ways than one. First, the state itself is no longer a party to the transaction and therefore cannot be held to have violated labor and employment laws with regard to the worker. More insidious is that consumer direction shifts the workers from being employees of an agency (likely an entity that employs enough workers to bring them under the coverage of many federal labor and employment laws) to being workers employed in private homes by individuals (who are much less well protected). As a result, paraprofessional workers who work in consumer directed settings will lose a number of fundamental workplace protections the state affords agency workers, thus making the workers even more vulnerable than before. For example, although agency-based long term care workers are generally (albeit poorly) protected by occupational health and safety regulation, those employed by a private individual in a home are not covered at all. Many state workers' compensation statutes do not cover workers employed in private households, while many cover domestic workers employed by an agency. Some state minimum wage and maximum hour laws cover agency-based long term care workers, while those same state laws may not cover workers employed in private homes. Workers in private homes also lose coverage under Title VII of the Civil Rights Act of 1965, the [Family and Medical Leave Act], and the [Fair Labor Standards Act]. This means that anti-discrimination laws do not protect them and they do not have a federally protected right to unpaid family or medical leave and do not have a right to unionize.

Family members who serve as consumer directed long term care workers find themselves with even fewer protections. For example, even in states where long term care workers employed by an individual are covered by workers' compensation, a family member might be excluded from coverage, even though they run the same high risks of on-the-job injury as other workers. Parents and spouses are not eligible to receive unemployment compensation if their family member lays them off. Family member workers may not be eligible for state disability programs.

QUESTIONS

1. Should individuals be permitted to use Medicaid funds to hire family members to serve as care providers?

2. As part of her discussion of consumer directed care, Kraiem argues that:

> [W]e are pretending that the interests of the consumer and the interests of the worker can be severed from each other and treated as oppositional. It means that we can imagine an arms-length transaction with a person

who is accepting the position not only for wages, but possibly in part out of love and/or obligation. It leads to seeing the two as entirely separate, rather than as inexorably linked. It elides how the relationship between caretaker and care recipient is just that: a relationship between real people with histories and futures and with shared economic interests. Economic reductionism also elides the love that some people feel for each other, the deep sorrow at the illness of a loved one, the extraordinary burden disability can place upon a family. It buries the guilt or negativity or exhaustion that are almost inevitable in caretaking relationships. It hides how the economic life of the family is inseparable from its emotional life.

Id. at 699.

Do you share her concern about the commodification of family labor? If so, is it a sufficient reason for states not to allow payment to relatives?

PROBLEM

Marguerite Martin is a 92-year-old woman with vascular dementia. Her daughter, Judy, is her agent pursuant to a validly executed durable power of attorney. If Judy hires a home health aide to work for Marguerite, is this consumer directed care? Could Judy hire herself to provide consumer directed care for her mother?

c. Protections for Home Care Workers

Home care workers are typically paid very low wages. On average, they earn just $7.25 per hour.

In addition to the disadvantage of low wages, home care workers lack many of the protections afforded to workers in other industries. For example, home care workers have historically not been protected by the Federal Labor Standards Act (FLSA) provisions setting a minimum wage or requiring overtime payments. This is because the Department of Labor had classified such workers as falling within the "companionship" exception to the FLSA, which does not provide these protections to workers who provide "companionship services for individuals who (because of age or infirmity) are unable to care for themselves." 29 U.S.C. §213(a)(15). The Department of Labor had defined companionship services broadly to include household tasks such as cooking and laundry, so long as such household work did not exceed 20 percent of the total weekly hours worked. 29 CFR §552.6.

In September 2013, however, the Obama Administration announced that it would extend additional protections to home care workers by changing the regulatory interpretation of "companionship services." Under the new regulations, which are set to take effect in January 2015, home care workers employed by agencies and other third parties would no longer fall under the companionship exemption, regardless of their duties. Home care workers employed directly by a member of the home in which they are employed, moreover, would only fall within the exemption if they provide primarily "fellowship" (i.e., engagement in social, physical, and mental activities") and "protection" (i.e., monitoring the care recipient by being present in the person's home or accompanying them outside the home). Under the new regulations, a home care worker would be able to spend up to 20 percent of his or her time providing assistance with personal care and still fall under the companionship exemption. However, the exemption will be forfeited if the worker provides domestic services primarily for the benefit of other household members or "medically related services" (i.e., those typically performed by trained personnel). While the Obama Administration's goal of improving the working conditions of home care workers is widely supported, these changes have been the subject of significant criticism from disability rights advocates who caution that they may unduly undermine the ability of persons with disabilities to pay for the care that they need to live in the community.

As might be expected given the low wages and difficult working conditions often faced by home care workers, there is significant turnover within the field. *See* Peggie R. Smith, *Aging and Caring in the Home: Regulating Paid Domesticity in the Twenty-First Century*, 92 Iowa L. Rev. 1835 (2007) (arguing that lack of workplace protections for home care workers, hard working conditions, and low pay contribute to a very unstable workforce in which approximately half of all home care workers quit their jobs annually). This can make it difficult to maintain continuity of care.

The move toward consumer directed care has been criticized for further undermining the rights of home care workers. For example, in the article excerpted earlier in this section, Daniela Kraiem expressed concern that it not only eliminates key workplace protections, but that it will decrease wages and make it harder for home care workers to use collective bargaining to further their interests. *See also* Peggie R. Smith, *Home Sweet Home? Workplace Casualties of Consumer-Directed Home Care for the Elderly*, 21 Notre Dame J.L. Ethics & Pub. Pol'y 537 (2007) (raising similar concerns).

NOTES

1. *Companionship interpretation upheld.* The Supreme Court upheld the Department of Labor's interpretation of the FLSA companionship exception in *Long Island Care at Home, Ltd., et al. v. Coke*, 551 U.S. 158 (2007).

2. *Debate over the proposed changes to the companionship rule.* For examples of articles calling for changes to the companionship rule, see Julia Lippitt, Note, *Protecting the Protectors: A Call for Fair Working Conditions for Home Health Care Workers*, 19 Elder L.J. 219 (2011) (arguing that improving conditions for home care workers requires, among other things, applying FLSA protections to home care workers); Peggie Smith, Direct Care Alliance, Inc., Direct Care Alliance Policy Brief No. 2: Protecting Home Care Workers Under the Fair Labor Standards Act (June 2009) (calling for revised regulations).

   By comparison, disability rights advocates, and especially those in the independent living movement, have raised serious concerns about the changes to the companionship rule, including concerns that the changes would significantly increase the cost of attendant services, thus undermining individuals' ability to obtain the care they need in the community and potentially resulting in otherwise avoidable institutionalization. Particular concern has also been raised about the wisdom and feasibility of the 20% limitation. For example, in a 2013 letter to the Department of Labor, the Chair of the National Council on Disability explained that:

> The disability and aging communities are concerned that the new definition of companionship services, especially the types of services that would be considered "incidental" and therefore limited to 20 percent of the caregiver's time, would reduce the availability of family and friend caregivers, increase the strain on state home care systems, and threaten the consumer's choice of provider. While we recognize DOL's view that tasks more aligned with "homemaking duties" are not intended to be the primary functions of a companion, such services are, nevertheless, central to the provision of "fellowship and protection." In fact, many of the services described by DOL as "incidental," or even entirely excluded from companionship support, are the very ones a family member or informal caregiver might need to provide. That is, family and friends who function as paid caregivers routinely perform tasks such as dressing, grooming, toileting, feeding, doing the laundry, bathing, wound care, injections, blood pressure testing, and turning and repositioning.

Letter from National Council on Disability to Department of Labor (Mar. 19, 2013), *available at* http://www.ncd.gov/publications/2013/03192013.

QUESTION

Professor Peggie Smith notes that:

> The average home-care worker is a low-income, forty-six-year-old woman. She is unmarried and a mother of children under the age of eighteen. There is a substantial likelihood that she is a woman of color, either African American or Hispanic. There is a twenty-percent chance that she is an immigrant and speaks a language other than English at home.

Peggie R. Smith, *Aging and Caring in the Home: Regulating Paid Domesticity in the Twenty-First Century*, 92 Iowa L. Rev. 1835, 1848 (2007).

How might ethnic, generational, and racial differences between home care workers and care recipients affect the quality and nature of care? Should such effects be taken into account in hiring decisions? May they be?

PROBLEMS

1. Randall, a 91-year-old widower, hired Tiffany to be his live-in caretaker. Tiffany shops for Randall, cooks his meals, does his laundry, sets out his medications, helps him bathe and dress, takes him to doctor's appointments and to social engagements, and provides in-home companionship. Must

Randall pay Tiffany minimum wage for her services? Would your answer differ if Tiffany did not live with Randall, but instead came into his home to provide care for him five days a week?

2. Mrs. Haverson, an elderly African-American woman who lives in her single-family residence, does not feel comfortable being cared for by Caucasian attendants. She has asked the home health care agency with which she contracts not to send her any Caucasian home health aides. May the agency comply with her request? If the agency refuses to do so and continues to send Mrs. Haverson Caucasian attendants, may Mrs. Haverson refuse their services on the basis of their race? In answering this question, consider looking ahead to the case of *Chaney v. Plainfield Healthcare Center*, 612 F.3d 908 (7th Cir. 2010), discussed in Section C.3.b of this chapter (see page 393).

d. Emerging Models of Service Coordination

Managing the services and providing the support that an older adult needs to remain safely and comfortably in the community can be an overwhelming task for many older adults and their families. Increasingly, families are turning to privately paid, professional *geriatric care managers* to guide them through the process of obtaining support and services. The National Association of Professional Geriatric Care Managers, a membership organization that certifies such professionals, defines a geriatric care manager as "a health and human services specialist who acts as a guide and advocate for families who are caring for older relatives or disabled adults." *See* www.caremanager.org.

Geriatric care managers come from a variety of disciplinary backgrounds, although nursing and social work backgrounds are common. The tasks performed by geriatric care managers vary depending on the manager and on the needs and desires of the older adult. Common tasks include arranging for needed housekeeping services (e.g., home repairs or shopping), arranging for home health and companionship services, managing finances, providing referrals to other professionals (including lawyers), scheduling appointments, and facilitating communication among family members. To be most effective, geriatric care managers should have a deep understanding of local resources, be skilled communicators, and be knowledgeable about aging processes.

Another emerging model for service coordination and referrals is the elder care "village." Elder care villages are local, nonprofit membership organizations designed to enhance the ability of members to successfully age in place. The first such village, Beacon Hill Village, was founded by friends living in an upscale neighborhood in Boston and began operating in 2002. By the organization's tenth anniversary, more than 60 such villages had been created.

In return for a membership fee, "villages" typically provide members with a combination of services and referrals for services. For example, Beacon Hill Village provides some services at no cost or nominal cost (e.g., an escort home when required by a doctor and grocery shopping services), as well as referrals to paid service providers (some of whom provide discounts to members) and volunteers. In addition, it offers its members opportunities for social engagement including fitness programs and talks with local notables.

e. Sources of Payment for Home Care

Consistent with the growing recognition of the importance of community-based care, today home health care can be paid for, and provided by, a variety of different sources depending on the care recipient's needs and finances. The following chart, prepared by the U.S. Department of Labor as part of proposed regulations covering home care workers, suggests the breadth of funding streams for in-home care.

Summary of Home Health Care Service Payers and Service Coverage

Payer	Description	Eligibility	[ ] Home Health Service Coverage
Public			
Medicare	Federal government program to provide health insurance coverage, including home health care, to eligible individuals who are disabled or over age 65	Individual is under the care of a doctor and receiving services under plan of care; has a certified need for intermittent skilled nursing care, physical therapy, speech-language pathology services, continued occupational therapy; and must be homebound	Intermittent skilled nursing care, physical therapy, speech-language pathology services, continued occupational therapy.
	The program pays a certified home health agency for a 60 day episode of care during which the agency provides services to the beneficiary based on the physician approved plan of care	HHA providing services is Medicare-certified; services needed are part-time or intermittent, and are required <7 days per week or <8 hours per day over 21 day period	Does not cover 24hr/day care at home; meals delivered to home; homemaker services when it is only service needed or when not related to plan of care; personal care given by home health aides when it is only care needed.
Medicaid	A joint federal-state medical assistance program administered by each state to provide coverage for low income individuals	Eligibility and benefits vary by state. In general, states must cover individuals who receive federally assisted income maintenance payments	

(Continued)

Payer	Description	Eligibility	[ ] Home Health Service Coverage
		such as Social Security, individuals who are eligible for Temporary Assistance for Needy Families and to other individuals defined as "categorically needy."—D Coverage of home health services must include part-time nursing, home care aide services, medical supplies and equipment. Optional state coverage may include audiology; physical, occupational, and speech therapies; and medical social services.	
	The program pays home health agencies and certified independent providers	Coverage is provided under: Medicaid Home Health, State Plan Personal Care Services benefit, and Home and Community-Based state plan services and waivers.	
Older Americans Act	Provides federal funding for state and local social service programs that provide services so that frail, disabled, older individuals may remain independent in their communities	Must be 60 yrs of age or older	Home care aides, personal care, chore, escort, meal delivery, and shopping services.
Veterans Administration	Home health care services provided through the VA's network of hospital-based home care units	Veterans who are at least 50% disabled due to service-related conditions	Home health care. Does not include nonmedical services provided by HCAs.
Social Services Block Grant	Federal block grants to states for state-identified service needs	Varies by state	Often includes program providing home care aide, homemaker, or chore worker services.
Community organizations	Some community organizations provide funds for home health and supportive care	Varies by program	Covers all or a portion of needed services. Vary by program.

(Continued)

Payer	Description	Eligibility	[ ] Home Health Service Coverage
Private			
Commercial Health Insurance Companies	Many policies cover home care services for acute, and less often, long-term needs	Varies by policy	Varies by insurance policy
Medigap Insurance	Covers some personal care services when a Medicare beneficiary is receiving covered home health services	Varies by policy	Focused on short-term personal care services in support of Medicare covered home health care skilled nursing services.
Self-Pay	The individual receiving the services pays "out of pocket."	Individuals who are not eligible for covered services under third-party public or private payers	Services that do not meet the eligibility criteria of other payers.

Application of the Fair Labor Standards Act to Domestic Service, 76 Fed. Reg. 81190-01 (Dec. 27, 2011).

4. Aging in Place Exercises

EXERCISE 7.1

ROLE-PLAYING

Ruth Badden is an 87-year-old former schoolteacher with an excellent sense of humor, a passion for backgammon, and an interest in politics. She also has cataracts, arthritis, mild confusion, and a recent hip replacement, and often feels unstable when walking. She lives in the village of Manlius, New York, in the house in which she raised her three children: Yvonne, Marty, and Oliver. She recently has come to the conclusion that although she wishes to live at home, she will need regular assistance if she is to do so safely. Although she keeps her car and has a current license, she knows her driving is "none too good" and she believes that she "shouldn't be on the road at my age and with my eyes." She also recognizes that "my hip's bad" and is reasonably worried about the possibility of falling. Even simple tasks like laundry and cooking dinner are becoming increasingly difficult. Ruth lives on a fixed income of $1,600 per month. Aside from her house and car, Ruth has approximately $50,000 in savings.

Ruth feels fortunate to have three children whom she loves dearly.

Yvonne, her youngest, is a 50-year-old branch manager at a bank in State College, Pennsylvania. Yvonne was married at a young age and has since divorced. Yvonne's only child is now a freshman at college, and Yvonne is enjoying the freedom of being an empty-nester. She likes her job, her town, and her active social life. She also enjoys her weekly conversations with her mother. Although they do not see each other often, Yvonne cares very much about Ruth and thinks of Ruth as "my best friend."

Marty, Ruth's middle child, lives in the city of Syracuse, which is adjacent to Manlius, with her husband and their three children (ages 17, 15, and 12). Marty works part-time as a paralegal in Syracuse; her husband works full-time as an accountant. When not working, Marty can be found shuttling her three children to sports and after-school activities nearly every day. Marty's youngest child was recently diagnosed with attention deficit disorder, and Marty is finding herself spending extra time trying to understand the diagnosis and getting her child the extra help he needs. Marty very much cares about her mother but finds it difficult to make the time to see her. Accordingly, most of Marty's contact with her mother is by cell phone. Whenever Marty has to wait for her children, or has a long drive to pick one of them up, she'll call Ruth to chat. Last month, at Ruth's request, she took Ruth for her annual check-up. The doctor was running late and, as a result, Marty was 45 minutes late picking up her middle son from lacrosse practice.

Oliver, Ruth's oldest, is 62 years old and also lives in Manlius. While Ruth loves Oliver, his life has been a bit of a disappointment to her. After returning from a period of active military services overseas, Oliver began to experience post-traumatic stress disorder. In part as a result, Oliver has bounced around from job to job. He has been divorced twice and, while he is currently in AA, he has had significant problems with alcoholism over the past 30 years. Last month, he took a 30-hour-a-week job as a line cook at a local restaurant. He is hopeful about the job and thinks it may be one he will be able to stick out. By contrast, Oliver finds dealing with his mother stressful as she is frequently trying to "improve" and "educate" him. He knows that she is disappointed by him and is bitter that she cannot seem to appreciate the challenges he faces. However, once a month, Ruth invites Oliver over for dinner, and he never misses it. She always makes his favorite meal: roast beef with potatoes and Yorkshire pudding. During these visits, Oliver feels he has little to say to his mother and often can't wait to leave. Still, he dutifully goes because he knows it matters to her and the food is always tasty.

Ruth also feels fortunate to have a very helpful neighbor, Ned. Ned is a schoolteacher who works in the neighboring town of Jamesville. Ned shares custody of his two children with his ex-wife. One of his favorite things about his job as a schoolteacher is the flexibility it allows him in the summer. He tries to plan at least two or three week-long camping trips with his children each year because he finds this to be important bonding time. Ned's own parents live in Florida, and he treats Ruth somewhat like a surrogate mother. When he sees her struggling to take out the garbage, he will do it for her. In the winter, he shovels her walk. In the fall, he rakes her leaves. He knows she must be lonely, so at least once a week he'll stop by her house to say hello, often bringing a treat or newspaper article with him.

Imagine that you are Yvonne, Marty, Oliver, or Ned. Who, if anyone, do you think should be helping Ruth meet her needs? What do you think the best arrangement for Ruth would be? What kind of care should each be providing, if any? Under what conditions should that care be provided?

Now imagine that you are Ruth. What help or care would you want others to provide for you or help you to obtain? Who would you want to provide that care? Why? How might you go about obtaining the help or care that you desire?

Now imagine that you are Ruth's attorney. What advice might you give her? What questions might you wish to ask Ruth or her family in order to provide helpful counsel?

EXERCISE 7.2

COUNSELING & RESEARCH

Charlie, a man in his 80s, has been diagnosed with Alzheimer's disease. He has been living alone with significant assistance from his son, Sheldon, and Sheldon's wife, Loraine, as well as several women from his church. This living arrangement, however, appears no longer to be safe for Charlie. He is unable to find his way home if he goes out (although he rarely attempts to leave because he has pain in his feet and therefore does not enjoy walking). He is unable to perform housekeeping functions safely. He is able to feed himself but unable to prepare his own food or remember to eat regular meals. Increasingly, he has difficultly with personal grooming and, if left on his own, generally fails to maintain his personal hygiene.

Communication is also becoming difficult for Charlie. His speech is highly anomic (he tends to substitute one word for another), his sentences are increasingly jumbled, and he tends to use vague terms such as "stuff" and "things." Fortunately, Charlie still remembers his name and vital information, knows he is a die-hard Yankees fan, and recognizes all of his immediate family members although he tends to confuse their names. In addition to Alzheimer's disease, Charlie has hypertension and a history of cardiac problems.

Charlie and his sons, Sheldon and Hugh, have agreed that it no longer makes sense for Charlie to live alone. Instead, they have jointly decided that he will move in with Sheldon and Loraine, who live in a two-story suburban home. Their two children are grown, and they have a spare bedroom and bathroom that they plan to fix up for Charlie.

Both Sheldon and Loraine are middle class professionals who currently hold full-time jobs. They are unsure who, if anyone, will or should provide care to Charlie while they are at work. Sheldon, 62, is considering taking early retirement but is concerned that doing so may not be financially prudent. Further complicating matters is the fact that although Sheldon and Loraine are determined to provide the care Charlie needs, neither has significant prior experience dealing with someone with dementia. And while they appreciate the emotional support that Sheldon's brother (and Charlie's only other child) provides them, they recognize that Hugh has his own serious health issues and is simply unable to provide any direct care for Charlie at this time.

Sheldon and Loraine would like your advice on the following issues:

a. What should they do to prepare for Charlie's move? What challenges should they anticipate and how can they prepare for those challenges?

b. How can they pay for the care Charlie needs? Charlie's income is limited to $1,450 a month. He has approximately $70,000 in savings.

c. What kinds of home care or assistance might be available to help them? With your professor's guidance, research what resources might be available in your area to help.

d. Finally, Sheldon and Lorraine wonder whether they are misguided in trying to make aging in place possible for Charlie. Should they be thinking about an institutional placement instead? What would you advise?

C. NURSING HOMES

The term "nursing home" is commonly used to refer to both *skilled nursing facilities* (SNFs) and *nursing facilities* (NFs). SNFs focus on rehabilitative care, whereas NFs focus on chronic care. Medicare therefore provides some coverage for SNF services, but no coverage for NF services. Other than this coverage difference, the two types of facilities are generally indistinguishable to consumers. Most nursing homes are certified as both SNFs and NFs. Accordingly, in discussing the regulatory framework governing nursing home care, this text simply uses the term nursing home to refer to both types of facilities.

While only approximately 1.6 million Americans live in a nursing home at any given time, a significant percentage of Americans will spend time in a nursing home over the course of their lifetime. A person who is 65 years of age has an approximately 40 percent chance of spending time in a nursing home at some point in their life, and approximately one in four Americans dies in a nursing home. Most of those who die in a nursing home do so after a relatively short stay. A 2010 study found that 65 percent of those who died in a nursing home had lived there for less than a year, and over half had died within six months of admission. *See* Anne Kelly et al., *Length of Stay for Older Adults Residing in Nursing Homes at the End of Life*, 58 J. AM. GERIATRICS SOC'Y 1701, 1701 (2010) (discussing the length of nursing home stays).

The likelihood of residing in a nursing home increases dramatically as people age. Only approximately 3 percent of people in their upper 70s are nursing home residents, compared to approximately 20 percent of those in their lower 90s, more than 30 percent in their upper 90s, and nearly 40 percent of centenarians. *See* WAN HE & MARK N. MUENCHRATH, U.S. CENSUS BUREAU, ACS-17, 90+ IN THE UNITED STATES: 2006-2008 (2011).

1. Nursing Home Admission: Reasons and Process

Nursing home placement typically occurs because a person has serious limitations in the ability to perform the *activities of daily living* (ADLs). ADLs are basic personal care tasks and include toileting, transferring, ambulating, bathing, dressing, and feeding. Nursing home residents are also typically limited in their ability to perform *instrumental activities of daily living* (IADLs). IADLs are basic domestic tasks including meal preparation, money management, shopping, housework, and using a telephone. IADL limitations alone, however, are not sufficient to warrant admission to a nursing home.

Although nursing home placement is often thought of as permanent, it is frequently temporary. A person may be in a nursing home while recovering from a serious illness or receiving rehabilitative care after experiencing an injury, such as breaking or fracturing a bone as a result of a fall. Similarly, some nursing homes provide *respite services*; individuals who are being cared for at home may temporarily reside in a nursing home in order to provide their caregivers with time off from caregiving so that the caregivers may go on vacation, rest, or attend to other needs.

The likelihood that any particular individual will become a nursing home resident varies not only on his or her health and age, but also on other demographic factors. Not all segments of the population have the same access to the resources and community-based supports that might help them avoid institutionalization. In general, women are more likely than men to become nursing home residents, a phenomenon which the evidence suggests cannot be explained merely by their longer life expectancies. Similarly, lower income and lower educational levels increase the likelihood of nursing home placement.

The decision to enter a nursing home is a difficult one, and older adults frequently fear that they will be "put" or "placed" in a nursing home by their families. Legally, however, nobody can be placed in a nursing home without his or her consent unless another person or entity has the specific legal authority to do so. There are two types of surrogate decision-makers who may have that authority. The first is an agent who the would-be resident has appointed to make such decisions for him or her. Notably, there is some disagreement as to whether such decisions should be considered "health care" decisions and thus the domain of persons appointed pursuant to a health care proxy, or "housing" decisions and thus the domain of persons appointed pursuant to a durable power of attorney for finances (see Note 3 on page 120 of Chapter 4). An appointed agent can only, however, consent to the admission of the principal in limited circumstances. This is because individuals with the cognitive capacity to do so may both (1) revoke the document appointing the agent, and (2) make decisions on their own behalf, including the decision not to move to a nursing home, even if their agent disagrees with those decisions. Thus, as a general matter, an agent can only force a nursing home admission where the person being admitted lacks capacity to object and doing so is otherwise consistent with the agent's fiduciary duties. The only type of surrogate who has authority to institutionalize an individual over his or her objection is a court-appointed guardian whose authority includes the right to institutionalize. Thus, unless the guardianship is plenary, the guardian's powers may not include the power to institutionalize a ward over the ward's objection.

Many older adults who move to nursing homes, however, lack either a legal surrogate with the authority to admit them to a home or the cognitive capacity to consent to becoming a nursing home resident. Nevertheless, facilities routinely admit such individuals and treat their admissions as voluntary. Although legally problematic and potentially concerning from a civil rights perspective, this practice is rarely questioned. Rather, when the older adult has some level of diminished cognitive capacity, families are frequently treated as having decision-making authority. As Professor Marshall Kapp has explained,

> In reality . . . it is routinely assumed by all key participants virtually without discussion or reflection that families will play a, if not the, dominant role in making decisions about the decisionally incapacitated person's residence . . . , whether or not any particular family member has formal legal authority to act as decision maker. Even in the absence of a valid DPOA or guardianship order, available family members are routinely turned to despite their lack of official standing, and their choices for the client are implemented. Indeed, especially when family members are functioning in essential caregiving roles, it is difficult to imagine them not being at the center of the decision making process.

Marshall B. Kapp, *Where Will I Live? How do Housing Choices Get Made for Older Persons*, 15 NAELA Q. 2, 4 (2002).

Moreover, many older adults feel pressured or forced to enter nursing homes when their families believe that placement is appropriate, even though their families do not have the legal authority to force such a move. Where family members who have been providing social support or care insist that an older adult move to a nursing facility, that older adult may feel that he or she does not have a meaningful choice.

2. The Statutory and Regulatory Framework Governing Nursing Homes

The primary source of regulation for nursing homes is the federal Nursing Home Reform Act of 1987 and its implementing regulations. The Act imposes a wide range of requirements on all nursing homes that are certified to receive either Medicaid or Medicare funding. The Act, passed in response to serious concerns about life inside America's nursing homes, sought to improve both residents' quality of care and quality of life. Among other provisions, it created a comprehensive resident assessment system, strengthened the process by which regulators engage in investigate surveys of homes, and set forth extensive resident rights. Because the Nursing Home Reform Act was part of the Omnibus Reconciliation Act of 1987, nursing home residents' federal rights are sometimes referred to as "OBRA 1987" rights.

While the Nursing Home Reform Act and its implementing regulations form the backbone of the regulatory system for protecting the rights and interests of America's nursing home residents, the Act is only one part of the regulatory structure for nursing homes. Indeed, states are responsible for inspecting nursing homes, licensing nursing home administrators and staff, and licensing the health care providers who work in nursing homes. In addition, nursing homes are subject to state laws regulating them specifically as well as to more general laws regulating aspects of their operations, for example, public health and physical plant requirements.

Under the Nursing Home Reform Act, nursing homes participating in Medicare and Medicaid are subject to an annual government inspection called a *survey*. Surveys are unannounced visits by professional inspectors (commonly employees of a state health department) who determine whether the nursing home is complying with federal requirements. If a compliance failure is found, it is called a *deficiency*, and the surveyors then assess the scope and severity of that deficiency.

The consequences of a deficiency finding vary depending on the severity and scope of the problem, as well as whether it is a repeat problem. Possible sanctions range from requiring the facility to provide additional staff training, to monetary fines, to a denial of Medicare and Medicaid payments for new admissions, to termination of the home from participation in Medicare and Medicaid. The latter two sanctions can have severe consequences for the financial viability of the nursing home and are rarely used. Indeed, regulators tend to be wary of penalties that would result in the potential closure of a nursing home in part because of the consequences for its existing residents. For example, there is concern that residents might suffer *transfer trauma*, stress associated with a change in living environment, as a result of a closure. In some areas where the demand for nursing home beds is high relative to supply, there may also be concerns that closing facilities will exacerbate the shortage of beds.

The Government Accountability Office (GAO) has found significant problems with the survey process, including significant inconsistencies among survey practices both within and between states, which result in some states reporting far more deficiencies then others under the same or similar circumstances. The GAO has also found underreporting of serious deficiencies, including those that pose an immediate threat to residents' health and safety. According to the GAO:

> CMS's nursing home survey data show a significant decrease in the proportion of nursing homes with serious quality problems, from about 29 percent in 1999 to about 16 percent by January 2005, but this trend masks two important and continuing issues: inconsistency among state surveyors in conducting surveys and understatement by state surveyors of serious deficiencies. Inconsistency in states' surveys is demonstrated by CMS data that reveal continued wide interstate variability in the proportion of homes found to have serious deficiencies. For example, in the most recent time period, one state found such deficiencies in about 6 percent of homes, whereas another state found them in about 54 percent of homes. . . . [C]onfusion about the definition of actual harm contributed to inconsistency and understatement in state surveys. In addition, state surveyors continue to understate serious deficiencies, as shown by the larger number of serious deficiencies identified in federal comparative surveys than in state surveys of the same homes. Although federal comparative surveys since October 1998 show an overall decline in the proportion that identify serious deficiencies not identified by state surveys, data for the two most recent periods show an increase in such discrepancies, from 22 percent to 28 percent of comparative surveys. In the five large states we reviewed, federal surveyors concluded that the state surveyors had missed serious deficiencies in from 8 percent to 33 percent of comparative surveys—that is, these deficiencies existed and should have been identified at the time of the state survey.

U.S. Gov't Accountability Office, GAO-06-117, Nursing Homes: Despite Increased Oversight, Challenges Remain in Ensuring High-Quality Care and Resident Safety (2005).

In addition, the GAO report found that surveys were excessively predictable in their timing. Predictability is problematic because it enables nursing homes to plan for their inspection such that their performance during the inspection is not representative of their overall performance. For example, a nursing home may increase its staffing levels when it anticipates that a survey is imminent.

The federal government makes the result of nursing home surveys publically available through its online tool Nursing Home Compare (www. medicare.gov/nursinghomecompare). Nursing Home Compare can be a useful tool for those choosing among nursing homes. In addition to providing information about deficiencies, Nursing Home Compare shows a nursing home's staffing ratios as well as the frequency of certain health conditions among residents. It may be difficult, however, for the public to know how much importance to place on various indicators. For example, the fact that many residents in a facility have a particular, negative health condition may reflect poor quality of care, or it may reflect that the home accepts a population that is particularly susceptible to that problem, or some combination of the two.

NOTE

The legal impact of transfer trauma. In *O'Bannon v. Town Court Nursing Home*, 447 U.S. 773 (1980), the Supreme Court ruled that nursing home residents did not have a right to a hearing before the nursing home in which they resided lost its Medicaid certification. In doing so, the majority assumed that the residents might face "transfer trauma," but found such injury would be too indirect to constitute a deprivation of any interest in life, liberty, or property. By comparison, transfer trauma arguments have been used by nursing homes to successfully obtain preliminary injunctions enjoining the government from terminating their participation in Medicare or Medicaid pending further proceedings. *See, e.g., Mediplex of Mass., Inc., v. Shalala*, 39 F. Supp. 2d 88 (D. Mass. 1999) (in granting a preliminary injunction enjoining termination of a nursing facility's status as medical services provider under Medicare and Medicaid, considering the potential harm to the facility's residents if reimbursements stopped and facility was shut down); *International Long Term Care, Inc. v. Shalala*, 947 F. Supp. 15 (D.D.C. 1996) (holding that transfer of residents would be a sufficient, irreparable harm to support a preliminary injunction prohibiting termination of nursing home's Medicare payments). *See also* Elias S. Cohen, *Legal Issues in Transfer Trauma and Their Impact*, 21 GERONTOLOGIST 520 (1981).

EXERCISE 7.3

Go to the Nursing Home Compare website and look up the nursing homes in your county. What information do you find? If you were looking for a nursing home for yourself or your loved one, would you use this site? What resources might you use instead or in addition?

3. Nursing Home Residents' Rights

Under the Nursing Home Reform Act, nursing home residents have significant federal rights. These include both positive rights (e.g., the right to quality care) and negative rights (e.g., the right to be free from certain types of restraints and limitations).

As a general matter, nursing homes are required to provide residents with care and services that allow them to "attain or maintain the highest practicable physical, mental, and psychosocial well-being." 42 CFR §483.25.

Nursing homes are also limited in their ability to control residents' choices and opportunities. As described in the excerpted regulations that follow, each resident "has a right to a dignified existence, self-determination, and communication with and access to persons and services inside and outside the facility." 42 CFR §483.10.

a. Statutory and Regulatory Framework

What follows are excerpts from the federal regulations governing nursing home quality of care. These regulations guarantee certain rights to nursing home residents residing in a facility that receives Medicare or Medicaid funding. Some focus on nursing home residents' rights and liberties, whereas others focus on nursing homes' duties regarding the quality of care they provide.

REQUIREMENTS FOR LONG-TERM CARE FACILITIES
42 CFR §483, SUBPART B (2013)

42 CFR §483.10 Resident Rights

The resident has a right to a dignified existence, self-determination, and communication with and access to persons and services inside and outside the facility. A facility must protect and promote the rights of each resident, including each of the following rights:

(a) Exercise of rights.

(1) The resident has the right to exercise his or her rights as a resident of the facility and as a citizen or resident of the United States.

(2) The resident has the right to be free of interference, coercion, discrimination, and reprisal from the facility in exercising his or her rights.

(3) In the case of a resident adjudged incompetent under the laws of a State by a court of competent jurisdiction, the rights of the resident are exercised by the person appointed under State law to act on the resident's behalf.

(4) In the case of a resident who has not been adjudged incompetent by the State court, any legal-surrogate designated in accordance with State law may exercise the resident's rights to the extent provided by State law.

(b) Notice of rights and services.

* * *

(2) The resident or his or her legal representative has the right . . . to access all records pertaining to himself or herself including current clinical records within 24 hours (excluding weekends and holidays); and . . . to purchase at a cost not to exceed the community standard photocopies of the records or any portions of them upon request and 2 working days advance notice to the facility.

(3) The resident has the right to be fully informed in language that he or she can understand of his or her total health status, including but not limited to, his or her medical condition;

(4) The resident has the right to refuse treatment, to refuse to participate in experimental research . . . ; and

* * *

(11) Notification of changes.

(i) A facility must immediately inform the resident; consult with the resident's physician; and if known, notify the resident's legal representative or an interested family member when there is—

(A) An accident involving the resident which results in injury and has the potential for requiring physician intervention;

(B) A significant change in the resident's physical, mental, or psychosocial status

(C) A need to alter treatment significantly . . . ; or

(D) A decision to transfer or discharge the resident from the facility . . . .

(ii) The facility must also promptly notify the resident and, if known, the resident's legal representative or interested family member when there is—

(A) A change in room or roommate assignment. . . .

* * *

(c) Protection of Resident Funds.

(1) The resident has the right to manage his or her financial affairs, and the facility may not require residents to deposit their personal funds with the facility.

* * *

(8) Limitation on charges to personal funds. The facility may not impose a charge against the personal funds of a resident for any item or service for which payment is made under Medicaid or Medicare (except for applicable deductible and coinsurance amounts). . . .

(i) Services included in Medicare or Medicaid payment. During the course of a covered Medicare or Medicaid stay, facilities may not charge a resident for the following categories of items and services:

(A) Nursing services as required at §483.30 of this subpart.

(B) Dietary services as required at §483.35 of this subpart.

(C) An activities program as required at §483.15(f) of this subpart.

(D) Room/bed maintenance services.

(E) Routine personal hygiene items and services as required to meet the needs of residents. . . .

(F) Medically-related social services as required at §483.15(g) of this subpart.

(ii) Items and services that may be charged to residents' funds. Listed below are general categories and examples of items and services that the facility may charge to residents' funds if they are requested by a resident, if the facility informs the resident that there will be a charge, and if payment is not made by Medicare or Medicaid:

(A) Telephone.

(B) Television/radio for personal use.

(C) Personal comfort items, including smoking materials, notions and novelties, and confections.

(D) Cosmetic and grooming items and services in excess of those for which payment is made under Medicaid or Medicare.

(E) Personal clothing.

(F) Personal reading matter.

(G) Gifts purchased on behalf of a resident.

(H) Flowers and plants.

(I) Social events and entertainment offered outside the scope of the activities program. . . .

(J) Noncovered special care services such as privately hired nurses or aides.

(K) Private room, except when therapeutically required (for example, isolation for infection control).

(L) Specially prepared or alternative food requested instead of the food generally prepared by the facility, as required by §483.35 of this subpart.

(iii) Requests for items and services.

(A) The facility must not charge a resident (or his or her representative) for any item or service not requested by the resident.

(B) The facility must not require a resident (or his or her representative) to request any item or service as a condition of admission or continued stay.

(C) The facility must inform the resident (or his or her representative) requesting an item or service for which a charge will be made that there will be a charge for the item or service and what the charge will be.

(d) Free choice. The resident has the right to—

(1) Choose a personal attending physician;

(2) Be fully informed in advance about care and treatment and of any changes in that care or treatment that may affect the resident's well-being; and

(3) Unless adjudged incompetent or otherwise found to be incapacitated under the laws of the State, participate in planning care and treatment or changes in care and treatment.

(e) Privacy and confidentiality. The resident has the right to personal privacy and confidentiality of his or her personal and clinical records.

(1) Personal privacy includes accommodations, medical treatment, written and telephone communications, personal care, visits, and meetings of family and resident groups, but this does not require the facility to provide a private room for each resident. . . .

(f) Grievances. A resident has the right to—

(1) Voice grievances without discrimination or reprisal. Such grievances include those with respect to treatment which has been furnished as well as that which has not been furnished; and

(2) Prompt efforts by the facility to resolve grievances the resident may have, including those with respect to the behavior of other residents.

(g) Examination of survey results. A resident has the right to—

(1) Examine the results of the most recent survey of the facility conducted by Federal or State surveyors and any plan of correction in effect with respect to the facility . . . ; and

(2) Receive information from agencies acting as client advocates, and be afforded the opportunity to contact these agencies.

* * *

(i) Mail. The resident has the right to privacy in written communications, including the right to—

(1) Send and promptly receive mail that is unopened; and

(2) Have access to stationery, postage, and writing implements at the resident's own expense.

(j) Access and visitation rights.

(1) The resident has the right and the facility must provide immediate access to any resident by [various government officials, the resident's physician, the State long-term care ombudsmen, relatives unless the resident denies or withdraws consent, others visiting with the consent of the resident].

(2) The facility must provide reasonable access to any resident by any entity or individual that provides health, social, legal, or other services to the resident, subject to the resident's right to deny or withdraw consent at any time.

(3) The facility must allow representatives of the State Ombudsman . . . to examine a resident's clinical records with the permission of the resident or the resident's legal representative, and consistent with State law.

(k) Telephone. The resident has the right to have reasonable access to the use of a telephone where calls can be made without being overheard.

(l) Personal property. The resident has the right to retain and use personal possessions, including some furnishings, and appropriate clothing, as space permits, unless to do so would infringe upon the rights or health and safety of other residents.

(m) Married couples. The resident has the right to share a room with his or her spouse when married residents live in the same facility and both spouses consent to the arrangement.

(n) Self-Administration of Drugs. An individual resident may self-administer drugs if the interdisciplinary team, as defined by §483.20(d)(2)(ii), has determined that this practice is safe. . . .

42 CFR §483.12 Admission, Transfer & Discharge Rights

(a) Transfer and discharge—

(1) Definition: Transfer and discharge includes movement of a resident to a bed outside of the certified facility whether that bed is in

the same physical plant or not. Transfer and discharge does not refer to movement of a resident to a bed within the same certified facility.

(2) Transfer and discharge requirements. The facility must permit each resident to remain in the facility, and not transfer or discharge the resident from the facility unless—

(i) The transfer or discharge is necessary for the resident's welfare and the resident's needs cannot be met in the facility;

(ii) The transfer or discharge is appropriate because the resident's health has improved sufficiently so the resident no longer needs the services provided by the facility;

(iii) The safety of individuals in the facility is endangered;

(iv) The health of individuals in the facility would otherwise be endangered;

(v) The resident has failed, after reasonable and appropriate notice, to pay for (or to have paid under Medicare or Medicaid) a stay at the facility. For a resident who becomes eligible for Medicaid after admission to a facility, the facility may charge a resident only allowable charges under Medicaid; or

(vi) The facility ceases to operate.

* * *

(b) Notice of bed-hold policy and readmission—
[Subsection 1 and 2 require nursing homes to provide notice of their bed hold policies before a transfer to a hospital or therapeutic leave.—ED.]

(3) Permitting resident to return to facility. A nursing facility must establish and follow a written policy under which a resident, whose hospitalization or therapeutic leave exceeds the bed-hold period under the State plan is readmitted to the facility immediately upon the first availability of a bed in a semi-private room if the resident—

(i) Requires the services provided by the facility; and

(ii) Is eligible for Medicaid nursing facility services.

* * *

(c) Equal access to quality care.

(1) A facility must establish and maintain identical policies and practices regarding transfer, discharge, and the provision of services under the State plan for all individuals regardless of source of payment;

* * *

(d) Admissions policy.

(1) The facility must—

(i) Not require residents or potential residents to waive their rights to Medicare or Medicaid; and

(ii) Not require oral or written assurance that residents or potential residents are not eligible for, or will not apply for, Medicare or Medicaid benefits.

(2) The facility must not require a third party guarantee of payment to the facility as a condition of admission or expedited admission, or continued stay in the facility. ...

(3) In the case of a person eligible for Medicaid, a nursing facility must not charge, solicit, accept, or receive, in addition to any amount otherwise required to be paid under the State plan, any gift, money, donation, or other consideration as a precondition of admission, expedited admission or continued stay in the facility. ...

42 CFR §483.13 Resident Behavior and Facility Practices

(a) Restraints. The resident has the right to be free from any physical or chemical restraints imposed for purposes of discipline or convenience, and not required to treat the resident's medical symptoms.

(b) Abuse. The resident has the right to be free from verbal, sexual, physical, and mental abuse, corporal punishment, and involuntary seclusion.

42 CFR §483.15 Quality of Life

A facility must care for its residents in a manner and in an environment that promotes maintenance or enhancement of each resident's quality of life.

(a) Dignity. The facility must promote care for residents in a manner and in an environment that maintains or enhances each resident's dignity and respect in full recognition of his or her individuality.

(b) Self-determination and participation. The resident has the right to—

(1) Choose activities, schedules, and health care consistent with his or her interests, assessments, and plans of care;

(2) Interact with members of the community both inside and outside the facility; and

(3) Make choices about aspects of his or her life in the facility that are significant to the resident.

(c) Participation in resident and family groups.

(1) A resident has the right to organize and participate in resident groups in the facility;

(2) A resident's family has the right to meet in the facility with the families of other residents in the facility;

(3) The facility must provide a resident or family group, if one exists, with private space;

(4) Staff or visitors may attend meetings at the group's invitation;

(5) The facility must provide a designated staff person responsible for providing assistance and responding to written requests that result from group meetings;

(6) When a resident or family group exists, the facility must listen to the views and act upon the grievances and recommendations of residents and families concerning proposed policy and operational decisions affecting resident care and life in the facility.

(d) Participation in other activities. A resident has the right to participate in social, religious, and community activities that do not interfere with the rights of other residents in the facility.

(e) Accommodation of needs. A resident has the right to—

(1) Reside and receive services in the facility with reasonable accommodation of individual needs and preferences, except when the health or safety of the individual or other residents would be endangered; and

(2) Receive notice before the resident's room or roommate in the facility is changed.

(f) Activities.

(1) The facility must provide for an ongoing program of activities designed to meet, in accordance with the comprehensive assessment, the interests and the physical, mental, and psychosocial well-being of each resident.

(2) The activities program must be directed by a qualified professional. . . .

(g) Social Services.

(1) The facility must provide medically-related social services to attain or maintain the highest practicable physical, mental, and psychosocial well-being of each resident.

(2) A facility with more than 120 beds must employ a qualified social worker on a full-time basis.

* * *

(h) Environment. The facility must provide—

(1) A safe, clean, comfortable, and homelike environment, allowing the resident to use his or her personal belongings to the extent possible; . . .

42 CFR §483.25 Quality of Care

Each resident must receive and the facility must provide the necessary care and services to attain or maintain the highest practicable physical, mental, and psychosocial well-being, in accordance with the comprehensive assessment and plan of care.

(a) Activities of daily living. Based on the comprehensive assessment of a resident, the facility must ensure that—

(1) A resident's abilities in activities of daily living do not diminish unless circumstances of the individual's clinical condition demonstrate that diminution was unavoidable. This includes the resident's ability to—

(i) Bathe, dress, and groom;

(ii) Transfer and ambulate;

(iii) Toilet;

(iv) Eat; and

(v) Use speech, language, or other functional communication systems.

(2) A resident is given the appropriate treatment and services to maintain or improve his or her abilities specified in paragraph (a)(1) of this section. . . .

(b) Vision and hearing. To ensure that residents receive proper treatment and assistive devices to maintain vision and hearing abilities, the facility must, if necessary, assist the resident—

(1) In making appointments, and

(2) By arranging for transportation to and from the office of a practitioner specializing in the treatment of vision or hearing impairment or the office of a professional specializing in the provision of vision or hearing assistive devices.

(c) Pressure sores. Based on the comprehensive assessment of a resident, the facility must ensure that—

(1) A resident who enters the facility without pressure sores does not develop pressure sores unless the individual's clinical condition demonstrates that they were unavoidable; and

(2) A resident having pressure sores receives necessary treatment and services to promote healing, prevent infection and prevent new sores from developing.

* * *

(e) Range of motion. Based on the comprehensive assessment of a resident, the facility must ensure that—

(1) A resident who enters the facility without a limited range of motion does not experience reduction in range of motion unless the resident's clinical condition demonstrates that a reduction in range of motion is unavoidable; and

(2) A resident with a limited range of motion receives appropriate treatment and services to increase range of motion and/or to prevent further decrease in range of motion.

(f) Mental and Psychosocial functioning. Based on the comprehensive assessment of a resident, the facility must ensure that—

(1) A resident who displays mental or psychosocial adjustment difficulty, receives appropriate treatment and services to correct the assessed problem, and

(2) A resident whose assessment did not reveal a mental or psychosocial adjustment difficulty does not display a pattern of decreased social

interaction and/or increased withdrawn, angry, or depressive behaviors, unless the resident's clinical condition demonstrates that such a pattern was unavoidable.

* * *

(h) Accidents. The facility must ensure that—

(1) The resident environment remains as free of accident hazards as is possible; and

(2) Each resident receives adequate supervision and assistance devices to prevent accidents.

(i) Nutrition. Based on a resident's comprehensive assessment, the facility must ensure that a resident—

(1) Maintains acceptable parameters of nutritional status, such as body weight and protein levels, unless the resident's clinical condition demonstrates that this is not possible; and

(2) Receives a therapeutic diet when there is a nutritional problem.

(j) Hydration. The facility must provide each resident with sufficient fluid intake to maintain proper hydration and health.

* * *

(l) Unnecessary drugs—

(1) General. Each resident's drug regimen must be free from unnecessary drugs. . . .

(2) Antipsychotic Drugs. Based on a comprehensive assessment of a resident, the facility must ensure that—

(i) Residents who have not used antipsychotic drugs are not given these drugs unless antipsychotic drug therapy is necessary to treat a specific condition as diagnosed and documented in the clinical record; and

(ii) Residents who use antipsychotic drugs receive gradual dose reductions, and behavioral interventions, unless clinically contraindicated, in an effort to discontinue these drugs.

NOTES

1. *State plans.* You will note that the regulations pertaining to bed hold policies make reference to a State Plan. Each state is required to create a State Plan, a comprehensive written statement describing the scope and nature of the Medicaid program, which outlines current Medicaid eligibility standards, policies, and reimbursement methodologies. *See generally* 42 U.S.C. §1396a (2013).

2. *Criticisms of the Nursing Home Reform Act.* The nursing home industry often cites the Nursing Home Reform Act as an example of over-regulation, and criticizes the Act for stifling innovation and creating a very institutional model of care. Public interest attorney and nursing home law expert Eric Carlson has responded as follows:

> Although . . . many nursing facility operators . . . blame the Nursing
> Home Reform Law for nursing facilities' institutional ambiance . . . [t]he
> blame should be placed squarely on nursing facility operators themselves,
> for it has been demonstrated numerous times in recent years that a nurs-
> ing facility can meet the quality of care standards of the Nursing Home
> Reform Law and allow residents to engage in meaningful activities. In
> nursing facilities ascribing to the "Eden Alternative," for example, resi-
> dents maintain gardens, and the facility's pets walk through the hallways.

Eric Carlson, *In the Sheep's Clothing of Resident Rights: Behind the Rhetoric
of "Negotiated Risk" in Assisted Living*, 3 NAELA Q. 4 (2003).

3. *Rights of LGBT nursing home residents.* LGBT nursing home residents may
face additional barriers to exercising their rights. A 2011 survey found that
LGBT nursing home residents face significant discrimination in nursing
homes—including harassment directed at them by both staff and other
residents—and that many hide their LGBT identity out of fear. *See* National
Senior Citizens Law Center in collaboration with Lambda Legal, National
Center for Lesbian Rights, National Center for Transgender Equality,
National Gay and Lesbian Task Force and Services & Advocacy for GLBT
Elders (SAGE), *LGBT Older Adults in Long-Term Care Facilities: Stories from
the Field* (2011), *available at* www.lgbtagingcenter.org.

PROBLEMS

1. Mrs. Fredericks is very dissatisfied with her nursing home. One of her chief
complaints is that there is no telephone in her room and that therefore she
must use the phone at the nurse's station whenever she needs or wants to
call her family. This bothers her in part because it means that the nursing
home's staff can hear almost everything she says to her family. In the past
week, she says she has noticed that nursing staff on the morning shift are
extremely slow to come when she rings her call bell (something she needs to
do in order to get the help she needs to toilet). She suspects this is because a
staff member overheard her complaining to her daughter on the telephone
about staff being rude to her.

   What federal rights, if any, are being denied Mrs. Fredericks in this
situation? Must the nursing home provide an alternative phone?

2. Mr. Walters, who has dementia and congestive heart failure, was admitted
to Harbor House Nursing Home after he shattered his hip in a fall at his
home. The fall left Mr. Walters weak and unable to safely walk without
supervision. Since Mr. Walters was admitted to Harbor House Nursing
Home, his health has deteriorated dramatically. He has become incontinent
of bowel and bladder, has grown increasingly withdrawn, and has become
almost entirely bed-bound.

   What federal rights are implicated in this situation?

3. In which of the following situations has the resident been unlawfully restrained?

   a. Two staff members fail to show up for duty, and, as a result, Shady Acres Nursing Home, where Mr. Klein lives, is understaffed. Mr. Klein has a history of wandering about the facility to visit other residents who may or may not want his visits. Because of insufficient staff to control or monitor Mr. Klein, staff place him for the afternoon in a chair with an attached tray that prevents him from getting up without assistance.

   b. Mrs. Smith, a nursing home resident, fell twice trying to get up in the middle of the night to use the bathroom. Nursing home staff therefore put bedrails on her bed to prevent her from doing so.

   c. Miss Prill, a nursing home resident, has contractures affecting her wrists, arms, and lower legs. Contractures are a form of joint dysfunction caused by shortened or distorted muscular or connective tissue, and they cause Miss Prill's body to appear contorted. Consistent with her doctor's orders, nursing home staff put her in body braces to prevent further stiffening.

   d. Mr. Johnson, a nursing home resident, complains loudly about the nursing home. He thinks staff is rude, the food tastes bad, and the other residents are just plain depressing. These complaints are annoying to staff and concerning to visitors. Mr. Johnson is given a mood-enhancing drug that significantly reduces this behavior.

   e. Mr. Donald, a nursing home resident, constantly goes to the nurses' station and makes sexually inappropriate comments to female staff members. Several times he has tried to grope them. This behavior was significantly reduced after the registered nurse for his unit prescribed a sedative.

4. Mr. and Mrs. Baxter, a married couple, reside in the same nursing home. Mr. and Mrs. Baxter both have extensive physical disabilities, and Mrs. Baxter is experiencing mild dementia. Mr. and Mrs. Baxter have expressed the desire to share a room in the nursing home, although the nursing home has a policy of not allowing members of the opposite sex to share a room. Mr. Baxter has, albeit indirectly, indicated that a shared room is critical because the couple wish to engage in intimate relations together. Must the nursing home permit them to share a room? Should the nursing home do anything to facilitate, discourage, or monitor relations between the couple? May it?

5. Mr. Anthony, who has Alzheimer's disease, has repeatedly exposed himself to female staff members and several times attempted to grab the breasts or buttocks of female nursing assistants attempting to provide him with personal care. The nursing home has placed him in a segregated, locked unit that primarily houses individuals with significant mental health issues. If you represented Mr. Anthony, what concerns might you have about this approach? What rights are implicated in this situation?

6. Melinda's mother, Betsey, resides in Hornsfield Nursing Home. Melinda is very worried that her mother's health is deteriorating. She is particularly worried that Betsey spends most of the day sitting in a recliner by the nurse's station, and rarely walks or gets any other form of exercise. Melinda visits regularly. When she does so, she urges Betsey to exercise and to walk, and she also talks extensively to Betsey's aides about her concerns and what she perceives to be their lazy refusal to help her mother get the exercise she needs. Hornsfield Nursing Home has informed Melinda that her visits to her mother are unduly upsetting Betsey, and that Melinda is therefore not permitted to visit more than twice a week. They have also requested that she only visit during the daytime. What rights are implicated in this situation? Can Hornsfield limit Melinda's visits? Could it ban visits from Melinda altogether?

EXERCISE 7.4

The University of Minnesota School of Public Health has compiled on online database of state nursing home regulations. *See* University of Minnesota School of Public Health, *NH Regulations Plus, available at* http://www.hpm.umn.edu/nhregsplus/index.html. Look up your state's regulations. How do its regulations interact with the federal regulations described in this chapter?

b. Balancing Competing Interests

At times, the rights and interests of residents may conflict with those of another resident or with those of nursing home staff. Since the Nursing Home Reform Act is a federal statute, in some cases, whose right takes precedence can be determined based on the doctrine of preemption: The federal rights granted by the Nursing Home Reform Act trump state statutory rights with which they conflict. At other times, the situation may require the courts to weigh the competing interests of the parties. The next case provides an example of one such situation.

Chaney v. Plainfield Healthcare Center

612 F.3d 908 (7th Cir. 2010)

WILLIAMS, Circuit Judge.

This case pits a health-care worker's right to a non-discriminatory workplace against a patient's demand for white-only health-care providers. Plainfield Healthcare Center is a nursing home that housed a resident who did not want assistance from black certified nursing assistants. Plainfield complied with this racial preference by telling Brenda Chaney, a black nursing assistant, in writing everyday [*sic*] that "no black" assistants should enter this resident's room or provide her with care.

Chaney brought this action under Title VII of the 1964 Civil Rights Act. She claims that Plainfield's practice of acceding to the racial biases of its residents is illegal and created a hostile work environment. She also asserts that Plainfield fired her because she was black. The Equal Employment Opportunity Commission, as amicus, agrees, and together they urge reversal of the district court's grant of summary judgment to Plainfield. Because the racial preference policy violates Title VII by creating a hostile work environment and because issues of fact remain over whether race motivated the discharge, we reverse the district court's order.

I. BACKGROUND

Since Plainfield Healthcare Center ("Plainfield") prevailed on summary judgment, we recount the facts in the light most favorable to Brenda Chaney, the non-movant. Plainfield hired Chaney as a nurse aide or certified nursing assistant ("CNA"). As a CNA, she was responsible for monitoring patients, responding to their requests for service, and generally assisting with their daily living needs. Plainfield detailed Chaney's daily shift duties on an assignment sheet that she and other employees received upon arriving at work. The assignment sheet listed the residents in Chaney's unit and their corresponding care needs. It also featured a column with miscellaneous notes about each resident's condition. In the case of Marjorie Latshaw, a resident in Chaney's unit, the sheet instructed nurse aides that Latshaw "Prefers No Black CNAs."

Plainfield acknowledges its policy of honoring the racial preferences of its residents in assigning health-care providers. Plainfield maintains it expected its employees to respect these racial preferences because it otherwise risked violating state and federal laws that grant residents the rights to choose providers, to privacy, and to bodily autonomy. Indeed, in its reply brief to the district court on summary judgment, Plainfield acknowledged that the assignment sheet for Chaney "banned" her from assisting Latshaw.

For fear of being fired, Chaney went along with the policy. Although Latshaw remained on her assignment sheet, Chaney reluctantly refrained from assisting her, even when she was in the best position to respond. Once, Chaney found Latshaw on the ground, too weak to stand. Despite wanting badly to help, Chaney had to search the building for a white CNA. Plainfield housed at least two other residents with a similar distaste for black CNAs. One refused Chaney's assistance in the shower, asking for a different nurse aide instead. On a separate occasion, a co-worker warned Chaney that another resident does not care for blacks. Emotionally, these race-based limitations depressed Chaney, who routinely left work "teary eyed."

Plainfield's practice of honoring the racial preferences of residents was accompanied by racially-tinged comments and epithets from co-workers. For instance, in the presence of a resident, a white nurse aide named Audria called Chaney a "black bitch." Another time, a white coworker looked directly at Chaney and asked why Plainfield "... keep[s] on hiring all of these black niggers? They're not gonna stay anyway." The epithets were reported to the unit supervisor, Loretta Askew, who promised to address them. Although the epithets ceased, co-worker Audria continued to remind Chaney that certain residents were off limits because she was black. Chaney reported these comments to Askew, who renewed her promise to take care of it. Audria eventually left Chaney alone, but Plainfield's racial preference policy remained in place and continued to surface in conversations with other employees.

* * *

The district court entered summary judgment in favor of Plainfield on the claim[] of hostile workplace. ... Although the court recognized that the comments from Chaney's co-workers had created a hostile work environment, it concluded that Plainfield avoided liability by responding promptly each time it received a complaint. Treating the racial preference policy as a separate claim of a hostile work environment, the court concluded that the note on Chaney's assignment sheet advising her of the "Prefers No Black CNAs" exclusion was reasonable given Plainfield's good-faith belief that ignoring the resident's preferences would have violated Indiana's patient-rights laws. ...

II. ANALYSIS

On appeal, Chaney and the EEOC argue that Plainfield's policy of acceding to the racial biases of its residents is an unlawful employment practice that, along with racial animosity from her co-workers, created an unremediated, racially hostile workplace. They also contend that she presented sufficient evidence to create a triable question of whether racial animus motivated her firing. We review the grant of summary judgment de novo, with the familiar standard that summary judgment should be granted if there is no genuine issue of material fact and the record shows that the law entitles the moving party to judgment.

A. Racially Hostile Workplace Claim

Title VII prohibits employers from discriminating against any individual "with respect to his compensation, terms, conditions, or privileges of employment, because of such individual's race. ..." 42 U.S.C. §2000e-2(a)(1). In order to impose Title VII liability for a racially hostile workplace, a plaintiff must show: (1) the work environment was both subjectively and objectively offensive; (2) that the harassment was based on membership in a protected class; (3) that the conduct was severe or pervasive; and (4) that there is a basis for employer liability.

We have no trouble finding that a reasonable person would find Plainfield's work environment hostile or abusive. ... Here, over the course of three months, coworkers called Chaney a "black bitch" and a "nigger" on multiple occasions. And in her deposition, Chaney alleges that more subtle racial slights and comments continued even after management was notified of the problem. Most importantly, Plainfield acted to foster and engender a racially-charged environment through its assignment sheet that unambiguously, and daily, reminded Chaney and her co-workers that certain residents preferred no black CNAs. Unlike white aides, Chaney was restricted in the rooms she could enter, the care that she could provide, and the patients she could assist.

Plainfield argues there is no basis for employer liability because its response to the racial epithets was adequate in stopping the harassment and that any subsequent comments were mere reminders of a particular resident's preference and not racially offensive. While it is true that Plainfield's actions stopped the use of the most vulgar racial epithets, we cannot agree that any further comments to Chaney about patients' racial preferences were innocent and objectively unoffensive. Nor can we agree that Plainfield's policy of acceding to patient preference, and expecting Chaney to adhere to its instructions, was reasonable. Plainfield claims this policy was necessary to comply with state and federal law.

It is now widely accepted that a company's desire to cater to the perceived racial preferences of its customers is not a defense under Title VII for treating employees differently based on race. Plainfield argues that this well-settled reading of Title VII does not apply—or should not apply—in the long-term care setting. It contends that long-term care facilities have obligations to their clients that place them in a different position from most employers. Plainfield is both a medical provider and a permanent home for hundreds of residents. The rights of those residents are secured by federal and state laws and a vast network of regulations that, according to Plainfield, it must honor before considering its Title VII obligations to its employees.

For support, Plainfield cites a line of Title VII cases permitting sex discrimination in the health-care setting. Taken together, they hold that gender may be a legitimate criterion—a bona fide occupational qualification ("BFOQ")—for accommodating patients' privacy interests. It does not follow, however, that patients' privacy interests excuse disparate treatment based on race. Title VII forbids employers from using race as a BFOQ, and Plainfield's cases allowing gender preferences in the health-care setting illustrate why. The privacy interest that is offended when one undresses in front of a doctor or nurse of the opposite sex does not apply to race. Just as the law tolerates same-sex restrooms or same-sex dressing rooms, but not white-only rooms, to accommodate privacy needs, Title VII allows an employer to respect a preference for same-sex health providers, but not same-race providers.

Plainfield argues that even if Title VII does not expressly contemplate a patient-preference defense to race-based work assignments, Plainfield's policy is a reasonable and good-faith effort to comply with Indiana law and should be excused on that basis. Under Indiana regulations governing long-term care facilities, residents have a right to "choose a personal attending physician and other providers of services." 410 Ind. Admin. Code 16.2-3.1-3(n)(1). If Plainfield's reading of the regulation (requiring it to instruct its employees to honor a patient's racial preferences) were correct, it would conflict with Title VII. When two laws conflict, one state, one federal, the Supremacy Clause dictates that the federal law prevails. Had a resident sued Plainfield under the patient's rights provision, Title VII would have supplied an affirmative defense. Title VII does not, by contrast, contain a good-faith "defense" that allows an employer to ignore the statute in favor of conflicting state law.

In any event, Indiana's regulations do not require Plainfield to instruct its employees to accede to the racial preferences of its residents. The regulations merely require Plainfield to allow residents access to health-care providers of their choice. If a racially-biased resident wishes to employ at her own expense a white aide, Indiana law may require Plainfield to allow the resident reasonable access to that aide. But the regulations do not say that a patient's preference for white aides that Plainfield employs trumps Plainfield's duty to its employees to abstain from race-based work assignments.

Plainfield's reading of Indiana regulations is also untenable because it puts Plainfield at risk of violating duties of medical care that it owes its residents. A potential violation could have occurred when Chaney, adhering to Plainfield's policy, reluctantly left Latshaw on the floor so she could search the building for a white nurse aide rather than immediately attend to her needs. Plainfield's claim of "good-faith" appears less than compelling as a factual matter as well. If Plainfield was worried that dishonoring race-based work preferences risked violating Indiana's regulations, it could have asked Indiana's State Department of Health whether state law required Plainfield to direct its employees to cater to its residents' racial preferences. The record does not show an attempt to seek such guidance.

Plainfield's next argument that the racial preference policy was required under federal law is also not persuasive. Plainfield relies primarily on three sections of the Medicare Act. The first, 42 U.S.C. §1395, states that "Nothing in this subchapter" shall interfere with the practice of medicine. "[T]his subchapter" refers to the Medicare Act, not, as Plainfield suggests, the federal employment-rights law. Similarly off the mark is Plainfield's reliance on 42 U.S.C. §1395a. That provision merely reminds Medicare beneficiaries that federal law does not preclude them from using providers that have opted out of Medicare. Finally, Plainfield relies on 42 U.S.C. §1395i, which provides that Medicare beneficiaries in long-term care facilities have a right to choose "a personal attending physician." The law is silent about a beneficiary's right to choose other service providers, such as CNAs. Moreover, as with the Indiana regulation, even if the law extended to other service providers, it would merely require Plainfield to allow residents access to them, rather than obligate Plainfield to institute race-based work practices.

Plainfield also defends the racial preference policy on a practical level: without it, Plainfield risks exposing black employees to racial harassment from the residents and, in turn, exposing itself to hostile workplace liability. It adds, without providing authority, that discharging a racially hostile resident to avoid exposing employees to the resident is illegal. But without resorting to discharging residents, a long-term care facility confronted with a hostile resident has a range of options.

It can warn residents before admitting them of the facility's nondiscrimination policy, securing the resident's consent in writing; it can attempt to reform the resident's behavior after admission; and it can assign staff based on race-neutral criteria that minimize the risk of conflict. Plainfield could have, for instance, advised its employees that they could ask for protection from racially harassing residents. That way, Plainfield would not be imposing an unwanted, race-conscious work limitation on its black employees; rather, it would be allowing all employees to work in a race-neutral, non-harassing work environment, as is commonly expected of employers. And even if all these efforts do not guarantee full racial harmony, they exemplify reasonable measures that an employer can undertake to avoid liability for known workplace harassment.

Plainfield, however, chose none of these options. Instead, Plainfield told Chaney that it was excluding her from work areas and residents solely on account of her race, thereby creating a racially-charged workplace that poisoned the work environment. In less than three months, Chaney reported at least three specific incidents of harassment, two of which . . . involved racial slurs directed toward her. Although the direct epithets stopped after Plainfield learned of them, the record does not show whether the lulls in harassment were fortuitous or the result of remedial action. More fundamentally, Plainfield never corrected the principle source of the racial hostility in the workplace—its willingness to accede to a patient's racial preferences. The hostility that Chaney described came from daily reminders that Plainfield was employing her on materially different terms than her white co-workers. Fueling this pattern was the racial preference policy, both a source of humiliation for Chaney and fodder for her co-workers, who invoked it regularly. It was, in short, a racially hostile environment, and the evidence presented at summary judgment allows a jury to conclude that Plainfield took insufficient measures to address it.

* * *

III. CONCLUSION

The judgment of the district court is REVERSED and REMANDED for further proceedings.

NOTE

Accommodating residents' gender preferences. As *Chaney* acknowledged, courts have permitted health care facilities to assign personal care staff based on gender on the grounds that under certain circumstances gender is a *bona fide occupational qualification* (BFOQ) within the meaning of Title VII. As Professor Kimani Paul-Emile has explained:

> The BFOQ defense may . . . be used as a defense against a charge of accommodating customer preferences in a very limited number of circumstances in which customer privacy is a concern. Thus, for example, although the BFOQ defense will not serve as a valid justification for an airline to hire only women

as flight attendants to comply with male customer preferences, the privacy interests of psychiatric patients can justify a BFOQ for personal hygiene attendants of the same sex. To this end, courts have held that for certain workers, such as nursing assistants, hospital delivery room nursing staff, and others involved in assisting individuals with dressing, disrobing, or bathing, gender may be a legitimate BFOQ for accommodating patients' privacy or modesty interests. In *Chaney*, however, the court correctly held that race is not a relevant factor to consider in addressing privacy concerns, nor is it relevant to the work of CNAs.

Kimani Paul-Emile, *Patients' Racial Preferences and the Medical Culture of Accommodation*, 60 UCLA L. Rev. 462, 486-87 (2012).

QUESTIONS

1. Under what other circumstances might residents' rights come into tension with those of nursing home staff? How should the law balance these competing interests?

2. Do you agree with Professor Paul-Emile's conclusion, stated in the preceding note, that *Chaney* "correctly held that race is not a relevant factor to consider" in addressing residents' privacy concerns?

3. In *Chaney*, the Seventh Circuit suggested that the nursing facility find alternative ways to address a potentially hostile working environment, such as warning prospective residents of the facility's nondiscrimination policy and obtaining the residents' written consent to that policy, or attempting to "reform" residents' behavior following admission. How might you critique these suggestions based on what you know about the demographics of the nursing home population? Could a nursing home evict a resident for failing to follow a nondiscrimination policy?

4. Enforcing Nursing Home Residents' Rights Through Informal Processes

When a nursing home resident experiences a problem, the first avenue for relief rarely is (and rarely should be) litigation. Rather, litigation should typically be a last resort, and the first step should usually be to speak with nursing home staff to try to informally resolve the problem.

Where the problem requires coordination or planning, it may be appropriate to seek a change in the resident's care plan and a care planning meeting to discuss such changes. Under the Nursing Home Reform Act, a nursing home is required to create a comprehensive *care plan* shortly after admission of each new resident. The care plan sets forth the resident's needs and preferences, as well as measureable objectives and timetables to meet those needs, and the services that are to be provided to do so. The care plan must be reviewed every three months and, if necessary, revised to reflect any changes in the resident's condition or care. Care planning is, by law, an interdisciplinary exercise: The attending physician, a registered nurse with responsibility for the resident, and staff from other disciplines reflecting the resident's needs must be included. Facilities are also required to involve both the resident and the resident's family or legal representative in the care planning process to the extent practicable. *See* 42 CFR §483.20(k).

As explained by attorney Eric Carlson in his treatise on long-term care advocacy,

> Care plans are the cornerstone of the Nursing Home Reform Law. Care plans should reflect the blending of medical expertise and resident preference. . . . If a care plan is prepared well—and followed faithfully—a resident will receive care that truly meets his individual physical, mental, and psychosocial needs.

Eric Carlson, *Long-Term Care Advocacy* §2.10 (LexisNexis 2011). Carlson cautions, however, that:

> The care planning at most facilities falls well short of this ideal. Most care plans exhibit a certain sameness, as if the same care plan were prepared for each resident—indeed, provider magazines contain advertisements for computer software than can generate care plans at the touch of a button.

Id. He therefore urges residents and their family members to reject "perfunctory" care plans, and instead to try to attend care planning meets so that they can help develop an individualized and specific care plans designed to document and to help meet particular residents' needs and preferences.

Another resource for informal problem resolution is the nursing home *ombudsman.* The Older Americans Act requires that each state establish and operate a long-term care ombudsmen program that, among other tasks, identifies, investigates, and resolves complaints related to resident well-being or resident rights that are made by or on behalf of residents. *See* 42 USCA §3058g. Consistent with these requirements, ombudsmen programs typically assign each nursing home an ombudsman, a neutral third party with whom nursing home residents and their families can communicate. The ombudsman can help inform residents and family members of their rights and can help them work with a facility to avoid or resolve a dispute. The level of engagement and skill of nursing home ombudsmen varies significantly from state to state and county to county. The majority of ombudsmen are volunteers who are trained and advised by professional ombudsmen staff.

5. Enforcing Nursing Home Residents' Rights Through Litigation

In response to a combination of serious quality of care problems at many nursing homes, and a number of large damage awards in cases involving nursing home neglect, nursing home litigation has become a small but significant area of practice among the plaintiffs' trial bar. Typical factual patterns involve nursing home residents suffering serious injury or death as a result of alleged negligence that resulted in a fall, malnutrition, or choking; neglect that allowed the resident to wander into danger; or an assault by a third party.

This section explores the types of legal claims that can be brought when a resident has experienced an adverse event as a result of a nursing home's allegedly improper act or omission. As part of this consideration, it examines the role that statutory violations play in such suits as well as the impact of arbitration clauses in nursing home admission contracts on nursing home litigation.

In considering these materials, it is important to keep in mind that litigation is rarely the only approach that advocates will take when trying to remedy rights violations. Advocates are likely to combine a litigation strategy with a strategy for informal enforcement, especially if the resident is still alive. In addition, advocates may seek to address concerns by reporting concerns to appropriate regulatory bodies.

a. Private Rights of Action

There is disagreement in the courts as to whether the Nursing Home Reform Act creates a private right of action (i.e., the right for an injured party to sue to directly enforce the Act's provisions). Until the Third Circuit's decision in *Grammer v. John J. Kane Regional Centers*, excerpted below, there was a strong trend away from finding a private right. The decision in *Grammer* is thus significant in part because it raises new questions as to whether additional circuits may come to recognize a private right of action, at least in publically operated facilities.

Grammer v. John J. Kane Regional Centers

570 F.3d 520 (3d Cir. 2009)

NYGAARD, Circuit Judge.

We are asked in this appeal to determine whether an action will lie under 42 U.S.C. §1983 to challenge the treatment Appellant's decedent received (or did not receive) at the Appellee nursing home—treatment Appellant argues violated the Federal Nursing Home Reform Amendments (FN[H]RA), 42 U.S.C. §1396r et seq. We answer that question in the affirmative and will reverse and remand the cause to the District Court.

In so holding, we conclude that the language of the FNHRA is sufficiently rights-creating and that the rights conferred by its various provisions are neither "vague and amorphous" nor impose upon states a mere precatory obligation. Further, we conclude that §1983 provides the proper avenue for relief because the Appellee has failed to demonstrate that Congress foreclosed that option by adopting another, more comprehensive enforcement scheme.

I.

Appellant's mother, Melviteen Daniels, was a resident of the John J. Kane Regional Center at Glen Hazel, in Pittsburgh, Pennsylvania. The Kane Center is a residential skilled nursing care and rehabilitation center for short-term and/or long-term needs, and is operated by Allegheny County. The Appellant maintains that, as a result of Kane Center's failure to provide proper care, her mother developed decubitus ulcers, became malnourished and eventually developed sepsis, from which she died.

Grammer sued Kane Center bringing claims under 42 U.S.C. §1983 for wrongful death (Count I) and survival (Count II). Grammer alleged that the Kane Center deprived Mrs. Daniels of her civil rights by breaching a duty to ensure quality care under the Omnibus Budget Reconciliation Act of 1987 (OBRA) and, more specifically, the FNHRA thereto. The Kane Center filed a motion to dismiss, arguing that neither the OBRA nor the FNHRA provide a right that is enforceable through §1983. The Kane Center maintained that the statutes merely set forth requirements a nursing facility must comply with to receive federal Medicaid funds. The District Court adopted the Magistrate Judge's recommendation finding no right of action under the statutes, and dismissed the case pursuant to Fed. R. Civ. P. 12(b)(6).

* * *

III.

* * *

Before Congress amended the Medicare and Medicaid Acts in 1987, only two sanctions were available against nursing homes for noncompliance with federal participation requirements. First, the Secretary of Health and Human Services or the states themselves could decertify the facility and terminate the nursing home's eligibility to receive Medicaid reimbursements. Second, if noncompliance was not an immediate and serious threat to the residents' health and safety, the Secretary or the states could deny payment for new admissions for up to eleven months. These sanctions were rarely invoked. As a result, the programs permitted too many substandard nursing homes to continue operations. . . .

In 1987, Congress passed the FNHRA, contained in OBRA, to provide for the oversight and inspection of nursing homes that participate in Medicare and Medicaid programs. The requirements for certification include satisfying certain standards in areas such as "quality of care" and "resident rights."

Grammer's complaint alleged claims under §1983 for wrongful death (Count I) and survival (Count II). Grammer contends that the Kane Center's failure to provide the standards of care delineated by the FNHRA deprived her mother of her civil rights. Grammer's complaint focuses on the following provisions of the FNHRA:

- A nursing home must care for its residents in such a manner and in such an environment as will promote maintenance or enhancement of the quality of life of each resident, 42 U.S.C. §1396r(b)(1)(A);
- A nursing facility must provide services and activities to attain or maintain the highest practicable physical, mental and psychosocial well-being of each resident in accordance with a written plan of care which (a) describes the medical, nursing and psychosocial needs of the resident and how such needs will be met; 42 U.S.C. §1396r(b)(2)(A);
- A nursing facility must conduct a comprehensive, accurate, standardized reproducible assessment of each resident's functional capacity, which assessment (i) describes the resident's capability to perform daily life functions and significant impairments in functional capacity; (iv) including identification of medical problems; 42 U.S.C. §1396r(b)(3)(A);
- To the extent needed to fulfill all plans of care described in paragraph (2), a nursing facility must provide (or arrange the provision of) dietary services that assure the meals meet the daily nutritional and special dietary needs of each resident. Services described in clause (iv) must be provided by qualified persons in accordance with each resident's written plan of care; 42 U.S.C. §1396r(b)(4)(A)(iv);
- A nursing facility must provide services and activities to attain or maintain the highest practicable physical, mental and psychosocial well-being of each resident in accordance with a written plan of care which (C) is periodically reviewed and revised after each assessment under paragraph (3)—such assessment must be conducted (i) promptly upon (but not later than 14 days after the date of) admission for each individual admitted on or after October 1, 1990; (ii) the nursing facility must examine each resident no less frequently than once every three months and, as appropriate, revise the resident's assessment to assure the continuing accuracy of the assessment; (D) the results of such an assessment shall be used in developing, reviewing and revising the resident's plan of care under paragraph (2); 42 U.S.C. §1396r(b)(2)(C), (b)(3)(C)(i)(*l*) & (ii), (b)(3)(D), (b)(4)(B);
- To the extent needed to fulfill all plans of care described in paragraph (2), a nursing facility must provide (or arrange the provision of) (ii) medically related services to attain or maintain the highest practicable physical, mental, and psychosocial well being of each resident; (v) an ongoing program, directed by qualified professional, of activities designed to meet the interests and the physical, mental and psychosocial well-being of each resident; 42 U.S.C. §1396r(b)(4)(A)(ii) & (v);
- A nursing facility must maintain clinical records on all residents, which records include the plans of care (described in paragraph (2)) and the

residents' assessments (described in paragraph (3)), as well as the results of any preadmission screening conducted under subsection (e)(7) of this section; 42 U.S.C. §1396r(b)(6)(C);

■ The right to be free from physical or mental abuse, corporal punishment, involuntary seclusion, and any physical or chemical restraints imposed for the purposes of discipline or convenience and not required to treat the resident's medical symptoms . . . 42 U.S.C. §1396r(c)(1)(A)(ii) & (c)(1)(D).

We are therefore presented with the question whether these various provisions of the FNHRA give Medicaid recipients like Melviteen Daniels rights whose violation can be remedied under §1983. As noted, we answer in the affirmative.

IV.

A.

42 U.S.C. §1983 is a vehicle for imposing liability against anyone who, under color of state law, deprives a person of "rights, privileges, or immunities secured by the Constitution and laws." *Maine v. Thiboutot*, 448 U.S. 1, 4-6 (1980). However, a plaintiff must assert the violation of a federal right—not merely a violation of a federal law—to seek redress. If a plaintiff alleges a violation of a federal right as the basis of a §1983 action, we must determine whether the applicable federal statute confers an individual right. *Blessing* [*v. Freestone*, 520 U.S. 329, 340 (1997)]. That is to say, whether a particular federal statute creates a federal right of the kind enforceable by an action for damages under §1983 requires that we determine "whether or not Congress intended to confer individual rights upon a class of beneficiaries." *Gonzaga Univ.* [*v. Doe*, 536 U.S. 273, 285 (2002)]. A plaintiff bears the burden of establishing that a statute gives rise to federal rights enforceable through §1983.

B.

In *Blessing*, the Supreme Court set forth three factors courts should use to determine whether a statute conferred a federal right upon an individual: first, courts should determine whether Congress intended that the statutory provision in question benefits the plaintiff; second, courts should decide whether the right asserted is so "vague and amorphous" that its enforcement would strain judicial competence; and lastly, courts should determine whether the statute unambiguously imposes a binding obligation on the states. The Supreme Court further instructed that if a plaintiff successfully meets these three requirements, she has established a rebuttable presumption that she has such a right. However, this presumption could be rebutted if Congress "specifically foreclosed a remedy under §1983."

* * *

C.

There is no question that the statutory provisions under which Grammer raises her claims meet the first *Blessing* factor. As both a Medicaid recipient and a nursing home resident, Grammer's mother was an intended beneficiary of 42 U.S.C. §1396r. . . . Moreover, unlike the statutes at issue in *Gonzaga Univ.* and *Blessing,* the FNHRA are directly concerned with "whether the needs of any particular person have been satisfied." . . .

The second *Blessing* factor is also met here. The rights Grammer asserts are not so "vague or amorphous" that their enforcement would strain judicial resources. The various rights are clearly delineated by the provisions at issue. The repeated use of the phrases "must provide," "must maintain" and "must conduct" are not unduly vague or amorphous such that the judiciary cannot enforce the statutory provisions. These provisions make clear that nursing homes must provide a basic level of service and care for residents and Medicaid patients.

Finally, the language unambiguously binds the states and the nursing homes as indicated by the repeated use of "must." This language is mandatory in nature and easily satisfies the third factor of the *Blessing* test.

D.

[M]eeting *Blessing's* "zone of interest" factor is not enough. In *Gonzaga Univ.,* the Supreme Court cautioned us to be careful to ensure that the statute at issue contains "rights-creating language" and to make certain that the language is phrased in terms of the persons benefitted, not in terms of a general "policy or practice." 536 U.S. at 287. While *Blessing* stands for the proposition that violations of rights, not laws, give rise to §1983 actions, nevertheless, the *Gonzaga Univ.* court warned against interpreting *Blessing* "as allowing plaintiffs to enforce a statute under §1983 so long as the plaintiff falls within the general zone of interest that the statute is intended to protect." *Gonzaga Univ.,* 536 U.S. at 283. Therefore, nothing short of an "unambiguously conferred [individual] right" as demonstrated through "rights-creating language" can support a §1983 action.

* * *

The FNHRA are replete with rights-creating language. The amendments confer upon residents of such facilities the right to choose their personal attending physicians, to be fully informed about and to participate in care and treatment, to be free from physical or mental abuse, to voice grievances and to enjoy privacy and confidentiality. 42 U.S.C. §1396r(c)(1)(A). Nursing homes are required to care for residents in a manner promoting quality of life, provide services and activities to maintain the highest practicable physical, mental and psychosocial well-being of residents, and conduct comprehensive assessments of their functional abilities. 42 U.S.C. §1396r(b)(1), (2) & (3). Further, the statute specifically guarantees nursing home residents the right to be free from physical or mental abuse, corporal punishment, involuntary seclusion, and any physical or chemical restraints imposed for the purposes of discipline or convenience and not required to treat their medical symptoms. 42 U.S.C. §1396r(1)(A)(ii).

* * *

Additionally, the FNHRA use the word "residents" throughout. Thus, its provisions are clearly "phrased in terms of the persons benefitted." *See Gonzaga Univ.*, 536 U.S. at 284. Moreover, no provision uses the word "resident" simply in passing. Instead, the FNHRA are constructed in such a way as to stress that these "residents" have explicitly identified rights, such as "the *right* to be free from physical or mental abuse, corporal punishment, involuntary seclusion, and any physical or chemical restraints imposed for the purposes of discipline or convenience and not required to treat the resident's medical symptoms." 42 U.S.C. §1396r(c)(1)(A) (emphasis added). These statutory provisions are, in other words, "concerned with 'whether the needs of any particular person have been satisfied,'" not solely with an aggregate institutional policy and practice.

* * *

The legislative history of the enactment of the FNHRA is likewise compelling when determining Congressional intent to create a right of action. [Discussion of legislative history omitted.]

. . . [W]e hold that Congress did use rights-creating language sufficient to unambiguously confer individually enforceable rights.

E.

We have one final step in our analysis. The Supreme Court instructs that we are to examine not only the text of the statute at issue, but also its structure to satisfy ourselves that it is sufficiently rights-creating. . . . The language used throughout the FNHRA is explicitly and unambiguously rights-creating, despite the countervailing elements of the statute. The larger statutory structure, therefore, does not neutralize the rights-creating language contained throughout the FNHRA.

F.

Accordingly, the various provisions of the FNHRA under which Grammer sues do confer individual rights that are presumptively enforceable through §1983. The burden shifts to the Kane Center to rebut the presumption of an enforceable right under §1983. The Kane Center has not satisfied its burden here, as it fails to argue that Congress precluded individual enforcement of the rights conferred by the FNHRA in any way. Moreover, our independent examination and assessment of the Medicaid Act disclosed no evidence of congressional intent to preclude enforcement of the rights created by the various provisions of this statute. This is so because no provision contains express terms to that effect and no comprehensive remedial scheme is established by the provisions at issue.

V.

In sum, it is clear enough that Congress intended to create individual rights in drafting and adopting §1396r, and that Appellant's mother falls squarely within the zone of interest these provisions are meant to protect. Hence, we hold that the statutory provisions which Grammer seeks to enforce under §1983 satisfy both *Gonzaga Univ.'s* insistence on rights-creating language as evidence of Congressional intent and *Blessing's* remaining factors. We will reverse the order of the District Court and remand the cause for further proceedings.

STAFFORD, District Judge, dissenting.

* * *

The Medicaid Act (the "Act"), which contains the statutory provisions allegedly violated by Appellee, is Spending Clause legislation. Spending Clause legislation rarely confers upon funding beneficiaries the right to bring private actions . . . against funding recipients. The Supreme Court has been explicit: "[U]nless Congress 'speak[s] with a clear voice,' and manifests an 'unambiguous' intent to confer individual rights, federal funding provisions provide no basis for private enforcement by §1983." *Gonzaga*, 536 U.S. at 280. In section 1396r, Congress did not speak with a "clear voice" or manifest an "unambiguous intent" to provide a basis for private enforcement of funding requirements under section 1983.

* * *

The Supreme Court in *Gonzaga* emphasized that "[s]tatutes that focus on the person regulated rather than the individuals protected create no implication of an intent to confer rights on a particular class of persons." *Gonzaga*, 536 U.S. at 287.[6]

Under the Medicaid Act, the federal government directs funding to states to assist them in providing medical assistance to certain eligible individuals. . . . [T]he focus is on what the nursing facility must do in return for federal funds; the focus is *not* on the individuals to whom the benefit of each provision flows.

---

6. . . . In the implied right of action context, federal courts have consistently held that no implied private right of action exists under the Medicaid Act, OBRA, or FNHRA. *See, e.g., Prince v. Dicker*, 29 Fed. Appx. 52, 54-55 (2d Cir. 2002) (holding, with no discussion, that 42 U.S.C. §1396r did not confer a private right of action that could be enforced against a private nursing home); *Brogdon v. Nat'l Healthcare Corp.*, 103 F. Supp. 2d 1322, 1330-32 (N.D. Ga. 2000) (finding that Congress did not intend to authorize nursing home residents to file suit against nursing facilities to enforce the section 1396r standards required for participation in the Medicaid program); *Sparr v. Berks County*, 2002 WL 1608243 *2-3 (E.D. Pa. July 18, 2002) (dismissing action brought by executor of patient's estate against the nursing home for violations of the FNHRA, finding that although the statute was enacted to benefit the plaintiff, there was nothing in the legislative purpose or history to suggest that Congress intended to create a private right of action).

...I do not agree that Congress intended to confer upon nursing home residents the right to invoke section 1983 to sue individual nursing homes for alleged violations of the non-monetary service requirements set forth in section 1396r. The district court properly dismissed the case, and we should affirm.

NOTES

1. *Wrongful death and survival actions.* As discussed above, *Grammer* involved both wrongful death and survival actions. A wrongful death action is an action brought on behalf of the decedents' survivors. By contrast, a survival action is an action based on the claim or claims the decedent would have had if he or she had survived.

2. *Reactions to* Grammer. The federal district courts have, so far, had a mixed reaction to *Grammer*. While some have followed it, others have explicitly refused to do so. Moreover, even among those courts that do not reject *Grammer* altogether, some read it narrowly. For example, in *Taormina v. Suburban Woods Nursing Homes, LLC*, 765 F. Supp. 2d 667 (E.D. Pa. 2011), the federal court for the Eastern District of Pennsylvania dismissed a Section 1983 suit brought against a private nursing home. It distinguished *Grammer* on the grounds that the defendant nursing home in *Grammer* was operated by a government entity and, therefore, there was no question that it was operating under color of state law. *See also Baum v. N. Dutchess Hosp.*, 764 F. Supp. 2d 410 (N.D.N.Y. 2011) (providing a lengthy critique of *Grammer*).

3. *Causes of action under state nursing home regulatory schemes.* Many states have significant state-based regulation of nursing home practices. In some cases, these regulations closely mirror the federal regulations. Whether such state-based statutes create a private right of action is also the subject of significant disagreement. Ultimately, courts look to legislative intent to determine whether a private right exists. For example, *Morisette v. Terence Cardinal Cooke Health Care Ctr.*, 797 N.Y.S.2d 856 (N.Y. Sup. Ct. 2005), involved a claim brought under New York State's Public Health Law §2801-d, which grants nursing home residents a variety of rights that largely parallel those set forth under the federal Nursing Home Reform Act. The plaintiff claimed that her mother died as the result of the nursing home's failure "to provide and implement an adequate and reasonable plan of care" as required under §2801-d and that this caused her mother to "'plug from mucous secretions' thereby leading to 'respiratory arrest, anoxic brain injury and death.'" The court found that the plaintiff, acting on behalf of her mother's estate, had stated a valid claim under the law. In doing so, it explained:

> The legislative history [of §2801-d] evinces an intent to provide an additional avenue of relief to the vulnerable nursing home population to insure

that their rights are enforced. . . . The legislative history demonstrates that the Legislature was aware that incentives were needed to induce attorneys to bring suits on behalf of injured patients, so as to deter future deprivations and compensate those who are injured. The reality is that many lawyers will decline a meritorious case when dealing with an individual who has a limited life expectancy, who is not a wage earner, and who is not supporting or providing services to others, and thus where damages are limited. This is precisely the case with many nursing home residents; hence the need for the enactment of incentives.

Id. at 862.

b. The Role of Statutory Violations Absent a Private Right of Action

Even where statutes do not create a private right of action, they can play a significant role in nursing home litigation. Statutory violations may be evidence of a pattern or practice. State or federal statutes may also establish the standard of care, and their violation may be treated as creating a presumption of negligence. The next case explores these different roles.

Estate of French v. Stratford House et al.

333 S.W.3d 546 (Tenn. 2011)

GARY R. WADE, J.

***

FACTS AND PROCEDURAL HISTORY

In 2000, Martha French ("Ms. French"), age 54, suffered a debilitating stroke, her second, and was admitted to total care at the Highland Manor Nursing Home ("Highland Manor") in Portland. Also afflicted with diabetes, arterial fibrillation, depression, hypertension, and anxiety, Ms. French periodically experienced pressure ulcers at Highland Manor. After Ms. French had been a patient at Highland Manor for approximately three years, her daughter, Kimberly S. French (the "Administratrix"), arranged for her transfer to the Stratford House, a long-term care facility in Chattanooga. At the time of her admittance on April 3, 2003, Ms. French had no pressure ulcers. Because of her immobility, however, Ms. French was at significant risk of developing ulcers. The facility's Patient Transfer Form, Resident Assessment Protocol ("RAP") Summary, and Care Plan all documented Ms. French's susceptibility to pressure ulcers. A course of treatment was prescribed in order to prevent a reoccurrence of the condition. According to the plan of care established at the facility, Ms. French had to be turned by nursing home personnel and repositioned frequently, kept clean and dry after incontinence, and provided with adequate hydration and nutrition.

Ms. French's condition deteriorated during her time at the Stratford House. By the middle of July 2003, she had both a low-grade fever and low blood pressure and, on July 23, the Administratrix arranged for a transfer to Erlanger Medical Center ("Erlanger"), where physicians attempted to increase her blood pressure by hydrating her intravenously. When she was admitted to Erlanger, Ms. French had a urinary tract infection and a number of pressure ulcers that had become infected. She developed pulmonary swelling after her admission, and medical devices were required to assist with her breathing. A feeding tube was inserted. Later, when the Administratrix discovered the gravity of her mother's condition, she instructed the physicians to halt the aggressive measures, including the breathing assistance and the use of a feeding tube. Ms. French died on July 26, 2003. Her death certificate lists sepsis (commonly known as blood poisoning) as the cause of her death.

On March 22, 2004, the Administratrix filed suit on behalf of Ms. French's estate against the Stratford House, OP Chattanooga, Inc., Tandem Health Care, Inc., Tandem Health Care of Ohio, Inc., Cookeville Long Term Facility, Inc., f/k/a Tandem Health Care of Tennessee, Inc., HP/Stratford House, Inc., and HP/Holding, Inc. (the "Defendants"). The Administratrix alleged (1) ordinary negligence; (2) negligence per se based upon violations of state and federal nursing home regulations; and (3) violations of the Tennessee Adult Protection Act ("TAPA"). The complaint sought both compensatory and punitive damages....

ANALYSIS

* * *

In addition to the claims for ordinary negligence and medical malpractice, the Administratix alleges negligence per se based upon violations of certain federal and state nursing home regulations. Specifically, the Administratix claims that the Defendants breached their duty of care to Ms. French by failing "[t]o comply with all standards of care required by the Federal Regulations, 42 CFR 483.10 et seq, including, but not limited to" nineteen enumerated but uncited standards, and also by failing "[t]o comply with all standards of care required by the Nursing Home Regulations of the Tennessee Department of Health, Rules of the Tennessee Department of Health Board for Licensing Health Care Facilities, Chapter 1200-8-6, et seq, including, but not limited to, Standards 1200-8-6.05, 1200-8-6-.06, 1200-8-6-.12 and 1200-8-6-.15." The Court of Appeals, having affirmed the trial court's holding that all of the claims in the complaint sounded in medical malpractice, "refuse[d] to use the federal regulations of nursing homes, or the state regulations based upon them, to create a cause of action separate and apart from a medical malpractice action." *Estate of French*, 2009 WL 211898, at *10.

This Court has summarized the doctrine of negligence per se as follows:

The standard of conduct expected of a reasonable person may be prescribed in a statute and, consequently, a violation of the statute may be deemed to be negligence per se. When a statute provides that under certain circumstances particular acts shall or shall not be done, it may be interpreted as fixing a standard of care . . . from which it is negligence to deviate. In order to establish negligence per se, it must be shown that the statute violated was designed to impose a duty or prohibit an act for the benefit of a person or the public. It must also be established that the injured party was within the class of persons that the statute was meant to protect.

The negligence per se doctrine may also be applied based upon violations of regulations or ordinances, as well as statutes.

The Court of Appeals followed the rationale set forth in *Conley* [*v. Life Care Ctrs. of Am., Inc.*, 236 S.W.3d 713 (Tenn. Ct. App. 2007)], another case in which the plaintiff had asserted negligence per se based upon the federal nursing home regulations found in 42 C.F.R. §483. In *Conley*, the court had rejected the negligence per se theory of recovery for two reasons. Initially, "[t]he federal regulations are simply too vague and general to constitute a standard of care by which a jury, or for that matter a court, can effectively judge the acts or omissions of health care providers and nursing home operators." *Id.* at 733. Further, the "claims that are based upon alleged violations of federal regulatory standards constitute a national standard of care that runs afoul [of] the" [Tennesee Medical Malpractice Act (TMMA)], and, more specifically, its "locality rule." *Id.* at 733-34.

As to the case before us, the Court of Appeals properly ruled that a negligence per se claim cannot co-exist with a medical malpractice claim. The Administratix may not, therefore, use the alleged violations of the federal and state regulations to prove a deviation in the standard of care as a component of the medical malpractice claim. There are good reasons for our conclusion.

First, the effect of declaring conduct negligent per se is to hold that conduct is negligent as a matter of law, thus requiring plaintiffs to prove only proximate and actual causation and damages. This conflicts with the TMMA's instruction that "there shall be no presumption of negligence on the part of the defendant" in a medical malpractice action except in cases where the res ipsa loquitur doctrine applies. . . .

Second, a finding of negligence per se based upon federal and state nursing home regulations would be inconsistent with our General Assembly's directive that the relevant standard of care for a medical malpractice claim is that existing "in the community in which the defendant practices or in a similar community at the time the alleged injury or wrongful action occurred." Tenn. Code Ann. §29-26-115(a)(1). . . .

Because not all of the Administratrix's claims sound in medical malpractice, however, this case is distinguishable from *Conley*, in which the Court of Appeals concluded that the TMMA was the exclusive remedy. We must determine, therefore, whether the Administratrix may proceed on a negligence per se theory in support of her claims of ordinary negligence. The two prerequisites for a negligence per se claim are present here: Ms. French belonged to the class of persons the federal and state nursing home regulations were designed to protect, and her injuries were the type that the regulations were designed to prevent. . . .

We recognize that an express private right of action was not created under either the Federal Nursing Home Reform Act ("FNHRA") or the corresponding Tennessee act, which establish the rights of residents, patients, and the public with regard to nursing home care. The establishment of a set of licensing requirements for nursing homes and a system of agency prosecution to ensure compliance does not create a new cause of action against nursing homes. As stated, however, our recognition that violations of the regulations may be deemed negligence per se does not create a new cause of action where one does not already exist. We are also mindful of the fact that ordinary negligence actions against nursing homes are classified as such (and are distinct from medical malpractice actions) because they can be assessed based upon ordinary, everyday experiences. Requiring the finder of fact to parse through voluminous regulations to determine the standard of care in an ordinary negligence action against a nursing home may not always be the most direct approach toward the establishment of a nursing home's negligence. Nevertheless, proof of violations of federal and state nursing home regulations is relevant in determining whether a defendant nursing home has breached the standard of care. For the reasons stated, the Administratrix may pursue a negligence per se theory with regard to her ordinary negligence claims based upon alleged violations of federal and state nursing home regulations. . . .

[Dissent omitted.]

NOTES

1. *Similar results.* For cases that reach similar conclusions to *Estate of French*, see *McLain v. Mariner Health Care, Inc.*, 631 S.E.2d 435, 437 (Ga. App. 2006) (in a wrongful death claim against a nursing home, reversing lower court's grant of defendant's motion to dismiss on the grounds that the plaintiff could use the nursing home's violation of provisions in the Nursing Home Reform Act to establish negligence per se); *McCain v. Beverly Health & Rehab. Serv.*, No. Civ. A. 02-657, 2002 WL 1565526 (E.D. Pa. July 15, 2002) (holding that an estate of a nursing home resident who allegedly died as a result of pressure sores caused by the home's alleged negligence could use provisions in the Nursing Home Reform Act to establish negligence per se).

2. *Causal connection requirement.* In order for negligence per se to apply, the statutory violation at issue must be causally related to the harm suffered by the plaintiff. Whether a particular violation can be said to be causally related to a resident's injury, however, may be a subject of dispute. For example, courts have reached different conclusions as to whether the failure to have a

license should be treated as causally related to harm caused by the person or entity who lacking the proper license. *Compare Flint City Nursing Home, Inc. v. Depreast*, 406 So. 2d 356 (Ala. 1981) (trial court erred by admitting evidence that a nursing home and nursing home administrator were not properly licensed), *with Deerings W. Nursing Ctr. v. Scott*, 787 S.W.2d 494 (Tex. App. 1990) (holding that there was sufficient evidence to establish that a nursing home aide's failure to have a license was the proximate cause of an injury to a nursing home visitor).

3. *Vagueness limitation.* Even if a court finds that certain provisions of the Nursing Home Reform Act or a related state statute set the standard of care in a tort claim, they may find that others are too vague to do so. *See, e.g., Makas v. Hillhaven*, 589 F. Supp. 736, 741-42 (1984) (finding that provisions in a state statute establishing a Nursing Home Patients' Bill of Rights were "so general and nebulous that a trier of fact could not determine whether the standard had been violated").

c. Types of Quality of Care Claims

When a nursing home resident is injured or otherwise harmed as a result of the home's failure to provide appropriate care, the resident and the resident's family may be able to use a variety of different legal theories to hold the home civilly liable. Some such claims can be brought pursuant to a particular state or federal statute. In addition to potential private rights of action under statutes regulating nursing homes, a resident who was been assaulted or neglected might, for example, bring a claim for elder abuse based on a state elder abuse statute.

Nursing home residents and their families may also bring a wide variety of common law claims based on allegedly improper and injurious acts or omissions. Some of these are claims sound in contract. For example, a resident may allege that the nursing home failed to provide the level of care it was contractually obligated to provide. The underlying contract at issue is typically the nursing home admission agreement.

Other claims against nursing homes are based in tort. Most commonly, a claim will be premised on negligence, arguing that the nursing home breached a duty to the resident and thereby proximately caused the resident a compensable injury. Intentional tort claims (e.g., battery or intentional infliction of emotional distress) may also be appropriate in some cases. In addition to tort claims brought by the resident or on behalf of the resident, most states have wrongful death statutes which provide a limited cause of action to certain relatives of someone who died as a result of tortious behavior. The viability of a wrongful death claim will depend in large part on whether the resident has survivors who fall within the categories of persons permitted to bring suit under the state's statute. For example, some states limit the cause of action to spouses and minor children. If the deceased resident did not have a legally recognized spouse, then most likely there will be no cause of action;

although many nursing home residents have adult children, few nursing home residents have minor children.

As *Estate of French* illustrated, a key issue in many negligence claims against nursing homes is whether or not the claim should be considered a claim for medical malpractice. This is because many states have adopted "tort reform" legislation that limits damage awards or otherwise constrains liability in medical malpractice cases. For example, as a result of tort reform efforts, Texas limits non-economic damages that a single claimant can recover in medical malpractice cases to $250,000 against all doctors and health care practitioners and $250,000 per institution against health care facilities such as hospitals and nursing homes, with an overall cap of $500,000 against health care institutions per claimant. *See* Tex. Civ. Prac. & Rem. Code Ann. §74.301 (2013). This creates, in effect, an overall limit on non-economic damages in medical malpractice cases of $750,000. According to Professor Michael Rustad, these reforms have virtually eliminated suits against nursing homes in Texas:

> Because the expenses for bringing a suit against a nursing home often exceed the potential recovery, nursing home cases are no longer being filed in large numbers in Texas. Plaintiffs [sic] counsel representing nursing home residents are "cherry-picking cases with well-off clients who can show economic damages," leaving most elderly nursing home victims without the possibility of legal representation.

Michael L. Rustad, *Neglecting the Neglected: The Impact of Noneconomic Damage Caps on Meritorious Nursing Home Lawsuits*, 14 Elder L.J. 331, 333 (2006).

The cases that follow explore the different types of claims brought against nursing homes. The first examines a situation in which a nursing home allegedly failed to provide a resident with adequate care to meet her needs. The second examines a situation in which a nursing home allegedly failed to adequately protect a resident from injuries caused by another resident.

Zaborowski v. Hospitality Care Center of Hermitage, Inc.

2002 WL 32129508 (Pa. Com. Pl. 2002)

Dobson, J.

The matter before this court for disposition is defendants['] preliminary objections to plaintiff Michael Zaborowski's complaint.

* * *

Hospitality is a skilled care nursing home facility licensed in Pennsylvania to provide services to those unable to independently care for themselves. Hospitality also participates in the Medicare/Medicaid program. As such, it is subject to various statutes applicable to Medicare and Medicaid, as well as provider agreements between itself and Medicare and Medicaid. Cassity and

Bible, at all relevant times to the instant matter, were directors and officers of Hospitality. In addition, Cassity and Bible are its sole shareholders.

On September 4, 1997, Zaborowski, acting as an agent for his mother Anna M. Zaborowski (plaintiff decedent), admitted plaintiff decedent as a resident to Hospitality pursuant to the terms and conditions of a written admissions agreement. . . . Plaintiff decedent remained a resident of Hospitality from the date of her admission until her death on April 15, 2001. Zaborowski maintains that the quality of care delivered by Hospitality was properly provided to plaintiff decedent until December 2000.

Around December 2000, Hospitality terminated its then president, Steven Bible, and director of nursing, Lori Bible. Following their discharge, Hospitality, at the direction of Cassity and Bible, retained the services of Nubridge Development Inc. to manage and operate Hospitality. Sometime thereafter, Hospitality sent a letter to plaintiff decedent informing her of the change in management and also representing that "[a]s always, [Hospitality's] priority is to provide quality care and to provide a safe and comfortable environment for [its] residents."

Hospitality failed to provide such an environment. Instead, under Cassity's and Bible's sole control and Nubridge's management, Hospitality failed to properly maintain plaintiff decedent's quality of care. As a result of the inadequate care provided by Hospitality, plaintiff decedent suffered various conditions and injuries, including but not limited to bleeding around the areas of the G-tube and lungs, significant weight loss, choking, dehydration, seizures, labored respiration, stage I pressure sores and death. Consequently, Zaborowski commenced the instant suit by filing a survival action and a wrongful death action against Hospitality, Nubridge, Bible and Cassity.

* * *

[Plaintiff brought a wide variety of claims against Defendant. This edited version only includes the court's ruling on a subset of these claims.—ED.]

BREACH OF CONTRACT

Hospitality filed a preliminary objection in the nature of demurrer to Count VI (breach of contract) of Zaborowski's complaint. Zaborowski alleges that Hospitality breached an admissions agreement with the plaintiff decedent to provide her "with safe and reasonable care in a safe environment, as well as services which would help or attain or maintain the highest practicable, physical, mental and psychosocial well being, in accordance with a written care plan." Hospitality contends that this type of language is mere puffery and that Zaborowski's claim is one sounding in tort, rather than contract. The court overrules Hospitality's objection.

Pennsylvania courts have not issued an opinion addressing the issue of whether a nursing home can be held liable to a resident for breach of contract. But, several other jurisdictions have held that a resident can maintain such a cause of action against a nursing home for breach of contract.

This court believes *Callens v. Jefferson County Nursing Home*, 769 So. 2d 273 (Ala. 2000), is persuasive. In *Callens*, the plaintiff brought a breach of contract action against a nursing home for failing to provide a "safe, clean and comfortable environment." *See id.* at 279. The Alabama Supreme Court rejected the nursing home's argument that the plaintiff's claim arises in tort, not in contract, and held that since "the duty to maintain sanitary conditions is expressed in the contract . . . a breach of that duty is actionable in contract." *Id.* at 279-80.

Instantly, Zaborowski has pled the existence of a contract between the plaintiff decedent and Hospitality. The language of the contract, as set forth in the complaint, imposes a duty to provide "safe and reasonable care in a safe environment," as well as "services which would . . . maintain the highest practicable, physical, mental and psychosocial well being." If the complaint is to be believed, Hospitality failed to meet these requirements and therefore breached the contract.

FRAUD

Hospitality, Cassity and Bible filed a preliminary objection in the nature of demurrer to Count IX (fraud) of Zaborowski's complaint. Zaborowski alleges that the defendants are liable for fraud because they made certain representations in a letter addressed to plaintiff decedent in order to induce her to remain a resident of Hospitality, and that the defendants had no intention of fulfilling these representations. Defendants contend that the language contained within the letter is mere puffery. The court sustains the defendants' objection.

* * *

Puffery is "an exaggeration or overstatement expressed in broad, vague and commendatory language." *Castrol Inc. v. Pennzoil Co.*, 987 F.2d 939, 945 (3d Cir. 1993). Such speech is "offered and understood as an expression of the seller's opinion only, which is to be discounted as such by the buyer, and on which no reasonable [person] would rely." W. Page Keeton, Prosser and Keeton on the Law of Torts §109 at 757 (5th ed. 1984). . . .

Instantly, plaintiff relies upon the defendants' representation in the letter that "[a]s always, our priority is to provide quality care and to provide a safe and comfortable environment for our residents." This representation is . . . so indefinite and elusive in meaning that the statement does not constitute a representation, but instead is mere puffery.

BREACH OF FIDUCIARY DUTY

. . . Count VIII alleges that Hospitality, Bible and Cassity breached their fiduciary duties to plaintiff decedent with respect to her care and treatment. Hospitality, Cassity and Bible assert that their relationship with plaintiff decedent was one of caregiver to patient and was not fiduciary in nature. The court overrules the defendants' objection with respect to Hospitality.

* * *

The court concedes, as defendants argue, that fiduciary relationships are most often found in financial dealings; however, the court believes that the relationship between a nursing home and its residents can be fiduciary in nature. This relationship was aptly described in *Schenck v. Living Centers-East Inc.*:

> "[M]any if not most nursing home residents are in a vulnerable physical and/or mental state. Placing a loved one in such a facility necessarily entails trust on the part of the family as well as the resident. Since the residents reside in the home, the family has comparatively limited access and opportunity to learn if the resident is neglected or otherwise mistreated. If entrusting one's money to a receiver or conservator created a business relationship, one would hope at least in principle that entrusting a valued family member to the care of a business entity such as a nursing home would carry similar responsibilities." 917 F. Supp. 432, 438 (E.D. La. 1996).

This court, however, is reluctant to broadly hold that a nursing home resident is always subject to the "overmastering dominance" of the nursing home. Instead, like other courts that have previously addressed this issue, this court holds that the nature of the relationship between the nursing home and its resident must be determined on a case by case basis and the burden of establishing such a relationship rests with the plaintiff.

* * *

Instantly, the court believes that Zaborowski's cause of action for breach of fiduciary duty survives a demurrer. Zaborowski alleged that plaintiff decedent "was entrusted for her care and treatment into the exclusive care, custody, and control of" Hospitality. As a result of this entrustment, a fiduciary duty was formed between plaintiff decedent and Hospitality, which Hospitality subsequently breached by "failing to use the highest standard of care in regard to the care and treatment of [plaintiff decedent]." But, Zaborowski will have the burden of proving that a fiduciary duty existed between the plaintiff decedent and Hospitality at trial. Zaborowski must adduce sufficient evidence showing that the plaintiff decedent was subject to the overmastering dominance of Hospitality or that her weakness, dependence or justifiable trust on Hospitality created a special confidence thereby imposing a fiduciary duty.

UNFAIR TRADE PRACTICES AND CONSUMER PROTECTION LAW

Hospitality, Cassity and Bible filed preliminary objections in the nature of demurrer to Count X (UTPCPL) of Zaborowski's complaint. Zaborowski alleges in ¶78 of his complaint:

> "[t]hat the conduct of defendant Hospitality, Cassity and Bible . . . constitutes an unfair and/or deceptive act or practice prohibited by the [UTPCPL] in any or all of the following respects:
> "(a) In representing that goods and services are of a particular standard, quality or grade or that goods are of a particular style or model if they are of another;

"(b) In failing to comply with the terms of any written guarantee or warranty given to the buyer at, prior to or after contract for the purchase of goods or services is made; and

"(c) In engaging in fraudulent conduct, as set forth in Count IX [fraud], which creates the likelihood of confusion or misunderstanding[.]"

Defendants Hospitality, Cassity and Bible collectively argue that the UTPCPL is inapplicable to the instant matter because the claim is based on statements regarding the medical services plaintiff decedent received while a resident of Hospitality. Cassity and Bible also argue that they cannot be held individually liable under the UTPCPL. The court sustains these objections.

The application of the UTPCPL to nursing homes is an issue of first impression. . . .

Although medical services are not expressly excluded under the UTPCPL, Pennsylvania courts have held that unfair or deceptive acts or practices pertaining to such services does not afford a private cause of action against providers of these services. . . .

Given the courts' interpretation of the UTPCPL, the statute does not create a private cause of action against a nursing home based upon its delivery of medical services. . . . Nursing homes are not one-dimensional business enterprises, but instead they are hybrid organizations, offering both medical and non-medical services. Thus, this court holds that a plaintiff can maintain a private cause of action against a nursing home under the UTPCPL based only upon the non-medical services provided by the nursing home.

Instantly, Zaborowski's complaint fails to differentiate between medical and non-medical services. Consequently, Zaborowski must file an amended complaint alleging that Hospitality's conduct constituting unfair or deceptive acts prohibited by the UTPCPL pertains to non-medical goods and services, and not those that are medical in nature. Zaborowski must also file an amended complaint alleging what unfair or deceptive acts prohibited by the UTPCPL did Cassity and Bible engage in as individuals. If Zaborowski fails to file an amended complaint in accordance with this opinion, then Count X will be stricken. . . .

Riley v. Maison Orleans II, Inc.

829 So. 2d 479 (La. Ct. App. 2002)

MAX N. TOBIAS, Jr., Judge.

Defendants, Maison Orleans II ("Maison Orleans"), and Scottsdale Insurance Company ("Scottsdale"), appeal the judgment of the district court in favor of plaintiffs, Queenester Banks Riley, Fredonia Banks Peters, and Sylvia T. Banks Robinson, individually and jointly on behalf of the estate of Lawrence Banks ("Mr. Banks"), in the amount of $854,729.00. . . .

FACTS

Lawrence Banks was a resident of Maison Orleans, a nursing home in New Orleans, Louisiana. On 16 February 1993 at approximately 4:30 A.M., Joseph Harris attacked Mr. Banks. Mr. Harris, also a resident of Maison Orleans, suffered from organic brain syndrome and was unable to care for himself or his needs. On this particular morning, Mr. Banks was awaiting his morning paper outside of his apartment when Mr. Harris beat him in the head and face with a steel pipe. At trial, Marquitta Patterson, a phlebotomist for Smith Kline Beecham, testified that she saw Mr. Harris hitting Mr. Banks and screamed. At the time of the incident, the attending aids [*sic*] were asleep in the recreational room near the nursing station and a worker from the other side of the building was the first to assist Mr. Banks. . . .

Prior to his admission to Maison Orleans, Mr. Harris was evaluated by Dr. Richard Richoux, an expert in general and forensic psychiatry. Dr. Richoux confirmed that Mr. Harris' history did not indicate violent behavior and he observed no violent or hostile propensities during the evaluation.

Dr. Richoux noted that Harris had "organic brain syndrome," a condition affecting 75-80% of all nursing home residents and "is pretty much synonymous" with dementia. Dr. Richoux testified that there was no reason to anticipate violent or aggressive behavior from Mr. Harris in the near future and he had no basis to believe that Mr. Harris did not belong in the nursing home. The fact that Mr. Harris was known to "preach" to walls and talk to nonexistent people did not indicate violent tendencies in the context of his condition. There was no reason to order restraints or confine Mr. Harris. Dr. Richoux testified that when he examined Mr. Harris, Mr. Harris was taking Ativan and Hydergine.

Dr. Richoux testified that "wandering behavior is sometimes a problem" among those suffering from organic brain syndrome, but Mr. Harris had not been known to wander. Dr. Richoux explained that such individuals do not normally require someone following them around twenty-four hours a day. . . .

When asked by the trial judge whether it would be normal for someone in Mr. Harris' condition to strike someone else with a lead pipe, Dr. Richoux responded:

> No, Your Honor. I would not consider it to be in a normal range. But I would consider it to be very unusual as a manifestation of what I perceive his psychiatric condition to be. It's not something that one expects of a person because they qualify for a diagnosis of Organic Brain Syndrome or Dementia. So, therefore, there's no way to put someone—if I diagnose Organic Brain Syndrome or Dementia I don't usually say either to a nursing home or to a care taker, for that matter, "Now, people with this condition frequently get violent so you better watch out."

Dr. Richoux conceded that had the nursing home placed Mr. Harris under twenty-four hour supervision, the incident might not have occurred. However, Dr. Richoux also explained that twenty-four hour supervision means that the patient should be checked frequently, not that the patient be literally followed around and/or kept under constant surveillance.

Eric Wilmore, the Assistant Administrator who ran the nursing home at the time of the incident, explained that the notation in Mr. Harris records, "Unable to care for self. Needs 24-hour supervision," refers to the basic reason that people are in a nursing home to begin with; it is meant "to ensure that they bathe, that they eat, that their medication is given. . . ."

Mr. Wilmore testified that the nursing home does not have the capacity to lock people down and restrain them. In fact, he noted that La. R.S. 40:2010.8A(10) mandates that nursing home residents be free from physical and chemical restraints with certain very limited exceptions inapplicable to the instant case. He stated that Mr. Harris was an appropriate resident for the nursing home:

> Actually, he was pretty typical of a nursing home patient. He was elderly; he suffered from a certain degree of senility, as a lot of nursing home patients do. He had no history of being violent, being combative or hostile.

Mr. Wilmore testified that Mr. Harris would have been able to get the pipe in the maintenance room and go to where he beat Mr. Banks without being seen by any of the employees even had they been awake. . . .

We note, however, that the record reflects that one of the nursing assistants, Regina Guillory, saw Mr. Harris with the pipe *before* the attack. She asked him for the pipe and he refused to give it up. He then ran though the courtyard and into the lobby where he proceeded to hit Mr. Banks several times in the head. Ms. Guillory claims that Mr. Harris then ran to his room and said, "I got you now, you f——er." Mr. Banks sustained numerous head injuries, lacerations, and fractures and underwent surgery in relation to the beating. Mr. Banks later died on 20 April 1993 of a heart attack.

PROCEDURAL HISTORY

On 30 August 1993, the plaintiffs filed suit against Maison Orleans, and its insurer, Scottsdale, asserting a survival action, wrongful death claim, negligence claim, and a claim for insurance coverage. An excess insurer, United National Insurance Company, was later added as a defendant. Both insurance companies filed motions for summary judgment asserting policy exclusions for "sexual and physical abuse." United National Insurance Company was dismissed from the suit and Scottsdale's motion was granted in part.

On 24 May 2000, the jury was dismissed after they were observed talking and passing notes. The matter continued as a bench trial. A final judgment was rendered in favor of the plaintiffs and against Maison Orleans and Scottsdale on the survival and negligence claims. . . .

In its reasons for judgment, the trial court stated:

> The harm encountered by Banks falls within the scope of protection afforded by Maison's duty which was breached by its negligence. Here, Maison had a duty to provide supervision of its residents at or about the time of the incident. Defendants do not refute this fact nor do they refute that their on duty staff members were asleep during the time of the incident. Furthermore, the availability of the steel pipe to Harris created an unreasonable risk of harm to Banks. As a result, it is reasonable to conclude that the risks and degree of harm suffered by Banks were not the result of his own actions and could have been significantly reduced if the defendant's staff members had been available.

. . . Maison Orleans' motion . . . appeals the judgment of the district court on the issues of liability and damages. Scottsdale moved for a new trial or, in the alternative, to modify the judgment, both of which were denied. . . .

DUTY-RISK ANALYSIS

In its first assignment of error, Maison Orleans argues that it did not breach the standard of care imposed on nursing homes, which is of reasonable care considering the patient's mental and physical condition. It further contends that it did not have a duty to furnish a nurse or attendant to supervise Mr. Harris at all times.

* * *

We agree with Maison Orleans's claim that the admission of Mr. Harris into the nursing home did not violate its standard of care. Dr. Richoux testified that that there was nothing in Mr. Harris' presentation to indicate that Maison Orleans would not be an appropriate facility for him. On the other hand, Mr. Banks and his family also expected some reasonable amount of protection for Mr. Banks while in the facility.

We disagree, however, that Maison Orleans' twenty-four hour supervision of Mr. Harris was proper and that sleeping aides in the recreational room that morning was not a direct cause of Mr. Banks' injuries. The uncontroverted evidence indicates that Mr. Harris should have been checked at least every two hours. Even Dr. Richoux testified that had the nursing home had Mr. Harris under twenty-four hour supervision, the accident might not have happened. In addition, had even one aide been awake and on the floor that morning, Ms. Guillory could have sought immediate help when she observed Mr. Harris with the pipe before the attack. Thus, we find that the obvious lack of supervision contributed to Mr. Banks' injuries. Further, had the aides not been asleep, it is reasonable to assume that Mr. Banks would have been afforded more protection at the time of the incident.

Mr. Harris was also a cause-in-fact of the injuries suffered by Mr. Banks. Mr. Harris and Mr. Banks were both under the custody and care of Maison Orleans, which had a duty to protect Mr. Banks against the attack upon him. We find that Maison Orleans breached its duty because Mr. Harris was able to retrieve a pipe from the premises and attack Mr. Banks while the attending aides were asleep. Thus, we agree with the trial court's imposition of liability upon Maison Orleans. This assignment of error lacks merit.

* * *

BYRNES, C.J., Concurring in part and dissenting in part.

... [A]s I find that there is no liability on the part of Maison Orleans II, Inc., I respectfully dissent from the balance of the majority opinion.

The Maison Orleans is not an insurer of Mr. Banks' safety. A nursing home has no duty to furnish a nurse or attendant at all times.

The trial court found that, "the availability of the steel pipe to Harris created an unreasonable risk of harm to Banks." However, it is not as though the steel pipe had been dropped carelessly in the hall outside of Harris' door. Mr. Wilmore testified that the pipe was used to prop open the door to a maintenance shed behind the kitchen, accessible only from the outside. Heavy door-stops are quite common. Harris could have struck Banks with any number of other objects that would have been reasonably available. Unlike a gun or a knife, the pipe was not intrinsically dangerous. It was only dangerous in the manner in which it was used. Even a bedpan, a hard-bound book, a telephone or any number of other common items readily available to nursing home residents could have been used by Mr. Harris to strike Mr. Banks.

* * *

As matter of law Mr. Harris had the right to privacy in his room and the right to retain personal possessions. In other words, Mr. Harris was entitled to have legal access to any number of objects, which could inflict bodily harm if wielded with the intention to do so. There are any number of conceivable and permissible personal possessions that could be used to strike another resident, for example, hardbound books, paper weights, mugs, clocks and telephones, just to name a few. In fact, there is an express statutory right to phone access. Mr. Harris[] was not an inmate, he was a resident. He was not interdicted or confined. *In other words, it was Mr. Harris' decision, however poorly arrived at, to cause harm and not the lead pipe that was the legal cause of Mr. Banks' injuries, because had he not had access to the lead pipe he would have had access to any number of other items. The lead pipe was not intrinsically dangerous, e.g., it was not a gun, poison, or highly combustible.*

* * *

The majority states that: "[H]ad even one aide been awake and on the floor that morning, Ms. Guillory could have sought immediate help when she observed Mr. Harris with the pipe before the attack." The record does not support this contention. ...

Everything in the record indicates that the incident happened so quickly that there is no reason to believe that had the employees been awake that they could have reacted and gotten down the 75 foot hall in time to prevent Joseph Harris from striking Mr. Banks.

The majority states that: "The uncontroverted evidence indicates that Mr. Harris should have been checked every two hours." Mr. Wilmore testified that being a nursing home operator did not give him the right to restrain Mr. Harris to his room or to lock him in his room. Mr. Harris had the right to be up and walk around the nursing home before 5:00 a.m. if he wished to do so. Remember, Mr. Banks was also up and about before 5:00 a.m. that same morning and no one suggests that this called for any special supervision. Had someone noticed Mr. Harris up at that hour they would have had no duty to follow him around, and to do so without reason would arguably be an intrusion on his rights to privacy. *No one patrols the halls and there is no evidence that the standard of care would require such patrols.* Mr. Harris was not interdicted and he was not a prisoner stripped of certain rights. *He was not in the custody of the nursing home and was free to leave whenever he wished. . . . To suggest liability under that article would exceed any case in the existing jurisprudence and would almost certainly add ruinous insurance costs to nursing home care which would be very bad policy in our aging society.* He was only a resident, not an inmate of a prison or a psychiatric facility. For Mr. Harris the nursing home was merely an apartment house or rooming house with a high level of service. . . .

[An additional opinion concurring in part and dissenting in part has been omitted.—ED.]

NOTE

Liability for elder abuse. Some states have adopted statutes that allow nursing homes to be held civilly liable specifically for elder abuse and neglect. Whether or not a nursing home can be held liable under such an act, however, may depend on whether the claim is characterized as medical malpractice. For example, in *Delany v. Baker*, 971 P.2d 98 (Cal. 1999), the California Supreme Court considered the application of the state's Elder Abuse Act to a claim involving nursing home neglect. The case involved an 88-year-old woman who died after developing multiple Stage III and IV bedsores as a result of frequently being "left lying in her own urine and feces for extended periods of time." The court found that the neglect was "the result, in part, of rapid turnover of nursing staff, staffing shortages, and the inadequate training of employees." At issue in the case was whether a nursing home that engaged in "reckless neglect" of a resident could be held liable for heightened penalties under the state's Elder Abuse Act, as the jury had determined the home should be, or whether such remedies were unavailable because the claim fell into the statute's exception for claims based on "professional negligence." In upholding a jury's finding that the nursing home was liable under the state's Elder Abuse Act, the court chose to narrowly interpret the phrase "based on professional negligence" in order to "enhance . . . the statute's remedial purpose [of] protecting elder and dependent adults who are residents of nursing homes and other health care facilities from reckless neglect and various forms of abuse" and to "avoid the anomaly of having health care professionals exempted from [the] heightened remedies for the very same misconduct for which nonprofessionals would be liable."

QUESTIONS

1. What should a plaintiff's attorney take into consideration when deciding whether to bring litigation against a nursing home that the attorney believes is responsible for preventable harm to the attorney's client? If the attorney pursues litigation, what considerations should shape which type of claim or claims the attorney brings on behalf of the client?

2. What should Maison Orleans have done to avoid Mr. Banks's injury? Do you believe that this was required by law?

3. Would you agree with Chief Judge Byrnes's characterization of a nursing home as being, from the resident's point of view, "merely an apartment house or rooming house with a high level of service"? What role does this characterization play in his opinion in *Riley*?

PROBLEMS

1. In a problem in Section C.3.a of this chapter (see page 391), you were asked about Mr. Walters, who has dementia and congestive heart failure and who was admitted to Harbor House Nursing Home after he shattered his hip in a fall at his home. The fall left him weak and unable to safely walk without supervision. Since he was admitted to Harbor House Nursing Home, his health has deteriorated dramatically. He has become incontinent of bowel and bladder, has grown increasingly withdrawn, and has become almost entirely bed-bound. Suppose Mr. Walter's family chose Harbor House nursing home because it advertised that it provided "high quality, individualized care for your loved one" and its brochures announced to prospective residents that "we do our best so you can be your best." Mr. Walter dies as a result of pneumonia, which his family claims was brought on by his weakened state. If his estate sues Harbor House, what legal claims might they bring? What would be the legal basis for those claims?

2. Plaintiff alleges that her mother, a resident of defendant's nursing home who suffered from physical and mental problems, died as a result of the nursing home's negligence. Specifically, plaintiff alleges that while attempting to light a cigarette in the nursing home's designated smoking area, her mother caught her nightgown on fire and suffered serious burns that ultimately caused her death. Plaintiff alleges that the nursing home was inadequately staffed, and that the injury could have been prevented if her mother had been adequately observed and supervised while smoking.

   a. Does plaintiff have a viable wrongful death claim against the nursing home? *See Taylor v. Vencor, Inc.*, 525 S.E.2d 201 (N.C. Ct. App. 2000) (holding that the trial court erred in granting defendant's motion to dismiss on these facts).

b. What should a nursing home do to avoid liability for such injuries? Can it ban smoking by residents?

d. The Impact and Enforceability of Mandatory Arbitration Clauses

Today, many nursing home contracts include clauses stating that if a dispute arises between the resident and the facility, it will be resolved through *arbitration*, a private process in which a neutral third party adjudicates in lieu of a judge. Such clauses are advantageous to nursing homes for several reasons, including that arbitration is typically confidential (thus reducing the risk of negative publicity) and, compared to court-based adjudication, is typically a less expensive process, involves a truncated discovery process, and is perceived as resulting in lower damage awards.

For much the same reasons, plaintiffs' attorneys often wish to avoid arbitration. In doing so, however, they run up against the Federal Arbitration Act (FAA), which establishes a public policy in favor of arbitration. Thus, in *Marmet Health Care Center v. Brown*, 132 S. Ct. 1201 (2012), the Supreme Court vacated a decision of the Supreme Court of Appeals of West Virginia that had held that all pre-dispute arbitration agreements that apply to claims alleging personal injury or wrongful death against nursing homes in West Virginia were unenforceable on public policy grounds. In so doing, the Court rejected the state court's reasoning that the FAA does not preempt state public policies against such agreements. The U.S. Supreme Court explained that the FAA does not contain any "exception for personal-injury or wrongful-death claims," but rather represents an "'emphatic federal policy'" in favor of arbitration; therefore, West Virginia was not free to refuse to enforce arbitration agreements based on the "categorical rule" the state court had adopted.

Accordingly, courts typically enforce binding arbitration agreements in nursing home contracts even if they are entered into before any dispute has arisen. The next two cases explore the conditions under which an exception to this general policy will be made.

Broughsville v. OHECC, LLC

2005 WL 3483777 (Ohio App. 9th Dist. 2005)

WHITMORE, Judge.

This cause was heard upon the record in the trial court. Each error assigned has been reviewed and the following disposition is made:

Plaintiff-Appellant Dovie Broughsville has appealed the decision of the Lorain County Court of Common Pleas granting the application of Defendant-Appellee OHECC, L.L.C., dba Ohio Extended Care Center ("OHECC") to stay trial pending results of arbitration. This Court affirms.

I.

On September 9, 2004, Appellant filed a complaint for negligence in the Lorain County Court of Common Pleas, alleging that Appellant sustained serious personal injury while in the exclusive care of OHECC, a nursing home/long term care facility located in Lorain, Ohio. The alleged injury occurred on September 11, 2003 while Appellant was a respite care resident of OHECC. OHECC answered Appellant's complaint on October 26, 2004. That same day, OHECC filed an application to stay trial pending results of arbitration pursuant to an arbitration provision found in the facility's admission agreement (the "Agreement").

On November 15, 2004, Appellant filed a brief in opposition to OHECC's application to stay trial pending results of arbitration. The brief argued that the arbitration provision contained in the Agreement was unenforceable and that the trial court must deny OHECC's application. On December 6, 2004, OHECC filed a reply to Appellant's brief in opposition to the application to stay trial pending results of arbitration. In its March 1, 2005 journal entry, the Lorain County Court of Common Pleas found the arbitration provision not to be unconscionable and granted OHECC's application to stay trial pending results of arbitration.

Appellant timely appealed, asserting one assignment of error.

II. ASSIGNMENT OF ERROR NUMBER ONE "THE TRIAL COURT ERRED IN GRANTING APPELLEE'S APPLICATION TO STAY TRIAL PENDING RESULTS OF ARBITRATION."

In her sole assignment of error, Appellant has argued that the Lorain County Court of Common Pleas' decision to grant OHECC's application to stay trial pending results of arbitration was in error. Specifically, Appellant has argued that the arbitration provision in the Agreement is unconscionable, that Appellant is not a signatory to the Agreement, . . . and that federal regulations preclude inclusion of arbitration provisions in admission agreements. We disagree with Appellant's contentions.

Apparent Authority

The first issue we must review is whether Appellant's daughter, Odarise McCall Wheeler ("Wheeler"), had the authority to bind Appellant to arbitration, effectively waiving her right to a jury trial. Appellant has argued that because Wheeler signed the Agreement, and because Appellant allegedly never gave her authority to sign an arbitration provision, that the arbitration provision is unenforceable as against her. We disagree.

In support of her argument that Wheeler did not have the authority to enter into an arbitration provision and waive the right to a jury trial, Appellant has relied solely on Wheeler's affidavit, in which she avers that Appellant "never provided [Wheeler] with the authority to agree to submit any claim for injury to arbitration and to waive the right to a jury trial." Even setting aside the arguably self-serving nature of this statement, the question is not whether Wheeler had *actual* authority to bind Appellant to arbitration, but whether she had apparent authority to do so.

... The present case is a classic example of apparent authority. Wheeler, by signing the Agreement on behalf of her mother, acted in such a way that a reasonable person could believe that that she had the necessary authority to make the contract. Regardless of actual authority, circumstances were such at the time of the signing that Wheeler's conduct could be interpreted as authority to enter into an agreement on Appellant's behalf.

To demonstrate apparent agency, the facts must establish "(1) That the principal held the agent out to the public as possessing sufficient authority to embrace the particular act in question, or knowingly permitted him to act as having such authority, and (2) that the person dealing with the agent knew of the facts and acting in good faith had reason to believe and did believe that the agent possessed the necessary authority." When determining the apparent power of an agent, we must scrutinize the conduct of the principal, not the actions of the agent.

In the instant matter, we think it clear that while Appellant may not have held Wheeler out to the public as her agent, she knowingly permitted her to act as having such authority by signing Appellant's name to the Agreement. Appellant was present at the signing of the Agreement and made no attempt to stop Wheeler, to ask questions of OHECC or to request to read the document. While it is averred that Appellant suffers from mild dementia, nowhere is it argued that she was incompetent at the time of the signing or was unable to vocalize an objection to Wheeler's actions. In fact, the only reason cited for Wheeler's intervention was that Appellant was suffering from contractures.

Furthermore, upon reviewing the record, we find it equally clear that OHECC, acting in good faith, had reason to believe that Wheeler possessed the authority to admit Appellant into the residence and to sign the Agreement. Arguably, OHECC knew of the relationship between Appellant and Wheeler, having provided respite care for them in the past. Additionally, Wheeler, by signing the document in the presence of Appellant and whereas Appellant acquiesced to such conduct, gave OHECC reason to believe that Wheeler acted under Appellant's authority.

The cases cited by Appellant to support her argument are inapposite. In *Pagarigan v. Libby Care Center, Inc.* (2002), 99 Cal. App. 4th 298, 120 Cal. Rptr. 2d 892, the resident lacked the mental competence to authorize her daughters to enter in an arbitration agreement at the time of admission. In *Phillips v. Crofton Manor Inn* (May 15, 2003), Cal. App. 2nd Dist., 2003 WL 21101478, the court held that although the daughter claimed to be father's representative, such a claim by daughter did not authorize her to sign an arbitration agreement on his behalf. Once again, at all times relevant to the case, the resident was incompetent and unable to authorize their representative to enter into an arbitration agreement. In both of these cases, due to incompetence, the residents could not explicitly authorize, hold out, or knowingly permit the agent to act in such a way, in satisfaction of element one of the doctrine of apparent authority.

While Appellant allegedly suffers from mild dementia which causes "periods of confusion," Appellant has not argued and nowhere in the record is it indicated that Appellant was incompetent at the time of admission or that she was suffering a period of confusion. To the contrary, Wheeler's affidavit clearly states that contractures, not dementia, was the reason she signed Appellant's name to the Agreement. Contractures is a physical ailment and there is no indication in the record that Appellant was unable to think lucidly, to understand the Agreement, to ask questions or to object to Wheeler's signing her name. Therefore, we find that Wheeler had the apparent authority to sign the Agreement and bind Appellant to the arbitration provision therein.

Unconscionability

Having resolved the question of whether Appellant is bound to the Agreement, we must next address the issue of unconscionability. Appellant contends that the arbitration provision in the Agreement is unenforceable as it is procedurally and substantively unconscionable. We disagree.

Generally, we review a trial court's disposition of a motion to stay trial pending arbitration under an abuse of discretion standard. However, the unconscionability of a contract and its provisions is purely a question of law. Therefore, we review the trial court's determination of unconscionability de novo. . . .

Initially we note that public policy in Ohio favors arbitration as a means to settle disputes. Accordingly, arbitration provisions are generally valid and enforceable. . . . In fact, when examining an arbitration clause, a court must "bear in mind the strong presumption in favor of arbitrability and resolve all doubts in favor of arbitrability." However, an arbitration provision may be held unenforceable under the statute on "grounds that exist at law or in equity for the revocation of any contract." One of those grounds is unconscionability. A party seeking to invalidate an arbitration clause on grounds of unconscionability must establish that the provision is both procedurally and substantively unconscionable.

Procedural unconscionability concerns the "formation of the agreement and occurs when no voluntary meeting of the minds is possible." This Court has held that when determining procedural unconscionability, a reviewing court must consider factors bearing directly to the relative bargaining position of the parties. Such factors include "'age, education, intelligence, business acumen, experience in similar transactions, whether terms were explained to the weaker party, and who drafted the contract.'" Substantive unconscionability goes to the terms of contract themselves. Contractual terms are substantively unconscionable if they are unfair and commercially unreasonable.

Having reviewed the applicable law, we turn our attention to the arbitration provision at issue and the circumstances surrounding Appellant's signing of it.

Procedural Unconscionability

Appellant has argued that the arbitration provision included in the Agreement is procedurally unconscionable and thereby unenforceable.

In reviewing the surrounding circumstances, we find that no procedural unconscionability existed at the time Appellant entered into the arbitration provision. While it is evident that Appellant was not on equal footing with OHECC in terms of bargaining power, mere inequality of bargaining power is not a sufficient reason to hold an arbitration provision unenforceable. . . .

In the instant case, Appellant was in a sound bargaining position. She was being admitted by her daughter voluntarily and of her own free will, for respite care. There was no apparent emergency or need for an expeditious admission. The record does not indicate there was any pressure exerted on Appellant, nor was haste imposed in reviewing and signing the Agreement. Furthermore, while Appellant was 85 years old at the time of the signing, the record does not indicate that she was suffering from dementia or confusion at the time and nowhere has Appellant averred that she was incompetent. Wheeler, who presumably read and signed the Agreement on Appellant's behalf, was competent, 54 years old, college educated and a registered nurse.

Furthermore, the arbitration provision was written in plain language and is in the same sized font as the rest of the Agreement. While the provision does appear on pages 12 and 13 of the Agreement, it is, contrary to Appellant's assertions, set out with a bold, capitalized heading "Resolution of Disputes." Additionally, the provision is divided into four categories, each with a bold and underlined descriptive title. Paragraph 2 clearly states that any dispute arising between the parties based on an alleged violation of a resident's rights shall be settled by binding arbitration as set forth in Paragraph 4. Appellant has argued that the term "arbitration" was foreign to her, and that may be the case, but nothing in the record indicates that Appellant or Wheeler were discouraged from asking questions concerning the terms of the Agreement or harried in any way.

Appellant also contends that the fact that she was not represented by an attorney should necessitate a finding of procedural unconscionability. We disagree. While having an attorney present is a factor to be considered, it is in no way dispositive of the issue. We think it common sense that most people do not hire lawyers to accompany them every time they are required to sign a form contract. Similarly, the fact that Appellant and Wheeler lacked particularized legal training has little bearing on our decision, as a vast majority of the population lack legal training, yet remain bound to contracts that they have signed. The record also reflects that Appellant had been admitted to the facility on a previous occasion and had signed an admissions agreement with an identical arbitration provision. Such experience with similar transactions tends to disfavor a finding of unconscionability.

Finally, the arbitration provision clearly states that the resident's agreement to arbitrate disputes is not a condition of admission. Appellant has argued that this clause is purely a pretext—that the Agreement provided no mechanism for rejecting the arbitration provision and therefore, the arbitration clause was presented on a take it or leave it basis. This argument is unpersuasive. An unconscionable contract is "one in which there is an absence of meaningful choice for the contracting parties[.]" Here, Appellant, through her agent, did not lack the opportunity to choose. As discussed *supra*, there was no emergency and Appellant could have chosen to forego signing the Agreement and found respite care with another facility. Furthermore, Appellant could have asserted her power as a paying customer and demanded removal of the arbitration provision in exchange for her business. Instead, she chose to sign the Agreement, not once, but on two separate occasions. Appellant did not lack meaningful choice.

Based on the foregoing, we find that the arbitration provision at issue was not procedurally unconscionable.

Substantive Unconscionability

... As Appellant has failed to show the existence of procedural unconscionability, this Court declines to address the issue of substantive unconscionability.

* * *

Federal Law Prohibits Arbitration Provisions

Appellant has argued that federal laws and regulations prohibit the inclusion of arbitration provisions in admission agreements. Specifically, Appellant has argued that nursing home admission contracts containing arbitration provisions constitute unauthorized additional consideration from the resident. Appellant has argued that by requiring a resident to waive a right to a jury trial in order to be admitted, the facility is garnering additional consideration that is impermissible under federal medical assistance programs. *See* 42 U.S.C. §1396r(c)(5)(A)(iii); 42 C.F.R. §483.12(d)(3).

We begin by reiterating that OHECC in no way required Appellant to waive her right to a jury trial in order to be admitted to the facility. The provision clearly stated that admission was not contingent upon agreement to arbitrate disputes. There is no evidence that OHECC would have denied admission to Appellant had she refused to agree to the arbitration provision. The primary reason for this lack of evidence is that at no time did Appellant refuse to agree to the arbitration provision, nor did she inquire as to the consequences of declining to arbitrate.

Furthermore, Appellant has cited no authority supporting her argument that agreeing to arbitration constitutes additional consideration in violation of federal law. We think that such a contention is problematic and we align with other jurisdictions in expressly rejecting the argument. In *Gainesville Health Care Center, Inc. v. Weston* (2003), 857 So. 2d 278, the First District Court of Appeal of Florida held that "[w]e have found no authority from any jurisdiction which holds that an arbitration provision constitutes 'consideration' in this sense; nor do we believe that the federal regulation was intended to apply to such a situation." *Id.* at 288. The Supreme Court of Alabama has followed a similar tact, holding that:

> "[R]equiring a nursing-home admittee to sign an arbitration agreement is not charging an additional fee or other consideration as a requirement to admittance. Rather, an arbitration agreement sets a forum for future

disputes; both parties are bound to it and both receive whatever benefits and detriments accompany the arbitral forum."

Owens v. Coosa Valley Health Care, Inc. (2004), 890 So. 2d 983, 989.

Based on the foregoing, we conclude that the inclusion of an arbitration provision in a nursing home admissions agreement does not constitute additional consideration and therefore is not precluded by 42 U.S.C. §1396r(c)(5)(A)(iii) nor 42 C.F.R. §483.12(d)(3).

* * *

III.

Appellant's sole assignment of error is overruled. The judgment of the trial court is affirmed. . . .

Howell v. NHC Healthcare-Fort Sanders, Inc.

109 S.W.3d 731 (Tenn. Ct. App. 2003)

OPINION

The Trial Court refused to enforce an Agreement for Mediation and Arbitration. On appeal, we [a]ffirm.

Defendants' Motion to Compel Mediation and Arbitration pursuant to Tenn. Code Ann. §29-5-303, was overruled by the Trial Court. We granted an interlocutory appeal, pursuant to Rule 9, Tenn. R. App. P.

This action was filed by the executor of the Estate of Orangie Howell, who died while residing in the NHC-Ft. Sanders Nursing Home in Knoxville. The Complaint charges the nursing home with abuse and neglect, and infliction of physical suffering and mental anguish upon the deceased, *inter alia*.

The defendants insist the admitting agreement signed by the deceased's husband is enforceable, and requires that these claims are subject to mediation and arbitration, because the agreement so provides.

The Trial Court conducted an evidentiary hearing on the Motion, and Paula Larkins, who presented the admitting contract to Howell, testified that the contract signed by Howell was the only one used by the nursing home at the time, and that a patient or their legal representative was required to sign the contract before being admitted to the facility. She testified that she remembered meeting with Howell and one or both of his daughters, and that she did not read the contract verbatim, but paraphrased it to Howell. She did not ask Howell to read the agreement, and she did not ask him if he could read.

Larkins testified that she explained the dispute resolution procedure to Howell, and that she explained that the arbitration was binding. She did testify that she did not explain to Howell that by signing the contract, he was giving up his wife's right to a jury trial. She further testified that Ms. Howell was too sick to return home from the hospital, and Mr. Howell had to sign the contract in order to have Ms. Howell admitted to the nursing home. Howell's daughter, Constance Davis testified that she accompanied her father to the nursing home, that her father could not read or write, but that it was his decision to make and she and her sister just accompanied him for support and that she understood that the papers had to be signed before her mother could be admitted to the nursing home.

Howell's other daughter testified that she also accompanied her father to the nursing home, and that the nursing home representative went through the paperwork and explained each page to her father. She testified that she did not see the papers and that she did not remember hearing the words "arbitration," "mediation," or "dispute resolution."

Howell testified that he was employed as a roofer for many years, and that he was now retired due to stomach cancer, that he was unable to read or write, but that he could sign his name. He testified that lady at the nursing home "pushed" the documents in front of him and asked him to sign them, and that she did not explain them. He testified that his daughters were there with him, but that they did not look at the document. He testified that he never asked what was in the document, he just knew that he was supposed to be signing a contract to get his wife in the nursing home, and he did not remember the lady at the nursing home telling him to come to her if he had any problems or concerns, and he did not remember anyone using the term "arbitration."

Howell testified he had never heard of arbitration, did not know what it was, and that it was not explained to him. He testified that the nursing home's representative never told him he was waiving his wife's right to a jury trial.

The Trial Court found that Ms. Larkins tried to explain the contract to Mr. Howell, but that she testified that she never explained to him that by signing the contract he was giving up his right or his wife's estate's right to a jury trial. The Trial Court found that the situation was sort of an emergency, or at least something that had to be done, and that the agreement was not enforceable against Mr. Howell. The Court then entered the Order denying defendants' Motion to arbitrate.

Appellants argue that the Trial Court erred in failing to compel arbitration based upon the arbitration clause contained in the admission agreement. The Trial Court ruled that the arbitration provision was not enforceable, based upon the following findings:

1) Mrs. Howell needed the care of a nursing home,

2) Mr. Howell and his daughters went to the NHC nursing home and were presented with the admission agreement,

3) The agreement provides for exclusive resolution of disputes by arbitration and mediation,

4) Mr. Howell is unable to read or write, and one would suspect this in talking to him,

5) The nursing home representative chose to explain the agreement to Mr. Howell rather than handing it to him to read for himself,

6) The nursing home representative said she explained mediation and arbitration, but said she never explained that he was giving up his right to jury trial,

7) Mr. Howell had to sign the agreement to have his wife admitted to the nursing home.

Tennessee has adopted the Uniform Arbitration Act, which provides in part:

> A written agreement to submit any existing controversy to arbitration or a provision in a written contract to submit to arbitration any controversy thereafter arising between the parties is valid, enforceable and irrevocable save upon such grounds as exist at law or in equity for the revocation of any contract;

... Tenn. Code Ann. §29-5-302; *see Buraczynski v. Eyring*, 919 S.W.2d 314 (Tenn. 1996).

This provision is substantially the same as that contained in the Federal Arbitration Act, codified at 9 U.S.C. §2. Since there is no dispute that this provision is in the contract which provides that the parties must submit to arbitration, the issue thus becomes whether any grounds exist which would require revocation. Further, while courts are required to give an arbitration agreement "as broad a construction as the words and intentions of the parties will allow", this applies to the scope of the agreement, and not whether grounds exist to deny enforceability of the agreement. . . .

Appellee argues that the Agreement is not enforceable because it was not signed by the decedent and that Mr. Howell was not authorized to sign an agreement waiving her rights. Appellees raise another interesting argument that a portion of the medicare/medicaid statute dealing with nursing homes, codified at 42 U.S.C. §1396r(c)(5)(A)(ii), specifically prohibits a nursing home from accepting any additional consideration from a medicare/medicaid patient aside from the standard rate paid by medicare/medicaid, and argue that our case law provides that an arbitration agreement or, indeed, any type of agreement must have consideration to be enforceable and that mutuality of promises can be a sufficient consideration for the same. Thus, the argument goes that if mutual promises to submit to arbitration are consideration for the agreement, then the agreement would run afoul of the federal statute.

While these arguments are not without appeal, we pretermit consideration because we believe the dispositive issue is set forth in the Trial Court's findings.

In *Buraczynski*, the Supreme Court addressed the issue of the enforceability of an arbitration agreement between a patient and doctor, and discussed the factors which should be analyzed in dealing with this issue. The Court said the agreement in that case was a contract of adhesion because it was offered to the patient on a "take it or leave it" basis, and because the doctor was in a position of greater bargaining power. The Court noted, however, that while contracts of adhesion are not favored, the simple fact that the contract was one of adhesion does not necessarily render it unenforceable. The Court then observed that enforceability "generally depends upon whether the terms of the contract are beyond the reasonable expectations of an ordinary person, or oppressive or unconscionable."

* * *

[*Buraczynski* and other Tennessee cases] support the Trial Court's determination that the arbitration clause should not be enforced under the circumstances. The Agreement is eleven pages long, and the arbitration provision is on page ten. Rather than being a stand-alone document, it is "buried" within the larger document. It is written in the same size font as the rest of the agreement, and the arbitration paragraph does not adequately explain how the arbitration procedure would work, except as who would administer it.

The facts surrounding the execution of the agreement militate against enforcement. The Trial Court found Ms. Howell had to be placed in a nursing home expeditiously, and that the admission agreement had to be signed before this could be accomplished. The agreement was presented to Mr. Howell on a "take-it-or-leave-it" basis. Moreover, Mr. Howell had no real bargaining power. Howell's educational limitations were obvious, and the agreement was not adequately explained regarding the jury trial waiver.

The fact that Howell cannot read does not excuse him from a contract he voluntarily signed. . . . But the circumstances here demonstrate that Larkin took it upon herself to explain the contract, rather than asking him to read it, and that her explanation did not mention, much less explain, that he was waiving a right to a jury trial if a claim was brought against the nursing home. As we have observed, the defendant who is seeking to enforce the arbitration provision has the burden of showing the parties "actually bargained over the arbitration provision or that it was a reasonable term considering the circumstances." *Brown [v. Karemor International Inc.,* 1999 WL 221799 (Tenn. Ct. App. 1999)]. Given the circumstances surrounding the execution of this agreement, and the terms of the agreement itself, appellant has not demonstrated that the parties bargained over the arbitration terms, or that it was within the reasonable expectations of an ordinary person.

We affirm the Judgment of the Trial Court and remand, with the cost of the appeal assessed to NHC Healthcare-Fort Sanders, Inc.

NOTES

1. *Approaches to avoiding arbitration.* In addition to arguing unconscionability, plaintiffs may seek to avoid arbitration by arguing that the arbitration agreement was not properly signed or was not signed by a person with sufficient authority to bind the resident, that the agreement does not apply to the claims being brought (e.g., claims by the resident's relatives or estate), that the agreement unlawfully limits statutory remedies otherwise available to the plaintiff, or that it otherwise contravenes state law. For example, in *Blankfeld v. Richmond Health Care Inc.,* 902 So. 2d 296 (Fla. Dist. Ct. App. 2005), the court held that the trial court erred by compelling arbitration in a case alleging that a nursing home had negligently cared for the plaintiff. The court held the arbitration procedure was void as a matter of public policy because it limited the remedies available to injured parties under Florida's Nursing Home Residents Act. Specifically, the offending clause required arbitration by an organization that barred its arbitrators from awarding certain types of damages absent "clear and convincing evidence" whereas the state Act used a "preponderance of

the evidence" standard. In addition, the court held that the arbitration clause was unenforceable because it had been agreed by the resident's health care agent (not the resident), and Florida law does not authorize agents acting pursuant to health care proxies to enter into binding arbitration agreements on behalf of patients.

2. *Critiques of mandatory arbitration.* The use of pre-dispute binding arbitration contracts in the long-term care context has come under significant criticism in the legal literature. *See, e.g.,* Lisa Tripp, *A Senior Moment: The Executive Branch Solution to the Problem of Binding Arbitration Agreements in Nursing Home Admission Contracts,* 31 CAMPBELL L. REV. 157 (2009) (arguing that that pre-dispute binding arbitration agreements in nursing home contracts should be considered unconscionable and that nursing homes receiving federal funding should be prohibited from using them).

3. *Arbitration clauses as part of a larger strategy.* The use of arbitration clauses in nursing home contracts can be seen as part of a broader effort on the part of nursing home operators to reduce litigation costs. In his book *Litigating the Nursing Home Case,* James O'Reilly describes the use of mandatory arbitration as one of four legal strategies the for-profit nursing home industry is advancing to control the costs associated with nursing home litigation. The three others he identifies are: (1) lobbying state legislatures to impose limits (or "caps") on damage awards; (2) creating a "web" of corporate entities designed to shield corporate profits from large damage awards; and (3) making the cost of bringing a nursing home lawsuit prohibitively expensive for many plaintiffs and their attorneys (e.g., by engaging in extensive discovery processes). *See* JAMES T. O'REILLY, LITIGATING THE NURSING HOME CASE 7 (2009).

QUESTIONS

1. Is *Howell* consistent with *Broughsville*?

2. Would you advise a client to sign a nursing home contract that contained a mandatory arbitration clause? Why or why not?

3. California prohibits nursing homes from: (1) presenting an arbitration agreement as part of the Standard Admission Agreement; or (2) requiring residents or their representatives to sign an arbitration agreement or any other document as a condition of admission or continued stay. In California, moreover, the top of any arbitration agreement must contain a prominent, bold-faced advisory alerting residents that they "shall not be required to sign this arbitration agreement as a condition of admission." CAL. CODE CIV. PROC. §1281.96.

   Is this law enforceable after the U.S. Supreme Court's decision in *Marmet,* discussed on page 425?

e. Summary Problem

Your client, Frank Williams, has decided to move to a nursing home on his doctor's advice. After visiting several homes with Dana, his daughter and health care agent, he selected Sunny Acres Nursing Home, a nearby facility with a reputation for having unusually good food. After a brief introduction and tour of the nursing home, the nursing home administrator offered Mr. Williams the below Admissions Agreement to sign. She explained that Mr. Williams's signature on the agreement is a condition of admission, and encouraged him to read it carefully and to ask any questions he may have. Although she was taken aback by the request to do so, she allowed Mr. Williams to take it with him to "read over" at home. He instead brought it directly to you. It reads as follows:

Admission Agreement

In consideration of Frank Williams (hereinafter "Patient") being admitted to Sunny Acres Nursing Home (hereinafter "Sunny Acres"), it is agreed as follows:

1. Patient and Sunny Acres agree that Sunny Acres and its agents shall be the exclusive providers of health care to Patient.

2. Patient and Sunny Acres agree that all medical and other records created or maintained by Sunny Acres and relating to Patient will be kept strictly confidential and will not be disclosed to any other individuals or entities at any time unless disclosure is required by a law enforcement entity.

3. Sunny Acres shall have the right to discharge the Patient if Patient is delinquent in paying monthly charges, violates the rules of patient conduct, or upon 60 days' written notice given by Sunny Acres.

4. Patient understands that Sunny Acres cannot guarantee his safety and well-being and that patient must take responsibility for his own actions. Patient further understands that a nursing home is a communal living setting and that this means that the interests of the group will be given priority over individual preferences.

5. Any disputes arising from the care of Patient or this agreement shall be subject to binding arbitration in accordance with the rules and procedures of the National Health Care Attorney Advocates' Association (NHCAAA).

Dated: _____

Patient's signature: _____

Sunny Acres representative's signature: _____

Based on the contract on the previous page, answer the following questions:

a. Which, if any, provisions in the Admissions Agreement might *not* be legally enforceable and why?

b. What concerns might the language in the Admissions Agreement raise? Why?

c. Would you advise Mr. Williams to sign the Agreement? Why or why not?

D. ASSISTED LIVING

1. Overview of Assisted Living

Over the past several decades, there has been a shift away from nursing homes and towards *assisted living* facilities instead. This shift reflects a preference for a less medicalized care setting as well as a belief, in many cases accurate, that assisted living facilities provide residents with a greater level of independence than is available in a nursing home setting.

The term "assisted living" is used to describe a wide variety of different types of housing environments. Typically, the term is used to refer to a facility that provides residents with a combination of private or semi-private housing, meals in a common dining room, and other services such as housekeeping, transportation, laundry, and exercise or other recreational activities. Personal care services such as help with ADLs or medication management may also be available, typically for an additional fee.

As the Assisted Living Consumer Alliance, a coalition comprised of organizations that advocate for older adults, has explained:

> Assisted living facilities tend to be very different from one another. An assisted living unit may be as grand as a small apartment with a tiny kitchen in a large complex or as modest as a shared room with little more than a bed and dresser for each resident. One can find an assisted living facility housing 100 residents and providing on-site nursing care two blocks away from another facility that houses six residents and employs a staff with no health-care expertise at all.

Assisted Living Consumer Alliance, *Finding an Assisted Living Facility, available at* http://www.assistedlivingconsumers.org/consumer-information.

Constant with this variability, the Assisted Living Federation of America, an association of assisted living providers and related businesses, very broadly defines assisted living as

> a long-term care option that combines housing, support services and health care, as needed. Assisted living is designed for individuals who require assistance with everyday activities such as meals, medication management or assistance, bathing, dressing and transportation. Some residents may have memory disorders including Alzheimer's, or they may need help with mobility, incontinence or other challenges.

Assisted Living Federation of America, *What Is Assisted Living?*, *available at* http://www.alfa.org/alfa/Assisted_Living_Information.asp.

By contrast, other definitions limit the term "assisted living" to facilities that provide around-the-clock supervision. For example, the American Association of Homes and Services for the Aging defines assisted living as a program that provides and/or arranges for daily meals, personal and other supportive services, health care, and 24-hour oversight to persons residing in a group residential facility who need assistance with the activities of daily living.

Despite the prevalence of the term, there is no single federal definition of "assisted living." The lack of a federal definition reflects the fact that, unlike nursing homes, which are subject to extensive regulation and regulatory oversight at both the state and federal levels, regulation of assisted living facilities occurs almost exclusively at the state level.

State definitions of assisted living vary widely, but tend to be fairly vague. For example, Vermont defines assisted living as

> a program which combines housing, health, and supportive services for the support of resident independence and aging in place. Within a homelike setting, assisted living units offer, at a minimum, a private bedroom, private bath, living space, kitchen capacity, and a lockable door. Assisted living promotes resident self-direction and active participation in decision-making while emphasizing individuality, privacy, and dignity.

VT. STAT. ANN. §7102 (2012). Texas loosely defines an assisted living facility as "an establishment that: (A) furnishes, in one or more facilities, food and shelter to four who are unrelated to the proprietor of the establishment; and (B) provides personal care services." TEX. HEALTH & SAFETY CODE ANN. §247.002. Consistent with such a broad definition, assisted living facilities in Texas can place as many as four residents in a single room, can have a few as one toilet per every six residents, and as little as one shower or tub for every ten residents. Moreover, no specific staffing ratio is required.

The extent of regulation of assisted living facilities also varies significantly from state to state, as do enforcement procedures. Overall, however, there is far less regulation of the assisted living industry than of the nursing home industry. This is, however, an area of policy that is experiencing rapid change.

Advocates for older adults have raised serious concerns about the relative lack of regulation of assisted living facilities and have argued that this results in inadequate protection for assisted living residents. Such lack of regulation is concerning to advocates in part because of the significant needs of the population served by assisted living facilities. Individuals who would in past times have been seen as candidates for nursing home placement are increasingly obtaining long-term care services in assisted living facilities. The result is that assisted living facilities are caring for many people with significant physical and cognitive disabilities who need extensive assistance to maintain their physical and mental well-being.

Assisted living residents—especially those who live in facilities that provide high levels of service, privacy, and resident control—are disproportionately white. Assisted living residents are also, on average, more affluent than nursing home residents. These socio-economic differences likely reflect, at least in part, differences in how nursing home care and assisted living are financed. Nearly 90 percent of assisted living residents pay for those services from their personal resources. By contrast, approximately two-thirds of nursing home residents are Medicaid beneficiaries. This may change as more federal and state monies are directed away from nursing home and towards assisted living facilities. Increasingly, states are allowing Medicaid funds to be used for assisted living—indeed, almost all states have *home and community-based services* (HCBS) waiver programs that allow low-income residents to live in assisted living facilities.

QUESTION

Should Congress extend the resident rights laid out in the Nursing Home Reform Act to residents of assisted living facilities? Why or why not?

2. Duties of Assisted Living Facilities

a. Level of Services

Assisted living facilities, by definition, typically provide residents with significantly fewer services relative to nursing homes. States vary in the extent to which they regulate the level of services provided by assisted living facilities. To prevent assisted living facilities from admitting individuals whose needs they are unable to meet, states can establish admission criteria that limit admission of new residents to those whose care needs the facility is equipped to meet. Similarly, states can create discharge criteria that require facilities to discharge residents whose needs exceed a state-established level.

Clear admission and discharge criteria are designed to protect residents of assisted living facilities from avoidable neglect. However, such criteria also limit residential choice and the ability of assisted living residents to age in place, and can effectively force residents to move to more restrictive settings such as nursing homes. In light of these concerns, some states have developed flexible admission and discharge criteria. For example, some states waive discharge requirements if the resident is able to independently obtain the assistance he or she needs. Other states explicitly permit assisted living facilities to enter into *negotiated risk* contracts.

Negotiated risk (sometimes referred to as *managed risk* or *shared responsibility*) is a term used to refer to an arrangement whereby assisted living residents agree to accept housing that may fall short of fully meeting their needs for health and safety in return for the opportunity to live in a certain type of housing setting. Negotiated risk agreements have been credited not only with protecting resident autonomy, but also with providing an opportunity for residents and facilities to explicitly discuss and figure out how to manage and reduce risks. *See, e.g.,* Ethel Mitty & Sandi Flores, *Aging in Place and Negotiated Risk Agreements,* 29 GERIATRIC NURSING 94 (2008). Negotiated risk contracts are, however, controversial. As Eric Carlson has noted, "In general, assisted living facility representatives argue that true negotiated risk is about honoring resident preferences and, in response, resident advocates claim that the resident autonomy argument is a Trojan horse for bringing liability waivers into assisted living." Eric M. Carlson, *Protecting Rights or Waiving Them? Why "Negotiated Risk" Should Be Removed From Assisted Living,* 10 J. HEALTH CARE L. & POL'Y 287, 294 (2007). Carlson himself takes the position that:

> [T]he negotiated risk agreement is a way for the assisted living provider to have his cake and eat it too. The facility provides assisted living services that do not meet the resident's needs, collects payment for those services, and is insulated from liability for any injury that may be caused by the inadequate level of care. The facility essentially sets the standard of care through contract, and that standard admittedly does not meet the resident's needs.

Eric Carlson, *In the Sheep's Clothing of Resident Rights: Behind the Rhetoric of "Negotiated Risk" in Assisted Living,* 3 NAELA Q. 4, 6 (2003).

The next case provides an opportunity to consider the nature and extent of assisted living facilities' duties, and the effect of a resident's decision to engage in risky behavior on those duties.

Storm v. NSL Rockland Place, LLC

898 A.2d 874 (Del. Super. 2005)

SLIGHTS, J.

I.

In this opinion, the Court considers whether an assisted living facility may advance the affirmative defense of primary assumption of the risk in response to a resident's claim that the facility provided negligent or reckless care to him. . . . To the Court's knowledge, the question of whether primary assumption of the risk is a viable defense in the healthcare context has not been decided in Delaware.

A. Paul Storm, Jr. ("Mr. Storm") was a resident of a licensed assisted living facility owned and operated by Defendant, NSL Rockland Place, LLC ("Rockland"). On February 9, 2002, two Rockland employees found Mr. Storm in his room at Rockland lying face-down on the floor. It was presumed that Mr. Storm had fallen while alone in his room. As a result of the fall, Mr. Storm allegedly suffered serious physical injuries.

Plaintiff, JoAnn Storm, Mr. Storm's wife (collectively "the Storms"), filed this action individually and as guardian ad litem of Mr. Storm alleging, inter alia, that Rockland was negligent, reckless and wanton in the care and services it rendered to Mr. Storm. Rockland answered by denying the allegations of wrongdoing and raising Mr. Storm's primary and secondary assumption of the risk as affirmative defenses.

Arguing that primary assumption of the risk would operate as a complete bar to recovery, Rockland now seeks summary judgment. Rockland contends that Mr. Storm was aware of and expressly consented to the risks involved when residents of an assisted living facility are given appropriate opportunities to exercise independence in their day-to-day living activities. Under such circumstances, Rockland argues that injuries sustained by Mr. Storm in the course of exercising his independence may not be the subject of a claim against the institutional care provider to the extent such injuries fall within the range of foreseeable risks expressly assumed by the resident. For the reasons that follow, the Court finds that Delaware "healthcare providers" may not, as a matter of law, invoke the affirmative defense of primary assumption of the risk in claims brought by patients alleging substandard care. In the healthcare context, key elements of the defense will always be missing. Specifically, the healthcare defendant will rarely be able to establish that the plaintiff knowingly and expressly consented to engage in inherently risky conduct and will never be able to establish that the plaintiff consented to allow the healthcare provider to exercise less than ordinary care during the course of treatment. Moreover, the Court is satisfied that it would be endorsing bad public policy if it were to allow a healthcare provider to escape liability for proven negligence in rendering care on the ground that the patient purportedly consented to the risk of negligent care and consequent injury by agreeing to receive the treatment or healthcare services in the first place. . . .

II.

In January 2002, the Storms approached the intake staff at Rockland to inquire whether Rockland could provide a full-time residence for Mr. Storm where he could receive individualized medical care and twenty four hour supervision. Prior to admitting Mr. Storm, Rockland arranged for him to receive a medical evaluation so that it could prepare an initial service assessment outlining the assistance that Mr. Storm would require. The pre-admission evaluation was performed by Dr. Bean, Mr. Storm's neurologist. Dr. Bean opined that Mr. Storm suffered from multiple sclerosis, alcoholism, hypertension and depression. He noted that Mr. Storm would require assistance with ambulation due to falls and poor judgment. He also was in need of psychological and drug and alcohol rehabilitation.

With the pre-admission evaluation in hand, Rockland created a Medical Service Agreement which outlined the assistance and services it would provide to Mr. Storm while he resided at Rockland. This agreement was to remain in effect until Rockland performed its own evaluation of Mr. Storm and determined whether Mr. Storm required additional or different services. On January 10, 2002, both Mr. Storm and Rockland executed the Medical Service Agreement. Thereafter, as a final step of establishing residency at Rockland, Mr. Storm and Rockland entered into a Residency Agreement on January 26, 2002.

Mr. Storm was a resident at Rockland from January 26 through February 9, 2002. During his first week, Mr. Storm was able to ambulate with a steady gate [*sic*] while using a cane, eat his meals, refrain from alcohol consumption, and take his prescribed medications. His conduct, however, soon changed for the worse.

On February 1, Mrs. Storm came to Rockland to take her husband out for dinner only to find that Mr. Storm had been drinking alcohol and was intoxicated. She immediately contacted Rockland and directed its staff not to permit Mr. Storm to leave the facility without informing her because he was likely to consume alcohol and then be a danger to himself or others. According to Mrs. Storm, Rockland agreed to pay extra attention to Mr. Storm to ensure that he was in compliance with his treatment plan. In the ensuing days, however, Mr. Storm continuously would leave Rockland's campus and return intoxicated and smelling of alcohol. He also refused to take his prescribed medication and to eat many of his meals. On one occasion, when prompted by Rockland employees to take his medication, Mr. Storm responded: "I'm not in prison—I'll do what I want." According to Mrs. Storm, Rockland did not inform her of her husband's recalcitrance.

On the morning of February 9, Mr. Storm again refused to eat and take his medication and instead told a certified nursing assistant to leave him alone and that he would not be coming to breakfast or lunch. He remained in his room throughout the day. As evening approached, the Rockland staff once again attempted to coax Mr. Storm to leave his room and eat dinner. Mr. Storm did not respond. When two certified nursing assistants were dispatched to check on Mr. Storm, they found him unresponsive lying facedown on the floor. Mr. Storm apparently had fallen while alone in his room. He allegedly sustained an acute subdural hematoma and severe anoxia resulting in irreversible brain damage and permanent physical and neurological impairments and disabilities.

Mrs. Storm subsequently filed a complaint individually and as guardian ad litem of Mr. Storm alleging medical negligence, reckless and wanton conduct, breach of statutory duties, breach of contract, and loss of consortium. Rockland's answer denied wrongdoing and alleged, inter alia, that Mr. Storm's claims were barred by the doctrine of primary assumption of the risk.

III.

Rockland has moved for summary judgment. It contends that Mr. Storm's conduct constitutes primary assumption of the risk and should operate to relieve Rockland from liability. According to Rockland, Mr. Storm was aware of, and consented to, the risks associated with the independent living environment at Rockland. He exercised his independence and was injured as a result of his own conduct. In this regard, Rockland relies primarily upon the exculpatory language contained in the Residency Agreement which provides, in pertinent part:

> [Rockland] is designed to provide residential living in an apartment setting combined with individualized personal assistance and 24 hour supervision. The objective of the assisted living program is to provide the supportive services needed by residents of [Rockland] to manage on their own in their daily lives and to ensure that each resident can exercise a maximum level of independence, control and choice in his or her daily life.
>
> The Resident acknowledges that these principles of independence, control, and choice will result in a higher quality of life for each resident in the community, recognizes the additional risk that results from the ability of the Resident to make such choices, and agrees to mutually accept and share this risk. . . .
>
> Resident agrees that [Rockland] shall not be liable to Resident for personal injuries or damage to property, even if resulting from the negligence of [Rockland] or its employees, unless resulting from its gross negligence or willful misconduct. Resident acknowledges that the independence, control and choice afforded within [Rockland] requires that the Resident assume responsibility for any loss, injury or damage resulting from Resident's personal actions and conduct.

As further support of its position, Rockland cites the "Resident Rights" section of the Residency Agreement which afforded Mr. Storm the right to leave and return to Rockland at reasonable times and the right to privacy of self and possessions. According to Rockland, Mr. Storm's execution of the Residency Agreement, coupled with Mr. Storm's clear exercise of his "Resident's Rights," as demonstrated when he exclaimed "I'm not in prison—I'll do what I want" and admonished Rockland staff to "leave [him] alone," all evidence his express acknowledgment and consent of the risks inherent in living at Rockland. Rockland argues that Mr. Storm expressly assumed the risk of injury and is barred, therefore, as a matter of law, from recovery.

* * *

IV.

The Court's principal function when considering a motion for summary judgment is to examine the record to determine whether genuine issues of material fact exist. Summary judgment will be granted if, after viewing the record in a light most favorable to the non-moving party, no genuine issues of material fact exist and the moving party is entitled to judgment as a matter of law. . . .

* * *

V.

A. Primary Assumption of the Risk As a Matter of Law

From a legal perspective, liability in negligence will first depend upon whether the defendant was under a legal obligation, or duty, "to protect the plaintiff from the risk of harm which caused his injuries." . . . If the Court finds that the defendant owed no duty of care to the plaintiff at the time he sustained his injuries, the defendant is entitled to summary judgment as a matter of law.

When a defendant invokes the affirmative defense of primary assumption of the risk, the Court must evaluate the viability of the defense as part of its duty analysis because primary assumption of the risk "obviates the duty owed by the defendant." Stated differently, a finding by the Court that a plaintiff expressly assumed a risk in a manner that would implicate primary assumption of the risk is tantamount to a finding that the defendant owed no duty to the plaintiff. Needless to say, if the defendant establishes that it owed no duty to the plaintiff, *ipso jure*, it has established that it is entitled to summary judgment as a matter of law.

B. Primary Versus Secondary Assumption of the Risk

Assumption of the risk historically has operated to bar recovery when a plaintiff voluntarily assumed a risk of harm arising from a defendant's negligent or reckless conduct. . . .

. . . It is now settled in Delaware that primary assumption of the risk is implicated when the plaintiff expressly consents "to relieve the defendant of an obligation of conduct toward him, and to take his chances of injury from a known risk arising from what the defendant is to do or leave undone." "Express consent," however, does not suggest that the plaintiff must utter specific words portraying his intent to consent to the risk. Instead, "[d]epending upon the situation at hand, express consent may be manifested by circumstantial words or conduct." In all, the resulting effect of a primary assumption of the risk defense "is that the defendant is relieved of legal duty to the plaintiff; and being under no legal duty, he cannot be charged with negligence."

Secondary assumption of risk, on the other hand, is generally implicated "where the plaintiff's conduct in encountering a known risk may itself be unreasonable, because the danger is out of proportion to the advantage which he is seeking to obtain[.]" The defense does not, however, relieve a defendant of legal duty to a plaintiff. The conduct of the plaintiff is instead considered a form of comparative negligence and his recovery is dependent upon the relative fault a fact-finder attributes to him. Hence the now generally accepted notion that secondary assumption of the risk is completely subsumed by the principles of comparative negligence.

C. Primary Assumption of the Risk Does Not Apply to Healthcare

Courts have allowed a primary assumption of the risk defense to negate a wide array of negligence claims. Having said that, the defense most frequently surfaces in cases of sports-related activities that "involv[e] physical skill and challenges posing significant risk of injury to participants in such activities, and as to which the absence of such a defense would chill vigorous participation in the sporting activity and have a deleterious effect on the nature of the sport as a whole." . . .

Two common themes appear in each instance where primary assumption of the risk has been deemed to be an appropriate affirmative defense. First, the plaintiff chooses to engage in the activity, not out of necessity but out of a desire to satisfy a personal preference, e.g., to participate or watch others participate in a sporting event. Second, when the plaintiff chooses to engage in the inherently risky activity, he acknowledges that he and others engaging in such activity may not act with "ordinary care." For instance, when the plaintiff signs up to play ice hockey in a community league, he is likely to sign a consent that advises him that there is physical contact inherent in the sport that may cause injury. If he is injured when another player checks him into the boards, he will have no claim sounding in negligence because the other player acted within the rules of the game and the plaintiff primarily assumed the risk of injury. If, on the other hand, that same plaintiff is hip checked into a parked car while walking down the street, the doctrine of primary assumption of the risk does not apply because the plaintiff has not consented to engage in such conduct or to have others engage in such conduct towards him.

Of the two themes prevalent in primary assumption of the risk scenarios, the first is rarely extant in the healthcare context and the second never is in play and could not be countenanced in any event. As to the first theme, it is rare that a consumer of healthcare services chooses to be sick or otherwise in need of care. Most people, with the exception of those who have elective or cosmetic surgery, seek out health care because they must. In this case, for example, Mr. Storm went to Rockland for healthcare services because he suffered from, among other conditions, multiple sclerosis and an alcohol addiction that required specialized care. One can safely say that he did not choose to suffer from those conditions and did not choose to be in need of care for them. The element of choice is missing.

As to the second theme, there is virtually no scenario in which a patient can consent to allow a healthcare provider to exercise less than "ordinary care" in the provision of services. Even if given, a patient's consent to allow a healthcare provider to exercise less than ordinary care would be specious when considered against the strict legal, ethical and professional standards that regulate the healthcare profession. Regardless of whether the patient elects to have healthcare or requires it, the patient appropriately expects that the treatment will be rendered in accordance with the applicable standard of care. This is so regardless of how risky or dangerous the procedure or treatment modality might be.

Rockland's attempt to invoke the primary assumption of the risk defense fails because it cannot demonstrate that Mr. Storm chose to be sick or that he consented to allow Rockland to exercise less than ordinary care when it provided healthcare services to him. Even assuming arguendo that Mr. Storm was aware of the risks associated with independent living, he accepted these risks only because he was in need of medical care. Moreover, by accepting the risks inherent in the Rockland treatment environment, he did not in any way consent to allow Rockland to exercise less than what the applicable standards of care required of it when providing services. Permitting a primary assumption of the risk defense under these circumstances would simply be unconscionable.

* * *

D. Plaintiff's Secondary Assumption of the Risk

Although primary assumption of the risk is not available to Rockland under the circumstances presented here, Rockland will be permitted to prosecute its affirmative defense of secondary assumption of the risk and to elicit evidence at trial that Mr. Storm's conduct contributed to his injuries. The issue of whether that conduct constitutes contributory negligence and, if so, the degree of fault that should be attributed to Mr. Storm, remain questions of fact for the jury to decide. These questions will be considered within the parameters established by Delaware's statutory comparative negligence scheme. Presumably, they will also be considered as questions secondary to Rockland's showcase defense, namely, that the Storms cannot establish that Rockland breached the standard of care in the provision of services to Mr. Storm. This threshold issue remains very much in dispute.

VI.

Based on the foregoing, the Court is satisfied that Rockland's legal status as a licensed assisted living facility and healthcare provider do not allow it to assert a primary assumption of the risk defense as a means to escape liability for allegedly substandard health care. Rockland's motion for summary judgment is DENIED. . . .

NOTE

Comparison to nursing home litigation. Many of the same issues arise in litigation over quality of care concerns at assisted living facilities and litigation over quality of care concerns at nursing homes. For example, there may be a question as to what should be the legal effect of a facility violating statutory requirements. For example, in *Apple Investment Properties, Inc. v. Watts*, 469 S.E.2d 356 (Ga. App. 1996), an assisted living facility was sued for negligent supervision by the estate of a resident who had suffered from Alzheimer's disease who died after he "wandered unsupervised into the cold" and "a passer-by found him, lying on the ground wearing only his underwear, and . . . he had to be hospitalized for hypothermia." The plaintiff sought to obtain records of similar incidents involving other residents, which the facility was required to keep under state law. The facility argued that such records were neither relevant nor could they be disclosed as doing so would deny the other residents confidentiality in their records. The court disagreed, finding evidence of similar conduct relevant to both the determination of negligence (including whether the facility was on notice that its employees were not adequately supervising residents) and to the issue of punitive damages. The court further found that disclosure could not be barred on privacy grounds noting that doing so would be counterproductive: "The one who is championing [the residents'] privacy right would gain by its protection, even more so if it hid acts of negligence against any of those same persons."

QUESTIONS

1. Should assisted living facilities be allowed to retain residents whose needs rise to a level that would render them ineligible for admission as a new resident?

2. In states that require an assisted living facility to discharge a resident whose needs exceed the facility's ability to provide care, should states waive the discharge requirement if the resident is able to obtain the assistance he or she needs by bringing in outside service providers (e.g., by contracting with a home health agency)?

3. Should assisted living providers be required to waive admission or discharge requirements to accommodate persons with disabilities where state law permits them to, or should this be left to the discretion of the facility? Consider revisiting this question after reviewing the materials on housing discrimination in Section F of this chapter.

b. Protecting Residents from One Another

One of the risks created when facilities have limited resources and services relative to the needs of their residents is that the facility will not meet their residents' needs. This is not only a potential problem for the individual whose needs are not met, but also for his or her fellow residents. The next case explores this form of risk.

Pollack v. CCC Investments, LLC d/b/a Tiffany House by Marriott

933 So. 2d 572 (Fla. App. 4th Dist. 2006)

KLEIN, J.

Appellant's mother, a resident of an assisted living facility, was murdered by another resident living at the facility. Appellant brought this action for her wrongful death which resulted in a verdict for the defense. We reverse because the court erred in not instructing the jury regarding statutes and regulations which may have been violated by the defendants.

The incident occurred at Tiffany House by Marriott, a minimum level assisted living facility managed by Marriott Senior Living Services, Inc. and owned by Marriott International, Inc., where the plaintiff's mother began living in June, 1998. Around three years later, in May 2001, another patient, Felix Freed, who had been living at Tiffany House for about eighteen months, murdered appellant's mother and then called the nurses' desk to report that he had killed another resident.

Plaintiff brought this suit alleging violations of Chapter 400, Florida Statutes, and that Tiffany House had acted negligently in admitting Freed and allowing him to continue to reside there. The evidence at trial showed that just before his admission to Tiffany House, Freed had been hospitalized in a psychiatric facility because he suffered from dementia and there were concerns that he could be dangerous to himself or others. When he was admitted to Tiffany House, he suffered from major depressive disorder, dementia, and psychosis. His medical evaluation indicated that he was in need of continuous licensed nursing care.

In March[] 2001, Freed informed employees of the defendants that he was concerned that he could hurt himself or others. He was then evaluated at a local hospital and, after reporting that these homicidal or suicidal tendencies had ceased, he returned to Tiffany House. Soon after that, according to his medical records, other residents had observed personality changes in Freed, including increased signs of frustration and lack of tolerance. His daughter reported that she was concerned about her father's increasing paranoia and his psychiatrist prescribed an antipsychotic medication. The psychiatrist's records reflect that on May 3, 2001, he ordered a psychiatric nurse to monitor Freed, but a nurse was never retained by the defendants nor was there any indication in the defendants' medical records of this order by the psychiatrist. The murder occurred seven days later.

Plaintiff requested several jury instructions involving state regulations and statutes pertaining to assisted living facilities. One of those instructions was a portion of Residency Criteria and Admission Procedures. Fla. Admin. Code 58A-5.0181.

> 1) Admission Criteria. An individual must meet the following minimum criteria in order to be admitted to a facility holding a standard, limited nursing or limited mental health license. [...]
>
> g) Not be a danger to self or others as determined by a physician, or mental health practitioner licensed under Chapters 490 or 491. [...]
>
> l) Not require 24-hour nursing supervision.

Another provided:

> Every facility shall be under the supervision of an administrator who is responsible for the operation and maintenance of the facility including the management of all staff and provision of adequate care to all residents . . .

§400.4176, Fla. Stat.; Fla. Admin. Code R. 58A-5.019(1).

A third provided:

> All staff shall be assigned duties consistent with his/her level of education, training, preparation, and experience. Staff providing services requiring licensing or certification must be appropriately licensed or certified. All staff shall exercise their responsibilities, consistent with their qualifications, to observe residents, to document observations on the appropriate resident's record, and to report the observations to the resident's health care provider in accordance with this rule chapter.

Fla. Admin. Code R. 58A-5.019(2)(b).

A fourth provided:

> (3) Staff Records. [. . .]
>   (b) Personal records for each staff member shall contain, at a minimum, a copy of the original employment application with references furnished and verification of freedom from communicable disease including tuberculosis. In addition as applicable: (listing numerous required licenses and certifications.)

Fla. Admin. Code R. 58A-5.024. There was evidence from which the jury could have found violations of all of the above.

* * *

Because . . . there was evidence from which the jury could have found violations of the statutes and regulations, plaintiff is entitled to a new trial. Reversed. . . .

QUESTIONS

1. Should Mr. Freed have been denied admission to the assisted living facility? Should he have been evicted?

2. If Mr. Freed could not live at Tiffany House, where should he have resided instead?

3. Would denying Mr. Freed residency at Tiffany House amount to impermissible discrimination on the basis of disability? Consider revisiting this question after reviewing the materials on housing discrimination in Section F of this chapter.

4. Suppose the same injury had befallen the appellant's mother when she was a resident in a skilled nursing facility. To what extent might the legal claim differ based on this fact? Why?

E. CONTINUING CARE RETIREMENT FACILITIES

Continuing care retirement communities (CCRCs) are housing organizations that are designed to provide residents with a continuum of care over their lifetimes. This continuum of care usually consists of independent living units, assisted living, and nursing home care. In the typical CCRC, all levels of care are provided at a single location, and the CCRC is designed to serve as the resident's home for the remainder of his or her lifetime. Although the CCRC model has been in existence for more than 100 years, the industry has grown significantly over the past several decades.

CCRCs can be an attractive option for older adults because they allow them to remain part of a familiar community as their care needs change over time. This may be particularly appealing for spouses who wish to remain in the same community when one needs a higher level of care than the other. For others, however, the CCRC arrangement may feel confining or even suffocating. For example, the large upfront fees charged by many CCRCs may result in the CCRC controlling a very substantial portion of residents' life savings, making it difficult—perhaps prohibitively difficult—for residents to ever move.

To join a CCRC, individuals enter into a long-term contract with the housing provider. The provider agrees to provide certain forms of housing, health care, services, and amenities in return for payment. This payment typically consists of a large up-front fee and a monthly occupancy fee. Consistent with this design, many CCRC residents finance their move into a CCRC by selling their homes and using the proceeds, sometimes in combination with other assets, to cover the cost.

CCRC residents often have a choice as to how they structure their financial arrangement with the facility. According to a comprehensive Government Accountability Office (GAO) study, there are three primary contractual arrangements from which CCRC residents select:

■ *Life Care Contracts*, in which the resident pays a substantial entrance fee and a monthly fee in return for a lifetime guarantee of housing, services, and amenities. In this arrangement, the level of care the resident receives has little or no effect on the monthly fee he or she pays.

■ *Modified Contracts*, in which the resident pays a substantial entrance fee as well as a monthly fee. The monthly fee is somewhat lower than that paid for a Life Care Contract and, as a result, only a limited set of services or amenities are included in the initial monthly fee. If the resident's needs increase, the resident will need to pay additional fees to pay for the services to meet those needs.

■ *Fee-for-Service Contracts*, in which the resident pays an entrance fee and a monthly fee. Both of these fees are lower than in the other two arrangements, but they do not cover health-related services. These services, in turn, must be purchased separately on an as-needed basis.

In addition, some CCRCs offer rental agreements that do not require entrance fees. *See* U.S. GOV'T ACCOUNTABILITY OFFICE, GAO-10-611, REPORT TO THE CHAIRMAN, SPECIAL COMMITTEE ON AGING, U.S. SENATE, OLDER AMERICANS: CONTINUING CARE RETIREMENT COMMUNITIES CAN PROVIDE BENEFITS, BUT NOT WITHOUT SOME RISK 5-6 (2010).

The entrance fees for CCRCs vary based on the community and on the type of contract. The 2010 GAO study found that such fees ranged from an average of $143,000 for Life Care Contracts, to $91,200 for Modified Care Contracts, to $97,749 for Fee-For-Service Contracts. Consistent with these figures, CCRC residents tend to be affluent and well-educated.

The federal government does not specifically regulate CCRCs, although it does regulate components of CCRCs such as nursing home facilities situated within CCRCs. By contrast, the majority of states have enacted CCRC-specific regulations. While regulatory provisions range significantly, a common requirement is that CCRCs make certain mandatory disclosures as to key policies. These requirements reflect the fact that, although CCRCs are often touted as a way to increase older adults' future security, those joining CCRCs actually face significant risks. As the GAO has noted:

> CCRC financial difficulties can lead to unexpected increases in residents' monthly fees. And while CCRC bankruptcies or closures have been relatively rare, and residents have generally not been forced to leave in such cases, should a CCRC failure occur, it could cause residents to lose all or part of their entrance fee. Residents can also become dissatisfied if CCRC policies or operations fall short of residents' expectations or there is a change in arrangements thought to be contractually guaranteed, such as charging residents for services that were previously free.

Id. (abstract). Other rights granted by some state statutes include the right to rescind a contract after a short period of time (e.g., a week or two). A few states also limit CCRCs' ability to raise the rates charged to existing residents, and CCRCs' ability to evict residents for non-payment of monthly charges.

A key issue for CCRC residents is how decisions about transitioning to higher levels of care are made. In some cases, a CCRC may require the resident to transfer to a higher level of care even when doing so is against the wishes of the resident. A resident may resist such a transition not only because he or she prefers the setting of the lower level of care, but because the higher level of care is more expensive. Increased costs may be due to higher monthly fees, or may reflect additional charges such as charges for meals, for maintaining an apartment while the resident is temporarily residing in a higher level of care, and for receiving off-site care not available within the

CCRC. Most state laws governing CCRCs either do not address resident rights regarding such transitions, or simply require the CCRC to disclose the conditions under which a transfer may be required. By contrast, a handful of states statutorily limit CCRCs' ability to require a transfer. For example, Maine permits an involuntary transfer to a residential care unit or a skilled nursing facility only if "the resident poses a health or safety danger to other residents or a change in a resident's health status or abilities necessitates a move to a higher level of care." ME. REV. STAT. ANN. tit. 24-A, §6228 (2013).

Another important issue for CCRC residents is whether the CCRC has an adequate number of skilled nursing home beds available for residents. CCRC contracts generally do not guarantee that residents who need nursing home care will receive that care in the CCRC's own nursing facility and, instead, allow the CCRC to place the resident in a nursing home that is not part of the CCRC. This can lead to an unpleasant surprise for some residents. As attorneys Michael Gilfix and Bernard Krooks have observed:

> A married couple moves into a CCRC largely because they want to be together for life. They believe that, if one spouse needs to be in the nursing home on the grounds, the other will be able to visit as often as he or she likes. The discovery that the facility can place a resident in another nursing home in the community can be nothing less than shattering. Yet virtually every CCRC contract allows for such placement. There may be guarantees about moving back to the CCRC facility when the next vacancy occurs, but this provides little consolation.

Michael Gilfix & Bernard A. Krooks, *Continuing Care Retirement Communities: Issues for Elder Law Attorneys*, 16 ELDER L. REP. 1, 4 (2006).

The case that follows provides an opportunity to explore some of the complications faced by CCRC residents and how CCRC contracts may attempt to address the possibility of such complications.

Seabrook Village v. Murphy

853 A.2d 280 (N.J. Super. Ct. App. Div. 2004)

FUENTES, J.A.D.

Petitioner John Murphy appeals from the final decision of the New Jersey Department of Community Affairs (DCA), Bureau of Homeowner Protection. In its decision, the DCA determined that Seabrook Village was legally entitled to cancel its Residence and Care Agreement with petitioner and discharge him from its facility for his (1) refusal to pay monthly service fees and (2) failure to execute a release of the Living Unit that he previously occupied.

* * *

We now hold that a resident of a continuing care facility appealing his or her dismissal or discharge from such facility to the DCA is legally entitled to a "plenary hearing," as defined in N.J.A.C. 1:1-2.1. Such a hearing must be conducted by either the Commissioner of the DCA or by the Office of

Administrative Law pursuant to the Commissioner's referral for adjudication. We further hold that a resident of a continuing care facility can be involuntarily discharged only upon the establishment of "just cause," as defined in N.J.S.A. 52:27D-344d and N.J.A.C. 5:19-6.5(c). Any waiver of "just cause" contained in an agreement entered into by a resident or any contractually crafted ground for removal not sanctioned by specific statutory or regulatory authority, is legally unenforceable and void as against public policy.

* * *

I

Erickson Retirement Communities, d/b/a Seabrook Village, operates a continuing care retirement community located in Tinton Falls. Seabrook offers three types of living arrangements for its residents: (1) Independent Living Units; (2) Assisted Living Units; and (3) Care Center Units. The latter two are housed in the Extended Care Center. . . .

Petitioner, in consultation with his son Michael Murphy [whom he had appointed as his attorney-in-fact pursuant to a durable power of attorney], decided to reside in one of Seabrook's Independent Living Units. Prior to signing any documents or making any payments, petitioner sought clarification as to the status of any deposit required. By letter dated February 17, 1999, Seabrook Executive Director Joan Carr assured petitioner that "[a]ll of these funds are fully refundable," both prior to and after petitioner moved into his unit.

On June 10, 1999, petitioner signed the Residence and Care Agreement with Seabrook and paid the required entrance fee of $149,000. In addition to the entrance fee, the Agreement also required petitioner to pay a Monthly Service Fee of $1,290. Michael signed as guarantor of his father's financial obligations to Seabrook.

In May 2001, petitioner agreed to a transfer from his Independent Living Unit to an Assisted Living Unit located in the Renaissance Gardens facility. This unit had been marketed as requiring an entrance fee of $150,000. When Michael inquired about the $1,000 deposit differential, he was told that his father's initial $149,000 would be sufficient.

After the move, Michael alleges that he discovered promotional materials from Seabrook offering Assisted Living Units to the general public with an entrance fee of only $99,000. He immediately contacted Seabrook to complain about a number of problems pertaining to the level and quality of care petitioner was receiving at the new unit and requested a $50,000 refund from the original $149,000 entrance fee deposit.

Seabrook refused to refund the excess funds, referring petitioner and his son to section 7.3 of the Agreement which specifically provides that the entrance fee shall not be refunded or decreased "due to any temporary or permanent transfer, [by a resident] for whatever reason, during the Term of this Agreement." In this light, by letter dated June 18, 2001, Michael wrote to Carr to document his complaints about the deficient conditions in the Assisted Living Unit and to reiterate his demand for a $50,000 refund. He concluded this letter by emphasizing that he: (1) would not sign the release for occupancy of his father's original Independent Unit; and (2) would not continue to pay the Monthly Service Fee, "until such time as the many concerns I have raised are adequately addressed and both my father and I feel absolutely comfortable that [Renaissance Gardens] is the best place for him to be."

On October 9, 2001, Michael and his counsel met with representatives of Seabrook in an attempt to amicably resolve the ongoing disagreement. By letter dated October 24, 2001, petitioner authorized Seabrook to re-subscribe the Independent Living Unit "with an entrance fee of not less than $149,000." According to petitioner's counsel, there were twenty individuals on the waiting list to subscribe. The unit had been vacant since June 12, 2001.

Despite this apparent resolution of the dispute, by letter dated February 14, 2002, Seabrook notified petitioner of its intention to terminate his residency effective sixty days from his receipt of the notice. The notice also attached a statement of account indicating an arrears of $47,255.64, noting that the last payment petitioner made was on June 14, 2001, for $5,355.27.

The termination notice cited section 12.2 of the Agreement as providing the legal authority for the removal. That section reads as follows:

12.2 Termination by SEABROOK VILLAGE.

SEABROOK VILLAGE may terminate this Agreement in the manner provided below. Resident may request a hearing to contest SEABROOK VILLAGE'S decision to terminate the Agreement. Such hearing shall be held pursuant to the New Jersey Administrative Procedure Act and the Uniform Administrative Practice Rules.

12.2.1 SEABROOK VILLAGE may terminate this Agreement by giving sixty (60) days notice to Resident of SEABROOK VILLAGE'S intention to terminate.

12.2.2 SEABROOK VILLAGE may terminate this Agreement by giving Resident less than sixty (60) days notice if there is "just cause" for termination. The term "just cause" shall mean, but shall not be limited to, a good faith determination in writing, signed by the Executive Director and Medical Director of the Community, that Resident is a danger to himself or others while remaining in the Community. The written determination shall state: (1) that the determination is made in good faith, (2) the reasons supporting the determination, (3) the basis for the conclusion that there is no less restrictive reasonable alternative to dismissal, discharge or cancellation for abating the danger posed by Resident, and (4) an explanation as to why the danger is such that a notice period of less than sixty (60) days is required.

It shall also be "just cause" if Resident is unable to pay the Monthly Service Fee and SEABROOK VILLAGE has used Resident's entire Entrance Fee to provide services to Resident. For purposes of determining whether SEABROOK VILLAGE has used Resident's entire Entrance Fee to provide services to Resident, SEABROOK VILLAGE shall determine the unused portion of Resident's Entrance Fee (if any), which is defined as the difference between the Entrance Fee paid and the lesser of (a) the fees generally charged by SEABROOK VILLAGE to provide services and care to Resident, or (b) based upon the per capita cost to the Community of providing services and care to Resident calculated as (i) no more than two percent (2%) of the Entrance Fee for each month Resident occupies, or is entitled to occupy, a Living Unit, (ii) no more than four percent (4%) of the Entrance Fee for each month Resident occupies, or is entitled to occupy, an Extended Care Unit at the Community, and (iii) no more than ten percent (10%) of the Entrance Fee as a one-time charge for processing and refurbishing. If the Entrance Fee is depleted within ninety (90) days of Resident's failure to pay the Monthly Service Fee, SEABROOK VILLAGE may not require Resident to vacate the Community before ninety (90) days from the date of failure to pay. During this time, Resident shall pay SEABROOK VILLAGE a reduced Monthly Service Fee based on Resident's income.

By letter dated March 25, 2002, Michael responded to Seabrook's termination notice disputing the alleged $47,255.64 delinquency in his father's account and reiterating his demand for a $50,000 credit based on the original $149,000 entrance fee. This prompted a response from Seabrook asserting, in part, that,

> [b]y operation of our contract, and previous sixty day notice, our Agreement will end on April 16 [2002]. You must pay your father's balance by 5:00 P.M. on April 16 or pick him up. If you do not, we will drive him to your home that evening and should arrive between the hours of 6:00 P.M. to 11:00 P.M. The cost of after-hours transportation will be added to the account.

Confronted with this impasse, petitioner appealed Seabrook's action to the DCA, demanding "a full administrative hearing" pursuant to N.J.A.C. 5:19-6.5(e). Seabrook agreed to permit petitioner to continue to reside at its facility pending the outcome of the administrative appeal.

At the request of the DCA, the parties submitted proposed adjudicatory facts. Thereafter, based only on the parties' written submissions, Stewart P. Palilonis, Manager of Planned Real Estate Development in the Bureau of Homeowner Protection, issued the Agency's Findings of Adjudicatory Facts, finding in pertinent part that: (1) petitioner had refused to pay the Monthly Service Fee from June 14, 2001 to February 14, 2002; (2) petitioner had violated the terms of the Agreement by failing or refusing to sign a release of the Independent Living Unit when he was transferred to the Assisted Living Unit; (3) Seabrook proved "just cause" for terminating the Agreement; and (4) Seabrook was justified in discharging petitioner.

Against this factual backdrop we will now address the legal issues presented.

II
Legal Grounds for Termination of Residency

Petitioner argues that Seabrook did not have the legal authority to terminate his residency because it failed to establish "just cause" within the meaning of N.J.S.A. 52:27D-344d and N.J.A.C. 5:19-6.5(c). Seabrook maintains, however, that N.J.S.A. 52:27D-334a(7), N.J.A.C. 5:19-6.4(a) 7 and section 12.2.1 of the Residence and Care Agreement authorize it to terminate petitioner's residency without "just cause," provided that the resident receives a sixty-day notice of Seabrook's intent to terminate the residency. The Attorney General, on behalf of the Commissioner of the DCA, urges us to reject Seabrook's argument and hold that a resident of a continuing care facility cannot be involuntarily discharged without the provider or operator establishing "just cause" under the Act.

* * *

In our view, subsection 344a(7) imposes a procedural requirement upon the provider or operator of a continuing care facility to notify a resident, at least sixty days in advance, of its intention to seek his or her involuntary removal from the facility. Subsection 344d sets out "just cause" as the only substantive legal basis for the resident's removal and provides for a notice period of less than sixty days under the appropriate circumstances. Thus, subsections 344a(7) and 344d are intended to operate in tandem, describing a resident's procedural and substantive rights. We are satisfied that the public policy underpinning the Act supports this conclusion.

In 1986, the Legislature adopted the Continuing Care Retirement Community Regulation and Financial Disclosure Act. N.J.S.A. 52:27D-330. In so doing, the Legislature recognized that "continuing care retirement communities [were then] ... becoming an important and increasingly preferred alternative for the long-term residential, social and health care needs of New Jersey's senior citizens." N.J.S.A. 52:27D-31. The Legislature therefore directed the DCA to establish a comprehensive regulatory scheme to monitor the operations of these facilities. *Ibid.* It did so because "tragic consequences can result to senior citizens when a continuing care provider becomes insolvent or unable to provide responsible care." *Ibid.*

Pursuant to this legislative charge, N.J.S.A. 52:27D-358, the Commissioner of the DCA regulates almost every aspect of the continuing care industry, i.e., requirements for and certification of operational authority, marketing, entrance and services fees, content and scope of residential agreements, financial responsibility standards and administrative structural requirements. N.J.A.C. 5:19-1.1 to -9.9. This regulatory framework compliments the equally comprehensive legislative scheme set out in N.J.S.A. 52:27D-330 to -360.

As we noted in *Starns v. American Baptist Estates of Red Bank,* 352 N.J. Super. 327, 337, 800 A.2d 182, 188 (App. Div. 2002), "[a] continuing care facility provides more for each resident than a place to live." The overarching public policy of the Continuing Care Act is the protection of our State's older citizens, who have reached a point in their lives when they are unable to fully function without some level of personal support and medical assistance. Although the Act's main thrust is the financial stability of these facilities, there is also a clear legislative preoccupation with ensuring that the residents of these facilities receive quality care commensurate with their personal needs and financial resources. A key component of that care is the provision of a stable, secure and safe environment where residents and their families can plan the remainder of the residents' lives without the looming prospect of displacement based on the unilateral actions of the provider or operator.

Construing N.J.S.A. 52:27D-344a(7) as conferring upon the operators or providers of these facilities the unfettered authority to disrupt this stability by involuntarily displacing a resident, merely by providing a sixty-day termination notice, runs directly counter to this legislative scheme and does violence to the Act's core purpose, the protection of the resident. This approach would also undermine the DCA's oversight role by permitting the removal of a resident without the due process protection envisioned in N.J.S.A. 52:27D-344d: "A resident may request a hearing to contest a facility's decision to dismiss or discharge the resident."

Conversely, requiring a provider or operator to establish "just cause" as a prerequisite for the involuntary removal of a resident, furthers the legislative policy of protection, while giving the provider or operator the authority to remove residents who are no longer capable of safely functioning within the facility's programs' parameters or otherwise endanger the safety or undermine the security of other residents or staff. N.J.S.A. 52:27D-344d.

Because the statutory requirement of "just cause" is intended to protect residents from arbitrary or ill-motivated displacement, any contractual provision that seeks to circumvent, waive or otherwise undermine this statutory protection by crafting an independent ground for removal, is unenforceable and void as against public policy. N.J.S.A. 52:27D-344f; N.J.A.C. 5:19-6.5(h).

Courts in our State have consistently reached similar conclusions in other areas where, as here, there is a clear public policy in favor of protecting a particularly vulnerable population. *Vasquez v. Glassboro Service Ass'n, Inc.*, 83 N.J. 86, 98, 415 A.2d 1156, 1162 (1980) (invalidating on public policy grounds a migrant worker contract that provided for the worker's summary ejection from employer-provided housing in the event of his discharge); *Sacks Realty Co. v. Shore*, 317 N.J. Super. 258, 269, 721 A.2d 1011, 1016-17 (App. Div. 1998) (invalidating waiver of statutory protections in connection with condominium conversion); *Cardona v. Eden Realty Co.*, 118 N.J. Super. 381, 288 A.2d 34 (App. Div.), *certif. denied*, 60 N.J. 354, 289 A.2d 799 (1972) (exculpatory clauses, void as against public policy in residential leases).

Against the backdrop of these legal principles, we now hold that a provider or operator of a continuing care facility, seeking to involuntarily remove or discharge a resident, must establish "just cause" as that term is defined in N.J.S.A. 52:27D-344d. We further hold that section 12.2.1 of the Seabrook Residence and Care Agreement, which authorizes Seabrook to discharge and remove a resident merely by giving a sixty-day advance notice violates the "just cause" provisions in N.J.S.A. 52:27D-344d and N.J.A.C. 5:19-6.5(c), and is legally void and unenforceable as against public policy.

The Actions of the DCA

Acting upon petitioner's appeal from Seabrook's decision to terminate his residency, the DCA determined that Seabrook had established "just cause" under N.J.S.A. 52:27D-344d and N.J.A.C. 5:19-6.5(c). This "decision" by the DCA was reached without conducting an evidentiary hearing and is facially devoid of legal analysis. In short, this "decision" constitutes an utter abdication of the DCA's responsibilities under the Continuing Care Act.

All parties in this appeal agree that the matter must be remanded to the DCA Commissioner for a full hearing as envisioned by the statute. N.J.S.A. 52:27D-344d. We now hold that this hearing must be conducted as a "plenary hearing," as that term is defined in N.J.A.C. 1:1-2.1. The Commissioner has the option of conducting the adjudicatory proceeding or referring the matter to the Office of Administrative Law.

The Commissioner's findings must be supported by specific references to the evidence in the record and conclusions of law must be supported by the appropriate authority.

Reversed and remanded. We do not retain jurisdiction.

QUESTIONS

1. *Seabrook* provides an example of a state choosing to specifically regulate senior housing facilities. Should states regulate senior care facilities differently from other housing providers?

2. Professor Katherine Pearson has advocated for a "Bill of Rights" for CCRC residents. One of the rights that Pearson argues residents should have is the right to have a fellow resident fill at least one seat on the governing board of their CCRC. Another is the right to sue to enforce their rights. *See Continuing Care Retirement Communities (CCRCs): Secure Retirement of Risky Investment? Hearing before the Special Committee on Aging, United States Senate, One Hundred Eleventh Congress, Second Session, July 21, 2010*, 111th Cong. 34 (2010) (statement of Katherine Pearson).

   Should residents have such rights? What other rights might you include in a Bill of Rights for CCRC residents?

3. What do you see as the primary advantages and disadvantages of living in a CCRC?

F. PROTECTION FROM DISABILITY DISCRIMINATION IN HOUSING

Individuals with disabilities, including those with aging-related disabilities, are the beneficiaries of significant federal protections from housing-related discrimination. The federal Fair Housing Act (FHA), 42 U.S.C. §§3601 et seq., prohibits discrimination on the basis of race, color, religion, sex, national original, and disability in the sale or rental of real property. Under the FHA, the refusal to make reasonable accommodations in rules, policies, practices, or services to make it possible for a person with a disability to reside in a dwelling can constitute impermissible discrimination.

The provisions of the FHA apply to all federal housing and housing directly supported by federal funding, as well as to private housing with two key exceptions: (1) single-family homes sold or rented by an owner who does not own more than three such single-family homes at any one time and who meets certain other criteria; and (2) a housing unit that is located in a dwelling occupied or intended to be occupied by no more than four families and the owner maintains and occupies one of the units as his or her own residence. *See* 42 U.S.C. §3603(b)(1)-(2) (2013). In addition to the FHA, the Rehabilitation Act, Section 504, as codified at 29 U.S.C. §794, prohibits discrimination solely by reason of disability as to participation in or benefits under programs or activities receiving federal financial assistance.

The cases that follow examine the protections that the FHA and related laws afford seniors. The first case examines the legitimacy of "independent living" requirements. The second two explore the circumstances under which a housing provider must provide a "reasonable accommodation" and the nature of such accommodations. Note that although the second case involves a Colorado state statute, the interpretation would, as the court indicates, be the same under the FHA.

Cason v. Rochester Housing Authority

748 F. Supp. 1002 (W.D.N.Y. 1990)

LARIMER, District Judge.

For over two hundred years our Country has prospered under the principle that all men and women should have an equal opportunity to enjoy "life, liberty and the pursuit of happiness."

There was a time when the disabled did not have the same opportunities and were relegated to a kind of second class status in employment, housing and transportation. That circumstance was caused more by the community's misinformation and thoughtlessness than by the individual's actual disabling condition. Much has been done to eliminate this situation but it would be simplistic to believe that problems do not remain. Public agencies must be especially vigilant to protect the disabled from all forms of discrimination-intentional as well as benign discrimination caused by the public's perception of what is "best" for the disabled.

This case revolves around claims that the Rochester Housing Authority ("Authority") discriminates against disabled applicants for public housing. Three applicants who have physical and mental disabilities and whose applications for public housing were denied, commenced this action seeking declaratory and injunctive relief on behalf of themselves and a class of similarly situated applicants.

Because I believe that the Authority uses eligibility criteria for public housing that tend to discriminate against those with handicaps and because I believe those requirements cause the Authority to consider handicapped applicants by a different standard than so-called able-bodied applicants, the eligibility standards are in clear violation of federal law and must be struck down.

PROCEDURAL BACKGROUND

Plaintiffs have brought this action under the Fair Housing Act of 1968, 42 U.S.C. §3601 *et seq.*, the Rehabilitation Act of 1973, 29 U.S.C. §794, and the United States Housing Act, 42 U.S.C. §1437 *et seq.* The three named plaintiffs claim that their applications for low-income public housing were denied by the Authority because of plaintiffs' handicaps in clear contravention of federal law, which makes it illegal to discriminate in housing based on the physical or mental disability of an applicant.

One of the plaintiffs is a 31 year-old woman who has been diagnosed as schizophrenic and the other two are elderly women, each of whom suffers from various physical handicaps and one of whom has also been diagnosed as schizophrenic. In spite of their handicaps, plaintiffs contend that they meet all of the legitimate eligibility requirements and that the denial of their application was based on an impermissible evaluation of their disabilities.

The matter was originally before me on plaintiffs' motion for a preliminary injunction and for class certification. At that initial appearance on the preliminary injunction motion, the parties agreed to consolidate the hearing on the motion for a preliminary injunction with trial on the merits as to some of the disputed issues. . . .

The complaint charges the Authority with several discriminatory practices in its application process. Plaintiffs claim that the Authority imposes an arbitrary and subjective "ability to live independently" standard in determining whether to approve an application for public housing by a disabled applicant. Plaintiffs claim that this standard violates several federal statutes and current federal regulations that were adopted concerning fair housing and the handicapped. The Authority's application process violates federal law because it authorizes and condones detailed inquiries into the nature and scope of the applicant's disabling condition and because it requires, in some cases, that the applicant release confidential medical information. Plaintiffs also claim that the Authority fails to give adequate and proper notice of actions taken on housing applications.

FACTS

The eligibility standards for public housing controlled by the Authority are set forth in the Rochester Housing Authority Rental and Occupancy Manual,

§124 at pp. 17-18. The Manual was promulgated in May, 1988. The "Standards for Tenant Selection Criteria" allow consideration of the following:

> a) an applicant's ability to live independently, or to live independently with minimal aid;
>
> b) an applicant's past performance in meeting financial obligations, especially rent, unless good cause can be shown for non-payment of rent;
>
> c) a record of disturbance of neighbors, destruction of property or of living or habits at prior residences which may adversely affect the health, safety and of other tenants (sic);
>
> d) a history of criminal activity involving crimes of physical violence to persons or property, or other criminal acts which would adversely affect the health, safety, and welfare of other tenants.

Plaintiffs challenge only the standard relating to the "ability to live independently" and the Authority's inquiries and procedures utilized to make that determination.

The "ability to live independently" is defined in the Manual as follows:

> Ability to live independently shall mean that an applicant is able to perform those basic functions of adult living for and by him/her self. These activities include: ability to understand and to sign contracts and legal agreements, ability to perform basic housekeeping and personal care; ability to perform necessary daily activities ability to understand and conform to applicable standards of safety. (sic)

The facts relating to the procedures utilized by the Authority in reviewing and assessing applications are largely undisputed and are set forth in the record by affidavit and deposition testimony. The Authority classifies all applicants for housing into two general categories. Into the first category fall families. Individual applicants, be they elderly or handicapped, are lumped into the second.

All *individual* applicants undergo an in-home evaluation, performed by an employee of the Authority. Prospective tenants in this category also are asked to complete a questionnaire, which contains many of the questions challenged in this action as discriminatory and intrusive. Each individual applicant signs a form consenting to the release of otherwise confidential medical information, although that information is not obtained in all cases.

The Authority employee who reviews the application then makes a subjective determination, based on her/his observations of the applicant and the answers to the questionnaire, whether circumstances exist to justify further inquiry into the applicant's ability to live independently in public housing. If such an investigation is deemed necessary, the application is referred to a social worker, who is in some cases employed by the Monroe County Health Department. In some instances, the social worker conducts a nursing evaluation, during which a variety of specific questions concerning the applicant's disability, personal hygiene and ability to live independently are asked.

Based on all this information, the Authority then makes a decision to accept or reject the application. In many instances concerning applications from handicapped individuals, the decision to deny housing is specifically based on the applicant's perceived inability to "live independently." There were no reported rejections of non-handicapped applicants for this reason.

Plaintiffs allege that the Authority denied their applications for housing solely on the basis of their handicaps.

In the case of plaintiff Cason, she received a letter dated February 6, 1990 from defendants, which stated that her application was denied because of her need for a wheelchair, because she is able only to walk short distances with the aid of a walker, because she is incontinent and relies on adult diapers, and because she would require 10 hours of daily aide service. The letter, attached to the complaint as exhibit "F," makes repeated reference to the Authority's conclusion that Cason is unable to live on an independent basis.

The evidence relating to the denial of plaintiff Doe's application consists of a short letter dated August 24, 1989 . . . and the deposition testimony of Donna Smith, a housing specialist employed by the Authority who testified that the decision to deny Doe's application was chiefly hers. The letter recommends that Doe attempt to live independently of her parents for a period of 18 months, after which time the Authority would re-evaluate her "independent skills."

Smith testified at her deposition that she rejected Doe's application because she exhibited an inability to live independently and because Smith feared Doe would be uncooperative and might have trouble fulfilling the obligations of tenancy, chiefly that she might fail to pay the rent on time. Smith reached her decision on the basis of her own personal observations of Doe's behavior during a home visit, as well as information provided by Doe's therapist. Smith testified that during the visit, Doe repeatedly complained about small matters unrelated to the visit and appeared unable to understand questions or directions, and that subsequent to the interview, Doe made repeated telephone calls to Smith's office regarding a variety of complaints. At her deposition, Smith denied that these calls were related to the fact that the Authority had "lost" Doe's application for *two years* prior to this time although an activity sheet relating to Doe's file indicated that several of the telephone calls were "about [Doe's] application."

Smith also testified that Doe's counselor at Rochester Mental Health voiced similar reservations about Doe's ability to live independently, and had recommended to Doe, apparently without success, that she move into a group home. Although Doe did submit a landlord reference stating that she had paid her rent and had created no other problems, Smith discounted the reference because the "landlords" were Doe's parents.

The only written communication to Doe concerning her rejection consists of the letter referred to above. Smith testified that in conversations with Doe, however, she told Doe that the main reason for the denial was her perceived inability to live independently.

Attached to the complaint as exhibit "J" is a December 1988 letter to Plaintiff Roe from Donna Smith, informing her that her housing application was being denied because she required a higher level of care than the Authority could offer. Exhibit "K" is a memo to Smith directing her to remove Roe's name from the waiting list for the Enriched Housing Program because of an "involved psych history."

Further evidence concerning the denial of plaintiff Roe's application can be gleaned from the deposition testimony of Kathleen Richards, a Social Services Assistant at the Authority. Richards apparently made the decision to deny Roe's application for a program known as Extended Shared Aid Program (ESAP) housing, to which Roe's application had been referred by the Tenant Selection Division of the Authority, after Roe was rejected for Enriched Housing.

Richards testified that she based her decision in part on documentation in the nursing evaluation file, which indicated that Roe was in need of support services and had a history of resistance to such services. The applicant's assessment questionnaire revealed that Roe had been hospitalized, had felt "depressed" at times, and was bothered by noises. Finally, Richards referred to a conversation with the director of the Enriched Housing Program, who stated that his file on Roe contained evidence that Roe had suffered for some time from a variety of physical and mental afflictions, had questionable hygiene habits, and had a history of non-cooperation with service providers.

Apparently no adverse information about plaintiff Roe was obtained from prior landlords. In fact, Donna Smith testified that Roe's prior landlord in New York City had experienced no difficulties with Roe's ability to comply with the terms of her lease.

DISCUSSION

A. Applicability of Statutes to the Authority.

Although the parties do not dispute the issue, there appears to be no question that the Fair Housing Act and the Rehabilitation Act apply to the Authority.

The Fair Housing Act, 42 U.S.C. at §3603, extends generally to dwellings provided in whole or in part with the aid of Federal monies. The Fair Housing Amendments Act of 1988 ("FHAA"), P.L. 100-430, for the first time extended the protections of the Fair Housing Act to the handicapped; prior to that time, it had prohibited discrimination only on the basis of race, color, religion, sex and national origin.

On the other hand, the Rehabilitation Act, §794 of Title 29, U.S.C., from its enactment in 1973, has prohibited discrimination against handicapped persons "under any program or activity receiving Federal financial assistance." In 1988, Congress amended this section, along with other civil rights legislation, via the Civil Rights Restoration Act, P.L. 100-259. The amendments added to §794 a definition of "program or activity," which definition appears to include the Authority. *See* 29 U.S.C. §794(b). It is clear, however, from the legislative history, that the amendments were not intended to extend the application of the act to entities such as the Authority, but merely to *clarify* what had from the beginning been Congress' intent to make the Rehabilitation Act broad and far-reaching in its application. The court is aware of no authority holding that the Rehabilitation Act of 1973 did not apply to the challenged practices before its amendment in 1988.

. . . Defendants' documentation . . . along with representations at argument concerning the extent to which HUD exerts control over the Authority, convinces the Court that the Authority receives some financial assistance from HUD and, therefore, must comply with all federal statutes that prohibit discrimination against the handicapped.

B. Fair Housing Act.

The court finds that the challenged practices violate the Fair Housing Act. The Fair Housing Amendments Act (FHAA), passed in 1988, extended the protections embodied in the Fair Housing Act to handicapped persons. Title 42 U.S.C. §3604(f)(1) now makes it unlawful "[t]o discriminate in the sale or rental, or to otherwise make unavailable or deny, a dwelling to any buyer or renter because of a handicap." Section 3602(h) defines "handicap" as including any "physical or mental impairment which substantially limits one or more . . . major life activities." The defendants do not dispute that the plaintiffs are handicapped as defined by the statute. *Huntington Branch, NAACP v. Town of Huntington*, 844 F.2d 926, 934 (2d Cir. 1988), *aff'd on other grounds*, 488 U.S. 15, 109 S. Ct. 276, 102 L. Ed. 2d 180 (1988) established that plaintiffs suing under the Fair Housing Act can succeed *either* by showing discriminatory impact or discriminatory treatment. Proof of the latter requires a showing of intent to discriminate. Plaintiffs allege only that the Authority's practices have the *effect* of discriminating against handicapped individuals.

Defendants point out that, since 1987, of 276 handicapped applicants for housing, only 17 have had their applications denied on the basis of conclusions reached from the application of the challenged "ability to live independently" criteria. They argue that this statistic proves that there is no discriminatory effect.

The Authority, however, improperly measures effect. A plaintiff makes out a prima facie case of disparate impact by showing that a given practice has a greater impact on handicapped applicants than on non-handicapped ones. . . . Thus, discriminatory effect is shown by proof that all persons negatively affected by an allegedly unlawful practice are handicapped. . . . In this case, defendants deny housing only to handicapped applicants on the basis of an inability to live independently; no non-handicapped persons apparently were denied housing on the basis of their inability to live independently. I therefore find that plaintiffs have sufficiently shown discriminatory effect.

Having determined the existence of adverse impact, the question remains whether defendant somehow may avoid liability under the Act. As phrased in *Town of Huntington*, 844 F.2d at 936, "the defendant must prove that its actions furthered, in theory and in practice, a legitimate, bona fide governmental interest and that no alternative would serve that interest with less discriminatory effect."

I find defendants' justifications for their actions to be without merit. Defendants contend that inquiring into a handicapped person's ability to live independently furthers the goal of ensuring that tenants will respect the property and rights of other residents. As discussed *infra*, the need to protect other tenants from physical dangers posed by destructive tenants surely is an important governmental interest. Nevertheless, I am not convinced that delving into an applicant's confidential medical history, or requiring that the applicant demonstrate an ability to live independently, are the least discriminatory methods of advancing that interest.

In enacting FHAA, Congress specifically considered the plight of housing applicants with mental illnesses. "In the case of a person with a mental illness . . . there must be objective evidence from the person's prior behavior that the person has committed overt acts which caused harm or which directly threatened harm." H.R. Rep. No. 711, 100th Cong. 2d Sess. 5, *reprinted in* 1988 U.S. Code Cong. & Admin. News 2173, 2190 ("House Report"). The landlord's determination must not rest on "unsubstantiated inferences." *See id.* at 2191. In my view, there is no *objective* evidence concerning threatened harm that justified rejecting Cason, Roe and Doe.

The court is sympathetic to the Authority's desire not to rent public housing to persons with objectively dangerous tendencies. Nevertheless, defendants have produced no evidence that the challenged practices allow the Authority to screen out potentially dangerous tenants, nor have they shown the court that less intrusive means of investigating applicants, such as requests for landlord references, would be ineffective in achieving the desired ends.

Presumably, in renting to a non-handicapped person, the Authority takes a similar, and perhaps in some cases a greater, risk that some harm will come to the property or to other tenants. Yet such applicants' ability to live independently is never questioned, and they are not required to disclose their medical history. It would thus seem that the authority is content to rely upon information of a less intrusive and personal nature to assess the threat posed by these non-handicapped tenants. Without any objective evidence to indicate otherwise, it appears that the difference in treatment of the handicapped stems from unsubstantiated prejudices and fears regarding those with mental and physical disabilities. This is precisely the sort of situation that the fair housing laws were designed to prohibit.

Another factor relevant to a Fair Housing Act challenge is whether there exists evidence of discriminatory intent. Plaintiffs here, to the extent they base their position on a showing of adverse impact, offer no evidence of intent. This, however, is not fatal to their case. . . . Surely, evidence of discriminatory intent would aid plaintiffs' position, but the absence of such proof weighs only slightly against granting relief.

The court in *Town of Huntington* followed *Arlington Heights* and ruled that the "balance should be struck more readily in favor of the plaintiff when it is seeking only to enjoin a municipal defendant from interfering with its own plans rather than attempting to compel the defendant itself to build housing." 844 F.2d at 940. Although the Second Circuit dealt with a challenge to a discriminatory zoning ordinance, its reasoning applies here as well. Plaintiffs seek not to compel the Authority to develop housing, but merely to change the procedure by which it selects tenants for its existing facilities.

C. Regulatory Violations.

The Authority's practice of making inquiry into an applicant's ability to live independently is clearly at odds with the regulations promulgated by the United States Department of Housing and Urban Development ("HUD"). Part 24 of the Code of Federal Regulations (C.F.R.), at §100.202(c), explicitly defines the permissible scope of inquiry allowed of a handicapped applicant for housing:

> (c) It shall be unlawful to make an inquiry to determine whether an applicant for a dwelling . . . has a handicap or to make inquiry as to the nature or severity of a handicap of such a person. However, this paragraph does not prohibit the following inquiries, provided these inquiries are made of all applicants, whether or not they have handicaps: (1) Inquiry into an applicant's ability to meet the requirements of ownership or tenancy. The remaining exceptions, which allow inquiries relating to specific types of housing, as well as those aimed at determining whether an applicant is a substance abuser or engages in other illegalities, are not at issue here.

The "requirements of tenancy" referred to above may be found at 24 C.F.R. §966.4. This section details various lease requirements related to public housing, and at subsection (f) lists 12 separate obligations that the lease may impose on tenants. Each concerns requirements that tenants not conduct themselves or treat the property in a manner that will interfere with other tenants' health, safety or enjoyment of the property. Tenants must, *inter alia*, avoid physical damage to the premises, keep them in a sanitary condition and comply with all applicable housing codes. Nowhere is there found a requirement that a resident be able to live "independently," rather than with the aid of others.[1]

Defendants do not deny that their conduct contravenes the current HUD regulations. Their position appears to be that because they annually send an outline of their procedures to HUD and that HUD has given at least tacit approval to those procedures that they are in compliance with HUD requirements.

It is clear, however, that the last "approval" of the Authority's policies was over two years ago, in 1988, and was apparently based on the 1987 HUD handbook. The applicable federal regulations that now control were

---

1. The Authority complains that it lacks the staff and resources to provide support services to tenants. Plaintiffs, however, stress that they require nothing of the sort from the Authority; rather, many handicapped applicants receive support from Medicaid or other assistance programs. A tenant who is able to meet the objective requirements of tenancy should not be denied housing simply because she receives medical assistance or other aid.

promulgated *after* these dates. In any event, the prior approval by HUD cannot excuse the Authority from complying with all requirements of federal statutes and regulations concerning discrimination in housing. Clearly, the federal regulations cited above now control and the Authority must follow them.

C.F.R. Part 24, §100.202(d), tracking the language of 42 U.S.C. §3604(f)(9), does permit the Authority to refuse to rent a dwelling to one whose tenancy will pose a direct threat to the health and safety of others, or will result in physical damage to the property. There is no evidence in the record, however, to indicate that an *inability* to live independently creates the type of threat contemplated by the statute. . . .

"Generalized perceptions about disabilities and unfounded speculations about threats to safety are specifically rejected as grounds to justify exclusion [from housing]." House Report, at 2179.

D. Class Certification Motion.

[After detailed analysis the court then granted the Plaintiffs' motion to certify this as a class action, "with the class composed of all individuals with handicaps, as defined by the Fair Housing Act and §504 of the Rehabilitation Act, who have in the past three years applied for, are presently applying for or will in the future apply for, low income public housing administered by defendant Rochester Housing Authority."—ED.]

CONCLUSION

Plaintiffs' motion for declaratory and injunctive relief is granted. The current procedures utilized by the Rochester Housing Authority to select tenants clearly violates federal law because the procedure has the effect of discriminating against handicapped applicants.

Specifically, that portion of the Authority's manual entitled "Standards for Tenant Selection Criteria" that requires an applicant to demonstrate an ability "to live independently" violates federal statutes and is contrary to federal regulations concerning discrimination in housing and must not be utilized in the tenant selection process. The Rochester Housing Authority is hereby enjoined from using this criteria in considering applications for housing. Furthermore, the Rochester Housing Authority is ordered to vacate the rejection of the applications of the three representative plaintiffs and those other members of the class that were denied housing on the basis of their inability to live independently and to immediately reconsider those applications under proper standards; and it is further

ORDERED that the Authority is to promulgate within sixty (60) days and obtain HUD approval for new standards for determining tenant eligibility that comply with all federal statutes and regulations that prohibit discrimination against the handicapped in housing.

IT IS SO ORDERED.

PROBLEMS

1. CCRCs typically require new residents to be capable of independent living. Is such a requirement lawful?

2. In 2012, the website of a real estate agency specializing in sales of units in Leisure World, a gated retirement community, stated that:

> It is the responsibility of the buyers to provide a Physician Letter stating "Health and the Ability to Care for Ones-Self." The Original Copy must be signed by your attending physician on letterhead and submitted before the opening of Escrow.

Leisure Living Resales, Details, *available at* http://www.leisurelivingresales .com/Pages/Details.aspx.

   a. Does this provision constitute impermissible discrimination on the basis of disability?
   b. Suppose that Leisure World frequently makes exceptions to this requirement when persons with disabilities request such exceptions. Does this change your answer to problem 2.a?

Weinstein v. Cherry Oaks Retirement Community

917 P.2d 336 (Colo. App. 1996)

Opinion by Judge HUME.

Respondents, Cherry Oaks Retirement Community, Cherry Oaks Company, Steve Shraiberg, Alfred S. Blum, Urban Property Management, Inc., d/b/a Urban, Inc., and June O'Neill (Cherry Oaks) appeal the order of the Colorado Civil Rights Commission (Commission) finding that their actions toward complainants, Miriam Weinstein and the estate and heirs of Hyman Weinstein, deceased, constituted discriminatory and unfair housing practices in violation of the Colorado Fair Housing Act (CFHA). We affirm.

Cherry Oaks Retirement Community is a privately-owned, residential care facility for senior citizens who have impaired capacity to live independently but are not totally bedfast or in need of 24-hour medical or nursing care. It is licensed as a "personal care boarding home," and is therefore subject to regulations promulgated by both the State of Colorado and the City and County of Denver departments of health. Department of Health Regulation No. 7.2, 6 Code Colo. Reg. 1011-1, requires a licensed facility to develop and implement criteria for the admission and discharge of its residents based upon the identified needs of residents that the facility is capable of meeting.

Prior to 1992, Cherry Oaks had implemented a policy requiring facility residents who use wheelchairs or walkers to transfer to ordinary chairs when taking meals in the dining room. The wheelchairs and walkers were then removed from the dining room and placed in another room. The purpose of this policy, according to the executive director of the facility, was to allow

Cherry Oaks' personnel an opportunity to observe residents regularly and to ensure that they were physically appropriate to remain at the boarding home.

In March 1992, Hyman and Miriam Weinstein visited the Cherry Oaks facility in the process of selecting a personal care residence. As part of their visit, they ate in the dining room, and Mr. Weinstein sat in his wheelchair during that meal. Later that same month, the Weinsteins entered into a one-year lease with Cherry Oaks. At that time Mr. Weinstein was ambulatory although he required the use of a walker and, occasionally, a wheelchair. He was able to transfer from his walker or wheelchair to an ordinary chair without assistance.

In June 1992, Mr. Weinstein's physical condition began to deteriorate as a result of amyotrophic lateral sclerosis (Lou Gehrig's disease). The transfer from wheelchair to dining room chair became increasingly difficult and painful. In late November or early December 1992, the Weinsteins asked that Mr. Weinstein be allowed to take his meals in his wheelchair.

For a short time, Mr. Weinstein was allowed to remain in his wheelchair at an isolated table. However, Cherry Oaks later discontinued that practice and offered instead to provide two aides at no cost to the Weinsteins to assist Mr. Weinstein in making the transfer.

The Weinsteins were told that wheelchairs did not look good in the dining room, that allowing wheelchairs in the dining room would be a violation of the city fire code, that regulations required such transfers, and that allowing one wheelchair in the dining room would lead to requests from others for the same treatment. At no time did Cherry Oaks tell the Weinsteins or their family that they were no longer eligible to remain as residents or inform them that Mr. Weinstein's failure to make the transfer at mealtimes could result in their discharge from the facility.

As a result of Cherry Oaks' refusal to allow Mr. Weinstein to take his meals while remaining in his wheelchair, the Weinsteins began taking all their meals in their apartment and moved out at the end of their lease term. There is no evidence in the record as to whether Mr. Weinstein was ever asked to demonstrate his ability to transfer after he quit coming to the dining room for meals.

The Weinsteins filed a complaint with the Commission alleging that Cherry Oaks' policies and conduct in refusing to allow Mr. Weinstein to remain seated in his wheelchair for meals constituted a discriminatory and unfair housing practice based on his disability in violation of §§24-34-502(1)(a), 24-34-502.2(1)(b), & 24-34-502.2(2)(b), C.R.S. (1995 Cum. Supp.). The complaint was pursued by Miriam Weinstein and Hyman Weinstein's heirs and estate after his death in May 1993.

Following a hearing, an Administrative Law Judge (ALJ) determined that Cherry Oaks' policies and conduct discriminated against Mr. Weinstein solely on the basis of his disability. The findings and conclusions of the ALJ were generally adopted by the Commission on appeal. The Commission's final decision altered only the amount of monetary sanctions that had been awarded by the ALJ's preliminary order.

Respondents contend that the Commission erred in determining that Cherry Oaks engaged in discriminatory practices in violation of the CFHA, arguing that the facility's policy requiring residents to transfer from their wheelchairs to dining room chairs for meals did not discriminate against Hyman Weinstein on the basis of his disability. We disagree.

According to §§24-34-502(1)(a) and 24-34-502.2(1)(b), the refusal or denial of equal terms, conditions, or privileges of housing, including rental housing, to individuals with a disability is prohibited. Discrimination under the CFHA includes the refusal to make reasonable accommodations in rules, policies, practices, or services when such accommodations may be necessary to afford disabled persons an equal opportunity to use and enjoy a dwelling. "Reasonable accommodation" may be defined as changing a rule that may be otherwise generally applicable so as to make its burden less onerous on a disabled individual. *See North Shore-Chicago Rehabilitation Inc. v. Skokie,* 827 F. Supp. 497 (N.D. Ill. 1993) (to avoid being found in violation of federal fair housing act, party accused of discrimination must show that no reasonable accommodation could be made).

* * *

Individuals are not admitted or permitted to remain as residents in a personal care boarding home if they have physical limitations that prevent ambulation unless such limitations are adequately compensated by artificial means. Further, residents must be able to enter and leave wheelchairs and walkers without assistance. Denver Department of Health & Hospitals Regulation 2.8 (1976).

In determining whether a regulatory agency's order should stand, the question is not whether a reviewing body would reach the identical conclusion upon the evidence but whether, based upon the entire record, the findings are supported by substantial evidence. . . .

Because the CFHA is almost identical to the federal Fair Housing Amendment Act, federal case authority is deemed persuasive in interpreting the provisions of the CFHA.

To prevail under the CFHA, a complainant may demonstrate that the challenged regulation discriminates against disabled persons on its face and serves no legitimate government interest. Alternatively, a complainant must show either discriminatory intent or discriminatory impact. Discriminatory intent is proved by showing that disabilities like those of the complainant were, in some part, the basis for the policy being challenged. . . .

Once a complainant demonstrates a prima facie case of discriminatory action, the burden shifts to the respondent to present legitimate, bona fide reasons for such action and to show that no less discriminatory alternative was available. If some basis is advanced in support of the legitimacy of challenged actions or policies, then the complainant may demonstrate that such basis is pretextual.

Here, the ALJ determined that Cherry Oaks' transfer policy violated the CFHA under both the discriminatory intent and the discriminatory impact tests. The ALJ found that Mr. Weinstein was denied the full use and enjoyment of the communal dining room by the unyielding enforcement of the facility's policy requiring him to transfer from his wheelchair in order to take meals there; that the "legitimate" reasons advanced by Cherry Oaks for disallowing wheelchairs in the dining room were pretextual; and that neither fire code regulations nor other state or local regulations prohibited the residents' use of wheelchairs in the dining room. The ALJ also determined that, because aides were present to help residents transfer to and from dining room chairs, the transfer policy was not an effective means of determining which individuals could not enter or leave their wheelchairs without assistance.

Further, in spite of the facility's transfer policy and requirement that persons not capable of remaining at Cherry Oaks be asked to leave, Mr. Weinstein was not asked to leave. In fact, respondent O'Neill testified that she thought Mr. Weinstein was still able to enter or leave his chair without assistance and thus was eligible to remain at Cherry Oaks even though his family refused to allow him to transfer at mealtimes.

The ALJ concluded that the real reason for the transfer policy was to maintain a "disability-free" atmosphere at Cherry Oaks rather than to determine eligibility to remain at the facility. O'Neill and the dining room manager both stated that wheelchairs in the dining room did not "look good." Corespondent Blum, who also was counsel for Cherry Oaks, wrote in respondents' brief that: "Cherry Oaks is designed to provide senior citizens a relaxing, comfortable atmosphere, *free from any semblances of a gloomy, septic hospital environment.*" (emphasis added).

The ALJ found that Cherry Oaks did not present a legitimate reason for the transfer policy. Respondents argue that the transfer policy was an appropriate means of gauging whether a resident had physical needs that exceeded those which the facility could provide. However, conditioning wheelchair or walker accommodated persons' dining room privileges on the arbitrary testing policy was not a reasonable method of determining appropriateness to remain in the facility.

On these findings, the ALJ concluded that because Mr. Weinstein's disability was in some part the basis of Cherry Oaks' application of and refusal to alter its transfer policy, discriminatory intent had been demonstrated.

We agree with the ALJ's determination that Cherry Oaks has not presented a legitimate reason for its transfer policy. Further, we agree that Cherry Oaks has not met its burden of establishing that no reasonable accommodation could have been made to allow Mr. Weinstein full use and enjoyment of the dining room unless or until his ineligibility to remain in the facility had been established.

Our review of the record satisfies us that sufficient evidence exists to support the ALJ's findings of fact and ultimate determination that Cherry Oaks engaged in discriminatory and unfair housing practices. Thus, we conclude that the Commission did not err in determining Cherry Oaks to be in violation of the Colorado Fair Housing Act as alleged in the Weinsteins' complaint.

The order is affirmed. . . .

PROBLEM

Hazel Anderson, an 83-year-old resident of Crosslands Retirement Community, was using a motorized cart for mobility when Crosslands implemented a new policy prohibiting the use of such carts in common areas during peak hours (11:00 A.M. to 1:30 P.M. and 4:00 P.M. to 6:00 P.M.). The stated purpose of the policy was to protect other residents from the dangers posed by such carts. To comply with the policy, Ms. Anderson initially used a walker or wheelchair to get to meals or other activities during peak times. After suffering a significant fall, Crosslands amended its policy to allow her to use her cart to enter and exit the dining room during peak times. There was some dispute as to whether, and to what extent, the rules limited Mrs. Anderson's ability to socialize with other residents.

    a. Could the management of Crosslands Retirement Community have addressed concerns about motorized carts in a less restrictive manner? If so, should the court have found that the failure to do so was unlawful?

    b. In *United States v. Hillhaven Corp.*, 960 F. Supp. 259 (D. Utah 1997), the federal district court held that Crosslands had not violated the Fair Housing Act based on these facts. Was that outcome consistent with that in *Weinstein*?

Herriot v. Channing House

2009 WL 225418 (N.D. Cal. 2009)

JEREMY FOGEL, District Judge.

I. BACKGROUND

Plaintiff Sally Herriot ("Herriot") seeks reconsideration of this Court's order dated August 26, 2008 ("the prior Order"), and reasserts her Fair Housing Amendments Act ("FHAA") claim and state-law claims. Defendant Channing House opposes reconsideration and moves separately for summary judgment with respect to Herriot's claims under the Americans with Disabilities Act ("ADA") and her negligence claim. The Court has considered the moving and responding papers, as well as the oral arguments presented at the hearing on November 21, 2008. For the reasons discussed below, the motion for reconsideration will be denied, and the motion for summary judgment will be granted.

A. Underlying Dispute

Herriot is a ninety-year-old resident of Channing House, a continuing care retirement community ("CCRC") where she has resided since 1992. As a CCRC, Channing House is licensed by the State of California to provide care and services to persons over the age of sixty-two. Residents of Channing House sign a contract that guarantees them lifetime care in the facility in exchange for an entrance fee and monthly payments. Channing House offers its residents a three-level continuum of care: independent living, assisted living and skilled nursing. Independent living residents occupy their own apartments without any restrictions on visitation. Assisted living and skilled nursing care are provided in shared facilities. Channing House transfers its residents to a higher level of care based on residents' health care needs.

In 2006, Herriot was hospitalized and Channing House determined that it was necessary to transfer Herriot permanently from her independent living unit to an assisted living or skilled nursing facility. Herriot, her family and her personal physician, Dr. Deidre Stegman ("Dr. Stegman"), objected to the transfer. Herriot returned to her apartment and retained private care for sixteen hours each day to assist her with hygiene, dressing and grooming activities. On April 25, 2006, Herriot received a letter from Channing House informing her that "[y]our physical condition and needs require that you be transferred to our on-site Assisted Living area. The level of care that you require exceeds that which may be lawfully provided in your current Independent Living Apartment." Channing House also contacted the California Department of Social Services ("DSS") regarding Herriot's case, indicating that Herriot was in need of twenty-four hour assistance and had limited ability to ambulate. The DSS instructed Channing House to "obtain an updated medical assessment of the resident." The DSS also warned that Channing House could be cited for failure to provide the basic services needed by its residents, and that "neither the licensee nor the resident can delegate the responsibility to another party or person." . . .

It is undisputed that Herriot requires twenty-four hour care, has limited ambulatory capacity and suffers from dementia. A report from Dr. Ami Laws ("Dr.[ ]Laws"), who conducted an independent medical examination of Herriot at the Court's request, confirms Herriot's need for twenty-four hour care, and states that she "needs help with all her ADL's including bathing, dressing, going to the toilet, transferring from bed to chair [and] feeding. . . ." The report is consistent with an assessment performed by Channing House dated April 9, 2007 and with Herriot's own admission that she requires assistance with the activities of daily living. However, both Dr. Laws and Dr. Stegman opine that Herriot likely would suffer physically and mentally from a transfer to a skilled nursing facility.

As a result of the instant litigation, Herriot has not been transferred. Channing House has offered Herriot several options, including a proposal that she move into a shared room on the assisted living floor but pay an additional $25.00 a day to convert the room to a private room that she could furnish with some of her own belongings. Herriot has not accepted any of these arrangements. Instead, she requests that she be permitted to remain in her independent living unit and receive private care at her own expense.

B. Procedural History

... On August 26, 2008, the Court issued its Order Denying Plaintiff's Motion for Partial Summary Judgment, Denying Defendant's Motion for Summary Judgment and Granting Defendant's Motion for Summary Adjudication. ...

On October 10, 2008, Herriot sought leave to file a motion for reconsideration of the prior Order. ... Channing House opposes reconsideration and moves separately for summary judgment with respect to Herriot's [claims for violation of the Americans with Disabilities Act and for negligence].

II. LEGAL STANDARD

A motion for summary judgment should be granted if there is no genuine issue of material fact and the moving party is entitled to judgment as a matter of law. ...

III. DISCUSSION

Herriot seeks reconsideration of this Court's adjudication of her FHAA and state-law claims in favor of Channing House, which in turn moves for summary adjustment on Herriot's remaining ADA claim and negligence claim. Essentially, Herriot alleges failure to accommodate and disability discrimination. She contends that Channing House should be required to modify its transfer policy, seek an exception to DSS regulations, and permit her to remain in her independent living apartment with the assistance of personally-funded private aides. She also asserts that the transfer policy discriminates against Channing House's residents on the basis of their disabilities. Channing House argues that it should not be required to seek an exception to its policy or the DSS regulations because legally it may not delegate its duty of care to private aides, and that even if an exception were granted, the requested accommodation would constitute a fundamental alteration of its continuing care program. Channing House asserts that it seeks to transfer Herriot not because of her disabilities but because as a matter of law Herriot may not remain in an independent living unit.

A. Failure to Accommodate Claims

The FHAA's definition of prohibited discrimination encompasses "a refusal to make reasonable accommodations in rules, policies, practices, or services, when such accommodations may be necessary to afford [the physically disabled] equal opportunity to use and enjoy a dwelling." *Giebeler v. M & B Assocs.*, 343 F.3d 1143, 1146 (9th Cir. 2003) (citing 42 U.S.C. §3604(f)(3)(B)). The definition of discrimination under Title III of the ADA includes "failing to make a reasonable modification in 'policies, practices, or procedures,' [...] necessary to accommodate [a person's] disability." *Fortyune v. American Multi-Cinema, Inc.*, 364 F.3d 1075, 1082

(9th Cir. 2004) (citing 42 U.S.C. §12182(b)(2)(A) (ii)) (internal citations omitted).

Both of Herriot's failure to accommodate claims turn on the question of whether her requested accommodation is reasonable. In its prior order, this Court held that "Herriot requires a type and degree of care that Channing House may not lawfully provide in an independent living unit." Order at 8 (citing 22 Cal. Code. Reg. §87455(c)(2) (resident requires 24-hour care); 22 Cal. Code. Reg. §87615(a)(5) (resident needs assistance with all activities of daily living)). As it noted in granting Herriot's request for leave to file a motion for reconsideration, the Court reached this conclusion without the benefit of briefing with respect to certain regulatory exceptions that permit variances "to a specific regulation based on the unique needs or circumstances of a specific resident." 22 Cal. Code Reg. §87101(e)(6). Herriot contends that if "the intent of the law [could] be met through alternative means," Channing House could (and in this case should) submit a written exception request on behalf of a resident who "has a prohibited and/or restrictive health condition." *Id.* §87616.

However, although there may be some circumstances where a facility's refusal to seek an exception on a resident's behalf would be actionable, that is not the case here. Channing House has a legal responsibility to be aware of its residents' conditions on an on-going basis so that it can respond to their changing needs and bring in medical interventions as necessary. To ensure that RCFE's "provide the services necessary to meet resident needs," DSS imposes extensive personnel training and supervision requirements, including a detailed training protocol for "[a]ll RCFE staff who assist residents with personal activities of daily living." *Id.* §87411. In its interpretation of this provision, the Community Care Licensing Division ("CCLD") has clarified that an RCFE may not delegate its duty of providing assistance with activities of daily living to privately paid personal assistants. CCLD Evaluator Manual, Regulation Interpretations and Procedures for Residential Care Facilities for the Elderly 61 (January 2002).

California law not only prohibits Channing House from delegating its care duties to private aides, but it also expressly authorizes Channing House's proposed transfer of Herriot to its staffed nursing floor. California Health and Safety Code §1788(a)(10)(A), which regulates continuing care contracts, provides an explicit statutory basis for transfer to a higher level of care when the care required by the resident exceeds that which lawfully may be provided in the living unit. As noted above, there does not appear to be a genuine dispute of material fact with respect to the type and degree of care required by Herriot. Although the regulations contemplate exceptions, Herriot requests an accommodation that unreasonably and impermissibly would require Channing House to violate its legal obligations.

Herriot's reasonable expectations upon entering Channing House also undermine her legal position. Herriot's Continuing Care Agreement expressly provides that at some point Herriot might be required to transfer to a higher level of care better equipped to address her care needs. Channing House is designed so that residents who no longer are able to live independently will receive more intensive care and supervision at either the assisted living or skilled nursing levels of care. The system serves the health and well-being of residents, while ensuring that Channing House can discharge its managerial responsibilities that it is obligated both legally and contractually to provide. Herriot remains free to choose both where she lives and what type of personal care she will receive by moving to a private residence apart from Channing House.

In addition, neither the FHAA nor the ADA impose liability on a provider for failing to provide an accommodation that fundamentally would alter the nature of its business. The CCRC model, which every resident accepts when they move into Channing House, offers a degree of certainty with respect to a resident's medical costs and contemplates transfers along a "continuum of care" designed to meet residents' healthcare needs. California law recognizes that CCRCs must have control over level-of-care decisions, and it expressly authorizes involuntary transfers within the continuum of care. Herriot argues that the presence of private personal care aides would not be remarkable in a facility providing residential life care for seniors. Although it likely would not be remarkable for aides to be present temporarily, it would be a fundamental alteration, and an unlawful accommodation as discussed above, to permit the private aides to provide all of the assistance required by a resident.

B. FHAA Discrimination Claim

Herriot next argues that the Court erroneously evaluated the *McDonnell Douglas* burden-shifting test because she presented direct rather than circumstantial evidence of disability discrimination. She notes correctly that the proper standard for challenging facially discriminatory policies is derived from *Johnson Controls*, 499 U.S. [187, 200-01 (1991)]. Under *Johnson Controls*, a plaintiff makes out a case of intentional discrimination by showing that the defendant's policy "on its face applies less favorably to a protected group." *Id.* at 1048. However, on its face the policy at issue here does not apply less favorably to disabled individuals as a group. The transfer policy does not result in differential treatment toward or exclude a specific class of persons. Herriot is being treated no differently than other residents, including residents with disabilities, who have agreed contractually to move through the continuum of care. Application of the transfer policy does not exclude all disabled persons from residing in independent living, but rather conforms with state regulations that require residents who need twenty-four hour care or assistance with their activities of daily living to reside in a level of care appropriate to their needs.

This Court thus appropriately applied the *McDonnell Douglas* burden-shifting framework to Herriot's disparate treatment claim under the FHAA and FEHA. *See Sanghvi v. City of Claremont*, 328 F.3d 532, 536 n.3 (9th Cir. 2003) (noting that *McDonnell Douglas* framework developed in the Title VII context extends to FHAA and ADA claims). Under *McDonnell Douglas*, once the plaintiff has established a prima facie case, the burden shifts to the defendant, which must articulate a legitimate nondiscriminatory reason for the application of its policies. *McDonnell Douglas Corp. v. Green*, 411 U.S. 792, 802-03 (1973). In light of the analysis above, the Court concludes that Channing House's compliance with state regulations and its legal and contractual right to uphold the fundamental nature of its continuing care program are legitimate nondiscriminatory reasons for its policy and decision to transfer Herriot.

C. ADA Discrimination Claim

"To prevail on a Title III discrimination claim, the plaintiff must show that (1) she is disabled within the meaning of the ADA; (2) the defendant is a private entity that owns, leases, or operates a place of public accommodation; and (3) the plaintiff was denied public accommodations by the defendant because of her disability." *Molski v. M.J. Cable, Inc.*, 481 F.3d 724 (9th Cir. 2007). It is undisputed here that Herriot has one or more disabilities within the definition of the ADA and that Channing House is an entity subject to the ADA. With respect to the third element, Herriot must show that her disability was one factor in the defendant's alleged discriminatory treatment. Channing House argues that its transfer policy and decision to transfer Herriot are based specifically on compliance with state regulations and upholding its continuum of care. Herriot argues that it is precisely her disabilities that trigger the state law obligation and contractual right to transfer. Confronted with a similar motivational issue, another district court has observed:

> While Plaintiff's arguments have some emotional appeal, they fail to account for the fact that acceptance into an assisted living facility presupposes that a resident has a physical or mental disability and needs assistance with daily activities of living. But there is a statutory ceiling on the level of care that assisted living facilities are both authorized and required to provide. Therefore, [Defendant] is entitled to assess whether Plaintiff's disabilities match the level of care [it] is authorized to provide. And [Defendant] only contracted to provided a limited level of care as an assisted living facility. The parties' agreement expressly permits [Defendant] to assess whether Plaintiff's needs and [Defendant's] resources are compatible.

Winters ex rel. Winters v. Chugiak Senior Citizens, Inc., 531 F. Supp. 2d 1075, 1081 (D. Alaska 2007). This reasoning is equally applicable here.

D. Remaining Claims

The foregoing analysis also disposes of Herriot's state-law claims. . . .

IV. ORDER

Good cause therefore appearing, IT IS HEREBY ORDERED that Herriot's motion for reconsideration is DENIED and Channing House's motion for summary judgment is GRANTED. Judgment shall be entered accordingly.

NOTES

1. *State agencies' anti-discrimination obligations.* Federal statutes, including the Rehabilitation Act and Title II of the Americans with Disabilities Act, prohibit state agencies from discriminating against persons with disabilities. In addition, the FHA applies to state agencies. Thus, certain state regulations of care facilities may be preempted by federal anti-discrimination law. For example, in *Buckhannon Board & Care Home, Inc. v. West Virginia Department of Health & Human Resources*, 19 F. Supp. 2d 567 (1998), the U.S. District Court of the District of West Virginia upheld against a motion to dismiss a claim brought by the operator and residents of a board and care home that alleged that the state had violated the FHA and the ADA by requiring residents of such facilities to be able to physically remove themselves from "situations involving imminent danger." Residents whose rights are threatened by such regulatory schemes may therefore be well-advised to seek relief from the state. *See* Melissa Morris & Kim Pederson, *Reasonable Accommodations in Assisted Living, Crafting Effective Requests to Promote Housing Choice*, CLEARINGHOUSE REV. J. OF POVERTY L. & POL'Y (Mar.-Apr. 2011) ("Ultimately, if an accommodation request implicates the state licensing scheme at all, our recommendation is to request the accommodation for the state or, if necessary, negotiate with the facility for the facility to seek an exception or waiver from the state.").

2. *Discrimination in nursing home admissions.* Individuals may also use anti-discrimination statutes such as the FHA and the Rehabilitation Act to challenge nursing home admissions policies. For example, in *Wagner v. Fair Acres*, 49 F.3d 1002 (3d Cir. 1994), the plaintiff was denied admission to a county home because of the behavioral manifestations of Alzheimer's disease. The Third Circuit held that the federal Rehabilitation Act prohibition against discrimination against the "handicapped" applies to nursing homes that receive federal funding. In addition, the court found that the plaintiff had presented sufficient evidence for a jury to find that she was unlawfully discriminated against because the nursing home had failed to make a reasonable accommodation for her. The court noted that "there was ample evidence that Mrs. Wagner's aggressive behaviors associated with her Alzheimer's disease clearly rendered her . . . 'a challenging and demanding patient.'" However, the court explained that:

   > We find that this fact alone cannot this fact alone cannot justify her exclusion from a nursing home that receives federal funds. Otherwise nursing homes would be free to "pick and choose" among patients, accepting and

admitting only the easiest patients to care for, leaving the more challenging and demanding patients with no place to turn for care.

Id. at 1015. The Third Circuit therefore vacated the district court's order granting the defendant's motion for a new trial and remanded the case to the district court for reconsideration.

QUESTIONS

1. Could a requested accommodation that conflicts with a state statutory scheme ever be found to be reasonable? If so, when?

2. Should Sally Herriot have sued the State of California instead of suing Channing House? Would the result have been different if she had?

PROBLEMS

1. In *Weinstein*, the court discussed a state law requiring residents of personal care boarding homes to be able to enter and leave a wheelchair or walker without assistance. Suppose that Mr. Weinstein became unable to do so, but he offered to privately pay to have a personal care assistant available 24 hours per day to assist him with such transferring. Could Cherry Oaks have lawfully evicted Mr. Weinstein because of this inability? Would it have been required to do so?

2. Mrs. North suffers from an anxiety disorder. Her psychiatrist suggested she might benefit from the soothing companionship of a pet. On this advice, Mrs. North adopted Princess, a large Persian cat. Princess brings Mrs. North great joy, and Mrs. North treats her like a child. When Mrs. North feels anxious, patting Princess calms her down. When she awakes in the middle of the night, or has difficulty sleeping, the presence of Princess napping at the foot of her bed comforts her. Mrs. North would like to move to Oakwood Retirement Community, an assisted living facility. The facility prohibits all animals. Must they make an exception for Princess?

3. Consider the following test questions developed by a group of prospective gerontology teachers for a quiz on senior housing. How would you critique the questions and answers based on what you have read?

   a. An older adult widower who has a chronic illness is able to care for most of his own needs. However, he does require transportation to his physician as well as help with his laundry and food preparation. He is lonely and has no nearby relatives. Which housing arrangement would be most appropriate to suggest to this client?
   (1) Assisted living facility
   (2) Nursing home
   (3) Skilled nursing facility
   (4) Single room occupancy hotel

   Correct answer: (1)

b. An older adult who lived alone prior to admission to the hospital now needs maximum assistance with ADLs (i.e., activities of daily living) and takes prescription medication twice a day. She is to be discharged from the hospital. Which facility could most appropriately meet this individual's needs?

(1) Adult daycare center

(2) Assisted-living facility

(3) Group home

(4) Skilled Nursing home

Correct answer: (4)

CHAPTER 8

Elder Abuse and Neglect

A. INTRODUCTION

Elder mistreatment is a complex phenomenon that includes physical, psychological, and sexual abuse, as well as financial exploitation, of older adults. The term is also frequently used to describe self-neglect, a phenomenon that occurs when individuals fail to meet their health, safety, or personal hygiene needs.

Although it is clear that elder abuse and neglect is not uncommon in later life, the overall prevalence of elder mistreatment remains unknown. A 2010 study of elder mistreatment in New York State estimated that 7.6 percent of non-institutionalized New York residents age 60 and older experience some form of abuse or neglect each year. *See* Lifespan of Greater Rochester, Inc., Weill Cornell Medical Center & NY Dep't for the Aging, Under the Radar: New York State Elder Abuse Prevalence Study (2011). A 2009 national telephone survey of non-institutionalized persons age 60 and older in the continental United States reported that 11 percent had experienced neglect or physical, emotional, or sexual abuse in the past year, and that 5 percent were being financially exploited by a family member. *See* Ron Acierno et al., National Elder Mistreatment Study (Mar. 2009). Notably, the study may have significantly underestimated the prevalence of mistreatment because it did not survey older adults with significant cognitive impairment, a group at heightened risk for such mistreatment.

Elder mistreatment is associated with significant declines in well-being and heightened rates of mortality. Older adults are likely to face more serious consequences of abuse and neglect than would younger adults subjected to parallel treatment. For example, an elder who is shoved may not only be more likely to fall because of reduced stability, but may also more easily break or fracture bones as a result because bones become more fragile with age.

This chapter explores different forms of elder mistreatment, how the law defines elder mistreatment, and the legal system's response to addressing elder mistreatment. In part because this is an area of the law that is very much in flux, the reader is encouraged to seek to not only understand the current state of the law, but also to think normatively about how the law should address these issues.

B. THE PHENOMENON OF ELDER MISTREATMENT

1. Types of Elder Mistreatment

Elder mistreatment can take many forms.

Physical elder abuse occurs when an older adult is subjected to physical violence. Such physical violence can range from overt acts of violence (e.g., hitting, shoving, or pinching), to improper handling (e.g., shattering bones or tearing tissues by dropping or roughly handling a frail individual), to improperly restraining an older adult either through the use of physical restraints (i.e., practices or devices that limit mobility) or chemical restraints (i.e., medications such as sedatives or antipsychotic drugs used to control behavior).

Psychological elder abuse occurs when another person subjects an older adult to mental or emotional anguish. Common forms of psychological elder abuse include intimidation, humiliation, and threats. Imposing isolation on an older adult or infantilizing an older adult can also constitute psychological elder abuse.

Sexual elder abuse occurs when another person subjects an older adult to non-consensual sexual contact or activity.

Financial exploitation occurs when another person misuses the funds or property of an older adult or, through wrongful behavior, causes the individual to use his or her funds or property in a way he or she otherwise would not use them.

Elder neglect, by contrast, is typically said to occur when someone in a caretaking relationship with the older adult fails to take reasonable efforts to meet that person's basic needs for health and safety.

There is, however, no single definition of elder mistreatment. Rather, different organizations and jurisdictions have adopted competing definitions of elder abuse and neglect. In many cases, the differences in definition are largely semantic. However, there is an active debate as to whether all mistreatment to which an older adult is subjected should be considered to be elder abuse or neglect, or whether the term "elder abuse and neglect" should be applied only to a certain sub-set of mistreatment experienced by older adults. Those who favor a more restrictive definition frequently limit the use of the term "elder abuse" to situations where the victim is in a trust relationship with the perpetrator, or where the victim was targeted for the mistreatment at least in part because of his or her age.

No matter how elder mistreatment is defined, it is clear that it occurs in both institutional settings and community-based settings. While research suggests that it is likely that most elder mistreatment is perpetrated by family members, elder abuse and neglect are also distressingly common in institutional settings such as nursing homes. A study released in the year 2000 by Health Care Financing Administration (now known as the Centers for Medicare and Medicaid Services or CMS) found that only 8 percent of the nation's nursing homes had sufficient staff to meet the minimum quality of care standards that the law requires them to meet in order to receive federal funding even though they did, in fact, receive it. The study further suggested that the majority of nursing homes have such insufficient levels of staffing that problems such as weight loss, bedsores, malnutrition, and dehydration are virtually unavoidable. *See* HEALTH CARE FINANCING ADMINISTRATION, REPORT TO CONGRESS: APPROPRIATENESS OF MINIMUM NURSE STAFFING RATIOS IN NURSING HOMES 14 (July 20, 2000 draft), *available at* http://phinational.org/sites/phinational.org/files/clearing house/Phase_I_VOL_I.pdf.

PROBLEMS

1. Joe, who lives with his elderly mother, has a drinking problem. About once a week he comes home drunk and yells at her, calling her names and telling her that one of these days he is going to kick her out and put her in a nursing home where she belongs.

   a. Is Joe's behavior elder abuse?
   b. To what extent should his mother's age affect how society judges his behavior? Legally? Morally?

2. Bobby, a mugger, likes to target elderly women because they carry cash and tend to be easy targets. He cases out a senior citizens center and sees an elderly woman, Vera, exiting the building. As she approaches the bus stop where he is standing, he grabs her pocketbook, slaps her to put her off balance, and takes off with the pocket book.

   a. Is Bobby's behavior elder abuse?
   b. To what extent should Vera's age affect how society judges his behavior? Legally? Morally?

2. Patterns in Elder Mistreatment

While there is significant debate over the causes of elder mistreatment, social isolation of older adults, caregiver stress, a history of domestic violence, perpetrator dependence on the victim and vice versa, perpetrator substance abuse, elder impairment, and ageist attitudes on the part of perpetrators are all correlated with increased risk of mistreatment. In addition, understaffing is associated with increased risk of mistreatment in institutional care settings.

While elder abuse affects older adults throughout the U.S. population, certain demographic groups are at a heightened risk for elder abuse. For example, the existing research indicates that elderly women are at greater risk than are elderly men for physical abuse, sexual mistreatment, and potential neglect. Other apparent risk factors for elder abuse victimization include social isolation, residence in a shared living arrangement, and, although the evidence is less conclusive, dementia.

There also appear to be distinct patterns in who perpetrates elder abuse. Elder abuse victims who are not living in institutional settings are most likely to have been victimized by family members (primarily adult children and spouses of the victims). Female victims are especially likely to have been victimized by a family member. Indeed, a significant portion of elder abuse, especially of elder abuse against women, is likely simultaneously domestic violence. Relative to the general population, perpetrators of elder abuse are also disproportionately likely to suffer from substance abuse, mental illness, and emotional problems, and are more likely to be financially dependent on their victim.

Notably, perpetrator gender and victim gender appear to be related to one another. Although men are more likely than women to perpetrate elder abuse against both older men and older women, they are disproportionately likely to offend against male victims.

3. Warning Signs

Given the prevalence of elder mistreatment, elder law attorneys can expect to regularly encounter older adults who are victims—or are at risk for becoming victims—of elder abuse or neglect. It is critical that lawyers be aware of potential warning signs of abuse and neglect. Otherwise, attorneys may not only miss an opportunity to help their clients meet their non-legal needs (e.g., by connecting clients to community resources that may be of assistance), but may also find that the legal strategies and techniques that they are employing are inappropriate given their clients' situations. Indeed, lawyers who are unaware of their clients' victimization or risk for victimization may ultimately be complicit in that victimization or even facilitate it by, for example, preparing legal documents that transfer control of the client's resources to his or her oppressor.

The following table summarizes some of the key warning signs of elder abuse or neglect. These are, of course, only warning signs. In many cases, older adults may exhibit these symptoms or conditions for reasons entirely unrelated to abuse or neglect.

Warning Signs of Elder Abuse and Neglect

Physical Warning Signs	Behavioral Warning Signs	Financial Warning Signs	Caregiver Behavior Warning Signs
Elder has bruises, welts, lacerations, or other injuries, especially if they • are in multiple stages of healing • include unexplained venereal disease or genital infection • include bruises on the trunk of the body • are reported by the elder to have been inflicted by another Elder exhibits poor personal hygiene Elder exhibits unexplained weight loss or skin deterioration Elder has untreated physical problems such as bedsores	Elder has significant changes in behavior Elder appears withdrawn, depressed, or agitated Elder hesitates to talk openly or speaks of not being "allowed" to do basic tasks or to have certain interactions Elder is non-compliant with medical regiment Elder is over- or under-medicated Elder expresses feelings of helplessness Elder has entered into a new relationship that is inconsistent with prior values or behavior	Elder's belongings are missing Elder's financial accounts show new patterns of activity, especially new patterns of bank withdrawals Numerous unpaid bills in elder's name Multiple new credit cards are opened in elder's name There is a discrepancy between elder's resources and his or her living condition Elder's mailing address has been changed to somewhere other than elder's residence Elder is receiving unnecessary services or goods	Caregiver blocks access to the elder Caregiver does not let the elder speak for him- or herself Caregiver is primarily concerned with the elder's financial situation Caregiver blames, belittles, or threatens the elder Caregiver has a substance abuse problem Caregiver has moved in with the elder and refuses to leave

Advocates for abused elders frequently recommend that attorneys working with older adults screen their clients for elder abuse. For example, in a 2007 article in the *NAELA Journal*, Betsy Abramson, Bonnie Brandl, Tess Meuer, and Jane Raymond recommended that elder law attorneys screen all of their clients for elder abuse. They suggested that:

> Informing clients that the attorney engages in universal screening removes a stigma or concern by clients that their status as a victim of domestic violence is somehow "showing." Victims of domestic violence often will not voluntarily disclose their situation, but will do so if sensitively and privately asked. To put the client at ease, the attorney can begin with a prefatory, "I always ask all of my clients these questions because I have found I cannot identify elder abuse on my own . . ." or "I want all of my clients to know that I care and can help." It also helps clients understand that even if they are not ready to take action at this moment, their attorney will be available later.

Betsy Abramson et al., *Isolation as a Domestic Violence Tactic in Later Life Cases: What Attorneys Need to Know*, 3 NAELA J. 47, 63 (2007).

NOTE

The debate over caregiver stress. One of the earliest explanations offered for elder abuse was that it was caused by "caregiver stress." Subsequent research has challenged this causal explanation, although caregiver stress does appear to be correlated with the incidence of elder abuse. Nevertheless, caregiver stress is often cited as a "cause" of elder abuse, and this explanation is a source of concern for many advocates for older victims. Advocates have expressed concern that if professionals responding to elder abuse consider caregiver stress to be a cause of that abuse, they may act in ways that are detrimental to the victims they aim to help, including by 1) failing to recognize that elder abuse can occur in situations in which an older adult is healthy and not a care recipient, 2) offering assistance to abusers and not victims (and thus potentially empowering abusers), 3) failing to hold perpetrators accountable because they are seen as having an excuse for their wrongful behavior, and 4) blaming victims for their own mistreatment. *See* BONNIE BRANDL ET AL., ELDER ABUSE DETECTION AND INTERVENTION: A COLLABORATIVE APPROACH 38-40 (2007) (raising these concerns, among others).

QUESTIONS

1. Should elder law attorneys screen their clients for elder abuse? If so, should they screen all clients or only those they believe to be at particular risk?

2. If elder law attorneys screen for elder abuse, how should they do so? What questions should they ask? Why?

3. The ABA Commission on Domestic Violence has recommended that attorneys integrate questions screening for domestic violence into the standard interview for all new clients. As examples of screening questions, the Commission suggests:
   - Has your intimate partner ever pushed, slapped or hit you in some way?
   - Has your intimate partner ever hurt or threatened you?
   - Has your intimate partner ever forced you to do something you did not want to do?
   - Is there anything that goes on at home that makes you feel afraid?
   - Does your intimate partner prevent you from eating or sleeping, or endanger your health in other ways?
   - Has your intimate partner ever hurt your pets or destroyed your clothing, objects in your home, or something you especially cared about?

   See AMERICAN BAR ASSOCIATION, COMMISSION ON DOMESTIC VIOLENCE, TOOL FOR ATTORNEYS TO SCREEN FOR DOMESTIC VIOLENCE.

   Would you recommend a similar approach to screening for elder abuse?

C. APPROACHES TO REMEDYING ELDER MISTREATMENT

Elder abuse was not considered a public concern until the middle of the 20th century. The issue first received meaningful governmental attention in the 1950s as part of a broader discussion of a need for protective services for physically or mentally challenged adults. In 1974, after several decades of advocacy and federally funded demonstration projects, Congress enacted Title XX of the Social Security Act, which effectively required all states to create Adult Protective Service (APS) units. Although APS units originally focused on issues related to self-care and dementia, elder mistreatment is currently considered central to their work. Today, APS agencies are typically seen as the "front-line responders" to elder abuse; they not only investigate reports of elder mistreatment, but they also offer services to victims of that mistreatment.

In the late 1970s, a series of Congressional hearings on elder abuse brought additional attention to the issue of elder mistreatment. It was at this point that the problem began to be clearly described as an issue of age—not merely vulnerability—and terms such as "granny bashing" and "elder abuse" became prominent. Consistent with this focus on victim age, policymakers interested in addressing the phenomenon looked to the existing set of laws designed to protect people of a particular age: those related to child abuse and neglect. To this day, child protection laws serve as a frame of reference for elder protection laws and exert a strong influence on policy related to elder mistreatment. For example, many states have adopted elder abuse reporting laws that mirror their child abuse reporting laws.

Although interest in elder mistreatment in the United States was sparked by federal legislative leadership, most of the statutes and regulations governing the governmental response to elder abuse can be found at the state level. Every state has now enacted at least some legislation designed to address elder mistreatment. The result, however, is that the legal framework for elder protection varies from state to state. Despite this variation, most laws designed to protect older adults fall into one of three categories: 1) laws that create and govern APS units, 2) laws that permit or require certain persons to report certain types of mistreatment to a government entity, typically APS, and 3) statutes that specifically penalize or prohibit certain treatment of older adults. This third category includes both laws that provide for civil sanctions against perpetrators, and those that provide for criminal sanctions. Of these, some create new crimes for which perpetrators of elder mistreatment can be held liable, while others simply create enhanced penalties for those convicted of crimes involving elderly or vulnerable victims. This subsection explores the second two types of laws.

1. Mandatory Reporting

In every state, elder abuse must be reported to the state if it occurs in certain types of residential facilities. Most states have adopted mandatory elder abuse reporting statutes that also require at least some categories of persons to report elder mistreatment regardless of residential setting. There is, however, significant variation in the requirements such statutes impose.

First, mandatory elder abuse reporting statutes differ based on who is required to report elder mistreatment. Some states limit the duty to report to certain categories of persons, whereas others require all persons with reason to suspect mistreatment to report. In states that selectively impose reporting requirements, health care professionals, social workers, bank employees, and law enforcement personnel are frequently targeted as reporters.

Second, statutes differ as to about whom reports are required. Some states require reporting suspected mistreatment of anyone above a certain age (commonly 60 or 65), regardless of that person's mental or physical condition. The Rhode Island statute excerpted below provides an example of this approach. In other states, reporting is only required if the victim is above a certain age and also meets other criteria (commonly the presence of a physical or cognitive disability). Still other states do not explicitly use a chronological age in defining the group of persons about whom reports must be made but, nevertheless, implicitly make age a factor by requiring reports about individuals who have "infirmities" or "impairments" associated with older age. Finally, some states do not use age-based criteria and instead mandate reporting about any adult with a particular vulnerability or set of vulnerabilities.

Third, states differ in how they define elder mistreatment. One significant distinction among the states is whether they require reporting of *self-neglect*, a phenomenon discussed in greater length in Section D.2.b of this chapter (see page 523).

Fourth, states differ in the consequences that they attach to violating reporting duties. In many states failure to report is a misdemeanor, and the penalty for it is limited to a monetary fine and licensure implications for certain categories of professionals. However, some states authorize imprisonment for failures to report, and a few states explicitly permit a failure to report to give rise to civil liability.

A final major distinction among mandatory reporting statutes is whether they provide exceptions to general reporting requirements in situations where the victim is not at imminent risk. While such exceptions are rare, they exist in several states. For example, as shown in the statutory excerpt that follows, Wisconsin limits reporting duties where the victim is not currently or imminently at risk. Similarly, Maine excuses professionals from reporting if their factual basis for suspecting mistreatment was obtained in the course of treating the suspected *abuser* for a related issue unless the victim's life or health is immediately threatened. Likewise, Maine excuses professionals from reporting if their factual basis for suspecting mistreatment was obtained in the course of treating the suspected *victim* for a related issue unless the victim's life or health is immediately threatened or the victim is incapacitated. *See* Me. Rev. Stat. Ann. tit. 22, §3477 (2013).

Mandatory elder abuse reporting laws are very popular. Mandatory reporting laws are promoted as a cost-efficient way to bring elder abuse, a problem that is often overlooked, to the attention of authorities who may be able to assist victims and prosecute perpetrators. Mandatory reporting laws are also promoted as a way to signal societal condemnation of elder mistreatment and respect for older adults. In addition, imposing mandatory reporting requirements on professionals is seen as a way to encourage those professionals to pursue the training they need to recognize elder abuse—if only to avoid professional discipline or other sanctions.

Mandatory reporting laws, however, have been extensively criticized by researchers. For example, scholars have expressed concern that such laws are not only ineffective at reducing elder abuse or increasing help for victims of elder abuse, but that they may also be counterproductive. Specifically, there is reason to be concerned that mandatory reporting laws discourage mistreated older adults and their caregivers from obtaining needed medical and other services. In addition, by increasing APS's investigatory obligation, they may undermine APS's ability to intervene in known cases of mistreatment by diverting the resources needed to do so to investigation instead. In addition to these functional critiques, mandatory elder abuse reporting laws have been criticized for unduly undermining the autonomy of older adults.

Below are excerpts from two states' mandatory elder abuse reporting laws. In addition, excerpts from Oregon's mandatory law can be found in Section D.2 of Chapter 3 of this book (see page 60). As you read them, consider the relative advantages and disadvantages of their competing approaches.

R.I. GEN. LAWS §42-66-8 (2013)

Any person who has reasonable cause to believe that any person sixty (60) years of age or older has been abused, neglected, or exploited, or is self-neglecting, shall make an immediate report to the director of the department of elderly affairs or his or her designee. In cases of abuse, neglect or exploitation, any person who fails to make the report shall be punished by a fine of not more than one thousand dollars ($1,000). Nothing in this section shall require an elder who is a victim of abuse, neglect, exploitation or who is self-neglecting to make a report regarding such abuse, neglect, exploitation or self-neglect to the director or his or her designee.

WIS. STAT. ANN. §46.90 (2013)

(4) Reporting.
    (ab) The following persons shall file reports as specified in par. (ad):
        1. An employee of any entity that is licensed, certified, or approved by or registered with the department.
        3. A health care provider, as defined in s. 155.01(7).
        4. A social worker, professional counselor, or marriage and family therapist certified under ch. 457.
    (ad) Except as provided in par. (ae), a person specified in par. (ab) who has seen an elder adult at risk in the course of the person's professional duties

shall file a report with the county department, the elder-adult-at-risk agency, a state or local law enforcement agency, the department, or the board on aging and long-term care if the elder adult at risk has requested the person to make the report, or if the person has reasonable cause to believe that any of the following situations exist:

1. The elder adult at risk is at imminent risk of serious bodily harm, death, sexual assault, or significant property loss and is unable to make an informed judgment about whether to report the risk.

2. An elder adult at risk other than the subject of the report is at risk of serious bodily harm, death, sexual assault, or significant property loss inflicted by a suspected perpetrator.

(ae) A person specified in par. (ab) to whom any of the following applies is not required to file a report as provided in par. (ad):

1. If the person believes that filing a report would not be in the best interest of the elder adult at risk. If the person so believes, the person shall document the reasons for this belief in the case file that the person maintains on the elder adult at risk.

2. If a health care provider provides treatment by spiritual means through prayer for healing in lieu of medical care in accordance with his or her religious tradition and his or her communications with patients are required by his or her religious denomination to be held confidential.

(ar) Any person, including an attorney or a person working under the supervision of an attorney, may report to the county department, the elder-adult-at-risk agency, a state or local law enforcement agency, the department, or the board on aging and long-term care that he or she believes that abuse, financial exploitation, neglect, or self-neglect of an elder adult at risk has occurred if the person is aware of facts or circumstances that would lead a reasonable person to believe or suspect that abuse, financial exploitation, neglect, or self-neglect of an elder adult at risk has occurred. The person shall indicate the facts and circumstances of the situation as part of the report.

NOTES

1. *Underreporting.* Despite mandatory reporting statutes, the vast majority of cases of elder mistreatment are never reported to the authorities. *See* Marie-Therese Connolly, *When Elder Abuse and the Justice System Collide: Police Power, Parens Patriae, and 12 Recommendations,* 22 J. ELDER ABUSE & NEGLECT 37, 54-55 (2010) (identifying competing estimates of the rates of underreporting, and suggesting factors that may increase reporting rates such as prosecutors being more willing to prosecute elder abuse when it is reported).

2. *Resources on mandatory reporting.* For a discussion of the privacy implications of mandatory reporting laws, see Nina A. Kohn, *Outliving Civil Rights,*

86 WASH. U. L. REV. 1053 (2009). For a discussion of the advantages and disadvantages of mandatory reporting from the perspective of domestic violence advocates as well as practical information for would-be reporters, see Bonnie Brandl, *Mandatory Reporting of Elder Abuse: Implications for Domestic Violence Advocates* (2005) (issue paper for the National Clearinghouse on Abuse in Later Life, *available at* www.ncall.us).

QUESTIONS

1. You have now seen three mandatory elder abuse reporting statutes (those from Rhode Island and Wisconsin highlighted in this section, as well as Oregon's law, excerpted in Chapter 3, on pages 60-61). Which approach is the best? Worst? Why?

2. Who, if anyone, should be a mandated reporter of elder abuse? Why?

3. Should lawyers be required to report elder abuse when they reasonably suspect a client is a victim of such abuse? When they reasonably suspect that a client is a perpetrator of such abuse? To what extent would such reporting be consistent with the traditional lawyer-client relationship?

4. Would you support parallel mandatory reporting requirements for victims of elder abuse and non-elderly abuse victims (e.g., middle-aged domestic violence victims)? Why or why not?

5. Professor Eve Brank and her colleagues have suggested that an alternative to mandatory reporting laws would be to empower older adults to report their own abuse by educating older adults about their rights and "appropriate expectations for care." *See* Eve M. Brank, Lindsey E. Wylie & Joseph A. Hamm, *Potential for Self-Reporting of Older Adult Maltreatment: An Empirical Examination,* 19 ELDER L.J. 351, 381 (2012). What might be the advantages of self-reporting over third-party reporting? Do you see self-reporting as a viable alternative to mandatory reporting? As a viable supplement to mandatory reporting?

2. Civil Sanctions

In certain situations, elder abuse may lead to civil liability. Some forms of elder abuse are tortious. For example, physical or sexual abuse of older adults may give rise to a tort claim sounding in battery (as in the case of an elder subjected to intentional physical violence) or false imprisonment (as in the case of an elder who is physically restrained). Psychological abuse may give rise to the tort of intentional infliction of emotional distress. Neglect may, in some situations, be found to give rise to a negligence claim. Tort claims based on elder abuse are probably most commonly filed against institutional care providers. As discussed in Chapter 7, such suits can be facilitated by the extensive federal and state regulations governing nursing home practices. Not only may such statutes establish a standard of care, but failure to comply with their mandates may serve as the basis for the government to bring a civil action against an offending institution.

Elder mistreatment may also give rise to claims that sound in contract or quasi-contract. For example, a family member or institution may be found to have breached a contractual agreement by failing to provide care that was promised to an older adult. Depending on the situation, a perpetrator of financial exploitation may potentially be held civilly liable on a variety of grounds, including that he or she committed a fraud or (as in the case of exploitation accomplished using a power-of-attorney) breached a fiduciary duty.

3. Criminal Sanctions

Historically, elder abuse has been treated as an issue to be addressed by social service providers, not the criminal justice system. However, over the past decade, this has begun to change and the criminal justice system is increasingly seen as having an important role to play in addressing elder mistreatment. The result has been a significant increase in the available resources for elder abuse prosecution. For example, attention has been focused on the creation of local multi-disciplinary teams (MDTs) that bring law enforcement and social service personnel together to create community-wide strategies to address elder mistreatment. Another important development has been the formation of specialized elder abuse prosecution units in several key U.S. Attorneys' offices. The prosecutors in these units have become role models and trainers for other criminal justice personnel, in part by demonstrating the potential for obtaining high rates of conviction in elder abuse prosecutions. Yet another key focus has been on the development of forensic resources and knowledge about elder abuse.

There are three primary ways that the criminal justice system can be used to prosecute elder abuse.

First, perpetrators of elder mistreatment can be prosecuted for a wide range of traditional common law crimes (e.g., battery, assault, rape, and manslaughter). In some cases, the criminal justice system may impose enhanced sentences or other penalties for such crimes because of the victim's elderly or vulnerable status.

Second, perpetrators of elder mistreatment may be prosecuted for statutory crimes that do not differentiate among victims based on age (e.g., fraud or predatory lending). For example, when a nursing home bills Medicaid for services to an individual to whom the facility neglected to provide required care, it may be prosecuted on the grounds that it committed fraud.

Third, perpetrators may also be prosecuted at the state level under criminal statutes that create new categories of crimes against elderly or otherwise vulnerable victims.

For example, in California it is a crime to willfully cause or permit a person age 65 or older to suffer "unjustifiable physical pain or mental suffering" or to inflict such suffering on a person age 65 or older. The statutory penalty for this crime is increased if the victim is 70 years of age or older and suffers great bodily injury or death. In addition, in California it is a misdemeanor for a person who has care or custody of an older adult to willfully cause or permit that adult "to be placed in a situation in which his or her person or health may be endangered." CAL. PENAL CODE §368 (2013).

Unlike California, some states that have created statutory crimes aimed at elder abuse do not require the victim to be elderly and instead criminalize the abuse of "vulnerable adults" or "dependent adults." However, a portion of those states that do not explicitly differentiate between victims based on age treat advanced age or age-related disability as a type of vulnerability that can support a criminal charge. For example, South Carolina makes it a crime to abuse a "vulnerable adult" but defines a "vulnerable adult" as any person who is unable to adequately care for him- or herself "because of the infirmities of aging" and treats "advanced age" as itself an infirmity of aging. *See* S.C. CODE ANN. §16-3-1050, §43-35-10(11) (2012).

The impact that such statutes will have is still largely unknown in part because most were adopted relatively recently. In general, advocates for older adults tend to view such statutes as a sign of valuable progress in the battle against elder mistreatment. Unfortunately, there has been little evaluation of the effects of such laws despite the fact that, as the excerpted article that follows suggests, there are reasons for concern.

Nina A. Kohn, Elder (In)Justice: A Critique of the Criminalization of Elder Abuse

49 Am. Crim. L. Rev. 1 (2012)

In a growing number of cases, . . . states are targeting elder abuse by criminalizing behavior that would otherwise be legally permissible. For example, a common trend is to criminalize the failure of a caregiver to meet the needs of an elderly or vulnerable person, even where no parallel crime would exist at common law. Another common approach is to make abuse of a durable power of attorney, which is a common form of elder financial exploitation, a separate crime.

A notable feature of many of the statutes that criminalize behavior that previously would not be the basis for criminal sanction is that they outlaw "abusive" behavior even in situations in which the victim may not see the behavior as abusive or may have consented to it. For example, as part of their attack on the financial exploitation of older adults, many states have adopted statutory provisions that make "undue influence" a crime. By specifically criminalizing undue influence, states can permit the prosecution of persons regarded as having taken unfair advantage of an older adult without requiring the prosecution to establish theft, coercion, fraud, or other more traditional grounds for finding that an agreement was not freely entered into, such as a showing of diminished cognitive capacity. . . . Other states single out "undue influence" as a form of exploitation that may constitute the crime of elder abuse. In general, such statutes do not specify what constitutes "undue influence" other than to make it clear that undue influence is something other than duress, coercion, fraud, or a variety of other forms of exploitation. One exception is Nevada, which states that "'undue influence' does not include the normal influence that one member of a family has over another." Another exception is Utah, which criminalizes undue influence of a vulnerable adult, and specifically defines "undue influence" as occurring "when a person uses the person's role, relationship, or power to exploit, or knowingly assist or cause another to exploit, the trust, dependency, or fear of a vulnerable adult, or uses the person's role, relationship or power to gain control deceptively over the decision making of the vulnerable adult."

Similarly, in the name of combating sexual abuse of older adults, some states have criminalized consensual sexual conduct that would otherwise be legally permissible. For example, in the state of Washington, it is a crime for a disabled person age sixty or older to engage in consensual sexual activity with someone who provides that person with paid transportation. In Vermont, it is a crime for anyone who works or volunteers at a caregiving facility or program to engage in sexual acts with any person whose ability to care for him or herself is impaired due to infirmities of aging.

Likewise, the Wisconsin Individual-at-Risk Restraining Order makes it possible to obtain a restraining order over someone—and hold them criminally liable for violating that restraining order—even where the "victim" neither lacks capacity nor objects to contact with the third party. The fact that an older adult is competent is not a basis for dismissal of the petition. Moreover, an order can be granted even if the respondent does not pose a risk to the older adult, but merely poses a threat to an investigation of alleged mistreatment, interferes with an offer of services to the older adult (regardless of whether the older adult wishes to obtain such services and regardless of whether those services have been found to be in the older adult's best interest), or threatens to mistreat or mistreats an animal owned by or in service to the older adult.

* * *

The move toward the criminalization of elder abuse parallels similar moves in other social policy domains. The United States is a highly legalistic society in which legal system responses to social problems are increasingly the norm, and in which the criminal justice system serves not only to punish and deter, but also to express social condemnation of acts deemed morally wrong. Moreover, the breadth of the crimes that states are creating in response to elder abuse, and the resulting prosecutorial discretion they demand, are emblematic of a larger trend in the American criminal justice system. The United States has experienced a vast proliferation of statutorily-created crimes which, by design, require law enforcement personnel to exercise significant discretion to enforce.

The way this trend plays out in the context of elder abuse is particularly concerning because of the extent to which the resulting laws threaten those they aim to protect. . . . [S]uch laws threaten to undermine older adults' civil rights and civil liberties by criminalizing certain forms of interaction with them. These laws also indirectly undermine older adults' rights because of their collateral consequences: . . . the most common consequences of state intervention in elder abuse cases are imposition of guardianship and institutionalization of the victim.

These consequences of the criminal justice system's embrace of elder abuse prosecution, while perhaps more dramatic and more expansive, are not unlike those facing domestic violence victims as a result of the criminal justice system's embrace of that problem. As such, those looking to understand and improve the criminal justice system's response to elder abuse have much to learn from the critiques of the criminal justice system's similarly heavy-handed response to domestic violence. Specifically, critiques of the criminal justice system response to domestic violence suggest that although a robust criminal justice response to elder abuse can play an important role in addressing specific instances of abuse and in shaping societal attitudes toward that abuse, the manner in which the response is structured will determine the extent to which it achieves these goals and the costs associated with their achievement. For example, policies that reduce victim involvement may increase general deterrence by encouraging and facilitating successful prosecution of abuse, and may simultaneously enhance the safety and security of many victims. At the same time, such policies may reinforce negative stereotypes about older adults, disempower older adults, create new forms of victim oppression, and even directly endanger some elder abuse victims. Moreover, they are particularly likely to do so in ways that entrench existing social attitudes and power structures.

Given these tensions, it is critical to reconsider the current criminal justice system response to elder abuse, and to ask whether fundamental changes are appropriate. It would be a mistake to abandon a criminal justice response to elder abuse altogether. The criminal justice system's involvement does serve to incapacitate and deter offenders, in part by expressing society's condemnation of elder abuse and suggesting that society values elder abuse victims—a message that may help shift attitudes that facilitate elder abuse much as focusing criminal justice system resources on domestic violence has helped shift societal norms about the acceptability of domestic violence. It would also, however, be a mistake to ignore the potential costs of the current autonomy-limiting criminal justice response to elder abuse, or to assume that there are not feasible, preferable alternative approaches that could afford older adults greater agency. . . .

NOTE

1. *Brooke Astor case.* In 2009, a New York jury convicted Anthony Marshall, son of the late philanthropist Brooke Astor, on 14 counts (including grand

larceny) based on his exploitation of his mother. The prosecution was criticized by some for prosecuting the case instead of leaving the matter to the probate court to consider as part of a will dispute. For an informative discussion of the case and the lessons attorneys can learn from it, see ABA Commission on Law and Aging, *The Brooke Astor Case: An Appalling Set of Circumstances, available at* www.americanbar.org/groups/law_aging.html.

2. *The importance of interdisciplinary collaboration.* As prosecutor Page Ulrey and elder abuse expert Bonnie Brandl have noted, "collaboration between agencies and systems is vital" to the successful prosecution of elder abuse because "elder abuse cases are often tremendously complicated." *See* Page Ulrey & Bonnie Brandl, *Collaboration Is Essential: King County's Response to a Case of Elder Abuse and Exploitation,* 36 GENERATIONS 73, 77 (2012). The extent and nature of such collaboration, however, varies significantly from one community to the next. In some communities such collaboration is primarily informal, with professionals from different agencies or disciplines informally consulting one another on cases or referring cases to one another. By contrast, "[i]n some communities, formalized teams have been organized to respond. Examples of these teams include interdisciplinary/multidisciplinary case review teams, financial abuse review teams, elder fatality review teams, and coordinated community response councils. These groups promote collaboration among various disciplines and, in some cases, address systemic issues that limit effective responses to victims." *Id.*

QUESTIONS

1. When, and to what extent, should elder abuse be prosecuted as a crime?

2. Should the state be permitted to prosecute elder abuse over the objection of the victim?

D. LEGAL DEFINITIONS OF ELDER MISTREATMENT

People of all ages experience problems. The question for the law is when should behavior that causes problems be considered unlawful (e.g., tortious or criminal), and, if so, how should that unlawfulness be classified. Thus, in the context of elder abuse, a key question is when should behavior that causes harm to older adults or their resources be deemed unlawful elder abuse, and when should it "merely" be considered unsavory or immoral. Accordingly, the next set of cases considers different types of behavior that cause harm to older adults or undermine their resources, and explores the legal consequences of those acts or omissions.

1. Malfeasance

State v. Maxon

79 P.3d 202 (Kan. App. 2003)

JOHNSON, P.J.

Christopher and Jodi Maxon were each convicted of two counts of theft and one count of mistreatment of a dependent adult. They appeal, challenging the sufficiency of the evidence and the imposition of Christopher's upward dispositional departure sentence. We affirm the mistreatment of a dependent adult convictions but reverse the theft convictions, thereby rendering the sentencing question moot.

* * *

The victim, Bea Bergman, lost her husband, Paul, to a heart attack in January 1999. Bea and Paul had lived modestly and accumulated substantial assets valued in the millions of dollars. Bea had relied on Paul to handle all their major financial decisions and, at his death, was even relying exclusively on him for transportation. After Paul's death, Bea was "[v]ery confused and very lost"; she experienced several episodes of anxiety for which she summoned emergency medical assistance. The month following Paul's death, Dr. Yvette Crabtree of the Kenyon Clinic examined Bea and prescribed an anti-anxiety medication and an antidepressant.

Also in the month following Paul's death, Bea called Maxon Moving to arrange for the hauling of Paul's personal effects to the Salvation Army. Maxon Moving was a family-owned operation and had been one of Paul's regular customers since the 1940s. Further, Paul and Bea had hired Maxon Moving to move their belongings on a number of occasions. Bea talked with Joyce Maxon and mentioned that she intended to give her husband, Ron Maxon, Sr., a marble-top table that Ron Sr. had admired during previous moves. The next day Ron Sr. went to Bea's house. Bea gave him the table, as well as a thank you card containing a $2,000 check.

Shortly thereafter, Joyce became a frequent visitor at Bea's house. She would transport Bea to antique shops, to the grocery store, to the doctor's office, and to church. Eventually, Joyce was spending weekday nights at Bea's house, and Bea would spend the weekend at Joyce's house. Bea became progressively integrated into the Maxon family, which, in addition to Ron Sr. and Joyce, included Ron Maxon, Jr., Christopher Maxon, Jodi Maxon, and Sharyl Ledom. Bea attended Maxon family functions and wanted the Maxons to call her "Aunt Bea." Coincidentally, as Bea was being welcomed into the Maxon family circle, she began writing checks to and purchasing property for the various Maxon family members. During the approximately 8-month long feeding frenzy, Bea dispersed over $600,000 to or for the benefit of the Maxons. However, during this same period, Bea also wrote checks to her daughter, her granddaughter, and a niece.

Specifically, the theft charges in this case involved: (1) the sale of Bea's house to Christopher and Jodi; and (2) Christopher's purchase of a new truck. In May 1999, Bea had listed her house for sale with her real estate agents, Linda and Charles Stanfield; the listing price was $177,500. Shortly after the listing, Bea moved into an apartment. The listing was cancelled in June 1999, and Christopher and Jodi moved into the house. In July, the new occupants fenced the yard, installed a hot tub, and built a new deck, albeit Bea footed the bill. In late July or early August, Christopher and Jodi contracted with Bea to purchase the house for $100,000, financed in part with a $99,500 promissory note which was to balloon upon the Maxons' sale of their La Cygne, Kansas, house. The note was paid in full within 3 or 4 months. There was some testimony that Bea had offered to give the house to Christopher and Jodi.

In October 1999, Christopher picked out a new Ford truck at a dealership in Olathe. He asked the salesman for permission to drive the truck to show his mother, because if she approved of the vehicle, she would give him the purchase money. Christopher drove to Bea's apartment, gave her a ride, and presented her with the bill. Bea wrote a $38,745.34 check, payable to Olathe Ford, and gave it to Christopher to purchase the truck. Bea was not sure, but she thought Jodi accompanied Christopher when this transpired. The truck was titled solely in Christopher's name.

In November 1999, Bea reconciled with her estranged son, Paul Thorpe. Thorpe and his wife subsequently moved into an apartment down the hall from Bea.

During the Christmas season of 1999, Bea severed her relationship with the Maxons. The rift was precipitated by the Maxons' Christmas gifts to Bea, which she considered to be miserly responses to her Christmas gifts to them of $25,000 checks. She was hurt by the Maxons' failure to reciprocate her generosity and had no further contact with the Maxons.

Subsequently, Bea's son examined her financial records and noted the checks that had been written to the Maxons. Bea and her son met with the attorney that was acting as Paul's executor, who referred them to another attorney, Harry Wigner. Wigner sent Bea to a psychiatrist for an examination and contacted the district attorney's office about the possibility of filing criminal charges.

The psychiatrist, Dr. Everette Sitzman, diagnosed Bea as suffering from bipolar disorder with episodes of hypomania and prescribed a mood stabilizing agent. The doctor opined that people with Bea's affliction are vulnerable to influence by others and often require a protective trust or conservatorship to protect their assets.

After a year-long investigation, the Johnson County District Attorney's office filed charges against Ron Sr., Joyce Maxon, Jodi Maxon, Christopher Maxon, Sharyl Ledom, and Ron Maxon, Jr. All of the defendants, except for Ron Jr., were tried together. The case before us involves the charges against Christopher and Jodi which were identical: (1) one count of felony theft of Bea's house; (2) one count of felony theft of United States currency (used to purchase the Ford truck); and (3) one count of misdemeanor mistreatment of a dependent adult. The thefts were charged in the alternative, alleging that they were committed by obtaining or exerting unauthorized control over the property or that they were committed by obtaining the property through deception. Further, the jury was given an aiding and abetting instruction. Christopher and Jodi were convicted on all counts; the jury found the thefts were committed in both alternative manners. The district court granted the State's motion for an upward dispositional departure sentence in Christopher's case based on Bea's vulnerability and sent him to prison for 38 months. Jodi received a presumptive probation sentence.

Appellants structure their appeal to first challenge the sufficiency of the evidence to support a conviction based upon K.S.A. 2002 Supp. 21-3701(a)(1), arguing they did not obtain or exert unauthorized control over any of Bea's property, i.e. no theft occurred. . . . Next, the Maxons argue the absence of any evidence to establish that any false statements or representations were made to induce Bea to transfer her property, negating the sufficiency of the evidence to support the theft by deception convictions under K.S.A. 2002 Supp. 21-3701(a)(2). . . . The third issue presented challenges the sufficiency of the evidence to support the convictions for mistreatment of a dependent adult, asserting that Bea was not a "dependent adult" in 1999 and that appellants did not mistreat her. . . .

MISTREATMENT OF DEPENDENT ADULT

In deciding appellants' challenge to the sufficiency of the evidence to support their convictions for mistreatment of a dependent adult, we review all of the evidence, viewed in the light most favorable to the prosecution, to determine if a rational jury could have found the defendants guilty beyond a reasonable doubt. . . .

The statute creating this crime is K.S.A. 21-3437, the relevant portions of which are:

> "(a) Mistreatment of a dependent adult is knowingly and intentionally committing one or more of the following acts:
>
> . . . .
>
> (2) taking unfair advantage of a dependent adult's physical or financial resources for another individual's personal or financial advantage by the use of undue influence, coercion, harassment, duress, deception, false representation or false pretense by a caretaker or another person. . . .
>
> . . . .
>
> "(c) For purposes of this section: 'Dependent adult' means an individual 18 years of age or older who is unable to protect their own interest."

* * *

Christopher and Jodi present two arguments: (1) The evidence does not establish that Bea was a dependent adult; and (2) no evidence was presented to establish undue influence, coercion, deception, or false pretense. . . .

Was the Victim a Dependent Adult?

* * *

In arguing the insufficiency of the evidence to establish Bea's inability to protect her own interest, appellants acknowledge that Dr. Sitzman provided direct testimony on that question. However, appellants urge us to discount Dr. Sitzman's testimony and look to the other evidence supporting their contention that Bea was a confident, assertive individual. Our standard of review precludes our making an assessment of Dr. Sitzman's credibility or weighing his testimony against that of the other medical professionals, no matter how qualified or persuasive the others might appear on the record. The jury viewed the witnesses firsthand and its factual determination must be respected.

Evidence of Mistreatment

Appellants persuasively argue that the evidence did not support a finding that they utilized coercion, deception, false representation, or false pretense to obtain money and property from Bea. However, the statute is drawn in the disjunctive; evidence of undue influence is sufficient to support a conviction.

* * *

The evidence was sufficient to establish that the Maxon family systematically preyed upon Bea's mental and emotional vulnerability to obtain her money. Joyce orchestrated the transfers, timing the gift requests to coincide with Bea's manic or "giving" periods and deciding who would be the next recipient of Bea's bounty. However, all family members, including Christopher and Jodi, participated in the scheme. Indeed, the siblings apparently squabbled about who should get the next distribution and the inequities in the amounts each was receiving.

The legislature, by enacting K.S.A. 21-3437, intended to criminalize the conduct in which Christopher and Jodi engaged in conjunction with other Maxon family members. The evidence was sufficient to support the convictions for mistreatment of a dependent adult.

* * *

THEFT BY DECEPTION

* * *

Appellants note that the record contains no evidence that they made an express or implied false statement or representation in conjunction with the house sale or the truck purchase. Further, they argue that Bea did not rely on any false statements or representations that may have been made. We agree.

The State's brief emphasizes the circumstances surrounding the two transactions but fails to identify any falsity upon which Bea relied. The representations which might have induced Bea's actions are either true or not shown to be false. As examples: Christopher's statement that he needed a new truck because the transmission was out of his existing truck is not refuted in the record; the representation that Christopher and Jodi were having difficulty selling their La Cygne house is supported in the record.

The only arguably false statement referred to by the State involved comments that certain Maxon family members had seen or heard from Bea's dead husband. While such statements may have been calculated to endear the Maxons to Bea or to further the general exploitation of the vulnerable widow, any inference of a causal connection between the statements and the specific transactions being prosecuted is too nebulous to support a criminal conviction.

The evidence was insufficient to support the convictions for theft by deception, and those convictions are reversed.

THEFT BY OBTAINING OR EXERTING UNAUTHORIZED CONTROL

Alternatively, Christopher and Jodi were alleged to have committed theft by the more commonly understood means of simply taking Bea's property without her permission. . . . The elements instruction identified the stolen property as: (1) the house and property at 11412 Flint, Overland Park, Johnson County, Kansas; and (2) United States currency in connection with the purchase of the Ford F-350 pickup.

The appellants point us to the obvious problem with defining their acts as a traditional theft, *i.e.* they obtained control over the property with Bea's permission. Bea not only authorized Christopher and Jodi to take control of the property, but she actively participated in effecting the transfers. Bea signed and acknowledged the execution of the warranty deed to transfer the residential real estate; Bea wrote the check, payable to Olathe Ford, and gave it to Christopher.

* * *

. . . On appeal, the State does not contend that Bea did not consent to the defendants' control over the property, but rather the argument is that Bea's consent was ineffective because she did not possess the necessary mental capacity to give her property to the defendants.

* * *

[O]ur statutes do not contain a specific provision that negates an individual's consent when the defendant knows or should know the donor lacks the mental capacity to give consent. On appeal, the State urges us to judicially create a definition of "unauthorized control" that includes a consensual transfer from a donor who has insufficient mental capacity to give a voluntary or intelligent consent.

* * *

The argument that the legislature intended felony theft, committed by obtaining or exerting unauthorized control over property, to be extended to embrace the act of obtaining a consensual transfer from a person with mental, emotional, or personality problems would be more persuasive if the legislature had not created the specific crime of mistreatment of a dependent adult to encompass that act. The State recognized that the mistreatment of a dependent adult crime applied to this scenario by prosecuting the Maxons for that crime for all of Bea's transfers, except for the two selected to be charged as felony thefts. Precedent teaches us that it is improper to prosecute a defendant for a general crime when the facts establish the violation of a specific statute. . . . Obviously, the theft statute is general while the mistreatment of a dependent adult statute is specific. Therefore, we decline to find that the legislature intended to make those acts constituting the specific crime of mistreating a dependent adult part of the general theft statute definition of obtaining or exerting unauthorized control.

Even if we were to redefine the theft statute, we would require that the victim's impairment be more than the poor business judgment exhibited by those suffering from mild hypomania. The evidence presented does not support a finding that Bea lacked the capacity to contract, lacked testamentary capacity, or was amenable to an involuntary conservatorship as a disabled or impaired person. At best, there was substantial competent evidence that Bea suffered from emotional, mental, or personality disorders that made her vulnerable to the Maxons' influence.

During the time frame of the alleged thefts, Bea was conducting her own business and apparently entering into contracts, *e.g.* she executed a listing agreement on her house and leased an apartment. She made gifts to her daughter of approximately $177,000 in 1999, as well as making substantial gifts to a granddaughter, a niece, and her son. None of these recipients were named as codefendants with the Maxons. Logically, if Bea had sufficient mental capacity to make gifts to her family, then she could consent to the transfers to the Maxons.

We are particularly concerned with the evidence to support the convictions for felony theft of the residential property. One of the State's own exhibits is the house deed, containing an acknowledgment which recites that Bea executed the document in the presence of the notary public and that the deed "was executed as a free and voluntary act and deed for the uses and purposes therein set forth." Further, the Maxons bought the property; they paid Bea $100,000. The elements instruction told the jury that it had to find that the Maxons obtained or exerted unauthorized control over the entire property. At most, the Maxons cheated Bea out of the difference between the sale price and the value of the property, whatever that might have been. At what point is a purchase price so inadequate that a good deal becomes a felony? The evidence was insufficient to support the charge that the Maxons exerted or obtained unauthorized control over the entire residential property, as per the jury instructions.

The mistreatment of a dependent adult convictions are affirmed; the felony theft convictions are reversed. . . .

State v. Stubbs

562 N.W.2d 547 (Neb. 1997)

WHITE, Chief Justice.

* * *

During the spring of 1993, Rick Stubbs, appellant, visited [Dale] Edmisten on numerous occasions and would offer to purchase various items from Edmisten. There is evidence that Edmisten sold items to Stubbs on more than one occasion.

Edmisten testified that after a visit from Stubbs, Edmisten would notice that items such as tools would be missing from his home. Edmisten, however, could not identify which items were missing and did not see Stubbs actually take any of his property.

In March 1993, [Edmisten's niece Janie] Knickerbocker visited Edmisten. While visiting her uncle, she observed that he could recall what had occurred in the past but had some difficulty with understanding what was occurring in the present. She noticed that Edmisten shuffled when he walked and that he had some difficulty moving. During that visit, Knickerbocker also noted items present in her uncle's home.

On March 26, 1993, Knickerbocker obtained power of attorney for both Edmisten's health and financial affairs. She testified that it appeared that Edmisten understood what he was signing.

While Knickerbocker at that time felt that Edmisten could not live by himself, she decided to postpone plans to put him into a nursing home until the end of May, and she returned to Colorado. Edmisten continued living by himself, cooking his own meals, dressing himself, and picking up his mail.

Knickerbocker returned to her uncle's home in May 1993. She noticed that several items which she had seen in March were now gone: an anvil, an oxbow, an Indian war ax, an antique dresser set, two trunks, a .22-caliber rifle, and a John Deere tractor. She then notified the county sheriff's office, reporting the items that were missing. Officer Mike Dye of the Lincoln County sheriff's office investigated the matter. Dye spoke to Stubbs, who allegedly said that he had spoken to Edmisten, that he had been to his house, and that he had purchased some items.

Stubbs was later charged by information on March 2, 1994. Specifically, Stubbs was charged with the knowing and intentional abuse of a vulnerable adult by exploitation. He was arraigned on April 11, and trial was held on March 21, 1995.

At trial, several witnesses testified as to the physical and mental health of Edmisten. Knickerbocker testified that Edmisten appeared confused after [an automobile] accident in 1992, that he shuffled when he walked, that such movement was difficult, that he needed assistance in getting groceries, and that he had a poor diet, consisting mainly of milk.

Sandra Bay, a neighbor of Edmisten's, testified that Edmisten would drive his truck to his mailbox. According to Bay, Edmisten would sometimes misjudge the distance to the mailbox and veer slightly off the roadway. She also testified that Edmisten's physical health was deteriorating, that is, he was having a difficult time walking and moving very well.

Kimberly Eckhoff and Melvin Eckhoff, longtime family friends, often brought Edmisten food because it appeared that he was not eating very well. Kimberly Eckhoff cleaned Edmisten's house on one occasion. She noted that the house was a mess on that occasion and testified that Edmisten would shuffle as he walked. Melvin Eckhoff took Edmisten to the grocery store at least once a week after learning that store employees were worried that Edmisten was having a difficult time maneuvering through their store. Melvin Eckhoff would also take Edmisten to the bank.

Ray Seifer, another neighbor, testified that he saw Edmisten once or twice a week. He described Edmisten as not being very mobile and noticed that because of his age, Edmisten was having problems remembering things.

Dr. George Cooper, a family practitioner in North Platte since 1962, was called by the State as an expert witness. In July 1993, Dr. Cooper examined Edmisten. Dr. Cooper found that Edmisten's lungs were clear, that he had normal arterial and venous circulation, that he did not have a deficit such as paralysis, and that his blood pressure was normal. Dr. Cooper diagnosed Edmisten as being mildly senile and having vertigo and proprioception deficit, which is the loss of a sense of balance. He reported that Edmisten was both physically and mentally active without full awareness of the consequences. He also concluded that it was very likely that Edmisten could be considered a vulnerable adult.

When Edmisten was asked whether he lived independently, he testified that he did not live with anyone, cooked his own meals, dressed himself, watched television, took care of his bills, bathed himself, and did not have any medical problems for which he was taking medicine. When asked whether he was in pretty good health, Edmisten answered, "I thought so." Edmisten testified that he would know where he was and what he was doing.

Evidence was also submitted to demonstrate Stubbs' alleged exploitation of Edmisten. Knickerbocker stated at trial that a lot of her uncle's property had disappeared: an oxbow, an anvil, an Indian war ax, a dresser set, two trunks, quilts, and the John Deere 4630 tractor. Bay testified that she observed a red and white pickup being driven past Edmisten's house and onto his driveway several times one day when Edmisten was gone. In addition, Bay testified that she noticed that a considerable number of items had disappeared from Edmisten's workshop. Kimberly Eckhoff and her husband, Randy, also observed a red pickup being driven past Edmisten's home one day. Melvin Eckhoff mentioned that he noticed items missing from Edmisten's workshop.

Edmisten stated at trial that he thought items which he owned had been taken by Stubbs. He could not, however, list specifically what had been taken. Finally, Edmisten, as well as Knickerbocker and Bay, testified that they had never actually seen Stubbs wrongfully take property from Edmisten.

Evidence was introduced to the effect that the John Deere tractor was in a general state of disrepair. Several individuals testified as to the value of the tractor. The witnesses concluded that the value was somewhere between $5,500 and $11,000.

Edmisten testified that he did not remember offering to sell the tractor to Stubbs. To the contrary, Stubbs' mother testified that Edmisten told her that he wanted $3,500 for the tractor and would not accept anything less. It appears as though Stubbs' mother submitted a check to Edmisten for $3,500 in April 1993 on Stubbs' behalf.

At the close of the evidence, the court held that there was sufficient evidence to sustain a verdict on the "substantial . . . functional impairment" portion of the vulnerable adult statute. Later on appeal, the State stipulated that the only issue was whether Edmisten suffered a "substantial functional impairment."

The jury found Stubbs guilty of abuse of a vulnerable adult, and he was subsequently sentenced. Stubbs appealed his conviction.

On appeal, the Nebraska Court of Appeals held that while the evidence supported a finding that Edmisten was physically and mentally aging, it did not support a finding that he suffered a substantial functional impairment which left him incapable of caring for himself or living independently. The court also held that the evidence did not show that Stubbs took Edmisten's property by means of undue influence, breach of a fiduciary relationship, deception, or extortion. Finally, the court held that the State failed to show a nexus between Edmisten's impairment and the alleged exploitation. The court reversed the trial court's judgment and vacated Stubbs' conviction and sentence. The State then petitioned this court for further review.

The State contends that the Court of Appeals erred in (1) finding that the evidence presented at trial was insufficient to prove that Stubbs exploited Edmisten; (2) finding that the evidence presented at trial was insufficient to prove that Edmisten was a "vulnerable adult" as defined by Neb. Rev. Stat. §28-371 (Reissue 1995); and (3) holding that the State must show a nexus between a vulnerable adult's impairment and the exploitation of a vulnerable adult when this showing is not required by the statute.

* * *

The State argues that the Court of Appeals erred in holding that there was insufficient evidence to demonstrate that Edmisten was a vulnerable adult as defined by §28-371. We disagree and affirm the Court of Appeal's decision with regard to this issue.

Stubbs was convicted under Neb. Rev. Stat. §28-386(1) (Reissue 1995), which states that a "person commits knowing and intentional abuse of a vulnerable adult if he or she through a knowing and intentional act causes or permits a vulnerable adult to be . . . (d) Exploited."

The initial step when determining whether such statute has been violated is to determine whether the victim was a vulnerable adult. A vulnerable adult is "any person eighteen years of age or older who has a substantial mental or functional impairment or for whom a guardian has been appointed under the Nebraska Probate Code." §28-371. In the instant case, assessment of whether Edmisten could be considered a vulnerable adult is limited to a finding of whether he had suffered a substantial functional impairment as stipulated to by the State. Pursuant to Neb. Rev. Stat. §28-368 (Reissue 1995), substantial functional impairment means a "substantial incapability, because of physical limitations, of living independently or providing self-care as determined through observation, diagnosis, investigation, or evaluation."

In this case, there is insufficient evidence to establish that Edmisten was incapable of living independently or providing self-care. Edmisten testified himself that he was living independently, cooking his own meals, bathing and dressing himself, paying his bills, and eating solid foods such as steak and pizza, and that he was in good health, experiencing no medical problems. Knickerbocker testified that she did not feel that it was necessary to move Edmisten into a nursing home until the end of May 1993. Dr. Cooper testified that Edmisten experienced no respiratory, circulatory, or heart problems and reported that his blood pressure was normal.

There is evidence that Edmisten was naturally aging. Such a process took a toll on Edmisten's body and mind. However, moving slowly and forgetting some things are not sufficient to support a finding that an individual is unable to live independently. Therefore, the State has failed to meet its burden of establishing that Edmisten suffered from a "substantial functional impairment." As a result, the State failed to adequately demonstrate that Stubbs violated §28-386. For these reasons, the Court of Appeals was correct in vacating Stubbs' conviction and sentence. Since the preceding analysis is dispositive of the instant case, the State's remaining assignments of error need not be addressed.

Affirmed.

QUESTIONS

1. What is the underlying rationale for making Stubbs's conviction turn on whether Edmisten suffered a substantial functional impairment? Do you find it compelling?

2. Compare the definition of "dependent adult" in the Kansas statute at issue in *Maxon* with the definition of "vulnerable adult" in the Nebraska statute at issue in *Stubbs.* How do they differ? Which approach is preferable and why?

3. Was the statutory definition of "substantial functional impairment" in *Stubbs* too limited? If you were writing the underlying statute, how would you define "substantial functional impairment"?

4. As Professor Martha Fineman has explored in her work on vulnerability, all people are vulnerable. *See, e.g.,* Martha Albertson Fineman, T*he Vulnerable Subject and the Responsive State,* 60 Emory L.J. 251, 257 (2010). By singling out some victims as vulnerable victims are laws such as those at issue in *Stubbs* and *Maxon* obfuscating this fact? If so, is that a problem?

2. Neglect

Sometimes, elder abuse takes the form not of a bad act, but of an omission—that is, a failure to provide needed care or support. Sometimes the failure is that of another person such as a family member, friend, or paid caregiver. In such situations, the law must determine when that individual will be treated as legally responsible for that failure, and when such omissions (while perhaps morally concerning) do not violate legal duties. Other times, the failure is an individual's own failure to provide for his or her own care. In such situations, there may be debate as to whether the failure should be considered a matter of public concern and whether the public should intervene to remedy the consequences of that failure.

a. Third-Party Neglect

People v. McKelvey

281 Cal. Rptr. 359 (Cal. App. 2d Dist. 1991)

GILBERT, Associate Justice.

Defendant Thomas L. McKelvey III appeals a judgment of conviction of neglect of a dependent adult. (Pen. Code, §368.) We affirm and hold section 368 provided fair warning of the conduct it prohibits as to defendant.

FACTS

Dolores McKelvey, a multiple sclerosis victim, lived at home with her daughter Theresa and her son, the defendant. Mrs. McKelvey was paralyzed and unable to walk or use a wheelchair. Theresa cared for Mrs. McKelvey's personal hygiene, and defendant cooked and maintained the family home. On November 28, 1988, Theresa permanently left home because her mother's care "overwhelmed" her. She informed her mother she was leaving.

Four days later defendant summoned emergency assistance for his mother. A fireman responding to the call testified he discovered Mrs. McKelvey in a hospital bed lying in excrement from her ankles to her shoulders. Maggots, ants and other insects crawled upon her. She had sores on her legs and complained of the insect bites. Her skin flaked when he brushed the insects away. The house strongly smelled of excrement.

Mrs. McKelvey appeared mentally alert, however, and asked not to be moved because she was in pain. The paramedics decided she required hospital attention and drove her to an emergency room.

Four days later Mrs. McKelvey died from heart failure due to multiple sclerosis, malnutrition, infections and neglect. A pathologist testified Mrs. McKelvey suffered from pressure sores, kidney and leg infections, dehydration, malnutrition, and bone fractures of the femur, pelvis and ribs due to osteoporosis. He opined the circumstances of her neglect were sufficient to cause great bodily harm or death.

The prosecutor charged Theresa and defendant with neglect of a dependent adult. At trial Theresa testified she attended to her mother's personal hygiene until she was defeated by her mother's needs and left home. She stated defendant complained, "'It's not my job'" during past arguments concerning Mrs. McKelvey's needs.

Defendant testified he did not care for his mother's personal hygiene due to their mutual embarrassment. He cooked for and fed her, and Theresa attended to her cleanliness. He added his mother could change her own diapers, and he would provide her with clean ones as needed. Despite her illness, defendant described Mrs. McKelvey as alert and in charge of the household. He expressed surprise and distress upon learning of her condition the day he summoned emergency assistance.

After a court trial, the trial judge convicted defendant of neglect of a dependent adult. He expressly found "overwhelming" evidence defendant was responsible for his mother's care and allowed her to suffer and become injured. He sentenced defendant to one-third the midterm of three years to be served consecutively to an unrelated conviction of driving under the influence. On appeal defendant contends 1) the first clause of section 368 is unconstitutionally vague, and 2) insufficient evidence supports his conviction.

DISCUSSION

I.

Defendant contends the trial court convicted him of violating this clause of section 368: "Any person who, under circumstances or conditions likely to produce great bodily harm or death, willfully . . . permits any . . . dependent adult, with knowledge that . . . she is . . . a dependent adult, to suffer. . . ." He argues this clause is unconstitutional because it does not afford fair warning to the class of actors falling within its reach. He asserts the clause is sufficiently broad to include visitors or bystanders who permit a dependent adult to suffer.

* * *

The constitutional commands of due process require that all citizens receive fair notice of potentially criminal conduct. A statute must be sufficiently definite to provide standards for those whose acts are proscribed as well as those who enforce the law and determine guilt. In reviewing a statute challenged for vagueness, courts focus upon defendant's act rather than hypothetical or conceivable acts falling within the statute.

When drafting section 368, the Legislature commendably displayed concern for the elderly and the dependent. Regrettably it displayed indifference to clarity. The second clause of section 368 is clear. It punishes those responsible for the custody or care of a dependent adult, who allow or cause the dependent adult to become injured.

The first clause of section 368 is uncertain. It does not describe those persons liable for permitting or causing a dependent adult to suffer. The clause appears to include within its reach any and all persons.

Nevertheless, the uncertainty as to the first clause is of no help to defendant. The trial court decided he was responsible for his mother's care. He was therefore included within the first as well as the second clause of section 368. We therefore need not review the statute further to decide whether a visitor or bystander would also be criminally liable.

II.

Defendant argues insufficient evidence supports the trial court's findings he had care of his mother and permitted her to suffer and become injured. He points out Theresa was responsible for his mother's cleanliness, and his mother refused to permit him to care for her hygiene. He adds his mother was alert and in command of the household and had a telephone beside her bed. She could have summoned assistance, he contends, had she been suffering.

In determining the sufficiency of evidence to support a criminal conviction, the reviewing court must decide whether a rational trier of fact could have found defendant guilty beyond a reasonable doubt. . . .

The deplorable condition in which emergency medical persons discovered Mrs. McKelvey belies defendant's contentions that she was in charge of the household, could summon assistance if necessary and could request clean diapers as needed. Theresa had been absent from the residence for four days, and the only reasonable inference from the evidence is that Mrs. McKelvey had no hygienic care during that time. Moreover, defendant was the only physically able, competent adult in the household after Theresa left. As such, he was responsible for the care of his paralyzed, incapacitated mother, including her cleanliness.

A pathologist testified at trial the circumstances of Mrs. McKelvey's neglect were sufficient to cause great bodily harm or death. These included urinary and kidney infections, leg infections from insects, and skin burns from urine and excrement. These conditions, added to her malnourished and dehydrated state due to multiple sclerosis, led to her death. Sufficient evidence supports the trial court's implied finding that defendant's conduct was a gross or culpable departure from the ordinary standard of due care and was criminally negligent within section 368.

People v. Heitzman

886 P.2d 1229 (Cal. 1994)

Lucas, Chief Justice.

Penal Code section 368, subdivision (a), is one component of a multi-faceted legislative response to the problem of elder abuse. The statute imposes felony criminal liability on "[a]ny person who, under circumstances or conditions likely to produce great bodily harm or death, willfully causes or permits any elder or dependent adult, with knowledge that he or she is an elder or dependent adult, to suffer, or inflicts thereon unjustifiable physical pain or mental suffering, or having the care or custody of any elder or dependent adult, willfully causes or permits the person or health of the elder or dependent adult to be injured, or willfully causes or permits the elder or dependent adult to be placed in a situation such that his or her person or health is endangered. . . ."[2]

In this case, we must decide whether the statute meets constitutional standards of certainty. As we shall explain, we conclude initially that, on its face, the broad statutory language at issue here fails to provide fair notice to those who may be subjected to criminal liability for "willfully . . . permit[ting]" an elder or dependent adult to suffer pain, and similarly fails to set forth a uniform standard under which police and prosecutors can consistently enforce the proscription against "willfully . . . permit[ting]" such suffering. Under these circumstances, section 368(a) would be unconstitutionally vague absent some judicial construction clarifying its uncertainties.

We conclude that the statute may properly be upheld by interpreting its imposition of criminal liability upon "[a]ny person who . . . permits . . . any elder or dependent adult . . . to suffer . . . unjustifiable pain or mental suffering" to apply only to a person who, under existing tort principles, has a duty to control the conduct of the individual who is directly causing or inflicting abuse on the elder or dependent adult. Because the evidence in this case does not indicate that defendant had the kind of "special relationship" with the individuals alleged to have directly abused the elder victim that would give rise to a duty on her part to control their conduct, she was improperly charged with a violation of section 368(a). We therefore reverse the judgment of the Court of Appeal.

I. FACTS

The egregious facts of this case paint a profoundly disturbing family portrait in which continued neglect of and apparent indifference to the basic needs of the family's most vulnerable member, an elderly dependent parent, led to a result of tragic proportion. Sixty-seven-year-old Robert Heitzman resided in the Huntington Beach home of his grown son, Richard Heitzman, Sr., along with another grown son, Jerry Heitzman, and Richard's three sons. On December 3, 1990, police were summoned to the house, where they discovered Robert dead in his bedroom. His body lay on a mattress that was rotted through from constant wetness, exposing the metal springs. The stench of urine and feces filled not only decedent's bedroom, but the entire house as well. His bathroom was filthy, and the bathtub contained fetid, green-colored water that appeared to have been there for some time.

---

2. "Elder" is defined as "any person who is 65 years of age or older." (§368, subd. (d).) Section 368, subdivision (e), defines "dependent adult" as any person between 18 and 64 years of age "who has physical or mental limitations which restrict his or her ability to carry out normal activities or to protect his or her rights. . . ."

Police learned that Jerry Heitzman was primarily responsible for his father's care, rendering caretaking services in exchange for room and board. Jerry admitted that he had withheld all food and liquids from his father for the three days preceding his death on December 3. Jerry explained that he was expecting company for dinner on Sunday, December 2, and did not want his father, who no longer had control over his bowels and bladder, to defecate or urinate because it would further cause the house to smell.

At the time of his death, decedent had large, decubitus ulcers, more commonly referred to as bed sores, covering one-sixth of his body. An autopsy revealed the existence of a yeast infection in his mouth, and showed that he suffered from congestive heart failure, bronchial pneumonia, and hepatitis. The forensic pathologist who performed the autopsy attributed decedent's death to septic shock due to the sores which, he opined, were caused by malnutrition, dehydration, and neglect.

Twenty years earlier, decedent had suffered a series of strokes that paralyzed the left side of his body. Defendant, 31-year-old Susan Valerie Heitzman, another of decedent's children, had previously lived in the home and had been her father's primary caregiver at that time. In return, defendant's brother Richard paid for her room and board. Richard supported the household by working two full-time jobs, and supplemented this income with decedent's monthly Social Security and pension checks.

One year prior to her father's death, defendant decided to move away from the home. After she moved out, however, she continued to spend time at the house visiting her boyfriend/nephew Richard, Jr. Since leaving to live on her own, she noticed that the entire house had become filthy. She was aware that a social worker had discussed with Jerry the need to take their father to a doctor. When she spoke to Jerry about it, he told her he had lost the doctor's telephone number the social worker had given him. She suggested to Jerry that he recontact the social worker. She also discussed with Richard, Jr., the need for taking her father to the doctor, but she never made the necessary arrangements.

In the last six weekends before her father died, defendant had routinely visited the household. She was last in her father's bedroom five weeks prior to his death, at which time she noticed the hole in the mattress and feces-soiled clothing lying on the floor. Another of decedent's daughters, Lisa, also visited the house that same day.

Two weeks prior to her father's death, defendant spent the entire weekend at the house. On Sunday afternoon, she saw her father sitting in the living room, and noticed that he looked weak and appeared disoriented. A week later, during Thanksgiving weekend, and several days prior to decedent's death, defendant again stayed at the house. Decedent's bedroom door remained closed throughout the weekend, and defendant did not see her father. On the day decedent died, defendant awoke mid-morning and left the house to return to her own apartment. Around one o'clock in the afternoon, Jerry discovered decedent dead in his bedroom.

In a two-count indictment, the Orange County District Attorney jointly charged Jerry and Richard, Sr., with involuntary manslaughter (§192), and Jerry, Richard, Sr., and defendant with violating section 368(a). At the preliminary examination, the magistrate determined that, although defendant did not have care or custody of decedent as did her brothers, there was probable cause to believe she owed a duty of care to her father and that she had been grossly negligent in failing to carry out that duty. She was therefore held to answer along with her brothers for willfully permitting an elder to suffer unjustifiable physical pain and mental suffering.

On November 4, 1994, an information was filed in superior court charging defendant with a violation of section 368(a). Thereafter, she moved to set aside the information pursuant to section 995 on the basis that the evidence presented at the preliminary hearing failed to establish probable cause she had committed a crime. In relevant part, defendant argued that the evidence that she knew of her father's deteriorating condition did not create a duty for her to act to prevent the harm suffered by him. In its opposition to her motion, the prosecution contended that defendant's duty of care was established by section 368(a) itself, which imposes a duty on every person to not permit any elderly or dependent adult to suffer unjustifiable pain.

. . . Defendant thereafter . . . argu[ed] that section 368(a) is unconstitutionally vague because, by purporting to punish any person for permitting the infliction of pain or mental suffering on any elder, the statute fails to adequately define the class of persons having a legal duty to protect elders from such abuse.

The superior court agreed with defendant that the statutory language at issue was unconstitutionally vague, sustained the demurrer and dismissed the case against her. The People appealed the court's order of dismissal, and the Court of Appeal reversed with directions to overrule the demurrer. It first determined that, because her alleged complicity in her father's death was solely one of inaction, defendant could be held criminally liable under section 368(a) only if she was under a duty to act. The court found that such a duty did exist, based on the special relationship between a parent and child codified in the financial support statutes, section 270c and Civil Code former sections 206 and 242, and thus rejected defendant's vagueness challenge. The court concluded that, as the daughter of a "pensioner" father, defendant was under a duty to act, without gross negligence, to repel a threat to her father's well-being, and that therefore she was properly charged with a violation of section 368(a).

Defendant and the People each sought review of the Court of Appeal's decision reversing the superior court's order sustaining the demurrer. Although the People prevailed below, they sought review on the ground that by construing the statute as incorporating the financial support statutes, the Court of Appeal had impermissibly added two elements to the crime of elder abuse, i.e., a filial relationship between the perpetrator and the victim, and an indigent victim. We granted both petitions.

II. DISCUSSION

A. Criminal Liability for a Failure to Act

Section 368(a) purportedly reaches two categories of offenders: (1) *any person* who willfully causes or permits an elder to suffer, or who directly inflicts, unjustifiable pain or mental suffering on any elder, and (2) the elder's *caretaker or custodian* who willfully causes or permits injury to his or her charge, or who willfully causes or permits the elder to be placed in a dangerous situation. The statute may be applied to a wide range of abusive situations, including within its scope active, assaultive conduct, as well as passive forms of abuse, such as extreme neglect. (*Cf. People v. Smith* (1984) 35 Cal. 3d 798, 806, 201 Cal. Rptr. 311, 678 P.2d 886 [construing identical language in felony child abuse statute].)

Defendant here was charged under section 368(a) with willfully *permitting* her elder father to suffer the infliction of unjustifiable pain and mental suffering. It was thus her *failure to act*, i.e., her failure to prevent the infliction of abuse on her father, that created the potential for her criminal liability under the statute. Unlike the imposition of criminal penalties for certain positive acts, which is based on the statutory proscription of such conduct, when an individual's criminal liability is based on the *failure* to act, it is well established that he or she must first be under an existing legal duty to take positive action.

A legal duty to act is often imposed by the express provisions of a criminal statute itself. . . .

When a criminal statute does not set forth a legal duty to act by its express terms, liability for a failure to act must be premised on the existence of a duty found elsewhere. A criminal statute may thus incorporate a duty imposed by another criminal or civil statute. . . .

A criminal statute may also embody a common law duty based on the legal relationship between the defendant and the victim, such as that imposed on parents to care for and protect their minor children. . . .

Accordingly, in order for criminal liability to attach under section 368(a) for willfully permitting the infliction of physical pain or mental suffering on an elder, a defendant must first be under a legal duty to act. Whether the statute adequately denotes the class of persons who owe such a duty is the focus of the constitutional question presented here.

B. Vagueness

The Fourteenth Amendment to the United States Constitution and article I, section 7 of the California Constitution, each guarantee that no person shall be deprived of life, liberty, or property without due process of law. This constitutional command requires "a reasonable degree of certainty in legislation, especially in the criminal law. . . ." . . .

It is established that in order for a criminal statute to satisfy the dictates of due process, two requirements must be met. First, the provision must be definite enough to provide a standard of conduct for those whose activities are proscribed. . . .

Second, the statute must provide definite guidelines for the police in order to prevent arbitrary and discriminatory enforcement. . . .

For several reasons, we reject the People's contention that the statute itself imposes a blanket duty on everyone to prevent the abuse of any elder. The wide net cast by a statutory interpretation imposing such a duty on every person is apparent when we consider that it would extend the potential for criminal liability to, for example, a delivery person who, having entered a private home, notices an elder in a disheveled or disoriented state and purposefully fails to intervene.

Under general principles of tort law, *civil* liability is not imposed for the failure to assist or protect another, absent some legal or special relationship between the parties giving rise to a duty to act. In the absence of any indication, express or implied, that the Legislature meant to depart so dramatically from this principle, well established at the time section 368(a) was enacted, it would be unreasonable to interpret the statute as imposing a more serious form of liability, indeed, *felony criminal liability*, on every person who fails to prevent an elder from suffering abuse, absent some legal or special relationship between the parties.

* * *

[L]ike the purpose underlying the felony child abuse statute from which it derives, section 368(a) was enacted in order to protect the members of a vulnerable class from abusive situations in which serious injury or death is likely to occur. The Legislature was presumably aware that, under the proposed legislation, some individuals would be subject to criminal liability for conduct not previously unlawful. How far the Legislature intended the potential reach of the new law to extend is not, however, entirely clear.

* * *

[D]ecisions construing either section 368(a) or the felony child abuse statute on which it was modeled do not provide a clear definition of those under a duty to protect either elders or children, respectively. Under these circumstances, section 368(a) fails to provide adequate notice as to the class of persons who may be under an affirmative duty to prevent the infliction of abuse. Of equal, if not greater, constitutional significance, police and prosecutors may lack sufficient standards under which to determine who is to be charged with permitting such abuse.

As noted above, whether or not the lack of statutory clarity has opened the door to arbitrary or discriminatory enforcement of the law is the second prong of our inquiry into the constitutionality of section 368(a).

* * *

Three of the decedent's adult children, Richard, Sr., Jerry, and defendant were jointly charged with a violation of section 368(a). At the preliminary hearing, the prosecutor argued that both Richard, Sr., and Jerry had the care and custody of decedent and could therefore be held to answer under that portion of the statute pertaining to caretakers or custodians. The prosecutor argued further that, although defendant was not responsible for the care or custody of her father, she was properly charged under the first clause of section 368(a) as "any person" who willfully permitted any elder to suffer abuse.

Richard, Sr., and Jerry were not the only family members residing with decedent. Richard, Sr.'s three sons also lived in the home. One of these individuals, Richard, Jr., was defendant's boyfriend. For the last six weekends before her father's death, defendant had routinely been in the house visiting with Richard, Jr. Approximately one month before her father died, defendant discussed with Richard, Jr., the possibility of his helping her take decedent to the doctor. The record therefore would appear to support an inference that whatever defendant knew about her father's deteriorating condition, Richard, Jr., knew as well. Under the prosecutor's reading of the statutory language, the first part of section 368(a) would also appear to be applicable to decedent's grandson, Richard, Jr. He was, however, neither arrested nor charged.

Lisa, a fourth Heitzman sibling who, like defendant, did not reside in the same house as her father and brothers, had visited the home five weeks before decedent's death. She was present in the home when defendant entered their father's room for the last time and discovered the hole where the mattress had rotted through. The record also indicates that at one point Lisa contacted the Orange County Department of Social Services concerning her father's condition, but that the agency did not follow up on her call. It would thus appear that Lisa, like defendant, was well aware of decedent's situation. Unlike defendant, however, Lisa was neither arrested for nor charged with a violation of section 368(a).

* * *

In sum, contrary to constitutional requirements, neither the language nor subsequent judicial construction of section 368(a) provides adequate notice to those who may be under a duty to prevent the infliction of abuse on an elder. Moreover, the statute fails to provide a clear standard for those charged with enforcing the law. Although the selective prosecution of defendant does not conclusively demonstrate the presence of arbitrary or discriminatory enforcement of the statute, it arguably lends support to the view that the potential exists for such impermissible enforcement.

[The court then discussed and rejected the People's argument that section 368(a) was not impermissibly vague because it only proscribed "criminal negligence."—ED.]

We have determined that the portion of section 368(a) purporting to impose on any person the duty to prevent the infliction of pain or suffering on an elder fails to meet the constitutional requirement of certainty. Before declaring a statute void for vagueness, however, we have an obligation to determine whether its validity can be preserved by "giv[ing] specific content to terms that might otherwise be unconstitutionally vague." . . .

[T]he statutory scheme . . . provides that a *caretaker* or *custodian* who causes or permits injury or physical endangerment will incur criminal liability with a lesser degree of harm or potential harm to the victim. By limiting potential criminal liability for the failure to prevent abuse of an elder to those under an existing legal duty to control the conduct of the person inflicting the abuse, the apparent relationship of culpability to harm inherent in the statutory structure is both recognized and maintained.

The statutory certainty provided by the construction set forth herein conveys fair notice to those already under a legal duty to control the conduct of another that their failure to carry out such duty may trigger felony criminal liability in the event an elder is physically abused at the hands of their charge. Clarifying and narrowing the scope of the statute also reduces the possibility that it will be enforced in an arbitrary or discriminatory manner by providing a standard for police, prosecutors and courts as to who might be liable for a failure to prevent the infliction of abuse on an elder. Such a standard serves to diminish the potential for those charged with the enforcement of section 368(a) to rely on personal notions of legal duties, rather than those created by established legal principle. In light of these conclusions, we hold that, as construed, section 368(a) is not unconstitutionally vague.

III. DISPOSITION

Based on their status as Robert Heitzman's caretakers, felony criminal liability was properly imposed on Richard, Sr., and Jerry pursuant to section 368(a) for the role they played in bringing about their father's demise. We observe that, had the events leading to Robert Heitzman's death occurred prior to the enactment of section 368(a), it is likely that prosecutors would have had great difficulty establishing a basis of criminal liability under which to successfully charge Richard, Sr., and Jerry. Because of this, and regardless of our disposition of defendant here, we believe the statute has well served its intended purpose in this distressing case.

Furthermore, given defendant's failure to intercede on her father's behalf under the egregious circumstances presented here, we can well understand the prosecution's decision to charge defendant under section 368(a). Because the People presented no evidence tending to show that defendant had a *legal duty* to control the conduct of either of her brothers, however, we reverse the judgment of the Court of Appeal with directions to reinstate the trial court's order dismissing the charges against defendant.

We emphasize that our disposition of this case in no way signifies our approval of defendant's failure to repel the threat to her father's well-being. The facts underlying this case are indeed troubling, and defendant's alleged indifference to the suffering of her father cannot be condoned. The desire to impose criminal liability on *this* defendant cannot be accomplished, however, at the expense of providing constitutionally required clarity to an otherwise vague statute.

The judgment of the Court of Appeal is reversed.

QUESTIONS

1. Are *Heitzman* and *McKelvey* consistent with one another? Why or why not?

2. Delores McKelvey's daughter Theresa pled guilty. Suppose the case against her had gone to trial. Could she have been found guilty under Section 368? How might you differentiate her behavior from that of Susan Heitzman?

3. The current version of the underlying statute in *Heitzman* and *McKelvey* reads:

   > Any person who knows or reasonably should know that a person is an elder or dependent adult and who, under circumstances or conditions likely to produce great bodily harm or death, willfully causes or permits any elder or dependent adult to suffer, or inflicts thereon unjustifiable physical pain or mental suffering, or having the care or custody of any elder or dependent adult, willfully causes or permits the person or health of the elder or dependent adult to be injured, or willfully causes or permits the elder or dependent adult to be placed in a situation in which his or her person or health is endangered, is punishable by imprisonment in a county jail not exceeding one year, or by a fine not to exceed six thousand dollars ($6,000), or by both that fine and imprisonment, or by imprisonment in the state prison for two, three, or four years.

   CAL. PENAL CODE §368(b)(1)(2013). If you were a member of your state's legislature, would you support your state adopting an identical statute? Why or why not?

Sieniarecki v. State of Florida

756 So. 2d 68 (Fla. 2000)

LEWIS, J.

We have for review a challenge to the constitutionality of section 825.102(3), Florida Statutes (1997), which, in pertinent part, penalizes "[a] caregiver's [culpably negligent] failure or omission to provide [a] ... disabled adult with the care, supervision, and services necessary to maintain the ... disabled adult's physical and mental health, including, but not limited to, food, nutrition, clothing, shelter, supervision, medicine, and medical services that a prudent person would consider essential for the well-being of the ... disabled adult." ...

MATERIAL FACTS AND PROCEEDINGS BELOW

In this case, the evidence at trial demonstrated that petitioner, Theresa Sieniarecki, was the oldest of decedent's four children. Until approximately two weeks before her death, the petitioner's mother, Patricia Sieniarecki, lived with petitioner, petitioner's boyfriend, and two of petitioner's brothers in the family home. Mrs. Sieniarecki's husband (petitioner's father) died from lung cancer shortly after Mrs. Sieniarecki had undergone two hip surgeries, and while she was recovering in a rehabilitation facility.

Following her second hip surgery and her husband's death, the mother's disposition changed dramatically. She appeared to be despondent and disoriented. She would ask her younger son where her dead husband was, calling that son by his older brother's name. It appeared that she had "given up," and that she "wouldn't do anything." Although apparently physically able to walk, she now would not walk at all. The children never left their mother alone at home, because she sometimes needed help or food. Always a picky eater, she ate and drank so little that, at the time of her death, even though she was five feet, three inches tall, she weighed only sixty-eight pounds.

It was also during this time that the family home was subjected to foreclosure. The children helped their mother with the sale of the home, and, with the little money left over after paying off the mortgage debt, the family moved into two separate apartments. Before moving, the children discussed with whom Mrs. Sieniarecki was to live. The record reflects that it was decided that the mother would live with petitioner—who had completed the tenth grade, but did not work—because petitioner "was able to take care of her," whereas, the two brothers (one of whom was at work "a lot," while the other worked and attended school) would not have had "that much time to spend with her." The two brothers moved into an efficiency apartment. Petitioner, her boyfriend, and her mother moved into a two-bedroom apartment.

The apartment manager testified that, at the time petitioner and her boyfriend were making arrangements to move into the apartment, the manager asked whether Mrs. Sieniarecki, who "looked like she was very weak," would be able to reach an upstairs apartment. Petitioner's boyfriend indicated to him that Mrs. Sieniarecki would be carried up when the three of them moved in, and "would not ever be coming back down the stairs anymore." In fact, when the three of them did move in, petitioner's boyfriend carried Mrs. Sieniarecki up to the apartment, because she was "tired."

Since Mrs. Sieniarecki would not walk (even to the bathroom), she required adult diapers. Petitioner testified that she bathed her mother and changed her diapers. She testified that she had no help from others with these tasks. Although she brought her mother food and liquids, if she tried to persuade her mother to eat, Mrs. Sieniarecki would "take a bite and then she'd throw it," or she would just "leave it there to sit all night." While, on one hand, petitioner testified that she spent time with her mother, and, except when her brother came to visit "every once in a while," all the responsibility fell on her, she also stated that she did not know whether her mother ate what she brought her or not. She stated that she was her mother's sole provider, except when her brother brought chili dogs for her mother to eat.

The mother's previous mattress—which was filthy—was kept in a utility room by the front door of the apartment. The new mattress on the mother's bed was not covered with a bottom sheet, because the old sheets got "messed up," and petitioner "threw them out with the old mattress." Petitioner testified that her mother would get feces on her hands from the adult diapers, and then scratch her legs and face, and touch the wall. Petitioner testified that she cleaned up after her mother, but never noticed any diaper rash on her.

She also stated that she never called anyone to obtain help, advice or medical care for her mother.

Mrs. Sieniarecki's children testified that, whenever it was suggested to their mother that she go to a doctor, the mother would yell, indicating her disagreement. Petitioner also testified that, if she suggested to her mother that she not smoke cigarettes, her mother would yell at her to bring cigarettes.

According to petitioner's testimony, at about 10 P.M. on the night before her mother died, petitioner put a new diaper on her, "because she was gross." At about midnight, her mother "bitched at me, she wanted water. She just yelled, Theresa, bring me some water." The next morning, at mid-morning, when petitioner went in to see her mother, she was dead. Police were called at about 11:50 A.M. that morning.

The detective who came to the scene found Mrs. Sieniarecki lying on the bare mattress with one sheet covering her. She was wearing nothing but a polo shirt, with one tennis shoe on her right foot. Her hair was disheveled and her body was smeared with feces. The mattress on which she was lying was filthy, soiled with urine and feces. He found feces smeared on the wall next to the bed.

Dr. Price, the physician who performed the autopsy (stipulated to be an expert in forensic pathology) testified regarding Mrs. Sieniarecki's condition and the cause of her death. Dr. Price indicated that she had no teeth, and that he found nothing other than bile in her stomach or digestive tract. Her eyes were deeply sunken in, indicative of severe dehydration. Her right foot was ulcerated in the heel area "clear down to the bone," and this decubitus ulcer was "covered by green pus." Her skin was reddened with external sores in the thigh and buttocks area, indicating antemortem irritation from feces or urine being left on her skin. Although in her fifties, Mrs. Sieniarecki appeared to be much older.

The cause of Mrs. Sieniarecki's death was, in Dr. Price's opinion, septicemia (an infection in her blood), occurring as a result of decubitus ulcers, a bladder infection and a vaginal infection. Dehydration and malnutrition contributed to the cause of death. . . . The infection not only involved her bladder and vagina, but had spread into her fat and abdominal cavity as well.

PROCEEDINGS BELOW

After a jury trial, petitioner was found guilty of neglect of a disabled adult, pursuant to section 825.102(3), Florida Statutes (1997). That section provides in pertinent part:

> (3)(a) "Neglect of an elderly person or disabled adult" means:
>   1. A caregiver's failure or omission to provide an elderly person or disabled adult with the care, supervision, and services necessary to maintain the elderly person's or disabled adult's physical and mental health, including, but not limited to, food, nutrition, clothing, shelter, supervision, medicine, and medical services that a prudent person would consider essential for the well-being of the elderly person or disabled adult; or

2. A caregiver's failure to make a reasonable effort to protect an elderly person or disabled adult from abuse, neglect, or exploitation by another person.

Neglect of an elderly person or disabled adult may be based on repeated conduct or on a single incident or omission that results in, or could reasonably be expected to result in, serious physical or psychological injury, or a substantial risk of death, to an elderly person or disabled adult.

. . .

c) A person who willfully or by culpable negligence neglects an elderly person or disabled adult without causing great bodily harm, permanent disability, or permanent disfigurement to the elderly person or disabled adult commits a felony of the third degree, punishable as provided in s. 775.082, s. 775.083, or s. 775.084.

"Caregiver" is defined in the statute as "*a person who* has been entrusted with or *has assumed responsibility for the care* or the property of an elderly person *or [a] disabled adult. 'Caregiver' includes,* but is not limited to, *relatives,* court-appointed or voluntary guardians, *adult household members,* neighbors, health care providers, and employee and volunteers of facilities as defined in subsection (7)." §825.101(2), Fla. Stat. (1997) (emphasis supplied). "Disabled adult" is defined as "a person 18 years of age or older who suffers from a condition of physical or mental incapacitation due to a developmental disability, organic brain damage, or mental illness, or *who has one or more physical or mental limitations that restrict the person's ability to perform the normal activities of daily living.*" §825.101(4), Fla. Stat. (1997) (emphasis supplied).

LAW AND ANALYSIS

On appeal, the Fourth District upheld petitioner's conviction in the face of a three-tiered constitutional challenge. First, petitioner asserted that the applicable provisions are "facially unconstitutional because they do not contain a specific intent requirement and thereby violate due process by imposing an affirmative duty upon [petitioner] to act, while penalizing [petitioner's] failure to comply." Next, she maintained that the provisions "are unconstitutionally vague." Finally, she urged that section 782.07(2), Florida Statutes (1997), "violates her mother's right to privacy embodied in Article I, section 23 of the Florida Constitution." . . . Consistent with the Fourth District's decision, we find that petitioner's arguments fail to overcome the presumption of constitutionality which applies.

DUE PROCESS

Petitioner's first claim is that the neglect provisions of the statute violate due process because they fail to contain a specific intent requirement. Although couched here in different terms (i.e., as a "due process" challenge, rather than an argument based on vagueness, overbreadth or indefiniteness), this assertion that the statute potentially criminalizes innocent conduct . . . has, in a slightly different context, been addressed before.

Twice, the constitutionality of certain Florida child protection statutes based upon negligence has been questioned before this Court. The first of these statutes, section 827.05, Florida Statutes (1975), which prohibited the "negligent treatment of children," was found to be unconstitutional. . . .

However, the second such statute, which proscribed "simple criminal child abuse" (defined, *inter alia*, as depriving a child of necessary food, clothing, shelter or medical treatment, either willfully or by culpable negligence) was upheld against a similar challenge. *See State v. Joyce*, 361 So. 2d 406, 407 (Fla. 1978) (upholding, in the face of a vagueness challenge, former section 827.04(2), Florida Statutes (1975), which prohibited the willful or *culpably negligent* deprivation of a child's necessary food, clothing, shelter or medical treatment). In *Joyce*, this Court rejected an argument . . . that the simple criminal child abuse statute was unconstitutional, reasoning:

> Appellees contend that the county courts' invalidation of Section 827.04(2), Florida Statutes (1975), is consistent with our decision in *State v. Winters*, 346 So. 2d 991 (Fla. 1977). There, Section 827.05, Florida Statutes (1975), which criminalized "negligent treatment of children," was declared unconstitutionally vague, indefinite and overbroad. . . . The basis for our holding there was that the negligent treatment statute made criminal acts of simple negligence-conduct which was neither willful nor culpably negligent. Section 827.04(2), in contrast, requires willfulness (scienter) or culpable negligence. . . . As we recently concluded in upholding Section 784.05, Florida Statutes (1975), the culpable negligence statute, the term "culpable negligence" does not suffer from the constitutional infirmity of vagueness. . . .

Here, similarly, the challenged provisions proscribe neglect which is caused either wilfully or by culpable negligence. . . .

VAGUENESS

As we explained . . . [t]he standard for testing vagueness under Florida law is whether the statute gives a person of ordinary intelligence fair notice of what constitutes forbidden conduct. . . .

Further, the traditional rule is that "a person to whom a statute may constitutionally be applied may not challenge that statute on the ground that it may conceivably be applied unconstitutionally to others in situations not before the Court." *New York v. Ferber*, 458 U.S. 747 (1982). . . .

Here, petitioner claims that it is not clear, within the meaning of the statute, that her mother had "one or more physical or mental limitations that restrict the person's ability to perform the normal activities of daily living," or that petitioner "assumed" responsibility to provide "care, supervision, and services necessary to maintain" her mother's "physical and mental health, including, but not limited to, food, nutrition, clothing, shelter, supervision, medicine, and medical services that a prudent person would consider essential for [her] well-being." As to petitioner's first point, it was undisputed that Mrs. Sieniarecki's behavior after her husband's death was disoriented, and that she "wouldn't do anything." While petitioner questions the degree to which a person's normal functions must be impaired in order to qualify as a "disabled person," when "measured by common understanding and practice," the de facto total impairment which her mother exhibited clearly falls within the statute's definition.

Next, petitioner questions whether she "assumed" responsibility to provide care, supervision and necessary services to her mother. In the absence of a statutory definition, words of common usage are construed in their plain and ordinary sense. . . . In the dictionary, the pertinent definition of the infinitive "to assume" is "to take to or upon oneself." Webster's Third New International Dictionary 133 (1993). Here, petitioner's own testimony reflected that she "took upon herself" the responsibility to care and provide for her mother. Petitioner, who was not otherwise employed, testified that she bathed her mother and changed her diapers (and no one else helped her with these tasks); that she brought her mother food and liquids; that all the responsibility fell on her; and that—except when her brother brought chili dogs for her mother to eat—she was her mother's sole provider. The evidence established that a joint decision was made as to where petitioner's mother would reside after sale of the family home and who would provide the day to day care. Petitioner also testified that she never called anyone to obtain help, advice or medical care for her mother.

Thus, it is clear, on the facts of this case, that the petitioner "assumed responsibility" for the care of her mother, a "disabled adult" within the plain meaning of the statute. Petitioner's resulting conduct in failing to adequately address her mother's most basic needs—either by providing for them herself or by seeking the assistance of others—squarely fell within the statute's proscriptions.

Therefore, not only is the statute not unconstitutional as applied, but petitioner also lacks standing to raise a facial vagueness challenge. . . .

MRS. SIENIARECKI'S PRIVACY RIGHT

Appellant's last claim is that section 825.102(3) violates her mother's right to privacy. See art. I, §23, Fla. Const. Specifically, she asserts that, because her mother had the right to refuse medical treatment, petitioner cannot be convicted of neglect for failing to provide proper medical attention. However, as the Fourth District observed in its decision below, constitutional rights are personal in nature and generally may not be asserted vicariously. . . . For this reason, petitioner's final challenge also fails.

For the foregoing reasons, the decision below is approved. . . .

QUESTIONS

1. Why does the court in *Sieniarecki* find that the defendant assumed a duty? Would the result have been the same if the defendant had been the

decedent's non-relative roommate? Would anyone who lived with the decedent have been found to have assumed a duty?

2. The statute at issue in *Sieniarecki* has been critiqued on the grounds that it unfairly penalizes people who take care of vulnerable people and that this is especially unfair because those held criminally responsible may not realize they have a legal duty and may not consider themselves to be caregivers. *See* Lindsey E. Wylie & Eve M. Brank, *Assuming Elder Care Responsibility: Am I a Caregiver?*, 6 J. EMPIRICAL LEGAL STUD. 899 (2009).

    a. Do you share this concern? Why or why not?

    b. To what extent could this concern be addressed by changing the statutory definition of "caregiver" or of "disabled adult"? If you were revising the statute, would you change either definition?

3. If Mrs. Sieniarecki had survived, to what extent would her privacy interests have been impacted by the state prosecuting her children for their neglect of her? Similarly, to what extent would Dolores McKelvey's and Robert Heitzman's privacy interests have been implicated by the prosecutions of their children if they had survived? Are these interests relevant after their deaths?

b. Self-Neglect

Self-neglect, which is estimated to occur at three times the rate of all other forms of elder mistreatment combined, occurs when an individual engages in behavior that threatens his or her own health or safety. This failure may reflect an unwillingness to provide for him- or herself, but it can also reflect an inability to do so. There is a fine distinction, of course, between self-neglect and eccentric behavior, although eccentric behavior is more likely to be consistent with the individual's underlying value system.

Self-neglect may occur either independently of other forms of elder abuse or simultaneously with abuse or neglect perpetrated by another person. Common symptoms include poor hygiene, a refusal of services, and unsafe or unsanitary housing. Relative to the general population, individuals who are self-neglecting are also disproportionately likely to suffer from other problems that affect their ability to engage in self-care, including alcoholism and hoarding.

There is some debate as to whether or not self-neglect should be considered a form of elder abuse and neglect. While many believe that it should, others see the term as failing to recognize the third-party behaviors and societal failures (e.g., failures to ensure that all people have the resources they need to live safe, healthy lives) that contribute to the symptoms associated with self-neglect. Yet others prefer to reserve the terms abuse and neglect—terms associated with a certain form of culpability—for acts or omissions of third parties.

A second point of disagreement is whether individuals with the cognitive capacity to understand the nature and consequences of their failure to provide for themselves can be said to be truly self-neglecting. While some believe it should (in part, often, because capacity can be fluid and hard to define), others would reserve the term self-neglect for situations in which individuals cannot be said to be making a fully aware choice as to their behavior.

There is significant disagreement as to what behaviors should be considered self-neglect and how the state, social service providers, and others should respond to the problem. Self-neglect raises difficult ethical issues not only for lawyers, but also for social service workers and health care providers. For example, health care providers working with patients who are self-neglecting may feel torn between their ethical obligation to respect their patients' autonomy and their ethical obligation of *beneficence*, that is, their ethical obligation to act in a way that benefits their patients.

Given the disagreements about the definition of self-neglect and the proper response to it, it is not surprising that states differ in their approach to addressing the problem of self-neglect. While responses vary significantly, states are increasingly including "self-neglect" in their definitions of elder abuse subject to mandatory reporting. This inclusion has been criticized as a form of social control that unduly limits individuals' ability to self-determine. Others have defended such reports not only on the grounds that they can help get vulnerable persons needed help, but also on the grounds that third-party neglect often masquerades as self-neglect.

NOTE

Further reading. For a review of the literature describing the phenomenon of self-neglect, see James G. O'Brien, *Self-Neglect in Old Age*, 7 AGING HEALTH 573 (2011) (providing an overview of literature on self-neglect). For a compelling argument as to the negative implications of undermining autonomy in later life, see ROBERT N. BUTLER, WHY SURVIVE? BEING OLD IN AMERICA (2002).

QUESTIONS

1. Should states require that third parties report self-neglect to a governmental agency?

2. How should states best address the problem of self-neglect?

3. Did Mrs. Sieniarecki have a privacy right that was implicated by the Florida statute in the above case of *Sieniarecki v. Florida*? If so, was it violated?

4. Do individuals have a "right" to engage in self-neglect?

PROBLEMS

1. Ancient Greek philosopher Diogenes of Sinope (also known as Diogenes the Cynic), a founder of Cynicism, is said to have publically demonstrated his disdain for materialism, common conceptions of decency, and the value

placed on reputation by, among other things, begging, sleeping in a jar in a marketplace, and defecating and eating in public settings. Was he self-neglecting? *Cf.* A.N.G. Clark et al., *Diogenes Syndrome: A Clinical Study of Gross Neglect in Old Age*, 1 LANCET 366 (1975) (coining the term "Diogenes syndrome" to describe a severe form of elder self-neglect).

2. Shelton is an 85-year-old man with two bad knees, which, due to his congestive heart failure, cannot be safely repaired or replaced. He lives alone in a small two-story home on the outskirts of a large city. Both his bedroom and his only bathroom are on the second floor of his house. He is unable, however, to safely ascend the stairs to the second story. He has been visited by a social worker who has suggested that he move to an assisted living facility, which Shelton has sufficient resources to pay for. Shelton refuses. He says that the house has always been his home, and that he will never move regardless of whether it would be safer for him to be elsewhere. He explains that all his possessions and memories are in the house.

   a. Suppose that Shelton nevertheless ascends the stairs to sleep and use the bathroom. He has fallen twice while doing so, once causing a minor pelvic fracture. Is Shelton self-neglecting? What, if anything, should the social worker do about Shelton and his living situation?

   b. Suppose that to avoid using the stairs, which he recognizes it is unsafe to do, Shelton uses his living room couch as a bed and urinates and defecates in jars, which he throws out with the rest of his trash. When there is snow or ice, he has trouble getting outside to take out the trash. The jars and his other waste can therefore accumulate for up to a month at a time. Is Shelton self-neglecting? What, if anything, should the social worker do about Shelton and his living situation?

CHAPTER 9

Death and Dying

A. INTRODUCTION

Although death can occur at any age and affects people of all ages, older adults typically face a more imminent death than younger ones. Elder law attorneys therefore need to be able to discuss issues surrounding death and dying, and they need an understanding of the law governing a person's ability to shape and direct the circumstances and timing of his or her death.

Accordingly, this chapter begins by exploring the practical and emotional challenges that elder law attorneys face when working with dying clients and discussing planning for end-of-life care. It then explores key legal rights related to end-of-life choices, including those related to affirmatively choosing to take measures that terminate life or hasten the dying process. Finally, it discusses hospice care and Medicare's hospice benefit.

B. COUNSELING TERMINALLY ILL CLIENTS

Elder law attorneys frequently work with clients who have been diagnosed with a terminal illness and are anticipating an imminent death. Working with such clients can be very rewarding, but it can also be emotionally intense, requiring the attorney to engage in conversations about topics often treated as taboo.

What follows are excerpts from two articles designed to provide guidance to attorneys working with dying clients on issues related to the end of life. The first, authored by probate judge Georgia Akers, considers how a dying individual's process of dealing with his or her impending death may affect the attorney-client relationship, especially in the context of estate planning. The second provides recommendations for how attorneys should talk with clients about planning for end of life decisions.

Georgia Akers, On Death and Dying: Counseling the Terminally Ill Client and the Loved Ones Left Behind

1 Est. Plan. & Community Prop. L.J. 1 (2008)

In 1969, Dr. Elisabeth Kubler-Ross published her book *On Death and Dying*, which brought death out of the closet and made death acceptable to discuss. Her research included interviewing hundreds of terminally ill patients, and she discovered that persons who are dying go through stages.

Most contemporary psychiatrists, however, do not agree that the terminally ill go through the phases in an orderly manner. Often a patient will return to a prior phase, have a mixture of phases, get stuck in one phase, or bypass a phase entirely.

A. DENIAL AND ISOLATION

Upon being confronted with the diagnosis of a terminal illness, the first reaction a client will have is often, "'No, not me, it cannot be true.'" This denial is present in patients who were told outright by their physicians of their terminal illness as well as those who were not explicitly informed but came to the conclusion on their own. This denial, however, "is more typical in a patient who is informed prematurely or abruptly" without taking into consideration the patient's readiness to hear this disclosure.

* * *

Denial should not be seen as an unhealthy manifestation. It is natural and "functions as a buffer after unexpected shocking news [and] allows the patient to collect himself." Patients in denial often seek second opinions in the hope that their treating physician is wrong.

A client in the denial stage will not want to meet with an attorney and will not be receptive to any estate planning, no matter how hard the family may plead and cajole the individual to "get his affairs in order." If dragged to your office, the patient will not cooperate and will consider the consultation a waste of time.

As the attorney, it may be best to listen but not ask a lot of estate planning questions. Keep the interview short and attempt to establish a rapport with the client. Likely the client will not be receptive and will not be completely tuning in to any advice offered. If clients do not want to discuss the illness or seem unrealistic about the situation, then do not push them. Since clients may be coming to you as a result of their recent diagnosis and poor prognosis, it is easy to base your attorney client relationship on their medical illness. To build a better relationship and better understand the needs of your client, spend some time getting to know the actual person.

B. ANGER

"When the first stage of denial cannot be maintained any longer, it is replaced by feelings of anger, rage, envy, and resentment. . . . The logical next question becomes: 'Why me?'"

The patient is very difficult to cope with from the view of family and medical staff as "anger is displaced in all directions and projected onto the environment . . . at random." Comments such as "the doctors are just no good" or "the proper tests have not been ordered" are common in the anger stage. The nursing staff is even more of a target, and the bell in the hospital room might ring frequently.

The family also receives the brunt of the anger. They are "received with little cheerfulness or anticipation." Naturally, the family responds with tears, guilt, and avoidance, which makes the patient even angrier.

Where is the anger coming from? The patient sees his life interrupted prematurely. The family's life continues on, and they will be enjoying things he will not. The patient will raise his voice, make demands, and complain. He provokes anger and rejection. The patient is in a desperate stage. Just like the family and medical staff, the attorney can also be a target of the displaced anger.

If a client is in the anger stage, then the attorney may see the client make cruel or unreasonable decisions regarding the client's family during the estate planning. The client may leave little of his estate to the family or place the estate in an income-only trust. The client may vocalize that he does not want his wife's next husband to enjoy his estate or that he does not want his wife to have a good time once he is dead.

Listen to the client and attempt to understand the anger. Does the client's action reflect on a lifelong pattern of behavior, or is his action in line with the values he has had throughout his life? If not, then the attorney can gently point out the contradictions and let the client make sense of them. If this fails, then it may be prudent to have the client go home to think about his plan for a few days.

C. BARGAINING

In the bargaining stage, the client may think, "God has not responded when I was angry with Him. Perhaps if I am nice, He will postpone the inevitable." In other words, the client hopes good behavior may be rewarded with an extension of life. The client is beginning to accept the fact that he is dying and is now hoping for more time on Earth. Bargaining is an attempt to postpone death where the client may promise a life dedicated to God or good works in exchange for more time.

At this stage, the attorney may see a request for an extraordinarily large bequest to a church or charity. The client's family may become aware of larger than normal gifts being made to a church or charity. The attorney should first determine if the client has had a pattern of charitable giving by asking whether it fits into the client's life history and values. If not, then ask the client to explain this discrepancy.

D. DEPRESSION

Once the surgeries, constant hospitalizations, symptoms, and weakened body reach a point where the terminally ill client can no longer deny the illness, he cannot simply whisk the illness away with a smile anymore. In place of the client's anger, rage, and attempts at bargaining will now stand a sense of great loss.

The weakening of the body is only a part of the client's losses. Increasing financial burdens take their toll, as luxuries and necessities may no longer be affordable. Funds previously set aside for a child's college education may need to be utilized for living expenses. An inability to function may cause the client to quit his job. When this happens, the other spouse often becomes the primary support, and the children may not get the attention they once expected. Depression is an emotion that the terminally ill client must undergo to prepare for death.

In order to facilitate the final stage of acceptance, no one should encourage the client to look at the brighter side because this prevents him from contemplating his impending death. The client needs to be allowed to express his sorrow. There is no need for words because acceptance is best treated by a familiar touch or quiet company. Too much interference from cheerful visitors at this time may hinder the client's emotional preparation.

If a client is depressed, then the attorney may need to prompt the client and be more active. If the client does not volunteer or request particular information, then the attorney should not assume the client lacks desire. It may be prudent to wait a few days if a client comes to your office in a depressed state. If the depression is severe and persistent for more than a couple of weeks, then refer the client to a mental health professional.

E. ACCEPTANCE

If a client has had enough time and received help working through the first four stages of death, then he will reach a stage where he is no longer depressed or angry about his fate. He will have expressed his envy for those living and his anger toward those who do not share his fate. The client will have mourned the approaching loss of so many people and places. The client will contemplate his fate with a degree of quiet expectation.

Acceptance is an unhappy stage, almost void of feelings. Acceptance makes it seem as if the pain is gone and the struggle is over. The client has found some peace, and his circle of interest has diminished. He wishes to be left alone and is not talkative. Communication becomes more nonverbal than verbal. Terminally ill clients can die easier if they are not prevented from detaching themselves slowly from all the meaningful relationships in their lives. During this stage, the family usually needs more support than the client needs in order to let go.

During the stage of acceptance, the client finds peace in his life and in his impending death. This is the ideal stage in which to do estate planning. However, it is unpredictable when and if acceptance will occur.

F. FINAL THOUGHTS

Attorneys need to be aware of these various stages of death and try to determine which stage the terminally ill client is going through. Emotional moments may cause meetings with the client to run longer than expected. Although attorneys are prone to thoroughly discussing matters, when dealing with a terminally ill client attorneys should be comfortable with silence and use it as a tool to help the client cope with the situation. If the client has an unusual request regarding his estate plan, then it is possible that the request is influenced by the client's current death stage.

There is no specific timetable as to how long a client might be in any given stage. When advising a client, the attorney comes to the client with his own experiences with loss and death. These personal experiences can either help or interfere with assisting the client. It may be necessary for the attorney to perform a quick self-assessment. If the attorney is not able to put his emotions aside, then he may need to refer the client to another attorney. . . .

As advocates, attorneys should be aware that a client who is severely ill is sometimes treated as a person with no right to an opinion. The client may be in the company of medical personnel who in their minds are assisting him, but none of them will stop to listen to him. He becomes a thing. We might need to remind the family and medical personnel that our client has feelings, wishes, opinions, and the right to be heard.

Ed de St. Aubin et al., Elders and End-of-Life Medical Issues: Legal Context, Psychological Issues, and Recommendations to Attorneys Serving Seniors

7 Marq. Elder's Advisor 259 (2006)

The elder law lawyer who broaches the subject of end-of-life decisions may be met with resistance and dismissed by the client who is not willing, ready, or able to deal with this matter. The lawyer may observe the client becoming anxious, withdrawn, angry, hostile, or sad by even the mention of the subject. The client may say or think, "It can't happen to me; I'm too healthy." Or, the client may say, "I can't think about this right now and not for many years to come." Lawyers must acknowledge and respect that some clients are not ready to face this issue. Some clients may need time to consider the issue perhaps in the privacy of their home, at a time they select, in a frame of mind that permits a more receptive acceptance of the end of their life on earth. The attorney may need to ask the client whether he needs time to think about what medical decisions he would like at the end of his life. The client may need to be invited back at a later date to discuss the issue further.

What cannot be stated with sufficient emphasis is that, as with other areas, the lawyer can counsel their client, but the lawyer should accept the client's decision for what it is: a decision made by a competent individual even though that decision may be at odds with what the lawyer believes is in the client's best interest. If the client indicates no intention to execute advanced directives, the lawyer must respect that decision. Further, if the lawyer observes that the client is in psychological distress or is experiencing profound death anxiety, a referral to a mental health professional should be offered. The American Psychological Association, state psychological associations, and local mental health associations are some sources the lawyer may want to consult for a list of mental health providers in their community. Lawyers should do what they do best, which is represent the interests of their client to the best of their ability. Lawyers are not therapists, but they are encouraged to be psychologically minded in their relationship with their client, especially at this delicate time period.

SO HOW SHOULD THE ELDER LAW ATTORNEY PROCEED IN THESE CONVERSATIONS?

Remember law school and recall one of the basic lessons: assume nothing. First, answer the question of who is the client. Is this a case of individual representation, joint representation or intermediary representation, to list just a few of the many options that exist? . . .

Second, educate the client about the advanced care directives and instruments available in which the client can articulate her preferences concerning medical-end-of-life-decisions. . . . Discuss the value of documenting how the client would like to be dealt with at times of vulnerability and distress. For example, make the client aware that there may be a considerable cost savings, both emotional and financial, to her and her loved ones if litigation can be avoided and the need for guardianship proceedings curtailed. The client's attention may be directed to emotional savings to family members and financial preservation if undesired medical treatment, as articulated in an advanced directive, is not undertaken. So too, make the client aware of the potential negative consequences of not documenting his end-of-life medical desires such as undergoing treatment or being sustained on artificial life support systems against his wishes.

Third, start a conversation with the client about his goals and interests in end-of-life medical treatment. Keep in mind the need for autonomy and the desire to achieve ego-integrity through generativity [i.e., creating a legacy that will benefit younger and future generations].

ASK THE CLIENT ABOUT HIS LIFE

Let the client speak about his life, current, past, and future. Encourage the client to talk about accomplishments, which, at some level, facilitates the client's own meaning-making, affording her the opportunity to accept both life and death. Listen to what the clients say. Ask follow up questions: What was it about that event or situation that was important to you? How do you want to be remembered? What do you most value about your life? To help the client speak in concrete terms, ask him to explore what their life would look like if he knew he had several weeks or a month to live. What would she do? Who would he be with? What would she say? Also, listen as much for what is not said as for what is said. Be sensitive, non-judgmental, empathic and creative in discussing the client's perception of these issues.

ASK FUNDAMENTAL THRESHOLD QUESTIONS

For example, what are the client's views about self-determination in health care decision-making? Is the question that they cannot make the decision or that they chose not to at this time? What role does the client's spirituality or religion play in her views? Let the client know that you understand that these are difficult topics for him. An attorney may offer to schedule another time to meet after the client has had an opportunity to give it some thought. Be willing to terminate the discussion and schedule another appointment.

ASK THE HARD QUESTIONS

An attorney should facilitate a discussion that allows the client to maintain autonomy as she makes end-of-life decisions for medical care. The client should be asked to imagine situations that may seem unimaginable, and given this imagined situation, what she would want to be done in terms of medical treatment. An attorney could present the following scenarios to determine if the client would desire medical treatment, and if so, what kind: (1) what if the client were in pain most of the time and that pain could not be adequately relieved; (2) what if the client could no longer care for their daily needs suffering from hardships such as incontinence and loss of bowel control; (3) what if the client could not recognize her loved ones; (4) what if the client was confined to a wheelchair or confined in his home; (5) what if the client could not think or was dependent on a machine to live, such as a feeding tube, dialysis machine or breathing machine? An attorney should introduce scenarios that prompt the client to consider specific directives.

NOTE

Cross-cultural conversations. For a discussion of how culture impacts individuals' decision-making processes with regards to end-of-life care, and how professionals might enhance their own sensitivity to these issues, see Marjorie Kagawa-Singer & Leslie J. Blackhall, *Negotiating Cross-Cultural Issues at the End of Life,* 286 JAMA 2993 (2001).

QUESTIONS

1. In discussing the experience of dying persons and how attorneys working in the area of trust and estates might respond to that experience, Judge Akers does not differentiate among dying people based on their age. How might the experience of dying vary based on age? How might it be different to represent an older person who is dying as opposed to a younger adult who is dying?

2. Akers advises attorneys working with terminally ill persons to try to determine what stage of dying their clients are in. Do you agree with this advice?

3. Akers recommends that "[i]f an attorney is not able to put his emotions aside, then he may need to refer the client to another attorney." Do you agree? What does it mean to put emotions to the side? Are there times when an attorney's emotional response to a client's situation is an asset?

4. Professor de St. Aubin et al. encourage attorneys to "be psychologically minded in their relationship with their clients." What does it mean to be psychologically minded? Is this encouragement consistent with their caution that lawyers are not therapists?

C. THE RIGHT TO REFUSE LIFE-SUSTAINING CARE

A competent individual has a constitutionally recognized legal right to refuse to engage in behavior or receive care that will prolong his or her life. This includes the right to refuse to eat or drink, even if doing so will lead to death. It includes the right to refuse treatment or services necessary to sustain life. It further extends to the right to terminate life-sustaining treatment once it has begun.

While the right to refuse life-sustaining treatment is clear, individuals may experience certain barriers to exercising that right.

First, they may face resistance from family members or medical providers who are personally uncomfortable with the decision to refuse care. As Kathryn Tucker, an attorney with Compassion & Choices (a nonprofit organization advocating, among other things, legalization of physician-assisted suicide) writes:

> There may be instances where a particular clinician is uncomfortable or unwilling, for reasons of personal conviction or religion, to withdraw treatment. In such instance the responsibility of the clinician is to inform the patient and refer to a clinician willing to respect the patient's choice. It is also the responsibility of the clinician to anticipate and treat prophylactically distressing symptoms that might arise related to the withdrawal of therapy. Unfortunately, despite the clarity of this professional duty, studies reveal that some clinicians will simply not inform patients of options which they do not

support. Accordingly, it may fall to the elder law advisor to share critical information about end-of-life care options with their clients. Further, it may be necessary for the attorney to undertake advocacy on their client's behalf to ensure that the client's decision is respected.

Kathryn L. Tucker, *Counseling Clients Who Are Terminally Ill: The Right to Make Decisions Regarding End-of-Life Care*, 261 ELDER L. ADVISORY 1 (2012).

Second, their capacity to make such a fundamental decision may be challenged, as is illustrated by the first case in this chapter, *In the Matter of Anna M. Gordy*, 658 A.2d 613 (Del. Ch. 1994).

Third, when the patient lacks the mental capacity to make the decision to refuse life-sustaining treatment, there may be a question as to whether there is sufficient evidence of the patient's wishes for a surrogate to make the decision on the patient's behalf.

1. Refusal of Life-Sustaining Care for Cognitively Incapacitated Persons

Since the Supreme Court's decision in *Cruzan v. Director, Missouri Department of Health*, 497 U.S. 261 (1990), in which the Court upheld a state law requiring clear and convincing evidence of a patient's wishes in order for a surrogate to authorize withdrawal of life support, it has been generally recognized that the U.S. Constitution protects not only the right of an individual to refuse life-sustaining treatment, but also the right to have that decision made by a surrogate. Nevertheless, to protect life and the interests of those who have cognitive incapacity, states can and have enacted a variety of schemes to govern how and when a surrogate may refuse life-sustaining treatment on behalf of a patient. The next case considers this issue.

In the Matter of Anna M. Gordy

658 A.2d 613 (Del. Ch. 1994)

ALLEN, Chancellor.

Pending is an application for the appointment of a guardian of the person of Anna M. Gordy, a 96 year-old resident of the Emily P. Bissell Hospital. The petitioner is James Davis, the elder of Mrs. Gordy's two children. Mr. Davis seeks his designation as guardian so that he may be legally enabled to deny to the Bissell Hospital consent to the surgical insertion in his mother's abdomen of a gastric feeding tube. Based upon a living will that Mrs. Gordy executed a few years ago, and on her statements over the years and currently, Mr. Davis believes that his mother does not or would not wish this step to be taken. The court appointed an attorney to serve as guardian ad litem for Mrs. Gordy. His report to the court recommends the granting of the relief that Mr. Davis seeks. The Attorney General, however, disagrees. He objects to Mr. Davis' proposal. While the Attorney General agrees that if Mrs. Gordy is legally competent her authority over her own health care decisions is conclusive, he asserts that she is not competent at this time. Moreover the Attorney General believes that in the circumstances presented it is in Mrs. Gordy's interest to have the gastric feeding tube inserted. Thus the Attorney General asks that this court appoint Mr. Davis guardian of his mother, but asserts that it should direct him to consent to the insertion of the gastric feeding tube.

The pending application thus raises two principal issues. The first is whether by reason of her advanced years and the deterioration that accompanies great age Mrs. Gordy is no longer competent to make decisions respecting her own health care. If she is determined not to be competent in this sense, then it is agreed that James Davis is an appropriate person to be granted legal power to make decisions respecting his mother's person. The second question assumes that a guardian is appointed. It is whether, in the circumstances, the guardian may, consistently with the best interests of the ward and with his legal obligations, refuse to authorize the insertion of a gastric feeding tube necessary to assure to Mrs. Gordy continued adequate nutrition.

* * *

I.

Anna M. Gordy has been a patient at the Emily P. Bissell Hospital for approximately two years. Despite her advanced age, and aside from the matter that caused this petition to be filed, Mrs. Gordy appears to enjoy good health for a person of her advanced years. Over recent years she has suffered some subdural hematomas as a result of falls and she has required the implantation of a pacemaker to deal with a heart problem, but she does not have a long list of medical problems as is often encountered with the very, very old. Mrs. Gordy has suffered some loss of cognitive ability in recent years, but continues to be sufficiently alert to engage in conversation with her sons, who regularly visit her, and with medical and nursing staff. It is the opinion of medical professionals that she suffers from Alzheimer's disease. This disease causes a loss of brain function gradually leading first to a change in personality and then to a loss of upper brain function. In its final stages (if another cause of death does not intervene) more primitive brain functions are lost as well. One of these primitive reflexes that are lost in the last stages of Alzheimer's disease is the swallowing reflex. Thus, unless something else intervenes, starvation may be a cause of death in end-stage Alzheimer's patients.[1]

---

1. Death by starvation no doubt seems to many of us an exceptionally cruel and painful lingering death. . . . In fact recent medical research suggests that where terminally ill patients are involved this supposition is incorrect. *See* Robert M. McCann et al., *Comfort Care for Terminally Ill Patients: The Appropriate Use of Nutrition and Hydration*, 272 J. Am. Med. Assn. 1263 (October 26, 1994). This study involved 32 terminal cancer patients all of whom expressed a desire not to be fed or given liquids through tubes. They were allowed to eat and drink as they chose but gradually chose to eat little. The study reports

Mrs. Gordy's Alzheimer's disease is not at that stage, however. She is at the earlier stage in which upper brain function is eroding. She is not, however, eating sufficiently to maintain her weight or to sustain her life.

Mrs. Gordy does eat, but only in limited quantities and with the aid of a nurse or other member of the hospital staff. She seems to have a very difficult time eating solid food and states that she is not hungry. Psychiatrists and a medical doctor proffered a variety of reasons for her inability or unwillingness to eat, ranging from her neurological disease, depression, to discomfort in chewing. If her nutritional deficiencies are not promptly remedied or reversed, she is expected to die soon, perhaps within a few weeks. If through the insertion of a gastric feeding tube or otherwise, she does begin to take sufficient nourishment and is rehydrated, the testimony is that she could live for a number of years. Increased nourishment would not be expected to alter the course of her Alzheimer's disease, however. Thus medical testimony indicates that at some point in the future, she would be in a completely vegetative state. At this point the gastric feeding tube could sustain her vegetative life for a further period than would otherwise occur.

Mrs. Gordy has repeatedly stated her desire not to be sustained through tube feeding. Within the last few weeks, she has voiced her opposition when asked questions concerning the insertion of a feeding tube by a psychiatrist, an attorney serving as her guardian *ad litem*, and a representative of the State Division of Aging, Ombudsman's office, all of whom made inquiries in connection with this action. More formally in 1990 Mrs. Gordy executed a document entitled "Living Will, Right To Natural Death" in which she expressly rejected the use of a feeding tube in the event that she had a terminal illness as diagnosed by two physicians. The same document expressly repudiates many other life support processes, including even cardiopulmonary resuscitation and antibiotics. Mrs. Gordy's determination to avoid a feeding tube is clearly manifested in her living will where she not only initialed that she did not want "artificial nutrition and hydration (nourishment provided by a feeding tube)" used, but took the further step of writing the word "No" next to her initials. The court has not been presented with any evidence indicating that Mrs. Gordy was not fully competent when she initialed and signed the living will.

Concerning the extent of Mrs. Gordy's current understanding, I note that when psychiatrist Gregory Villabona asked her about the nature of the tube to be inserted, she replied "It is like a hose that they put in you to put food in. . . ." When Dr. Villabona asked her why the doctors wanted to insert the tube, she replied "I don't want to eat and they think it is the wise thing to do."

---

that while these patients lost their appetites, the resulting starvation seemed to ease their pain and suffering. The report of this study published in the New York Times quoted Dr. Ann Marie Groth-Juncker, one of the authors of the study: "People dying of diseases other than cancer, Alzheimer's among them, have the same experience," said Dr. Groth-Juncker. . . . "This is, of course, how people have always died, before there were hospitals with IV's and feeding tubes." N.Y. Times, Oct. 26, 1994, p. 20 col. 1.

When he asked what would happen if they did not insert the tube, she responded "I might die." And finally when he asked if she wanted the tube to be inserted, she said "No, I don't." Likewise when attorney William L. Garrett, Jr., Mrs. Gordy's guardian *ad litem*, visited her and asked whether she would want a tube to feed her if she needed to be fed by that method to stay alive, she responded "I don't." When asked if she was certain of this response, she said "I'm sure. I know what I want to eat and I eat what I want." There is no evidence that Mrs. Gordy ever has retracted her statements that she does not want a feeding tube or ever has contradicted her position.

She has stated, however, that she wants to live. I do not regard these two statements as inconsistent. Rather I interpret them consistently to mean that Mrs. Gordy wants to live but not at the price of being fed through a gastric feeding tube. I accept for these purposes that if no feeding tube is implanted into Mrs. Gordy that she is likely to die as a result of starvation within a relatively short time.

Two psychiatrists, Drs. Cantrell and Dhanjani, who questioned Mrs. Gordy concluded that she is incompetent to give "informed consent" at this time to the withholding of a gastric feeding tube. These opinions were based principally upon the conclusion that Anna Gordy suffers from depression, from organic brain syndrome or from Alzheimer's disease resulting in diminished cognition and frequent confusion, and upon the view that Mrs. Gordy's statement that she would prefer to live is inconsistent with her expressed desire to resist the insertion of a gastric feeding tube. Dr. Villabona, on the other hand, expresses the view that Mrs. Gordy "demonstrated that she understood the consequences of her refusal not only of the procedure but of her limited food intake" and that she "has made an informed decision when she refuses tube placement." . . . Finally, Dr. Sherwood, the medical director of the Bissell Hospital, testified that he considered Mrs. Gordy to be terminally ill due to her neurological disease; that he considered Mrs. Gordy to be severely ill-suited for a gastric tube because her dementia would likely cause her to painfully rip the tube out of her body; and that he would *not* recommend insertion of the tube.

II.

The first question presented is whether Mrs. Gordy is, by reason of "mental incapacity, . . . in danger of substantially endangering [her] health." 12 Del. C. §3901 (1994). On this question, as the foregoing indicates, the evidentiary record is in conflict. Certainly on such a question the burden of proof and the burden of persuasion must be upon that party attempting to deprive another of the basic liberty entailed in one's control over the medical treatment that one undergoes.

* * *

[N]o party has demonstrated (1) that Mrs. Gordy's decision to refuse the insertion of a gastric feeding tube is the result of an inability to recognize facts relevant to or consequences of that decision; (2) that she is unable to reason with respect to that simple if profound decision; or (3) that there is a substantial likelihood that her diagnosed Alzheimer's condition has affected that decision. The last of these conclusions is the one that is most contestable. The testimony that Mrs. Gordy has lost a great deal of her cognitive competency is strong, and the seriousness of her decision is such that the effects of that loss should be carefully considered. Nevertheless I find Dr. Villabona's expressed view that Mrs. Gordy was capable of giving informed consent to the surgical procedure to be the more persuasive medical view. Most important in corroborating that view is the fact that Mrs. Gordy has maintained that position for some years, clearly expressing in her 1990 living will the direction that no gastric feeding tube be implanted in her. Moreover the testimony of the representative of the State Ombudsman's office, the affidavit of the guardian *ad litem*, and the testimony of the petitioner all in different respects support Dr. Villabona's conclusion. All of these witnesses no doubt took into account the fact that Mrs. Gordy's decision appears in the circumstances to be neither irrational or uninformed.

Based upon my evaluation of the evidence I conclude that Anna Gordy is not presently suffering from a "mental incapacity" that is endangering her health. Rather I conclude that she has made a rational choice concerning her medical treatment at the end of her very long life that deserves to be respected. . . .

QUESTION

Despite finding that Mrs. Gordy had capacity to make her own decisions, the court appointed her son as her guardian. The court explained that it did so because at "some point, perhaps very soon, she will no longer have sufficient residual mental capacity to make decisions that deserve respect concerning her own care and it is clear in this case that the appropriate person to make those decisions, under the appropriate legal standard, is the petitioner." Was this a wise approach for the court to take? Was the appointment legally sound?

PROBLEM

Sara Tornado has been in a persistent vegetative state (PVS) for approximately eight years since she collapsed in her home. Her husband, Ned Tornado, has been appointed as her guardian. Last month, convinced that Sara had no chance of improvement, Ned petitioned the County Court to allow him to remove Sara's feeding tube. Sara's parents, Robert and Mary Binder, object to Ned's petition. They argue that Sara is unconscious and that removal of the feeding tube is contrary to the religious tradition in which Sara was raised.

How should the Court proceed?

2. Refusal of Nutrition and Hydration

As *Cruzan* implicitly recognized, the right to terminate life-sustaining treatment includes the right to refuse artificial nutrition and hydration. If an individual is not receiving artificial nutrition and hydration, however, he or she may still wish to hasten death by refusing to eat or drink. Doing so is referred to as *voluntarily stopping eating and drinking* (VSED) or alternatively by related names such as *voluntary refusal of food and fluid*, *voluntary terminal dehydration*, *voluntary death by dehydration*, or *terminal dehydration*. Unlike individuals receiving artificial nutrition and hydration, individuals engaging in VSED are capable of receiving food and hydration orally, either by feeding themselves or by being fed by another person.

While it is generally assumed that terminally ill individuals have a legal right to engage in VSED, that right is less clearly established than the right to refuse artificial nutrition and hydration and is sometimes disputed. In the excerpted article that follows, Professor Thaddeus Pope and attorney Lindsey Anderson describe VSED and explain why, even when accomplished with the assistance of a medical provider, VSED should be recognized as conceptually distinct from physician-assisted suicide.

Thaddeus Pope & Lindsey Anderson, Voluntarily Stopping Eating and Drinking: A Legal Treatment Option at the End of Life

17 Widener L. Rev. 363 (2011)

VSED entails deliberately ceasing the (self or assisted) oral intake of all food and fluids, except for those small amounts of fluids necessary for mouth comfort or for the administration of pain medication. The patient remains physically capable of taking oral sustenance but chooses not to do so in order to hasten his or her death. For patients with the capacity to make healthcare decisions, the decision to stop eating and drinking can be made at any time and is completely voluntary. The patient could simply refuse food and fluids. This causes a peaceful death by dehydration.

VSED might be confused with, and therefore should be carefully distinguished from, two similar mechanisms. First, VSED applies specifically to patients who choose to stop eating and drinking orally. These are patients who are physically able to take food and fluid by mouth, but choose not to do so. VSED does not apply to persons dependent upon a feeding tube or upon any other form of artificial nutrition and hydration.

Second, VSED applies specifically to patients who deliberately choose to stop eating and drinking in order to hasten death. It does not apply to patients who lack the capacity to make a contemporaneous (or advance) choice to VSED. It does not include those patients who cease to eat or drink spontaneously, perhaps because of a condition (such as a tooth abscess or gastric reflux) that interferes with their appetite or swallowing.

* * *

Ongoing debates surrounding when to use or to stop use of many types of end-of-life treatment, such as CPR and ventilators, date only to the 1960s. The option to hasten death by withholding or withdrawing these types of treatment did not exist (and could not have existed) prior to their development. In contrast, VSED is a method of hastening death that dates back thousands of years.

Jainism, for example, is an Indian religion dating to the ninth century B.C. In one of its rituals, Santhara (or Sallekhana), a Jain stops eating with the intention of preparing for death. The intention is to purify the body and to remove all thought of physical things from the mind: "The supreme goal is to minimize the damage [that] one does to their environment." Santhara is undertaken only when the body is no longer capable of serving its owner as an instrument of spirituality and when the inevitability of death is a matter of undisputed certainty. Santhara is seen as the ultimate way to expunge all sins, liberating the soul from the cycle of birth, death and rebirth. Starvation prevents the accumulation of karma, and ascendance is achieved through strict asceticism.

Hundreds of Jains use Santhara each year. But widespread attention was focused on the practice in 2006. Sixty-one-year-old Vimli Devi Bansali, a resident of the Indian state of Rajasthan, was suffering from incurable brain cancer. In September 2006, she observed Santhara, and died after not eating or drinking for fourteen days. Her fast led to a petition being filed in the state's high court seeking to ban the practice as tantamount to suicide. The case has not yet been heard.

Hinduism includes a similar practice called Prayopavesa. While it also entails fasting to death, Prayopavesa is limited to those: (a) who are unable to perform normal bodily purification; (b) whose death appears imminent or whose condition is so bad that life's pleasures are nil; and (c) who engage in the ritual under community regulation. The process allows one to settle differences with others and to ponder life. Notably, it is distinguished from "sudden suicide," which is prohibited as disturbing the cycle of death and rebirth.

* * *

When a person voluntarily stops eating and drinking, death occurs by dehydration. Terminal dehydration occurs by a complicated physiological process over a seven to fourteen day period. As humans, we constantly lose water through sweating, respiration, and urination. The only way to compensate for this water loss is intake via food and fluids. Once a person stops eating and drinking, there is only water loss and no water gain, causing dehydration.

* * *

The ultimate cause of death in a dehydrated person is usually a cardiac arrhythmia. A cardiac arrhythmia is any type of irregular heartbeat. In many circumstances, arrhythmias have little to no impact on the human body. However, in some situations, an arrhythmia can cause death. Cardiac tissue relies on electric potentials to make the heart pump. During dehydration, the body loses the ability to generate these electric impulses because of ion imbalances, making the heart unable to pump normally. This inability to pump causes missed heart beats, which, by definition, are cardiac arrhythmias.

* * *

Death by VSED involves very little pain, if any. In fact, "[t]he general impression among hospice clinician[s] is that starvation and dehydration do not contribute to suffering among the dying and might actually contribute to a comfortable passage from life."

Expectedly, many patients do report feelings of hunger and thirst in the first few days. These appear to be the only true side effects of VSED. To address these symptoms, the medical profession calls for excellent oral care. Specifically, care-givers of patients who choose VSED should provide mouth care involving swab-bing the mouth, giving ice chips, and applying lip balm to keep lips supple and free from cracks. This type of care prevents and remedies the symptom of thirst, the symptom most notably associated with dehydration.

In addition to oral care, patients who choose VSED are likely to need two other forms of palliative care. First, for the many VSED patients who are physically ill, pain medication may be necessary to alleviate the pain of their underlying illness. Medical professionals who specialize in palliative care may provide sufficient medication to patients at this stage, especially considering the patient's choice to hasten death. The ability to have palliative care readily available throughout the VSED process contributes to the overall quality of death for people who choose VSED.

Second, competent and incompetent patients also require comfort care during the course of VSED. This comfort care is similar to the typical care given to the elderly or sick. It varies from patient to patient, but can certainly include turning, bathing, and attending to the requests of the person.

* * *

[T]here are four important distinctions between VSED and [Physician Assisted Suicide (PAS)]. Individually and cumulatively, these distinctions overwhelmingly establish that VSED is not suicide. Therefore, assisting VSED cannot be assisted suicide. First, . . . hand feeding is a form of medical treatment. As such, its refusal is specifically and expressly defined, usually statutorily, as not constituting suicide. Moreover, equating the removal of [artificial nutrition and hydration (ANH)] with suicide has been rejected. Given the similarity of hand feeding and ANH, the equation of VSED with suicide should similarly be rejected.

Second, VSED does not constitute "suicide" as that term is used in pro-hibitions of assisted suicide. . . . The patient's natural state is to dehydrate unless fluids are affirmatively introduced. VSED does not entail the acceler-ation of this process, but rather the mere absence of action to slow or stop it.

Admittedly, the active-passive distinction has been widely attacked. But the distinction has been endorsed by the United States Supreme Court. And it was endorsed by the Supreme Court specifically because it has been consis-tently accepted by courts and legislatures across the United States. The act-omission distinction is, as the Court explained, deeply embedded in "our Nation's history, legal traditions, and practices." Third, the distinction between VSED and assisted suicide comports with the legal principle of intent. A healthcare provider who honors a patient's request for VSED "intends, or may so intend, only to respect his patient's wishes." In the ordinary case of murder by positive act of commission, the consent of the victim is no defense. But where the charge is one of murder by omission to do an act, and the act omitted could only be done with the consent of the patient, refusal by the patient of consent to the doing of such act does, indirectly, provide a defense to the charge of murder. The doctor cannot owe to the patient any duty to maintain his life where that life can only be sustained by intrusive medical care to which the patient will not consent.

While the physician need not honor a request for affirmative assistance ("making [the] patient die"), the physician must honor the patient's refusal ("letting [the] patient die"). Unlike a request for PAS, a request for VSED is grounded "on well-established traditional rights to bodily integrity and freedom from unwanted touching."

Fourth, the distinction between VSED and assisted suicide comports with the legal principle of causation. When "a patient ingests lethal medication prescribed by a physician, he is killed by that medication." But, according to the way in which the refusal of ANH has been traditionally explained, when a patient refuses nutrition and hydration, "he dies from an underlying fatal disease or pathology."

The lives of those patients with a terminal or irreversible illness are obviously already endangered. But VSED causation works the same way for other patients too. The typical person loses 2.5 liters of water each day: through the kidneys as urine, through the skin as sweat, and through the lungs as water vapor. This is a natural and automatic process that will, as described above, eventually lead to the person's death. VSED does not cause this process; it is simply the omission of action to reverse it. Moreover, the intent and consequence of the provider's actions are to provide comfort and reduce suffering. Death is an incidental byproduct, a double effect.

NOTE

Medical futility. Disputes over termination of life-sustaining treatment can also arise when the patient or the patient's surrogate demands life-sustaining treatment that the medical provider believes to be futile. Some states have statutes that specifically permit providers to refuse to provide care that is ethically or medically inappropriate, such as futile care. Even in states that do not have such statutes, courts have permitted providers to refuse to provide—or terminate provision of—medically futile care such as life-sustaining treatment for individuals who are brain dead. Notably, when the dispute proceeds to court, it may do so in the form of an action to remove the surrogate. *See, e.g., In re Guardianship of Mason*, 669 N.E.2d 1081 (Mass. App. Ct. 1996) (discussed in Chapter 4). Of course, not all such disputes are resolved through legal battles. Frequently, they are resolved through discussion or mediation or by transferring the patient to a facility willing to provide the requested care. For further discussion of the law as it relates to medical futility, see Thaddeus Pope, *Involuntary Passive Euthanasia in U.S. Courts: Reassessing the Judicial Treatment of Medical Futility Cases*, 9 Marq. Elder's Advisor 229 (2008).

QUESTION

In 1991, the American Medical Association's Council on Judicial and Ethical Affairs issued a report on decisions at the end of life that stated: "There is no such thing as a 'natural' death. Somewhere along the way for just about every patient, death is forestalled by human choice and human action, or death is allowed to occur because of human choice." *See* AMERICAN MEDICAL ASSOCIATION, CEJA REPORTS, *available at* www.ama-assn.org. Do you agree? Should the extent to which a death is or is not "natural" be of any legal consequence?

D. THE RIGHT TO DIE AND RECEIVE AID IN DYING

The United States is currently deeply divided on the issue of whether individuals should be able to end their own lives. The key constitutional challenges and legislative efforts around the right to die have, however, focused not on the right to suicide itself but rather on whether individuals should be able to receive assistance from others in ending their own lives.

1. The Constitutional Approach to the Right to Die

The Supreme Court has never ruled on whether or not there is a constitutional right to commit suicide. At common law, suicide was a felony—the felony of murder. Although there has been a move toward decriminalizing suicide, some states still consider it a crime and some even still consider it to be a felony. Indeed, as recently as 1996, the Mississippi Supreme Court affirmed that suicide is a crime in that state (*see Nicholson on Behalf of Gollott v. State*, 672 So. 2d 744 (Miss. 1996)). However, even in states where suicide remains a crime, it may not be a punishable crime because some state legislatures have rescinded punishment for suicide without decriminalizing the act itself.

The Supreme Court has, by contrast, considered the question of whether there is a constitutional issue to physician-assisted suicide in the next case.

Washington v. Glucksberg

521 U.S. 702 (1997)

Chief Justice REHNQUIST delivered the opinion of the Court.

The question presented in this case is whether Washington's prohibition against "caus[ing]" or "aid[ing]" a suicide offends the Fourteenth Amendment to the United States Constitution. We hold that it does not.

* * *

Petitioners in this case are the State of Washington and its Attorney General. Respondents Harold Glucksberg, M.D., Abigail Halperin, M.D., Thomas

A. Preston, M.D., and Peter Shalit, M.D., are physicians who practice in Washington. These doctors occasionally treat terminally ill, suffering patients, and declare that they would assist these patients in ending their lives if not for Washington's assisted-suicide ban.... In January 1994, respondents, along with three gravely ill, pseudonymous plaintiffs who have since died and Compassion in Dying, a nonprofit organization that counsels people considering physician-assisted suicide, sued in the United States District Court, seeking a declaration that Wash. Rev. Code §9A.36.060(1) (1994) is, on its face, unconstitutional.

The plaintiffs asserted "the existence of a liberty interest protected by the Fourteenth Amendment which extends to a personal choice by a mentally competent, terminally ill adult to commit physician-assisted suicide." Relying primarily on *Planned Parenthood of Southeastern Pa. v. Casey*, 505 U.S. 833 (1992), and *Cruzan v. Director, Mo. Dept. of Health*, 497 U.S. 261 (1990), the District Court agreed and concluded that Washington's assisted-suicide ban is unconstitutional because it "places an undue burden on the exercise of [that] constitutionally protected liberty interest." ... The District Court also decided that the Washington statute violated the Equal Protection Clause's requirement that "'all persons similarly situated ... be treated alike.'"

A panel of the Court of Appeals for the Ninth Circuit reversed. ... The Ninth Circuit reheard the case en banc, reversed the panel's decision, and affirmed the District Court. Like the District Court, the en banc Court of Appeals emphasized our *Casey* and *Cruzan* decisions. The court also discussed what it described as "historical" and "current societal attitudes" toward suicide and assisted suicide and concluded that "the Constitution encompasses a due process liberty interest in controlling the time and manner of one's death—that there is, in short, a constitutionally-recognized 'right to die.'" After "[w]eighing and then balancing" this interest against Washington's various interests, the court held that the State's assisted-suicide ban was unconstitutional "as applied to terminally ill competent adults who wish to hasten their deaths with medication prescribed by their physicians." ... The court did not reach the District Court's equal protection holding. We granted certiorari and now reverse.

I.

We begin, as we do in all due process cases, by examining our Nation's history, legal traditions, and practices. In almost every State—indeed, in almost every western democracy—it is a crime to assist a suicide. ... The States' assisted-suicide bans are not innovations. Rather, they are longstanding expressions of the States' commitment to the protection and preservation of all human life. Indeed, opposition to and condemnation of suicide—and, therefore, of assisting suicide—are consistent and enduring themes of our philosophical, legal, and cultural heritages.

More specifically, for over 700 years, the Anglo-American common-law tradition has punished or otherwise disapproved of both suicide and assisting suicide. ...

II.

* * *

Our established method of substantive-due-process analysis has two primary features: First, we have regularly observed that the Due Process Clause specially protects those fundamental rights and liberties which are, objectively, "deeply rooted in this Nation's history and tradition," and "implicit in the concept of ordered liberty," such that "neither liberty nor justice would exist if they were sacrificed[]." Second, we have required in substantive-due-process cases a "careful description" of the asserted fundamental liberty interest. Our Nation's history, legal traditions, and practices thus provide the crucial "guideposts for responsible decisionmaking," that direct and restrain our exposition of the Due Process Clause. As we stated recently in *Flores*, the Fourteenth Amendment "forbids the government to infringe . . . 'fundamental' liberty interests at all, no matter what process is provided, unless the infringement is narrowly tailored to serve a compelling state interest."

* * *

We now inquire whether this asserted right has any place in our Nation's traditions. Here . . . we are confronted with a consistent and almost universal tradition that has long rejected the asserted right, and continues explicitly to reject it today, even for terminally ill, mentally competent adults. To hold for respondents, we would have to reverse centuries of legal doctrine and practice, and strike down the considered policy choice of almost every State.

Respondents contend, however, that the liberty interest they assert is consistent with this Court's substantive-due-process line of cases, if not with this Nation's history and practice. . . . According to respondents, our liberty jurisprudence, and the broad, individualistic principles it reflects, protects the "liberty of competent, terminally ill adults to make end-of-life decisions free of undue government interference." The question presented in this case, however, is whether the protections of the Due Process Clause include a right to commit suicide with another's assistance. . . .

In *Cruzan*, we considered whether Nancy Beth Cruzan, who had been severely injured in an automobile accident and was in a persistive vegetative state, "ha[d] a right under the United States Constitution which would require the hospital to withdraw life-sustaining treatment" at her parents' request. We began with the observation that "[a]t common law, even the touching of one person by another without consent and without legal justification was a battery." We then discussed the related rule that "informed consent is generally required for medical treatment." After reviewing a long line of relevant state cases, we concluded that "the common-law doctrine of informed consent is viewed as generally encompassing the right of a competent individual to refuse medical treatment." Next, we reviewed our own cases on the subject, and stated that "[t]he principle that a competent person has a constitutionally protected liberty interest in refusing unwanted medical treatment may be inferred from our prior decisions." Therefore, "for purposes of [that] case, we assume[d] that the United States Constitution would grant a competent person a constitutionally protected right to refuse lifesaving hydration and nutrition." We concluded that, notwithstanding this right, the Constitution permitted Missouri to require clear and convincing evidence of an incompetent patient's wishes concerning the withdrawal of life-sustaining treatment.

Respondents contend that in *Cruzan* we "acknowledged that competent, dying persons have the right to direct the removal of life-sustaining medical treatment and thus hasten death," and that "the constitutional principle behind recognizing the patient's liberty to direct the withdrawal of artificial life support applies at least as strongly to the choice to hasten impending death by consuming lethal medication." Similarly, the Court of Appeals concluded that "*Cruzan*, by recognizing a liberty interest that includes the refusal of artificial provision of life-sustaining food and water, necessarily recognize[d] a liberty interest in hastening one's own death."

The right assumed in *Cruzan*, however, was not simply deduced from abstract concepts of personal autonomy. Given the common-law rule that forced medication was a battery, and the long legal tradition protecting the decision to refuse unwanted medical treatment, our assumption was entirely consistent with this Nation's history and constitutional traditions. The decision to commit suicide with the assistance of another may be just as personal and profound as the decision to refuse unwanted medical treatment, but it has never enjoyed similar legal protection. Indeed, the two acts are widely and reasonably regarded as quite distinct. In *Cruzan* itself, we recognized that most States outlawed assisted suicide—and even more do today—and we certainly gave no intimation that the right to refuse unwanted medical treatment could be somehow transmuted into a right to assistance in committing suicide.

* * *

The history of the law's treatment of assisted suicide in this country has been and continues to be one of the rejection of nearly all efforts to permit it. That being the case, our decisions lead us to conclude that the asserted "right" to assistance in committing suicide is not a fundamental liberty interest protected by the Due Process Clause. The Constitution also requires, however, that Washington's assisted-suicide ban be rationally related to legitimate government interests. This requirement is unquestionably met here. . . .

First, Washington has an "unqualified interest in the preservation of human life." . . .

Respondents admit that "[t]he State has a real interest in preserving the lives of those who can still contribute to society and have the potential to enjoy life." The Court of Appeals also recognized Washington's interest in protecting life, but held that the "weight" of this interest depends on the "medical condition and the wishes of the person whose life is at stake." Washington, however, has rejected this sliding-scale approach and, through its assisted-suicide ban, insists that all persons' lives, from beginning to end, regardless of physical or mental condition, are under the full protection of the law. As we have previously affirmed, the States "may properly decline to make judgments about the 'quality' of life that a particular individual may enjoy," . . . even for those who are near death.

Relatedly, all admit that suicide is a serious public-health problem, especially among persons in otherwise vulnerable groups. The State has an interest in preventing suicide, and in studying, identifying, and treating its causes.

Those who attempt suicide—terminally ill or not—often suffer from depression or other mental disorders. Research indicates, however, that many people who request physician-assisted suicide withdraw that request if their depression and pain are treated. The New York Task Force, however, expressed its concern that, because depression is difficult to diagnose, physicians and medical professionals often fail to respond adequately to seriously ill patients' needs. Thus, legal physician-assisted suicide could make it more difficult for the State to protect depressed or mentally ill persons, or those who are suffering from untreated pain, from suicidal impulses.

The State also has an interest in protecting the integrity and ethics of the medical profession. . . . [T]he American Medical Association, like many other medical and physicians' groups, has concluded that "[p]hysician-assisted suicide is fundamentally incompatible with the physician's role as healer." And physician-assisted suicide could, it is argued, undermine the trust that is essential to the doctor-patient relationship by blurring the time-honored line between healing and harming.

Next, the State has an interest in protecting vulnerable groups—including the poor, the elderly, and disabled persons—from abuse, neglect, and mistakes. . . . We have recognized . . . the real risk of subtle coercion and undue influence in end-of-life situations. . . . If physician-assisted suicide were permitted, many might resort to it to spare their families the substantial financial burden of end-of-life health-care costs.

The State's interest here goes beyond protecting the vulnerable from coercion; it extends to protecting disabled and terminally ill people from prejudice, negative and inaccurate stereotypes, and "societal indifference." The State's assisted-suicide ban reflects and reinforces its policy that the lives of terminally ill, disabled, and elderly people must be no less valued than the lives of the young and healthy, and that a seriously disabled person's suicidal impulses should be interpreted and treated the same way as anyone else's.

Finally, the State may fear that permitting assisted suicide will start it down the path to voluntary and perhaps even involuntary euthanasia. The Court of Appeals struck down Washington's assisted-suicide ban only "as applied to competent, terminally ill adults who wish to hasten their deaths by obtaining medication prescribed by their doctors." Washington insists, however, that the impact of the court's decision will not and cannot be so limited. . . . [W]hat is couched as a limited right to "physician-assisted suicide" is likely, in effect, a much broader license, which could prove extremely difficult to police and contain. Washington's ban on assisting suicide prevents such erosion.

* * *

We need not weigh exactingly the relative strengths of these various interests. They are unquestionably important and legitimate, and Washington's ban on assisted suicide is at least reasonably related to their promotion and protection. We therefore hold that Wash. Rev. Code §9A.36.060(1) (1994) does not violate the Fourteenth Amendment, either on its face or "as applied to competent, terminally ill adults who wish to hasten their deaths by obtaining medication prescribed by their doctors."

* * *

Justice SOUTER, concurring in the judgment [concurrence omitted].

Justice O'CONNOR, concurring. [Justice Ginsburg joined in the O'Connor concurrence; Justice Breyer joined in the O'Connor concurrence "except insofar as it joins the opinions of the Court."—ED.]

* * *

In sum, there is no need to address the question whether suffering patients have a constitutionally cognizable interest in obtaining relief from the suffering that they may experience in the last days of their lives. There is no dispute that dying patients in Washington and New York can obtain palliative care, even when doing so would hasten their deaths. The difficulty in defining terminal illness and the risk that a dying patient's request for assistance in ending his or her life might not be truly voluntary justifies the prohibitions on assisted suicide we uphold here.

Justice STEVENS, concurring in the judgments.

The Court ends its opinion with the important observation that our holding today is fully consistent with a continuation of the vigorous debate about the "morality, legality, and practicality of physician-assisted suicide" in a democratic society. I write separately to make it clear that there is also room for further debate about the limits that the Constitution places on the power of the States to punish the practice.

* * *

Today, the Court decides that Washington's statute prohibiting assisted suicide is not invalid "on its face," that is to say, in all or most cases in which it might be applied. That holding, however, does not foreclose the possibility that some applications of the statute might well be invalid.

* * *

In *Cruzan v. Director, Mo. Dept. of Health*, 497 U.S. 261 (1990), the Court assumed that the interest in liberty protected by the Fourteenth Amendment encompassed the right of a terminally ill patient to direct the withdrawal of life-sustaining treatment. As the Court correctly observes today, that assumption "was not simply deduced from abstract concepts of personal autonomy." Instead, it was supported by the common-law tradition protecting the individual's general right to refuse unwanted medical treatment. We have recognized, however, that this common-law right to refuse treatment is neither absolute nor always sufficiently weighty to overcome valid countervailing state interests. . . . In most cases, the individual's constitutionally protected interest in his or her own physical autonomy, including the right to refuse unwanted medical treatment, will give way to the State's interest in preserving human life.

Cruzan, however, was not the normal case. Given the irreversible nature of her illness and the progressive character of her suffering. Nancy Cruzan's interest in refusing medical care was incidental to her more basic interest in controlling the manner and timing of her death. In finding that her best interests would be served by cutting off the nourishment that kept her alive, the trial court did more than simply vindicate Cruzan's interest in refusing medical treatment; the court, in essence, authorized affirmative conduct that would hasten her death. When this Court reviewed the case and upheld Missouri's requirement that there be clear and convincing evidence establishing Nancy Cruzan's intent to have life-sustaining nourishment withdrawn, it made two important assumptions: (1) that there was a "liberty interest" in refusing unwanted treatment protected by the Due Process Clause; and (2) that this liberty interest did not "end the inquiry" because it might be outweighed by relevant state interests. I agree with both of those assumptions, but I insist that the source of Nancy Cruzan's right to refuse treatment was not just a common-law rule. Rather, this right is an aspect of a far broader and more basic concept of freedom that is even older than the common law. . . . This freedom embraces not merely a person's right to refuse a particular kind of unwanted treatment, but also her interest in dignity, and in determining the character of the memories that will survive long after her death. . . . In recognizing that the State's interests did not outweigh Nancy Cruzan's liberty interest in refusing medical treatment, *Cruzan* rested not simply on the common-law right to refuse medical treatment, but—at least implicitly—on the even more fundamental right to make this "deeply personal decision[]."

Thus, the common-law right to protection from battery, which included the right to refuse medical treatment in most circumstances, did not mark "the outer limits of the substantive sphere of liberty" that supported the Cruzan family's decision to hasten Nancy's death. Those limits have never been precisely defined. They are generally identified by the importance and character of the decision confronted by the individual. Whatever the outer limits of the concept may be, it definitely includes protection for matters "central to personal dignity and autonomy." It includes "the individual's right to make certain unusually important decisions that will affect his own, or his family's, destiny. The Court has referred to such decisions as implicating 'basic values,' as being 'fundamental,' and as being dignified by history and tradition. . . ."

The *Cruzan* case demonstrated that some state intrusions on the right to decide how death will be encountered are also intolerable. The now-deceased plaintiffs in this action may in fact have had a liberty interest even stronger than Nancy Cruzan's because, not only were they terminally ill, they were suffering constant and severe pain. . . .

While I agree with the Court that *Cruzan* does not decide the issue presented by these cases, *Cruzan* did give recognition, not just to vague, unbridled notions of autonomy, but to the more specific interest in making decisions about how to confront an imminent death. Although there is no absolute right to physician-assisted suicide, *Cruzan* makes it clear that some individuals who no longer have the option of deciding whether to live or to die because they are already on the threshold of death have a constitutionally protected interest that may outweigh the State's interest in preserving life at all costs. The liberty interest at stake in a case like this differs from, and is stronger than, both the common-law right to refuse medical treatment and the unbridled interest in deciding whether to live or die. It is an interest in deciding how, rather than whether, a critical threshold shall be crossed.

* * *

The state interests supporting a general rule banning the practice of physician-assisted suicide do not have the same force in all cases. . . .

. . . Although as a general matter the State's interest in the contributions each person may make to society outweighs the person's interest in ending her life, this interest does not have the same force for a terminally ill patient faced not with the choice of whether to live, only of how to die. Allowing the individual, rather than the State, to make judgments "'about the "quality" of life that a particular individual may enjoy,'" does not mean that the lives of terminally ill, disabled people have less value than the lives of those who are healthy. Rather, it gives proper recognition to the individual's interest in choosing a final chapter that accords with her life story, rather than one that demeans her values and poisons memories of her.

Similarly, the State's legitimate interests in preventing suicide, protecting the vulnerable from coercion and abuse, and preventing euthanasia are less significant in this context. I agree that the State has a compelling interest in preventing persons from committing suicide because of depression or coercion by third parties. But the State's legitimate interest in preventing abuse does not apply to an individual who is not victimized by abuse, who is not suffering from depression, and who makes a rational and voluntary decision to seek assistance in dying. . . .

Relatedly, the State and *amici* express the concern that patients whose physical pain is inadequately treated will be more likely to request assisted suicide. Encouraging the development and ensuring the availability of adequate pain treatment is of utmost importance; palliative care, however, cannot alleviate all pain and suffering. An individual adequately informed of the care alternatives thus might make a rational choice for assisted suicide. For such an individual, the State's interest in preventing potential abuse and mistake is only minimally implicated.

The final major interest asserted by the State is its interest in preserving the traditional integrity of the medical profession. The fear is that a rule permitting physicians to assist in suicide is inconsistent with the perception that they serve their patients solely as healers. But for some patients, it would be a physician's refusal to dispense medication to ease their suffering and make their death tolerable and dignified that would be inconsistent with the healing role. For doctors who have longstanding relationships with their patients, who have given their patients advice on alternative treatments, who are attentive to their patient's individualized needs, and who are knowledgeable about pain symptom management and palliative care options, heeding a patient's desire to assist in her suicide would not serve to harm the physician-patient relationship. Furthermore, because physicians are already involved in making decisions that hasten the death of terminally ill patients—through termination of life support, withholding of medical treatment, and terminal sedation—there is in fact significant tension between the traditional view of the physician's role and the actual practice in a growing number of cases.

As the New York State Task Force on Life and the Law recognized, a State's prohibition of assisted suicide is justified by the fact that the "'ideal'" case in which "patients would be screened for depression and offered treatment, effective pain medication would be available, and all patients would have a supportive committed family and doctor" is not the usual case. Although, as the Court concludes today, these potential harms are sufficient to support the State's general public policy against assisted suicide, they will not always outweigh the individual liberty interest of a particular patient. Unlike the Court of Appeals, I would not say as a categorical matter that these state interests are invalid as to the entire class of terminally ill, mentally competent patients. I do not, however, foreclose the possibility that an individual plaintiff seeking to hasten her death, or a doctor whose assistance was sought, could prevail in a more particularized challenge. Future cases will determine whether such a challenge may succeed.

* * *

... In my judgment, however, it is clear that the so-called "unqualified interest in the preservation of human life," *Cruzan*, 497 U.S., at 282, is not itself sufficient to outweigh the interest in liberty that may justify the only possible means of preserving a dying patient's dignity and alleviating her intolerable suffering.

Justice GINSBURG, concurring in the judgments.

I concur in the Court's judgments in these cases substantially for the reasons stated by Justice O'Connor in her concurring opinion. ...

Justice BREYER, concurring in the judgments.

I believe that Justice O'Connor's views, which I share, have greater legal significance than the Court's opinion suggests. I join her separate opinion, except insofar as it joins the majority. And I concur in the judgments. I shall briefly explain how I differ from the Court.

I agree with the Court in *Vacco v. Quill*, 521 U.S. 793, that the articulated state interests justify the distinction drawn between physician assisted suicide and withdrawal of life-support. I also agree with the Court that the critical question in both of the cases before us is whether "the 'liberty' specially protected by the Due Process Clause includes a right" of the sort that the respondents assert. I do not agree, however, with the Court's formulation of that claimed "liberty" interest. The Court describes it as a "right to commit suicide with another's assistance." But I would not reject the respondents' claim without considering a different formulation, for which our legal tradition may provide greater support. That formulation would use words roughly like a "right to die with dignity." But irrespective of the exact words used, at its core would lie personal control over the manner of death, professional medical assistance, and the avoidance of unnecessary and severe physical suffering—combined.

* * *

I do not believe, however, that this Court need or now should decide whether or a not such a right is "fundamental." That is because, in my view, the avoidance of severe physical pain (connected with death) would have to constitute an essential part of any successful claim and because . . . the laws before us do not *force* a dying person to undergo that kind of pain. Rather, the laws of New York and of Washington do not prohibit doctors from providing patients with drugs sufficient to control pain despite the risk that those drugs themselves will kill. And under these circumstances the laws of New York and Washington would overcome any remaining significant interests and would be justified, regardless.

* * *

This legal circumstance means that the state laws before us do not infringe directly upon the (assumed) central interest (what I have called the core of the interest in dying with dignity). . . .

Were the legal circumstances different—for example, were state law to prevent the provision of palliative care, including the administration of drugs as needed to avoid pain at the end of life—then the law's impact upon serious and otherwise unavoidable physical pain (accompanying death) would be more directly at issue. . . .

NOTES

1. *Equal protection challenge.* On the same day that *Glucksberg* was decided, the Court also decided the case of *Vacco v. Quill*, 521 U.S. 793 (1997). In *Vacco*, the Court considered the permissibility of a New York state law that made it a felony for a physician to assist a patient in committing suicide, but permitted a physician to discontinue life-saving treatment without which a patient would die. The Court found that although the law created two different classes of terminally ill people who were then subjected to different treatment, the classification was constitutionally permissible.

2. *Terminology.* The term *euthanasia* is derived from the Greek words "eu" and "thanatos," meaning "good death." Euthanasia, also referred to as "mercy killing," is an act or omission intended to cause the death of another and which is justified by beneficence. By contrast, with physician assisted suicide the patient is the person who decides to terminate his or her own life, and the doctor's involvement may be indirect (e.g., the doctor provides lethal medication but does not administer it).

3. *Double effect.* Regardless of whether a state permits physician-assisted suicide, a health care provider may legally administer opioids or sedatives that hasten an individual's death if the purpose of administering the drug(s) is to relieve the patient's pain and suffering. In such situations, the medication is said to have a "double effect."

4. *Terminal sedation. Glucksberg* makes reference to the practice of *terminal sedation.* Terminal sedation (also called *palliative sedation*) occurs when a dying patient is given a sedative designed to ease the pain of dying and cause the individual to sleep or enter a state of unconsciousness that he or she is expected to remain in until death arrives. Terminal sedation is generally recognized as legal and consistent with medical ethics because its goal is to ease symptoms causing suffering, not to hasten death.

QUESTIONS

1. How did the right asserted by Nancy Cruzan differ from the rights at issue in *Glucksberg*? Do these differences, in your opinion, justify the different outcomes of *Cruzan* and *Glucksberg*?

2. If you had been on the Supreme Court at the time *Glucksberg* was decided, which opinion would you have been most likely to join? Why?

3. The *Glucksberg* case addresses the concerns of doctors working with terminally ill patients who wish to commit suicide. In many cases, lawyers also work with such clients. To what extent should attorneys be permitted to counsel their clients as to committing suicide? How do the concerns raised by such counseling differ from those in *Glucksberg*?

4. To what extent does *Glucksberg* preclude future constitutional challenges to physician-assisted suicide?

5. What types of actions should be considered to be "assistance" with suicide? Consider the following possibilities:
   ■ Reassuring someone contemplating suicide that you will love him no matter what he does;
   ■ Telling someone that you support her decision to end her life;
   ■ Writing a book with instructions for how to end one's life;
   ■ Giving a gun to someone knowing that he intends to use it to commit suicide;
   ■ Placing lethal medication in the mouth of another individual that that individual then voluntarily swallows.

PROBLEM

Your client has retained you to update his will. He informs you that he is terminally ill and is in tremendous pain. He tells you that he plans to commit suicide with the help of his wife. How should you proceed? What are you permitted to do or required to do under the Model Rules of Professional Conduct? Would your answer be any different if the wife were your client instead?

2. The Statutory Approach to the Right to Die

As of the date of publication, only three states (Oregon, Washington, and Vermont) had adopted legislation permitting physician-assisted suicide. The supreme court of a fourth state, Montana, has held that physician-assisted suicide is not a crime in that state. In all other states, physician-assisted suicide should be assumed to be unlawful at the current time.

In states that do not permit physician-assisted suicide, physicians who assist patients with dying—like other persons who provide such assistance—risk criminal liability for unlawfully aiding or abetting suicide and potentially even for murder. Moreover, they may risk liability even though they do not directly kill a patient (i.e., they do not inject a lethal drug but, rather, provide medication that the patient then voluntarily ingests). Quite simply, individuals have been found criminally liable for assisted suicide even where they did not perform the act that directly killed the individual (e.g., where the person assisting provided the individual committing suicide with a loaded gun for that purpose).

Even in the states that have legislatively permitted physician-assisted suicide, it is only permitted in certain, limited situations. The following pages contain excerpts from the Oregon statute and excerpts from a report on its impact and implementation. Notably, the statutory regimes in Washington and Oregon are substantially similar.

THE OREGON DEATH WITH DIGNITY ACT
OR. REV. STAT. §§127.800 ET SEQ. (2013)

127.800 §1.01. Definitions.

The following words and phrases, whenever used in ORS 127.800 to 127.897, have the following meanings:

(1) "Adult" means an individual who is 18 years of age or older.

(2) "Attending physician" means the physician who has primary responsibility for the care of the patient and treatment of the patient's terminal disease.

(3) "Capable" means that in the opinion of a court or in the opinion of the patient's attending physician or consulting physician, psychiatrist or psychologist, a patient has the ability to make and communicate health care decisions to health care providers, including communication through persons familiar with the patient's manner of communicating if those persons are available.

(4) "Consulting physician" means a physician who is qualified by specialty or experience to make a professional diagnosis and prognosis regarding the patient's disease.

(5) "Counseling" means one or more consultations as necessary between a state licensed psychiatrist or psychologist and a patient for the purpose of determining that the patient is capable and not suffering from a psychiatric or psychological disorder or depression causing impaired judgment.

(6) "Health care provider" means a person licensed, certified or otherwise authorized or permitted by the law of this state to administer health care or dispense medication in the ordinary course of business or practice of a profession, and includes a health care facility.

(7) "Informed decision" means a decision by a qualified patient, to request and obtain a prescription to end his or her life in a humane and dignified manner, that is based on an appreciation of the relevant facts and after being fully informed by the attending physician of:

(a) His or her medical diagnosis;

(b) His or her prognosis;

(c) The potential risks associated with taking the medication to be prescribed;

(d) The probable result of taking the medication to be prescribed; and

(e) The feasible alternatives, including, but not limited to, comfort care, hospice care and pain control.

(8) "Medically confirmed" means the medical opinion of the attending physician has been confirmed by a consulting physician who has examined the patient and the patient's relevant medical records.

(9) "Patient" means a person who is under the care of a physician.

(10) "Physician" means a doctor of medicine or osteopathy licensed to practice medicine by the Board of Medical Examiners for the State of Oregon.

(11) "Qualified patient" means a capable adult who is a resident of Oregon and has satisfied the requirements of ORS 127.800 to 127.897 in order to obtain a prescription for medication to end his or her life in a humane and dignified manner.

(12) "Terminal disease" means an incurable and irreversible disease that has been medically confirmed and will, within reasonable medical judgment, produce death within six months.

127.805 §2.01. Written Request for Medication to End One's Life

(1) An adult who is capable, is a resident of Oregon, and has been determined by the attending physician and consulting physician to be suffering from a terminal disease, and who has voluntarily expressed his or her wish to die, may make a written request for medication for the purpose of ending his or her life in a humane and dignified manner in accordance with ORS 127.800 to 127.897.

(2) No person shall qualify under the provisions of ORS 127.800 to 127.897 solely because of age or disability.

127.810 §2.02. Form of the Written Request.

(1) A valid request for medication under ORS 127.800 to 127.897 shall be in substantially the form described in ORS 127.897, signed and dated by the patient and witnessed by at least two individuals who, in the presence of the patient, attest that to the best of their knowledge and belief the patient is capable, acting voluntarily, and is not being coerced to sign the request.

(2) One of the witnesses shall be a person who is not:

(a) A relative of the patient by blood, marriage or adoption;

(b) A person who at the time the request is signed would be entitled to any portion of the estate of the qualified patient upon death under any will or by operation of law; or

(c) An owner, operator or employee of a health care facility where the qualified patient is receiving medical treatment or is a resident.

(3) The patient's attending physician at the time the request is signed shall not be a witness.

(4) If the patient is a patient in a long term care facility at the time the written request is made, one of the witnesses shall be an individual designated by the facility and having the qualifications specified by the Department of Human Services by rule.

127.815 §3.01. Attending Physician Responsibilities.

(1) The attending physician shall:

(a) Make the initial determination of whether a patient has a terminal disease, is capable, and has made the request voluntarily;

(b) Request that the patient demonstrate Oregon residency pursuant to ORS 127.860;

(c) To ensure that the patient is making an informed decision, inform the patient of:

(A) His or her medical diagnosis;

(B) His or her prognosis;

(C) The potential risks associated with taking the medication to be prescribed;

(D) The probable result of taking the medication to be prescribed; and

(E) The feasible alternatives, including, but not limited to, comfort care, hospice care and pain control;

(d) Refer the patient to a consulting physician for medical confirmation of the diagnosis, and for a determination that the patient is capable and acting voluntarily;

(e) Refer the patient for counseling if appropriate pursuant to ORS 127.825;

(f) Recommend that the patient notify next of kin;

(g) Counsel the patient about the importance of having another person present when the patient takes the medication prescribed pursuant to ORS 127.800 to 127.897 and of not taking the medication in a public place;

(h) Inform the patient that he or she has an opportunity to rescind the request at any time and in any manner, and offer the patient an opportunity to rescind at the end of the 15 day waiting period pursuant to ORS 127.840;

(i) Verify, immediately prior to writing the prescription for medication under ORS 127.800 to 127.897, that the patient is making an informed decision;

(j) Fulfill the medical record documentation requirements of ORS 127.855;

(k) Ensure that all appropriate steps are carried out in accordance with ORS 127.800 to 127.897 prior to writing a prescription for medication to enable a qualified patient to end his or her life in a humane and dignified manner; and

(l) (A) Dispense medications directly, including ancillary medications intended to facilitate the desired effect to minimize the patient's discomfort, provided the attending physician is registered as a dispensing physician with the Board of Medical Examiners, has a current Drug Enforcement Administration certificate and complies with any applicable administrative rule; or

(B) With the patient's written consent:

(i) Contact a pharmacist and inform the pharmacist of the prescription; and

(ii) Deliver the written prescription personally or by mail to the pharmacist, who will dispense the medications to either the patient, the attending physician or an expressly identified agent of the patient.

(2) Notwithstanding any other provision of law, the attending physician may sign the patient's death certificate.

127.820 §3.02. Consulting Physician Confirmation.

Before a patient is qualified under ORS 127.800 to 127.897, a consulting physician shall examine the patient and his or her relevant medical records and confirm, in writing, the attending physician's diagnosis that the patient is suffering from a terminal disease, and verify that the patient is capable, is acting voluntarily and has made an informed decision.

127.825 §3.03. Counseling Referral.

If in the opinion of the attending physician or the consulting physician a patient may be suffering from a psychiatric or psychological disorder or depression causing impaired judgment, either physician shall refer the patient for counseling. No medication to end a patient's life in a humane and dignified manner shall be prescribed until the person performing the counseling determines that the patient is not suffering from a psychiatric or psychological disorder or depression causing impaired judgment.

127.830 §3.04. Informed Decision.

No person shall receive a prescription for medication to end his or her life in a humane and dignified manner unless he or she has made an informed decision as defined in ORS 127.800 (7). Immediately prior to writing a prescription for medication under ORS 127.800 to 127.897, the attending physician shall verify that the patient is making an informed decision.

127.835 §3.05. Family Notification.

The attending physician shall recommend that the patient notify the next of kin of his or her request for medication pursuant to ORS 127.800 to 127.897. A patient who declines or is unable to notify next of kin shall not have his or her request denied for that reason.

127.840 §3.06. Written and Oral Requests.

In order to receive a prescription for medication to end his or her life in a humane and dignified manner, a qualified patient shall have made an oral request and a written request, and reiterate the oral request to his or her attending physician no less than fifteen (15) days after making the initial oral request. At the time the qualified patient makes his or her second oral request, the attending physician shall offer the patient an opportunity to rescind the request.

127.845 §3.07. Right to Rescind Request.

A patient may rescind his or her request at any time and in any manner without regard to his or her mental state. No prescription for medication under ORS 127.800 to 127.897 may be written without the attending physician offering the qualified patient an opportunity to rescind the request.

127.850 §3.08. Waiting Periods.

No less than fifteen (15) days shall elapse between the patient's initial oral request and the writing of a prescription under ORS 127.800 to 127.897. No less than 48 hours shall elapse between the patient's written request and the writing of a prescription under ORS 127.800 to 127.897.

127.855 §3.09. Medical Record Documentation Requirements.

The following shall be documented or filed in the patient's medical record:

(1) All oral requests by a patient for medication to end his or her life in a humane and dignified manner;

(2) All written requests by a patient for medication to end his or her life in a humane and dignified manner;

(3) The attending physician's diagnosis and prognosis, determination that the patient is capable, acting voluntarily and has made an informed decision;

(4) The consulting physician's diagnosis and prognosis, and verification that the patient is capable, acting voluntarily and has made an informed decision;

(5) A report of the outcome and determinations made during counseling, if performed;

(6) The attending physician's offer to the patient to rescind his or her request at the time of the patient's second oral request pursuant to ORS 127.840; and

(7) A note by the attending physician indicating that all requirements under ORS 127.800 to 127.897 have been met and indicating the steps taken to carry out the request, including a notation of the medication prescribed.

127.860 §3.10. Residency Requirement.

Only requests made by Oregon residents under ORS 127.800 to 127.897 shall be granted. Factors demonstrating Oregon residency include but are not limited to:

(1) Possession of an Oregon driver license;

(2) Registration to vote in Oregon;

(3) Evidence that the person owns or leases property in Oregon; or

(4) Filing of an Oregon tax return for the most recent tax year.

127.865 §3.11. Reporting Requirements.

(1) (a) The Health Services shall annually review a sample of records maintained pursuant to ORS 127.800 to 127.897.

(b) The division shall require any health care provider upon dispensing medication pursuant to ORS 127.800 to 127.897 to file a copy of the dispensing record with the division.

(2) The Health Services shall make rules to facilitate the collection of information regarding compliance with ORS 127.800 to 127.897. Except as otherwise required by law, the information collected shall not be a public record and may not be made available for inspection by the public.

(3) The division shall generate and make available to the public an annual statistical report of information collected under subsection (2) of this section.

127.870 §3.12. Effect on Construction of Wills, Contracts and Statutes.

(1) No provision in a contract, will or other agreement, whether written or oral, to the extent the provision would affect whether a person may make

or rescind a request for medication to end his or her life in a humane and dignified manner, shall be valid.

(2) No obligation owing under any currently existing contract shall be conditioned or affected by the making or rescinding of a request, by a person, for medication to end his or her life in a humane and dignified manner.

127.875 §3.13. Insurance or Annuity Policies.

The sale, procurement, or issuance of any life, health, or accident insurance or annuity policy or the rate charged for any policy shall not be conditioned upon or affected by the making or rescinding of a request, by a person, for medication to end his or her life in a humane and dignified manner. Neither shall a qualified patient's act of ingesting medication to end his or her life in a humane and dignified manner have an effect upon a life, health, or accident insurance or annuity policy.

127.880 §3.14. Construction of Act.

Nothing in ORS 127.800 to 127.897 shall be construed to authorize a physician or any other person to end a patient's life by lethal injection, mercy killing or active euthanasia. Actions taken in accordance with ORS 127.800 to 127.897 shall not, for any purpose, constitute suicide, assisted suicide, mercy killing or homicide, under the law.

127.885 Immunities; Basis for Prohibiting Health Care Provider from Participation; Notification; Permissible Sanctions.

Except as provided in ORS 127.890:

(1) No person shall be subject to civil or criminal liability or professional disciplinary action for participating in good faith compliance with ORS 127.800 to 127.897. This includes being present when a qualified patient takes the prescribed medication to end his or her life in a humane and dignified manner.

(2) No professional organization or association, or health care provider, may subject a person to censure, discipline, suspension, loss of license, loss of privileges, loss of membership or other penalty for participating or refusing to participate in good faith compliance with ORS 127.800 to 127.897.

(3) No request by a patient for or provision by an attending physician of medication in good faith compliance with the provisions of ORS 127.800 to 127.897 shall constitute neglect for any purpose of law or provide the sole basis for the appointment of a guardian or conservator.

(4) No health care provider shall be under any duty, whether by contract, by statute or by any other legal requirement to participate in the provision to a qualified patient of medication to end his or her life in a humane and dignified manner. If a health care provider is unable or unwilling to carry out a patient's request under ORS 127.800 to 127.897, and the patient

transfers his or her care to a new health care provider, the prior health care provider shall transfer, upon request, a copy of the patient's relevant medical records to the new health care provider.

(5) (a) Notwithstanding any other provision of law, a health care provider may prohibit another health care provider from participating in ORS 127.800 to 127.897 on the premises of the prohibiting provider if the prohibiting provider has notified the health care provider of the prohibiting provider's policy regarding participating in ORS 127.800 to 127.897. . . .

* * *

127.890 §4.02. Liabilities.

(1) A person who without authorization of the patient willfully alters or forges a request for medication or conceals or destroys a rescission of that request with the intent or effect of causing the patient's death shall be guilty of a Class A felony.

(2) A person who coerces or exerts undue influence on a patient to request medication for the purpose of ending the patient's life, or to destroy a rescission of such a request, shall be guilty of a Class A felony.

(3) Nothing in ORS 127.800 to 127.897 limits further liability for civil damages resulting from other negligent conduct or intentional misconduct by any person.

(4) The penalties in ORS 127.800 to 127.897 do not preclude criminal penalties applicable under other law for conduct which is inconsistent with the provisions of ORS 127.800 to 127.897.

* * *

127.897 §6.01. Form of the Request.

A request for a medication as authorized by ORS 127.800 to 127.897 shall be in substantially the following form:

REQUEST FOR MEDICATION
TO END MY LIFE IN A HUMANE
AND DIGNIFIED MANNER

I, _____, am an adult of sound mind.

I am suffering from _____, which my attending physician has determined is a terminal disease and which has been medically confirmed by a consulting physician.

I have been fully informed of my diagnosis, prognosis, the nature of medication to be prescribed and potential associated risks, the expected result, and the feasible alternatives, including comfort care, hospice care and pain control.

I request that my attending physician prescribe medication that will end my life in a humane and dignified manner.

INITIAL ONE:

_____ I have informed my family of my decision and taken their opinions into consideration.

_____ I have decided not to inform my family of my decision.

_____ I have no family to inform of my decision.

I understand that I have the right to rescind this request at any time.

I understand the full import of this request and I expect to die when I take the medication to be prescribed. I further understand that although most deaths occur within three hours, my death may take longer and my physician has counseled me about this possibility.

I make this request voluntarily and without reservation, and I accept full moral responsibility for my actions.

Signed: _____

Dated: _____

DECLARATION OF WITNESSES

We declare that the person signing this request:

(a) Is personally known to us or has provided proof of identity;

(b) Signed this request in our presence;

(c) Appears to be of sound mind and not under duress, fraud or undue influence;

(d) Is not a patient for whom either of us is attending physician.

_____ Witness 1/Date

_____ Witness 2/Date

NOTE: One witness shall not be a relative (by blood, marriage or adoption) of the person signing this request, shall not be entitled to any portion of the person's estate upon death and shall not own, operate or be employed at a health care facility where the person is a patient or resident. If the patient is an inpatient at a health care facility, one of the witnesses shall be an individual designated by the facility.

Oregon Department of Health & Human Services' Fifteenth Annual Report on Oregon's Death with Dignity Act (excerpts)

January 2013

Oregon's Death with Dignity Act (DWDA), enacted in late 1997, allows terminally-ill adult Oregonians to obtain and use prescriptions from their physicians for self-administered, lethal doses of medications. The Oregon Public Health Division is required by the Act to collect information on compliance and to issue an annual report. The key findings from 2012 are listed below. The number of people for whom DWDA prescriptions were written (DWDA prescription recipients) and deaths that occurred as a result of ingesting prescribed DWDA medications (DWDA deaths) reported in this summary are based on paperwork and death certificates received by the Oregon Public Health Division as of January 14, 2013. For more detail, please view the figures and tables on our web site: http://www.healthoregon.org/dwd.

* * *

▪ As of January 14, 2013, prescriptions for lethal medications were written for 115 people during 2012 under the provisions of the DWDA, compared to 114 during 2011. At the time of this report, there were 77 known DWDA deaths during 2012. This corresponds to 23.5 DWDA deaths per 10,000 total deaths.

▪ Since the law was passed in 1997, a total of 1,050 people have had DWDA prescriptions written and 673 patients have died from ingesting medications prescribed under the DWDA.

▪ Of the 115 patients for whom DWDA prescriptions were written during 2012, 67 (58.3%) ingested the medication; 66 died from ingesting the medication, and one patient ingested the medication but regained consciousness before dying of underlying illness and is therefore not counted as a DWDA death. The patient regained consciousness two days following ingestion, but remained minimally responsive and died six days following ingestion.

▪ Eleven (11) patients with prescriptions written during the previous year (2011) died after ingesting the medication during 2012.

▪ Twenty-three (23) of the 115 patients who received DWDA prescriptions during 2012 did not take the medications and subsequently died of other causes.

* * *

▪ Of the 77 DWDA deaths during 2012, most (67.5%) were aged 65 years or older; the median age was 69 years. As in previous years, most were white (97.4%), well-educated (42.9% had at least a baccalaureate degree), and had cancer (75.3%).

▪ Most (97.4%) patients died at home; and most (97.0%) were enrolled in hospice care either at the time the DWDA prescription was written or at the time of death. Excluding unknown cases, all (100.0%) had some form of health care insurance, although the number of patients who had private insurance (51.4%) was lower in 2012 than in previous years (66.2%), and the number of patients who had only Medicare or Medicaid insurance was higher than in previous years (48.6% compared to 32.1%).

▪ As in previous years, the three most frequently mentioned end-of-life concerns were: loss of autonomy (93.5%), decreasing ability to participate in activities that made life enjoyable (92.2%), and loss of dignity (77.9%).

▪ . . . Prescribing physicians were present at the time of death for seven patients (9.1%) during 2012 compared to 17.3% in previous years.

QUESTIONS

1. What is the justification for limiting the right to physician-assisted suicide to the terminally ill? Should the right be extended to anyone who is experiencing significant suffering as a result of permanent illness? Should it be extended to any competent person who sincerely believes he or she would be better off dead?

2. As Oregon's report on utilization of its Death with Dignity Act indicates, a large portion of those who are prescribed lethal prescriptions in accordance with the Act never take them. What might explain this phenomenon?

PROBLEMS

1. Judith Berger, an Oregon resident, has been diagnosed with pancreatic cancer. Her favorite aunt died of pancreatic cancer a decade ago and suffered great emotional and physical pain in her final months. Judith does not wish to go through what her aunt went through and has decided to choose the timing of her own death as provided for by Oregon's Death with Dignity Act. Judith's closest living relative is her only child, a son. Although she loves her son dearly, she suspects he would not approve of her choice to end her own life and does not wish to tell him of her plans. Should Judith be required to tell her son of her intentions? Under Oregon law, must she tell him?

2. Jerry Illardo is an Oregon resident with a terminal illness. One of the effects of the illness is that he has great difficulty swallowing. He does not think he will be capable of swallowing the lethal medication that his doctor has prescribed him in accordance with Oregon's Death with Dignity Act. He has requested that his doctor instead inject him with a lethal medication. May the doctor do so?

3. Saint Jerome's Hospital is located in the state of Oregon. In accordance with the hospital's religious tradition, the Board of Directors of Saint Jerome's opposes physician-assisted suicide. Can Saint Jerome's Hospital prohibit doctors that work for it from participating in physician-assisted suicide?

4. Steve Jacoby is a primary care doctor who practices in Oregon. He feels that assisting patients to end their own lives is inconsistent with his role as a doctor. Can he refuse to do so? Can he refuse to inform his patients about the options provided by Oregon's Death with Dignity Act?

EXERCISE 9.1

You are the legislative aide to Senator Maude Milton, Chair of the Health and Human Services Committee of the West Carolina House of Representatives. Senator Milton wishes to introduce a bill that would legalize assisted suicide in the state of West Carolina. She asks you to draft the bill. What provisions would you include? In answering this questions, consider the following sub-issues:

■ Would you limit the bill's coverage to persons who are terminally ill? If so, how would you define terminally ill?
■ Would you limit the bill's coverage to assistance by physicians?
■ What types of "assistance" would you permit or prohibit?

Once you have decided upon your approach, draft a proposed statute for the Senator's consideration.

E. HOSPICE CARE

Hospice is a form of specialized care for people who are dying and their families. Hospice care does not aim to cure the person's underlying lethal condition. Rather, it focuses on providing for the comfort and well-being of the dying person and his or her family members, and the alleviation of the negative symptoms associated with the patient's condition. A key aspect of hospice care therefore is *palliative care*. Palliative care is medical care focused on alleviating suffering and improving quality of life for seriously ill patients. Hospice care can be provided in a variety of different settings—from a hospital, to a specialized residence, to a person's home.

Hospice care provides significant benefits to both terminally ill patients and their families. As Professor Kathy Cerminara has explained:

> Hospice care provides well-documented benefits to patients, families and caregivers when patients near the end of life. It permits patients to exercise more control over their circumstances near the end of life, which benefits them psychologically. Through a team-based, interdisciplinary approach, individual hospice care providers "act as guides into death, offering information, support, and guidance from the perspectives of persons who are familiar with the dying process" to patients, families, and caregivers. Families and caregivers can benefit from services such as counseling and respite care, which is short-term, inpatient care designed to give patients' caregivers short breaks from the stresses of caregiving. For patients, the psychological benefits of hospice care can result in physical benefits, such as lower blood pressure, increased efficacy of medications intended to relieve physical pain, and stronger immune systems.

Kathy L. Cerminara, *Hospice and Health Care Reform: Improving Care at the End of Life*, 17 WIDENER L. REV. 443, 449 (2011).

The Medicare program includes a significant hospice benefit. Medicare covers hospice services for Medicare Part A beneficiaries who have a life expectancy of six months or less (and eligibility can be renewed if the person outlives the six-month life expectancy but still has six months or less to live). Nevertheless, the Medicare hospice benefit is dramatically underused. Very few individuals utilize the benefit for anywhere near six months. Rather, the average hospice patient receives hospice care for less than three weeks, a third receive hospice care only during the last week of their lives, and one in ten receives hospice benefits for only the very last day of life.

What follows are key excerpts from the regulations governing the Medicare hospice benefit. As you read the excerpts, consider how knowledge of these provisions might help you to advise a dying client or a client whose loved one is dying.

MEDICARE'S HOSPICE REGULATIONS
42 CFR §418 (2013)

§418.3 Definitions.

For purposes of this part—

* * *

Hospice means a public agency or private organization or subdivision of either of these that is primarily engaged in providing hospice care as defined in this section.

Hospice care means a comprehensive set of services described in [this Act], identified and coordinated by an interdisciplinary group to provide for the physical, psychosocial, spiritual, and emotional needs of a terminally ill patient and/or family members, as delineated in a specific patient plan of care.

* * *

Terminally ill means that the individual has a medical prognosis that his or her life expectancy is 6 months or less if the illness runs its normal course.

Subpart B. Eligibility, Election and Duration of Benefits

§418.20 Eligibility Requirements.

In order to be eligible to elect hospice care under Medicare, an individual must be—

(a) Entitled to Part A of Medicare; and

(b) Certified as being terminally ill in accordance with §418.22[, which requires, among other things, that the physician or a medical director certify that "the individual's prognosis is for a life expectancy of 6 months or less if the terminal illness runs its normal course"].

* * *

§418.24 Election of Hospice Care.

(a) *Filing an election statement.* An individual who meets the eligibility requirement of §418.20 may file an election statement with a particular hospice. If the individual is physically or mentally incapacitated, his or her representative (as defined in §418.3) may file the election statement.

(b) *Content of election statement.* The election statement must include the following:

(1) Identification of the particular hospice that will provide care to the individual.

(2) The individual's or representative's acknowledgement that he or she has been given a full understanding of the palliative rather than curative nature of hospice care, as it relates to the individual's terminal illness.

(3) Acknowledgement that certain Medicare services, as set forth in paragraph (d) of this section, are waived by the election.

(4) The effective date of the election, which may be the first day of hospice care or a later date, but may be no earlier than the date of the election statement.

(5) The signature of the individual or representative.

(c) *Duration of election.* An election to receive hospice care will be considered to continue through the initial election period and through the subsequent election periods without a break in care as long as the individual—

(1) Remains in the care of a hospice;

(2) Does not revoke the election; and

(3) Is not discharged from the hospice under the provisions of §418.26.

(d) *Waiver of other benefits.* For the duration of an election of hospice care, an individual waives all rights to Medicare payments for the following services:

(1) Hospice care provided by a hospice other than the hospice designated by the individual (unless provided under arrangements made by the designated hospice).

(2) Any Medicare services that are related to the treatment of the terminal condition for which hospice care was elected or a related condition or that are equivalent to hospice care except for services—

(i) Provided by the designated hospice;

(ii) Provided by another hospice under arrangements made by the designated hospice; and

(iii) Provided by the individual's attending physician if that physician is not an employee of the designated hospice or receiving compensation from the hospice for those services.

* * *

§418.28 Revoking the Election of Hospice Care.

(a) An individual or representative may revoke the individual's election of hospice care at any time during an election period.

(b) To revoke the election of hospice care, the individual or representative must file a statement with the hospice that includes the following information:

(1) A signed statement that the individual or representative revokes the individual's election for Medicare coverage of hospice care for the remainder of that election period.

(2) The date that the revocation is to be effective. (An individual or representative may not designate an effective date earlier than the date that the revocation is made.)

(c) An individual, upon revocation of the election of Medicare coverage of hospice care for a particular election period—

(1) Is no longer covered under Medicare for hospice care;

(2) Resumes Medicare coverage of the benefits waived under §418.24(e)(2); and

(3) May at any time elect to receive hospice coverage for any other hospice election periods that he or she is eligible to receive.

* * *

§418.56 Condition of Participation—Interdisciplinary Group.

The hospice must designate an interdisciplinary group or groups as specified in paragraph (a) of this section which, in consultation with the patient's attending physician, must prepare a written plan of care for each patient. The plan of care must specify the hospice care and services necessary to meet the patient and family-specific needs identified in the comprehensive assessment as such needs relate to the terminal illness and related conditions.

(a) *Standard: Approach to service delivery.*

(1) The hospice must designate an interdisciplinary group or groups composed of individuals who work together to meet the physical, medical, psychosocial, emotional, and spiritual needs of the hospice patients and families facing terminal illness and bereavement. . . . The interdisciplinary group must include, but is not limited to, individuals who are qualified and competent to practice in the following professional roles:

(i) A doctor of medicine or osteopathy (who is an employee or under contract with the hospice).

(ii) A registered nurse.

(iii) A social worker.

(iv) A pastoral or other counselor.

* * *

(b) *Standard: Plan of care.* All hospice care and services furnished to patients and their families must follow an individualized written plan of care established by the hospice interdisciplinary group in collaboration with the attending physician (if any), the patient or representative, and the primary caregiver in accordance with the patient's needs if any of them so desire. The hospice must ensure that each patient and the primary care giver(s) receive education and training provided by the hospice as appropriate to their responsibilities for the care and services identified in the plan of care.

(c) *Standard: Content of the plan of care.* The hospice must develop an individualized written plan of care for each patient. The plan of care must reflect patient and family goals and interventions based on the problems identified in the initial, comprehensive, and updated comprehensive assessments. The plan of care must include all services necessary for the palliation and management of the terminal illness and related conditions. . . .

(d) *Standard: Review of the plan of care.* The hospice interdisciplinary group (in collaboration with the individual's attending physician, if any) must review, revise and document the individualized plan as frequently as the patient's condition requires, but no less frequently than every 15 calendar days. . . .

§418.200 Requirements for Coverage.

To be covered, hospice services must . . . be reasonable and necessary for the palliation or management of the terminal illness as well as related conditions. . . .

§418.202 Covered Services.

. . . The following services are covered hospice services:

(a) Nursing care provided by or under the supervision of a registered nurse.

(b) Medical social services provided by a social worker under the direction of a physician.

(c) Physicians' services performed by a physician as defined in §410.20 of this chapter except that the services of the hospice medical director or the physician member of the interdisciplinary group must be performed by a doctor of medicine or osteopathy.

(d) Counseling services provided to the terminally ill individual and the family members or other persons caring for the individual at home. Counseling, including dietary counseling, may be provided both for the purpose of training the individual's family or other caregiver to provide care, and for the purpose of helping the individual and those caring for him or her to adjust to the individual's approaching death.

(e) Short-term inpatient care. . . .

Inpatient care may also be furnished as a means of providing respite for the individual's family or other persons caring for the individual at home. . . .

(f) Medical appliances and supplies, including drugs and biologicals. . . .

(g) Home health aide or hospice aide services. . . . Home health aides (also known as hospice aides) may provide personal care services as defined in §409.45(b) of this chapter. Aides may perform household services to maintain a safe and sanitary environment in areas of the home used by the patient, such as changing bed linens or light cleaning and laundering essential to the comfort and cleanliness of the patient. . . . Homemaker services may include assistance in maintenance of a safe and healthy environment and services to enable the individual to carry out the treatment plan.

(h) Physical therapy, occupational therapy and speech-language pathology services . . . provided for purposes of symptom control or to enable the patient to maintain activities of daily living and basic functional skills.

(i) Effective April 1, 1998, any other service that is specified in the patient's plan of care as reasonable and necessary for the palliation and management of the patient's terminal illness and related conditions and for which payment may otherwise be made under Medicare.

§418.204 Special Coverage Requirements.

(a) *Periods of crisis.* Nursing care may be covered on a continuous basis for as much as 24 hours a day during periods of crisis as necessary to maintain an individual at home. Either homemaker or home health aide services or both may be covered on a 24-hour continuous basis during periods of crisis but care during these periods must be predominantly nursing care. A period of crisis is a period in which the individual requires continuous care to achieve palliation or management of acute medical symptoms.

(b) *Respite care.*

(1) Respite care is short-term inpatient care provided to the individual only when necessary to relieve the family members or other persons caring for the individual.

(2) Respite care may be provided only on an occasional basis and may not be reimbursed for more than five consecutive days at a time.

(c) *Bereavement counseling.* Bereavement counseling is a required hospice service but it is not reimbursable.

NOTES

1. *Palliative care versus hospice care.* While palliative care is typically a hallmark of hospice care, it can be provided regardless of whether a patient is terminally ill. As medical doctors Laura Gelfman and Diane Meier have explained:

> Whereas hospice delivery is dependent on prognosis, palliative care is available to patients with serious, complex, and life-threatening illness independent of their prognosis and is offered simultaneously with life-prolonging and curative therapies. Experts advocate that when a patient is diagnosed with a serious illness, palliative care should be started and continue simultaneously with curative or disease-modifying treatments. Patients and families are vulnerable at the time of diagnosis of serious illness and the introduction of palliative care at this time allows for providers with expertise in communication to ensure that the goals of the patient and family are at the forefront of the medical care.

Laura P. Gelfman, M.D. & Diane E. Meier, M.D., *Making the Case for Palliative Care: An Opportunity for Health Care Reform*, 8 J. HEALTH & BIOMEDICAL L. 57, 59 (2012) (discussing the differences between palliative care and hospice, how this affects Medicare eligibility, and health care spending).

2. *Should hospice patients be required to renounce curative care?* Professor Cerminara suggests that Medicare should reconsider its requirement that those receiving the hospice services agree not to seek curative care. She writes:

> Studies have demonstrated that healthcare professionals fail to recommend hospice care as soon as they could, at least partly because of the confusion resulting from the current payment system's false dichotomy between curative and palliative treatment. Nurses, nurse managers, and social workers treating patients with end-stage renal disease, for example, have been shown to be confused about the Medicare rules requiring patients to renounce curative treatment to receive the hospice benefit, and that confusion has affected referrals to hospice care. One physician has attributed late referral to hospice care, in part, to the false dichotomy inherent in Medicare's payment structure as well as to "the mistaken view that patients [in hospice] must have a do-not-resuscitate order," which could be related to the requirement that patients must renounce curative treatment.
>
> On the patient side as well, having to renounce all curative efforts before Medicare will pay for hospice care may result in patient delay in accessing hospice care even if healthcare professionals have discussed that option in a timely fashion. Elisabeth Kubler-Ross identified five stages of dying, with the final one being acceptance; yet some patients never reach acceptance at all. To renounce curative treatment would require accepting impending death, so requiring patients to reach acceptance before accessing hospice care, at best, postpones their initial election of Medicare payment for such services. Due to a variety of cultural influences, some Hispanic and African-American patients may never be willing to renounce curative care, even after they have accepted impending death. In other words, the current Medicare payment system, which requires Medicare beneficiaries to accept the inevitability of their deaths before Medicare will pay for hospice care, deprives patients of valuable physical and psychological benefits at a time those benefits could greatly help ease the dying process.
>
> * * *
>
> . . . Eliminating the false dichotomy between curative and palliative treatment is likely very beneficial. First, it is the most efficient path to early hospice care for most patients. Second, removing the dichotomy may encourage hospice utilization among patients in racial and ethnic groups that traditionally have not embraced hospice care. Moreover, the healthcare system as a whole could benefit because, although it seems paradoxical, providing both curative and palliative care at the beginning of patients' hospice care experiences can reduce overall health care spending near the end of life.

Kathy L. Cerminara, *Hospice and Health Care Reform: Improving Care at the End of Life*, 17 Widener L. Rev. 443, 449-50, 455 (2011) (arguing that permitting concurrent care is unlikely to increase Medicare costs because "facilitating earlier access to hospice care in this way is likely to result in a decrease in costs associated with aggressive end-of-life interventions").

QUESTIONS

1. What services does Medicare provide as part of its hospice benefit that it does not provide as part of its home care benefit? In considering this question, you may wish to refer back to the discussion of the Medicare home health benefit in Section B.6 of Chapter 6 (see pages 266-273).

2. What are the primary benefits of hospice care as opposed to other forms of end-of-life care?

3. To what extent would increasing the rate of participation in hospice care improve end-of-life care for Americans?

4. What factors do you think account for the Medicare hospice benefit's low usage rate?

PROBLEM

Edith Abrams was admitted to Hope Hospice two weeks ago after being diagnosed with terminal cancer. She understands that this means that she is choosing not to pursue a cure for the cancer and that her life expectancy is very short. Nevertheless, she refuses to execute a *do-not-resuscitate* (DNR) order as recommended by her doctor. She says that she understands that the cancer will kill her, but she is not willing to die "early" from a heart attack if it is avoidable. Must she agree to the DNR in order to receive hospice services? Can the hospice resuscitate Ms. Abrams if she goes into cardiac arrest?

CHAPTER 10

Grandparenting and Grandparents' Rights

A. INTRODUCTION

Grandparents play a wide variety of roles in the lives of their grandchildren—from absent relative, to friendly visitor, to caregiver, to de facto parent. The roles that grandparents perform depend on a variety of factors, such as the needs of the child and of his or her parents and the cultural expectations of the family. The role of grandparents also varies over time as children age and their needs, along with those of their parents and grandparents, evolve.

This chapter explores key legal issues grandparents face in each of these roles, as well as legal issues related to adult grandchildren caring for their aging grandparents.

B. GRANDPARENTS AS VISITORS

Relationships with grandparents are often a very valuable and meaningful part of an individual's life experience, both during childhood and later in adulthood. In part for this reason, parents often try to actively foster relationships between their children and their children's grandparents. However, there are times when a parent may not wish for his or her child to have the type of relationship with a grandparent that the grandparent desires or, for that matter, for the child to have any relationship at all with the grandparent.

When grandparents are deprived of their desired relations with grandchildren, they may seek a court order requiring the parent or parents to permit visitation. Such court disputes are particularly likely to arise when the grandparent's own child is deceased and thus unable to provide his or her parents with direct access to the child. The question for the law then becomes whether, under what conditions, and to what extent, the parent may limit the grandparent's relationship with, and access to, the grandchild. The next two cases explore the answer to this question.

Troxel v. Granville

530 U.S. 57 (2000)

Justice O'CONNOR announced the judgment of the Court and delivered an opinion, in which THE CHIEF JUSTICE, Justice GINSBURG, and Justice BREYER join.

Section 26.10.160(3) of the Revised Code of Washington permits "[a]ny person" to petition a superior court for visitation rights "at any time," and authorizes that court to grant such visitation rights whenever "visitation may serve the best interest of the child." Petitioners Jenifer and Gary Troxel petitioned a Washington Superior Court for the right to visit their grandchildren, Isabelle and Natalie Troxel. Respondent Tommie Granville, the mother of Isabelle and Natalie, opposed the petition. The case ultimately reached the Washington Supreme Court, which held that §26.10.160(3) unconstitutionally interferes with the fundamental right of parents to rear their children.

I

Tommie Granville and Brad Troxel shared a relationship that ended in June 1991. The two never married, but they had two daughters, Isabelle and Natalie. Jenifer and Gary Troxel are Brad's parents, and thus the paternal grandparents of Isabelle and Natalie. After Tommie and Brad separated in 1991, Brad lived with his parents and regularly brought his daughters to his parents' home for weekend visitation. Brad committed suicide in May 1993. Although the Troxels at first continued to see Isabelle and Natalie on a regular basis after their son's death, Tommie Granville informed the Troxels in October 1993 that she wished to limit their visitation with her daughters to one short visit per month.

In December 1993, the Troxels commenced the present action by filing, in the Washington Superior Court for Skagit County, a petition to obtain visitation rights with Isabelle and Natalie. The Troxels filed their petition under two Washington statutes, Wash. Rev. Code §§26.09.240 and 26.10.160(3) (1994). Only the latter statute is at issue in this case. Section 26.10.160(3) provides: "Any person may petition the court for visitation rights at any time including, but not limited to, custody proceedings. The court may order visitation rights for any person when visitation may serve the best interest of the child whether or not there has been any change of circumstances." At trial, the Troxels requested two weekends of overnight visitation per month and two weeks of visitation each summer. Granville did not oppose visitation altogether, but instead asked the court to order one day of visitation per month with no overnight stay. . . . In 1995, the Superior Court issued an oral ruling and entered a visitation decree ordering visitation one weekend per month, one week during the summer, and four hours on both of the petitioning grandparents' birthdays.

Granville appealed, during which time she married Kelly Wynn. Before addressing the merits of Granville's appeal, the Washington Court of Appeals remanded the case to the Superior Court for entry of written findings of fact and conclusions of law. On remand, the Superior Court found that visitation was in Isabelle's and Natalie's best interests:

> "The Petitioners [the Troxels] are part of a large, central, loving family, all located in this area, and the Petitioners can provide opportunities for the children in the areas of cousins and music.
> "... The children would be benefitted from spending quality time with the Petitioners, provided that that time is balanced with time with the childrens' [sic] nuclear family...."

Approximately nine months after the Superior Court entered its order on remand, Granville's husband formally adopted Isabelle and Natalie.

The Washington Court of Appeals reversed the lower court's visitation order and dismissed the Troxels' petition for visitation, holding that nonparents lack standing to seek visitation under §26.10.160(3) unless a custody action is pending. Having resolved the case on the statutory ground, however, the Court of Appeals did not expressly pass on Granville's constitutional challenge to the visitation statute.

The Washington Supreme Court granted the Troxels' petition for review and ... affirmed.... The court rested its decision on the Federal Constitution, holding that §26.10.160(3) unconstitutionally infringes on the fundamental right of parents to rear their children. In the court's view, there were at least two problems with the nonparental visitation statute. First, according to the Washington Supreme Court, the Constitution permits a State to interfere with the right of parents to rear their children only to prevent harm or potential harm to a child. Section 26.10.160(3) fails that standard because it requires no threshold showing of harm. Second, by allowing "'any person' to petition for forced visitation of a child at 'any time' with the only requirement being that the visitation serve the best interest of the child," the Washington visitation statute sweeps too broadly....

We granted certiorari, and now affirm the judgment.

II

The demographic changes of the past century make it difficult to speak of an average American family. The composition of families varies greatly from household to household. While many children may have two married parents and grandparents who visit regularly, many other children are raised in single-parent households. In 1996, children living with only one parent accounted for 28 percent of all children under age 18 in the United States.... Understandably, in these single-parent households, persons outside the nuclear family are called upon with increasing frequency to assist in the everyday tasks of child rearing. In many cases, grandparents play an important role.

For example, in 1998, approximately 4 million children—or 5.6 percent of all children under age 18—lived in the household of their grandparents.

The nationwide enactment of nonparental visitation statutes is assuredly due, in some part, to the States' recognition of these changing realities of the American family. Because grandparents and other relatives undertake duties of a parental nature in many households, States have sought to ensure the welfare of the children therein by protecting the relationships those children form with such third parties. The States' nonparental visitation statutes are further supported by a recognition, which varies from State to State, that children should have the opportunity to benefit from relationships with statutorily specified persons—for example, their grandparents. The extension of statutory rights in this area to persons other than a child's parents, however, comes with an obvious cost. For example, the State's recognition of an independent third-party interest in a child can place a substantial burden on the traditional parent-child relationship. . . .

The Fourteenth Amendment provides that no State shall "deprive any person of life, liberty, or property, without due process of law." We have long recognized that the Amendment's Due Process Clause, like its Fifth Amendment counterpart, "guarantees more than fair process." *Washington v. Glucksberg*, 521 U.S. 702 (1997). The Clause also includes a substantive component that "provides heightened protection against government interference with certain fundamental rights and liberty interests." *Id.*, at 720.

The liberty interest at issue in this case—the interest of parents in the care, custody, and control of their children—is perhaps the oldest of the fundamental liberty interests recognized by this Court. . . .

Section 26.10.160(3), as applied to Granville and her family in this case, unconstitutionally infringes on that fundamental parental right. The Washington nonparental visitation statute is breathtakingly broad. According to the statute's text, "*[a]ny person* may petition the court for visitation rights *at any time*," and the court may grant such visitation rights whenever "visitation may serve *the best interest of the child*." §26.10.160(3) (emphases added). That language effectively permits any third party seeking visitation to subject any decision by a parent concerning visitation of the parent's children to state-court review. Once the visitation petition has been filed in court and the matter is placed before a judge, a parent's decision that visitation would not be in the child's best interest is accorded no deference. Section 26.10.160(3) contains no requirement that a court accord the parent's decision any presumption of validity or any weight whatsoever. Instead, the Washington statute places the best-interest determination solely in the hands of the judge. Should the judge disagree with the parent's estimation of the child's best interests, the judge's view necessarily prevails. Thus, in practical effect, in the State of Washington a court can disregard and overturn any decision by a fit custodial parent concerning visitation whenever a third party affected by the decision files a visitation petition, based solely on the judge's determination of the child's best interests. . . .

Turning to the facts of this case, the record reveals that the Superior Court's order was based on precisely the type of mere disagreement we have just described and nothing more. The Superior Court's order was not founded on any special factors that might justify the State's interference with Granville's fundamental right to make decisions concerning the rearing of her two daughters. To be sure, this case involves a visitation petition filed by grandparents soon after the death of their son—the father of Isabelle and Natalie—but the combination of several factors here compels our conclusion that §26.10.160(3), as applied, exceeded the bounds of the Due Process Clause.

First, the Troxels did not allege, and no court has found, that Granville was an unfit parent. That aspect of the case is important, for there is a presumption that fit parents act in the best interests of their children. . . . Accordingly, so long as a parent adequately cares for his or her children (i.e., is fit), there will normally be no reason for the State to inject itself into the private realm of the family to further question the ability of that parent to make the best decisions concerning the rearing of that parent's children.

The problem here is not that the Washington Superior Court intervened, but that when it did so, it gave no special weight at all to Granville's determination of her daughters' best interests. More importantly, it appears that the Superior Court applied exactly the opposite presumption. . . . In effect, the judge placed on Granville, the fit custodial parent, the burden of disproving that visitation would be in the best interest of her daughters. . . .

The decisional framework employed by the Superior Court directly contravened the traditional presumption that a fit parent will act in the best interest of his or her child. In that respect, the court's presumption failed to provide any protection for Granville's fundamental constitutional right to make decisions concerning the rearing of her own daughters. In an ideal world, parents might always seek to cultivate the bonds between grandparents and their grandchildren. Needless to say, however, our world is far from perfect, and in it the decision whether such an intergenerational relationship would be beneficial in any specific case is for the parent to make in the first instance. And, if a fit parent's decision of the kind at issue here becomes subject to judicial review, the court must accord at least some special weight to the parent's own determination.

Finally, we note that there is no allegation that Granville ever sought to cut off visitation entirely. . . .

Considered together with the Superior Court's reasons for awarding visitation to the Troxels, the combination of these factors demonstrates that the visitation order in this case was an unconstitutional infringement on Granville's fundamental right to make decisions concerning the care, custody, and control of her two daughters. . . . Accordingly, we hold that §26.10.160(3), as applied in this case, is unconstitutional.

Because we rest our decision on the sweeping breadth of §26.10.160(3) and the application of that broad, unlimited power in this case, we do not consider the primary constitutional question passed on by the Washington

Supreme Court—whether the Due Process Clause requires all nonparental visitation statutes to include a showing of harm or potential harm to the child as a condition precedent to granting visitation. We do not, and need not, define today the precise scope of the parental due process right in the visitation context. . . .

Accordingly, the judgment of the Washington Supreme Court is affirmed. It is so ordered.

[Concurrence of Justice Souter and dissenting opinions of Justices Stevens and Scalia omitted.]

Justice KENNEDY, dissenting.

[After concluding that the State Supreme Court was in error in finding that the best interests of the child standard is never appropriate in third-party visitation cases, and therefore should reconsider the case in light of this legal correction, Justice Kennedy explained that:]

My principal concern is that the holding seems to proceed from the assumption that the parent or parents who resist visitation have always been the child's primary caregivers and that the third parties who seek visitation have no legitimate and established relationship with the child. That idea, in turn, appears influenced by the concept that the conventional nuclear family ought to establish the visitation standard for every domestic relations case. As we all know, this is simply not the structure or prevailing condition in many households. For many boys and girls a traditional family with two or even one permanent and caring parent is simply not the reality of their childhood. This may be so whether their childhood has been marked by tragedy or filled with considerable happiness and fulfillment.

Cases are sure to arise—perhaps a substantial number of cases—in which a third party, by acting in a caregiving role over a significant period of time, has developed a relationship with a child which is not necessarily subject to absolute parental veto. Some pre-existing relationships, then, serve to identify persons who have a strong attachment to the child with the concomitant motivation to act in a responsible way to ensure the child's welfare. As the State Supreme Court was correct to acknowledge, those relationships can be so enduring that "in certain circumstances where a child has enjoyed a substantial relationship with a third person, arbitrarily depriving the child of the relationship could cause severe psychological harm to the child," 137 Wash. 2d, at 20, 969 P.2d, at 30; and harm to the adult may also ensue. In the design and elaboration of their visitation laws, States may be entitled to consider that certain relationships are such that to avoid the risk of harm, a best interests standard can be employed by their domestic relations courts in some circumstances.

Indeed, contemporary practice should give us some pause before rejecting the best interests of the child standard in all third-party visitation cases, as the Washington court has done. The standard has been recognized for many years as a basic tool of domestic relations law in visitation proceedings. Since 1965 all 50 States have enacted a third-party visitation statute of some sort. Each of these statutes, save one, permits a court order to issue in certain cases if visitation is found to be in the best interests of the child. While it is unnecessary for us to consider the constitutionality of any particular provision in the case now before us, it can be noted that the statutes also include a variety of methods for limiting parents' exposure to third-party visitation petitions and for ensuring parental decisions are given respect. Many States limit the identity of permissible petitioners by restricting visitation petitions to grandparents, or by requiring petitioners to show a substantial relationship with a child, or both. The statutes vary in other respects—for instance, some permit visitation petitions when there has been a change in circumstances such as divorce or death of a parent and some apply a presumption that parental decisions should control. Georgia's is the sole state legislature to have adopted a general harm to the child standard. . . .

In light of the inconclusive historical record and case law, as well as the almost universal adoption of the best interests standard for visitation disputes, I would be hard pressed to conclude the right to be free of such review in all cases is itself "'implicit in the concept of ordered liberty.'" In my view, it would be more appropriate to conclude that the constitutionality of the application of the best interests standard depends on more specific factors. In short, a fit parent's right vis-à-vis a complete stranger is one thing; her right vis-à-vis another parent or a de facto parent may be another. . . .

It must be recognized, of course, that a domestic relations proceeding in and of itself can constitute state intervention that is so disruptive of the parent-child relationship that the constitutional right of a custodial parent to make certain basic determinations for the child's welfare becomes implicated. . . . We owe it to the Nation's domestic relations legal structure, however, to proceed with caution.

It should suffice in this case to reverse the holding of the State Supreme Court that the application of the best interests of the child standard is always unconstitutional in third-party visitation cases. Whether, under the circumstances of this case, the order requiring visitation over the objection of this fit parent violated the Constitution ought to be reserved for further proceedings. Because of its sweeping ruling requiring the harm to the child standard, the Supreme Court of Washington did not have the occasion to address the specific visitation order the Troxels obtained. More specific guidance should await a case in which a State's highest court has considered all of the facts in the course of elaborating the protection afforded to parents by the laws of the State and by the Constitution itself. Furthermore, in my view, we need not address whether, under the correct constitutional standards, the Washington statute can be invalidated on its face. This question, too, ought to be addressed by the state court in the first instance.

In my view the judgment under review should be vacated and the case remanded for further proceedings.

QUESTIONS

1. In *Troxel*, the Court noted that there was "no allegation that Granville ever sought to cut off visitation entirely." Would the outcome of the case have been different if she had attempted to do so?

2. After *Troxel*, may a state use a "best interests" standard to determine whether or not to grant visitation with a child over a parent's objection?

Blixt v. Blixt

774 N.E.2d 1052 (Mass. 2002)

GREANY, J.

The plaintiff, John D. Blixt, is the maternal grandfather of the minor child of the defendants, a boy born on June 10, 1993. The defendants have never married each other, but the defendant Paul Sousa has been adjudicated the child's father. The child resides with his mother, the defendant Kristin Blixt (mother), and the defendants share legal custody of the child. The plaintiff filed a complaint in the Probate and Family Court seeking visitation with the child under G.L. c. 119, §39D, the so-called grandparent visitation statute (statute). The statute reads, in pertinent part, as follows:

> "If the parents of an unmarried minor child are divorced, married but living apart, under a temporary order or judgment of separate support, or if either or both parents are deceased, or if said unmarried minor child was born out of wedlock whose paternity has been adjudicated by a court of competent jurisdiction or whose father has signed an acknowledgement of paternity, and the parents do not reside together, the grandparents of such minor child may be granted reasonable visitation rights to the minor child during his minority by the probate and family court department of the trial court upon a written finding that such visitation rights would be in the best interest of the said minor child; provided, however, that such adjudication of paternity or acknowledgment of paternity shall not be required in order to proceed under this section where maternal grandparents are seeking such visitation rights. No such visitation rights shall be granted if said minor child has been adopted by a person other than a stepparent of such child and any visitation rights granted pursuant to this section prior to such adoption of the said minor child shall be terminated upon such adoption without any further action of the court."

The mother moved ... to dismiss the grandfather's complaint on the ground that the statute was unconstitutional on its face because it violated her substantive due process rights under the Fourteenth Amendment to the United States Constitution and cognate provisions of the Massachusetts Declaration of Rights. She also argued that the statute violated the equal protection provisions of both the Federal and State Constitutions. A judge in the Probate and Family Court, with respect to the mother's due process challenge, concluded that the statute was unconstitutional because it infringed on the defendants' "fundamental right to make decisions concerning the care, custody, and control of their child[ ]." The judge reasoned that the statute "contains no presumption that [the defendants] are acting in [the child's] best interest in denying visitation, nor . . . a requirement that the [p]laintiff demonstrate how [the child] is harmed by the denial of visitation." The grandfather appealed, and we granted the mother's application for direct appellate review. We conclude that the statute survives a facial challenge on due process grounds and also does not violate equal protection insofar as the mother's statutory classification is concerned. We, therefore, vacate the judgment and remand the case for further proceedings.

1. *Due process.* The mother's claim is to be decided under certain well-established principles governing a facial constitutional challenge as well as under the considerations stated by the United States Supreme Court in *Troxel v. Granville*, 530 U.S. 57 (2000). . . .

. . . It cannot be disputed that the State has a compelling interest to protect children from actual or potential harm. . . . As we shall explain more fully below, the statute can be interpreted to require a showing of harm to the child if visitation is not allowed. So interpreted, the statute furthers a compelling and legitimate State interest in mitigating potential harm to children in non-intact families, an area in which the State has been traditionally and actively involved.

. . . Contrary to the Washington statute under review in the *Troxel* case, which the plurality found to be "breathtakingly broad," *Troxel, supra* at 67, the Massachusetts statute, enacted before the *Troxel* decision, itself limits standing to seek visitation to grandparents in certain classes and circumstances. The mother readily acknowledges that the statute is not as broad as the Washington statute reviewed in the *Troxel* case, but she argues nonetheless that it cannot withstand any measure of constitutional scrutiny. We reject the mother's argument.

The statute adopts the "best interests of the child" standard as the test for determining visitation. This standard has long been used in Massachusetts to decide issues of custody and visitation and other issues relating to child welfare. The statute, however, uses the standard in a new context, and, based on the reasoning in the *Troxel* case, the standard, left unspecified, cannot survive a due process challenge. The interpretive role of an appellate court now comes into play. . . . [A]n appellate court may, in an appropriate case, construe a statute to render it constitutional. . . . We conclude that, operating with the guidance of the *Troxel* case and our case law in related areas, and law from other jurisdictions, the traditional best interests considerations (of which the Legislature is presumed to have been aware when it enacted the statute) can, and should, be construed to fit the statute's context and, thereby, satisfy due process.

To accord with due process, an evaluation of the best interests of the child under the statute requires that a parental decision concerning grandparent visitation be given presumptive validity. . . . To obtain visitation, the grandparents must rebut the presumption. The burden of proof will lie with them to establish, by a preponderance of the credible evidence, that a decision by the judge to deny visitation is not in the best interests of the child. More specifically, to succeed, the grandparents must allege and prove that the failure to grant visitation will cause the child significant harm by adversely affecting the child's health, safety, or welfare. The requirement of significant harm presupposes proof of a showing of a significant preexisting relationship between the grandparent and the child. In the absence of such a relationship, the grandparent must prove that visitation between grandparent and child is nevertheless necessary to protect the child from significant harm. Imposition of the standards just stated, as explained in specific written findings by the judge ensures a careful balance between the possibly conflicting rights of parents in securing their parental autonomy, and the best interests of children in avoiding actual harm to their well-being.

* * *

We conclude, in rejection of the facial due process challenge made by the mother, that the statute satisfies strict scrutiny because our construction narrowly tailors it to further the compelling State interest in protecting the welfare of a child who has experienced a disruption in the family unit from harm.

2. *Equal protection.* The mother claims that the statute violates equal protection because its classifications impermissibly burden parents of "non-traditional families" with litigation affecting their parental decisions. She correctly states that the statute does not apply to grandparents of a minor child whose parents are living together. The mother maintains that "[t]here are no distinguishing characteristics of widowed, divorced or otherwise single parents relevant to any interest of the [S]tate in promoting grandparent visitation under any standard of review." Essentially, the mother argues that the statute is both "underinclusive," because it does not burden biological parents of minor children who are living together at the time the petition is filed, and "overinclusive," because it burdens a single parent, or any two parents living separately, but who are, nonetheless, fully capable of making decisions in their children's best interest.

(a) Because the statute's classifications implicate fundamental parental rights, "strict scrutiny" analysis is again appropriate to evaluate the mother's equal protection challenge. . . .

(b) We review the validity of the statute on equal protection grounds only as it pertains to the class in which the mother belongs, that is, a parent of a nonmarital child born out of wedlock, living apart from the child's other parent, in this case, the child's father. . . . There is no reason in this case to depart from the established rule, followed both in Massachusetts and Federal courts, that, "[o]rdinarily one may not claim standing . . . to vindicate the constitutional rights of some third party." . . .

(c) Although it does not address equal protection concerns, the *Troxel* decision instructs us that it may be constitutionally permissible for a State to authorize court-ordered visitation in some situations, and not in others, as long as the visitation is ordered in carefully limited circumstances. Classifications within statutes authorizing some form of grandparent visitation grant standing depending on, in some States, the existence of a preexisting relation-ship with the child or, the domestic situation of the child's parents.[21] The mother asserts that classifications based on the living arrangements of a child's parents unfairly intrude into the lives of single parents, such as herself, and constitute "an outmoded notion of their capabilities as parents."

However, the mother mistakes the focus of our grandparent visitation statute. The statute's intent, as we have stated, is not to penalize parents but to safeguard children. . . .

The Legislature has long recognized, as it may, consistent with our Federal and State Constitutions, that children whose parents are unmarried and live apart may be at heightened risk for certain kinds of harm when compared with children of so-called intact families. . . . That children whose unmarried parents live apart may be especially vulnerable to real harm from the loss or absence of a grandparent's significant presence is a permissible legislative con-clusion, drawn from social experience and consistent with the State's com-pelling interest in protecting minors from harm. As *Troxel* recognizes, studies show that, in the over one-quarter of households in which children are raised by single parents, grandparents may play an increasingly important role in child rearing. Thus, grandparents may play an increasingly important role in a child's development. This important role, when it does develop, does not arise by accident, but by a parent's deliberate choice to invite the grandparent into the family fold, and to permit (or encourage) a bond between grandparent and grandchild that may then become crucial to the child's physical or emo-tional security. In such situations, the State's intervention may be necessary to secure the child's well-being from traumatic separation from the grandparent. Such intervention has nothing to do with appeasing a grandparent's hurt feelings, castigating a parent's lifestyle, or perpetuating an illusion of family unity. It has everything to do with protecting the child, insofar as possible, by preserving the fruits of significant developmental attachment whose seeds were planted by a parent.

Moreover, the Legislature may, within its narrow field of action under our equal protection guarantees, presume that the burden of the traumatic loss of a grandparent's significant presence may fall most heavily on the child whose unmarried parents live apart and who may not have or be able to draw on the resources of two parents in coping with his or her loss. Such a child may already be vulnerable to the feelings of loss, inadequacy, and insecurity that our society still often visits on those children whose family structure departs from an idealized two-parent norm. This is not to say that every child whose parents are unmarried and live apart is particularly vulnerable

---

21. This approach is one taken by a large number of States. . . . *See, e.g.,* Ariz. Rev. Stat. Ann. §25-409(A)(1) and (2) (West 2000) (when marriage of child's parents dissolved, or one parent deceased or missing, for three months); Ark. Code Ann. §9-13-103(a)(1)(A) (LexisNexis 2002) (when marital relationship between parents severed by death, divorce, or legal separation); Fla. Stat. Ann. §752.01(1) (West Supp. 2002) (when marriage of parents of child dissolved, one parent has deserted child, or child born out of wedlock). . . .

to the harm of a grandparent's absence, or that every child in a two-parent household will be shielded from such harm. We merely hold that the Legislature does not offend the principles of equal protection, as seen through the narrow lens of strict scrutiny, by confining the reach of the grandparent visitation statute, as we construe it today, to a discrete class of children within the discrete class of households at issue.

* * *

. . . The judgment dismissing the complaint is vacated, and the case is to stand for further proceedings in the Probate and Family Court consistent with this opinion.

So ordered.

COWIN, J. (dissenting in part) [dissent omitted].

SOSMAN, J. (dissenting, with whom IRELAND, J., joins).

The grandparent visitation statute at issue in today's opinion, G.L. c. 119, §39D, infringes on parents' fundamental right to make decisions concerning the upbringing of their children. It also creates classifications of parents, subjecting some of them to State interference in parental decision-making while leaving others free of such interference. As drafted, the statute violates both due process and equal protection guarantees, as neither its substantive provisions nor its classifications satisfy the requirement that they be narrowly tailored to serve a compelling State interest. Recognizing that the statute as drafted cannot withstand strict scrutiny, the court has simply substituted for the statute's actual provisions a general statement articulating the minimum constitutional requirements for such a statute and, for good measure, invented a special rule of pleading for grandparent visitation cases. This overhaul of the statute cannot be justified as mere "interpretation." Where, as here, the statute is unconstitutional on its face, it is our job to say so and to let the Legislature rewrite the statute if and as it wishes.

* * *

1. Substantive due process. The court acknowledges, as it must, that a statute impinging on parental decision-making implicates a fundamental right. . . .

a. Compelling State interest. The State's interest in "protecting the well-being of children" qualifies as a compelling State interest. The State's legitimate and compelling interest in the welfare of children, however, does not encompass all things that might be beneficial to children and does not confer on the State a power to mandate, over the objection of a fit, competent parent, anything that might be viewed as desirable for young people. Rather, in context, what has been recognized within the sphere of a compelling State interest to protect the "well-being of children" is an interest to prevent injury, abuse, trauma, exploitation, severe deprivation, and other comparable forms of significant harm.

* * *

Healthy relationships with grandparents are unquestionably of benefit to children. That such relationships are good for children does not allow the

State to force such relationships on them contrary to the wishes of their parents. . . .

Of course, when something is necessary to a child's "well-being," the State may intervene to make sure that the child is not deprived of that necessity. Grandparents, as wonderful as they are, are not a necessity. Children can and do grow up to be healthy, stable, productive members of society without them. Depriving children of relationships with their grandparents is not the equivalent of depriving them of health care, food, shelter, security, or a basic education. *See Santi v. Santi*, 633 N.W.2d 312, 318 (Iowa 2001) (no compelling State interest served by grandparent visitation statute, noting that "the case before us is not about car seats or vaccinations").

* * *

Consistent with considerable precedent from other States, both pre- and post-*Troxel*, today's decision appropriately recognizes that visitation orders would be unconstitutional absent a showing of significant harm to the child.[1]

* * *

As drafted, our grandparent visitation statute allows a judge to determine a child's "best interest" and, predicated solely on that determination, to countermand the decision of the child's fit, competent parents. The statute operates on the simple but erroneous assumption that judges are best equipped to resolve these intra-family disputes, and assumes that judges can therefore best decide whether and on what terms children should visit with their grandparents.[2] The statute is not limited to cases where significant harm from the parent's decision has been demonstrated. It does not even require any showing of a preexisting relationship between the grandparent and the child. It does not require any showing of parental unfitness or even some parental shortcoming akin to or suggesting a risk of unfitness. As such, it is not narrowly tailored to serve any compelling State interest, and therefore does not withstand strict scrutiny.

b. Redrafting the statute. Recognizing that our grandparent visitation statute's reliance on the "best interest" of the child standard "cannot survive a due process challenge" in the wake of *Troxel*, 437 Mass. at 657, 774 N.E.2d at 1060, the court today seeks to salvage its constitutionality by "interpreting"

---

1. Today's opinion does not seek to justify the visitation statute on the ground that it protects any "right" of grandparents. Grandparents have no constitutional "right" to visit their grandchildren, nor was any such "right" recognized at common law. . . . A grandparent's desire to enjoy a relationship with a grandchild, no matter how intense, is not a "right" to have such a relationship. No one has a "right" to associate with other people's children, and the mere fact that a person is a blood relative of those children does not confer any such "right." As such, today's opinion wisely declines to identify protection of a nonexistent "right" as a justification for this statute.

2. It also assumes that relationships with grandparents that are forced in this manner can confer a benefit on children. This is at best a dubious proposition. The warm, nurturing, and loving relationships we had with our grandparents were not the product of divisive intrafamily litigation and court orders that undermined our parents' authority. . . .

the term "best interest" to include the requirement that a fit parent's decision on visitation be given "presumptive validity" and allowing grandparents to overcome that presumption only if they establish, by a preponderance of the evidence, that the denial of visitation will "cause the child significant harm by adversely affecting the child's health, safety, or welfare." 437 Mass. at 658, 774 N.E.2d at 1060. . . . This is not "interpretation," or at least it is not a form of "interpretation" that comports with our judicial role. Rather, it is legislation masquerading as interpretation in order to salvage an admittedly unconstitutional statute.

* * *

This is not only legislation—the court does not even pretend that this is "interpretation"—but it is ineffective legislation at that. The affidavit requirement imposed by today's decision will do little (if anything) to relieve parents of the burdens of this kind of litigation. Parents will still have to hire a lawyer in order to pursue a motion to dismiss; and, as long as the grandparent can file a complaint or affidavit that alleges any disruption of a prior relationship with the child (and therefore a basis for claiming that the child will be "harmed" by the severance of that relationship), the motion to dismiss will not succeed in promptly terminating what has proved to be a protracted form of litigation. Fit, competent parents will still be hauled into court, and required to pay legal fees, to explain to a judge their reasons for deciding not to let their child visit with a particular grandparent on particular terms. In order to defeat the request for visitation, they may have to "expose what can only be described as the family's 'dirty linen.'" . . .

. . . As noted in today's opinion, all fifty States have adopted some form of grandparent visitation statute, and those statutes "vary considerably." There is a vast array of options amongst the differing provisions, both substantive and procedural, that States have enacted. It is not up to this court to pick and choose from among that vast array simply to rescue this statute. Such choices are the essence of legislation, not judicial interpretation.

* * *

3. *Equal protection.* The grandparent visitation statute also suffers glaring equal protection defects. It makes some parents and children subject to complaints for grandparent visitation, but exempts others, predicated entirely on the parents' living arrangements. Because the statute implicates a fundamental liberty interest, the statute's classifications must also be subjected to strict scrutiny. . . .

This distinction between parents whose fundamental rights are to be infringed cannot withstand strict scrutiny. Where the compelling State interest at stake is the prevention of significant harm to children, the classifications must be narrowly tailored to serve that interest, i.e., to identify children who are more likely to be harmed by, or who will suffer greater harm from, the denial of visitation with grandparents. There may be some defining characteristics that would operate, in a narrowly tailored way, to identify such children, but the mere fact that the child's biological parents do not live in the same household does not identify a category of at-risk children with anything approaching the requisite degree of precision. The mother correctly contends that the classifications in the statute are both overinclusive, in that they sweep into the statute large numbers of children at no greater risk of harm from the denial of visitation, and underinclusive, in that they exclude many common domestic situations that do expose children to an increased risk of harm from the denial of visitation.

Invoking principles governing representative standing and the requirement that only someone injured by a statute may challenge its constitutionality, the court concludes that it can essentially ignore the mother's equal protection arguments, and addresses only the claim of overinclusiveness at issue in the precise category into which these parents are assigned (i.e., never married and not living together). . . .

Under the court's approach . . . no one could ever bring an equal protection challenge based on the underinclusiveness of a statute burdening fundamental rights, even though underinclusiveness would be one way in which a statute may fail to be narrowly tailored. Persons who have escaped the burdens of such a statute are not going to bring suit asking that those burdens be placed on them, and, according to the court today, those who have been unfairly singled out for such infringement of their rights may not complain that the statute unfairly fails to reach others who are at least as deserving of the statute's burdens. And, under the court's approach, claims of overinclusiveness will be looked at in the isolation of the plaintiff's own category under a statute, ignoring the actual "tailoring" of the statute as a whole and pretending that the statute was addressed at only that single category. . . . Rather than endorse the court's cramped view of equal protection guarantees, . . . I would consider whether this statute, as a whole, qualifies as narrowly tailored to serve the identified compelling State interest that it ostensibly serves. . . . [T]he statute fails that test.

* * *

Essentially all parents raising children in nontraditional families are pulled into this statutory scheme. Many gay and lesbian couples raising children will be subject to this form of judicial interference, as the gay or lesbian parent of the child is no longer residing with the child's other biological parent. Divorced, single, or widowed parents who move in with other family members, and raise their children in an extended family, are subject to complaints under the statute, as are all parents who later live with or even marry someone other than a biological parent of the child. And, by definition, any parent who is raising his or her child single-handedly is subject to such proceedings. Rather than recognize the wealth of diversity in today's American family, this statute casts a slur on the parenting abilities of anyone whose family living arrangements deviate from the traditional, nuclear family consisting of father, mother, and their biological children.

Looking solely at the category of parents who were never married to each other and who are not presently living together, the court resorts to vague generalizations verging on pure stereotypes of families that are not "intact" to justify subjecting such parents, but not others, to the intrusive burdens of the visitation statute. . . .

The court does correctly point out that parents who are trying to raise a child single-handedly more often make a "deliberate choice" to foster a "bond" between the child and a grandparent, such that State intervention "may be necessary to secure the child's well-being from traumatic separation from the grandparent." 437 Mass. at 664, 774 N.E.2d at 1064. Again, however, the classification at issue not only fails as a narrowly tailored definition of single-parent households where such reliance on a grandparent may have developed, but the statute does not even require as a predicate that there be any prior relationship with the grandparent, let alone one that has become "crucial to the child's physical or emotional security." 437 Mass. at 664, 774 N.E.2d at 1064. A parent may, from the child's birth, have prohibited any contact with the grandparent, yet the completely estranged grandparent may, based solely on the parents' living arrangements, bring a claim for visitation. If the objective is to reach a category of children who have developed a "crucial" relationship with a grandparent, a category of children of unwed parents living apart is not a narrowly tailored definition of children who have such relationships, and the statute could easily articulate the category that is now proffered as the justification for the overbroad category into which these parents fall.

What is also puzzling about this justification is its somewhat circular logic. If single parents have voluntarily fostered a bond between child and grandparent, why would they then be more likely than other parents to harm the child by severing that bond? To the contrary, single parents have a greater, not a lesser, incentive to maintain the relationships on which they have deliberately led the child to rely. . . . Put bluntly, grandparents provide "free babysitting," a precious commodity to any single parent, and a commodity they are unlikely to refuse absent some compelling reason. It is not surprising that in such households, as a purely voluntary matter, "grandparents may play an increasingly important role in child rearing," 437 Mass. at 663, 774 N.E.2d at 1064, but there is nothing to indicate that, having done so, single parents are more likely to make an irrational about-face and banish the grandparent who has provided that assistance to date.

Finally, the court's justification for this distinction relies on a great deal of what "may" be the case—grandparents "may" play an important role for such children, such children "may be especially vulnerable" or "may be at heightened risk." 437 Mass. at 663, 774 N.E.2d at 1064. . . . However, the requirement that a statute be narrowly tailored to serve a compelling State interest requires more than a mere possibility, more than just rough approximations and tenuous assumptions, to justify burdening some parents' fundamental rights while exempting other parents from those burdens. The distinctions drawn must be "necessary" to promote the identified compelling interest, not just rationally related to it. Here, the approximations, possibilities, and assumptions invoked by the court do not suffice for purposes of the strict scrutiny to which this statute must be subjected.

* * *

[T]hese classifications were drawn for the express purpose of protecting "grandparents' rights." The obvious concern underlying each of these classifications is that the parents of the absent or deceased parent no longer have anyone in the child's household with whom they have a blood relationship and, lacking such a relationship, they understandably fear that the remaining parent will be less accommodating of their desire to see the grandchildren. From the grandparents' point of view, this is unquestionably a heart-wrenching situation, and their worries are well founded. It is readily apparent that the desire to "balance the scales" for such dispossessed grandparents is the true basis for the statute's classifications. Indeed, throughout the statute's history, the various enactments that comprise G.L. c. 119, §39D, have been referred to as promoting "grandparents' visitation rights," not as promoting the welfare of children, with each successive enactment identifying yet another category of grandparents who might be "frozen out" of their grandchildren's lives because of the departure or death of one parent. . . .

As such we are now dealing with legislation that was designed, and its categories created, for the purpose of serving a nonexistent "right" that does not qualify as a compelling State interest. . . . Here, the categories of grandparents whose "rights" are to be protected serve to identify those grandparents who are the least able to exert influence over the grandchild's remaining natural, custodial parent. Those same categories do not serve to identify children with a greater need for grandparent visitation. Trying to justify a statute designed to further the interests of grandparents on the theory that it narrowly defines a category of grandchildren in need is the equivalent of saying that a square peg is narrowly tailored to fit a round hole.

I would hold that the statute's equal protection infirmities must also be addressed by the Legislature, and that they cannot be cured by resort to vague generalizations about families that are not "intact." . . . Classifications that identify children at greater risk can surely be drawn with greater precision than the classifications in this statute. As the statute stands, however, the one characteristic that results in parents being subject to this infringement on family autonomy is not a characteristic that is a narrowly tailored predictor of children at risk. . . .

NOTES

1. *Status of grandparent visitation statutes. Troxel* encouraged a spate of constitutional challenges to grandparent visitation statutes. Some of these have been successful. As a result, although all 50 states have enacted grandparent visitation statutes, not all states have such a statute in effect. *See* Michael K. Goldberg, *A Survey of the Fifty States' Grandparent Visitation Statutes*, 10 Marq. Elder's Advisor 245 (2009).

2. *Uncertainty in the law related to grandparent visitation.* There remains significant uncertainty as to what is required for visitation statutes to survive constitutional scrutiny after *Troxel*. For example, courts have differed on whether a showing of the probability of harm to the child is required before visitation can be ordered against a parent's wishes. *See* Daniel R. Victor & Keri L. Middleditch, *Grandparent Visitation: A Survey of History, Jurisprudence, and Legislative Trends Across the United States in the Past Decade*, 22 J. Am. Acad. Matrim. Law. 391, 401-05 (2009) (exploring how different jurisdictions interpret *Troxel*).

3. *Factors relevant to a child's best interest.* Courts typically consider a broad array of factors in determining a child's best interest. For example, in *Walker v. Blair*, 382 S.W.3d 862 (Ky. 2012), the Kentucky Supreme Court held that to withstand constitutional scrutiny after *Troxel*, Kentucky's grandparent visitation statute should be interpreted as requiring grandparents to prove by clear and convincing evidence that requested visitation is in the best interest of the child. The court explained that this meant that:

> The grandparent petitioning for visitation must rebut this presumption [that a fit parent acts in the child's best interest] with clear and convincing evidence that visitation with the grandparent is in the child's best interest. In other words, the grandparent must show that the fit parent is clearly mistaken in the belief that grandparent visitation is not in the child's best interest. If the grandparent fails to present such evidence to the court, then parental opposition alone is sufficient to deny the grandparent visitation.
>
> A trial court can look at several factors to determine whether visitation is clearly in the child's best interests . . . including:
> 1) the nature and stability of the relationship between the child and the grandparent seeking visitation;
> 2) the amount of time the grandparent and child spent together;
> 3) the potential detriments and benefits to the child from granting visitation;
> 4) the effect granting visitation would have on the child's relationship with the parents;
> 5) the physical and emotional health of all the adults involved, parents and grandparents alike;
> 6) the stability of the child's living and schooling arrangements; . . .
> 7) the wishes and preferences of the child[; and]
> 8) the motivation of the adults participating in the grandparent visitation proceedings.
>
> * * *
>
> [T]he trial court should not attempt to determine whether the parent is actually fit before presuming that the parent is acting in the child's best interest. The trial court must presume that a parent adequately cares for his or her child (i.e., is fit) and acts in the child's best interest.

Id. at 871.

4. *Who is a grandparent?* In *Peters v. Costello*, 891 A.2d 705 (Pa. 2005), Daniel and Maryann Costello sought visitation under Pennsylvania's Grandparent

Visitation Act with a preschool-age girl whom they viewed as their grand-daughter. The child was the daughter of Francesca Szypula, who the Costellos had raised since Francesca was less than a year old. The girl's father, who had been granted primary physical custody of her, objected to the Costellos' petition and alleged that the Costellos lacked standing under the visitation statute because they were not related to the child either by blood or by adoption. The trial court and superior court disagreed, and the Pennsylvania Supreme Court affirmed, finding that the Costellos had standing because they stood *in loco parentis* to Francesca, the child's mother. The court explained that since the visitation statute failed to define the term "grandparent," the court would look to the "'common and approved usage' of the term 'grandparent'" and that persons acting *in loco parentis* to a parent fell within that meaning.

QUESTIONS

1. Assuming that the statute at issue in *Blixt* was unconstitutional without further interpretation, are there alternative ways that the court could have construed it to render it constitutional?

2. In finding that the state did not have a compelling interest in her dissent in *Blixt*, Justice Sosman explained that grandparents are not a necessity. To support her conclusion, Justice Sosman cited an Iowa case that distinguished the state's interest in grandparent visitation from the state's interest in ensuring that children are not deprived of necessities such as "car seats and vaccinations." Do you agree with Sosman's characterization of the role of grandparents? Can a state ever have a compelling interest in permitting grandparent visitation if grandparents are not a necessity?

3. Are grandparents' interests in visitation derivative of their child's right to such visitation, or may grandparents have a legally privileged interest in visitation with a grandchild even if their child would not have such an interest? For example, should grandparents have a right to visitation with children conceived using their son's donor sperm? Grandparents' rights advocate Jolyn Rudelson has argued that, as a result of sperm donation, "Grandparents are losing out on one of their most important roles, connecting their family generations: those who came before and those who will follow. In addition the paternal grandfathers are losing the right to have their name passed on, their only hope for immortality." Jolyn Rudelson, *Grandparents Deprived of Their Donor Grandchildren, available at* http://familyscholars.org/2011/06/23/grandparents-deprived-of-their-donor-grandchildren. Do you agree?

PROBLEM

Consider the facts of *Walker v. Blair*, 283 S.W.3d 862 (Ky. 2012):

> Michelle Walker ("Walker") and Steve Blair ("Steve") had one child in common, B.B. Steve committed suicide. And a few months later, Steve's

mother, Donna Blair ("Blair"), filed a petition . . . to establish grandparent visitation with five-year-old B.B. Walker opposed Blair's visitation petition and filed a motion to dismiss. . . . The trial court held an evidentiary hearing in which Walker, Blair, and Martin Blair testified. Martin Blair is Blair's ex-husband and B.B.'s paternal grandfather.

Blair testified that she and B.B. had a close, loving relationship. And she exhibited pictures of B.B.'s baptism, birthdays, holidays, and other occasions. Blair claimed that she often babysat B.B. and took him swimming, to the movies, and on outings to Rough River. She and Walker got along well for most of B.B.'s life. But, after Steve's death, Blair called Walker and asked if Steve's suicide made her happy. She testified that she thinks Walker and her husband contributed to Steve's suicide but claimed that she no longer feels animosity toward them. At the time of the hearing, Blair was divorced from Martin Blair but still saw him once or twice weekly. Blair also had a history of depression. At the time of the hearing, she was taking three different antidepressant medications. She received counseling before and after Steve's death but had not seen her therapist for several months before the evidentiary hearing. She testified that her mental condition is stable.

Martin Blair also testified at the hearing. He acknowledged that an active domestic violence order (DVO) prohibited him from all contact with Walker. A court issued the DVO when, following Steve's suicide, Martin threatened to kill Walker and her husband. Martin, who is an alcoholic, was arrested for violating the DVO shortly after it was entered. He testified that he believes Walker contributed to Steve's suicide. And Martin acknowledged that he would not be allowed to see B.B. if Blair is granted visitation. Walker testified that Blair had infrequent contact with B.B. According to Walker, Blair saw B.B. only when Steve exercised his right to see B.B. Walker placed B.B. in counseling after his father's suicide. Walker stated that B.B. has not asked to see or call his grandparents, and he does not recognize pictures of his grandparents. Although Walker opposed a court-ordered visitation schedule, she testified that she would follow the recommendation of B.B.'s therapist regarding his contact with Blair.

Id. at 866-67.

Should the court have granted Donna Blair visitation? Would doing so be constitutional? What facts should be considered most (or least) relevant to the court's determination?

EXERCISE 10.1

You are the counsel to the State of East Arizona's Senate Committee on Children and Families. The Chair of the Committee believes that the state's current child visitation statute is unlawful after *Troxel.* He wants you to draft a new statute that is both constitutional and, in his words, "good for families."

> a. Working alone or in a small group, draft a proposed statute for the Chair. As part of your work, please address whether grandparents should be granted greater rights to visitation than other potential visitors.
> b. Once you have drafted your proposed statute, write a memo to the Chair explaining why your statute is constitutional, the policy choices it reflects, and the rationale behind those policy choices.

C. GRANDPARENTS AS SUPPLEMENTAL CARE PROVIDERS

Most grandparents will, at some point in time, provide unpaid care for a grandchild. In many families with young children, parents rely on grandparents to provide significant amounts of childcare. Indeed, grandparents are the primary source of childcare for 30 percent of working mothers with children under the age of five. In a 2013 article, Professor Jessica Dixon Weaver described the prevalence and experience of grandparents caring for grandchildren, writing:

> Seventy-two percent of grandparents . . . take care of their grandchildren on a regular basis, and thirteen percent are primary caregivers for their grandchildren. The discrepancy in these statistics illustrates several tenets. First, there is a large segment of American parents who either have no other better option for affordable, quality care for their children, or like the First Lady [Michelle Obama], prefer to have their children cared for by a grandparent. Second, there is a large segment of American grandparents who are either willing or coerced to care for their grandchildren, typically without pay. Third, . . . something altruistic drives them to take on the responsibility of caregiving for a second generation.
>
> Whether amenable or coerced, a grandparent's choice to provide child care has a major socio-legal impact on their lives and on society. Grandparents who serve as full-time or part-time caregivers provide approximately $39.2 billion worth of unpaid service to their grandchildren. Most of this work is borne by women, the burden carriers in most family units, who typically give of themselves sacrificially until an accident, disease, or old age catches up with them. . . .
>
> . . . Grandparents' roles in the lives of their families have been increasing over the last decade. A record forty-nine million Americans (16.1 percent) live in a family household that contains at least two adult generations, or a grandparent and at least one other generation. The return of the

multigenerational family represents a sharp reversal from the past; between 1940 and 1980, the number of Americans living in such households declined from twenty-five percent to twelve percent. There are several reasons for the growth in multigenerational households since 1980, including an increase in the population of immigrants and the rising median age of first marriage of all adults. The main reason for the sudden spike in the last five years, however, is the Great Recession. During poor economic times the multigenerational family has reemerged, driven partly by job losses and home foreclosures. In some cases, adult children are moving back home with their parents, often with their nuclear families in tow. In other instances, grandparents are moving in with their adult children and grandchildren. For the most part, the grandparents are not in need of physical care—the choice is made for both financial and social reasons.

Today, there are various types of multigenerational living, as well as caretaking arrangements, among family members. For example, forty-nine percent of parents have one of their own parents living thirty minutes or less from them, and ten percent have a parent living with them in their home. Sixty-one percent of parents of two-year-olds to seventeen-year-olds say that grandparents assist with rearing their children. . . .

The sense of stability that grandparents offer is well documented. From an anthropological standpoint, a grandmother's presence and help have been shown to influence the reproductive success of kin. Beyond that, multigenerational housing can serve important social policy goals such as strengthening family ties and promoting age integration. The presence of grandparents in the home promotes sharing of parenting responsibilities, decreases involvement of children in delinquent activities, reduces episodes of depression among children, and improves children's academic performance. Another benefit includes increasing generational solidarity, which helps erode ageism.

Jessica Dixon Weaver, *Grandma in the White House: Support for Intergenerational Caregiving*, 43 SETON HALL L. REV. 1, 7, 10-11, 18 (2013).

Despite the economic and social benefits that grandparent caregivers provide, grandparents who provide such care can face significant economic disadvantages. For example, they may forgo paid employment, which may result not only in an immediate loss of income but also in a subsequent decrease in Social Security and pension benefits. Similarly, grandparents are not entitled to take leave to care for an ill grandchild under the federal Family and Medical Leave Act (FMLA) unless they are *in loco parentis* (i.e., standing in the place of parents).

NOTES

1. *Leave for the birth of a grandchild.* A grandparent generally cannot use the FMLA to obtain leave to attend or provide care associated with the birth of a grandchild. The FMLA does not cover leave to care for a grandchild under most circumstances, and an adult child's pregnancy is not in itself sufficient

to give rise to the right to leave. As the court explained in *Cruz v. Publix Super Markets, Inc.*, 428 F.3d 1379, 1383 (11th Cir. 2005):

> [B]eing pregnant, as opposed to being incapacitated because of pregnancy, is not a 'serious health condition' within the meaning of the FMLA. Thus, the protections of the FMLA do not extend to an employee taking leave to care for his or her adult child simply because that child is pregnant, unless, for example, that child is incapacitated due to the pregnancy.

2. *Further reading.* For further discussion of the disadvantages faced by grandparent caregivers, see Professor Weaver's article excerpted in this subsection, which explores how employment, tax, and housing laws fail to support, as well as negatively impact, the ability of grandparents to care for their grandchildren.

PROBLEM

Pamela, an elementary school teacher in her late 50s, has begun to think about retiring. She enjoys teaching, but she feels worn out from the constant disciplinary demands of her job and would like to have more time for herself. Her daughter and son-in-law, Sara and Mike, recently welcomed their third child. Both Sara and Mike are employed full-time outside of the home. They have asked Pamela if she would consider being the nanny for their new infant and also providing after-school care to the other two children. Pamela is intrigued by the possibility, as it would allow her to spend more time with all three grandchildren, but is unsure whether it is right for her. What should Pamela consider when deciding whether or not to take on this new role?

D. GRANDPARENTS AS PARENTS

As of the 2010 census, there were 4.9 million children residing in grandparent-headed households. Of these, approximately 20 percent (or more than 964,000) were being raised by their grandparents with neither of their parents present.

The majority of grandparents raising grandchildren are not elderly. Indeed, only approximately 28 percent of them are over age 65. However, grandparents raising grandchildren face other vulnerabilities. For example, grandparents raising grandchildren are more likely to be living below the poverty line than are other types of families raising children, and tend to be in poorer physical and mental health than their peers who do not have caretaking roles. Children being raised by grandparents, in turn, disproportionately lack health insurance, and frequently have experienced significant family problems. Divorce, parental drug abuse, and child abuse are the three most common reasons for grandparents raising grandchildren, followed by teen pregnancy, parental incarceration, and the death or disability of a parent.

Unfortunately, grandparents raising grandchildren often lack critical knowledge about their legal rights and entitlements. Elder law attorneys can help grandparents with these issues.

1. Financial Support

A variety of types of financial support may be available to a grandparent raising his or her grandchild. Sources of financial assistance include:

- *TANF grants.* Grandparents can apply for Temporary Assistance to Needy Families (TANF), often called "welfare." They can apply either for a family grant (eligibility for which will depend on their resources as well as the grandchild's) or a child-only grant (eligibility for which will not depend on the grandparent's resources). To obtain TANF monies, a grandparent must generally agree to cooperate with state efforts to collect child support from the grandchild's parents.
- *Foster care payments.* Foster care payments can be made to grandparent caregivers. However, because only approximately one-fourth of the children being raised by grandparents are in formal foster families, most grandparent-headed households do not receive this assistance.
- *Adoption assistance payments.* The federal government helps states to pay adoptive parents who adopt a child with special needs. Such payments may therefore be available to grandparents who adopt their grandchild with special needs.
- *Social Security payments.* Disabled grandchildren may be eligible for SSI. Grandchildren with retired or disabled parents may be eligible for OASDI benefits. In addition, grandchildren who are dependents of the grandparent can be eligible for OASDI benefits on their grandparent's earning record if the grandparent is raising the grandchild because of a death of a parent, the grandchild began living with the grandparent before age 18, and the child received at least one-half of his or her support from the grandparent during the year prior to the grandparent becoming eligible for OASDI benefits.
- *Payments for grandparent guardians.* Some states have begun programs that provide financial assistance to grandparents who are the legal guardian of a grandchild.
- *Child support.* A child's entitlement to child support from his or her parents does not end simply because he or she lives with a grandparent.

For further discussion of financial supports for grandparents raising grandchildren, see Carole B. Cox, *Policy and Custodial Parents*, 11 Marq. Elder's Advisor 281 (2010).

2. Custody and Decision-Making Authority for Grandchildren

Some grandparents become the primary caregiver for a grandchild as a result of the state placing the grandchild with the grandparent. All states now give some preference to placing children who are removed from the care of their parents (typically because of abuse or neglect) with family members instead of unrelated persons. As a result of this preference for *kinship care*, states frequently look to grandparents to care for children who would otherwise be placed in foster care with non-blood relatives. Kinship care is seen as desirable because, among other things, it promotes continuity of family relationships and preserves cultural and community ties.

Over the past several decades, there has been a large increase in the rate at which states place grandchildren with grandparents; however, grandparents most often come to serve as primary caregivers as a result of private arrangements with the child's parent or parents. Relatively little is known about the frequency or structure of these "voluntary" or "private" kinship care arrangements, although it is likely that most are the result of informal understandings.

Thus, many grandparents raising a grandchild have no formal legal relationship with that grandchild. This informality can create significant difficulties because in order to have authority to make decisions on behalf of a child, an individual typically must be the child's legal guardian or custodian. The extent to which lack of decision-making authority poses a problem, however, depends on the state and the type of decision that the grandparent wishes to make. In an effort to facilitate decision-making for children, the majority of states have enacted policies that empower relative caregivers to consent to a child's medical care even if they have only informal custody of the child. Similarly, almost half of the states have legislation empowering relative caregivers without formal custody arrangements to enroll a child in school or to consent to the child's participation in extracurricular activities. *See* Meredith Minkler, Grandparents & Other Relatives Raising Children: Characteristics, Needs, Best Practices, & Implications for the Aging Network (2001).

Nevertheless, in many cases, obtaining formal guardianship or custody of a grandchild will be of significant help to a grandparent who is raising his or her grandchild. The cases that follow explore how courts respond to a grandparent's request for custody against the competing claim of a parent.

In re Paternity of V.M.

790 N.E.2d 1005 (Ind. App. 2003)

Kirsch, Judge.

Victor Benavides appeals the trial court's decision denying his request for modification of permanent custody of his two minor children, V.M. and V.B., which had been previously placed with the children's maternal grandfather

Phillip Moore. Benavides raises two issues for review, which we consolidate and rephrase as: whether the trial court erred in denying his petition for modification of custody and continuing permanent custody with Moore on the basis that doing so was in the best interests of the children.

We affirm.

FACTS AND PROCEDURAL HISTORY

Benavides is the biological father of V.M., age 9, and V.B., age 7, and although Benavides assumed a parental role of A.M., age 11, he is not her biological father or her stepfather. All three children were born out of wedlock. Approximately seven years ago, the children's mother agreed to relinquish the care and custody of the children to her father. She has never expressed a real interest in the children and has had very little contact with them. She currently lives in Arizona and did not attend the custody hearing. Because of his lack of fitness and willingness to parent the children, due in large part to his past drinking problems and criminal behavior, Benavides also voluntarily relinquished custody of the children to Moore. It is undisputed that neither parent could then provide for the needs of the children.

Benavides is now married and has a biological child with his wife and two stepchildren. Until two or three years ago, Benavides had only sporadic contact with V.M. and V.B. Since then, he quit drinking and using drugs, attends church regularly, has consistent visitation with the children on alternate weekends, and pays child support to Moore.

In November 2001, Moore filed a petition with the trial court to make the temporary custody order a permanent order. Benavides did not dispute this at the time. After Moore and his wife moved the three children to Pittsboro from Lebanon, where Benavides resides, Benavides filed a petition for modification of custody of the children. A hearing was held on December 27, 2002, and the trial court denied the modification of custody on January 21, 2003, but awarded liberal visitation with all three children. Benavides appeals from this order.

DISCUSSION AND DECISION

Indiana law has traditionally recognized that "natural parents are entitled to the custody of their minor children, except when they are unsuitable persons to be entrusted with their care, control, and education." *Gilmore v. Kitson*, 165 Ind. 402, 406, 74 N.E. 1083, 1084 (1905). . . .

Because appellate courts defer to the trial court's discretion, we disturb the judgment only where there is no evidence supporting the findings or where the findings fail to support the judgment. . . .

. . . [I]t is presumed that it was in the best interest of the children to be placed in the custody of their natural father. The Moores had the burden to overcome that presumption. Here, the trial court concluded that staying with the Moores was in the children's best interests, and it articulated specific reasons for its conclusion. In pertinent part, the trial court entered the following order maintaining custody of the children with the Moores:

> 19. The issues before the Court are not just stability and consistency or whether or not Mr. Benavides is capable of caring for the children. Of course, he is now capable of caring for the children. He has made dramatic changes, for the better, to his life. He and [his wife] are making a very good life together. The issues before the court are much more complicated. . . .

> 24. Mr. Benavides previously consented to the present arrangement. The children are doing well in their new school. They like their new school. Mr. Benavides already has a household with a young daughter and two step-sons. [The other three children] are in a home where they are the focal point of Mr. and Mrs. Moore's affection and attention. The children have a new home, a larger home and more privacy. The children['s] mental, emotional, and financial needs are all being met.

> 25. The Court is exercising its sound discretion in this area to do what is best and what is right for the children at the present time. This is not an easy, flippant decision. The Court does not wish to separate the children as such a decision would (not) [sic] be advantageous to the children and certainly not in their best interest, any of them.

> 26. The Court understands that Mr. Benavides disparately [sic] wants to fulfill his responsibilities as a parent. However, he already has his hands full and Mr. and Mrs. Moore have been doing a very good job in his absences. The primary concern then becomes the children.

> 27. Thus, the best interests of the three children are the paramount consideration of this Court. Mr. Benavides consented to the present arrangement. Nothing has changed to such a degree to warrant a modification of custody.

> 28. Upon careful consideration of the testimony, including the in-camera interviews, the Court further concludes that the relationship and affections between Mr. Moore and the children have become so interwoven that to sever them, by modifying custody (and therefore removing the children from the only home they have known for many years and uprooting them from their new school and friends) would seriously mar and endanger the future happiness of the children. The mental and emotional well being of the children must be considered and giv[en] great deference by everyone.

> 29. The best interests of each of the children demand that they remain in the custody of Mr. Moore. Clear and convincing evidence has been provided to the Court that this is what is best and right for the children. There is a substantial and significant benefit to the children by remaining in the custody of Mr. Moore.

Our review of the record before us on appeal supports the conclusion that the presumption in favor of Benavides having custody of the children was rebutted by evidence of Benavides' past unfitness, voluntary abandonment of the children, long acquiescence of the Moore's custody, and other factors that would rebut the strong presumption in favor of Benavides. While sympathetic to the relationship that has developed between the children and Benavides, we acknowledge the upheaval that a change in custody in this case would undoubtedly involve. The trial court[] properly considered whether the presumption in favor of Benavides having custody had been rebutted and concluded that the children's best interests were served by continued placement with the maternal grandparents.

Affirmed.

Penland v. Harris

520 S.E.2d 105 (N.C. App. 1999)

MARTIN, Judge.

Plaintiffs filed this action on 20 April 1998 seeking joint custody of defendant's minor child. In their complaint, plaintiffs alleged that plaintiff, Brenda Penland, is defendant's mother and the natural maternal grandmother of the minor child; plaintiff David Penland is Brenda Penland's husband. Plaintiffs alleged that the minor child was born to defendant out of wedlock on 15 July 1992 and that the child's natural father is not named on the birth certificate. Plaintiffs alleged that defendant and the minor child lived in plaintiffs' home from the child's birth until 3 April 1998, when defendant married Andrew Harris and took the child to live with her in Harris' apartment. During the time when the minor child lived with plaintiffs, they alleged that they assumed parental roles and provided the child with food, health care, private schooling, and an overall healthy and stable environment while defendant earned a nursing degree. Since defendant's marriage to Harris, however, plaintiffs have been allowed only very limited contact and visitation with the minor child, to the detriment of the child's well being. Plaintiffs asserted that it was in the best interests of the child that they be awarded joint custody and "that her care, custody, and control be with the Plaintiffs at least 50% of the time." Plaintiffs also sought an *ex parte* order awarding them custody pending a hearing on the merits.

Defendant's motion to dismiss the complaint was granted by the trial court. Plaintiffs appeal.

* * *

[I]n *Price v. Howard*, 346 N.C. 68, 484 S.E.2d 528 (1997), our Supreme Court . . . held that a natural parent has a constitutionally protected paramount right in the care, custody, and control of his or her children which rises to the level of a liberty interest and is protected by the Due Process Clause of the Fourteenth Amendment. *Id.* The right is not absolute, however, and there is a corollary obligation on the part of the parent to care for his or her child and act in the child's best interest. Where a parent has acted in a manner inconsistent with his or her constitutionally protected custody right, that right must give way to a "best interest of the child" analysis. . . .

There is no bright line rule to determine what conduct on the part of a natural parent will result in a forfeiture of the constitutionally protected status and trigger application of a "best interest" analysis. Unfitness, abandonment, and neglect are certainly so egregious that a parent who engages in such behavior forfeits constitutional protections. On the other hand, raising a child out of wedlock does not constitute such behavior. The fact that the third party is able to offer the minor child a higher standard of living does not overcome a natural parent's paramount interest in the custody and control of the child. And, parental control over a child's associations is not behavior inconsistent with parental responsibilities; it is instead a fundamental part of the parent's right to custody.

We read *Price* as . . . requiring that a third party, including a grandparent, who seeks custody of a minor child as against the child's natural parent, must allege facts sufficient to show that the natural parent has acted in a manner inconsistent with his or her constitutionally protected status. . . .

The complaint in the present case falls far short of that requirement. Plaintiffs allege virtually no facts which would support a finding that defendant has engaged in conduct inconsistent with her parental responsibility. Plaintiffs allege their disapproval of defendant's choice of spouse, place of residence, and babysitters, and their fear that defendant will not permit the child to attend the school and church which plaintiffs desire that she attend. The primary focus of the complaint is upon plaintiffs' loving relationship with the minor child and their ability to provide her with a higher standard of living if she were in their custody.

Plaintiffs' dissatisfaction with defendant's husband and the couple's residence does not allege conduct so egregious as to be inconsistent with defendant's parental duties and responsibilities. Their assertion that they would be able to afford the minor child a higher standard of living is not relevant to the issue of defendant's constitutionally protected parental interest. Nor are plaintiffs' concerns as to defendant's decisions regarding which school and church the child will attend; decisions regarding the child's associations, education and religious upbringing are squarely within parental rights and responsibilities. Thus, we hold the complaint in the present case insufficient to state a claim . . . for custody of the minor child of defendant.

* * *

The order of the trial court is affirmed.

NOTES

1. *Debate over kinship care.* Family law scholars have debated whether, and the extent to which, the state should favor kinship care. Many commentators have argued that a preference for kinship care serves the interests of children by, among other things, reducing disruption, promoting continuity of family relationships, preserving cultural and community ties, and protecting children's identities. For example, Professor Dorothy Roberts has argued that:

> Compared to nonkin foster care, kinship foster care has many advantages for children. It usually preserves family, community, and cultural ties. For most people, staying in the extended family is in and of itself a benefit for children.

> Children are more likely to maintain contact with their parents and to remain with siblings if they are living with relatives than if they are placed in nonrelative foster care. It is likely that children are already familiar with the kin caregiver, so the placement avoids that trauma of moving in with strangers. Kinship foster care usually allows children to stay in their communities and to continue the cultural traditions their parents observe. Kinship foster care is more stable: children living with relatives are less likely to be moved to multiple placements while in substitute care. There is also evidence that children are better cared for by relatives than by strangers: more children in kinship foster care reported that they felt loved and happy, and fewer are abused while in state custody.

Dorothy E. Roberts, *Kinship Care and the Price of State Support for Children*, 76 CHI.-KENT L. REV. 1619, 1625 (2001). Scholars have argued that even if a child's relationship with his or her parents cannot be preserved, there is value in preserving relationships with other family members. *See, e.g.,* Naomi R. Cahn, *Children's Interests in a Familial Context: Poverty, Foster Care, and Adoption*, 60 OHIO ST. L.J. 1189, 1210 (1999) ("A family includes not just parent(s) and a child, but also siblings, grandparents, and other relatives. In determining removal, foster care placement, reunification, and adoption, the child's interests must include a consideration of her relationships with these other people.").

However, kinship care preferences are not without their critics. For example, Professor Elizabeth Bartholet has criticized kinship care preferences on the grounds that their use is often inconsistent with children's best interests, noting that:

> Child maltreatment is very often an intergenerational problem, so grandparents and other relatives are a risky population to look to for parenting. Kinship care providers are quite low on the socioeconomic scale and are generally much older than the parenting norm, often suffering related physical limits. There is no research to date that can really tell us whether the level of kinship preference currently at work serves or disserves children's interests.

Elizabeth Bartholet, *Creating a Child-Friendly Child Welfare System: Effective Early Intervention to Prevent Maltreatment and Protect Victimized Children*, 60 BUFF. L. REV. 1323, 1366-67 (2012).

2. *Choosing not to obtain custody.* While a lack of legal formality can make it difficult for grandparents providing private kinship care to act for the benefit of their grandchildren, many grandparents nevertheless choose not to pursue formal custody. Reasons for not doing so include concern about government intrusion into the family, the time and expense required to do so, and fear of causing conflict with the child's parent or parents. Such concerns may be particularly prevalent in certain communities. *See* Sonia Gipson Rankin, *Note, Why They Won't Take the Money: Black Grandparents and the Success of Informal Kinship Care*, 10 ELDER L.J. 153 (2002) (discussing why African-American grandparents tend not to seek a formal legal relationship with grandchildren in their care, despite the additional

resources and other advantages such relationship might provide). *See also* Dorothy E. Roberts, *Kinship Care and the Price of State Support for Children*, 76 Chi.-Kent L. Rev. 1619 (2001) (discussing why formalizing kinship care through kinship foster care may harm black families).

QUESTIONS

1. Should grandparents be given preference for child placement over non-relatives?

2. Should grandparents be given preference for child placement over other relatives (e.g., aunts, cousins, older siblings)?

PROBLEMS

1. When Mira was six months old, the state placed her with a foster mother after Mira's biological mother was found to have neglected her. Mira's mother has since died. Mira's foster mother, Freeda, has formed a deep bond with Mira and wishes to continue to care for her. Mira's biological grandmother, Georgia, however, wishes to obtain custody. Georgia is currently raising Mira's two older brothers, but has had only limited contact with Mira. In determining who should have legal custody over Mira, should the grandmother's status as a grandmother privilege her over the foster mother? If so, to what degree? *See S.M. v. A.W.*, 656 A.2d 841 (N.J. Super. 1995) (addressing this question).

2. Three years ago, Ella's daughter, Sharon, showed up at her door with her sons, Jeremy and Justin, in tow. Sharon explained that she was between jobs and needed someplace to stay. Several months later, Sharon found a job as a waitress at a local restaurant. There she met a cook who became her new boyfriend. Soon Sharon was spending most of her time at her new boyfriend's apartment. Ella, a retired office worker, found herself becoming her grandsons' primary caretaker. About a year and a half ago, Sharon became addicted to meth. After unsuccessfully trying to get Sharon treatment, Ella asked Sharon to move out. Sharon did so and has been living with her boyfriend ever since. The grandsons remain with Ella. Occasionally, Sharon will send them a card or drop by to take them out for ice cream. Last fall, Ella got into a heated argument with the principal at her grandsons' school when he told her that she did not have authority to enroll them. She eventually enrolled both boys, but now Justin has been diagnosed with asthma and she is worried she won't have the authority to get him the medical care he needs. Ella has come to you for legal advice. What would you advise Ella?

3. When Jeanne's daughter, Valerie, gave birth six years ago, Jeanne was thrilled. The child, a baby boy whom Valerie named Tyler, was Jeanne's first grandchild. Jeanne's husband of 15 years, Marshall, was also pleased to have a grandchild, in part because he did not have children of his own.

For the first few years of Tyler's life, Jeanne and Marshall saw very little of him. Valerie broke up with her then boyfriend, Tyler's father, and thereafter had a series of relationships with other men. A little over two years ago, a visibly pregnant Valerie showed up at Jeanne and Marshall's door with Tyler and her fiancé, Matt. Valerie explained that she and Matt were currently unemployed and needed someplace to stay until the baby was born. Jeanne and Marshall agreed to let them stay.

Soon after the baby, Kayla, was born, Valerie and Matt moved to a small apartment about ten minutes away from Jeanne and Marshall. Valerie was diagnosed with bipolar disorder and was prescribed medication, but she rapidly became non-compliant with her medication regimen and started drinking excessively. Less than two months after Kayla's birth, Matt left because "he couldn't handle Valerie's crap anymore." It soon became clear to Jeanne that Valerie was struggling with alcohol abuse and was unfit to care for either Kayla or Tyler. Worried for the children's safety, Jeanne encouraged Valerie to let her "help out."

When Kayla was four months old and Tyler was six years old, Valerie began dropping them off at Jeanne and Marshall's house for days at a time. By the time Kayla was seven months old, Jeanne and Marshall had become the primary caregivers for both children. As Jeanne put it, she went from being a "lady of leisure" to being "back to diaper duty, getting up at 6 A.M., and sleepless nights." Marshall has been supportive and actively helps out with both children, but Jeanne worries about the stress the situation is causing Marshall, who began experiencing chronic back pain shortly after the children moved in.

Kayla is now two years old; Tyler is eight; Jeanne is 64; and Marshall is 69. Jeanne and Marshall are finding raising Tyler and Kayla both emotionally and financially draining. While Valerie comes by once or twice a week to play with Kayla, Jeanne and Marshall provide all of her other care and support. They are also busy parenting Tyler, who has been diagnosed by the school psychologist with Attention Deficit Hyperactivity Disorder (ADHD) and whom Jeanne refers to as "high energy and increasingly disrespectful." While Tyler's official address is still Valerie's apartment and he often stays there on the weekends, the school bus driver knows to pick him up and drop him off at Jeanne and Marshall's home.

Jeanne feels very conflicted about her new role. Prior to Tyler and Kayla coming to live with them, Jeanne and Marshall had been newly retired and looking forward to having fun together. Marshall had just bought a new Harley-Davidson and the two were planning on making biking a regular part of their lives. Jeanne adores Kayla and Tyler. She says that she finds them to be a comfort to her and that she would not hesitate to take them in again, but she mourns the life she and Marshall had built together. She feels ashamed of her daughter, and—although she does not like to admit it—resents Valerie for getting pregnant with Kayla when she couldn't care for the child.

Jeanne is also worried that she and Marshall won't be able to continue to afford to care for Kayla and Tyler. While they own their own home, Jeanne and Marshall live on a fixed income (they both receive Social Security, and Marshall also has a small pension). Although Valerie gets small child support payments from Matt for Kayla, she does not share them with Jeanne and Marshall. Nor does Valerie have a job that provides health insurance for the children. Jeanne and Marshall wonder who will pay if one of the children breaks a bone or becomes very sick.

A few months ago, Jeanne finally "got up the nerve" and asked Valerie to contribute to the cost of raising Kayla and Tyler. Valerie became furious and yelled: "If you don't love your grandchildren enough to care for them—if all you want is money—I'll take them back. I can you know." Since then, Jeanne has been "walking on eggshells" around Valerie. This is particularly stressful for Jeanne because she has no formal legal authority to make decisions for either Tyler or Kayla. Indeed, last Wednesday, when she took Tyler to the doctor, the doctor insisted on obtaining Valerie's consent to treat him. Fortunately, Jeanne was able to reach Valerie by phone to get her consent, but she found the process "demeaning" and worries about what would happen if Tyler needed urgent care.

Jeanne finally decided she needed help after an incident last weekend when Valerie failed to drop off Tyler after his weekend at her apartment. Jeanne went by the apartment to look for Tyler and found Valerie drunk and the refrigerator nearly empty. Jeanne was furious at Valerie for disregarding Tyler's safety and told her so. In response, Valerie threw a beer bottle at Jeanne. Jeanne left, taking Tyler with her.

Based on the above fact pattern, consider the following questions:

a. Jeanne has come to see you to ask for your advice. What concerns do you have based on the above fact pattern? What advice would you give?

b. Since Jeanne last talked with you, Matt has also called a few times, asking to see Kayla. Jeanne and Marshall have refused to allow him any unsupervised visits with Kayla. They are still angry with Matt for abandoning Kayla and, moreover, suspect that he may be dealing meth. However, Matt's calls are becoming increasingly frequent, and last month he swore violently at Jeanne when she denied him "permission" to see Kayla. What concerns do you have based on these new facts? What advice would you give?

c. Three years have passed since Jeanne last spoke with you. Since that time, Matt turned his life around, is completely sober, and has been holding a steady job (complete with insurance benefits) for a year and a half. Ten months ago, over Jeanne and Marshall's objection, Matt was granted formal custody of Kayla. Matt is angry with Jeanne and Marshall for objecting to his petition for custody, being suspicious of him (he claims—persuasively—never to have been involved with illicit drugs), and for "badmouthing" him around Kayla. Despite

Jeanne and Marshall's pleas, Matt has flatly refused to allow either of them to see or speak to Kayla since he gained custody of her. What advice would you give Jeanne in light of these new developments?

E. GRANDPARENTS AS CARE RECIPIENTS

The Elizabethan Poor Law of 1601 (discussed in Chapter 5 in the context of filial responsibility statutes) required grandchildren to support indigent grandparents. While a few states retain such a duty, in most states grandchildren have no duty to support their grandparents unless they have affirmatively assumed that duty (in which case, an unreasonable failure to continue to provide care might lead to charges of neglect as discussed in Chapter 8).

Regardless of whether they have a legal duty to care for their grandparents, adult grandchildren may wish to do so or feel obligated to provide such care. Adult grandchildren who voluntarily assume care for grandparents, however, do not have the same employment protections as adult children have in such situations. Specifically, the federal Family and Medical Leave Act (FMLA) (discussed earlier in this chapter in the context of grandparents seeking leave to care for grandchildren) gives adult children the right to take unpaid leave to care for an ailing parent if, among other requirements, they have worked for at least 12 months for a public agency or a private employer with 50 or more employees. The same right is not, however, extended to adult grandchildren wishing to take such leave. The next case explores the contours of this limitation.

Dillon v. Maryland-National Capital Park & Planning Commission

382 F. Supp. 2d 777 (D. Md. 2005)

CHASANOW, District Judge.

Presently pending and ready for resolution in this action brought under the Family and Medical Leave Act ("FMLA"), 29 U.S.C. §§2601 et seq., are the cross-motions for summary judgment by Plaintiff Cynthia Dillon and Defendant Maryland-National Capital Park and Planning Commission ("MNCPPC"). The issues have been fully briefed and the court now rules, no hearing being deemed necessary. For the following reasons, Plaintiff's motion for summary judgment will be denied, and Defendant's motion for summary judgment will be denied in part and granted in part.

* * *

[Defendant contended that Plaintiff was lawfully terminated for being absent without leave.] Plaintiff contends that . . . she was entitled to leave under the FMLA in order to take care of her ailing grandmother, whom she asserts "basically raised [her] as a child." . . .

"[T]he FMLA creates both substantive and proscriptive rights." *Taylor v. Progress Energy, Inc.*, 415 F.3d 364 (4th Cir. 2005). The substantive rights include an employee's right to take up to twelve weeks of unpaid leave in any one-year period in order to care for a parent who has a serious health condition. 29 U.S.C. §2612(a)(1)(C). "The proscriptive rights include an employee's right not to be discriminated or retaliated against for exercising substantive FMLA rights or for otherwise opposing any practice made unlawful by the Act." *Taylor*, 415 F.3d at 364. Under the FMLA, "parent" is defined as "the biological parent of an employee or an individual who stood in loco parentis to an employee when the employee was a son or daughter." 29 U.S.C. §2611(7). Although the statute does not define the term "in loco parentis," the relevant Department of Labor regulations provide, "Persons who are 'in loco parentis' include those with day-to-day responsibilities to care for and financially support a child, or, in the case of an employee, who had such responsibility for the employee when the employee was a child. A biological or legal relationship is not necessary." 29 C.F.R. §825.113(c)(3).

As the plain language of the FMLA does not authorize FMLA leave for the care of grandparents, Plaintiff could only be entitled to FMLA leave to care for her grandmother if she stood in loco parentis to Plaintiff. Thus, Plaintiff bears the burden of putting forth sufficient evidence demonstrating that her grandmother qualifies as her "parent" under the FMLA.

* * *

[F]or purposes of this litigation, Plaintiff made the following declaration:

I was very close to my grandmother because she had basically raised me as a child. My mother was only 16 years old and still living at home when she was pregnant with me, and my grandmother was the one who financially provided for both of us. I was much closer to my grandmother than my mother during my formative years and slept in the same bed with her for the first 12 years. With the exception of spending a year living with my dad (when I was about 4 years old) and then while attending high school, when my mother and I lived separately from my grandmother, I spent my entire growing up period with my grandmother, who was the one who financially provided for me. I also returned to live with her after I too became pregnant at age 16 when my mother kicked me out of her residence because of my pregnancy. As the latter incident evinces, my grandmother was the one who I relied upon most for emotional and financial support as I was growing up and I love her as dearly as if she were my own mother.

This declaration, however, dramatically expands the information provided to Defendant during the time Plaintiff was seeking FMLA leave. Defendant contends that "the information supplied in support of her request did not demonstrate that her grandmother qualified as her 'parent' within the meaning of the FMLA," and that it was "devoid of facts demonstrating that her grandmother 'stood in place of' her mother, particularly in light of her mother's admitted presence in the home."

Because Plaintiff relies on information not previously presented to her employer, a potentially critical question in this case is whether Plaintiff may support her claim with evidence not shared with her employer at the time leave was requested and, thus, prior to it concluding that she did not qualify for FMLA leave, or whether she will be limited only to that evidence which she provided to Defendant prior to its making its decision. Defendant suggests that Plaintiff's burden is to establish that the information provided to it at the time it made its decision demonstrates that her grandmother stood in loco parentis to her. . . . However, even if Defendant's position is correct, and, therefore, Plaintiff must prove that the information provided to Defendant at the time it made its decision demonstrates her entitlement to FMLA leave, the court concludes that that evidence is enough to create a triable issue as to whether she was entitled to FMLA leave in order to care for her grandmother. Conversely, even with the new information provided by Plaintiff in her declaration and deposition testimony, the evidence is not so conclusive as to require a finding, as a matter of law, that Plaintiff's grandmother stood in loco parentis to her.

"The term 'in loco parentis,' according to its generally accepted common law meaning, refers to a person who has put himself in the situation of a lawful parent by assuming the obligations incident to the parental relation without going through the formalities necessary to legal adoption. It embodies the two ideas of assuming the parental status and discharging the parental duties." *Niewiadomski v. United States*, 159 F.2d 683, 686 (6th Cir. 1947). Black's Law Dictionary defines the phrase "in loco parentis" as "[i]n the place of a parent; instead of a parent; charged, factitiously, with a parent's rights, duties, and responsibilities." The mere fact of being a grandparent does not necessarily give rise to in loco parentis status. Indeed, a grandparent may assume the care and custody of a grandchild under circumstances which are consistent with the existence of the natural relationship between parent and child without any intention to sever that relationship.

"The key in determining whether the relationship of in loco parentis is established is found in the intention of the person allegedly in loco parentis to assume the status of a parent toward the child." 28 Am. Jur. 2d Proof of Facts 545, §2. The intent to assume such parental status can be inferred from the acts of the parties. "Other factors which are considered in determining whether in loco parentis status has been assumed are (1) the age of the child; (2) the degree to which the child is dependent on the person claiming to be standing in loco parentis; (3) the amount of support, if any, provided; and (4) the extent to which duties commonly associated with parenthood are exercised." *Id.*

Here, Plaintiff's evidentiary support for her proposition that she has established as a matter [of] law an in loco parentis relationship with her grandmother is not "sufficient for the court to hold that no reasonable trier of fact could find other than for" Plaintiff on this issue. However, as stated above, she has put forth enough at this stage to create a genuine issue of material fact as to whether her grandmother stood in loco parentis to her. Not only had Plaintiff informed Defendant that her grandmother had "raised" her as a child, but she had also informed it that her grandmother "fed" her and that she slept with her, indicating that Plaintiff indeed resided with her grandmother during her childhood and that her grandmother provided certain necessities for her. . . . Although these statements may not undisputedly demonstrate that her grandmother stood in loco parentis to her, the court cannot say, as a matter of law, that they fall short. The definitions of the term "in loco parentis" are often context specific, and no court—or regulation—has defined the term exhaustively. For some purposes, the presence of a biological parent in the home may foreclose another from holding the status of "in loco parentis." But for others, such as this case, the presence of Plaintiff's mother in the home is not fatal to Plaintiff's claim. In that home, as Plaintiff describes it, it is possible that her grandmother also stood "in loco parentis" at least for some portion of Plaintiff's childhood. Neither the language of the FMLA, nor the relevant regulations, put a minimum time requirement on the status. On the other hand, Plaintiff's mother was present and there is no evidence that she abandoned her role as a parent. While Plaintiff's grandmother provided shelter and financial support, the tasks described by Plaintiff may fall somewhat short of taking on a parental role.

Congress made clear that one of the purposes of the FMLA was "to balance the demands of the workplace with the needs of families, . . . and to promote national interests in preserving family integrity." 29 U.S.C. §2601(b)(1). Although Plaintiff has not removed all doubt from the issue, she has put forth sufficient evidence to create a triable issue as to whether the information provided to Defendant, or that provided in discovery, demonstrates a relationship that falls within the ambit of the rights accorded under the FMLA. Thus, neither party is entitled to summary judgment on this issue and both motions on this issue will be denied. . . .

QUESTIONS

1. Should adult grandchildren have any legal duty to provide—either financially or otherwise—for their grandparents? If so, what should be the scope of that duty?

2. Should FMLA coverage be extended to adult grandchildren who wish to care for ailing grandparents? Should there be any requirements for such leave beyond what is required of adult children?

Table of Cases

Principal cases appear in italics.

Index